NEGLIGENCE PURPOSE, ELEMENTS, AND EVIDENCE: THE ROLE OF FORESEEABILITY IN THE LAW OF EACH STATE

EDITOR IN CHIEF

Vicki Lawrence MacDougall

Professor of Law
Director of the Health Law Certificate Program
Faculty Advisor of the Oklahoma City University Law Review
Oklahoma City University School of Law

EXECUTIVE EDITOR

Gregg Luther

Oklahoma Trial Lawyer
Oklahoma City University Law Review Member
Alumni, Oklahoma City University School of Law

EXECUTIVE EDITOR

Lee F. Peoples

Frederick Charles Hicks Professor of Law
Interim Dean
Oklahoma City University School of Law
Member of the Oklahoma Bar

AUTHORS

Michael Blue	Jim Fitzsimmons	Jon Moore
Meg Butler	Allan L. Galbraith	Savanna Nolan
Connie Calvert	Timothy Gatton	Paige L. Pahlke
Joe Custer	Narendra K. Ghosh	Michael Panesar
Brian Davis	Matt Granda	Lee Peoples
Sabrina Davis	Justin Huckaby	Paul Petro
Andrew G. Deiss	Christine Iaconeta	Jennifer Prilliman
Casey Duncan	Matthew Kane	Steve Stevens
Danny Ellis	Gregg Luther	Vernon Sumwalt
Amy Emmerson	Vicki Lawrence MacDougall	

All Rights Reserved
Copyright © 2018 by Balloon Press, New York, NY

ISBN-13: 978-0-9980073-3-5

Library of Congress Cataloging-in-Publication Data
MacDougall, Vicki Lawrence
Negligence Purpose, Elements, and Evidence:
The Role of Foreseeability in the Law of Each State
p. cm.

ISBN-10: 0-9980073-3-1

Printed by: Bookmasters
Printed and Bound in Ashland, Ohio

Balloon Press, 250 Park Avenue, 7th Floor
New York, NY 10177

ACKNOWLEDGMENTS

The Editor in Chief and Executive Editors wish to thank the following individuals for their legal research, editorial, and clerical contributions to this text.

Vickey Cannady
Administrative Assistant
Oklahoma City University School of Law

Cindy Elbah
Administrative Assistant
Oklahoma City University School of Law

Kathryn L. Bautista
Oklahoma City University School of Law
Class of 2018

Brooke Ballard
Oklahoma City University School of Law
Class of 2018

Aimee Phillips
Oklahoma City University School of Law
Class of 2018

CONTENTS

FOREWORD

By the Honorable. Robert H. Henry
Former United States Circuit Judge for the
10th Circuit Court of Appeals
President—Oklahoma City University

The concept for this book was brought to my attention by a former mentor and long-time friend. The idea of creating a compendium of the foreseeability law of every state seemed daunting. However, after discussion with Dean Peoples, I recognized the benefits such a book would bring to the bench, the bar, and academia from my experiences as a practicing lawyer, State Attorney General, Dean of a Law School, United States Circuit Judge, and University President. I knew that bringing such a concept to a successful finished product would require a knowledgeable and skilled Editor In Chief. Our suggestion was Vicki Lawrence MacDougall. I was delighted to learn she accepted the challenge.

Foreseeability remains the major underpinning of American Tort jurisprudence. The recent publication of the RESTATEMENT (THIRD) OF TORTS has rekindled the interest and importance of foreseeability in negligence law. Under Professor MacDougall's guidance, this book follows the "sentence/citation format," which removes author opinion and commentary. This seeks to present the Black Letter Law from every state on foreseeability—exactly the kind of reference members of the bench demand.

Negligence Purpose, Elements, and Evidence: The Role of Foreseeability in the Law of Each State is an essential, timely, invaluable tool for the bench, bar, and academia. The answer to admissibility of evidence, relevance, sufficiency of evidence, question of law vs. fact, probative value, and many others are all answered with this book. Simple. Easy. Accurate.

I commend the editors and authors, and Dean Peoples
for this accomplishment.

INTRODUCTION

THE RESTATEMENT (THIRD) and Foreseeability "What Does It All Mean?"[1]

Vicki Lawrence MacDougall[2]
Editor-in-Chief

Negligence Purpose, Elements, and Evidence: The Role of Foreseeability in the Law of Each State serves three main purposes. The first goal is to provide a brief refresher in basic tort law. The second is the hope that this book will be a useful, basic research tool for the bench and the bar. And the third, and last purpose of this tome is to observe the role of foreseeability in each state and illustrate that the attempts of the Restatement (Third) of Torts, Liability for Physical and Emotional Harm (2010/2012) to remove foreseeability from the analyses of duty and proximate cause are out-of-step with the practical application of tort law in the vast majority of jurisdictions. Before discussing each goal of this book, I express my appreciation to the project's contributors for the considerable effort expended toward this undertaking.

Negligence Purpose, Elements, and Evidence: The Role of Foreseeability in the Law of Each State would have been impossible without the committed efforts of the authors of each chapter addressing the law of an individual state or the District of Columbia. The authors include practicing attorneys, law professors, and law librarians from throughout the country, and this book would not have become a reality without the effort of these individuals from across the nation. *Negligence Purpose, Elements, and Evidence: The Role of Foreseeability in the Law of Each State* would have remained a dream if not for the efforts of two people who turned the idea into a reality. Recognition must be made to the architect of the project, Gregg W. Luther, Oklahoma trial lawyer and alumni of the Oklahoma City University Law Review and School of Law, for proposing and fighting for the creation of this book. Further, a special acknowledgment goes to Interim Dean and Professor Lee F. Peoples, Frederick Charles Hicks Professor of Law and Law Library Director, Chickasaw Nation Law Library, Oklahoma City University School of Law, for handling author assignments and the multitude of organizational details that were necessary for this book to go to press.

---

[1] The subtitle of this introduction is borrowed from Thomas Nagel, *What Does It All Mean? A Very Short Introduction to Philosophy* (Oxford Univ. Press 1987).

[2] Professor of Law, Director of the Health Law Certificate Program, Faculty Advisor of the Oklahoma City University Law Review, Oklahoma City University School of Law. The author acknowledges the editorial expertise of Christopher M. Calvert, J.D., M.S., B.S., B.S., 2016-2017 Articles Editor, Oklahoma City University Law Review, whose editing improved this Introduction.

As previously mentioned, *Negligence Purpose, Elements, and Evidence: The Role of Foreseeability in the Law of Each State* has three main goals. First, this bench-book is a byproduct of concerns that arose from litigating cases. One major concern was that the basic premise and policies underlying tort law were being forgotten in an era consumed with the quest for tort reform. Another concern was the unfamiliarity with basic tort doctrine by some members of the profession and empathy toward judges who are normally assigned crowded dockets covering a multitude of topics, such as divorce, property disputes, probate, criminal matters, or the Uniform Commercial Code. Accordingly, there was a true need for a description of basic tort doctrine to refresh recollections that perhaps had faded since the first year of law school. Further, there was no basic research tool for exploring and comparing basic negligence laws among the states. *Negligence Purpose, Elements, and Evidence: The Role of Foreseeability in the Law of Each State* addresses these concerns with a concise statement of the general policy or purpose of tort law followed by a discussion of the elements of the negligence cause of action under the law of each state. A cursory description of helpful evidence accompanies the discussion of each state's law.

Second, *Negligence Purpose, Elements, and Evidence: The Role of Foreseeability in the Law of Each State* is also a research tool for judges, clerks, attorneys, and law students. It is a starting point when researching the law of negligence. Additionally, an attorney or court confronted with an undecided issue in his or her state could quickly review other states' laws on the unresolved point. This book could be a researcher's starting point when building arguments on cases of first impression. The organization of this book, with its concise summaries of law on a state-by-state basis, will assist those researching according to preferred jurisdictions as some courts favor following the jurisprudence of a particular jurisdiction when looking for guidance. For example, Alaska might be more influenced by California precedent, whereas Oklahoma prefers authority from Kansas. Furthermore, the breakdown of the law according to each state will assist the out-of-state attorney when confronted with a conflicts-of-law issue or when representing a client in a case from another jurisdiction. Although this book is not intended as an exhaustive statement of the law, hopefully *Negligence Purpose, Elements, and Evidence: The Role of Foreseeability in the Law of Each State* will assist in litigating negligence cases and growing tort doctrine throughout the country.

The third and overarching purpose of *Negligence Purpose, Elements, and Evidence: The Role of Foreseeability in the Law of Each State* is to show the current role of "foreseeability" in each state and how "foreseeability" crafts negligence law. As stated by Professor Owen, "[f]oreseeability is the dark matter of tort."[3] "Like celestial dark matter, foreseeability swirls throughout the law of tort, permeating, connecting, and providing moral strength to the elements of negligence."[4] The Restatement (Third) of Torts, Liability for Physical and Emotional Harm (2012) [hereinafter Restatement (Third) PEH][5] retains the concept of foreseeability only

---

[3] David G. Owen, *Figuring Foreseeability*, 44 WAKE FOREST L. REV. 1277, 1277 (2009).

[4] *Id.* at 1306.

[5] On the *Restatement (Third) PEH, see generally* W. Jonathan Cardi, *Purging Foreseeability: The New Vision of Duty and Judicial Power in the Proposed Restatement (Third) of Torts,* 58 VAND. L. REV. 739 (2005); David G. Owen, *Figuring Foreseeability*, 44 WAKE FOREST L. REV. 1277 (2009); Mike Steenson, *Minnesota Negligence Law and the Restatement (Third) of Torts: Liability for Physical and Emotional Harms*, 37 WILLIAM MITCHELL L.

in the breach of duty element of a negligence cause of action.[6] Provisions of the Restatement (Third) PEH attempt to eliminate foreseeability as a relevant consideration in establishing a duty of care and in the area of proximate cause.[7] Indeed, the Restatement (Third) PEH attempts to delete the term "proximate cause" and the "substantial factor" test used for cause-in-fact[8] altogether. Hopefully, this book will establish that the concepts of foreseeability and proximate cause are still predominate throughout the country and that the power of stare decisis is clearly behind both doctrines in the vast majority of states throughout the country. No other treatise details the status of foreseeability in each state. *Negligence Purpose, Elements, and Evidence: The Role of Foreseeability in the Law of Each State* illustrates the unique way each state uses "foreseeability" in the determination of duty, breach of duty, causation, both cause-in-fact and proximate cause (or "scope of liability"), and damages and that most states' current law is contra to select provisions of the Restatement (Third) PEH.[9]

Rev., 1055 (2011); Tory A. Weigand, *Duty, Causation and Palsgraf: Massachusetts and the Restatement (Third) of Torts*, 96 Mass. L. Rev. 55 (2015); Benjamin C. Zipursky, *Foreseeability in Breach, Duty and Proximate Cause*, 44 Wake Forest L. Rev. 1247 (2009); Thomas B. Read, et al., *The Restatement (Third), Duty, Breach of Duty and "Scope of Liability,"* 14, No. 3, *Iowa Defense Counsel Assoc., Defense Update*, 1 (Summer 2012).

[6] Section 3 of the Restatement (Third) of Torts, Liability for Physical and Emotional Harm § 3 (2012) provides, as follows: "A person acts negligently if the person does not exercise reasonable care under all the circumstances. Primary factors to consider in ascertaining whether the person's conduct lacks reasonable care are the foreseeable likelihood that the person's conduct will result in harm, the foreseeable severity of any harm that may ensue, and the burden of precautions to eliminate or reduce the risk of harm." "The Reporters are eager to maintain the role [of foreseeability] in breach, albeit reshaped by the Hand formula." Benjamin C. Zipursky, *Foreseeability in Breach, Duty, and Proximate Cause*, 44 Wake Forest L. Rev. 1247, 1275 (2009). "As to breach, foreseeability needs to be taken more seriously apart from its role in the Hand formula." *Id.*

[7] Tory A. Weigand, *Duty, Causation and Palsgraf: Massachusetts and the Restatement (Third) of Torts*, 96 Mass. L. Rev. 55 (2015). "Reduced to its bones, the *Third Restatement* views the fact-intensive nature of foreseeability unsuitable for the lofty work of duty and questions of law for judges, and mutes its traditional place in causation determinations. Stripped of its former and long-standing role as both a duty and causative workhorse, foreseeability is otherwise relegated to the issue of breach and the work of fact finders." *Id.* at 56.

[8] The Restatement (Third) of Torts, Liability for Physical and Emotional Harm § 26 (2012) embraces the "but-for" causation test. *Section 26* provides, as follows: "Tortious conduct must be a factual cause of harm for liability to be imposed. Conduct is a factual cause of harm when the harm would not have occurred absent the conduct. Tortious conduct may also be a factual cause of harm under § 27." Section 27 imposes liability for duplicative causation. Despite recognition that the substantial factor test "originated in the *Restatement of Torts* and was replicated in the Restatement (Second) of Torts," the *Restatement (Third) PEH* opines that the "substantial factor test has not, however, withstood the test of time, as it has proved confusing and been misused." Restatement (Third) of Torts, Liability for Physical and Emotional Harm § 26 cmt. j (2012). According to the *Restatement (Third)*, "the substantial-factor rubric tends to obscure, rather than to assist," explain, and clarify causation deliberations. *Id.* The substantial factor test is well established in case-law throughout the country and, it is unclear if courts will be eager to displace precedence. "Elimination of the substantial factor usage would be a significant change" and is "currently ingrained in . . . causative law and jury presentation." Tory A. Weigand, *Duty, Causation and Palsgraf: Massachusetts and the Restatement (Third) of Torts*, 96 Mass. L. Rev. 55, 79 (2015). Further, "legitimate criticism of section 27 is its omission of the requirement that a defendant's conduct alone be sufficient and substantial, and that any standard less than but-for represents a decision to impose liability without causation." *Id.* at 79.

[9] Benjamin C. Zipursky, *Foreseeability in Breach, Duty, and Proximate Cause*, 44 Wake Forest L. Rev. 1247, 1275 (2009). "In today's courts, foreseeability plays a role in breach, duty, and proximate cause." *Id.*

The main purpose of any Restatement is to restate, not create, the law.[10] However, in the tort arena, the Restatement, at times, has had a tendency to depart from its mission and attempt to change or create the law. This occasional quest to change the law is perhaps a longing to re-create the success of the Restatement (Second) of Torts, § 402A (1964). Section 402A is the "holy grail" of products liability law and was instrumental in the creation of strict products liability in tort in almost every state, and it literally shaped the development of that doctrine throughout the country. Obviously, it is easier to shape and create law in the absence of law, where precedent and stare decisis does not hinder the adoption of new doctrinal law. Typically, each jurisdiction has a well-defined body of substantive law on the issues of duty, proximate cause, and foreseeability.[11] However, proximate cause is an area of tort law that both the Restatement (Second) of Torts and the Restatement (Third) PEH have targeted for change.

Granted, the concept of proximate cause is amorphous. "The term 'proximate cause' is applied by the courts to those more or less undefined considerations which limit liability even where the fact of causation is clearly established. The word 'proximate' is a legacy of Lord Chancellor Bacon, who in his time committed other sins."[12] Arguably, it is a misguided term because proximate cause is "neither about proximity nor about causation."[13] The Restatement (Second) Of Torts, § 430 (1964) attempted to clarify the doctrine of proximate cause by changing the doctrine's name to "legal cause." However, the term "legal cause" was omitted from the Restatement (Third) PEH because "despite 75 years of Torts Restatement commitment to legal cause, its acceptance in the vocabulary of tort law is quite limited."[14] The pre-existing state law prevailed, and the terminology of proximate causation persevered. The Restatement (Third) PEH acknowledges that the term "'proximate cause' has been in widespread use in judicial opinions, treatises, casebooks, and scholarship." Despite this fact, the Restatement (Third) PEH simply does not "employ" the term "because

---

[10] Arguably, this is a myopic view. The American Law Institute believes that the *Restatements* have a broader purpose. "*Restatements* are not simply a 'restatement' of what courts have done. In many cases they attempt to synthesize decisions that seem disparate or confused. Sometimes, they attempt to rationalize a doctrine that has developed by accretion over time. Sometimes they are prescriptive rather than descriptive, providing rules that the Institute believes are an improvement." At times, the *Restatements* can be "an attempt to lead courts to a more appropriate rule of law." Michael D. Green, William C. Powers, Jr., Reporters, *Introduction, Part C*, The Restatement Third of Torts: Liability For Physical and Emotional Harm (2012).

[11] When urged to adopt the "scope of the liability" principles of *the Restatement (Third) PEH*, the Texas Supreme Court stated, as follows: "While we applaud any effort to bring greater clarity to this difficult area of the law, we must decline the invitation to abandon decades of case law." Dew v. Crown Derrick Erectors, Inc., 208 S.W. 3d 448, 452 at n. 4 (2006). Further, the Court of Appeals of Kansas observed that the "*Third Restatement* view may one day gain acceptance, but even its authors concede that they have staked out a basis of analysis that is different than the one actually employed by the courts today (or for the past 100 years for that matter). The *Restatement* reporters recognized that they have proposed a scope-of-risk analysis B rather than the standard foreseeability test applied . . . [in most states] for proximate cause." Hale v. Brown, 167 P. 3d 363, 365 (Kan. Ct. App. 2007).

[12] Prosser and Keeton on Torts § 41 (5th ed. 1984).

[13] Michael D. Green, William C. Powers, Jr., Reporters, *Introduction, Part C*, The Restatement Third of Torts: Liability For Physical and Emotional Harm (2012).

[14] *Special Note on Proximate Cause*, Restatement (Third) of Torts: Liability For Physical and Emotional Harm ch. 6 (2012).

it is an especially poor one to describe the idea to which it is connected."[15] Instead, the concept of proximate cause is entitled "Scope of Liability."[16] It is hard to argue that "scope of liability" properly describes the concept of proximate cause. However, proximate cause is firmly entrenched in the language of lawyers and the courts, so ridding the term "proximate cause" from case law and substituting the term "scope of liability" will prove a formidable task. The gift of precognition would likely reveal the continued use of the term proximate cause in the "vocabulary of tort law" and that the Restatement (Third) PEH's attempt to clarify through terminology will meet the same fate as the Restatement's (Second)'s attempt by utilizing the term "legal cause."

The test for "scope of liability (proximate cause)" the Restatement (Third) PEH adopts is "an actor's liability is limited to those harms that result from the risks that made the actor's conduct tortious."[17] According to the Restatement (Third) PEH,[18] "[c]ourts have increasingly moved toward adopting a foreseeability test" and "virtually all jurisdictions" currently "employ a foreseeability (or risk) standard for some range of scope-of-liability issues."[19] However, the Restatement (Third) PEH opines that the risk standard is "preferable to a foreseeability standard."[20] The Restatement (Third) PEH admits that the risk test and the foreseeability test are functionally equivalent and that both tests "exclude liability for harms that were sufficiently unforeseeable at the time of the actor's tortious conduct."[21] However, according to the Restatement (Third) PEH, the risk standard is "preferable because it provides greater clarity, facilitates clearer analysis in a given case, and better reveals the reason for its existence."[22] "A foreseeability test for negligence cases risks being misunderstood because of uncertainty about what must be foreseen, by whom, and at what time."[23] While that may be true, applying the risk standard could prove to be equally unclear and difficult to understand. The scope-of-risk test should "consider all of the range of harms risked by the defendant's conduct that the jury could find as the basis for determining that conduct tortious. Then, the court can compare the plaintiff's harm with the range of harms risked by the defendant to determine whether a reasonable jury might find

---

[15] Restatement (Third) of Torts: Liability For Physical and Emotional Harm, *Special Note on Proximate Cause*, ch. 9 (2010/ 2012).

[16] *Id.*

[17] Restatement (Third) of Torts: Liability For Physical and Emotional Harm § 29 (2012). The risk test has its origins in Overseas Tankship (UK) Ltd. v. Morts Dock & Eng'g Co. Ltd., [1961] AC 388 (PC).

[18] On the "risk test" and the "scope of liability" under the *Restatement (Third) PEH*, see generally David G. Owen, *Figuring Foreseeability*, 44 Wake Forest L. Rev. 1277 (2009); Mike Steenson, *Minnesota Negligence Law and the Restatement (Third) of Torts: Liability for Physical and Emotional Harms*, 37 William Mitchell L. Rev. 1055 (2011); Tory A. Weigand, *Duty, Causation and Palsgraf: Massachusetts and the Restatement (Third) of Torts*, 96 Mass. L. Rev. 55 (2015); Benjamin C. Zipursky, *Foreseeability in Breach, Duty and Proximate Cause*, 44 Wake Forest L. Rev. 1247 (2009); Thomas B. Read. *The Restatement (Third), Duty, Breach of Duty and "Scope of Liability,"* 14, No. 3, Iowa Defense Counsel Assoc., Defense Update, 1 (Summer 2012).

[19] Restatement (Third) of Torts: Liability For Physical and Emotional Harm § 29 cmt. e (2012).

[20] *Id.*

[21] *Id.* at cmt. j.

[22] *Id.*

[23] *Id.*

the former among the latter."[24] Clarity will, at times, be equally difficult under the risk test.[25] Listing potential risks of harm that could arise from tortious behavior will likely vary significantly upon the insight, imagination, and foresight of the author of the list. Uncertainty could haunt the risk test as easily as a test that considers foreseeability. Quite frankly, regardless of terminology or the test utilized, proximate cause is simply a murky, albeit fascinating, area of the law. The scope of liability will still give room to argue for the imposition of liability under almost any given set of facts under the risk theory. As previously noted, most jurisdictions utilize the concept of foreseeability in proximate cause.[26] The risk theory is a very useful tool in proximate cause analysis; however, it is unlikely to replace the current jurisprudence that is entrenched throughout the various states.[27]

The Restatement (Third) PEH recommends that jury instructions requiring that the tortious behavior "cause harm in a natural and continuous sequence" or "that the causal sequence 'be unbroken by any efficient intervening causes' should not be given because such language does "not reflect the risk standard adopted in this Section."[28] Once again, this language is very common in current jury instructions, a common definition of proximate cause,[29] and frequently repeated in appellate decisions. When confronted with a proximate cause, or scope-of-liability, issue, appellate courts, attorneys, and jury instructions will likely continue using those phrases.[30]

---

[24] *Id.* at cmt. d.

[25] "[T]here is concern whether the causation approach of the *Third Restatement* truly clarifies. The 'scope of liability' terminology is awkward and would result in substantial discomfort for jurists and litigants alike." Tory A. Weigand, *Duty, Causation and Palsgraf: Massachusetts and the Restatement (Third) of Torts,* 96 Mass. L. Rev. 55, 79 (2015).

[26] Only a very few courts have adopted the "risk test" of the *Restatement (Third) PEH*, such as Iowa, Thompson v. Kaczinski, 774 N.W. 2d 829 (Iowa 2009) and two federal courts that utilized the test without discussion. Drumgold v. Callaham, 707 F. 3d 28, 49 (1st Cir. 2013); Jo Ann Howard & Assoc., P.C. v. Cassity, No. 4:09CV01252, 2014 WL 7408884 (E.D. Mo. Dec. 31, 2014). Both Kansas and Texas have specifically rejected the "risk test" from the *Restatement (Third) PEH.* Dew v. Crown Derrick Erectors, Inc., 208 S.W. 3d 448, 452, n. 4 (Tex. 2006); Hale v. Brown, 167 P.3d 362, 365 & 367 (Kan. Ct. App. 2007).

[27] Mike Steenson, *Minnesota Negligence Law and The Restatement (Third) of Torts: Liability for Physical and Emotional Harms,* 37 William Mitchell L. Rev. 1055 (2011). Professor Steenson observes that four states have adopted the *Restatement (Third) PEH* and "purged foreseeability" from either the duty or proximate cause analysis. Those states are, as follows: Arizona, Gipson v. Kasey, 150 P.3d 228, 231 (Ariz. 2007) (duty); Iowa, Thompson v. Kaczinski, 774 N.W. 2d 829 (Iowa 2009) (duty and scope of liability); Nebraska, A.W. v. Lancaster County School District, 784 N.W. 2d 907 (Neb. 2010) (duty); and Wisconsin, Behrendt v. Gulf Underwriters Ins. Co., 768 N.W. 2d 568 (Wisc. 2009) (duty). Tennessee "specifically decided that foreseeability is pivotal in the resolution of duty issues without directly considering section 7." Mike Steenson, *Minnesota Negligence Law and The Restatement (Third) of Torts: Liability for Physical and Emotional Harms,* 37 William Mitchell L. Rev. 1055, 1062 (2011) (citing Satterfield v. Breeding Insulation Co., 266 S.W. 3d 347, 362-63 (Tenn. 2008)). Delaware rejects *the Restatement (Third) PEH.* Mike Steenson, *Minnesota Negligence Law and The Restatement (Third) of Torts: Liability for Physical and Emotional Harms,* 37 William Mitchell L. Rev. 1055, 1063 (2011) (citing Riedel v. ICI Ams. Inc., 968 A.2d 17, 20-21 (Del. 2009)).

[28] Restatement (Third) of Torts: Liability For Physical and Emotional Harm § 29 cmt. g (2012).

[29] *See, e.g.,* Hale v. Brown, 167 P.3d 362, 363 (Kan. Ct. App. 2007).

[30] *Id.*

Arguably, the most dramatic proposal of the Restatement (Third) PEH is its position on duty and foreseeability, or to be precise, the declaration that foreseeability should be ignored in ascertaining if a duty of care is owed.[31] The Restatement (Third) PEH observed that "[d]espite widespread use of foreseeability in no-duty determinations, this Restatement disapproves that practice and limits no-duty rulings to articulated policy or principle in order to facilitate more transparent explanations of the reasons for a no-duty ruling and to protect the traditional function of the jury as factfinder."[32] The Restatement (Third) PEH attempts to draw a bright line between questions of law for the court and questions of fact for the jury.[33] According to the Restatement (Third) PEH, there is an important difference between scope-of-liability (proximate cause) and duty because the "no-duty rules are matters of law decided by the courts, while the defendant's scope of liability is a question of fact for the factfinder."[34] Because foreseeability, as admitted by the Restatement (Third) PEH, is a valid, if not critical, factor throughout the country in duty analysis, eliminating foreseeability from the duty analysis is a bold approach. "If Judge Cardozo's Palsgraf opinion really was, as the Second Restatement's Reporter once said, a 'bombshell burst' that 'stated the issue of foreseeability in terms of duty,'" then today's ALI could be described as having . . . launched a retaliatory bombshell that states, in so many words, 'not in our Third Restatement.'"[35]

The Restatement (Third) PEH assumes that a duty is owed in the vast majority of cases.[36] As stated in Section 7 (a), an "actor ordinarily has a duty to exercise reasonable care when the actor's conduct creates a risk of physical harm."[37] Foreseeability of a risk of harm is critical in determining if the actor was negligent; however, the Restatement (Third) PEH's position is antithetical and provides that determinations of duty should be made without the use of the concept of foreseeability.[38] In most cases, there is a presumption of a duty if the actor created a risk of

---

[31] On *Restatement (Third) PEH* and duty, *see* W. Jonathan Cardi, *Purging Foreseeability: The New Vision of Duty and Judicial Power in the Proposed Restatement (Third) of Torts*, 58 VAND. L. REV. 739 (2005); W. Jonathan Cardi & Michael D. Green, *Duty Wars*, 81 S. CAL. L REV. 671 (2008); Alani Golanski, *A New Look at Duty in Tort Law: Rehabilitating Foreseeability and Related Themes*, 75 ALB. L. REV. 227 (2012); John H. Marks, *The Limit to Premises Liability for Harms Caused by "Known or Obvious" Dangers: Will it Trip and Fall Over the Duty-Breach Framework Emerging in the Restatement (Third) of Torts?* 38 TEX. TECH. L. REV. 1 (2005); Mike Steenson, *Minnesota Negligence Law and the Restatement (Third) of Torts: Liability for Physical and Emotional Harms*, 37 WILLIAM MITCHELL L. REV., 1055 (2011); Aaron D. Twerski, *The Cleaver, The Violin, and the Scalpel: Duty and the Restatement (Third) of Torts*, 60 HASTINGS L.J. 1 (2008); Thomas B. Read, et al., *The Restatement (Third), Duty, Breach of Duty and "Scope of Liability,"* 14, No. 3, *Iowa Defense Counsel Assoc., Defense Update*, 1 (Summer 2012).

[32] RESTATEMENT (THIRD) OF TORTS: LIABILITY FOR PHYSICAL AND EMOTIONAL HARM § 7 cmt. j (2012).

[33] *Id.* at cmt. a.

[34] *Id.*

[35] John H. Marks, *The Limit to Premises Liability for Harms Caused by "Known or Obvious" Dangers: Will it Trip and Fall Over the Duty-Breach Framework Emerging in the Restatement (Third) of Torts?* 38 TEX. TECH. L. REV. 1, 70 (2005).

[36] This approach is very similar to Justice Andrews's opinion in Palsgraf where he concluded that a duty was owed to the world at large to refrain from negligent conduct. Palsgraf v. Long Island R.R. Co., 162 N.E. 99 (N.Y. 1928) (Andrews, J., dissenting).

[37] RESTATEMENT (THIRD) OF TORTS: LIABILITY FOR PHYSICAL AND EMOTIONAL HARM § 7 (a) (2012).

[38] RESTATEMENT (THIRD) OF TORTS: LIABILITY FOR PHYSICAL AND EMOTIONAL HARM § 7 cmt. j (2012).

harm. Inasmuch as a duty does exist in the vast majority of cases, a presumption of duty is not an extraordinary concept. For example, the driver of a car owes a duty toward others on the road in most car accidents. Indeed, the academic study of the law of duty concentrates on those cases where there could be a problem with the duty issue, such as in no-duty-to-rescue, special relationship, protection against the actions of third parties, or entrants upon land cases. However, there is criticism that the approach of the Restatement (Third) PEH will "open the floodgates of plaintiffs' suits"[39] with its presumption of a duty in all cases where someone creates a risk of harm. Further, there is "no sound reason to abandon the duty analysis . . . which requires that some legally significant relationship exist between the parties for a duty of care to flow between them, in favor of the Third Restatement's novel, untested and impractical approach."[40]

Some members of the defense bar have expressed concerns regarding what could be considered an expansive view of duty.

> The Restatement 3rd PEH § 7 eliminates "foreseeability" of harm as one of the factors in the duty analysis. Rather, "An actor ordinarily has a duty to exercise reasonable care when the actor's conduct creates a risk of physical harm." REST 3d TORTS § 7 (a). Although this simplifies the duty analysis, it arguably establishes the existence of a duty in a wider variety of circumstances and situations, and this should be a concern to defendants. It no longer matters whether the physical harm to a particular person or class of people is foreseeable. Simply put, if the actor's conduct creates a risk of physical harm, the actor must exercise reasonable care.[41]

In other words, the presumption of duty could be perceived as "creating duties in areas of law where the court previously found no duty."[42]

Arguably, the most controversial provision regarding duty is eliminating foreseeability from consideration when deciding whether one owes a duty. Section 7(b) provides, as follows: "In exceptional cases, when an articulated countervailing principle or policy warrants denying or limiting liability in a particular class of cases, a court may decide that the defendant has no duty or that the ordinary duty of reasonable care requires modification."[43] Under this approach, a no-duty determination can only be made to a "class of cases,"[44] and

---

[39] Mike Steenson, *Minnesota Negligence Law and The Restatement (Third) of Torts: Liability for Physical and Emotional Harm*, 37 WILLIAM MITCHELL L. REV. 1055, 1085 (2011).

[40] *Id.*

[41] Thomas B. Read, et al., *The Restatement (Third), Duty, Breach of Duty and "Scope of Liability*," 14, No. 3, *Iowa Defense Counsel Assoc., Defense Update*, 3 (Summer 2012) (emphasis in original).

[42] Mike Steenson, *Minnesota Negligence Law and The Restatement (Third) of Torts: Liability for Physical and Emotional Harms*, 37 WILLIAM MITCHELL L. REV. 1055, 1085 (2011) (citing Riedel v. ICI Americas Inc., 968 A.2d 17, 20 (Del. 2009)).

[43] RESTATEMENT (THIRD) OF TORTS: LIABILITY FOR PHYSICAL AND EMOTIONAL HARM § 7 (b) (2012) (emphasis added).

[44] This approach would mean that there would be a duty owed to Helen Palsgraf or to the unforeseeable plaintiff. Justice Cardozo concluded based on the facts of the *Palsgraf* case that no duty was owed to Mrs. Palsgraf. Palsgraf v. Long Island R.R. Co., 162 N.E. 99 (N.Y. 1928). This approach was endorsed by the *Restatement (Second)*. RESTATEMENT (SECOND) OF TORTS § 281 (b) (1965). It would be disallowed under the *Restatement (Third) PEH*.

a no-duty determination in an individual case is prohibited.[45] "A no-duty ruling represents a determination, a purely legal question, that no liability should be imposed on actors in a category of cases."[46] Because duty is presumed if a risk of harm is created, a "defendant has the procedural obligation to raise the issue of whether a no-duty rule" would be applicable and whether the case falls within a category of cases wherein the court has concluded or will conclude it is appropriate for a no-duty rule.[47]

In a "purely legal question," the court concludes if there is no duty in a "class of cases" based on articulated policies. "These reasons of policy and principle do not depend on the foreseeability of harm based on the specific facts of a case. They should be articulated directly without obscuring references to foreseeability."[48] The Restatement (Third) PEH articulates principles or policies that courts should use when deciding whether a duty is owed in a category of cases. The considerations include conflicts with social norms,[49] conflicts with other areas of the law,[50] relational limitations,[51] institutional competence and administrative difficulties,[52] and deference to "discretionary decisions of another branch of government."[53] Contrary to most states when deciding duty issues, foreseeability is not among the factors considered. As stated by the Restatement (Third) PEH,

> These reasons of policy and principle do not depend on the foreseeability of harm based on the specific facts of a case. They should be articulated directly without obscuring reference to foreseeability. . . .
>
> Despite widespread use of foreseeability in no-duty determinations, this Restatement disapproves that practice and limits no-duty rulings to articulated policy or principle in order to facilitate more transparent explanations of the reasons for a no-duty ruling and to protect the traditional function of the jury as factfinder.[54]

The counter argument is that application of various factors could be manipulated or obscure explanations just as easily as the concept of foreseeability. Clarity could remain elusive, and transparency stay an unrealized dream.

---

[45] "When liability depends on factors specific to an individual case, the appropriate rubric is scope of liability. On the other hand, when liability depends of factors applicable to categories of actors or patterns of conduct, the appropriate rubric is duty. No-duty rules are appropriate only when a court can promulgate relatively clear, categorical, bright-line rules of law applicable to a general class of cases." RESTATEMENT (THIRD) OF TORTS: LIABILITY FOR PHYSICAL AND EMOTIONAL HARM § 7 (b) cmt. a (2012).

[46] *Id.* at cmt. j.

[47] *Id.* at cmt. b.

[48] *Id.* at cmt. j.

[49] *Id.* at cmt. c.

[50] *Id.* at cmt. d.

[51] *Id.* at cmt. e.

[52] *Id.* at cmt. f.

[53] *Id.* at cmt. g.

[54] *Id.* at cmt. j.

Currently, most courts use foreseeability as a key factor in duty cases. For example, a court deciding whether a shopkeeper has a duty to protect customers from criminal acts typically hinges on the court, at least, considering the foreseeability of a criminal act under the circumstances. The Restatement (Third) PEH would ask if the case fell within a category of cases in which no duty was owed, failing to examine the particular facts of the case. If policy and principle did not justify a no-duty rule for a class of cases, then a duty is presumed if there was a risk of harm. Consider alternately a case where a driver negligently causes a noisy automobile collision. The noise frightens a horse in a nearby field, causing the horse to stampede and run five miles. Then, the runaway horse strikes its owner, knocking her unconscious, and throwing the owner twenty feet into a pond. Alas, the owner drowns. Most courts would examine foreseeability in ascertaining whether the driver of the car owed a duty to the owner of the horse. The Restatement (Third) PEH would presume there was a duty. Examining if there is a duty in an individual case is prohibited. Only if the facts of the case fit into a "class of cases" where there is no-duty due to policy and principle[55] could a court conclude that there was no duty.[56]

The scholarly debate regarding duty and the Restatement (Third) PEH's proposal will likely continue.[57] The judicial reaction to the Restatement's (Third) PEH's approach has been lukewarm.[58] It is safe to say that most courts have not been faced with the question of whether to adopt the approach of the Restatement (Third) PEH, and slightly more courts

[55] This case really doesn't conflict with social norms or other areas of the law. There would not appear to be a relationship limitation nor would it interfere with another branch of government. This scenario would not appear to call into play institutional competence or administrative difficulties. The policies and principles outlined in the *Restatement (Third) PEH* would not appear to justify a no-duty rule to a "class of cases." RESTATEMENT (THIRD) OF TORTS: LIABILITY FOR PHYSICAL AND EMOTIONAL HARM § 7 cmts. c, d, e, f, & g (2012).

[56] Although the *Restatement (Third) PEH* would not decide this case under duty, it would be appropriate to consider "scope of liability," which would be a question of fact for the jury. The driver would be liable if the risk was included within the risks created by his behavior. The immediate response might be drowning is not within the risk created by a car accident. However, the precise details of an accident or manner of occurrence is not considered significant. Death by downing or death by collision is still death. Death is a risk that falls within the cluster of risks that are created by negligently causing a car accident. Again, results could still be equally arguable or obscure under the *Restatement (Third) PEH.*

[57] On *Restatement (Third) PEH* and duty, *see* W. Jonathan Cardi, *Purging Foreseeability: The New Vision of Duty and Judicial Power in the Proposed Restatement (Third) of Torts*, 58 VAND. L. REV. 739 (2005); W. Jonathan Cardi & Michael D. Green, *Duty Wars*, 81 S. CAL. L REV. 671 (2008); Alani Golanski, *A New Look at Duty in Tort Law: Rehabilitating Foreseeability and Related Themes,* 75 ALB. L. REV. 227 (2012); John H. Marks, *The Limit to Premises Liability for Harms Caused by "Known or Obvious" Dangers: Will it Trip and Fall Over the Duty-Breach Framework Emerging in the Restatement (Third) of Torts?* 38 TEX. TECH. L. REV. 1 (2005); Mike Steenson, *Minnesota Negligence Law and the Restatement (Third) of Torts: Liability for Physical and Emotional Harms*, 37 WILLIAM MITCHELL L. REV., 1055 (2011); Aaron D. Twerski, *The Cleaver, The Violin, and the Scalpel: Duty and the Restatement (Third) of Torts*, 60 HASTINGS L.J. 1 (2008); Thomas B. Read, et al., *The Restatement (Third), Duty, Breach of Duty and "Scope of Liability,"* 14, No. 3, *Iowa Defense Counsel Assoc., Defense Update*, 1 (Summer 2012).

[58] For states adopting the *Restatement (Third) PEH* § 7, *see, e.g.,* Gipson v. Kasey, 214 Ariz. 141, 150 P.3d 228, 231 (2007); Thompson v. Kaczinski, 774 N.W. 2d 829 (Iowa 2009); Latzel v. Bartek, 288 Neb. 1, 846 N.W. 2d 153, 162 (2014).

have rejected it than accepted it when specifically confronted with the issue.[59] Simply said, "foreseeability plays a role in the analysis of duty."[60] "Duty to foresee is often the most salient policy issue constituent within the larger duty determination."[61] Foreseeability "clarifies duty's parameters and helps send to the jury those cases in which enforcing an obligation to foresee is deemed normatively desirable."[62] Respect for precedent, stare decisis, and familiarity will likely be the winning arguments. "[T]he role of foreseeability gives courts appropriate gatekeeping responsibilities consistent with the traditions and policy of negligence law, and . . . it is a familiar system to judges and lawyers who understand it and know how to apply it."[63] Even if the Restatement (Third) PEH does not develop an enthusiastic throng, its most lasting contribution to the development of tort law may be "inviting courts to evaluate their own negligence law to determine whether it is structured in a clear way that judges and lawyers can understand and apply with consistency and that achieves proper balance in the judge-jury relationship."[64]

Courts will continue to be confronted with arguments to endorse the position of the Restatement (Third) PEH and adopt "scope of liability" instead of proximate cause, apply the "risk test" rather than foreseeability to resolve proximate cause issues, abandon the substantial factor test in favor of "but-for" causation, adopt the presumption of duty, and only apply no-duty rules to a category of cases based on solid principles that do not include foreseeability as a factor. Hopefully, this book, *Negligence Purpose, Elements, and Evidence: The Role of Foreseeability in the Law of Each State*, illustrates the continued importance of the concept of foreseeability and its use in the law of the vast majority of jurisdictions, and that the position of the Restatement (Third) PEH is the arguable outlier. If this book also proves useful to the legal profession as both a basic research tool and also as a refresher on basic tort law, then *Negligence Purpose, Elements, and Evidence: The Role of Foreseeability in the Law of Each State* will be a successful publication. It will have attained its intended purposes.

---

[59] *See, e.g.,* Wilson v. Moore Freightservice, Inc., No. 4:14-CV-00771, 2015 WL 1345261, at *5 (Pa. D. Mar. 25, 2015); Goodwin v. Yeakle's Sports Bar & Grill, Inc., 62 N.E. 3d 384, 390 (Ind. 2016); Cannizzaro v. Marinyak, 57 A.3d 830, 837 (Conn. Ct. App. 2012); Cullum v. McCool, 432 S.W. 3d 829 (Tenn. 2013); Tesar v. Anderson, 789 N.W. 2d 351, 357, n.13 (Wisc. Ct. App. 2010). In *Cullum,* the concurring judge urged the use of the *Restatement (Third) PEH. Cullum,* 432 S.W. 3d at 839 (Holder, J., concurring & dissenting). The Wisconsin Court of Appeals asked the question, "Why mess with success?" *Tesar,* 789 N.W. 2d at 357, n.13.

[60] Goodwin v. Yeakle's Sports Bar & Grill, Inc., 62 N.E. 3d 384, 390 (Ind. 2016).

[61] Alani Golanski, *A New Look at Duty in Tort Law: Rehabilitating Foreseeability and Related Themes,* 75 ALB. L. REV. 227, 278 (2012).

[62] *Id.* "Foreseeability in duty is a resilient hybrid factor tending to meld duty A (whether the protected group should be deemed closely enough situated to warrant defendant's consideration) and duty B (whether the defendant should be vigilant or investigate) concerns." *Id.*

[63] Mike Steenson, *Minnesota Negligence Law and the Restatement (Third) of Torts: Liability for Physical and Emotional Harms,* 37 WILLIAM MITCHELL L. REV., 1055, 1058 (2011).

[64] *Id.* at 1133.

CHAPTER 1

ALABAMA

ALABAMA
Michael M. Blue[1]

I. Purpose of Tort Law

The policy of Alabama's common law is to protect people's safety, the safety of families, and the safety of the general public. "The purpose of tort law, at least since the beginning of the 20th Century, has been to provide a civil remedy in situations where the plaintiff's legally protected interests have been injured by the defendant's violation of publicly imposed duties."[2] "The historical and traditional purpose of tort law has been to protect persons against unreasonable risks."[3]

Tort liability has been imposed to protect public policy, deter wrongdoing, and compensate those injured by violations of public policy. "Liability . . . attaches solely because the defendant has exposed" the public "to unreasonable risks."[4] "This is morally and legally correct."[5] "[T]he settled policy of our system of tort law is to place the responsibility for compensation for an injury on the party that proximately causes the injury."[6] "Compensatory damages are designed to make the plaintiff whole by reimbursing him or her for the loss or harm suffered."[7]

It is an accepted public policy to deter wrongdoing through civil actions and imposition of civil damages.[8]

---

[1] Personal Injury & Wrongful Death Attorney, BLUE LAW, Oklahoma City, OK, Member, Oklahoma Bar Association.

[2] Geohagan v. Gen. Motors Corp., 291 Ala. 167, 180, 279 So.2d 436, 448 (1973).

[3] Casrell v. Altec Indus., Inc., 335 So.2d 128, 131 (Ala. 1976); *see also* Atkins v. Am. Motors Corp., 335 So.2d 134, 140 (Ala. 1976) ("The historical and traditional purpose of tort law has been to protect individuals against" . . . "an unreasonable risk of harm.").

[4] Atkins v. Am. Motors Corp., 335 So.2d 134, 141 (Ala. 1976).

[5] *Id.*; *see also* W. KEETON, D. DOBBS, R. KEETON, & D. OWEN, PROSSER AND KEETON ON THE LAW OF TORTS 37 (5th ed. 1984) ("There is a definite tendency to impose greater responsibility upon a defendant whose conduct was intended to do harm, or was morally wrong.").

[6] King v. Nat'l Spa & Pool Inst., Inc., 607 So.2d 1241, 1247 (Ala. 1992); *see also* First Nat'l Bank of Auburn v. Dowdell, 275 Ala. 622, 625, 157 So.2d 221, 223 (1963) (recognizing that a company, corporation or association "must be held accountable for its torts").

[7] *Ex parte* Moebes, 709 So.2d 477, 478 (Ala. 1997); *see also* RESTATEMENT (FIRST) OF TORTS § 901 (1939) discussing some of the purposes for which tort actions are maintainable: "(a) to give compensation, indemnity or restitution for harms; (b) to determine rights; (c) to punish wrongdoers and deter wrongful conduct; and (d) to vindicate parties and deter retaliation or violent and unlawful self-help."

[8] *See, e.g.,* United States v. Stanley, 483 U.S. 669, 695, n.13, 107 S. Ct. 3054, 3071, 97 L. Ed. 2d 550 (1987) (in discussing the issue of qualified immunity for governmental officials, the Court stated: "Civil damages compensate victims of wrongdoing and deter tortious conduct . . ."); Carey v. Piphus, 435 U.S. 247, 256-7, 98 S.Ct. 1042, 1048-9, 55 L.Ed.2d 252 (1978) (recognizing the "formidable" deterrent effect "inherent in the award of compensatory damages.").

II.   Duty to Exercise Reasonable Care

A.   *Question of Law*

"The duty to use due care not to harm the person or property of another is of common law origin."[9] "In general, 'every person owes every other person a duty imposed by law to be careful not to hurt him.'"[10] "A duty of care arises when it is foreseeable that harm may result if care is not exercised."[11] Alabama has also recognized a duty to foreseeable third parties, based on a general "obligation imposed in tort to act reasonably."[12] It is a right of property or of life and liberty safeguarded by due process and other features of the Alabama Constitution.[13]

In determining whether a duty exists in a given situation, however, courts will consider a number of factors, including public policy, social considerations, and foreseeability.[14] "The key factor is whether the injury was foreseeable by the defendant."[15]

The duty to prevent harm to others is embodied within Alabama's negligence law. Duty "is essentially a public policy question, *i.e.*, whether the law should impose a requirement on the defendant that it do or refrain from doing some act for the safety and well-being of the plaintiff."[16] A duty of care arises when it is foreseeable that harm may result if care is not exercised.[17] Alabama recognizes that a negligence claim may be based upon "a common-law duty arising from the foreseeability of physical harm resulting from the defendant's failure to follow its policies concerning the safety of the public."[18]

Whether the defendant has a duty to exercise care towards the plaintiff is a question of law for the court to determine.[19] "In determining whether a duty exists in a given situation . . . courts should consider a number of factors, including public policy, social considerations, and foreseeability. The key factor is whether the injury was foreseeable by the defendant."[20]

---

[9] Pickett v. Matthews, 238 Ala. 542, 546, 192 So 261, 264 (1939).

[10] Smitherman v. McCafferty, 622 So.2d 322, 324 (Ala. 1993) (quoting Se. Greyhound Lines v. Callahan, 244 Ala. 449, 453, 13 So.2d 660, 663 (1943)).

[11] Lance, Inc. v. Ramanauskas, 731 So.2d 1204, 1208 (Ala. 1999).

[12] Berkel & Co. Contractors, Inc. v. Providence Hosp., 454 So.2d 496, 502 (Ala.1984).

[13] Pickett v. Matthews, 238 Ala. 542, 546, 192 So 261, 264 (1939); ALA. CONST. art I, § 10 ("That no person shall be barred from prosecuting or defending before any tribunal in this state, by himself or counsel, any civil cause to which he is a party."); ALA. CONST. art I, § 11 ("That the right of trial by jury shall remain inviolate."); Ala. Const. art. I, § 13 ("That all courts shall be open; and that every person, for any injury done him, in his lands, goods, person, or reputation, shall have a remedy by due process of law; and right and justice shall be administered without sale, denial, or delay.").

[14] Patrick v. Union State Bank, 681 So.2d 1364, 1368 (Ala. 1996) (quoting Smitherman v. McCafferty, 622 So.2d 322, 324 (Ala. 1993)).

[15] *Id.*

[16] Buchanan v. Merger Enters., Inc., 463 So.2d 121, 125 (Ala. 1984).

[17] Hannah v. Gregg, Bland & Berry, Inc., 840 So.2d 839, 857 (Ala. 2002).

[18] Armstrong Bus. Servs., Inc. v. AmSouth Bank, 817 So.2d 665, 680 (Ala. 2001).

[19] Pritchett v. ICN Med. All., Inc., 938 So.2d 933, 937 (Ala. 2006) (quoting Taylor v. Smith, 892 So.2d 887, 891–92 (Ala. 2004) ("In Alabama, the existence of a duty is a strictly legal question to be determined by the court.")).

[20] Patrick v. Union State Bank, 681 So.2d 1364, 1368 (Ala. 1996) (quoting Smitherman v. McCafferty, 622 So.2d 322, 324 (Ala. 1993)).

"The ultimate test of a duty to use care is found in the foreseeability that harm may result if care is not exercised."[21] The defendant's "knowledge of a dangerous condition may establish foreseeability."[22] In addition to the key factor of foreseeability of the injury, Alabama courts look to a number of factors to determine whether a duty exists, including: "(1) the nature of the defendant's activity; (2) the relationship between the parties; and (3) the type of injury or harm threatened."[23] The essential question is "whether the plaintiff's interests are entitled to legal protection against the defendant's conduct."[24]

"Where the facts upon which the existence of a duty depends, are disputed, the factual dispute is for resolution by the jury."[25] The jury must decide how a reasonably careful or prudent person must act in the same or similar situation.[26] The reasonableness determination considers, indeed balances, the burden on the defendant of preventing the harm against the severity and likelihood of the injury the plaintiff faces. Primary factors to consider in ascertaining whether the person's conduct lacks reasonable care are the foreseeable likelihood that the person's conduct will result in harm, the foreseeable severity of any harm that may ensue, and the burden of precautions to eliminate or reduce the risk of harm.[27]

B. Question of Fact

i. Elements

"It has long been held that the amount of care required by the standard of reasonable conduct is commensurate with the apparent risk or danger."[28] "The jury determines what level

---

[21] Bush v. Ala. Power Co., 457 So.2d 350, 353 (Ala.1984) (citing Havard v. Palmer & Baker Eng'rs, Inc., 293 Ala. 301, 302 So.2d 228 (1974)). "[T]he eye of vigilance perceives the risk of damage. . . . The risk reasonably to be perceived defines the duty to be obeyed, and risk imports relation; it is risk to another or to others within the range of apprehension." King v. Nat'l Spa & Pool Inst., Inc., 570 So.2d 612, 616 (Ala. 1990) (quoting Palsgraf v. Long Island R.R., 248 N.Y. 339, 344, 162 N.E. 99, 100 (1928)).

[22] DiBiasi v. Joe Wheeler Elec. Membership Corp., 988 So.2d 454, 462-63 (Ala. 2008).

[23] Taylor v. Smith, 892 So.2d 887, 892 (Ala. 2004) (quoting Morgan v. South Cent. Bell Tel. Co., 466 So.2d 107, 114 (Ala. 1985)).

[24] Smitherman v. McCafferty, 622 So.2d 322, 324 (Ala. 1993) (quoting W. Page Keeton et al., Prosser and Keeton on the Law of Torts § 53, at 357 (5th ed. 1984)).

[25] Ala. Power Co. v. Brooks, 479 So.2d 1169, 1175 (Ala. 1985) (quoting Ala. Power Co. v. Alexander, 370 So.2d 252, 254 (Ala. 1979)).

[26] Galaxy Cable, Inc. v. Davis, 58 So.3d 93, 99 (Ala. 2010) ("The duty of care is an objective standard determined by what an ordinary careful and prudent person would have done under the same or similar circumstances."); Bullen v. Roto Finishing Sys., 435 So.2d 1256, 1259 (Ala. 1983) ("Where not only the facts constituting the conduct of parties, but also the standard of care which they should have exercised, are to be determined, the case is entirely one of fact to be decided by the jury."). The jury will be instructed: "You must decide if the defendant (name of defendant) was negligent in this situation." APJI (3d) 28.00, 28.01.

[27] 1 Restatement (Third) of Torts: Liability for Physical and Emotional Harm § 3 (2010). In his classic formulation, Judge Learned Hand wrote that whether a person is negligent "is a function of three variables: (1) The probability [of injury]; (2) the gravity of the resulting injury, if [it occurs]; (3) the burden of adequate precautions." United States v. Carroll Towing Co., 159 F.2d 169, 173 (2d Cir. 1947). Thus, to exercise reasonable care one must take a precaution if the cost of doing so is less than the probability of injury times the magnitude of the potential injury. Id.

[28] Indus. Chem. & Fiberglass Corp. v. Chandler, 547 So.2d 812 (Ala. 1988); McClusky v. Duncan, 216 Ala. 388, 113 So. 250 (1927); see also King v. Nat'l Spa & Pool Inst., Inc., 570 So.2d 612, 615-16 (Ala. 1990)

of care is required to satisfy the duty to exercise ordinary care under the circumstances.[29] "In other words, where not only the facts constituting the conduct of the parties, but also the standard of care which they should have exercised, are to be determined the case is entirely one of fact to be decided by the jury."[30] "Reasonable care requires conduct commensurate with the danger to be reasonably apprehended."[31] Reasonableness is a fact question for the jury.[32]

ii.   Evidence

The plaintiff must present evidence of the level of care required. Evidence of how others would act in the same or similar circumstances is admissible to establish the level of care required.[33] Evidence of the foreseeable frequency and severity of the harm is also admissible to determine the level of care required.[34]

In closing, counsel may remind the jury that they are "setting a standard" for everyone, or "sending a message" to a class of defendants, when they determine how a reasonably careful person would have acted under the circumstances.[35]

Industry standards, practices and codes; ordinances; statutes; regulations; safety rules; manuals; and other technical materials are relevant to the issue of duty, lack of due care, reasonable care and negligence.[36] "Such evidence is not conclusive on this issue, but

---

("In *Palsgraf*, . . . Justice Cardozo wrote: '[T]he eye of vigilance perceives the risk of damage. . . . The risk reasonably to be perceived defines the duty to be obeyed, and risk imports relation; it is risk to another or to others within the range of apprehension.' 248 N.Y. at 344, 162 N.E. at 100."); Bobo v. Tenn. Valley Auth., 138 F. Supp. 3d 1285, 1311, n. 173 (N.D. Ala. 2015) ("[T]he orbit of the danger as disclosed to the eye of reasonable vigilance would be the orbit of the duty. . . . The risk reasonably to be perceived defines the duty to be obeyed, and risk imports relation; it is risk to another or to others within the range of apprehension.") (quoting Palsgraf v. Long Island R. Co., 248 N.Y. 339, 343–44, 162 N.E. 99, 100 (N.Y. Ct. App. 1928)).

[29] Adams v. Coffee Cty., 596 So.2d 892, 895 (Ala. 1992) ("[T]he question whether a person has exercised due care is still normally a question of fact for the jury to determine."); Senn v. Ala. Gas Corp., 619 So.2d 1320, 1322 (Ala. 1993) ("Whether a person involved in an accident acted reasonably in operating his motor vehicle depends on all of the circumstances surrounding the accident; the question is ordinarily one for the jury.").

[30] Patterson v. Seibenhener, 273 Ala. 204, 206-7, 137 So.2d 758, 760 (1962).

[31] Mobile & O.R. Co. v. Williams, 221 Ala. 402, 407, 129 So 60, 64 (1930).

[32] Simpson v. Wolf Ridge Corp., 486 So.2d 418, 420 (Ala. 1986).

[33] King v. Nat'l Spa & Pool Inst., Inc., 570 So.2d 612, 616 (Ala.1990) ("In Alabama, evidence that a defendant manufacturer complied with or failed to comply with industry standards, such as the standards promulgated by the trade association in this case, is admissible as evidence of due care or the lack of due care."); Dunn v. Wixom Bros., 493 So.2d 1356, 1360 (Ala.1986) (Although "[p]roof of industry practices . . . cannot conclusively establish the defendant's duty," they are "admissible for the jury's consideration in its application of the 'reasonable care' standard.").

[34] Taylor v. Smith, 892 So.2d 887, 892 (Ala. 2004); Indus. Chem. & Fiberglass Corp. v. Chandler, 547 So.2d 812, 818, n. 1 (Ala. 1988); Mobile & O.R. Co. v. Williams, 221 Ala. 402, 407, 129 So. 60, 64 (1930).

[35] Precise Eng'g, Inc. v. LaCombe, 624 So.2d 1339, 1343 (Ala. 1993) (Objections to arguments suggesting the jury's verdict would "send a message" to the defendant's industry were sustained by the trial judge. The Alabama Supreme Court held counsel's remarks in closing argument were not reversible error. "[W]e fail to see how any argument about sending a message to the industry probably prejudiced [defendant].").

[36] Galaxy Cable, Inc. v. Davis, 58 So.3d 93, 99 (Ala. 2010) ("We recognize that evidence of a defendant's compliance with applicable industry standards may be relevant and admissible for purposes of determining whether a defendant breached a duty of care it owed an injured plaintiff."); Standard Plan, Inc. v. Tucker, 582 So.2d 1024

is evidence of due care or lack of due care, to be evaluated by the trier of fact with other evidence on this issue."[37]

Statutes, rules and regulations, safety codes, and other laws which protect people's safety create a duty of reasonable care which can be enforced in a common law negligence action. "[I]t has been held that generally any violation of a statute is a *delict*, and that a violation of a penal statute may also constitute a civil tort."[38] Rules and regulations enacted by administrative agencies and boards pursuant to the powers delegated to them have the force and effect of law, and are relevant to the applicable standard of care.[39] Rules and regulations are highly material and relevant to the issue of the level of care required.[40] Alabama Courts must take judicial notice of any such rules.[41]

Violation of a rule, regulation, ordinance or statute may be used to establish negligence by showing (1) that the rule, regulation, ordinance or statute the defendant is charged with violating was enacted to protect a class of persons to which the plaintiff belonged; (2) that the plaintiff's injury was the kind of injury contemplated by the rule, regulation, ordinance or statute; (3) that the defendant violated the rule, regulation, ordinance or statute; and (4) that the defendant's violation of the rule, regulation, ordinance or statute proximately caused the plaintiff's injury.[42]

(Ala.1991) (holding that expert's opinion as to insurance-industry standard was admissible as long as a proper foundation was laid); King v. Nat'l Spa & Pool Inst., Inc., 570 So.2d 612 (Ala.1990) ("In Alabama, evidence that a defendant manufacturer complied with or failed to comply with industry standards, such as the standards promulgated by the trade association in this case, is admissible as evidence of due care or the lack of due care."); Dunn v. Wixom Bros., 493 So.2d 1356, 1360 (Ala.1986) (Although "[p]roof of industry practices . . . cannot conclusively establish the defendant's duty," they are "admissible for the jury's consideration in its application of the 'reasonable care' standard."); Knight v. Burns, Kirkley & Williams Const. Co., 331 So.2d 651, 654 (Ala. 1976) ("Under proper circumstances Occupational Safety and Health Act provisions and regulations may be admissible for a jury to consider in determining the standard of care that a defendant should have followed . . ."); City of Dothan v. Hardy, 237 Ala. 603, 188 So. 264 (1939) (upholding the admission into evidence of "Safety Rules For the Installation and Maintenance of Electrical Supply and Communication Lines from the 'Handbook of The Bureau of Standards, No. 10,' for the jury to consider in determining whether a defendant was negligent or not. These safety rules were promulgated by an agency of the United States Government.").

[37] King v. Nat'l Spa & Pool Inst., Inc., 570 So.2d 612, 616 (Ala. 1990).

[38] Tenneco Oil Co. v. Clevenger, 363 So.2d 316, 318 (Ala. Civ. App. 1978) (emphasis added).

[39] Hand v. State Dep't of Human Res., 548 So.2d 171, 173 (Ala. Civ. App. 1988) ("[R]egulations are regarded as having the force of law and, therefore, become a part of the statutes authorizing them."); Thompson v. West, 883 F. Supp. 1502, 1506 (M.D. Ala. 1995) ("Regulations, properly promulgated, have the force and effect of law.").

[40] Rice v. Merritt, 549 So.2d 508, 511 (Ala. Civ. App. 1989) (holding the "State Fire Code promulgated by statutory authority" had "the force and effect of state law" and served as the yardstick to measure the defendant's acts.).

[41] Parsons v. State, 251 Ala. 467, 475, 38 So.2d 209, 214 (1948) ("'[A] regulation by a department of government, addressed to and reasonably adapted to the enforcement of an act of Congress, the administration of which is confided to such department, has the force and effect of law . . .'" "And the courts take judicial notice of them."); State v. Friedkin, 244 Ala. 494, 497, 14 So.2d 363, 366 (1943) ("We prefer to accept the principle that the rules and regulations validly adopted by the board under this Act have the force and effect of law, of which courts take judicial knowledge.").

[42] Cook's Pest Control, Inc. v. Rebar, 28 So.3d 716, 726 (Ala. 2009) (quoting Dickinson v. Land Developers Constr. Co., 882 So.2d 291, 302 (Ala. 2003). "Violation of statutes or ordinances may be negligence. . . . If the statute or ordinance violated was enacted or promulgated for the protection of the person claiming to have been injured by reason of the violation, the violation of the statute may be negligence per se or negligence as

Safety rules are relevant and admissible to show the level of care required.[43] Safety rules, including those in published textbooks, treatises, periodicals, bulletins, pamphlets, essay, or other literature, are admissible through an expert witness to establish the standard of care.[44]

Company policies of the defendant are also proper evidence as proof of the level of care required.[45]

---

a matter of law." Proctor v. Classic Auto., Inc., 20 So.3d 1281, 1287 (Ala. Civ. App. 2009) (quoting Keeton v. Fayette County, 558 So.2d 884, 887 (Ala. 1989)); *but see* Parker Bldg. Servs. Co. v. Lightsey *ex rel.* Lightsey, 925 So.2d 927 (Ala. 2005) (Violation of building code adopted by city ordinance did not constitute negligence per se because building code was adopted for the benefit of "general public" and not for benefit of a distinguishable class of persons).

[43] Watkins v. City of Montgomery, 930 F. Supp. 2d 1302, 1310 (M.D. Ala. 2013), *aff'd sub nom.* Watkins v. City of Montgomery, Ala., 775 F.3d 1280 (11th Cir. 2014) (recognizing relevance of "safety rules of major significance and workplace conduct rules."); *Ex parte* Spivey, 846 So.2d 322, 326 (Ala. 2002) (recognizing that "safety rules, regulations, and procedures," such as "safety rules including regulations promulgated by the Occupational Safety and Health Administration" are standards reflecting "good practice."); Hawkins v. Miller, 569 So.2d 335, 338 (Ala. 1990) (plaintiff's claim that his employer failed "to provide a reasonably safe place to work" was based, in part, upon the employer's failure to "implement safety rules."); Ala. Power Co. v. Capps, 519 So.2d 1328, 1329 (Ala. 1988) (agreeing "Alabama Power Company, was on notice of a dangerous condition and, in violation of their own and the industry's accepted safety rules, took no action to inspect or correct the problem and the resulting low hanging uninsulated wire caused the death of (plaintiff's decedent)."); *see also* Magee v. Williams, 17 So.3d 687, 689 (Ala. Civ. App. 2009) (concluding it was not error for the jurors to consider "safety rules" for pedestrians and drivers outlined in the Alabama Safety Institute Driver Education Course Manual).

[44] Price v. Mgmt. Safety, Inc., 485 So.2d 1093, 1097, n. 1 (Ala. 1986). The court stated, as follows:

Federal safety regulations for plants such as (defendant's) operation (placed into evidence in this case by the report of (plaintiff's) expert in opposition to (defendant's) motion for summary judgment) are "for the jury to consider in determining whether a defendant was negligent or not," and we have written of them: "These safety rules were promulgated by an agency of the United States Government. Under proper circumstances Occupational Safety and Health Act provisions and regulations may be admissible for a jury to consider in determining the standard of care that a defendant should have followed, if properly introduced in accordance with the requirements of [City of Dothan v. Hardy, 237 Ala. 603, 188 So. 264 (1939)]."

Knight v. Burns, Kirkley & Williams Constr. Co., 331 So.2d 651, 654 (Ala.1976); *see also* City of Dothan v. Hardy, 237 Ala. 603, 607, 188 So. 264, 266 (1939) (treatises, codes and excerpts from books to which "sworn evidence of an expert witness that such treatise is esteemed by the professions as good authority on the subject," may be considered as proof relevant to the question of negligence.); Hrynkiw v. Trammell, 96 So.3d 794, 808 (Ala. 2012) ("Alabama has long been in the minority of jurisdictions in permitting the admissibility of learned treatises as substantive evidence in the case."); Ozment v. Wilkerson, 646 So.2d 4, 6 (Ala. 1994) (upholding the trial court's conclusion that "the FDA bulletin would be admitted only if it was shown to qualify as a learned treatise."); Ala. R. Evid. 803 (18): "**Learned Treatises.** To the extent called to the attention of an expert witness upon cross-examination or relied upon by the expert witness in direct examination, statements contained in published treatises, periodicals, or pamphlets on a subject of history, medicine, or other science or art, established as a reliable authority by the testimony or admission of the witness or by other expert testimony or by judicial notice. If admitted, the statements may be read into evidence but may not be received as exhibits.").

[45] Armstrong Bus. Serv., Inc. v. AmSouth Bank, 817 So.2d 665, 680 (Ala. 2001) (Under Alabama law, a duty can be created out of a company's own internal policies, where "the duty that supported the negligence claim was a common-law duty arising from the foreseeability of physical harm resulting from the defendant's failure to follow its policies concerning the safety of the public.").

It should also be pointed out, that even though a defendant has complied with a minimum standard of care, does not mean that defendant's conduct was reasonable. "Under the totality of the circumstances in a particular case, a defendant's conduct, although technically in compliance with a minimal standard, may be unreasonable—even so unreasonable as to constitute wantonness or willfulness."[46]

III.   Breach of Duty

A.   Elements

Negligence is defined as: "The failure to do what an ordinarily prudent person would have done under the circumstances, or the doing of that which an ordinarily prudent person would not have done."[47] "Negligence may consist in the omission to act, as well as in acting."[48] In other words, negligence is any conduct or omission "which falls below the standard established by law for the protection of others against unreasonable risk of harm."[49]

"To establish negligence, the plaintiff must prove: (1) a duty to a foreseeable plaintiff; (2) a breach of that duty; (3) proximate causation; and (4) damage or injury."[50] A plaintiff must prove that a defendant committed an act that would "probably injuriously affect him."[51] "The duty of care is an objective standard determined by what an ordinary careful and prudent person would have done under the same or similar circumstances."[52] The degree of care that an ordinary prudent person would exercise in the situation is decided by the jury.[53]

---

[46] Henderson v. Ala. Power Co., 627 So.2d 878, 880 (Ala. 1993), *abrogated on other grounds,* Ex parte Apicella, 809 So.2d 865 (Ala. 2001), *abrogated on other grounds,* Betterman v. Montana, 136 S. Ct. 1609, 194 L. Ed. 2d 723 (2016) (citing W. KEETON, D. DOBBS, R. KEETON, and D. OWEN, PROSSER AND KEETON ON THE LAW OF TORTS § 36, at 233 (5th ed.)).

[47] Alabama City, G. & A. Ry. Co. v. Bullard, 157 Ala. 618, 623, 47 So. 578, 580 (1908) (quoting WORDS AND PHRASES, vol. 5, p. 4744); *see also* Shanklin v. New Pilgrim Towers, L.P., 58 So.3d 1251, 1256 (Ala. Civ. App. 2010) ("Alabama law defines 'negligence' as 'the omission to do something which a reasonable man, guided by those considerations which ordinarily regulate the conduct of human affairs, would do, or doing something which a prudent and reasonable man would not do, with reference to the situation and knowledge of the parties under all of the attendant circumstances.'").

[48] Lewy Art Co. v. Agricola, 169 Ala. 60, 75, 53 So. 145, 150 (1910).

[49] United States v. Waterman S.S. Corp., 190 F.2d 499, 503 (5th Cir.—Ala. 1951).

[50] Hilyer v. Fortier, No. 1140991, 2017 WL 65346, at *7 (Ala. Jan. 6, 2017) (quoting Lemley v. Wilson, 178 So.3d 834 (Ala. 2015)); *see also* Ala. Power Co. v. Guy, 281 Ala. 583, 591, 206 So.2d 594, 599 (1967) ("Every action in tort consists of three elements: (1) the existence of a legal duty by defendant to plaintiff; (2) a breach of that duty; (3) damage as the proximate result.").

[51] Macrum v. Sec. Trust & Sav. Co., 221 Ala. 419, 422, 129 So. 74, 76 (1930) ("It would seem that the underlying principle (the basis of all actionable torts) is that one owes another the duty fixed by law not negligently or willfully or wrongfully to do an act which will probably injuriously affect him, unless there be legal justification."). Some acts will be deemed to be negligence as a matter of law. *See* Atkins v. Am. Motors Corp., 335 So.2d 134, 141 (Ala. 1976) ("We simply hold that selling a dangerously unsafe product is negligence as a matter of law.").

[52] Galaxy Cable, Inc. v. Davis, 58 So.3d 93, 99 (Ala. 2010) (citing Standifer v. Pate, 291 Ala. 434, 439, 282 So.2d 261, 266 (1973) ("Negligence is the want of such care as an ordinary or reasonably prudent and careful man would exercise under similar circumstances.")).

[53] Morgan Hill Paving Co. v. Fonville, 222 Ala. 120, 125, 130 So. 807, 812 (1930) ("Whether or not in these circumstances . . . the defendant was guilty of negligence, to be judged by what would be the conduct of a reasonably prudent man so circumstanced and with like responsibility, was a question for jury decision.").

B. *Evidence*

Evidence must be presented to show a breach of duty on the part of the defendant.[54] Evidence of the actions taken by the defendant in the situation is essential for the jury to consider in determining whether the defendant exercised due care in the situation.[55] Evidence of breach of duty can be direct or circumstantial.[56] The jury may consider all evidence presented in determining whether the defendant breached the duty of care.[57]

IV. Causation

A. *Elements*

A plaintiff must prove that their injuries were proximately caused by the defendant's failure to exercise due care.[58] "The proximate cause of an injury is the primary moving cause without which it would not have occurred, but which, in the natural and probable sequence of events, produces the injury."[59] Alabama's jury instruction defines "proximate causation" as follows: "naturally and probably brought about the harm," and that "the harm would not have happened without the conduct."[60]

In order to prevail, the plaintiff "must make it appear that it is [1] more likely than not that the conduct of the defendant was [2] a substantial factor in bringing about the harm."[61] "Negligence need not be the sole cause of injury in order to hold the negligent person liable."[62] It is sufficient that his or her negligence, "concurring with one or more

---

[54] Hilyer v. Fortier, No. 1140991, 2017 WL 65346, at *7 (Ala. Jan. 6, 2017); Ala. Power Co. v. Guy, 281 Ala. 583, 591, 206 So.2d 594, 599 (1967).

[55] Morgan Hill Paving Co. v. Fonville, 222 Ala. 120, 125, 130 So. 807, 812 (1930); *see also* Marshall Durbin Co. v. Hartley, 392 So.2d 240, 241 (Ala. Civ. App. 1980) ("When a plaintiff brings a suit and bases his right of recovery upon the negligence of another, he must show a state of facts from which the negligence charged may be reasonably inferred.").

[56] Elba Wood Prod., Inc. v. Brackin, 356 So.2d 119, 123 (Ala. 1978) ("Proof of negligence may be established completely through circumstantial evidence, and if there is evidence that points to any plausible theory of causation, there is a basis for recovery.").

[57] Morgan Hill Paving Co. v. Fonville, 222 Ala. 120, 125, 130 So. 807, 812 (1930).

[58] Lingefelt v. Int'l Paper Co., 57 So.3d 118, 122–23 (Ala. Civ. App. 2010) ("Proximate cause is an act or omission that, in a natural and continuous sequence, unbroken by any new independent causes, produces the injury and without which the injury would not have occurred.") (quoting Martin v. Arnold, 643 So.2d 564, 567 (Ala.1994)); Vines v. Plantation Motor Lodge, 336 So.2d 1338, 1339 (Ala.1976) ("Liability will be imposed only when negligence is the proximate cause of injury; injury must be a natural and probable consequence of the negligent act or omission which an ordinarily prudent person ought reasonably to foresee would result in injury."); City of Mobile v. Havard, 289 Ala. 532, 268 So.2d 805, 810 (1972) ("For an act to constitute actionable negligence, there must be not only some causal connection between the negligent act complained of and the injury suffered, but also the connection must be by a natural and unbroken sequence, without intervening, efficient causes, so that, but-for the negligence of the defendant, the injury would not have occurred.").

[59] City of Mobile v. Havard, 289 Ala. 532, 268 So.2d 805 (1972), *appeal after remand,* Havard v. Palmer & Baker Eng'rs, Inc., 293 Ala. 301, 302 So.2d 228 (1974).

[60] 2 Alabama Pattern Jury Instructions—Civil § 33.00 (3d ed. 2013).

[61] Sheffield v. Owens-Corning Fiberglass Corp., 595 So.2d 443, 450 (Ala. 1992) (quoting RESTATEMENT (SECOND) OF TORTS § 433B, *comment* a (1965)).

[62] Marshall Cty. v. Uptain, 409 So.2d 423, 426 (Ala. 1981).

efficient causes . . . is the proximate cause of the injury."[63] To recover, the plaintiff must show that some general harm, injury or consequence (not the exact injury sustained) to someone in plaintiff's position was foreseeable.[64] Foreseeability for proximate cause is the specific factual showing that establishes the conduct as a cause of the injury. Ordinarily, foreseeability that the defendant's conduct would cause some general harm or consequence is a question of fact for the jury.[65] "Whether or not the defendant's conduct was negligent under the particular circumstances and conditions here involved is best decided by a jury after a full trial."[66]

B.   Evidence

The question of foreseeability on the issue of causation is for the trier of fact.[67] "The question must go to the jury if reasonable inferences from the evidence support the theory of the complaint."[68] Evidence of the foreseeability of harm from the defendant's conduct is probative on the issue of causation and admissible.[69] The jury decides the weight to be given evidence of foreseeability of harm in determining whether the breach of duty caused the harm.[70]

---

[63] Lawson v. Gen. Tel. Co. of Ala., 289 Ala. 283, 267 So.2d 132 (1972) (quoting Shepard v. Gardner Wholesale, Inc., 288 Ala. 43, 256 So.2d 877 (1972)); Chambers v. Cox, 222 Ala. 1, 130 So. 416 (1930).

[64] Smith v. AmSouth Bank, Inc., 892 So.2d 905, 910 (Ala.2004) (Under Alabama law, in determining foreseeability, "it is not necessary to anticipate the *specific* event that occurred, but only that some general harm or consequence would follow.") (emphasis in original); Thetford v. City of Clanton, 605 So.2d 835, 840 (Ala. 1992) ("Foreseeability does not require that the particular consequence should have been anticipated, but rather that some general harm or consequence could have been anticipated.").

[65] Thetford v. City of Clanton, 605 So.2d 835, 840 (Ala.1992) ("Foreseeability is an issue for the jury to resolve.").

[66] Standifer v. Pate, 291 Ala. 434, 439, 282 So.2d 261, 266 (1973); *see also* Whataburger, Inc. v. Rockwell, 706 So.2d 1220, 1224 (Ala. Civ. App. 1997) ("We note that the issues of negligence and proximate cause are normally questions of fact to be determined by a jury.").

[67] Vesta Fire Ins. Corp. v. Milam & Co. Const., 901 So.2d 84, 100 (Ala. 2004) ("The settled rule that the question of proximate cause is usually a question of fact for the jury."); Lance, Inc. v. Ramanauskas, 731 So.2d 1204, 1209-10 (Ala. 1999) ("However, the test is not what [defendant] in fact knew, but whether it was reasonably foreseeable that a failure to maintain the vending machine in a safe condition could cause injury to a third party. . . . Viewing the evidence in the light most favorable to the parents, as we must, we hold that the evidence was sufficient to submit the question of foreseeability to the jury."); Garner v. Covington County, 624 So.2d 1346, 1349 (Ala. 1993) ("The question of proximate causation is ordinarily one for the jury, if reasonable inferences from the evidence support the plaintiff's theory."); *see also* Marshall County v. Uptain, 409 So.2d 423, 425 (Ala. 1981) ("The question of proximate cause is almost always a question of fact to be determined by the jury."); Green v. Ala. Power Co., 597 So.2d 1325 (Ala. 1992); Cain v. Sheraton Perimeter Park South Hotel, 592 So.2d 218 (Ala. 1991).

[68] Lawson v. Gen. Tel. Co. of Ala., 289 Ala. 283, 267 So.2d 132 (1972); Union Cent. Life Ins. Co. v. Scott, 286 Ala. 10, 236 So.2d 328 (1970).

[69] Ala. R. Evid. Rule 401, 402.

[70] Smith v. AmSouth Bank, Inc., 892 So.2d 905, 910 (Ala.2004); Thetford v. City of Clanton, 605 So.2d 835, 840 (Ala. 1992).

V. Damages

A. Elements

The damages in a negligence case caused by defendant's failure to exercise ordinary care are the amount that will compensate the plaintiff for all harm "so he may be made whole again."[71] Alabama allows the following elements of damages for bodily injury: Physical pain and suffering; mental anguish; mental anguish when in the zone of danger; permanent injuries, disabilities and disfigurement; aggravation of pre-existing condition; injury aggravated by disease or other cause; medical expenses, and loss of earnings including impairment to plaintiff's ability to earn.[72] "[T]he jury must award substantial compensation for substantial injuries."[73]

B. Evidence

"A jury determination of the amount of damages is the essence of the right to trial by jury."[74] Assessment of the compensatory damages proven by plaintiff lies squarely in the jury's province and "sacred domain."[75] "Juries are allowed to act upon probable and inferential, as well as direct and positive proof. And when, from the nature of the case, the amount of the damages cannot be estimated with certainty, or only a part of them can be so estimated, we can see no objection to placing before the jury all the facts and circumstances of the case, *having any tendency* to show damages, or their probable amount; so as to enable them to make the most intelligible and probable estimate which the nature of the case will permit.'"[76]

---

[71] Mason v. City of Albertville, 276 Ala. 68, 71, 158 So.2d 924, 927 (1963) ("'Damage' is a species of loss. 'Loss' signifies the act of losing or the thing lost. 'Damage,' in French dommage; Latin, damnum, from demo, take away, signifies the thing taken away, the lost thing which a party is entitled to have restored to him *so that he may be made whole again*. 'Loss' is not a word of limited, hard and fast meaning, and may mean either the act of losing or the thing lost. The term has been held to be synonymous with, or equivalent to, other terms, as for instance, damage, damages, deprivation, detriment, injury, privation.") (emphasis added); Birmingham Waterworks Co. v. Keiley, 2 Ala.App. 629, 637, 56 So. 838, 841 (1911) ("*Actual* damages are recoverable at law, out of a wrongdoer by the injured party *as a matter of right* as *compensation* for the actual loss sustained by him by reason of such wrong.") (emphasis in original).

[72] *Alabama Pattern Jury Instructions 3d* 11.09-11.17.

[73] Stone v. Echols, 351 So.2d 902, 903 (Ala. 1977).

[74] Indus. Chem. & Fiberglass Corp. v. Chandler, 547 So.2d 812, 818, n.1 (Ala. 1988).

[75] Daniels v. E. Ala. Paving, Inc., 740 So.2d 1033, 1044 (Ala.1999) ("[T]his Court has long held that '[t]here is no fixed standard for ascertainment of compensatory damages recoverable . . . for physical pain and mental suffering' and that 'the amount of such [an] award is left to the sound discretion of the jury, subject only to correction by the court for clear abuse or passionate exercise of that discretion.'") (quoting Ala. Power Co. v. Mosley, 294 Ala. 394, 401, 318 So.2d 260, 266 (1975)); Delchamps, Inc. v. Bryant, 738 So.2d 824, 837 (Ala.1999) ("There is no fixed standard for determining the amount of compensatory damages a jury may award for mental anguish. The amount of the damages award is left to the jury's sound discretion, subject only to review by the court for a clear abuse of that discretion."); Cent. Ala. Elec. Co-op. v. Tapley, 546 So.2d 371, 553-56 (Ala.1989) ("[I]n the typical case involving noneconomic damages and punitive damages, once the jury has been instructed on and determines liability, the amount of compensation to be awarded and the extent of punishment to be meted out are subjects unquestionably within the sacred domain of the jury's discretion.").

[76] Am. Life Ins. Co. v. Shell, 265 Ala. 306, 312, 90 So.2d 719, 723 (1956) (emphasis in original) (quoting Story Parchment Co. v. Paterson Parchment Co., 282 U.S. 555, 51 S.Ct. 248, 250, 75 L.Ed. 544 (1931)).

Furthermore, permitting a wrongdoer to avoid paying the full amount of a victim's damages on the grounds that those damages are difficult to calculate or determine with precision, "[w]ould enable the wrongdoer to profit by his wrongdoing at the expense of his victim."[77] "The most elementary conceptions of justice and public policy require [that] the wrongdoer shall bear the risk of the uncertainty which his own wrong has created."[78]

---

[77] Smith v. Atkinson, 771 So.2d 429, 438 (Ala. 2000) (quoting Petrik v. Monarch Printing Corp., 150 Ill.App.3d 248, 261-2, 501 N.E.2d 1312, 1321, 103 Ill.Dec. 774, 783 (1986)).

[78] *Id.*

CHAPTER 2

ALASKA

ALASKA

Gregg W. Luther[1]

I. Purpose of Tort Law

The Alaskan Supreme Court has stated that the purpose of Alaska's tort law is to provide just compensation to the tort victim[2], and that those responsible for the wrongdoing should bear the cost.[3] This purpose shall not be changed.[4] Alaska tort law is designed to achieve social objectives to allow innocent people an avenue of redress against wrongdoers.[5] Tort liability has been imposed to protect public policy, deter wrongdoing,[6] and compensate the innocent.[7]

II. Duty to Exercise Ordinary Care

A. Question of Law

To establish negligence, a plaintiff must prove that the defendant owed a duty to protect the plaintiff from harm.[8] Duty is determined by policy considerations "which lead the law to say a particular plaintiff is entitled to protection."[9] The existence of a duty is a question of law.[10]

The court looks at seven factors to determine whether a duty to exercise care exists. These are: (1) foreseeability of the harm to the plaintiff; (2) the degree of certainty that the plaintiff suffered injury; (3) the closeness of the connection between the defendant's conduct and the injury suffered; (4) the moral blame attached to the defendant's conduct; (5) the policy of preventing future harm; (6) the extent of the burden to the defendant and the consequences to the community of imposing a duty to exercise care with resulting liability for

---

[1] Trial Attorney Alumni, Oklahoma City University Law Review and School of Law.

[2] State Farm Mutual Automobile Insurance Co. v. Weiford, 831 P.2d 1264, 1266 (Alaska 1992); Anderson v. State *ex rel.* Central Bering Sea Fishermen's Ass'n, 78 P.3d 710, 717 (Alaska 2003) (Matthews, J., concurring, joined by Eastbaugh, J.).

[3] Mattingly v. Sheldon Jackson Coll., 743 P.2d 356, 360 (Alaska 1987).

[4] *Id.*

[5] *Id.*

[6] General Motors Corp. v. Farnsworth, 965 P.2d 1209, 1218 (Alaska 1998).

[7] Alaska Placer Co. v. Lee, 553 P.2d 54, 61 (Alaska 1976).

[8] Schumacher v. City & Borough of Yakutat, 946 P.2d 1255, 1257 (Alaska 1997).

[9] Bolieu v. Sisters of Providence in Washington, 953 P.2d 1233, 1235 (Alaska 1988) (quoting PROSSER, THE LAW OF TORTS).

[10] *Id.*

the breach; and (7) the availability, cost and prevalence of insurance for the risk involved.[11] The most important of these factors in imposing duty to exercise care is foreseeability of harm.[12] To be foreseeable, the "manifested harm need only be one of the cluster of harms in a generally foreseeable category."[13] A defendant owes a duty of due care to "all persons who are foreseeably endangered by his conduct, with respect to all risks which make the conduct unreasonably dangerous."[14] With regard to the fifth factor (preventing future harm) the Alaska Supreme Court has stated that its policy is to encourage the enforcement of rules that prevent harm to others.[15]

B. Question of Fact

i. Elements

The jury determines what level of care is required to satisfy the duty to exercise ordinary care in any given situation.[16] The degree of care required for the act undertaken is a question of fact.[17] Conduct is negligent "only if it creates an unreasonable risk of harm to a class of persons which includes the plaintiff."[18] The jury must decide how a reasonably careful person would have acted in the defendant's circumstances to prevent harm to others.[19]

ii. Evidence

The plaintiff must present evidence of the level of care required. To prove that a defendant was negligent, the plaintiff must show that the defendant failed to do what a reasonably prudent person would have done under like circumstances.[20] Violation of a statute, regulation, or ordinance may be considered in determining whether the defendant exercised reasonable care.[21] Where a legislative enactment commands or prohibits action for the safety of others, that enactment established a duty and its violation is negligence *per se*.[22]

---

[11] *Id.*

[12] Id. at 1236.

[13] Hurn v. Greenway, 293 P.3d 480, 487 (Alaska 2013).

[14] Winschel v. Brown, 171 P.3d 142, 146 (Alaska 2007).

[15] Alaskan Village, Inc. v. Smalley, 720 P.2d 945, 948 (Alaska 1986).

[16] Alaska Civil Pattern Jury Instruction § 03.03A (2008).

[17] Williams v. Municipality of Anchorage, 633 P.2d 248, 251 (Alaska 1981).

[18] State v. Guinn, 555 P.2d 530, 536 (Alaska 1976).

[19] Alaska Civil Pattern Jury Instruction § 03.03A (2008) provides: "Negligence is the failure to use reasonable care to prevent harm to oneself or to others. A person can be negligent by acting or by failing to act. A person is negligent if he or she does something that a reasonably careful person would not do in the same situation or fails to do something that a reasonably careful person would do in the same situation. The law does not require exceptional caution or skill, only reasonable care. You must decide how a reasonably careful person would have acted in [plaintiff's] [defendant's] situation."

[20] Mitchell v. Knight, 394 P.2d 892, 894 (Alaska 1964).

[21] Alaska Civil Pattern Jury Instruction § 03.04B (2008).

[22] Bachner v. Rich, 554 P.2d 430, 442 (Alaska 1976).

III. Breach of Duty

A. Elements

Negligence is the failure to use reasonable care to prevent harm to others.[23] The jury must weigh the actions of the defendant "against the standard of conduct of a reasonable prudent person in the same circumstances."[24]

B. Evidence

The plaintiff must establish a breach of duty by the defendant.[25] Alaska courts have permitted experts to testify that a defendant's actions constituted a major life and safety violation, making injury foreseeable.[26] The jury is bound to evaluate the reasonableness of the defendant's actions in light of the evidence of the situation.[27]

IV. Causation

A. Elements

A plaintiff must prove that the defendant's negligence was a substantial factor in causing the plaintiff's harm.[28] This is a two-part test. First, the plaintiff must show that the harm would not have happened "but-for" the defendant's negligence. Second, the defendant's conduct must have been so important that a reasonable person would regard it as the cause and attach responsibility to it.[29] The second part of this test is regarded as proximate cause.[30] Proximate cause is a question of fact, unless reasonable minds cannot differ based on the evidence.[31] Proximate cause requires that the general kind of harm suffered be foreseeable from the defendant's conduct.[32] Whether the negligence is causally connected to the harm is a question of fact.[33]

---

[23] Alaska Civil Pattern Jury Instruction § 03.03A (2008).

[24] Wilson v. Sibert, 535 P.2d 1034, 1036-37 (Alaska 1975).

[25] Silvers v. Silvers, 999 P.2d 786, 793 (Alaska 2000); *see also* Alaska Civil Pattern Jury Instruction § 03.01 (2008), which provides, as follows: "In order to find that the plaintiff is entitled to recover, you must decide it is more likely true than not true that: (1) the defendant was negligent; (2) the plaintiff was harmed; and (3) the defendant's negligence was a substantial factor in causing the plaintiff's harm."

[26] Hinman v. Sobocienski, 808 P.2d 820, 822 (Alaska 1991).

[27] *Wilson*, 535 P.2d at 1037.

[28] Alaska Civil Pattern Jury Instruction § 03.01 (2008).

[29] Robles v. Shoreside Petroleum, Inc., 29 P.3d 838, 841 (Alaska, 2001); s*ee also,* Alaska Civil Pattern Jury Instruction § 03.01 (2008), providing, as follows: "Negligence is a substantial factor in causing harm if: (1) the harm would not have occurred without the negligence; and (2) the negligence was important enough in causing the harm that a reasonable person would hold the negligent person responsible. The negligence cannot be a remote or trivial factor".

[30] *Robles*, 29 P.3d at 841.

[31] Winschel v. Brown, 171 P.3d 142, 148 (Alaska 2007).

[32] *Id.* at 149.

[33] Saddler v. Alaska Marine Lines, Inc., 856 P.2d 784, 789 (Alaska 1993).

B. *Evidence*

Circumstantial evidence, expert testimony, or common knowledge are proper evidence to establish causation.[34] The question of whether harm is foreseeable from the evidence is one of fact for the jury.[35]

V. Damages

A. *Elements*

The damages in a negligence case are the amount that will put the plaintiff, as nearly as possible, in the position that the plaintiff would have been in if the negligence had not occurred.[36]

B. *Evidence*

The party seeking damages bears the burden of proof to establish such damages.[37] The plaintiff must provide the jury with evidence establishing a reasonable basis for computing the award.[38]

---

[34] *Hinman*, 808 P.2d at 823.

[35] P.G. v. State, Dep't of Health & Human Servs., Div. of Family & Youth Servs., 4 P.3d 326, 334-35 (Alaska 2000).

[36] Beaulieu v. Elliott, 434 P.2d 665, 670-71 (Alaska 1967).

[37] Conam Alaska v. Bell Lavalin, Inc., 842 P.2d 148, 154 (Alaska 1992).

[38] *Id.*

CHAPTER 3

ARIZONA

ARIZONA
Sabrina A. Davis[1]

I. Purpose of Tort Law

Arizona courts have identified two primary purposes of tort law: safety and compensation. First, the courts describe the safety aspect in multiple ways, stating that objectives of tort law are to: (1) promote safety,[2] (2) deter careless or negligent conduct,[3] and (3) prevent future harm.[4] This includes "a duty to take affirmative measures to control or avoid increasing the danger from the conduct of others."[5] The second purpose of tort law is to compensate "victims for their actual harm."[6] There are two, sometimes conflicting, principles of tort law in Arizona that further clarify this purpose. They are, as follows: (1) compensation to the injured party is limited "to the amount necessary to make him whole"; and (2) one should avoid "a windfall to the tortfeasor if a choice must be made between him and the injured party."[7]

II. Duty to Exercise Ordinary Care

A. Question of Law

To establish a claim for negligence, a plaintiff must establish there is "a duty requiring the defendant to conform to a certain standard of care."[8] The Arizona Supreme Court defines "duty" as an "obligation, recognized by law, which requires the defendant to conform to a particular standard of conduct in order to protect others against unreasonable risks of harm."[9] Whether a duty exists is a question of law for the court to decide.[10]

The general standard of care in negligence actions is "what a reasonable prudent person would or would not do under the circumstances."[11] However, "those with special skills or

---

[1] Law Library Professor and Reference Librarian, Oklahoma City University School of Law Chickasaw Nation Law Library.

[2] Salt River Project Agr. Imp. & Power Dist. v. Westinghouse Elec. Corp., 694 P.2d 198, 211 (Ariz. 1984).

[3] Marquez v. Rapid Harvest Co., 405 P.2d 814, 817 (Ariz. App. 1965).

[4] Diggs v. Arizona Cardiologists, Ltd., 8 P.3d 386, 390 (Ariz. App. 1st Div. 2000).

[5] Ontiveros v. Borak, 667 P.2d 200, 208-09 (Ariz. 1983).

[6] Carstens v. City of Phoenix, 75 P.3d 1081, 1084 (Ariz. App. 1st Div. 2003).

[7] Hall v. Olague, 579 P.2d 577, 578 (Ariz. App. 2d Div. 1978).

[8] Gipson v. Kasey, 150 P.3d 228, 230 (Ariz. 2007).

[9] *Id.*

[10] *Id.*

[11] Morris v. Ortiz, 437 P.2d 652, 654 (Ariz. 1968).

training [have] the higher obligation to act in light of that skill, training, or knowledge."[12] The court may look at different sources to determine whether a duty to exercise care exists, including controlling case law, state statutes, administrative regulations, and public policy.[13] Some of the factors Arizona courts may consider in their duty analysis include "the reasonable expectations of parties and society generally, the proliferation of claims, the likelihood of unlimited or insurer-like liability, disproportionate risk and reparation allocation, and public policies affecting the expansion or limitation of new channels of liability."[14]

Until 2007, there was conflicting Arizona case law regarding the role of foreseeability in the legal determination of duty. This was resolved by the Arizona Supreme Court in *Gipson v. Kasey*, in which it expressly held "foreseeability is not a factor to be considered by courts when making determinations of duty."[15] The court reasoned that foreseeability is "more properly applied to the factual determinations of breach and causation than to the legal determination of duty."[16]

B.   Question of Fact

i.   Elements

The existence of a duty of care is separate from the standard of care (i.e., what the defendant must do or not do to satisfy the duty).[17] How a defendant must act to satisfy the duty is a jury determination.[18] Foreseeability of harm is a proper consideration for the jury in determining how a defendant must act.[19]

ii.   Evidence

To demonstrate what "reasonable care" requires in a circumstance, the plaintiff must show that "the defendant's conduct presented a foreseeable, unreasonable risk of harm."[20] Evidence of custom and usage is generally admissible as evidence of what level of care is required.[21] A defendant's policies are admissible as evidence of standard of care.[22] Safety rules are also admissible to establish what a defendant must do to satisfy the duty of care.[23] A statute or regulation enacted for public safety that mandates certain conduct is admissible to establish the level of care required.[24]

---

[12] Stanley v. McCarver, 92 P.3d 849, 854 (Ariz. 2004).

[13] *Id.* at 851; Lombardo v. Albu, 14 P.3d 288, 291–92 (Ariz. 2000); *Gipson*, 150 P.3d at 232.

[14] Wertheim v. Pima Cty., 122 P.3d 1, 6 (Ariz. App. 2d Div. 2005).

[15] *Gipson*, 150 P.3d at 231.

[16] *Id.*

[17] Rossell v. Volkswagen of Am., 709 P.2d 517, 521-22 (Ariz. 1985).

[18] *Gipson*, 150 P.3d at 230-31.

[19] *Id.*

[20] *Rossell*, 709 P.2d at 523.

[21] *Id.*

[22] Bell v. Maricopa Med. Cent., 755 P.2d 1180, 1184 (Ariz. App. 1988).

[23] S. Pac. Transp. Co. v. Lueck, 535 P.2d 599, 605 (Ariz. 1975).

[24] Brand v. J.H. Rose Trucking Co., 427 P.2d 519, 523 (Ariz. App. 1967).

III. Breach of Duty

A. Elements

To establish negligence, a plaintiff must also show that the defendant breached his or her duty to conform to the standard of care (that of a reasonable and prudent person).[25] Breach of duty is a factual issue for the jury to decide.[26] This inquiry includes considering "whether there is a foreseeable risk of injury from the conduct."[27]

B. Evidence

Whether there has been a breach of duty is an issue of fact.[28] The jury may consider the details of the defendant's conduct when determining if a breach of duty has occurred.[29] When the plaintiff pleads specific acts of negligence, only evidence limited to those grounds is admissible; i.e., the jury may not consider the doctrine of res ipsa loquitur.[30]

IV. Causation

A. Elements

Arizona case law establishes two standards for causation in a negligence claim, but it does not reconcile when one standard should be used versus the other. First, a defendant may be liable for negligence if his or her conduct contributed to the plaintiff's injuries and the injuries would not have occurred "but-for" the "defendant's conduct, even if that conduct contributed 'only a little' to plaintiff's injuries."[31] Second, a plaintiff can show "it is more likely than not that defendant's conduct was a substantial factor in bringing about the result."[32]

Further, the plaintiff must demonstrate that the defendant's negligent conduct proximately caused the plaintiff's injuries, which is established if "the plaintiff's injury was a foreseeable consequence of the [defendant's] act."[33] A foreseeable event has been defined as one reasonably "expected to occur now and then, and would be recognized as not highly unlikely if it did suggest itself to the actor's mind."[34] Arizona courts have further stated that,

---

[25] *Gipson*, 150 P.3d at 230.

[26] *Id.*

[27] Markowitz v. Ariz. Parks Bd., 706 P.2d 364, 369 (Ariz. 1985).

[28] *Gipson*, 150 P.3d at 230.

[29] *Markowitz*, 706 P.2d at 367.

[30] Martinez v. Jordan, 553 P.2d 1239, 1242 (Ariz. App. 1st Div. 1976). The only Arizona appellate cases expressly permitting consideration of circumstantial evidence in determining breach of duty are those that involve res ipsa loquitur; *see, e.g.,* Jackson v. H. H. Robertson Co., 574 P.2d 822 (Ariz. 1978); Sanchez v. Old Pueblo Anesthesia, P.C., 183 P.3d 1285 (Ariz. App. 2d Div. 2008).

[31] *Ontiveros*, 667 P.2d at 205.

[32] Wisener v. State, 598 P.2d 511, 513 (Ariz. 1979).

[33] Ritchie v. Krasner, 211 P.3d 1272, 1282 (Ariz. App. 1st Div. 2009).

[34] Hill v. Safford Unified Sch. Dist., 952 P.2d 754, 759 (Ariz. App. 2d Div. 1997).

"[t]he proximate cause of an injury is that which, in a natural and continuous sequence, unbroken by any efficient intervening cause, produces an injury, and without which the injury would not have occurred."[35]

B. Evidence

Arizona follows the Restatements, in absence of any law to the contrary.[36] Arizona courts have cited to § 433 of the Restatement (Second) of Torts for factors for the jury to consider when determining if the defendant's actions were a substantial factor in causing the plaintiff's injuries.[37] These factors include: (1) "the number of other factors that contribute in producing the harm and the extent of the effect they have in producing it"; (2) "whether the actor's conduct created a force or series of forces that were in continuous and active operation up to the time of the harm or created a harmless situation unless acted upon by other forces for which the actor was not responsible"; and (3) "lapse of time."[38]

The question of proximate cause is usually reserved for the jury.[39] However, the plaintiff "need only present probable facts from which the causal relationship reasonably may be inferred."[40]

V. Damages

A. Elements

The plaintiff must prove actual damages in order to recover on a negligence claim.[41] The damages awarded should "fairly and adequately compensate" the plaintiff for his or her personal injuries.[42] The goal is to put the plaintiff in the position he or she was in before the injury occurred.[43]

There are two categories of damages, special and general. "[S]pecial damages are those which are the natural but not the necessary consequence of the act complained of and usually stem from the particular circumstances of the case."[44] General damages are those that cannot be computed mathematically[45] and are presumed as a result of the alleged negligent act.[46]

---

[35] Robertson v. Sixpence Inns of Am., Inc., 789 P.2d 1040, 1047 (Ariz. 1990).

[36] Webster v. Culbertson, 761 P.2d 1063, 1066 (Ariz. 1988).

[37] See, e.g., Thompson v. Better-Bilt Aluminum Prods. Co., 832 P.2d 203, 207, n.6 (Ariz. 1992); Barrett v. Harris, 86 P.3d 954, 961, n. 7 (Ariz. App. 1st Div. 2004).

[38] Id.

[39] Markowitz, 706 P.2d at 370.

[40] Robertson, 789 P.2d at 1047.

[41] Gipson, 150 P.3d at 230.

[42] Myers v. Rollette, 439 P.2d 497, 503 (Ariz. 1968).

[43] Strawberry Water Co. v. Paulsen, 207 P.3d 654, 665 (Ariz. App. 1st Div. 2008).

[44] S. Ariz. Sch. for Boys, Inc. v. Chery, 580 P.2d 738, 741 (Ariz. App. 2d Div. 1978).

[45] Palmer v. Kelly, 97 P.2d 209, 210 (Ariz. 1939).

[46] S. Ariz. Sch. for Boys, 580 P.2d at 741.

Special damages must be pled with specificity,[47] but general damages do not require specificity in pleading.[48]

B.   *Evidence*

The plaintiff must show the amount of damages with "reasonable certainty," which requires a "basis for estimating loss that [does] not rest upon 'conjecture or speculation.'"[49] The amount of an award for damages is reserved for the jury, and "such award will not be overturned or tampered with unless the verdict was the result of passion and prejudice" such that it shocks the conscience of the court.[50] Arizona "law does not fix precise rules for the measure of damages," but instead leaves the assessment of damages to the "jury's good sense and unbiased judgment."[51]

---

[47] Ariz. R. Civ. P. 9(g).

[48] *S. Ariz. Sch. for Boys*, 580 P.2d at 741.

[49] Cty. of La Paz v. Yakima Compost Co., 233 P.3d 1169, 1186 (Ariz. App. 1st Div. 2010).

[50] Larriva v. Widmer, 415 P.2d 424, 430 (Ariz. 1966).

[51] Meyer v. Ricklick, 409 P.2d 280, 282 (Ariz. 1965).

CHAPTER 4

ARKANSAS

ARKANSAS
Gregg W. Luther[1]

I. Purpose of Tort Law

The Arkansas Supreme Court has stated that the tort system's primary objectives are compensation and deterrence.[2] It is the policy of Arkansas tort law that people should conduct themselves in a manner to avoid injury to the public.[3] Tort liability is imposed when someone fails to do what is required to protect another from harm.[4] Wrongdoers are held accountable for their actions by bearing responsibility to those harmed.[5] Arkansas tort law seeks to compensate those injured by another's wrongful conduct.[6] The jury acts as the conscience of the community when making its decision.[7]

II. Duty to Exercise Ordinary Care

A. *Question of Law*

The law of negligence requires that the plaintiff show the defendant owed a duty to exercise ordinary care.[8] To be negligent, the defendant's conduct must be one from which a reasonably careful person would foresee an appreciable risk of harm to others.[9] To prove foreseeability of harm, the harm must be "within the range of probability."[10] The concept of risk is an aspect of foreseeability.[11] To recover, a plaintiff must show that they were within a foreseeable group of persons that might be injured by defendant's conduct.[12] It is only necessary that the defendant be able to reasonably foresee an appreciable risk of harm to

---

[1] Trial Attorney, Oklahoma City University Law Review and School of Law alumni.

[2] Georgia-Pacific Corp. v. Carter, 265 S.W.3d 107, 303 (Ark. 2007).

[3] Strange v. Bodcaw Lumber Co., 96 S.W. 152, 154 (Ark. 1906).

[4] *Id.*

[5] Thompson v. Sanford, 663 S.W.2d 932, 934 (Ark. 1984).

[6] Ciba-Geigy Corp. v. Alter, 834 S.W.2d 136, 145 (Ark. 1992).

[7] Williams v. O'Neal Ford, Inc., 668 S.W.2d 545, 546 (Ark. 1984).

[8] Weisker v. Harvest Mgmt. Sub., LLC, 489 S.W.3d 696, 698 (Ark. Ct. App. 2016).

[9] Ethyl Corp. v. Johnson, 49 S.W.3d 644, 648 (Ark. 2001).

[10] *Id.* (quoting Larson Mach., Inc. v. Wallace, 600 S.W.2d 1, 9 (Ark. 1980)).

[11] *Id.* at 648-49 (quoting Wallace v. Broyles, 961 S.W.2d 712 (Ark. 1998)).

[12] Coca-Cola Bottling Co. v. Gill, 100 S.W.3d 715, 725 (Ark. 2003) (quoting Palsgraf v. Long Island R.R., 162 N.E. 99, 99 (N.Y. 1928)).

others, not the precise harm that occurred.[13] Whether a defendant owed the plaintiff a duty to exercise ordinary care is a question of law.[14]

B.   *Question of Fact*

i.   **Elements**

The jury determines what level of care is required to satisfy the duty to exercise ordinary care under similar circumstances.[15]

ii.   **Evidence**

The plaintiff must present evidence of what a reasonably prudent person would do in the same situation to avoid foreseeable risk of harm to others.[16] A plaintiff may establish this with direct or circumstantial evidence, but cannot rely on inferences based on conjecture or speculation.[17] A statute which is designed to protect a class of people may be used as evidence of due care under the circumstances.[18] Industry safety standards are also proper evidence of what a reasonably careful person would do under the circumstances to prevent foreseeable harm to others.[19] Safety rules are proper evidence to establish due care.[20] Where conduct in a circumstance required by a safety rule is relied upon as evidence of due care, the existence and/or evidence of the safety rule must be presented at trial.[21]

III.   **Breach of Duty**

A.   *Elements*

Breach of duty requires a determination by the triers of fact.[22]

B.   *Evidence*

A negligent act is one from which an ordinary prudent person in the actor's position—in the same or similar circumstances—would foresee an appreciable risk of harm to

---

[13] *Coca-Cola Bottling Co.*, 100 S.W.3d at 724.

[14] *Id.*

[15] Wiles v. Webb, 946 S.W.2d 685, 689 (Ark. 1997) (quoting AMI Civ. 3rd 303: "A failure to exercise ordinary care is negligence. When I use the words 'ordinary care,' I mean the care a reasonably careful person would use under circumstances similar to those shown by the evidence in this case. It is for you to decide how a reasonably careful person would act under those circumstances.")

[16] City of Caddo Valley v. George, 9 S.W.3d 481, 486 (Ark. 2000).

[17] *Id.*

[18] Cent. Okla. Pipeline, Inc., v. Hawk Field Servs., LLS, 400 S.W.3d 701, 712 (Ark. 2012).

[19] Ivory v. Woodruff Elec. Coop. Corp., 460 S.W.3d 805, 809 (Ark. Ct. App. 2015).

[20] Missouri Pc. R. Co. v. Davis, 186 S.W.3d 20, 25 (Ark. 1945).

[21] Williams v. First Sec. Bank of Searcy, 738 S.W.2d 99, 101 (Ark. 1987).

[22] Stacks v. Ark. Power & Light Co., 771 S.W.2d 754, 755-56 (Ark. 1989).

others as to cause him to not do an act, or be more careful.[23] Evidence must be presented to show a breach of duty on the part of the defendant.[24]

IV.   Causation

A.   Elements

The uniform rule established by the Arkansas Supreme Court for proximate cause requires that a person of reasonable intelligence be able to foresee that damage might result.[25] To determine whether the defendant's act was the proximate cause, the injury must have been the natural and probable consequence of the act, and such a consequence ought to have been foreseen by the defendant as a likely result.[26] A defendant cannot be liable unless in the exercise of ordinary care, it could have been anticipated or foreseen that the injury might have occurred.[27] However, in 1959 the Arkansas Supreme Court—while differentiating between proximate cause in the context of "the highest degree of care" and "ordinary care"—made the statement that "[f]oreseeability is an element in the determination of whether a person is guilty of negligence and has nothing to do with proximate cause."[28] This quote, without any context, is included in the Comment Section to the Arkansas Model Instruction for Proximate Cause.[29] Two years later, the Arkansas Supreme Court—in deciding whether a defendant's behavior was "merely" a condition, rather than a cause—revived the "ought to have been foreseen" language in the definition of proximate cause.[30] Ironically, the 1961 case is also quoted in the Comment Section of the Arkansas Proximate Cause Instruction, again without any context.[31] In 2001, the Arkansas Supreme Court eliminated all doubt that in order to establish proximate cause the consequences of the negligent act "ought to have been foreseen."[32]

B.   Evidence

The question of whether the negligent act was the proximate cause of the injury is ordinarily a question for the trier of fact.[33] However, where the plaintiff cannot present proof

---

[23] Hill v. Wilson, 224 S.W.2d 797, 800 (Ark. 1949).

[24] Wagner v. Gen. Motors Corp., 258 S.W.3d 749, 753 (Ark. 2007).

[25] Langston v. Moseley, 265 S.W.2d 697, 700 (Ark. 1954).

[26] Id. (citing Gage v. Harvey, 48 S.W. 898 (Ark. 1898)).

[27] Id. (citing LaGrand v. Ark. Oak Flooring Co., 245 S.W. 38 (Ark. 1922)).

[28] Collier v. Citizens Coach Co., 330 S.W.2d 74, 76 (Ark. 1959).

[29] See Comment Section, AMI 501—Proximate Cause—Concurring Proximate Cause—Definition.

[30] Ben M. Hogan & Co. v. Krug, 351 S.W.2d 451, 454-56 (Ark. 1961).

[31] See Comment Section, supra note 28.

[32] "Foreseeability is required. In Arkansas, negligence is the proximate cause only if the injury is the natural and probable consequence of the negligent act and ought to have been foreseen in light of the attending circumstances." Regions Bane & Trust v. Stone Co. Skilled Nursing Facility, Inc., 49 S.W.3d 107, 116 (Ark. 2001) (citing Lindle Shows v. Shibley, 460 S.W.2d 779 (Ark. 1970)). "Foreseeability is an element of a negligence cause of action in Arkansas." Regions Bank & Trust, 49 S.W.3d at 116 (Ark. 2001) (citing Benson v. Shuler Drilling Co., 871 S.W.2d 552 (Ark. 1994)).

[33] Stacks v. Ark. Power & Light Co., 771 S.W.2d 754, 756 (Ark. 1989).

that the consequences of the negligent act were foreseeable, a question of fact on proximate cause has not been created.[34]

V. Damages

A. Elements

The damages in a negligence case must be reasonable and fair.[35]

B. Evidence

Damages must be supported by substantial evidence.[36]

---

[34] Schmoll v. Hartford Cas. Ins., 290 S.W.3d 41, 45 (Ark. Ct. App. 2008).

[35] AMI 2201 Measure of Damages—General Instruction.

[36] Vaccaro Lumber v. Fesperman, 267 S.W.3d 619, 623 (Ark. 2007).

CHAPTER 5

CALIFORNIA

CALIFORNIA

Steven B. Stevens[1]

I. Purpose of Tort Law

Tort law, in its broadest sense, defines the obligations that individuals and entities owe to each other in society. "[T]ort law is primarily designed to vindicate social policy."[2] Social policy promotes safety and deters unreasonable conduct. "One of the purposes of tort law is to deter future harm."[3]

II. Duty to Exercise Ordinary Care

A. *Question of Law*

The existence of a legal duty of care is a question of law for the court.[4] To establish this legal duty, the plaintiff must produce facts which show a duty to exercise ordinary care (to avoid a foreseeable risk of harm) owed by the alleged wrongdoer to the plaintiff, or the "class of which he is a member."[5] The public policies of safety, prevention of injury, and accountability are not only embedded in California law; they are concepts that have centuries-old common law and civil law roots.[6] The California Legislature, in 1872, articulated the public policy of ordinary care towards others in Civil Code sections 1708 and 1714:

> Every person is bound, without contract, to abstain from injuring the person or property of another, or infringing upon any of his or her rights.[7]
> Everyone is responsible, not only for the result of his or her willful acts, but also for an injury occasioned to another by his or her want of ordinary care or skill in the management of his or her property or person, except

---

[1] Certified Specialist, ABPLA, Medical Professional Liability Law, State Bar of California Board of Legal Specialization, Appellate Advocacy.

[2] Foley v. Interactive Data Corp., 47 Cal.3d 654, 682, 254 Cal.Rptr. 211, 765 P.2d 373, 389 (Cal. 1988) (*internal quotations omitted*).

[3] Burgess v. Superior Court, 2 Cal. 4th 1064, 1080, 9 Cal.Rptr.2d 615, 831 P.2d 1197, 1206 (Cal. 1992).

[4] Delgado v. Am. Multi-Cinema, Inc., 72 Cal.App.4th 1403, 1405, 85 Cal.Rptr.2d 838, 840 (Cal. Ct. App. 1999).

[5] Beauchamp v. Los Gatos Golf Course, 273 Cal.App.2d 20, 32, 77 Cal.Rptr. 914, 922 (Cal. Ct. App. 1969).

[6] *See* Mitchil v. Alestree, 86 Eng. Rep. 190, 1676 WL 150 (1676) (affirming verdict against defendant. Defendant brought a wild horse to a place frequented by pedestrians and the plaintiff was injured as a result. "It was the defendant's fault, to bring a wild horse into such a place where mischief might probably be done, by reason of the concourse of people.").

[7] Civ. Code § 1708 (West 2016).

so far as the latter has, willfully or by want of ordinary care, brought the injury upon himself or herself.[8]

Whether, in a particular type of case, a court should depart from Section 1714's articulation of a duty of care depends on several factors which were announced in *Rowland v. Christian*.[9]

> [T]he major ones are the foreseeability of harm to the plaintiff, the degree of certainty that the plaintiff suffered injury, the closeness of the connection between the defendant's conduct and the injury suffered, the moral blame attached to the defendant's conduct, the policy of preventing future harm, the extent of the burden to the defendant and consequences to the community of imposing a duty to exercise care with resulting liability for breach, and the availability, cost, and prevalence of insurance for the risk involved.[10]

The *Rowland* factors are evaluated "at a relatively broad level of factual generality."[11]

"As a general principle, a defendant owes a duty of care to all persons who are foreseeably endangered by his conduct, with respect to all risks which make the conduct unreasonably dangerous."[12] "'The risk reasonably to be perceived defines the duty to be obeyed.' . . . Defendant owes a duty, in the sense of a potential liability for damages, only with respect to those risks or hazards whose likelihood made the conduct unreasonably dangerous, and hence negligent, in the first instance."[13]

Although foreseeability is the most important consideration,[14] it is not the only consideration. *Raymond v. Paradise Unified School District of Butte County*[15] expounded on *Rowland* in a case holding that a school district had a duty to supervise young children who were waiting for a school bus, despite denials that it was aware that they were using a bus stop frequented by older students. *Raymond* articulated other public policy factors, including: "[t]he social utility of the activity out of which the injury arises, compared with the

---

[8] CIV. CODE § 1714(a) (West 2016). *Civil Code* §1714 is a "basic policy of this state." Escola v. Coca Cola Bottling Co. of Fresno, 150 P.2d 436, 440441 (Cal. 1944) (Traynor, J., concurring) (applying principle to product liability law: "public policy demands that responsibility be fixed wherever it will most effectively reduce the hazards to life and health inherent in defective products that reach the market. It is evident that the manufacturer can anticipate some hazards and guard against the recurrence of others, as the public cannot.").

[9] Rowland v. Christian, 69 Cal.2d 108, 116, 70 Cal.Rptr. 97, 103, 443 P.2d 561, 567 (Cal. 1968).

[10] *Rowland*, 70 Cal.Rptr. at 100.

[11] Cabral v. Ralphs Grocery Co., 51 Cal.4th 764, 770, 122 Cal.Rptr.3d 313, 248 P.3d 1170, 1174 (Cal. 2011).

[12] Tarasoff v. Regents of Univ. of Calif., 17 Cal.3d 425, 433, 131 Cal.Rptr. 14, 22, 551 P.2d 334, 342 (Cal. 1976) (citations and internal quotations omitted).

[13] Dillon v. Legg, 441 P.2d 912, 919-20 (Cal. 1968) (quoting Palsgraf v. Long Island R.R., 162 N.E. 99, 100 (N.Y. 1928)).

[14] *Tarasoff*, 551 P.2d at 342.

[15] Raymond v. Paradise Unified Sch. Dist. of Butte County, 218 Cal.App.2d 1, 31 Cal.Rptr. 847 (Cal. App. Ct. 1963).

risks involved in its conduct; the ability to adopt practical means of preventing injury; the *prophylactic effect* of a rule of liability; and the *moral imperatives* which judges share with their fellow citizens."[16]

B.   *Question of Fact*

i.   Elements

How a reasonably prudent person must act under the given circumstances of the case is a question of fact for the jury.[17]

ii.   Evidence

Determining the risks which are "reasonably foreseeable" in a case is a question of fact for the jury.[18] The care required under the circumstances is determined by the proportion of the danger to be avoided, and the consequences that can be reasonably anticipated.[19] To establish "foreseeability of harm," a plaintiff must show the general character of the event or harm was foreseeable, not the precise nature and manner of the harm that occurred.[20] Foreseeability of harm to establish "ordinary care" under the same or similar conditions may be shown by knowledge of prior similar incidents, or the lack thereof.[21] Statistics may also be admissible to show existence or nonexistence of an unreasonable risk of harm to others.[22] A statute or regulation may be used to establish the level of care required where the injury was the type the statute was designed to prevent and the injured party was one of the class of persons protected by the statute.[23]

III.   Breach of Duty

A.   *Elements*

California Civil Instruction (CACI) 401 articulates this principle:

Negligence is the failure to use reasonable care to prevent harm to oneself or to others.

A person can be negligent by acting or by failing to act. A person is negligent if he or she does something that a reasonably careful person would

---

[16] *Raymond*, 218 Cal. App. 2d at 8, 31 Cal.Rptr. at 851852 (emphasis added) (citations omitted).

[17] Francis v. City & County of S.F., 44 Cal.2d 335, 342, 282 P.2d 496, 501 (Cal. 1955).

[18] Bigbee v. Pac. Tel. & Tel. Co., 34 Cal.3d 49, 55, 192 Cal.Rptr. 857, 860, 665 P.2d 947, 950 (Cal. 1983).

[19] Crowe v. McBride, 25 Cal.2d 318, 320, 153 P.2d 727, 728 (Cal. 1944).

[20] *Bigbee*, 665 P.2d at 952.

[21] Beauchamp v. Los Gatos Golf Course, 273 Cal.App.2d 20, 37-38, 77 Cal. Rptr. 914, 926 (Cal. Ct. App. 1969).

[22] *Id.*, 273 Cal.App.2d at 37, 77 Cal.Rptr. at 925-926.

[23] Jacobs Farm/Del Cabo, Inc. v. W. Farm Serv., Inc., 190 Cal.App.4th 1502, 1524, 119 Cal.Rptr.3d 529, 546 (Cal. Ct. App. 2010).

not do in the same situation or fails to do something that a reasonably careful person would do in the same situation.

You must decide how a reasonably careful person would have acted in [name of plaintiff/defendant]'s situation.[24]

Once the court decides defendant owes a duty to exercise ordinary care to avoid harm to the plaintiff, "the jury then considers the case-specific foreseeability of the plaintiff's injury in assessing whether the defendant breached the duty of ordinary care."[25]

B.   *Evidence*

Violations of custom and usage are admissible as evidence of negligence.[26] Safety regulations and their violation are admissible as evidence of duty and its breach.[27] Safety rules are admissible as evidence of the ordinary care required under the circumstances and whether the duty to exercise ordinary care was breached.[28]

"The jury represent the ideal prudent man whose assumed course of conduct under given circumstances constitutes ordinary care, and whether such care was used in view of the facts of a particular case the question having been submitted to a jury is necessarily determined by the sense and experience of the individual jurors collectively expressed in the verdict."[29] Justice Mosk, in his concurring opinion in *Ballard v. Uribe*,[30] expressed the same philosophy and characterized it with the familiar shorthand, the "conscience of the community":

> A jury has also been frequently described as "the conscience of the community." . . . In addition, courts have long recognized that in our heterogeneous society jurors will inevitably belong to diverse and often overlapping groups defined by race, religion, ethnic or national origin, sex, age, education, occupation, economic condition, place of residence, and political affiliation . . . The very purpose of the right to trial by a jury drawn from a representative cross section of the community is to achieve an overall impartiality by allowing the interaction of the diverse beliefs and values the jurors bring from their group experiences.[31]

---

[24] *Judicial Council of California Civil Jury Instruction* (CACI) 401 (2016).

[25] Huang v. Bicycle Casino, Inc., 4 Cal.App.5th 329, 341, 208 Cal.Rptr.3d 591, 601 (Cal. Ct. App. 2016).

[26] Scott v. John E. Branagh & Son, 234 Cal.App.2d 435, 440-41, 44 Cal.Rptr. 384, 387-88 (Cal. Ct. App. 1965).

[27] AmeriGas Inc. v. Landstar Ranger, Inc., 230 Cal.App.4th 1153, 1168, 179 Cal.Rptr.3d 330, 342 (Cal. Ct. App. 2014).

[28] Dillenbeck v. City of L.A., 69 Cal.2d 472, 481, 72 Cal.Rptr. 321, 327, 446 P.2d 129, 135 (Cal. 1968).

[29] Chalmers v. Hawkins, 78 Cal.App. 733, 741, 248 P. 727, 731 (Cal. Ct. App. 1926) (internal quotations omitted) (motorist struck pedestrian; jury instructed to place themselves in pedestrian's position; *held*, no error).

[30] Ballard v. Uribe, 41 Cal.3d 564, 224 Cal.Rptr. 664, 715 P.2d 624 (Cal. 1986).

[31] *Ballard*, 224 Cal.Rptr. at 672, 715 P.2d 624 (J. Mosk, concurring) (citations and internal quotations omitted).

IV.   Causation

A.   *Elements*

A plaintiff must prove that the defendant's negligence was a cause-in-fact of his injuries.[32] To establish a fact question for causation, plaintiff must show "a reasonable basis for the conclusion that it was more likely than not that the conduct of the defendant was a substantial factor in the result."[33] The proximate cause determination involves an element of foreseeability.[34] Foreseeability of harm for purposes of causation is a question of fact.[35]

B.   *Evidence*

A plaintiff must present "substantial evidence" of causation, which may be through direct or circumstantial evidence, to remove the causation determination from "mere speculation and conjecture."[36] "[F]oreseeability of harm may be relevant to the jury's determination of whether the defendant's negligence was a proximate or legal cause of the plaintiff's injury."[37]

V.   Damages

"The overall policy of preventing future harm is ordinarily served, in tort law, by imposing the costs of negligent conduct upon those responsible."[38] Civil Code section 3281, enacted in 1872, embodies this principle: "Every person who suffers detriment from the unlawful act or omission of another, may recover from the person in fault a compensation therefor in money, which is called damages."[39]

Under California law, a tortfeasor is liable for all of the damage proximately caused by their negligence.[40] This rule of law is given to the jury in California's pattern instruction, CACI 3900:

> The amount of damages must include an award for each item of harm that
> was caused by [name of defendant]'s wrongful conduct, even if the particu-
> lar harm could not have been anticipated.[41]

---

[32] Pedeferri v. Seidner Enters., 216 Cal.App.4th 352, 371-372, 163 Cal.Rptr.3d 55, 66 (Cal. Ct. App. 2013).

[33] Lysick v. Walcom, 258 Cal.App.2d 136, 153, 65 Cal.Rptr. 406, 418 (Cal. Ct. App. 1968).

[34] Parker v. City & County of S.F., 158 Cal.App.2d 597, 605, 323 P.2d 108, 114 (Cal. Ct. App. 1958).

[35] *Id.*, 323 P.2d at 115-116.

[36] Leslie G. v. Perry & Assocs., 43 Cal.App.4th 472, 484, 50 Cal.Rptr.2d 785, 792-93 (Cal. Ct. App. 1996).

[37] Ballard v. Uribe, 41 Cal.3d 564, 572, 224 Cal.Rptr. 664, 669 n.6, 715 P.2d 624, 635 n.6 (Cal. 1986).

[38] Cabral v. Ralphs Grocery Co., 51 Cal.4th 764, 781, 122 Cal.Rptr.3d 313, 327, 248 P.3d 1170, 1182 (Cal. 2011).

[39] Civ. Code § 3281 (West 2016).

[40] Stone v. Foster, 106 Cal.App.3d 334, 348, 164 Cal.Rptr. 901, 909 (Cal. Ct. App. 1980).

[41] *Judicial Council of California Civil Jury Instruction* (CACI) 3900 (2016).

CHAPTER 6

COLORADO

COLORADO

Jennifer S. Prilliman[1]

I. Purpose of Tort Law

Colorado common law provides that "the primary purpose of tort law is to compensate [a victim] for injuries wrongfully suffered at the hands of others."[2] Tort law protects the public from injury to their person or property.[3] Tort law provides society a way to distinguish between "acceptable and unacceptable non-criminal behavior,"[4] and serves an important deterrent function. Liability is created when "the defendant breaches a duty to the plaintiff."[5] The duty is established by the court or by statute.[6] The courts may consider a number of factors when determining if a defendant owes a plaintiff a duty, none of which are controlling.[7] The finding of a duty is based on "fairness under contemporary standards—whether reasonable people would recognize a duty and agree that it exists."[8] Reasonableness is based on what a "person of ordinary prudence would or would not do under the same or similar circumstances."[9] Colorado courts recognize that "jurors collectively represent a cross-section of the conscience of the community" and "will anticipate the consequences of their" verdict.[10]

II. Duty to Exercise Ordinary Care

A. Question of Law

To establish negligence, a plaintiff must prove that a "defendant owed a legal duty to protect the plaintiff from injury."[11] Generally, a "legal duty to use reasonable care

---

[1] Law Library Professor and Associate Law Library Director, Oklahoma City University School of Law Chickasaw Nation Law Library.

[2] Coats v. Dish Network, L.L.C., 2013 COA 62, ¶ 34, 303 P.3d 147, 154; *see also* Hoyal v. Pioneer Sand Co., 188 P.3d 716, 719 (Colo. 2008).

[3] Town of Alma v. AZCO Const., Inc., 10 P.3d 1256, 1262 (Colo. 2000) (en banc).

[4] Denver Pub. Co. v. Bueno, 54 P.3d 893, 897-98 (Colo. 2002).

[5] *Id.* at 898.

[6] *Town of Alma*, 10 P.3d at 1262 (Colo. 2000).

[7] Cary v. United of Omaha Life Ins., 68 P.3d 462, 465 (Colo. 2003), *as modified on denial of reh'g* (May 19, 2003).

[8] *Id.*; *see also* Taco Bell, Inc. v. Lannon, 744 P.2d 43, 46 (Colo. 1987).

[9] United Blood Servs. v. Quintana, 827 P.2d 509, 519 (Colo. 1992).

[10] Simpson v. Anderson, 517 P.2d 416, 418 (Colo. App. 1973).

[11] Raleigh v. Performance Plumbing & Heating, 130 P.3d 1011, 1015 (Colo. 2006) (en banc); *see also* HealthONE v. Rodriguez ex rel. Rodriguez, 50 P.3d 879, 888 (Colo. 2002) (*distinguished on other grounds by*, Moffett v. Life Care Ctrs. of Am., 219 P.3d 1068, 1078 (Colo. 2009)).

arises in response to a foreseeable and unreasonable risk of harm to others."[12] Whether the defendant has a duty to exercise care is a question of law[13] and it is "not a matter to be submitted to or decided by a jury."[14] The court examines "(1) the nature of the relationship between the parties and (2) a particular set of public policy factors. Either or both may confer a duty or inform the scope of the duty."[15] The jury or trier of fact will determine if the duty was breached.[16]

The court weighs a number of factors when considering if a duty exists including, but not limited to: "(1) the risk involved . . . ; (2) the foreseeability and likelihood of injury weighed against the social utility of the [actor's] conduct; (3) the magnitude of the burden of guarding against the injury; and (4) the consequences of placing that burden on the [actor]."[17] The court may also consider "any other relevant factors based on the competing individual and social interests implicated by the facts of the case."[18] Foreseeability of a risk of injury is a critical factor.[19] The foreseeable "zone of danger" is construed broadly.[20] If an injury is potentially foreseeable, there is a duty to avoid causing the injury.[21] "For an injury to be a foreseeable consequence of a negligent act, it is not necessary that the tortfeasor be able to foresee the exact nature and extent of the injuries or the precise manner in which the injuries occur, but only that some injury will likely"[22] occur. Additionally, foreseeability alone will not always create a duty of care.[23] While a special relationship between a defendant and a potential plaintiff is not required, it is a factor that "weighs in favor" of finding a duty.[24] The purpose of the imposition of a duty in Colorado is "to protect all citizens from the risk

---

[12] *United Blood Servs.*, 827 P.2d at 519.

[13] Westin Operator, LLC v. Groh, 2015 CO 25, ¶ 18, 347 P.3d 606, 611, *distinguished by,* Raup v. Vail Summit Resorts, Inc., 160 F. Supp. 3d 1285, 1289 (D. Colo. 2016) (Federal District Court in Colorado found that the duty in *Westin* only applied when a duty did not already exist by statute.); *HealthONE*, 50 P.3d at 888 (Colo. 2002).

[14] White v. Pines Enters., Inc., 728 P.2d 759, 760 (Colo. App. 1986); *see also* Turner v. Grier, 608 P.2d 356, 358 (1979).

[15] *Westin*, ¶ 25, 347 P.3d at 612.

[16] Observatory Corp. v. Daly, 780 P.2d 462, 466 (Colo. 1989), *distinguished by,* Build It & They Will Drink, Inc. v. Strauch, 253 P.3d 302, 306 (Colo. 2011) (finding that the foreseeability analysis applied in *Observatory* was not relevant to the Court's discussion of dram-shop liability).

[17] *Westin*, ¶ 33, 347 P.3d at 613-14; *HealthONE*, 50 P.3d at 888; *see also Observatory*, 780 P.2d at 466 (Colo. 1989). (These four factors are the ones most often described by the Colorado Supreme Court when establishing what factors will be considered.)

[18] Perreira v. State, 768 P.2d 1198, 1209 (Colo. 1989) (en banc); *HealthONE*, 50 P.3d at 888.

[19] *Westin*, ¶ 33, 347 P.3d at 614 n.5; *see also Taco Bell, Inc.*, 744 P.2d at 46.

[20] *See* Samuelson v. Chutich, 529 P.2d 631, 634 (Colo. 1974); *see* Moore v. Standard Paint & Glass Co. of Pueblo, 358 P.2d 33, 36 (1960) (generally applying foreseeability); 7 COLO. PRAC., PERSONAL INJURY TORTS AND INSURANCE § 12:8 (3d ed.).

[21] *See* Lindeman v. The Corp. of the President of the Church of Jesus Christ of Latter-Day Saints, 43 F. Supp. 3d 1197, 1210 (D. Colo. 2014) (citing Keller v. Koca, 111 P.3d 445, 446 (Colo. 2005)).

[22] *HealthONE,* 50 P.3d at 889 (Colo. 2002).

[23] Solano v. Goff, 985 P.2d 53, 54 (Colo. App. 1999) (Court declined to impose a duty on sheriff supervising inmates when one inmate murdered another).

[24] *Id.*

of physical harm to their persons or to their property."[25] Therefore a duty may be imposed, "without regard to any agreement or contract."[26]

B. Question of Fact

i. Elements

Early jurisprudence in Colorado holds that a defendant must exercise the care that "a reasonably prudent and cautious person under the same or similar circumstances"[27] would exercise. "What constitutes [reasonable conduct] under the circumstances is . . . a question of fact for the jury."[28] The nature of the activity will determine the standard of care, and the "care required increases as the danger does."[29] This standard is reflected in the *Colorado Civil Jury Instructions*.[30]

ii. Evidence

The victim has the burden of proof to establish that a tortfeasor had knowledge that a risk existed.[31] Evidence can be direct or circumstantial.[32] Rules and guidelines, such as an employer's safety rules, may be admissible to prove the standard of care employees must exercise.[33] A statute or regulation may be used to establish the level of care required where the injury was the type the statute was designed to prevent and the injured party was one of the class of persons protected by the statute.[34] Where the jury could conclude from the evidence produced that the defendant's conduct was not what a reasonably prudent person would have done under the circumstances, the issue of negligence is a question of fact for the jury.[35]

---

[25] *Town of Alma*, 10 P.3d at 1262 (Colo. 2000).

[26] *Id.*

[27] Denver Consol. Elec. Co. v. Simpson, 41 P. 499, 501 (1895); *see also* Blankette v. Pub. Serv. Co. of Colorado, 10 P.2d 327, 329 (1932) (en banc). These cases continue to be cited by modern courts. *See also* Imperial Distrib. Servs., Inc. v. Forrest, 741 P.2d 1251, 1254 (Colo. 1987) (en banc).

[28] Vaccaro v. Am. Family Ins., 2012 COA 9M, ¶ 42, 275 P.3d 750, 759; *see also* Hesse v. McClintic, 176 P.3d 759, 764 (Colo. 2008).

[29] *Blankette*, 10 P.2d at 329; *see also Imperial*, 741 P.2d at 1254 n.5.

[30] COLO. JURY INSTR., CIVIL § 9:8 Reasonable Care—Defined (2016).

[31] *See* Keller v. Koca, 111 P.3d 445, 448 (Colo. 2005*), as modified on denial of reh'g,* (May 16, 2005) *distinguished on other grounds by,* Lindeman v. The Corp. of the President of the Church of Jesus Christ of Latter-Day Saints, 43 F. Supp. 3d 1197, 1211, (D. Colo. 2014*).* The court in *Keller* noted that "where a plaintiff asserts a claim for negligent supervision, the question of whether the employer owes a duty of care to the injured third party boils down to issues of knowledge and causation."

[32] Bodeman v. Shutto Super Mkts., Inc., 593 P.2d 700, 701 (Colo. 1979) (en banc).

[33] City & Cty. of Denver v. DeLong, 545 P.2d 154, 155-56 (1992), *distinguished by,* Four Corners Helicopters, Inc. v. Turbomeca, S.A., 979 F.2d 1434, 1437 (10th Cir. 1992). (The Tenth Circuit found a presumption of due care is inapplicable in a wrongful death action where comparative negligence is at issue.)

[34] Lombard v. Colo. Outdoor Educ. Cent., 187 P.3d 565, 573 (Colo. 2008).

[35] *Hesse*, 176 P.2d at 765.

III. Breach of Duty

A. Elements

The jury determines whether in fact a defendant has breached a duty to the plaintiff.[36] The jury determines whether a breach of the duty to exercise care to protect the plaintiff from injury occurred by finding that the defendant acted unreasonably under the circumstances.[37]

B. Evidence

The plaintiff bears the burden of proof in a negligence action, and the defendant bears the same burden when asserting contributory negligence.[38] There must be substantial evidence and it will be viewed in the most favorable light against the defendant.[39] For example, in cases involving negligent supervision, the plaintiff must prove an employer knew or "should have known that the employee would cause harm."[40] Violating a statute can be used as evidence of a breach of duty.[41] The Supreme Court notes "that a person of ordinary prudence would generally follow the law."[42] Therefore, evidence of violation of a statute or ordinance,[43] or in some cases professional rules of conduct, may be used as evidence that a duty of care was breached.[44] "Evidence of a defendant's compliance with applicable industry standards in a tort case is both relevant and admissible for purposes of determining whether the defendant either breached, or satisfied, the duty of care it owed to an injured plaintiff."[45] An employer's safety rules may be admissible to prove the standard of care employees must exercise.[46] Evidence of breach of duty can be direct or circumstantial.[47]

IV. Causation

A. Elements

Causation is a central element of a negligence action.[48] Foreseeability is the "touchstone" of proximate cause.[49] A plaintiff must prove that their injuries were caused by the

---

[36] Metro. Gas Repair Serv. v. Kulik, 621 P.2d 313, 318 (Colo. 1980).

[37] *Hesse*, 176 P.2d at 764.

[38] Coakley v. Hayes, 215 P.2d 901, 902 (1950).

[39] *Id.*

[40] *Lindeman*, 43 F. Supp. 3d at 1210.

[41] *Lombard*, 187 P.3d at 573.

[42] *Id.* at 574.

[43] *Id.*

[44] *Id.*

[45] Yampa Valley Elec. Ass'n v. Telecky, 862 P.2d 252, 257 (Colo. 1993) (en banc).

[46] *City & Cty.*, 545 P.2d at 155.

[47] *Bodeman*, 593 P.2d at 701.

[48] City of Aurora v. Loveless, 639 P.2d 1061, 1063 (Colo. 1981) (en banc).

[49] *Build It*, 253 P.3d at 306 (citations omitted).

defendant's failure to exercise reasonable care.[50] To recover, the plaintiff must show an injury to someone in the plaintiff's position was reasonably foreseeable.[51] For liability to be imposed, the defendant is not required to foresee the specific injury, only that some injury could occur.[52] Foreseeability, for causation, is a specific factual showing that establishes the conduct as the cause of the injury.[53] Whether an injury was reasonably foreseeable is a question for a jury.[54]

B. Evidence

A "plaintiff must prove causation . . . by a preponderance of the evidence[55] and establish that the injury was a "natural and probable" consequence of defendant's action.[56] There must be some connection between the defendant's action and the plaintiff's injury. To establish proximate cause, a plaintiff must show it is foreseeable that some injury to others will likely result as a consequence of the negligent act, but a plaintiff is not required to show "the exact nature and extent of" the actual injury was a likely result.[57] Colorado uses the "but-for" test of causation.[58] A plaintiff must show that "but-for" defendant's negligent act or omission, the injury would not have occurred.[59] Either direct or circumstantial evidence is sufficient to prove causation.[60]

V. Damages

A. Elements

An injured party has the right to recover "damages which naturally and probably result from the negligence of another."[61] The aim of the awarded damages is to make the "injured party whole."[62] Damages are a measure of the loss or harm from an injury caused by the "unlawful act, omission, or negligence of another."[63]

---

[50] *Observatory*, 780 P.2d at 469.

[51] Vanderbeek v. Vernon Corp., 50 P.3d 866 (Colo. 2002) (en banc).

[52] *HealthONE*, 50 P.3d at 889.

[53] *City of Aurora*, 639 P.2d at 1063.

[54] *Id.*

[55] Reigel v. SavaSeniorCare L.L.C., 292 P.3d 977, 985 (Colo. App. 2011).

[56] *City of Aurora*, 639 P.2d at 1063 (upholding jury instructions defining proximate cause as "that cause which in natural and probable sequence produced the claimed injury. It is the cause without which the claimed injury would not have been sustained").

[57] *Build It*, 253 P.3d at 306 (citations omitted).

[58] *Reigel*, 292 P.3d at 985.

[59] *Id.*

[60] Boatright v. Berkley United Methodist Church, 518 P.2d 309, 310 (Colo. App. 1974).

[61] Cope v. Vermeer Sales & Serv. of Colo., Inc., 650 P.2d 1307, 1308 (Colo. App. 1982).

[62] *Id.* at 1309.

[63] Wilcox v. Clark, 42 P.3d 29, 30 (Colo. App. 2001).

B. *Evidence*

The jury will determine the award for damages.[64] The amount is "within the sole province of the jury" and appellate courts are reluctant to overturn the amount unless the award is "completely unsupported by the record."[65] "Difficulty or uncertainty in determining the precise amount does not prevent an award of damages."[66] If the jury determines there are damages, they may make a "reasonable estimation" of the amount of damages.[67]

---

[64] Houser v. Eckhardt, 506 P.2d 751, 756 (Colo. App. 1972).

[65] Jackson v. Moore, 883 P.2d 622, 625-26 (Colo. App. 1994).

[66] *Cope*, 650 P.2d at 1309.

[67] Margenau v. Bowlin, 12 P.3d 1214, 1218 (Colo. App. 2000).

CHAPTER 7

CONNECTICUT

CONNECTICUT

Amy Emerson[1]

I. Purpose of Tort Law

In Connecticut, tort law seeks to compensate plaintiffs for losses and to deter wrongful conduct.[2] "The fundamental policy purposes of the tort compensation system [is] compensation of innocent parties, shifting the loss to responsible parties or distributing it among appropriate entities, and deterrence of wrongful conduct."[3] The Connecticut courts also note that the primary function of tort law is to prevent future harm.[4] A defendant may be held liable for a breach of the a duty of care "for those harms that are reasonably foreseeable and within the scope of the risk created by their negligent conduct."[5] "[I]f it is not foreseeable to a reasonable person in the defendant's position that harm of the type alleged would result from the defendant's actions to a particular plaintiff,"[6] a duty does not exist and a defendant cannot be held liable.[7]

II. Duty to Exercise Ordinary Care

A. Question of Law

The first issue to be resolved in an alleged case of negligence is whether the defendant owed a duty of care to the plaintiff.[8] Its determination is a question of law, and until a duty has been established, the trier of fact may not consider whether it has been breached.[9] The Supreme Court of Connecticut defines duty as "a legal conclusion about relationships between individuals, made after the fact, and imperative to a negligence case of action."[10]

---

[1] Director of the Legal Research Clinic, Adjunct Clinical Professor of Law, Cornell Law School

[2] Rizzuto v. Davidson Ladders, Inc., 905 A.2d 1165, 1173-74 (Conn. 2006).

[3] Mendillo v. Bd. of Educ. of Town of E. Haddam, 717 A.2d 1177, 1190 (Conn. 1998). *overruled on unrelated grounds by,* Campos v. Coleman, 123 A.3d 854 (Conn. 2015).

[4] *Rizzuto,* 905 A.2d at 1173-74.

[5] Lodge v. Arett Sales Corp., 717 A.2d 215, 226 (Conn. 1998).

[6] RK Constructors, Inc. v. Fusco Corp., 650 A.2d 153, 156 (Conn. 1994).

[7] *Id.*

[8] McDermott v. Conn., 113 A.3d 419, 425 (Conn. 2015); Grenier v. Comm'r of Transp., 51 A.3d 367, 379 (Conn. 2012); RK Constructors, Inc. v. Fusco Corp., 650 A.2d 153, 155 (Conn. 1994).

[9] McDermott v. Conn., 113 A.3d 419, 425 (Conn. 2015); Grenier v. Comm'r of Transp., 51 A.3d 367, 379 (Conn. 2012); Lodge v. Arett Sales Corp., 717 A.2d 215, 219 (Conn. 1998); Jaworski v. Kiernan, 696 A.2d 332, 335 (Conn. 1997).

[10] McDermott v. Conn., 113 A.3d 419, 425 (Conn. 2015); Ruiz v. Victory Props., LLC, 107 A.3d 381, 388 (Conn. 2015); Cannizzaro v. Marinyak, 93 A.3d 584, 587 (Conn. 2014); Grenier v. Comm'r of Transp., 51 A.3d 367, 379 (Conn. 2012); Sic v. Nunan, 54 A.3d 553, 558 (Conn. 2012); Jaworski v. Kiernan, 696 A.2d 332, 335 (Conn. 1997).

The circumstances surrounding the conduct of the defendant shall be considered in determining the nature of the duty and the specific persons to whom it is owed.[11] Duty is "an expression of the sum total of those considerations of policy which lead the law to say the plaintiff is entitled to protection."[12]

In Connecticut, the threshold consideration in determining whether a duty exists is always whether the harm caused would have been foreseeable by a reasonable person in the defendant's position such that he would have, or should have, known that harm of the nature suffered by the plaintiff was likely to occur.[13] The test is an objective one; the defendant himself need not have foreseen the harm.[14] In addition, only the general nature of the harm need be foreseeable, not its exact nature.[15] *Connecticut Civil Jury Instruction* 3.6-7 explains that "If harm of the same general nature as that which occurred here was foreseeable, it does not matter if the manner in which the harm that actually occurred was unusual, bizarre or unforeseeable."[16]

Upon establishing foreseeability, the court thereafter employs an analysis of public policy considerations and balances other "pragmatic concerns" to determine the extent of the defendant's responsibility under the particular circumstances of each case.[17] Four factors that must be weighed in conducting a public policy analysis are: (1) identifying the "normal expectations" of those involved in the activity; (2) balancing safety concerns with "encouraging participation" in the activity; (3) avoiding a rise in litigation; and (4) decisions from other jurisdictions.[18]

It should be noted that the Connecticut Supreme Court has employed a "totality of the circumstances" rule to address the question of duty in instances involving property owners and invitees who are attacked by third parties.[19] Further, the Connecticut Supreme Court has only found a duty to help another person when there is a "special relationship of custody or control,"[20] including circumstances in which the defendant's own conduct created or increased the risk of harm.[21]

---

[11] Lodge v. Arett Sales Corp., 717 A.2d 215, 219 (Conn. 1998); Jaworski v. Kiernan, 696 A.2d 332, 336 (Conn. 1997); Waters v. Autuori, 676 A.2d 357, 361 (Conn. 1996); RK Constructors, Inc. v. Fusco Corp., 650 A.2d 153, 155 (Conn. 1994).

[12] Jaworski v. Kiernan, 696 A.2d 332, 336 (Conn. 1997).

[13] *Id.*

[14] *Id.*

[15] Lodge v. Arett Sales Corp., 717 A.2d 215, 220 (Conn. 1998); RK Constructors, Inc. v. Fusco Corp., 650 A.2d 153, 156 (Conn. 1994).

[16] *Connecticut Judicial Branch Civil Jury Instructions* 3.6-7 *Duty* (2016) (citing Coburn v. Lenox Homes, Inc., 186 Conn. 370, 375 (Conn. 1982); Pisel v. Stamford Hosp., 180 Conn. 314, 332-33 (Conn. 1980); Orlo v. Conn. Co., 128 Conn. 231, 237 (Conn. 1941)).

[17] McDermott v. Conn., 113 A.3d 419, 425 (Conn. 2015); Lawrence v. O & G Indus., 126 A.3d 569, 575 (Conn. 2015); Grenier v. Comm'r of Transp., 51 A.3d 367, 379-80 (Conn. 2012); Jaworski v. Kiernan, 696 A.2d 332, 336 (Conn. 1997) (contains the quote); Ruiz v. Victory Props., LLC, 107 A.3d 381, 388 (Conn. 2015); Cannizzaro v. Marinyak, 93 A.3d 584, 587 (Conn. 2014).

[18] Lawrence v. O & G Indus., 126 A.3d 569, 575 (Conn. 2015); Monk v. Temple George Assoc., LLC, 869 A.2d 179, 187 (Conn. 2005); Jaworski v. Kiernan, 696 A.2d 332, 337 (Conn. 1997).

[19] Monk v. Temple George Assoc., LLC, 869 A.2d 179, 188 (Conn. 2005).

[20] Cannizzaro v. Marinyak, 93 A.3d 584, 587 (Conn. 2014).

[21] Doe v. Saint Francis Hosp. & Med. Ctr., 72 A.3d. 929, 946 (Conn. 2013).

B.   *Question of Fact*

i.   Elements

Upon establishing that a duty exists, the court will next turn its attention to the scope of that duty, in order words, the standard of care.[22] The standard of care is determined by the jury.[23]

The Connecticut Supreme Court has held that "due care is always predicated on the existing circumstances."[24] Specifically, where there is no legislatively prescribed standard of care, the current standard is that of the "reasonably prudent person under the circumstances."[25] Older cases described the standard as that of the "ordinarily prudent person."[26] Connecticut courts have not applied a one-size-fits-all definition to the standard, but instead the courts look for "support in the facts that appear on the record."[27]

In determining the standard of care, Connecticut juries may consider industry standards, but such standards are not binding upon the court.[28] The same is true for custom in the trade.[29] Each must be considered "in light of the totality of the evidence presented in the case."[30]

ii.   Evidence

The burden of proof in a Connecticut negligence case rests upon the plaintiff, who must prove all of the elements of a negligence cause of action.[31] Plaintiffs are held to the standard generally applied in civil actions, under which they must prove the elements of the action by a preponderance of the evidence.[32] A statute or regulation may be used to establish the level of care required where the injury was the type the statute was designed to prevent and the injured party was one of the class of persons protected by the statute.[33]

---

[22] McDermott v. Conn., 113 A.3d 419, 425 (Conn. 2015); Mirjavadi v. Vakilzadeh, 74 A.3d 1278, 1287 (Conn. 2013).

[23] Lodge v. Arett Sales Corp., 717 A.2d 215, 219 (Conn. 1998); Ciarlelli v. Romeo, 699 A.2d 217, 220 (Conn. Ct. App. 1997), *cert denied*, 701 A.2d 657 (Conn. 1997); Steinhaus v. Steinhaus, 139 A.2d 55, 57 (Conn. 1958); Howe v. Neal, 140 A.2d 318, 319 (Conn. 1958).

[24] Lodge v. Arett Sales Corp., 717 A.2d 215, 221 (Conn. 1998); Roy v. Friedman Equip. Co., 157 A.2d 599, 601 (Conn 1960).

[25] Rawls v. Progressive N. Inc., 83 A.3d 576, 583 (Conn. 2014).

[26] Steinhaus v. Steinhaus, 139 A.2d 55, 57 (Conn. 1958); Howe v. Neal, 140 A.2d 318, 319 (Conn. 1958).

[27] Lodge v. Arett Sales Corp., 717 A.2d 215, 220 (Conn. 1998).

[28] McDermott v. Conn., 113 A.3d 419, 428 (Conn. 2015); Coburn v. Lenox Homes, Inc., 441 A.2d 620, 626 (Conn. 1982).

[29] McDermott v. Conn., 113 A.3d 419, 428 (Conn. 2015); Coburn v. Lenox Homes, Inc., 441 A.2d 620, 626 (Conn. 1982).

[30] McDermott v. Conn., 113 A.3d 419, 428 (Conn. 2015); Coburn v. Lenox Homes, Inc., 441 A.2d 620, 620 (Conn. 1982).

[31] Perry v. Conn., 894 A.2d 367, 371 (Conn. App. Ct. 2006), *cert denied*, 899 A.2d 621 (Conn. 2006).

[32] Kruck v. Conn. Co., 80 A. 162, 163 (Conn. 1911).

[33] Vt. Mut. Ins. v. Fern, 140 A.3d 278, 283-84 (Conn. Ct. App. 2016).

III. Breach of Duty

A. Elements

If a duty exists, the plaintiff must establish, by a preponderance of the evidence, that the duty was breached.[34] This is a question for the trier of fact.[35] The Supreme Court of Connecticut has defined breach as a failure to exercise reasonable care under the circumstances.[36] In determining the level of care required, *Connecticut Civil Jury Instruction* 3.6-4 provides that the jury should:

> consider all of the circumstances which were known or should have been known to the defendant at the time of the conduct in question. Whether care is reasonable depends upon the dangers that a reasonable person would perceive in those circumstances. It is common sense that the more dangerous the circumstances, the greater the care that ought to be exercised.[37]

B. Evidence

Expert testimony is permitted in many instances, but is required "when the question involved goes beyond the field of ordinary knowledge and experience of judges and jurors."[38] Common examples include cases involving professional competence and malpractice.[39] On the other hand, examples of cases in which expert testimony was not required involve the safe operation of a gas station, the lack of an existing porch railing, inadequacy of a fence to protect against the effects of blasting, and whether materials were obscene to minors.[40]

IV. Causation

A. Elements

The plaintiff bears the burden of proving that the defendant's negligence caused the plaintiff's injuries.[41] In Connecticut, "[l]egal cause is a hybrid construct, the result of balancing philosophic, pragmatic and moral approaches to causation."[42] First, the plaintiff must prove causation in fact, meaning that the "injury would not have occurred but-for the actor's

---

[34] Gaudio v. Griffin Health Serv. Corp., 733 A.2d 197, 206 (Conn. 1999); Kruck v. Conn. Co., 80 A. 162, 163 (Conn. 1911).

[35] Lawrence v. O & G Indus., 126 A.3d 569, 574 (Conn. 2015).

[36] Rawls v. Progressive N. Inc., 83 A.3d 576, 583 (Conn. 2014).

[37] *Connecticut Judicial Branch Civil Jury Instructions* 3.6-4 *Reasonable Care* (2016) (citing Galligan v. Blais, 364 A.2d 164, 166 (Conn. 1976); Pleasure Beach Park Co. v. Bridgeport Dredge & Dock Co., 165 A. 691, 693 (Conn. 1933); Geoghegan v. G. Fox & Co., 132 A. 408, 409 (Conn. 1926)).

[38] Ciarlelli v. Romeo, 699 A.2d 217, 220 (Conn. Ct. App. 1997), *cert. denied*, 701 A.2d 657 (Conn. 1997).

[39] *Ciarlelli v. Romeo,* 699 A.2d 217, 220 (Conn. Ct. App. 1997), *cert. denied*, 701 A.2d 657 (Conn. 1997).

[40] *See generally Id.* at 220-21.

[41] Rawls v. Progressive N. Inc., 83 A.3d 576, 583 (Conn. 2014).

[42] Suarez v. Sordo, 685 A.2d 1144, 1148 (Conn. Ct. App. 1996), *cert denied*, 688 A.2d 334 (Conn. 1997).

conduct."[43] If the injury would have occurred notwithstanding the defendant's conduct, then causation may not be attributed to the defendant.[44]

Next, the plaintiff must prove proximate cause. The purpose of proximate cause is to limit the potential for expansive liability.[45] It "establishes a reasonable connection between an act or omission of a defendant and the harm suffered by the plaintiff."[46] Proximate cause is defined by the Supreme Court of Connecticut as "[a]n actual cause that is a substantial factor in the resulting harm. . . ."[47] Determining proximate cause requires applying the "substantial factor" test, which determines "whether the harm which occurred was of the same general nature as the foreseeable risk created by the defendant's negligence."[48] In other words, proximate cause "requires that 'the defendant's conduct [was] a substantial factor in bringing about the plaintiff's injuries' and that there was 'an unbroken sequence of events that tied [the plaintiff's] injuries to the [defendant's conduct].'"[49] The Supreme Court of Connecticut has stated that "the meaning of the term "substantial factor" is so clear as to need no expository definition. . . . Indeed, it is doubtful if the expression is susceptible of definition more understandable than the simple and familiar words it employs."[50]

A plaintiff need not disprove all other potential causes of the accident, but must "establish that it is *more likely than not* that the cause on which the plaintiff relies was in fact a proximate cause of the accident," thereby ensuring that the "causal connection . . . [is] based [on] more than conjecture and surmise."[51]

Intervening intentional or criminal acts relieve negligent defendants of liability, "except where the harm caused by the intervening act is within the 'scope of risk' created by the defendant's conduct or where the intervening act is reasonably foreseeable."[52] Known as the superseding cause doctrine, this principle has been limited by the Connecticut Supreme Court to instances "in which an unforeseeable intentional tort, force of nature or criminal event supersedes the defendant's tortious conduct."[53]

B.   *Evidence*

Proximate cause is a question of fact for the jury, although it may "become a conclusion of law when the mind of a fair and reasonable [person] could reach only one conclusion. . . ."[54]

---

[43] Rawls v. Progressive N. Inc., 83 A.3d 576, 583 (Conn. 2014); *see also* Suarez v. Sordo, 685 A.2d 1144, 1148 (Conn. Ct. App. 1996), *cert denied*, 688 A.2d 334 (Conn. 1997).

[44] *Suarez*, 685 A.2d at 1148.

[45] *Id.*

[46] *Id.*

[47] *Id.*

[48] *Id.* at 1148-49.

[49] Rawls v. Progressive N. Inc., 83 A.3d 576, 583 (Conn. 2014).

[50] Mather v. Griffin Hosp., 540 A.2d 666, 669 (Conn. 1988) (citing Pilon v. Alderman, 152 A. 157 (Conn. 1930)).

[51] *Id.*

[52] Suarez v. Sordo, 685 A.2d 1144, 1149 (Conn. Ct. App. 1996), *cert denied*, 688 A.2d 334 (Conn. 1997).

[53] Archambault v. Soneco/Ne., Inc., 946 A.2d 839, 855 (Conn. 2008).

[54] Suarez v. Sordo, 685 A.2d 1144, 1151 (Conn. Ct. App. 1996), *cert denied*, 688 A.2d 334 (Conn 1997).

Both direct and circumstantial evidence are allowed and are considered equally probative.[55] "Circumstantial evidence need not be so conclusive as to exclude every other hypothesis, but must only create a 'reasonable belief in the probability of the existence of the material fact' in the mind of the trier."[56]

Evidence should be considered not as individual pieces in isolation, but in the "context of the whole."[57]

V.   Damages

A.   Elements

According to the Supreme Court of Connecticut, "[d]amages are 'intended to provide a victim with monetary compensation for an injury to his person, property or reputation.'"[58] Further, "[i]nherent in any action for money damages is a plaintiff's claim that the defendant has harmed the plaintiff, and that the plaintiff's injury can be remedied by a monetary award."[59]

The purpose of compensatory damages, "to restore an injured party to the position he or she would have been in if the wrong had not been committed," guides the proper measure of damages.[60]

B.   Evidence

The question of the amount of damages falls within the province of the jury.[61] There is no rule or mathematical computation for determining the amount of an award of non-economic damages, such as an award for pain and suffering, and the calculation of such an award is within the discretion of the trier of the facts.[62] It is the burden of the plaintiff to provide sufficient evidence for the trier to make a "fair and reasonable estimate."[63] Therefore, the amount of damages is dependent upon the facts and circumstances of each case.[64] The jury must "use human experience and apply sound common sense in determining" the amount of the verdict.[65] A jury verdict shall not be set aside by a court unless the award is "plainly excessive or exorbitant." More specifically, the award does not meet the court's test of "whether the jury's award falls somewhere within the necessarily uncertain limits of just damages or whether the size of the verdict so shocks the sense of justice as to compel the conclusion that the jury [was] influenced by partiality, prejudice, mistake or corruption."[66]

---

[55] Rawls v. Progressive N. Inc., 83 A.3d 576, 583 (Conn. 2014).

[56] *Id.* at 584.

[57] *Id.* at 780 n.8.

[58] Town of New Hartford v. Conn. Res. Recovery Auth., 970 A.2d 592, 614 (Conn. 2009).

[59] Blakeslee Arpaia Chapman, Inc. v. EI Constructors, Inc., 687 A.2d 506, 532 (Conn. 1997).

[60] Rizzuto v. Davidson Ladders, Inc., 905 A.2d 1165, 1181 (Conn. 2006).

[61] Duncan v. Mill Mgmt. Co. of Greenwich, Inc., 60 A.3d 222, 243 (Conn. 2013); Saleh v. Ribeiro Trucking, LLC, 32 A.3d 318, 322 (Conn. 2011).

[62] Saleh v. Ribeiro Trucking, LLC, 982 A.2d 178, 183 (Conn. Ct. App. 2009), *affirmed,* 32 A.3d 318, 322 (Conn. 2011).

[63] *Id.*

[64] Wochek v. Foley, 477 A.2d 1015, 1019 (Conn. 1984).

[65] *Connecticut Judicial Branch Civil Jury Instructions* 3.4-1 *Damages* (2016).

[66] Mahon v. B.V. Unitron Mfg. Inc., 935 A.2d 1004, 1015 (Conn. 2007).

CHAPTER 8

DELAWARE

DELAWARE
Amy Emerson[1]

I. Purpose of Tort Law

Delaware identifies a tort as any act "done, or omitted to be done, contrary to the obligation of the law."[2] The obligation is in the defendant's duty of care to the plaintiff,[3] and that "duty must arise by operation of law and not by the mere agreement of the parties."[4] In negligence actions, the duty is breached when there "is the failure to use such care as a reasonably prudent and careful person would exercise under similar circumstances."[5] Additionally, Delaware courts focus on the foreseeability of the harm to the injured party.[6] Damages are awarded to provide plaintiffs compensation for their "injury or loss."[7]

II. Duty to Exercise Ordinary Care

A. Question of Law

Negligence occurs when one fails to meet the standard of care required by the law.[8] Liability for negligence depends upon whether one party owes a duty of care to another, as well as the scope of that duty with respect to the interest involved.[9] Whether a duty exists is a question of law for the court.[10] The Delaware Supreme Court has looked closely at the *Restatement (Second) of Torts* for guidance in determining whether a duty exists.[11]

The *Restatement* predicates, and the Supreme Court of Delaware agrees, that negligent conduct falls into one of two categories. The categories are, as follows: (1) "an act which the actor as a reasonable man should recognize as involving an unreasonable risk of causing an invasion of an interest of another," also known as "misfeasance;" or (2) "a failure

---

[1] Director of the Legal Research Clinic, Adjunct Clinical Professor of Law, Cornell Law School.

[2] Garber v. Whittaker, 174 A. 34, 36 (Del. Super. Ct. 1934).

[3] *Id.*

[4] *Id.*

[5] Garrett v. People's Ry., 64 A. 254, 256 (Del. Super. Ct. 1906).

[6] Jardel Co. v. Hughes, 523 A.2d 518, 529 (Del. 1987).

[7] *Id.* at 528.

[8] Rogers v. Christina Sch. Dist., 73 A.3d 1, 6 (Del. 2013).

[9] *Id.* at 7.

[10] Price v. E.I. DuPont de Nemours & Co., 26 A.3d 162, 166 (Del. 2011); Riedel v. ICI Ams., Inc, 968 A.2d 17, 20 (Del. 2009); Pipher v. Parsell, 930 A.2d 890, 892 (Del. 2007).

[11] Rogers v. Christina Sch. Dist., 73 A.3d 1, 7 (Del. 2013); Price v. E.I. DuPont de Nemours & Co., 26 A.3d 162, 166-167 (Del. 2011).

to do an act which is necessary for the protection or assistance of another and which the actor is under a duty to do," also known as "nonfeasance."[12]

The *Restatement* further clarifies that, "A negligent act or omission may be one which involves an unreasonable risk of harm to another through either: (a) the continuous operation of a force started or continued by the act or omission, or (b) the foreseeable action of the other, a third person, an animal, or a force of nature."[13]

The Delaware Supreme Court notes that the *Comment* to the *Restatement* differentiates between the duties created by one who commits an affirmative act, versus one created by a failure to act.[14] One who commits an affirmative act, "is under a duty to others to exercise the care of a reasonable man to protect them against an unreasonable risk of harm to them arising out of the act."[15] On the other hand, one who fails to act "generally has no duty to act, *unless* "there is a special relation between the actor and the other which gives rise to the duty."[16]

Where an actor realizes, or should realize, that another's aid depends upon his action, this does not give rise to a duty, with the exception of circumstances in which one is required by law, or voluntarily takes custody of another, such that the other is deprived of "normal opportunities for protection."[17] Examples include common carriers, innkeepers, and possessors of land.[18] This duty also applies to the parent-child relationships.[19]

The Delaware Supreme Court summarizes, "Generally, the duty to act is 'largely confined to . . . situations in which there was some special relation between the parties, on the basis of which the defendant was found to have a duty to take action for the aid or protection of the plaintiff.'"[20]

Ultimately, "in a case involving misfeasance, the defendant's duty is automatic, whereas in a case involving nonfeasance, the defendant's duty arises only if there is a legally significant 'special relationship' between the parties."[21]

---

[12] RESTATEMENT (SECOND) OF TORTS § 284 (1965.), (citing Rogers v. Christina Sch. Dist., 73 A.3d 1, 7 (Del. 2013); Price v. E.I. DuPont de Nemours & Co., 26 A.3d 162, 167 (Del. 2011); Riedel v. ICI Ams., Inc, 968 A.2d 17, 22 (Del. 2009)).

[13] RESTATEMENT (SECOND) OF TORTS § 302 (1965), (citing Rogers v. Christina Sch. Dist., 73 A.3d 1, 7 (Del. 2013); Riedel v. ICI Ams., Inc, 968 A.2d 17, 22 (Del. 2009)).

[14] RESTATEMENT (SECOND) OF TORTS § 302 *cmt.* a (1965), (citing Rogers v. Christina Sch. Dist., 73 A.3d 1, 7 (Del. 2013)).

[15] RESTATEMENT (SECOND) OF TORTS § 302 *cmt.* a (1965), (citing Rogers v. Christina Sch. Dist., 73 A.3d 1, 7 (Del. 2013); Price v. E.I. DuPont de Nemours & Co., 26 A.3d 162, 167 (Del. 2011)).

[16] RESTATEMENT (SECOND) OF TORTS § 302 *cmt.* a (1965), (citing Rogers v. Christina Sch. Dist., 73 A.3d 1, 7 (Del. 2013); Price v. E.I. DuPont de Nemours & Co., 26 A.3d 162, 167 (Del. 2011); Riedel v. ICI Ams., Inc, 968 A.2d 17, 22 (Del. 2009)).

[17] RESTATEMENT (SECOND) OF TORTS § 314 (1965), (citing Rogers v. Christina Sch. Dist., 73 A.3d 1, 7-8 (Del. 2013)).

[18] RESTATEMENT (SECOND) OF TORTS § 314A (1965), (citing Rogers v. Christina Sch. Dist., 73 A.3d 1, 7 (Del. 2013)).

[19] RESTATEMENT (SECOND) OF TORTS § 316-320 (1965), (citing Rogers v. Christina Sch. Dist., 73 A.3d 1, 8 (Del. 2013)).

[20] Riedel v. ICI Ams., Inc, 968 A.2d 17, 23 (Del. 2009), (citing Rogers v. Christina Sch. Dist., 73 A.3d 1, 8 (Del. 2013)).

[21] Price v. E.I. DuPont de Nemours & Co., 26 A.3d 162, 167 (Del. 2011).

Under the *Restatement*, and according to Delaware case law, it is possible to assume a duty of care where one "undertakes, gratuitously or for consideration, to render services to another which he should recognize as necessary for the protection of the other's person or things."[22] In such an instance that party is "subject to liability to the other for physical harm resulting from his failure to exercise reasonable care to perform his undertaking, if: (a) his failure to exercise such care increases the risk of such harm, or (b) the harm is suffered because of the other's reliance upon the undertaking."[23]

Delaware does not recognize a duty to control the conduct of a third person in order to prevent harm to another, except where, "(a) a special relation exists between the actor and the third person which imposes a duty upon the actor to control the third person's conduct, or (b) a special relation exists between the actor and the other which gives to the other a right to protection."[24]

It should be noted that, in 2009, the Delaware Supreme Court considered adopting the *Restatement (Third) of Torts*, but declined to do so because, "[t]he drafters of the *Restatement (Third) of Torts* redefined the concept of duty in a way that is inconsistent with this Court's precedents and traditions. The *Restatement (Third) of Torts* creates duties in areas where we have previously found no common law duty and have deferred to the legislature to decide whether or not to create a duty."[25] The Court explained that the legislature, not the courts, should be responsible for deciding matters of social policy and that, "[t]his Court's charge does not include "articulating general social norms of responsibility."[26] The Court concluded, that "[w]hether the expansive approach for creating duties found in the *Restatement (Third) of Torts* is viewed as a step forward or backward in assisting courts to apply the common law of negligence, it is simply too wide a leap for this Court to take. Therefore, at the present time we continue to follow the *Restatement (Second) of Torts*."[27]

B. Question of Fact

i. Elements

The *Restatement (Second) of Torts*, adopted by the Supreme Court of Delaware, defines negligence as "conduct which falls below the standard established by law for the protection of others against unreasonable risk of harm," not including "conduct recklessly disregardful of an interest of others."[28]

The standard of care required of defendants is that of a "reasonably prudent person."[29] As stated by the Delaware Supreme Court, "[t]he inquiry in all cases is what a reasonable person would have done under the circumstances—a determination that necessarily will depend

---

[22] RESTATEMENT (SECOND) OF TORTS § 323 (1965), (citing Rogers v. Christina Sch. Dist., 73 A.3d 1, 8 (Del. 2013)).

[23] *Id.*

[24] Naidu v. Laird, 539 A.2d 1064, 1072 (Del. 1988), (citing Riedel v. ICI Ams., Inc, 968 A.2d 17, 24 (Del. 2009)).

[25] Riedel v. ICI Am.s, Inc, 968 A.2d 17, 20 (Del. 2009).

[26] *Id.* at 21.

[27] *Id.*

[28] RESTATEMENT (SECOND) OF TORTS § 282 (1965), (citing Rogers v. Christina Sch. Dist., 73 A.3d 1, 7 (Del. 2013)).

[29] Sears, Roebuck & Co. v. Midcap, 893 A.2d 542, 554 (Del. 2006).

on the particular facts of each case."[30] In another case, the Delaware Supreme Court defined the "duties owed in terms of reasonableness. One's duty is to act reasonably, as a reasonably prudent man (or entity) would. One breaches that duty by not protecting against an event that a reasonably prudent man would protect against. Stated differently, one's duty encompasses protecting against reasonably foreseeable events."[31] The question of liability is one for the jury.[32]

ii. Evidence

The plaintiff bears the burden of establishing, by a preponderance of the evidence, that the defendant failed to meet the legal standard of care.[33]

Although the Delaware Supreme Court has recently ruled that evidence of custom or practice in a particular industry may be used to show what is reasonable under the circumstances,[34] it has also taken the position in the past that custom may not necessarily establish the standard of care for a reasonable person under particular facts or circumstances.[35] This question is one for the jury.[36] A statute or regulation may be used to establish the level of care required where the statute was designed to protect a class of persons from harm or injury and the plaintiff is a member of that class.[37]

In addition, a Delaware court has ruled that expert testimony may not be used to establish a duty; rather, an expert may establish a standard of care. After an expert establishes the standard of care, the trier of fact determines whether a duty was breached.[38]

III. Breach of Duty

A. Elements

It is the responsibility of the plaintiff to show by a preponderance of the evidence that the defendant's negligent act or omission violated the duty owed to the plaintiff.[39]

B. Evidence

Whether the defendant beached its duty of care is a question for the jury.[40] In Delaware, demonstrating a breach of duty is closely linked to proving that the defendant caused the plaintiff's harm.[41]

---

[30] *Id.*

[31] Sirmans v. Penn, 588 A.2d 1103, 1107 (Del. 1990).

[32] Drejka v. Hitchens Tire Serv. Inc., 15 A.3d 1221, 1225 (Del. 2010).

[33] Jones v. Crawford, 1 A.3d 299, 302 (Del. 2010); Cuonzo v. Shore, 958 A.2d 840, 844 (Del. 2008).

[34] Sears, Roebuck & Co. v. Midcap, 893 A.2d 542, 554 (Del. 2006).

[35] Kuyper v. Gulf Oil Corp., 410 A.2d 164, 165 (Del. 1979).

[36] Roberts v. Daystar Sills, Inc., C.A. No. 05C-04-189 CLS, 2008 WL 8203205, at *2 (Del. Oct. 6, 2008).

[37] Harden v. Allstate Ins., 883 F.Supp. 963, 969 (D. Del. 1995).

[38] Roberts v. Delmarva Power & Light Co., 2 A.3d 131, 137 (Del. 2009).

[39] Culver v. Bennett, 588 A.2d 1094, 1096-97 (Del. 1991); Reid v. Hindt, 976 A.2d 125, 132 (Del. 2009).

[40] Pipher v. Parsell, 930 A.2d 890, 892 (Del. 2007).

[41] Reid v. Hindt, 976 A.2d 125, 132 (Del. 2009); Pipher v. Parsell, 930 A.2d 890, 892 (Del. 2007); Campbell v. DiSabatino, 947 A.2d 1116, 1117 (Del. 2008); Roache v. Charney, 38 A.3d 281, 286 (Del. 2012).

IV. Causation

A. Elements

It is necessary for the Delaware plaintiff to prove "a reasonable connection between the negligent act or omission of the defendant and the injury which the plaintiff has suffered."[42] The Supreme Court of Delaware refers to this connection as "proximate" or "legal cause."[43] In another case, the Supreme Court of Delaware framed the question of causation as one involving "issues of foreseeability, knowledge and the credibility of opposing witnesses and evidence."[44] The issue of causation is a question of fact to be submitted to the jury.[45]

Although many jurisdictions adhere to the "substantial factor" test for determining proximate cause, Delaware does not.[46] Instead, it defines proximate cause using the "but-for" rule.[47] Specifically, a proximate cause is one "which in natural and continuous sequence, unbroken by any efficient intervening cause, produces the injury and without which the result would not have occurred."[48] There may be more than one proximate cause of an injury.[49]

The Delaware Supreme Court further recognizes that, "an intervening cause involving abnormal, unforeseeable, or extraordinary negligence" may "break the chain of proximate causation."[50] Intervening acts are often described by Delaware courts as "superseding or supervening," in recognition of the policy of relieving the defendant from liability in such circumstances.[51] Whether an intervening cause would supersede the defendant's liability is a question for the jury.[52]

B. Evidence

Negligence is never presumed and must be proven before a plaintiff is entitled to recover.[53] The mere fact that an accident occurred is not enough.[54]

The Delaware Supreme Court states that it is well settled law that a claim which requires proof of facts that are "not within the common knowledge of laymen," "must be presented through competent expert testimony."[55] For example, in a case involving bodily

---

[42] Culver v. Bennett, 588 A.2d 1094, 1097 (Del. 1991)

[43] *Id.*

[44] Lynch v. Athey Prods. Corp., 505 A.2d 42, 49 (Del. 1985).

[45] *Id.*; Russell v. K-Mart Corp., 761 A.2d 1, 5 (Del. 2000); Jones v. Crawford, 1 A.3d 299, 303 (Del. 2010); Pipher v. Parsell, 930 A.2d 890, 892 (Del. 2007).

[46] Culver v. Bennett, 588 A.2d 1094, 1097 (Del. 1991); Russell v. K-Mart Corp., 761 A.2d 1, 5 (Del. 2000).

[47] Culver v. Bennett, 588 A.2d 1094, 1097 (Del. 1991); Russell v. K-Mart Corp., 761 A.2d 1, 5 (Del. 2000); Jones v. Crawford, 1 A.3d 299, 302 (Del. 2010); Spencer v. Goodill, 17 A.3d 552, 554 (Del. 2011).

[48] Russell v. K-Mart Corp., 761 A.2d 1, 5 (Del. 2000).

[49] Jones v. Crawford, 1 A.3d 299, 302 (Del. 2010).

[50] *Id.*

[51] *Id.* at 303.

[52] *Id.*

[53] DEL. P.J.I. CIV. §5.4 *No Presumption of Negligence* (2000).

[54] *Id.*

[55] Campbell v. DiSabatino, 947 A.2d 1116, 1118 (Del. 2008).

injuries, "the causal connection between the defendant's alleged negligent conduct and the plain-tiff's alleged injury must be proven by the direct testimony of a competent medical expert."[56]

V. Damages

A. Elements

The amount of damages to be awarded to the plaintiff shall be determined by the injuries which are caused by the defendant.[57] The purpose of awarding compensatory damages is to "impose satisfaction for an injury done" and "correct private wrongs."[58] Compensatory damages are often in the form of a monetary award, and "the size of the award is directly related to the harm caused by the defendant."[59] "The goal in fixing damages is just and full compensation, with the focus on the plaintiff's injury or loss."[60] Delaware courts have awarded damages to serve "the policy of deterring negligent conduct by making tortfeasors bear the full cost of their acts"[61]

Punitive damages may also be awarded where "the defendant's conduct, though unintentional, has been particularly reprehensible, *i.e.* reckless, or motivated by malice or fraud."[62]

Damages for future consequences of an injury, such as pain and suffering, may be awarded where it is "reasonably probable" that plaintiff will sustain such injuries.[63]

It is the duty of the injured party to "take all reasonable steps" to mitigate the damages caused by the defendant.[64]

B. Evidence

Compensatory and punitive damages are a question for the trier of fact.[65] The amount of compensatory damages awarded is controlled by the facts of the case.[66] "The amount of punitive damages shall be considered in light of the amount of compensatory damages, as well as the tortious conduct which caused the injury, while keeping always in mind that the compensatory damages have already made the victim 'whole.'"[67]

---

[56] Roache v. Charney, 38 A.3d 281, 286 (Del. 2012).

[57] Kane v. Reed, 101 A.2d 800, 802 (Del. 1954).

[58] Jardel Co. v. Hughes, 523 A.2d 518, 528 (Del. 1987).

[59] *Id.*

[60] *Id.*

[61] State Farm Mut. Auto. Ins. v. Nalbone, 569 A.2d 71, 74 (Del. 1989).

[62] Jardel Co. v. Hughes, 523 A.2d 518, 529 (Del. 1987).

[63] Kane v. Reed, 101 A.2d 800, 803 (1954); Laskowski v. Wallis, 205 A.2d 825, 826 (Del. 1964); Gannett Co. v. Kanaga, 750 A.2d 1174, 1188 (Del. 2000).

[64] Gulf Oil Corp. v. Slattery, 172 A.2d 266, 270 (Del. 1961).

[65] Jardel Co. v. Hughes, 523 A.2d 518, 527 (Del. 1987); Burkett-Wood v. Haines, 906 A.2d 756, 764 (Del. 2006).

[66] Kane v. Reed, 101 A.2d 800, 803 (Del. 1954).

[67] Malcolm v. Little, 295 A.2d 711, 714 (Del. 1972).

CHAPTER 9

DISTRICT OF COLUMBIA

DISTRICT OF COLUMBIA

Vicki Lawrence MacDougall[1]

I. Purpose of Tort Law

According to the law of the District of Columbia, the "primary purpose of tort law is to compensate plaintiffs for injuries they have sustained due to the wrongful conduct of others."[2] Other purposes of the negligence cause of action include deterrence of negligent behavior and the creation of an incentive to encourage due care.[3] To remain vital, tort law should reflect "contemporary community values and ethics."[4] Furthermore, the District of Columbia is one of the few jurisdictions that retains contributory negligence as an affirmative defense and a total bar to any and all recovery on the part of the injured plaintiff.[5] Accordingly, the policy of tort law is to allow full recovery to the totally innocent victim from the wrongdoer who has caused the loss and to deny recovery to one partially at fault in causing his or her own injuries.[6]

II. Duty to Exercise Ordinary Care

In order to recover for a negligence cause of action, a plaintiff must establish "a duty of care owed by the defendant to the plaintiff, a breach of that duty by the defendant, and damage to the interests of the plaintiff, proximately caused by the breach."[7] Before a defendant owes a duty to protect the plaintiff from harm, the defendant must be able to foresee a risk of injury to the plaintiff.[8] "The risk reasonably to be perceived defines the duty

---

[1] Professor of Law, Director, Health Law Certificate Program, Law Review Faculty Advisor, Oklahoma City University School of Law, Member, California and Oklahoma Bar Associations.

[2] Haymon v. Wilkerson, 535 A.2d 880, 885 (D.C. 1987).

[3] Reid v. District of Columbia, 391 A.2d 776, 778 (D.C. 1978), quoting Gypsum Carrier, Inc. v. Handelsman, 307 F.2d 525 (9th Cir. 1962).

[4] Rong Yao Zhou v. Jennifer Mall Restaurant, Inc., 534 A.2d 1268, 1274 (D.C. 1987).

[5] Massengale v. Pitts, 737 A.2d 1029 (D.C. 1999); Wingfield v. Peoples Drug Store, Inc., 379 A.2d 685 (D.C. 1977); Phillips v. D.C. Transit System, Inc., 198 A.2d 740 (D.C. 1964). The District of Columbia also retains the doctrine of last clear chance. Phillips v. D.C. Transit System, Inc., 198 A.2d 740, 741-42 (D.C. 1964).

[6] Massengale v. Pitts, 737 A.2d 1029 (D.C. 1999); Wingfield v. Peoples Drug Store, Inc., 379 A.2d 685 (D.C. 1977); Phillips v. D.C. Transit System, Inc., 198 A.2d 740 (D.C. 1964). The District of Columbia also retains the doctrine of last clear chance. Phillips v. D.C. Transit System, Inc., 198 A.2d 740, 741-42 (D.C. 1964).

[7] District of Columbia v. Harris, 770 A.2d 82. 87 (D.C. 2001), citing Turner v. District of Columbia, 532 A.2d 662, 666 (D.C. 1987); Sullivan v. AboveNet Communications, Inc., 112 A.3d 347, 354 (D.C. Ct. App. 2016).

[8] Munson v. Otis, 396 A.2d 994, 996 (D.C. 1979). The defendant had no duty to warn because the defendant had no reason to "believe that someone might suffer injury by failing to recognize that the sheet-rock panel would not hold his weight." Id. at 997.

to be obeyed."[9] As stated by Justice Oliver Wendall Holmes, "Unless my act is of a nature to threaten others, unless under the circumstances a prudent man would have foreseen the possibility of harm, it is no more justifiable to make me indemnify my neighbor against the consequences, than to make me do the same thing if I had fallen upon him in a fit, or to compel me to insure him against lightning."[10]

A.   Question of Law

The judicial branch normally defines the "contours of common law liability, including the duty that may have been breached in a negligence case."[11] It is a question of law whether a duty of care is owed in a particular case.[12]

A defendant's failure to comply with a criminal statute designed to protect the public from harm "is to fall short of the standard of diligence to which those who live in organized society are under a duty to conform."[13] Furthermore, the "decision to adopt from a penal statute a standard of care to be applied in determining common law negligence is purely a judicial one, for the court to make."[14] The standard of care established by a criminal statute can be borrowed to establish the standard of care in a civil cause of action "if by creating the hazard which the ordinance was intended to avoid it brings about the harm which the ordinance was intended to prevent."[15] Many factors are considered by the court in ascertaining whether a duty of care was owed by the defendant toward the plaintiff.

---

[9] Munson v. Otis, 396 A.2d 994, 997 (D.C. 1979), quoting Palsgraf v. Long Island R. Co., 248 N.Y. 339, 344,162 N. E. 99, 100 (1928).

[10] Ray v. American Nat. Red Cross, 696 A.2d 399, 404 (D.C. 1996), quoting Oliver W. Homes, The Common Law 95-96 (1881).

[11] Rong Yao Zhou v. Jennifer Mall Restaurant, Inc., 534 A.2d 1268, 1274 (D.C. 1987).

[12] Presley v. Commercial Moving & Rigging, Inc., 25 A.3d 873, 883 (D.C. 2011). An injured party in an automobile accident may avoid the recovery allowed under no-fault insurance and bring a negligence cause of action if the "injury directly results in substantial permanent scarring or disfigurement, substantial and medically demonstrable permanent impairment which has significantly affected the ability of the victim to perform his or her professional activities or usual and customary daily activities, or a medically demonstrable impairment that prevents the victim from performing all or substantially all of the material acts and duties that constitute his or her usual customary daily activities for more than 180 continuous days." Mark V. Holden, *The 1985 Amendments to the District of Columbia's No-Fault Motor Vehicle Insurance Act of 1982: The Future of No-Fault Insurance in the District*, 36 Cath. U. L. Rev. 777, 788-89, n. 81 (1987), citing D.C. Code Ann. § 35-2105(b)(1) (Supp. 1986). "It is a threshold question of law for the court to decide whether [an injured plaintiff] has met the strict statutory requirements . . . to overcome the Act's restrictions against tort actions for noneconomic losses." Smith v. WMATA, 631 A.2d 387, 391 (D.C. 1993).

[13] Rong Yao Zhou v. Jennifer Mall Restaurant, Inc., 534 A.2d 1268, 1274 (D.C. 1987).

[14] *Id.*

[15] Ross v. Hartman, 78 U.S. App. D.C. 217, 218, 139 F. 2d 14, 15 (Ct. App. D.C. 1943). The defendant's agent violated an ordinance by leaving a truck unattended, unlocked and with keys in the ignition. A thief stole the truck and ran over the plaintiff. Defendant was potentially liable for the plaintiff's injuries under the concept of negligence *per se. Ross,* 78 U.S. App. D.C. at 217, 139 F. 2d at 14.

[A] defendant is liable to a plaintiff for negligence only when the defendant owes the plaintiff some duty of care. [A] determination of whether a duty exists is the result of a variety of considerations and not solely the relationship between the parties. In the absence of contractual privity with an unrelated third party, whether a party should have foreseen that its contractual undertaking was necessary for the protection of the third party is important. Thus, even in the absence of contractual privity, we still look to the contract to determine the scope of the undertaking as it relates to the protection of the third party. In addition, [t]he existence of a duty is also shaped by considerations of fairness and results ultimately from policy decisions made by the courts and the legislatures.[16]

Two key factors, foreseeability of the harm and the relationship between the parties, along with policy considerations are critical in any analysis to ascertain if the interests of the plaintiff are "entitled to legal protection from the conduct of the defendant."[17]

In determining the existence of a duty owed to a plaintiff, [courts] have applied a "foreseeability of harm" test, which is based on the recognition that duty must be limited to avoid liability for unreasonably remote consequences. . . . Inherent also in the concept of duty is the relationship between the parties out of which the duty arises. . . . [U]ltimately, the determination of whether a duty should be imposed is made by weighing the various policy considerations and reaching a conclusion that the plaintiff's interest[s] are, or are not, entitled to legal protection against the conduct of the defendant.[18]

B.   Question of Fact

The District of Columbia has many of the same rules regarding duty that are present throughout the country, many inherited from the common law. For example, generally there is no duty to rescue or render aid absent special circumstances.[19] One exception to the no duty to rescue rule is if the actor has been involved in a car accident. Then, the driver does have a duty to investigate whether another person has been injured and summon aid.[20] Another no-duty rule is that there is no duty to warn about or to guard against obvious dangers.[21]

---

[16] Presley v. Commercial Moving & Rigging, Inc., 25 A.3d 873, 888 (D.C. 2011) (internal citations omitted). In *Presley*, a consultant on a construction project did not owe a duty to a construction worker who fell from a tower and hence was not liable as a matter of law for the death. *Presley*, 25 A.3d at 898.

[17] Odemns v. District of Columbia, 930 A.2d 137, 143 (D.C. 2007).

[18] Hedgepeth v. Whitman Walker Clinic, 22 A.3d 789,794 (D.C. 2011), quoting Odemns v. District of Columbia, 930 A.2d 137, 143 (D.C. 2007) (alterations in original)(quoting W.C. & A.N. Miller Co. v. United States, 963 F. Supp. 1231, 1243 (D.D.C. 1997)).

[19] Sullivan v. Yellow Cab Co., 212 A.2d 616, 618 (D.C. 1965).

[20] Sandwick v. District of Columbia, 21 A.3d 997, 1000 (D.C. 2011).

[21] Holland v. Baltimore & O. R. Co., 431 A.2d 597, 603 (D.C. App. 1981). The great weight of authority holds that a moving train is an obvious danger. *Id.* at 602. "Nothing could be more pregnant with warning of danger than the noise and appearance of a huge, rumbling string of railroad cars." *Id.* at 603.

An owner and occupier of land owes certain duties to the entrant upon land. However, the District of Columbia abolished the common law categories of invitee and licensee to ascertain the level of the duty owed to an entrant upon the land. Instead, a duty to used reasonable care under the circumstances is owed to the entrant if the entrant is lawfully on the premises.[22] However, the category of trespasser is retained and the landowner only owes a duty to not injure someone unlawfully on the premises through intentional or willful and wanton misbehavior.[23] A landowner may also be liable to a trespasser if the owner or occupier of land maintained a "hidden engine of destruction," such as a trap or spring gun.[24] Tempering the no-duty owed to a trespasser rule is a special rule toward trespassing children, the attractive nuisance doctrine.[25] The District of Columbia adopts the attractive nuisance doctrine as embodied within the *Restatement (Second) of Torts, § 339.*[26] *Section 339* provides, as follows:

> A possessor of land is subject to liability for physical harm to children trespassing thereon caused by an artificial condition upon the land if
>
> (a) the place where the condition exists is one upon which the possessor knows or has reason to know that children are likely to trespass, and
> (b) the condition is one of which the possessor knows or has reason to know and which he realizes or should realize will involve an unreasonable risk of death or serious bodily harm to such children and
> (c) the children because of their youth do not discover the condition or realize the risk involved in intermeddling with it or coming within the area made dangerous by it, and
> (d) the utility to the possessor of maintaining the condition and the burden of eliminating the danger are slight as compared with the risk to children involved, and
> (e) the possessor fails to exercise reasonable care to eliminate the danger or otherwise to protect the children.[27]

It is important to remember that even under the attractive nuisance doctrine that the duty imposed upon the owner or occupier of land is still only one of reasonable care under the circumstances; strict liability is not imposed upon the possessor.

---

[22] Boyrie v. E & G Property Services, 58 A.3d 475, 477 (D.C. 2013); Sandoe v. Lefta Associates, 559 A.2d 732, 738 (D.C. App. 1988).

[23] Boyrie v. E & G Property Services, 58 A.3d 475, 477 (D.C. 2013).

[24] Toomer v. William C. Smith & Co., Inc., 112 A.3d 324, 326 (D.C. 2015).

[25] Estrada v. Potomac Elec. Power Co., 488 A.2d 1359, 1360-61, at n. 1 (D.C. App. 1985).

[26] Holland v. Baltimore & O. R. Co., 431 A.2d 597, 601 (D.C. App. 1981).

[27] Restatement (Second) of Torts § 339 (1965).

The District of Columbia has adopted the undertaking theory and the *Restatement (Second) of Torts, § 324A* and imposes a duty upon the defendant to use reasonable care if the defendant undertakes services that the defendant knows or should know are necessary to protect a third party.[28] *Section 324A* provides, as follows:

> One who undertakes, gratuitously or for consideration, to render services to another which he should recognize as necessary for the protection of a third person or his things, is subject to liability to the third person for physical harm resulting from his failure to exercise reasonable care to protect his undertaking, if
>
> > (a) his failure to exercise reasonable care increases the risk of such harm, or
> > (b) he has undertaken to perform a duty owed by the other to the third person, or
> > (c) the harm is suffered because of reliance of the other or the third person upon the undertaking.[29]

The existence of a special relationship can create a duty of care to protect the plaintiff from the behavior of a third party. Special relationships include landlord/tenant, landowner/invitee, employer/employee, school district/pupil, hospital/patient, common carrier/passenger, and businessperson/patron.[30] Control is the common feature that ties together special relationships. Because "ability of one of the parties to provide for his own protection has been limited in some way by his submission to the control of the other, a duty should be imposed upon the one possessing control (and thus the power to act) to take reasonable precautions to protect the other one from assaults by third parties which, at least could reasonably have been anticipated."[31] In the landmark case of *Kline v. 1500 Massachusetts Avenue Apartment Corporation*,[32] the court imposed a duty on the landlord to protect tenants from foreseeable criminal acts committed on the premises, particularly the common areas under the landlord's control.[33]

---

[28] Presley v. Commercial Moving & Rigging, Inc., 25 A.3d 873, 888 (D.C. 2011).

[29] *Id.* at 889, quoting Restatement (Second) of Torts § 324A (1965).

[30] Kline v. 1500 Mass. Ave. Apart. Corp., 141 U.S. App. D.C. 370, 376-377, 439 F. 2d 477, 483-84 (Ct. App. D.C. Cir. 1970).

[31] *Kline.*, 141 U.S. App. D.C. at 376, 439 F. 2d at 482.

[32] 141 U.S. App. D.C. 370, 439 F. 2d 477 (Ct. App. D.C. Cir. 1970).

[33] *Kline,* 141 U.S. App. D.C. at 374-75, 439 F. 2d at 481-82.

III Breach of Duty

The time-honored test for breach of duty in the District of Columbia is the "uniform standard of conduct; that of reasonable care under the circumstances."[34] As aptly stated:

> Thus, our modern rule of negligent liability proceeds from a balance struck between an actor's freedom of choice and another's security in person and property: that one whose act unintentionally causes injury to another is generally liable to compensate the other only if the act was not reasonable under the circumstances—that is, only if the act created a foreseeable risk that could have been mitigated at a cost not disproportionate in light of the gravity and probability of the foreseeable harm. As Holmes suggested, the rule is the result of a balance among many conflicting policies, including those favoring private activity, compensation of persons injured through no fault of their own, and conservation of government and private resources that must be expended in proceedings to shift losses among individuals. Those considerations and others, however, and therefore the balance struck, may vary with the context of the claim.[35]

Negligence liability hinges on proof of a breach of the duty to use reasonable care. Although the District of Columbia has adopted no-fault insurance and most victims of car accidents receive compensation outside the negligence framework through no-fault insurance,[36] proof of a failure to use reasonable care is still mandated in any action pursued under a negligence framework.

A.   *Elements*

The overall standard of care is that of reasonableness under the circumstances of a given case and the query of how a reasonable person would behave. Requiring action of reasonable care is often conditioned on knowledge or notice of the danger[37] and the opportunity accompanied by sufficient time to remedy the condition or avoid the injury.[38] The District of Columbia has adopted Justice Learned Hand's calculus of risk and focuses on three elements to establish the standard of care in a given case. "The factors to be weighed in the determination of the degree of care demanded in a specific situation are 'the likelihood that conduct will injure others, taken with the seriousness of the injury if it happens, and balanced against the interest which must sacrifice to avoid the risk.'"[39]

---

[34] Ray v. American Nat. Red Cross, 696 A.2d 399, 402 (D.C. 1996).

[35] *Id.* at 404.

[36] Monroe v. Foreman, 540 A.2d 736 (1988); Smith v. WMATA, 631 A.2d 387 (D.C. 1993); Mark V. Holden, *The 1985 Amendments to the District of Columbia's No-Fault Motor Vehicle Insurance Act of 1982: The Future of No-Fault Insurance in the District*, 36 Cath. U. L. Rev. 777 (1987).

[37] Croce v. Hall, 657 A.2d 307, 310-11 (D.C. App. 1995); see also Tolu v. Ayodeji, 945 A.2d 596, 603-04 (D.C. 2008).

[38] Youssef v. 3636 Corp., 777 A.2d 787 (D.C. 2001).

[39] Conway v. O'Brien, 111 F.2d 611, 612 (2nd Cir. 1940), cited in Sandoe v. Lefta Associates, 559 A.2d 732, 740 (D.C. App. 1988); Smith v. Arbaugh's Restaurant, Inc., 152 U.S. App. D.C. 86, 89, 469 F.2d 97, 100 (1972).

B. *Evidence*

The burden is on the plaintiff to establish the standard of care and the departure from that standard by the defendant. "Admissibility and sufficiency, of course, present different issues; an item of evidence may be relevant and admissible, but insufficient, standing alone, to support a finding of negligence."[40] If the standard in question involves science, a profession, or an occupation that would be "beyond the keen of the average layperson," then expert testimony is required.[41]

The case must be submitted to the jury if there is some evidence from which the jury could find negligence, or there are disputed facts, or credibility of witnesses are in question. "Under that standard, cases are rare where issues of negligence and proximate cause can be taken from the jury and decided by the court as a matter of law."[42]

Violations of statutes may be used to establish negligence *per se* "if the statute is meant to promote safety, if the plaintiff is a member of the class to be protected by the statute, and if the defendant is a person upon whom the statue imposes specific duties."[43] The statute must set forth "specific guidelines to govern behavior," not simply a general guideline to use reasonable care.[44]

Although custom evidence is admissible to establish the standard of care, conformity to custom is not an absolute defense.[45] However, in professional negligence or malpractice cases, the "standard is measured by the course of action that a reasonably prudent [professional] with the defendant's specialty would have taken under the same or similar circumstances."[46] Professionals with special training are held to the standard of conduct "commensurate with such attributes. It is this notion of specialized knowledge and skill which animates the law of professional negligence."[47] The exception to this principle is the doctrine of inform consent which measures a physician's duty to disclose based on the material risk test, not by comparing the physician's behavior with that of his or her peers.[48] The material risk test mandates that the physician disclose all risks that a "reasonable person, in what the physician knows or should know to be the patient's position, would be likely to attach significance to the risk or cluster of risks in deciding whether or not to forego the proposed therapy."[49]

In the District of Columbia, "evidence of subsequent remedial measure is not admissible to prove negligence."[50] However, if the feasibility of safety precautions, either technical

[40] Bahura v. S.E.W. Investors, 754 A.2d 928, 945 (D.C. 2000).

[41] District of Columbia v. Harris, 770 A.2d 82. 91 (D.C. 2001).

[42] *Id.* at 89.

[43] Night & Day Management, LLC v. Butler, 101 A.3d 1033, 1039 (D.C. 2014).

[44] *Id.* at 1040. A statutory requirement to submit a security plan as part of a liquor license application requirement did not meet the required level of specificity. *Id.*

[45] Ray v. American Nat. Red Cross, 696 A.2d 399, 403 (D.C. 1996).

[46] *Id.* at 404, quoting Meek v. Shepard, 484 A.2d 579, 581 (D.C. 1984).

[47] *Ray*, 696 A.2d at 404, quoting Washington v. Washington Hosp. Ctr., 579 A.2d 177, 182 (D.C. 1990).

[48] Canterbury v. Spence, 150 U.S. App. D.C. 263, 464 F.2d 772 (Ct. App. D.C. Cir. 1972).

[49] Id., 150 U.S. App. D.C. at 279, 464 F.2d at 787.

[50] Ray v. American Nat. Red Cross, 696 A.2d 399, 408 (D.C. 1996).

possibility or effectiveness of alternatives, is controverted, then the subsequent remedial measures may be admissible.[51] Further, the defendant who sets a standard of care for himself to protect others from foreseeable harms may be found negligent if the defendant departs from the standard that the defendant has set for himself.[52]

Accident reports may be inadmissible hearsay. If the employee who prepared the accident report does not remember who provided the information contained in the report or did not witness the incident, then the accident report may be properly excluded from evidence as hearsay offered to establish the truth of the matter asserted therein.[53]

IV   Causation

The District of Columbia courts have defined proximate cause as "that cause which, in natural and continual sequence, unbroken by any efficient intervening cause, produces the injury and without which the result would not have occurred."[54] If a cause "contributes only slightly or possibly to the result," then the defendant's behavior is not the proximate cause.[55] Further, a cause is still a proximate cause even though the precise injury or the method in which the harm would occur could not have been foreseen if the "possibility of harm was clear to the ordinary prudent eye."[56]

A.   Elements

Proximate cause is divided into two elements, cause-in-fact and the policy element of proximate cause.[57] "The cause-in-fact requirement assures that no defendant will be liable unless he has in fact caused the plaintiff's harm."[58] Courts in the District of Columbia opine that the substantial factor test is the best guide to resolve the cause-in-fact issue and that "the test is of considerable assistance."[59] On the other hand, proximate causation is the "policy element" and "includes various liability-limiting considerations which relieve the defendant of liability for harm he actually caused where the chain of events appears highly extraordinary in retrospect."[60]

"The Supreme Court has emphasized that proximate cause is a generic label for the 'judicial tools used to limit a person's responsibility for the consequences of that person's own acts. . . . Accordingly, among the many shapes this concept took at common law was a demand

[51] Id.

[52] Kline v. 1500 Mass. Ave. Apart. Corp., 141 U.S. App. D.C. 370, 379, 439 F. 2d 477, 486 (Ct. App. D.C. Cir. 1970).

[53] Presley v. Commercial Moving & Rigging, Inc., 25 A.3d 873, 892 (D.C. 2011).

[54] District of Columbia v. Zukerberg, 880 A.2d 276, 281 (D.C. 2005), citing St. Paul Fire & Marine Ins. Co. v. James G. Davis Constr. Corp., 350 A.2d 751, 752 (D.C. App. 1976).

[55] Lacy v. District of Columbia, 424 A.2d 317, 321 (D.C. 1980).

[56] District of Columbia v. Harris, 770 A.2d 82. 91 (D.C. 2001).

[57] Lacy v. District of Columbia, 424 A.2d 317, 320 (D.C. 1980).

[58] Id.

[59] Id. at 321.

[60] Id. at 320-21, citing Restatement (Second) of Torts § 433, Reporter's Notes (1966).

for some direct relation between the injury asserted and the injurious conduct alleged.'"[61] The following six factors are utilized in analyzing a proximate cause issue in a case:

> (1) the causal connection between the defendant's wrongdoing and the plaintiff's harm; (2) the specific intent of the defendant to harm the plaintiff; (3) the nature of the plaintiff's alleged injury and whether it relates to the purposes of tort law; (4) whether the claim for damages is highly specula- tive; (5) the directness or indirectness of the alleged injury; and (6) the aim of keeping the scope of complex trials within judicially manageable limits, *i.e.*, avoiding the risks of duplicative recoveries and the danger of complex apportionment.[62]

Furthermore, a "defendant may not be held liable for harm actually caused where the chain of events leading to the injury appears *highly* extra-ordinary in retrospect."[63]

B. *Evidence*

To establish that the defendant's behavior was a proximate cause of the plaintiff's injury, the plaintiff must "present evidence from which a reasonable juror could find that there was a direct and substantial causal relationship between the defendant's breach of the standard of care and the plaintiff's injuries and that the injuries were foreseeable."[64] Gen- erally, causation including proximate cause is a question of fact to be decided by the jury.[65] However, proximate cause "becomes a question of law when the evidence adduced at trial will not support a rational finding of proximate cause."[66] A directed verdict for the defen- dant is appropriate "[w]hen the question of the defendant's causation 'remains one of pure speculation or conjecture, or the probabilities are at best evenly balanced.'"[67] Either direct or circumstantial evidence may be used to meet the burden to prove causation.[68]

Evidence of an intervening cause, even the criminal action of a third party, may or may not break the chain of causation. The defendant will be liable for the plaintiff's dam- ages, "despite the intervention of another's act in the chain of causation, '[i]f the danger of

---

[61] District of Columbia v. Beretta U.S.A. Corp., 2002 WL 31811717, 23 (D.C. Sup. Ct.), quoting Holmes v. Securities Investor Protection Corp., 503 U.S. 258, 268, 112 S.Ct. 1311, 117 L.Ed. 2d 532 (1992).

[62] District of Columbia v. Beretta U.S.A. Corp., 2002 WL 31811717, 23 (D.C. Sup. Ct.), quoting City of Phila- delphia v. Beretta, U.S.A. Corp., 277 F.3d 415, 423 (3rd Cir. 2002).

[63] Morgan v. District of Columbia, 468 A.2d 1306, 1318 (1983), quoting Lacy v. District of Columbia, 424 A.2d 317, 320-21 (D.C. 1980)(emphasis original).

[64] District of Columbia v. Zukerberg, 880 A.2d 276, 281 (D.C. 2005), citing District of Columbia v. Wilson, 721 A.2d 591, 600 (D.C. 1998).

[65] Reeves v. Washington Metropolitan Area Transit Authority, 135 A.3d 807, 811 (D.C. Ct. App. 2016).

[66] District of Columbia v. Zukerberg, 880 A.2d 276, 281 (D.C. 2005), citing Majeska v. District of Columbia, 812 A.2d 948, 950 (D.C. 2002).

[67] Bragg v. Owens-Corning Fiberglas Corp. 734 A.2d 643 (D.C. 1999), quoting W. Page Keeton, *et al.*, Prosser & Keeton on the Law of Torts *§ 41, at 268-69 (*5th ed. 1984).

[68] District of Columbia v. Zukerberg, 880 A.2d 276, 281 (D.C. 2005), citing District of Columbia v. Savoy Constr. Co., 515 A.2d 698, 708 (D.C. 1986).

an intervening negligent or criminal act should have been reasonably anticipated and pro-tected against.'"[69] Conversely, the "plaintiff may not look beyond the intervening act for his recovery" if the intervening act "could not have reasonably been anticipated."[70] Although a defendant does not normally have to foresee the precise nature of the injury to be held liable, the plaintiff must precisely prove that the defendant could have foreseen the risk of harm if the plaintiff's injury is caused by the intervening act of a criminal.[71]

V. Damages

The requirement that a negligent defendant pay for the injury his or her mis-behav-ior has caused to another springs from "the notion of the actor's culpability" and that the defendant's departure "from the accepted norms of behavior" and the steps that defendant should have taken to avoid the injury justifies shifting the plaintiff's loss onto the shoulders of the defendant for recompense.[72] Recovery in a negligence cause of action is the amount of damages proximately cause by the defendant's actions.[73]

A. Elements

Generally, the plaintiff can not recover more in compensatory damages than the ac-tual loss suffered.[74] The primary purpose is to make the plaintiff whole.[75] The award may in-clude medical bills, loss wages and mental suffering.[76] Damages for the future consequences caused by the tort, including loss of future earnings, are recoverable so long as the amount is reasonably certain.[77] Therefore, an injured plaintiff can recover future suffering, additional medical expenses and loss of future income so long as the loss is demonstrated and is not speculative.[78] A plaintiff within the zone of danger may recover for negligent infliction of emotional distress so long as the damages are serious and verifiable.[79]

---

[69] Lacy v. District of Columbia, 424 A.2d 317, 320, 323 (D.C. 1980), quoting St. Paul Fire & Marine Ins. Co. v. James G. Davis Constr. Corp., 350 A.2d 751, 752 (D.C. App. 1976); see also Board of Trustees of the Univ. of D.C. v. DiSalvo, 974 A. 2d 868, 872 (D.C. 2009).

[70] Lacy v. District of Columbia, 424 A.2d 317, 320, 323 (D.C. 1980).

[71] Lacy v. District of Columbia, 424 A.2d 317, 320, 323 (D.C. 1980), citing Kendall v. Gore Properties, Inc., 98 U.S. App. D.C. 378, 387, 236 F.2d 673, 682 (Ct. App. D.C. Cir. 1956); District of Columbia v. Harris, 770 A.2d 82. 92 (D.C. 2001).

[72] Munson v. Otis, 396 A.2d 994, 996 (D.C. 1979).

[73] District of Columbia v. Harris, 770 A.2d 82. 93 (D.C. 2001); Haymon v. Wilkerson, 535 A.2d 880, 885 (D.C. 1987).

[74] Doe v. Georgetown Center (II), Inc., 708 A.2d 255, 258 (D.C. 1998).

[75] Croley v. Republican Nat. Committee, 759 A.2d 682, 689 (D.C. 2000).

[76] Doe v. Georgetown Center (II), Inc., 708 A.2d 255, 257-58 (D.C. 1998).

[77] Otis Elevator Co. v. Tuerr, 616 A.2d 1254, 1260-61 (D.C. 1992).

[78] Croley v. Republican Nat. Committee, 759 A.2d 682, 690 (D.C. 2000).

[79] Bahura v. S.E.W. Investors, 754 A.2d 928, 937 (D.C. 2000).

B.   *Evidence*

The jury in a negligence case examines the evidence to calculate the measure of the damage award. Courts should not set aside the award of damages or order a new trial on the amount of damages unless the award is "contrary to all reason," "the verdict evidences prejudice, passion or partiality on the part of the jury, or appears to be the result of oversight, mistake, or consideration of an improper element."[80]

The District of Columbia adheres to the collateral source rule. Accordingly, "payments should not be reduced by the injured person's obtaining money or care from a collateral source. It is better that the injured party receive a double recovery than for the wrongdoer to be relieved of its liability for damages."[81]

Lapse of time between the negligent conduct and the onset of damages may be considered in the jury's determination that the alleged damages were a product of the defendant's behavior. "Close proximity in time between an accident and a plaintiff's subjective symptoms of physical injury may render unnecessary the presentation of expert testimony as to causation."[82] The connection simply has the "ring of truth."[83]

> Rain on the day the war ends does not prove that peace will not brook sunshine. In other words, if something happens after an occurrence (*post hoc)*, it has not necessarily happened on account of that occurrence (*propter hoc*); hence the *post hoc ergo propter hoc* fallacy. But neither obeisance to Latin phrases nor our more general obligation to exercise caution before converting "after" into "because" requires us to be blind to common-sense inferences from the timing of the . . . plaintiffs' symptoms. On the contrary, "the lapse of time which may exist between the time of negligent [behavior] . . . and eventual injury is a factor for the jury to consider in determining the causal connection between the negligence and the injury."[84]

If the negligence of the defendant aggravates a plaintiff's pre-existing injury, the plaintiff may only recover for the "increased or augmented" suffering.[85] Expert testimony may be required if the aggravated injury creates a "medically complicated question."[86] "In the absence of complicated medical questions, the plaintiff's own testimony, without need for supporting expert medical testimony, will suffice to prove causation of injury."[87]

---

[80] District of Columbia v. Harris, 770 A.2d 82. 93 (D.C. 2001), quoting Romer v. District of Columbia, 449 A.2d 1097, 1099 (D.C. 1982).

[81] Reid v. District of Columbia, 391 A.2d 776, 778 (D.C. 1978), quoting Gypsum Carrier, Inc. v. Handelsman, 307 F.2d 525 (9th Cir. 1962).

[82] Bahura v. S.E.W. Investors, 754 A.2d 928, 942 (D.C. 2000).

[83] *Id.* at 943.

[84] *Id.* at 943, quoting American Reciprocal Insurers v. Bessonette, 235 Or. 507, 384 P.2d 223, 224 (1963).

[85] Williams v. Patterson, 681 A.2d 1147, 1150 (D.C. App. 1996).

[86] *Id.*

[87] *Id.* quoting International Sec. Corp. of Va. v. McQueen, 497 A.2d 1076, 1080 (D.C. 1985).

Proof of loss of future income is complicated. "[T]he trier of fact must have evidence pertaining to the age, sex, occupational class, and probable wage increases over the remainder of the working life of the plaintiff. Furthermore, it is well settled that the task of projecting a person's lost earnings lends itself to clarification by expert testimony because it involves the use of statistical techniques and requires a broad knowledge of economics."[88] Loss of earnings for a self-employed person may be established by several factors, "including loss of profits from the business, the cost of substitute labor, the value of the plaintiff's services, and plaintiff's draw against profits."[89] Evidence is admissible to show the amount of business the plaintiff was able to generate.[90] The plaintiff's age, sex, and educational background are also relevant.[91] If a capacity to generate business is established, "it is not improper for a calculation [of lost future earnings] to be based upon earning potential rather than demonstrated earning capacity."[92]

---

[88] Croley v. Republican Nat. Committee, 759 A.2d 682, 690 (D.C. 2000).

[89] *Id.* at 692.

[90] *Id.*

[91] *Id.*

[92] *Id.* at 694, quoting Butera v. District of Columbia, 83 F. Supp. 2d 25, 35 (D.D.C. 1999).

CHAPTER 10

FLORIDA

FLORIDA
Jennifer S. Prilliman[1]

I. Purpose of Tort Law

The purpose of tort law in Florida is to compensate injured parties for their injuries, and to insure that tortfeasors "bear the cost of their tortious conduct."[2] The Florida Supreme Court notes that the common law and tort law "must keep pace with changes in our society,"[3] and "may be altered when the reason for the rule of law ceases to exist, or when change is demanded by public necessity or required to vindicate fundamental rights."[4] Liability for a tort rises out of a breach of duty to a plaintiff and seeks to both deter wrongful conduct and "encourage socially beneficial conduct."[5]

II. Duty to Exercise Ordinary Care

A. Question of Law

To establish a claim for negligence the injured party must show that the defendant (1) owed a duty, (2) did not conform to that duty, (3) there was a connection between the nonconforming conduct and the claimant's injury, and (4) actual harm was suffered.[6] Generally, everyone is required to exercise reasonable care for the "safety of others."[7] Whether the defendant has a duty to exercise care is a question of law.[8] Duty "is a minimal threshold legal requirement for opening the courthouse doors."[9] "The legal threshold for imposing a duty on a defendant is, however, crossed only when it is established that the defendant 'more likely

---

[1] Law Library Professor and Associate Law Library Director, Oklahoma City University School of Law Chickasaw Nation Law Library, member of the Oklahoma Bar.

[2] Jews for Jesus, Inc. v. Rapp, 997 So.2d 1098, 1105 (Fla. 2008) (quoting Clay Elec. Coop. v. Johnson, 873 So.2d 1182, 1190 (Fla. 2003)).

[3] Gates v. Foley, 247 So.2d 40, 43 (Fla. 1971).

[4] United States v. Dempsey, 635 So.2d 961, 964 (Fla.1994); *see also* Jews for Jesus, Inc. v. Rapp, 997 So.2d 1098, 1104 (Fla. 2008).

[5] Jews for Jesus, Inc. v. Rapp, 997 So.2d 1098, 1104 (Fla. 2008) (quoting *Denver Publ'g Co. v. Bueno,* 54 P.3d 893, 897–98 (Colo. 2002)).

[6] Williams v. Davis, 974 So.2d 1052, 1056 (Fla. 2007).

[7] Green v. Atl. Co., 61 So.2d 185, 186 (Fla. 1952).

[8] McCain v. Fla. Power Corp., 593 So.2d 500, 503 (Fla. 1992).

[9] *Id.* at 502.

than not' created a foreseeable zone of risk."[10] The jury, or trier of fact, will determine if the duty was breached.[11]

Foreseeability is an essential element of any negligence action.[12] In Florida, foreseeability is required to both establish a duty and when evaluating proximate cause.[13] If an injury is potentially foreseeable, there is a duty to avoid causing the injury.[14]

B. *Question of Fact*

i. **Elements**

What constitutes reasonable conduct under the circumstances is a question of fact for the jury.[15] The standard of care is reasonable care, or "that which a reasonably careful, prudent, and cautious person would use under the circumstances."[16] "The scope of the zone of risk is determined by the foreseeability of a risk of harm to others,"[17] and is based on the specific circumstances of the case.[18] The "reasonable specific foreseeability of a general zone of risk . . . is an objective test that necessarily involves Public policy considerations. It is a test that recognizes that more is required than the mere general risk of injury."[19] The ultimate issue for the jury "is whether the defendant's conduct created a foreseeable zone of risk, *not* whether the defendant could foresee the specific injury that actually occurred."[20]

ii. **Evidence**

A duty can be created by "(1) legislative enactments or administration regulations; (2) judicial interpretations of such enactments or regulations; (3) other judicial precedent; and (4) a duty arising from the general facts of the case."[21] A statute or regulation may be used to establish the level of care required where the injury was the type the statute was designed to prevent and the injured party was one of the class of persons protected by the statute.[22] A party's own policies may be used as evidence of the level of care required in a

---

[10] Smith v. Fla. Power & Light Co., 857 So.2d 224, 229 (Fla. Dist. Ct. App. 2003).

[11] Chirillo v. Granicz, 199 So.3d 246, 249 (Fla. 2016).

[12] Smith's Bakery, Inc. v. Jernigan, 134 So.2d 519, 520 (Fla. Dist. Ct. App. 1961).

[13] *McCain,* 593 So.2d at 502.

[14] *Smith*, 857 So.2d at 229.

[15] *See* Hall v. Billy Jack's, Inc., 458 So.2d 760, 762 (Fla. 1984).

[16] Hensley v. United States, 728 F. Supp. 716, 721 (S.D. Fla.1989).

[17] *Smith*, 857 So.2d at 230.

[18] *Id.*

[19] Gath v. St. Lucie City-Fort Pierce Fire Dist., 640 So.2d 138, 140 (Fla. Dist. Ct. App. 1994).

[20] Roos v. Morrison, 913 So.2d 59, 64 (Fla. Dist. Ct. App. 2005) (emphasis in original) (citations omitted).

[21] Williams v. Davis, 974 So.2d 1052, 1056 (Fla. 2007).

[22] deJesus v. Seaboard Coast Line R.R., 281 So.2d 198, 201 (Fla. 1973).

circumstance.[23] Evidence that the duty was breached may be direct or circumstantial,[24] but "negligence may not be inferred from the mere happening of an accident."[25] Additionally, if circumstantial evidence is relied on, "the initial inference must be established to the exclusion of any other reasonable theory or inference."[26]

The victim has the burden of proof to establish that the risk was foreseeable,[27] and they must prove that "defendant's conduct created or controlled the risk."[28]

III. Breach of Duty

A. Elements

The jury determines whether a breach of the duty of care to protect the plaintiff occurred.[29] "The duty element of negligence focuses on whether the defendant's conduct foreseeably created a broader 'zone of risk' that poses a general threat of harm to others."[30]

Individuals who create a risk are expected to "exercise prudent foresight."[31] "This requirement of reasonable, general foresight is the core of the duty element."[32]

B. Evidence

The plaintiff must "[make] at least a *prima facie* showing of negligence on the part of the defendant,"[33] and they must prove their case by a preponderance of the evidence.[34] Violating a statute can be used as prima facie evidence of a breach of duty.[35] The Florida courts recognize that it is reasonable for people to abide by the law.[36] Failure to comply with professional or industry standards may also be used as evidence of a breach of duty.[37]

---

[23] Marks v. Mandel, 477 So.2d 1036, 1038-39 (Fla. Dist. Ct. App. 1985).

[24] Nunez v. G.F. Car Ctr., Inc., 877 So.2d 31, 33 (Fla. Dist. Ct. App. 2004).

[25] *Id.* at 32.

[26] *Id.* at 33.

[27] *Smith*, 857 So.2d at 230.

[28] Levine v. Wyeth Inc., 684 F. Supp. 2d 1338, 1344 (M.D. Fla. 2010).

[29] *Roos*, 913 So.2d at 64.

[30] *McCain*, 593 So.2d at 502.

[31] *Id.* at 503.

[32] *Id.*

[33] Green v. Loudermilk, 146 So.2d 601, 603 (Fla. Dist. Ct. App. 1962) (emphasis in original).

[34] Fla. Motor Lines v. Ward, 137 So. 163, 166 (Fla. 1931) (en banc).

[35] Alford v. Meyer, 201 So.2d 489, 491 (Fla. Dist. Ct. App. 1967).

[36] *Id.*

[37] *See* City of Miami v. Ameller, 472 So.2d 728, 729 (Fla. 1985) (the city's failure to adhere to its own standards for playground equipment safety was used as evidence of a breach of duty).

IV. Causation

A. Elements

Causation is the central element of a negligence action.[38] Foreseeability is the key factor when determining if proximate cause exists.[39] Foreseeability for proximate cause differs from the foreseeability requirement for duty.[40] For proximate cause, "foreseeability is concerned with the specific, narrow factual details of the case, not with the broader zone of risk the defendant created."[41] For liability to be imposed, the defendant is not required to foresee the specific injury, only that some injury could occur.[42] "The law does not impose liability for freak injuries that were utterly unpredictable in light of common human experience," even if the injury occurred in the "zone of risk."[43] Whether an injury was reasonably foreseeable is generally a question for a jury.[44] However, the court may remove the question from the jury "where the facts are unequivocal, such as where the evidence supports no more than a single reasonable inference."[45]

B. Evidence

Florida uses the "more likely than not" standard for determining causation.[46] The plaintiff must prove, with a "reasonable basis" and substantial evidence, that the defendant's negligence "probably caused" the injury.[47] The "mere possibility" of causation will not be sufficient.[48] Either direct or circumstantial evidence may be used to prove causation.[49]

V. Damages

A. Elements

"A cause of action in negligence requires proof of actual loss or damage," often phrased as "actual harm."[50] The aim of compensatory damages awarded in negligence cases

---

[38] Asgrow-Kilgore Co. v. Mulford Hickerson Corp., 301 So.2d 441, 444 (Fla. 1974).

[39] *McCain*, 593 So.2d at 502.

[40] *Id.*

[41] *Id.* at 503.

[42] *Id.*

[43] *Id.*

[44] *Id.* at 504.

[45] *Id.*

[46] Cox v. St. Josephs Hosp., 71 So.3d 795, 799 (Fla. 2011).

[47] *Id.*

[48] Gooding v. Univ. Hosp. Bldg., Inc., 445 So.2d 1015, 1018 (Fla. 1984) (quoting Prosser, Law of Torts § 41 (4th ed. 1971)).

[49] Kincaid v. World Ins., 157 So.2d 517, 517 (Fla. 1963).

[50] Lucarelli Pizza & Deli v. Posen Const., Inc., 173 So.3d 1092, 1094 (Fla. Dist. Ct. App. 2015).

is to make the "injured party whole."[51] Actual harm "does not require a precise technical level or particular threshold of injury or impairment symptom that a plaintiff must satisfy to file an action."[52] However, the Florida courts emphasize the need for a plaintiff to prove "personal injury or property damage" in order to recover.[53] The Supreme Court of Florida holds that "the common law of Florida has *never* required individuals who have suffered an injury to meet an arbitrarily-drawn threshold of physical impairment for a cause of action to accrue."[54]

B.   *Evidence*

"It is a matter for the jury to decide whether there has in fact been an injury and damage."[55] The jury will determine the award for damages.[56]

---

[51] Nichols v. State Farm Mut., 851 So.2d 742, 753 (Fla. Dist. Ct. App. 2003), *approved sub nom.*, State Farm Mut. Auto. Ins. v. Nichols, 932 So.2d 1067 (Fla. 2006), *distinguished on other grounds by*, Wallen v. Tyson, 174 So.3d 1058, 1060 (Fla. Dist. Ct. App. 2015), *review denied*, No. SC15-1798 (Fla. Aug. 9, 2016).

[52] Am. Optical Corp. v. Spiewak, 73 So.3d 120, 127 (Fla. 2011).

[53] *Id.*

[54] *Id.* (emphasis in original); 21 Fla. Prac., Elements of an Action § 1401:1 (2015-2016 ed.).

[55] *Am. Optical Corp.*, 73 So.3d at 127.

[56] McIntyre v. McCloud, 334 So.2d 171, 171 (Fla. Dist. Ct. App. 1976) (per curium); *Am. Optical Corp.*, 73 So.3d at 129.

CHAPTER 11

GEORGIA

GEORGIA

Margaret (Meg) Butler[1]

I. Purpose of Tort Law

In codifying tort law in Georgia, the Georgia legislature defined "tort" as "the unlawful violation of a private legal right other than a mere breach of contract, express or implied. A tort may also be the violation of a public duty if, as a result of the violation, some special damage accrues to the individual."[2] In its infancy, tort liability in Georgia was "based upon prevailing concepts of fault, moral culpability, and deterrence of the wrongdoer."[3] The Georgia Supreme Court has elaborated, "It is generally recognized, as stated in *Prosser & Keeton, Torts,* 5th ed., § 4 at p. 25, that '[t]he "prophylactic" factor of preventing future harm has been quite important in the field of torts. The courts are concerned not only with compensation of the victim, but with admonition of the wrongdoer. When the decisions of the courts become known, and the defendants realize that they may be held liable, there is of course a strong incentive to prevent the occurrence of the harm.'"[4] The goal of preventing future harm is most seen in the explanation that "negligence is conduct which falls below the standard established by law for the protection of others against unreasonable risk of harm."[5]

Further, "[d]amages are given as compensation for injury," as where the measure of damage can be estimated in money.[6] Nominal damages only are awarded when the "injury is small or the mitigating circumstances are strong."[7] Georgia law presumes that general damages flow from tortious acts, and damages for those acts "may be recovered without proof of any amount."[8]

---

[1] Associate Director for Public Services, Georgia State University College of Law Library.

[2] O.C.G.A. § 51-1-1 (2000).

[3] Hatch v. O'Neill, 231 Ga. 446, 451, 202 S.E.2d 44, 48 (1973). "Tort liability was, like the criminal law, based upon moral responsibility, the ability of an individual to recognize the moral consequences of his own act and to will the consequences of such act."

[4] Denton v. Con-Way S. Express, Inc., 261 Ga. 41, 402 S.E.2d 269 (1991) (changes in original) (disagreed with on other grounds by Grissom v. Gleason, 262 Ga. 374, 418 S.E.2d 27 (1992)).

[5] Dupree v. Keller Industries, Inc., 199 Ga. App. 138, 142-143, 404 S.E.2d 291, 295 (1991) (quoting RESTATEMENT (SECOND) OF TORTS, § 282 (1965); Bradley Ctr. v. Wessner, 250 Ga. 199, 296 S.E.2d 693 (1982)).

[6] O.C.G.A. § 51-12-4 (2000).

[7] O.C.G.A. § 51-12-4 (2000).

[8] O.C.G.A. § 51-12-2 (2000); Georgia Power Co. v. Womble, 150 Ga. App. 28, 256 S.E.2d 640 (1979) (citing Alexander v. Holmes, 85 Ga. App. 124, 68 S.E.2d 242 (1951)).

II.   Duty to Exercise Ordinary Care

A.   *Question of Law*

Whether, and to what extent the defendant owes a legal duty to the plaintiff is a question of law.[9] In fact, "the threshold issue in a negligence action is whether and to what extent the defendant owes a legal duty to the plaintiff."[10] A legal duty can arise in a number of ways. On a negligence claim, a legal duty may arise from "the general duty one owes to all the world not to subject them to an unreasonable risk of harm."[11] Alternatively, a legislative enactment can give rise to a duty, or a duty may "be imposed by a common law principle recognized in the case law."[12] An action for negligence cannot be maintained if no duty is owed to the plaintiff.[13] "The [question of] duty is defined by the law,"[14] and "[t]he existence of a legal duty is a question of law for the court."[15]

Under Georgia's statutory scheme governing torts, "ordinary diligence" is defined as "the degree of care which is exercised by ordinarily prudent persons under the same or similar circumstances. . . . The absence of such diligence is termed ordinary negligence."[16] Extraordinary diligence corresponds with the duty of care associated with a tort claim based on slight negligence.[17] Failure to exercise slight diligence, on the other hand, corresponds with gross negligence claims.[18] "Slight diligence or care is the degree of care that persons of common sense, however inattentive they may be, use under the same or similar circumstances."[19]

The duty of care owed can be affected by several factors. First, the level of apparent risk can affect the amount of care required to meet the standard of reasonable conduct, "in

---

[9] Wilcher v. Redding Swainsboro Ford Lincoln Mercury, Inc., 321 Ga. App. 563, 566, 743 S.E.2d 27, 30 (2013) (citing Perkins v. Kranz, 316 Ga. App. 171, 172, 728 S.E.2d 804 (2012)).

[10] *Id.*

[11] Underwood v. Select Tire, Inc., 296 Ga. App. 805, 808, 676 S.E.2d 262, 267 (2009) (quoting Bradley Ctr. v. Wessner, 250 Ga. 199, 200, 296 S.E.2d 693, 695 (1982)).

[12] Rasnick v. Krishna Hosp., Inc., 289 Ga. 565, 566-67, 713 S.E.2d 835, 837 (2011) (citing Murray v. Ga. Dep't of Transp., 284 Ga. App. 263, 272, 644 S.E.2d 290, 298 (2007); *see also* O.C.G.A. § 51-1-1 (2016) (defining tort to include the violation of a public duty); O.C.G.A. § 51-1-8 (2000) (recognizing breach of private duties right of action).

[13] Scrocca v. Ashwood Condominium Ass'n, Inc., 326 Ga. App. 226, 230, 756 S.E.2d 308, 312 (2014) (quoting Anderson v. Atlanta Comm. for the Olympic Games, 273 Ga. 113, 118, 537 S.E.2d 345, 350 (2000)).

[14] Feise v. Cherokee Cty., 207 Ga. App. 17, 21, 427 S.E.2d 294, 298 (1992) (brackets in original) (quoting Shockley v. Zayre of Atlanta, 118 Ga. App. 672, 673, 165 S.E.2d 179, 181 (1968)).

[15] Fletcher v. Water Applications Distribution Grp., Inc., 333 Ga. App. 693, 697, 773 S.E.2d 859, 863 (2015) (citing Rasnick v. Krishna Hosp., Inc., 289 Ga. 565, 567, 713 S.E.2d 835, 837 (2011)).

[16] O.C.G.A. § 51-1-2 (2000).

[17] O.C.G.A. § 51-1-3 (2000). The slight negligence duty of care arises most commonly in cases involving common carriers who have "a duty of extraordinary care in the transportation of their passengers." GA. L. OF TORTS *Section* 3:3; *see also* Williamson v. Central of Georgia Ry. Co., 127 Ga. 125, 56 S.E. 119 (1906) (abrogated on issue of whether emotional distress is recoverable if resulting in foreseeable physical or mental impairment, even though there was no physical impact).

[18] O.C.G.A. § 51-1-4 (2000).

[19] 1 Council of Superior Court Judges of Georgia, *Suggested Pattern Jury Instructions: Civil Cases* § 60.030 (5th ed. July 2016).

proportion to the apparent risk. As the danger becomes greater, the actor is required to exercise caution commensurate with it."[20] If a person creates a dangerous condition or situation, even if the danger is created without any negligence, the person "is under a duty to remove the hazard or give warning of the danger so as to prevent others from being injured where it is reasonably foreseeable that this will occur."[21] For one who agrees to control and supervise a child, "even without compensation,"[22] there is "the duty to use reasonable care to protect the child from injury."[23] The level of care should be reasonably commensurate with the reasonably foreseeable risk of harm."[24] Foreseeability alone is not a basis for a duty of care;[25] Georgia has recognized that duty may be bounded by logic, science, and policy.[26]

Tort claims may also arise from breach of private duties, whether the duties arise from statute or are created by contract.[27] A claim for breach of private duties created by a contract may not be based merely on a breach of the contract itself.[28] Instead, the tort claim may be based on a special or confidential relationship that may give rise to private duties.[29] "'Some confidential relationships are created by law and contract (*e.g.*, partners), others may be created by the facts of the particular case.' The existence of a confidential relationship is generally a jury question."[30] However, "[w]here the facts are patent, unambiguous, and undisputed, the trial court may decide the issue of a confidential relationship as a matter of law."[31]

In the context of claims arising from professional negligence, the standard of duty may reflect the norms established in the professional's community. "[W]ith respect to the 'ordinary care, skill, and diligence' element [of a negligence claim], 'the law imposes upon persons performing professional services the duty to exercise a reasonable degree of skill and

[20] Millar Elevator Serv. Co. v. O'Shields, 222 Ga. App. 456, 458, 475 S.E.2d 188, 191 (1996) (quoting Prosser and Keaton on Torts §34, p. 208 (5th ed. 1984)).

[21] CSX Transp., Inc. v. Williams, 278 Ga. 888, 891, 608 S.E.2d 208, 210 (2005), quoting United States v. Aretz, 248 Ga. 19, 25, 280 S.E.2d 345, 350-51 (1981) (*CSX* indicates that "the concepts [*Aretz*] sets forth have no applicability to the issues presented in this case," suggesting that for *Aretz* to apply, the defendant would have had to "spread . . . asbestos dust among the general population, thereby creating a dangerous situation in the world beyond the workplace").

[22] Bunn v. Landers, 230 Ga. App. 744, 745, 498 S.E.2d 109, 112 (1998) (quoting Wallace v. Boys Club, etc., 211 Ga. App, 534, 535, 438 S.E.2d 746, 748 (1993).

[23] *Id.*

[24] *Id.*

[25] CSX Transp., Inc. v. Williams, 278 Ga. 888, 890, 608 S.E.2d 208, 209 (2005) (citing City of Douglasville v. Queen, 270 Ga. 770, 514 S.E.2d 195 (1999).

[26] *Id.*

[27] O.C.G.A. § 51-1-8 (2000).

[28] Odem v. Pace Acad., 235 Ga. App. 648, 656, 510 S.E.2d 326, 333 (1998) (citing Hanson v. Aetna Life & Cas., 625 F.2d 573 (5th Cir. 1980).

[29] TechBios, Inc. v. Champagne, 301 Ga. App. 592, 595-96, 688 S.E.2d 378, 382 (2009) (citing O.C.G.A. § 51-1-8 (2000)).

[30] Tidikis v. Network for Med. Commc'ns & Research LLC, 274 Ga. App. 807, 810, 619 S.E.2d 481, 485 (2005) (quoting Cochran v. Murrah, 235 Ga. 304, 306, 219 S.E.2d 421, 423 (1975) (citing Middleton v. Troy Young Realty, Inc., 257 Ga. App. 771, 773, 572 S.E.2d 334, 337 (2002)).

[31] Middleton v. Troy Young Realty, Inc., 257 Ga. App. 771, 773, 572 S.E.2d 334, 337 (2002) (quoting Williams v. Dresser Indus., 120 F.3d 1163, 1168 (11th Circ. 1997)).

care, *as determined by the degree of skill and care ordinarily employed by their respective professions under similar conditions and like surrounding circumstances.*"[32]

It is also possible to assume a duty of care. "Where one undertakes an act which he has no duty to perform and another reasonably relies upon that undertaking, the act must generally be performed with ordinary and reasonable care."[33]

B.   *Question of Fact*

i.   **Elements**

"The question of duty is defined by the law; the breach of that duty is determined by the particular facts. . . . *This is usually a question to be referred to the jury, and should always be so referred, unless the allegations (or evidence) show beyond controversy that there was no such breach of duty.*"[34] It is well-settled that the jury determines "questions of negligence, diligence, contributory negligence and proximate cause . . . except in plain and undisputable cases."[35] When determining whether a defendant has breached the duty of care, "[t]he question for the jury is whether danger should have been recognized by common experience, or by the special experience of the alleged wrongdoer, or by a person of ordinary prudence and foresight."[36]

Negligence, or the duty to protect from the unreasonable risk of harm, "is the failure to use that degree of care which it is the duty of persons to use under the circumstances."[37] Although Georgia's codification of tort law provides for claims based on "slight"[38] and "gross negligence,"[39] the standard of "'ordinary care' is that degree of care which is exercised by ordinarily prudent persons under the same or similar circumstances."[40] Under Georgia law, "'due care,' 'ordinary care,' and 'ordinary diligence' are *interchangeable terms*."[41] A plaintiff owes a general duty "to all the world not to subject them to an unreasonable risk of harm."[42]

---

[32] Allen v. Lefkoff, Duncan, Grimes & Dermer, P.C., 265 Ga. 374, 375, 453 S.E.2d 719, 720 (1995) (emphasis original) (quoting Housing Auth. of Savannah v. Greene, 259 Ga. 435, 436, 383 S.E.2d 867, 868 (1989); Peters v. Hyatt Legal Servs., 220 Ga. App. 398 (1996) (awarding punitive damages for professional malpractice, declining to extend the holding in *Allen)*.

[33] Stelts v. Epperson, 201 Ga. App. 405, 406, 411 S.E.2d 281, 282 (1991) (citing 57A Am. Jur. 255, *Negligence* § 208).

[34] Feise v. Cherokee Cty., 207 Ga. App. 17, 21, 427 S.E.2d 294, 298 (1992) (emphasis original) (quoting Shockley v. Zayre of Atlanta, 118 Ga. App. 672, 673, 165 S.E.2d 179, 181 (1968)).

[35] Bussey v. Dawson, 224 Ga. 191, 192, 160 S.E.2d 834, 835 (1968) (citing Howard v. Savannah Elec. Co., 140 Ga. 482, 73 S.E. 112, 114 (1913); Blanton v. Doughty, 107 Ga. App. 91, 95, 129 S.E.2d 376, 379 (1962)).

[36] Mixson v. Dobbs Houses, Inc., 149 Ga. App. 481, 483, 254 S.E.2d 864, 865 (1979) (citations omitted).

[37] Georgia Elec. Co. v. Smith, 108 Ga. App. 851, 854, 134 S.E.2d 840, 843 (1964) (citations omitted).

[38] O.C.G.A. § 51-1-3 (2000); *see also* 1 Council of Superior Court Judges of Georgia, *Suggested Pattern Jury Instructions: Civil Cases* § 60.020 (5th ed. July 2016).

[39] O.C.G.A. § 51-1-4 (2000); *see also* 1 Council of Superior Court Judges of Georgia, *Suggested Pattern Jury Instructions: Civil Cases* § 60.030 (5th ed. July 2016).

[40] Johns v. Marlow, 252 Ga. App. 79, 80, 555 S.E.2d 756, 757 (2001) (quoting O.C.G.A. § 51-1-2 (2000)).

[41] McDuffie v. Tanner, 108 Ga. App. 213, 216, 132 S.E.2d 675, 678 (1963) (emphasis original) (citing Criswell Baking Co. v. Milligan, 7 Ga. App. 861, 868, 50 S.E.2d 136, 141 (1948)).

[42] Peterson v. Reeves, 315 Ga. App. 370, 373, 727 S.E.2d 171, 174 (2012), quoting Bradley Ctr. v. Wessner,

However, "[r]easonable foresight does not require of a plaintiff or a defendant that he anticipate exactly that which will happen and exercise perfect judgment to prevent injury."[43] Further, "one is not liable for injury to another where his duty is that of ordinary care merely because of failure to exercise that degree of care which would have absolutely prevented injury."[44]

"The law of negligence protects innocent parties to whom a duty is owed from foreseeable harm, and foresight requires the ability to anticipate a risk of harm from the allegedly negligent conduct."[45] Liability for negligent performance of undertaking arises when a person negligently changes, or causes a change to, a nonhazardous condition.[46]

ii. Evidence

In a negligence action, the plaintiff bears the burden of proving the existence of "a legal duty to conform to a standard of conduct raised by the law for the protection of others against unreasonable risks of harm."[47] "Duty cannot be divorced from foreseeability, and thus, it follows that, to establish a breach of the applicable standard of conduct to support a negligence action, there must be evidence that the act (or omission to act) alleged to be negligent created a *foreseeable* unreasonable risk of harm."[48] It is not necessary for the event underlying a claim to have been specifically foreseeable by the defendant. Instead, to support a claim, "the act or omission complained of must be such that a person using ordinary care would have foreseen that the event, or *some similar event*, might reasonably result therefrom."[49]

The plaintiff bears the burden of proving the existence of "a legal duty to conform to a standard of conduct raised by the law for the protection of others against unreasonable risks of harm."[50] Stated another way, "[t]he question of negligence is solely for the jury in a case where the law has established no fixed measure of care imposed on the parties.[51]

---

250 Ga. 199, 201, 296 S.E.2d 693, 696 (1982) (declining to extend the rule stated in *Bradley Center* to medical malpractice claims).

[43] Ellington v. Tolar Const. Co., 237 Ga. 235, 238, 227 S.E.2d 336, 339 (1976).

[44] Lunsford v. Childs, 107 Ga. App. 210. 212, 129 S.E.2d 398, 400 (1963) (citing Richardson v. Pollard, 57 Ga. App. 777, 781, 196 S.E. 199, 203 (1938)).

[45] Worthy v. Beautiful Restaurant, Inc., 252 Ga. App. 479, 481, 556 S.E.2d 185, 188 (2001) (citing Amos v. City of Butler, 242 Ga. App. 505, 506, 529 S.E.2d 420, 422 (2000)).

[46] Herrington v. Deloris Gaulden, 294 Ga. 285 (2013) (citing Huggins v. Aetna Cas. & Sur. Co., 245 Ga. 248, 249, 264 S.E.2d 191, 192 (1980); Restatement (Second) of Torts, Section 324A (1965)).

[47] Martin v. Dempsey Funeral Servs. of Georgia, Inc., 319 Ga. App. 343, 348, 735 S.E.2d 59, 64 (2012) (citations omitted).

[48] Love v. Morehouse College, Inc., 287 Ga. App. 743, 744-45, 652 S.E.2d 624, 626 (2007) (emphasis original, punctuation omitted) (citing Watson v. Gen. Mechanical Servs., 276 Ga. App. 479, 481, 623 S.E.2d 679, 681 (2005)).

[49] 1 Council of Superior Court Judges of Georgia, *Suggested Pattern Jury Instructions: Civil Cases* § 60.020 (5th ed. July 2016) (emphasis original).

[50] Martin v. Dempsey Funeral Servs. of Georgia, Inc., 319 Ga. App. 343, 348, 735 S.E.2d 59, 64 (2012) (citing Freeman v. Eicholz, 308 Ga. App. 18, 20, 705 S.E.2d 919, 922 (2011)).

[51] City of Milledgeville v. Wood, 114 Ga. 370, 40 S.E. 239, 239 (1901) (citing Wright v. R.R. Co., 34 Ga. 330 (1866)).

The plaintiff must show affirmative evidence of negligence to meet the burden; otherwise the "court presumes performance of duty and freedom from negligence."[52] The burden of proof is to establish by a legal preponderance of evidence material allegations of the petition.[53]

Evidence of negligence regarding the duty owed by the defendant may take many forms. For example, evidence that a private entity has failed to follow or comply with its own standards or recommendations is admissible as illustrative of negligence, though it does not establish negligence.[54] Government rules and regulations may also be considered by the jury in determining whether a defendant exercised ordinary care,[55] although compliance with governmental regulations does not determine the issue of negligence liability.[56] A statute or regulation may be used to establish the level of care required where the injury was the type the statute was designed to prevent and the injured party was one of the class of persons protected by the statute.[57] Note, however, that the defendant may rebut the plaintiff's case with evidence "that the plaintiff failed to use ordinary care and that this failure was the sole proximate cause of the plaintiff's injury."[58]

Expert evidence is required to establish the ordinary standard of care in the context of professional negligence claims.[59] The obligation of the professional or skilled person is "to exercise a reasonable degree of care, skill, and ability, which generally is taken and considered to be such a degree of care and skill as, under similar conditions and like surrounding circumstances, is ordinarily employed by their respective professions."[60] Cases requiring such expert evidence include those involving engineering,[61] medical malpractice, architects, attorneys, certified public accountants, land surveyors, marriage and family therapists, clinical social workers, and veterinarians.[62] A claim based on an administrative, clerical, or routine act demanding no special expertise falls in the realm of simple negligence and thus does not require an expert affidavit.[63]

---

[52] Neal v. Miller, 194 Ga. App. 231, 232, 390 S.E.2d 125, 126 (1990) (quoting Collins v. Ralston & Ogletree, Inc., 186 Ga. App. 583, 584, 367 S.E.2d 861, 863 (1988)).

[53] Patillo v. Thompson, 106 Ga. App. 808, 811, 128 S.E.2d 656, 659 (1962) (citing Morgan v. Reeves, 84 Ga. App. 41, 46, 65 S.E.2d 453, 457 (1951)).

[54] Muller v. English, 221 Ga. App. 672, 678, 472 S.E.2d 448, 454 (1996) (quoting Manley v. Gwinnett Place Assocs., 216 Ga. App. 379, 380-81, 454 S.E.2d 577, 579 (1995) (overruled on other grounds)).

[55] Sinclair Disposal Serv., Inc. v. Ochoa, 265 Ga. App. 172, 173, 593 S.E.2d 358, 360 (2004).

[56] Id.

[57] Womack v. Oasis Goodtime Emporium I, Inc., 705 S.E.2d 199, 203 (Ga. App. 2010).

[58] 1 Council of Superior Court Judges of Georgia, *Suggested Pattern Jury Instructions: Civil Cases* § 60.110 (5th ed. July 2016).

[59] Covil v. Robert & Co. Assocs., 112 Ga. App. 163, 166-67, 144 S.E.2d 450, 453-54 (1965).

[60] Marquis Towers, Inc. v. Highland Grp., 265 Ga. App. 343, 346, 593 S.E.2d 903, 906 (2004) (quoting Dep't of Transp. v. Mikell, 229 Ga. App. 54, 58, 493 S.E.2d 219, 222 (1997)).

[61] Id.

[62] O.C.G.A. § 9-11-9.1 (2015).

[63] O.C.G.A. § 9-11-9.1 (2015). *See also* Upson Cty. Hosp., Inc. v. Head, 246 Ga. App. 386, 389, 540 S.E.2d 626, 630 (2000).

III.   Breach of Duty

A.   *Elements*

Negligence is conduct falling below the standard established by law for the protection of others against an unreasonable risk of harm.[64] "A 'legal duty' in context of negligence is one arising from contract between the parties or the operation of the law."[65] "Duty imposed by law" as a basis for action *ex delicto* for breach of a duty growing out of contractual relations means either a duty imposed by valid legislative enactment or a duty imposed by recognized common-law principles declared and reported in decisions of reviewing courts of justice.[66] "No matter how innocent the plaintiff may be, he is not entitled to recover unless the defendant did something that it should not have done, or failed to do something that it should have done pursuant to the duty owed to the plaintiff."[67]

B.   *Evidence*

"It is accepted generally as settled law that negligence, like any other fact, may be proved by circumstantial evidence as well as by direct testimony."[68] The negligence plaintiff bears the burden to present "specific facts establishing a breach of duty, as well as the other elements of negligence, and may not rest upon generalized allegations."[69] However, the plaintiff cannot recover "where the inference of negligence depends on circumstantial evidence and direct, unimpeached testimony shows defendant was without negligence."[70] If "the circumstantial evidence is as consistent with the theory that the defendant was not negligent as it is with the theory that he was, a jury is not allowed to guess. . . . A verdict for the plaintiff in such a case 'could only be the product of surmise, speculation, and conjecture.'"[71] "Negligence is not to be presumed, but is a matter of affirmative proof; in the absence of affirmative proof of negligence, the court presumes performance of duty and freedom from negligence."[72]

---

[64] Weller v. Blake, 315 Ga. App. 214, 219, 726 S.E.2d 698, 702 (2012) (quoting Lowry v. Cochran, 305 Ga. App. 240, 246, 699 S.E.2d 325, 331 (2010)).

[65] Coogle v. Jahangard, 271 Ga. App. 235 (2005) (quoting Ferrell v. Haas, 136 Ga. App. 274, 276-77, 220 S.E.2d 771, 773 (1975)).

[66] Sutker v. Pennsylvania Ins. Co., 115 Ga. App. 648, 651, 115 S.E.23 694, 697 (1967).

[67] City of Douglasville v. Queen, 270 Ga. 770, 771, 514 S.E.2d 195, 197-98 (1999) (punctuation omitted) (quoting Veterans Organization of Forth Oglethorpe v. Potter, 111 Ga. App. 201, 205, 141 S.E.2d 230, 232-33 (1965)).

[68] Cagle v. Atchley, 127 Ga. App. 668, 675, 194 S.E.2d 598, 603 (1972) (quoting Arnold Servs., Inc. v. Sullins, 110 Ga. App. 19, 20-21, 137 S.E.2d 727, 729 (1964) (citing PROSSER, THE LAW OF TORTS, 200 (2d ed.)).

[69] Shornacy v. North Atlanta Internal Medicine, P.C., 252 Ga. App. 321, 325, 556 S.E.2d 209, 213 (2001) (citing Bradley Ctr. v. Wessner, 250 Ga. 199, 296 S.E.2d 693 (1982)).

[70] Emory University v. Bliss, 35 Ga. App. 752, 754, 134 S.E. 637, 638 (1926).

[71] Harrelson v. United States, 420 F. Supp. 788, 794 (D.Ga.1976) (internal citations omitted) (citing Nash v. Raun, 149 F.2d 885, 888 (3rd Cir. 1945); quoting Calvert v. Katy Taxi, Inc., 413 F.2d 841, 844 (2nd Cir. 1969)).

[72] Neal v. Miller, 194 Ga. App. 231, 232, 390 S.E.2d 125, 126 (1990) (citing *Collins*, 186 Ga. App. at 584, 367 S.E.2d at 862 (1988)).

There is a presumption "that every man obeys the mandates of law and performs all of his social and official duties."[73] That presumption holds "until the contrary is shown."[74] "Neither duty nor negligence exists in a vacuum—they are entirely dependent upon circumstances involving others or their property."[75] "To prove a claim of negligence, of course, a plaintiff must prove that the defendant did something that it should not have done or failed to do something that it should have done pursuant to the duty owed the plaintiff."[76]

The burden of proof in civil actions in Georgia is the preponderance of the evidence, which "means 'greater weight,' and as it is used [in civil jury instructions] 'preponderance of the evidence' means 'the greater weight of evidence upon the issues involved.'"[77] "The weight of the evidence must be sufficient to incline a reasonable and impartial mind to one side of the issue rather than to the other."[78] Under the revised Evidence Code, "the jury may consider all the facts and circumstances of the case, the witnesses' manner of testifying, their intelligence, their means and opportunity for knowing the facts to which they testified, the nature of the facts to which they testified, the probability or improbability of their testimony, their interest or want of interest, and their personal credibility so far as the same may legitimately appear from the trial."[79]

In actions based on an injury to a child who is in the care of a childcare provider, the injury, "without more, does not create the presumption of negligence on the part of the provider."[80] Evidence demonstrating that a defendant has violated "'privately set guidelines' for industry standards is admissible and probative of negligence, but does not conclusively establish negligence or duty owed."[81] Similarly, "[a]n actor will not be allowed to show conformity with his own individual habits in order to prove due care."[82]

When considering whether a defendant exercised ordinary care, compliance with governmental rules and regulations may be considered.[83]

---

[73] Beavers v. LeSueur, 188 Ga. 393, 403 3 S.E.2d 667, 673-4 (1939) (citing Georgia Casualty Co. v. McRitchie, 45 Ga. App. 697, 166 S.E. 49, 51 (1932)).

[74] *Id.*

[75] *Underwood*, 296 Ga. App. at 809, 676 S.E.2d at 267 (2009), quoting Sims. v. American Cas. Co., 131 Ga. App. 461, 468, 206 S.E.2d 121, 127 (1974), *aff'd sub nom.*, Providence Washington Ins. Co. v. Sims, 232 Ga. 787, 209 S.E.2d 61 (1974).

[76] B-T Two, Inc. v. Bennett, 307 Ga. App. 649, 654, 706 S.E.2d 87, 91 (2011) (quoting Parker v. Hovers, 255 Ga. App. 184, 186, 564 S.E.2d 795, 798 (2002)).

[77] 1 Council of Superior Court Judges of Georgia, *Suggested Pattern Jury Instructions: Civil Cases* § 00.040 (5th ed. July 2016).

[78] 1 Council of Superior Court Judges of Georgia, *Suggested Pattern Jury Instructions: Civil Cases* § 00.040 (5th ed. July 2016).

[79] O.C.G.A. § 24-14-4 (2013) (formerly O.C.G.A. § 24-4-4).

[80] Persinger v. Step by Step Infant Dev. Ctr., 253 Ga. App. 768, 769, 560 S.E.2d 333, 336 (2002) (citations omitted in original).

[81] Kraft Reinsurance Ireland, Ltd. v. Pallets Acquisitions, LLC, 845 F. Supp. 2d 1342, 1353 (2011) (citing Spearman v. Georgia Bldg. Auth., 224 Ga. App. 801, 803, 482 S.E.2d 463, 465 (1997)).

[82] Welsh v. Fowler, 124 Ga. App. 369, 371, 183 S.E.2d 574, 577 (1971) (quoting Dawkins v. Jones, 119 Ga. App. 796, 798, 168 S.E.2d 881, 883 (1969)).

[83] *Sinclair Disposal Serv., Inc.*, 265 Ga. App. at 173, 593 S.E.2d at 360.

IV. Causation

A. *Elements*

    "Proximate cause is a limit on legal liability; it is a policy decision that, for a variety of reasons, the defendant's conduct and the plaintiff's injury are too remote for the law to allow recovery."[84] Proximate cause is distinct from "cause-in-fact," and a factfinder may find a defendant's conduct to have been a cause-in-fact, but not proximate cause, of a plaintiff's injury.[85] Proximate cause is an element of the negligence claim, and it "is that which, in the natural and continuous sequence, unbroken by other causes, produces an event, and without which the event would not have occurred."[86] Georgia has applied the "but-for" rule described by Professor Prosser, as follows; "The defendant's conduct is not a cause of the event, if the event would have occurred without it."[87] Another way to state the proximate cause rule in Georgia is that the alleged wrongful act is the proximate cause of the injury when the injury can be directly traced to the act, and the injury would not have resulted "but-for" the act.[88] Proximate cause is distinguished from a cause "which is merely incidental." An incidental cause is not the proximate and responsible cause.[89]

    Causation also includes an element of foreseeability. To be considered "proximate cause of injury," the injury must naturally arise from and be a probable consequence of the injurious act, and the wrongdoer should have foreseen the consequence as likely to flow from his actions.[90] Intervening acts will not break the chain of causation between the original act and the harm, so long as the intervening act "could reasonably have been anticipated, apprehended, or foreseen by the original wrong-doer."[91] Otherwise, the defendant is insulated by lack of proximate causation for the injury, as the injury would not have occurred without the unforeseeable intervening and independent act.[92]

---

[84] Snellgrove v. Hyatt Corp., 277 Ga. App. 119, 122, 625 S.E.2d 517, 521 (2006) (citing Atlanta Obstetrics & Gynecology Grp. v. Coleman, 260 Ga. 569, 398 S.E.2d 16, 17 (1990)).

[85] Atlanta Obstetrics & Gynecology Grp. v. Coleman, 260 Ga. 569, 398 S.E.2d 16, 17 (1990) (Weltner, Smith, & Bell, J.J., concurring).

[86] Zwiren v. Thompson, 276 Ga. 498, 500, 578 S.E.2d 862, 865 (1990) (citing T.J. Morris Co. v. Dykes, 197 Ga. App. 392, 395-396, 398 S.E.2d 403, 406 (1990)), *see also* Georgia Dep't of Transp. v. Owens, 330 Ga. App. 123, 766 S.E.2d 569 (2014).

[87] General Motors Corp. v. Davis, 141 Ga. App. 495, 496, 233 S.E.2d 825, 827 (1977) (quoting W. Prosser, Law of Torts 239 (4th ed. 1971)).

[88] Pettigrew v. Citizens Trust Bank, 229 B.R. 39, 42 (Bankr. N.D. Ga.1998) (citing Parris v. Pledger Ins. Agency, Inc., 180 Ga. App. 437, 439, 348 S.E.2d 924, 926 (1986); Housing Auth. of Atlanta v. Famble, 170 Ga. App. 509, 512, 317 S.E.2d 853, 857 (1984)).

[89] Standard Oil Co. v. Harris, 120 Ga. App. 768, 771, 172 S.E.2d 344, 347 (1969) (citing Savannah Electric Co. v. Wheeler, 128 Ga. 550, 562, 58 S.E. 38, 43 (1907); Dunbar v. Davis, 32 Ga. App. 192, 122 S.E. 895 (1924)).

[90] Lyons v. Georgia Power Co., 78 Ga. App. 445, 449, 51 S.E.2d 459, 462 (1949) (quoting Wright v. Southern Ry. Co., 62 Ga. App. 316, 320, 7 S.E.2d 793, 797 (1940)).

[91] Ontario Sewing Mach. Co., Ltd. v. Smith, 275 Ga. 683, 686, 572 S.E.2d 533, 536 (2002) (citing Williams v. Grier, 196 Ga. 327, 336, 26, S.E.2d 698 (1943)).

[92] *Id.* at 686-87.

In cases involving multiple tortfeasors, Georgia has refused "to endorse the additional hurdle that each individual tortfeasor's conduct must constitute a 'substantial' contributing factor in the plaintiff's injury in order to be considered a proximate cause thereof."[93]

B.   Evidence

The determination of the proximate cause of an injury is a fact-specific inquiry.[94] Questions of proximate cause are questions of fact for the jury, to be decided by the court only "in plain and undisputed cases."[95] When making its determination, the jury evaluates the facts "upon mixed considerations of logic, common sense, justice, policy, and precedent."[96] In evaluating the facts, there is a presumption that all persons "anticipate or foresee the reasonable and natural consequences of their conduct."[97] To succeed, the plaintiff's evidence must show "a reasonable basis for the conclusion that it is more likely than not that the conduct of the defendant was the cause-in-fact of the result."[98]

On the issue of causation, the plaintiff bears the burden of proof.[99] The plaintiff may show negligence by both circumstantial evidence and direct testimony.[100] Once negligence is established, the defendant has the "burden of explaining the cause of the occurrence."[101] If the defendant alleges that the plaintiff's acts or omissions were the sole proximate cause of the injury and presents evidence to support this theory, the burden shifts to the plaintiff to present evidence demonstrating that the defendant's negligence was at least a concurrent cause.[102]

V.   Damages

A.   Elements

Damages compensate for injury.[103] Damages are meant to compensate, rather than enrich, plaintiffs.[104] General damages flow or arise from the tortious act and proof of a spe-

---

[93] John Crane, Inc. v. Jones, 278 Ga. 747, 751, 604 S.E.2d 822, 826 (2004).

[94] Eidson v. Felder, 68 Ga. App. 188, 191-92, 22 S.E.2d 523, 525 (1942) (quoting Georgia Ry. & Power Co. v. Ryan, 24 Ga. App. 288, 100 S.E. 713 (1919)).

[95] *Ontario Sewing Mach. Co., Ltd.*, 275 Ga. at 687, 572 S.E.2d 533 (citing *Atlanta Obstetrics & Gynecology Grp.*, 260 Ga. at 570, 398 S.E.2d at 17).

[96] Bills v. Lowery, 286 Ga. App. 301, 304, 648 S.E.2d 779, 782 (2007) (quoting McCannon v. Wilson, 267 Ga. App. 815, 818, 600 S.E.2d 796, 799 (2004).

[97] Parsons v. Grant, 95 Ga. App. 431, 439, 98 S.E.2d 219, 225 (1957) (citing Terrel v. J.F. Giddings & Son, 28 Ga. App. 697, 112 S.E. 914 (1922)).

[98] Gay v. Redland Baptist Church, 288 Ga. App. 28, 29, 653 S.E.2d 779, 780 (2007) (citations omitted in original).

[99] Hardnett v. Silvey, 285 Ga. App. 424, 426, 646 S.E.2d 514, 516 (2007) (citations omitted in original). *See also* O.C.G.A. § 24-14-1 (2013).

[100] McCann v. Lindsey, 109 Ga. App. 104, 135 S.E.2d 519, 520 (1964).

[101] W. & Atl. R. R. v. Fowler, 77 Ga. App. 206, 214, 47 S.E.2d 874, 880 (1948).

[102] Kecskes v. City of Mt. Zion, 300 Ga. App. 348, 350, 695 S.E.2d 329, 332 (2009) (quoting Howard v. Gourmet Concepts Intl., 242 Ga. App. 521, 523, 529 S.E.2d 406, 409 (2000)).

[103] O.C.G.A. § 51-12-4 (2000).

[104] MCI Commc'ns Servs. v. CMES, Inc., 291 Ga. 461, 463, 728 S.E.2d 649, 651 (2012).

cific amount is not required in compensating the plaintiff for the injury.[105] Nominal damages are awarded when there is no actual damage from an injury, so long as some small or nominal injury is present.[106] The award of damages is a jury question.[107]

B.   Evidence

The plaintiff bears the burden of proving the amount of loss to the jury such that the amount can be calculated "with a reasonable degree of certainty."[108] The jury cannot be left to speculation, conjecture, or guesswork in calculating damages.[109] However, the jury has great discretion in determining a damage award.[110] Pain and suffering is determined by the "enlightened conscience of impartial jurors."[111]

The plaintiff bears the burden of furnishing the jury with sufficient data to estimate damages.[112] Direct testimony regarding market value of property need not be provided by an expert.[113] The jury may fix the value of personal property either higher or lower than the evidence produced, as the jury is not required to accept opinion evidence.[114]

---

[105] Alexander v. Holmes, 85 Ga. App. 124, 126, 68 S.E.2d 242, 245 (1951) (quoting Home Ins. Co v. North River Ins. Co., 192 Ga. App. 551, 558, 385, S.E.2d 736, 742 (1989)).

[106] O.C.G.A. § 51-12-4 (2000).

[107] O.C.G.A. § 51-12-12 (2000).

[108] Big Builder, Inc. v. Evans, 126 Ga. App. 457, 458, 191 S.E.2d 290, 291 (1972).

[109] Turner v. Connor, 192 Ga. App. 348, 349, 385 S.E.2d 19, 20 (1989) (quoting Bennett v. Associated Food Stores, Inc.,118 Ga. App. 711, 716, 165 S.E.2d 581, 585 (1968)).

[110] See Childs v. United States, 923 F. Supp. 1570, 1579 (S.D. Ga. 1996) (quoting Collins v. McPherson, 91 Ga. App. 347, 85 S.E.2d 552, 555 (1954)).

[111] Aretz v. United States, 456 F. Supp. 397, 401 (S.D. Ga. 1973).

[112] Moultrie Farm Ctr., Inc. v. Sparkman, 171 Ga. App. 736, 740, 320 S.E.2d 863, 867-8 (1984).

[113] Barking Hound Vill., LLC v. Monyak, 299 Ga. 144, 152, 787 S.E.2d 191, 197–98 (2016); see O.C.G.A. § 24–7–701 (b) (2013).

[114] Id.

CHAPTER 12

HAWAII

HAWAII
Sabrina A. Davis[1]

I. Purpose of Tort Law

According to the Hawai'i Supreme Court, "tort law is primarily designed to vindicate social policy."[2] The two social policies highlighted by the court include: (1) compensating those "injured through the unreasonable conduct of others," and (2) preventing "injury where possible by providing incentive to deter negligent acts."[3]

II. Duty to Exercise Ordinary Care

A. *Question of Law*

i. Elements

To prevail on a negligence claim, a plaintiff must prove there is a "duty, or obligation, recognized by the law, requiring the defendant to conform to a certain standard of conduct, for the protection of others against unreasonable risks."[4] The existence of such a duty is purely a question of law[5] and is decided on a case-by-case basis.[6] A duty "may be defined by common law or by statute."[7] In addition, "courts may adopt the requirements of a statute as the standard of care when the purpose of the statute is to protect a class of persons which includes the one whose interest is invaded."[8]

Foreseeability, within "the context of determining the existence and scope of a duty," is also a matter of law reserved for the courts.[9] In this context, foreseeability relates to "the knowledge of the risk of injury to be apprehended. The risk reasonably to be perceived defines the duty to be obeyed; it is the risk reasonably within the range of apprehension, of injury to another person, that is taken into account in determining the existence of the duty to

---

[1] Law Library Professor and Reference Librarian, Oklahoma City University School of Law, Chickasaw Nation Law Library.

[2] Francis v. Lee Enters., Inc., 971 P.2d 707, 712 (Haw. 1999).

[3] Steigman v. Outrigger Enters., Inc., 267 P.3d 1238, 1247 (Haw. 2011) (internal citations omitted).

[4] Molfino v. Yuen, 339 P.3d 679, 682 (Haw. 2014).

[5] Bidar v. Amfac, Inc., 669 P.2d 154, 158 (Haw. 1983).

[6] *Molfino*, 339 P.3d at 683.

[7] Lee v. Corregedore, 925 P.2d 324, 342 (Haw. 1996).

[8] *Id.* at 343 (internal citations omitted).

[9] Pulawa v. GTE Hawaiian Tel, 143 P.3d 1205, 1215 (Haw. 2006).

exercise care."[10] To test for foreseeability, the court considers from the defendant's perspective "whether there is some probability of harm sufficiently serious that a reasonable and prudent person would take precautions to avoid it."[11] Further, this "does not mean foreseeability of *any* harm whatsoever, and it is not sufficient that injury is merely possible."[12]

ii. Evidence

In determining whether a duty exists, the court weighs "the nature of the risk, the magnitude of the burden of guarding against the risk, and the public interest in the proposed solution."[13] Although expert witness testimony is usually reserved for issues of fact, "in the context of duty, expert testimony might be relevant to help establish some underlying fact on which duty may ultimately rest."[14]

III. Breach of Duty

A. Elements

A plaintiff must also prove a breach of the defendant's duty of care, also described as "failure on the defendant's part to conform to the standard required," to establish a claim for negligence.[15] This is a question for the trier of fact, as is the foreseeability of the danger.[16] To make this determination, the jury should consider "what is reasonable and unreasonable and whether the defendant's conduct was reasonable in the circumstances," i.e., "what a reasonable and prudent person would have done under the circumstances."[17] This is determined within the context of the "foreseeable range of danger."[18]

B. Evidence

The jury may consider as evidence of breach of duty "[p]roof of the failure of the defendant to conform his conduct to standards established by law for the protection of the class to which the injured party belongs, when shown to have a legitimate connection to the issue."[19] In general, opinion testimony on the standard of reasonable care is not permitted.[20]

---

[10] *Id.* at 1218, 1219 (emphasis omitted).

[11] *Id.* at 1218, 1219 (emphasis omitted).

[12] *Id.* at 1219 (emphasis in original).

[13] Molfino v. Yuen, 339 P.3d 679, 682–83 (Haw. 2014).

[14] Pulawa v. GTE Hawaiian Tel, 143 P.3d 1205, 1217 (Haw. 2006) (internal citations omitted).

[15] *Molfino*, 339 P.3d at 682.

[16] Bidar v. Amfac, Inc., 669 P.2d 154, 159 (Haw. 1983).

[17] Knodle v. Waikiki Gateway Hotel, Inc., 742 P.2d 377, 384 (Haw. 1987) (internal citations omitted).

[18] *Id.* at 384-385.

[19] State v. Tabigne, 966 P.2d 608, 615 (Haw. 1998).

[20] Sherry v. Asing, 531 P.2d 648, 657 (Haw. 1975), *disapproved of on other grounds by* Murakami v. Maui Cty., 730 P.2d 342 (Haw. Ct. App. 1986).

IV. Causation

A. *Elements*

The plaintiff must prove a "reasonably close causal connection between the conduct and the resulting injury" to succeed on a claim for negligence.[21] The Hawai'i Supreme Court adopted the following test (from the *Restatement of Torts*) to establish proximate cause: "The actor's negligent conduct is a legal cause of harm to another if (a) his conduct is a substantial factor in bringing about the harm, and (b) there is no rule of law relieving the actor from liability because of the manner in which his negligence has resulted in the harm."[22]

Foreseeability in the context of proximate cause "relates to the question of whether the specific act or omission of the defendant was such that the ultimate injury to the plaintiff reasonably flowed from defendant's breach of duty."[23] As with breach of duty, causation and foreseeability are questions for the trier of fact.[24]

B. *Evidence*

The jury may consider circumstantial evidence when determining causation in a negligence action.[25]

V. Damages

A. *Elements*

Finally, the plaintiff must prove "actual loss or damage" to prevail on a negligence claim.[26] In general, a plaintiff is "entitled to recover damages for all the natural and proximate consequences of the defendant's wrongful act or omission."[27] There are two categories of damages, general and special.[28] General damages "necessarily result from a legal wrong done" and can include "physical or mental pain and suffering, inconvenience, and loss of enjoyment which cannot be measured definitively in monetary terms."[29] In contrast, "[s]pecial damages are often considered to be synonymous with pecuniary loss and include such items as medical and hospital expenses, loss of earnings, and diminished capacity to work."[30] By

---

[21] Molfino v. Yuen, 339 P.3d 679, 682 (Haw. 2014).

[22] Montalvo v. Lapez, 884 P.2d 345, 351 (Haw. 1994) (internal citations omitted). This is sometimes referred to as the *Mitchell* test, as it was stated in Mitchell v. Branch, 363 P.2d 969, 973 (Haw. 1961) (*see, e.g.,* Taylor-Rice v. State, 979 P.2d 1086, 1100 (Haw. 1999)).

[23] Pulawa v. GTE Hawaiian Tel, 143 P.3d 1205, 1215 (Haw. 2006).

[24] Bidar v. Amfac, Inc., 669 P.2d 154, 159 (Haw. 1983).

[25] Wagatsuma v. Patch, 879 P.2d 572, 588 (Haw. Ct. App. 1994).

[26] Molfino v. Yuen, 339 P.3d 679, 682 (Haw. 2014).

[27] Dunbar v. Thompson, 901 P.2d 1285, 1294 (Haw. Ct. App. 1995).

[28] *Id.*

[29] *Id.*

[30] *Id.*

statute, "noneconomic damages which are recoverable in tort actions include damages for pain and suffering, mental anguish, disfigurement, loss of enjoyment of life, loss of consortium, and all other nonpecuniary losses or claims."[31]

B. *Evidence*

The jury should consider the following factors when determining the amount of a plaintiff's damages: (1) extent, nature, and permanency of plaintiff's injuries; (2) any resulting deformity, scars, or disfigurement, and the permanency of same; (3) reasonable value of past and "reasonably probable" future medical services; (4) past, current, and "reasonably probable" future pain, emotional suffering, and disability; and (5) past and "reasonably probable" future loss of income.[32]

---

[31] Montalvo v. Lapez, 884 P.2d 345, 364 (Haw. 1994) (citing HAWAI'I REVISED STATUTES § 663-8.5(a) (Supp.1992)).

[32] HI R CIV JURY *Instr.* 8.9 Elements of Damages.

CHAPTER 13

IDAHO

IDAHO
Sabrina A. Davis[1]

I. Purpose of the Tort Law

The Idaho Supreme Court has stated that "[t]ort actions are created to protect the interest in freedom from various kinds of harm."[2] Further, the court identified the primary purpose of tort law as "compensating plaintiffs for the injuries they have suffered wrongfully at the hands of others."[3]

II. Duty to Exercise Ordinary Care

A. *The Question of Law*

i. Elements

To establish a claim for negligence, a plaintiff must prove the existence of "a duty, recognized by law, requiring a defendant to conform to a certain standard of conduct."[4] More specifically, the duty is "to exercise ordinary care to prevent unreasonable, foreseeable risks of harm to others."[5] Whether a duty exists is a question of law for the court to decide.[6]

ii. Evidence

The court considers multiple factors when determining whether a duty exists, including the following factors:

> foreseeability of harm to the plaintiff, the degree of certainty that the plaintiff suffered injury, the closeness of the connection between the defendant's conduct and the injury suffered, the moral blame attached to the defendant's conduct, the policy of preventing future harm, the extent of the burden to the defendant and consequences to the community of imposing a duty to exercise care with resulting liability for breach, and the availability, cost, and prevalence of insurance for the risk involved.[7]

[1] Law Library Professor and Reference Librarian, Oklahoma City University School of Law, Chickasaw Nation Law Library.
[2] Bishop v. Owens, 272 P.3d 1247, 1255 (Idaho 2012).

[3] Blake v. Cruz, 698 P.2d 315, 322 (Idaho 1984).

[4] Morrison v. St. Luke's Regl. Med. Ctr., Ltd., 377 P.3d 1062, 1069 (Idaho 2016).

[5] Turpen v. Granieri, 985 P.2d 669, 672 (Idaho 1999) (internal citations omitted).

[6] *Id.* at 672.

[7] *Id* at 672.

B.   The Question of Fact

i.   Elements

Although the existence of a duty is a question of law, "[w]hether the duty attaches is largely a question for the trier of fact as to the foreseeability of the risk."[8] With regard to foreseeability, "only the general risk of harm need be foreseen, not the specific mechanism of injury."[9] However, the degree of foreseeability required "varies with the circumstances of each case."[10] According to the Idaho Supreme Court, "[w]here the degree of result or harm is great, but preventing it is not difficult, a relatively low degree of foreseeability is required. Conversely, where the threatened injury is minor but the burden of preventing such injury is high, a higher degree of foreseeability may be required."[11]

ii. Evidence

The jury should judge the defendant's conduct "against that of an ordinarily prudent person acting under the same conditions and circumstances."[12] A statute or regulation may be used to establish the level of care required where the injury was the type the statute was designed to prevent and the injured party was one of the class of persons protected by the statute.[13]

III.   Breach of Duty[14]

A.   Elements

A plaintiff must also prove a breach of duty in order to prevail on a negligence claim,[15] and this is a question for the jury.[16] Breach of duty, or "negligence," consists of "conduct which falls below the standard established by law for the protection of others against unreasonably great risk of harm."[17] The unreasonable risk must be "one that a reasonable man similarly situated would have foreseen," which "should be determined on the basis of what the defendant knew or could reasonably have known at the time of the alleged tort."[18]

---

[8] Sharp v. W.H. Moore, Inc., 796 P.2d 506, 509 (Idaho 1990).

[9] *Id*. at 510.

[10] *Id*. at 509-510.

[11] Sharp v. W.H. Moore, Inc., 796 P.2d 506, 509–10 (Idaho 1990) (internal citations omitted).

[12] Sorensen v. St. Alphonsus Regl. Med. Ctr., Inc., 118 P.3d 86, 93 (Idaho 2005).

[13] Orthman v. Idaho Power Co., 7 P.3d 207, 210 (Idaho 2000).

[14] The Idaho appellate courts appear to sometimes refer to the breach of duty element generally as "negligence." *See, e.g.*, Splinter v. City of Nampa, 256 P.2d 215, 220 (Idaho 1953); Curtis v. Dewey, 475 P.2d 808, 810 (Idaho 1970).

[15] Morrison v. St. Luke's Regl. Med. Ctr., Ltd., 377 P.3d 1062, 1069 (Idaho 2016).

[16] Curtis v. Dewey, 475 P.2d 808, 810 (Idaho 1970).

[17] *Id.* at 810.

[18] *Id.* at 810.

B. *Evidence*

The jury may consider circumstantial evidence when deciding if a duty was breached.[19]

IV. Causation

A. *Elements*

The third element of the negligence cause of action requires that a plaintiff demonstrate "a causal connection between the defendant's conduct and the resulting injuries."[20] Further, a plaintiff "may recover only for harm that was proximately caused by a breach of the duty of care."[21] Proximate cause consists of both actual cause (also referred to as "cause-in-fact") and legal cause (also referred to as legal responsibility);[22] both must be present for a plaintiff to recover.[23]

Actual cause refers to "whether a particular event produced a particular consequence" and is a factual question.[24] To fulfill the actual cause element, the alleged negligent act may satisfy either the "but-for" or the "substantial factor" test.[25] The "but-for" test is employed "when there is a single possible cause of the injury," whereas the "substantial factor" test is used "when there are multiple possible causes of injury."[26] On the other hand, legal cause "is satisfied if at the time of the defendant's negligent act the [plaintiff's] injury was reasonably foreseeable as a natural or probable consequence of the defendant's conduct."[27]

B. *Evidence*

Proximate cause is a factual inquiry that is "almost always for the jury."[28] The jury may consider circumstantial evidence when determining if proximate cause exists.[29]

V. Damages

A. *Elements*

Finally, a plaintiff must prove "actual loss or damage" to recover in a negligence action.[30] Both special and general damages are recoverable.[31] Special damages are described

---

[19] Splinter v. City of Nampa, 256 P.2d 215, 220 (Idaho 1953).

[20] Morrison v. St. Luke's Regl. Med. Ctr., Ltd., 377 P.3d 1062, 1069 (Idaho 2016).

[21] Johnson v. McPhee, 210 P.3d 563, 575 (Idaho App. 2009) (internal citations omitted).

[22] *See, e.g.*, Newberry v. Martens, 127 P.3d 187, 191 (Idaho 2005); Hayes v. Union Pac. R.R., 141 P.3d 1073, 1077 (Idaho 2006).

[23] Doe v. Sisters of Holy Cross, 895 P.2d 1229, 1234 (Idaho App. 1995).

[24] Newberry v. Martens, 127 P.3d 187, 191 (Idaho 2005).

[25] Doe v. Sisters of Holy Cross, 895 P.2d 1229, 1234 (Idaho App. 1995).

[26] Garcia v. Windley, 164 P.3d 819, 823 (Idaho 2007).

[27] Hayes v. Union Pac. R.R., 141 P.3d 1073, 1077 (Idaho 2006) (internal citations omitted).

[28] Cramer v. Slater, 204 P.3d 508, 515 (Idaho 2009).

[29] Splinter v. City of Nampa, 256 P.2d 215, 220 (Idaho 1953).

[30] Morrison v. St. Luke's Regl. Med. Ctr., Ltd., 377 P.3d 1062, 1069 (Idaho 2016).

[31] Taylor v. Neill, 326 P.2d 391, 393 (Idaho 1958).

as the natural but not necessary consequences of the negligent act, whereas general damages "are the immediate, direct, and proximate result" of the negligent act.[32]

B.   *Evidence*

It is within the sole province of the jury "to estimate [damages] as best they can by reasonable probabilities, based upon their sound judgment as to what would be just and proper under all the circumstances."[33] The Idaho Supreme Court has held that evidence of damages "is sufficient if it proves the damages with reasonable certainty."[34] Further, "[r] easonable certainty requires neither absolute assurance nor mathematical exactitude; rather, the evidence need only be sufficient to remove the existence of damages from the realm of speculation."[35]

---

[32] Stoddard v. Ploeger, 247 P. 791, 793 (Idaho 1926).

[33] Shrum v. Wakimoto, 215 P.2d 991, 993 (Idaho 1950).

[34] Griffith v. Clear Lakes Trout Co., 200 P.3d 1162, 1167 (Idaho 2009).

[35] Griffith v. Clear Lakes Trout Co., 200 P.3d 1162, 1167 (Idaho 2009).

CHAPTER 14

ILLINOIS

ILLINOIS
Jennifer S. Prilliman[1]

I. Purpose of Tort Law

Illinois defines the two fundamental purposes of tort law as (1) holding "wrongdoers liable for injuries that are proximately caused by their actions" and (2) providing "just compensation to the injured parties."[2] In addition, an appellate court stated that an "underlying purpose of tort law is to provide for public safety through deterrence of negligent designers and builders."[3]

Most of the relevant case law is devoted to the discussion of "just compensation." According to the Illinois Supreme Court, "[t]here is universal agreement that the compensatory goal of tort law requires that an injured plaintiff be made whole."[4] The Court elaborated on this, finding that, "[d]amages are recoverable to the extent necessary to place the injured party in the position he would have occupied if the wrong had not been committed."[5]

II. Duty to Exercise Ordinary Care

A. Question of Law

To establish negligence, a plaintiff must prove that the defendant owed a duty to the plaintiff, that the defendant breached their duty, and that the breach was the proximate cause of the plaintiff's injuries.[6] "A duty requires a person to conform to a certain standard of conduct for the protection of another against an unreasonable risk of harm."[7] Whether the defendant has a duty to exercise care is a question of law,[8] and it "must be resolved by the court."[9] The jury or trier of fact will determine if there was a breach.[10] Illinois courts consider the following five public policy factors when determining if a duty was owed: "(1) the reasonable foreseeability of the injury, (2) the likelihood of the injury, (3) the magnitude of

---

[1] Law Library Professor and Associate Law Library Director, Oklahoma City University School of Law Chickasaw Nation Law Library.

[2] Williams v. Rosner, 7 N.E.3d 57, 68 (Ill. App. Ct. 2014), *reh'g denied* (Apr. 10, 2014).

[3] Johnson v. Equip. Specialists, Inc., 373 N.E.2d 837, 843 (Ill. App. Ct. 1978).

[4] Best v. Taylor Mach. Works, 689 N.E.2d 1057, 1076 (Ill. 1997).

[5] Clark v. Children's Mem'l Hosp., 955 N.E.2d 1065, 1073-74 (Ill. 2011).

[6] Mieher v. Brown, 301 N.E.2d 307, 308 (Ill. 1973).

[7] Widlowski v. Durkee Foods, Div. of SCM Corp., 562 N.E.2d 967, 968 (Ill. 1990).

[8] *Mieher*, 301 N.E.2d at 308.

[9] *Widlowski*, 562 N.E.2d at 968.

[10] Iseberg v. Gross, 879 N.E.2d 278, 284 (Ill. 2007).

the burden of guarding against the injury, (4) the consequences of placing that burden on the defendant, and (5) the public policy and social requirements of the time and community."[11] The weight each factor is given will depend on the circumstances of the case.[12] Foreseeability of a risk of injury is always an important factor.[13]

When establishing the presence of a duty of care, the Illinois courts closely examine the relationship between the parties.[14] The Illinois Supreme Court explains that, "every person owes a duty of ordinary care to all others to guard against injuries which naturally flow as a reasonably probable and foreseeable consequence of an act."[15] This duty to exercise ordinary care does not require, "privity of interest or the proximity of relationship, but extends to remote and unknown persons."[16] The Court recognizes that, "hindsight makes virtually every occurrence foreseeable"[17] and does not impose a general "duty to the world at large."[18] "The court must also consider the likelihood of injury, the magnitude of the burden of guarding against it, and the consequences of placing that burden on the defendant."[19] "An independent 'direct relationship' between parties may help to establish the foreseeability of the injury" to a plaintiff or class of plaintiffs.[20] Furthermore, though a direct or special relationship is not required, finding a relationship is a factor that may tip the scales.[21]

B. *Question of Fact*

i. **Elements**

Illinois jurisprudence has long held that a defendant must exercise "the standard of care of a reasonably prudent person under the circumstances of a case."[22] What constitutes reasonable conduct under the circumstances is a question of fact for the jury.[23] Under Illinois jurisprudence, people are "presumed to know those things which are matters of common knowledge," and to anticipate consequences reasonable people would expect to occur.[24] The nature of the activity will determine what a jury considers ordinary care. Some activities require "a high degree;" other activities, a "low degree" of care.[25]

---

[11] Marshall v. Burger King Corp., 856 N.E.2d 1048, 1057 (Ill. 2006).

[12] O'Hara v. Holy Cross Hosp., 561 N.E.2d 18, 21 (Ill. 1990).

[13] *Id.*; Hooper v. Cty. of Cook, 851 N.E.2d 663, 669 (Ill. App. Ct. 2006).

[14] Cunis v. Brennan, 308 N.E.2d 617, 618 (Ill. 1974); Widlowski v. Durkee Foods, Div. of SCM Corp., 562 N.E.2d 967, 968 (Ill. 1990).

[15] *Id.*

[16] *Id.*

[17] O'Hara v. Holy Cross Hosp., 561 N.E.2d 18, 21 (Ill. 1990).

[18] Simpkins v. CSX Transp., Inc., 965 N.E.2d 1092, 1097 (Ill. 2012).

[19] *O'Hara*, 561 N.E.2d at 21.

[20] *Simpkins*, 965 N.E.2d at 1097.

[21] *Id.*

[22] Griffin v. Darda, 329 N.E.2d 245, 248 (Ill. App. Ct. 1975).

[23] *Id.*

[24] Kahn v. James Burton Co., 126 N.E.2d 836, 840 (Ill. 1955).

[25] Chi. Anderson Pressed Brick Co. v. Sobkowiak, 38 Ill. App. 531, 539 (Ill. App. Ct. 1890).

ii. Evidence

The plaintiff has the burden of proving the defendant owed the plaintiff a duty of care.[26] Injured parties can use either direct or circumstantial evidence to prove the existence of a duty.[27] "Where the law does not impose a duty, one will not generally be created by a defendant's rules or internal guidelines."[28] A statute or regulation may be used to establish the level of care required where the injury was the type the statute was designed to prevent and the injured party was one of the class of persons protected by the statute.[29] Evidence of standards, safety rules, regulations, and codes are admissible to aid the factfinder in deciding reasonable care.[30] Custom is also relevant in determining the standard of care.[31]

III. Breach of Duty

A. Elements

Whether the defendant breached his or her duty, is a finding of fact.[32] If "an ordinarily prudent person" would anticipate an "injury will reasonably and probably result from his failure to exercise ordinary care," liability may be imposed.[33] The defendant does not have to anticipate the specific nature of the injury or how it will occur.[34] "What is ordinary care depends upon the circumstances."[35]

B. Evidence

The plaintiff bears the burden of proof in a negligence action,[36] and the defendant bears the same burden when asserting the plaintiff's comparative negligence.[37] Industry standards may be used to demonstrate the standard of care required.[38] "A violation of a statute designed

---

[26] Leonardi v. Loyola Univ. of Chi., 658 N.E.2d 450, 455 (Ill. 1995).

[27] Pfeifer v. Canyon Const. Co., 628 N.E.2d 746, 749 (Ill. App. Ct. 1993); Mort v. Walter, 457 N.E.2d 18, 21 (Ill. 1983).

[28] Rhodes v. Ill. Cent. Gulf R.R., 665 N.E.2d 1260, 1272 (Ill. 1996).

[29] McCarthy v. Kunicki, 823 N.E.2d 1088, 1097 (Ill. App. Ct. 2005).

[30] Marshall v. Burger King Corp., 824 N.E.2d 661, 665 (Ill. App. Ct. 2005).

[31] *Id.* at 666.

[32] Griffin v. Darda, 329 N.E.2d 245, 248 (Ill. App. Ct. 1975).

[33] Cunis v. Brennan, 308 N.E.2d 617, 621 (Ill. 1974).

[34] *Id.*

[35] Peterson v. Cochran & McCluer Co., 31 N.E.2d 825, 830 (Ill. App. Ct. 1941); *see also* Ill. Cent. R.R. v. Keegan, 112 Ill. App. 28, 36 (Ill. App. Ct. 1904).

[36] Leonardi v. Loyola Univ. of Chi., 658 N.E.2d 450, 455 (Ill. 1995).

[37] Casey v. Baseden, 490 N.E.2d 4, 7 (Ill. 1986); 28 Ill. Law & Prac. Negligence § 72 (Illinois follows a modified comparative negligence rule and does not follow the common law contributory negligence rules.).

[38] Murphy v. Messerschmidt, 355 N.E.2d 78, 81 (Ill. App. Ct. 1976), *aff'd and remanded*, 368 N.E.2d 1299 (Ill. 1977).

to protect human life and property may be used as *prima facie* evidence of negligence."[39] A violation alone will "not constitute negligence *per se*" if the defendant can demonstrate that they acted reasonably."[40] An Illinois appellate court explained,

> The difference between deeming a violation negligence *per se* as opposed to merely *prima facie* evidence of negligence is that under the negligence *per se* approach when the plaintiff shows the violation of a statute designed to protect human life and also shows that he was of the class it was intended to protect, a conclusive presumption of duty and breach of duty is established, while under the latter approach the violation of the statute is only evidence of duty and breach, nonbinding on the jury.[41]

A plaintiff injured by a defendant's violation of statute must show, "(1) the violation proximately caused the injury; (2) the statute or ordinance was intended to protect the class of persons to which the party belongs; and (3) the injury suffered was of the type that the statute or ordinance was designed to protect against."[42] Evidence of breach of duty can be direct or circumstantial.[43]

IV.   Causation

A.   *Elements*

"Proximate cause is an essential element of a negligence claim."[44] "There are two requirements for a showing of proximate cause: cause-in-fact and legal cause."[45] Cause-in-fact requires "reasonable certainty that a defendant's acts caused the injury or damage."[46] Legal cause requires that the harm was foreseeable and "that a reasonable person" would expect the result to happen because of their conduct.[47] Whether an injury was reasonably foreseeable is a question for a jury.[48] For purposes of causation, the defendant is not required to foresee the specific injury, only that some injury could occur.[49]

---

[39] Cooney v. Chi. Pub. Sch., 943 N.E.2d 23, 28 (Ill. App. Ct. 2010).

[40] Bier v. Leanna Lakeside Prop. Ass'n, 711 N.E.2d 773, 783 (Ill. App. Ct. 1999), *as modified on denial of reh'g* (May 19, 1999).

[41] *Id.*

[42] Janis v. Graham, 946 N.E.2d 983, 987 (Ill. App. Ct. 2011).

[43] Thomas v. Smith, 137 N.E.2d 117, 121 (Ill. App. Ct. 1956).

[44] Berke v. Manilow, 63 N.E.3d 194, 203 (Ill. App. Ct. 2016); *see also* Sycamore Pres. Works v. Chicago & N.W. Ry., 7 N.E.2d 740, 742 (Ill. 1937).

[45] Hooper v. Cty. of Cook, 851 N.E.2d 663, 669 (Ill. App. Ct. 2006).

[46] City of Chi. v. Beretta U.S.A. Corp., 821 N.E.2d 1099, 1127 (Ill. 2004).

[47] Robinson v. Boffa, 930 N.E.2d 1087, 1092 (Ill. App. Ct. 2010); El-Zoobi v. United Airlines, Inc., 50 N.E.3d 1150, 1156 (Ill. App. Ct. 2016).

[48] Heastie v. Roberts, 877 N.E.2d 1064, 1083 (Ill. 2007).

[49] *Hooper*, 851 N.E.2d at 669.

B. *Evidence*

A plaintiff must prove causation by a preponderance of the evidence and establish that the injury, with "reasonable certainty," was a consequence of defendant's action.[50] "The mere fact that an injury has occurred, in and of itself, is insufficient to show proximate cause."[51] "[L]iability cannot be predicated on surmise or conjecture as to the cause of the injury."[52] There must be some connection between the defendant's action and the plaintiff's injury. Either direct or circumstantial evidence is sufficient to prove causation.[53]

V. **Damages**

A. *Elements*

An injured party has the right to "recover all damages which naturally flow from the commission of a tort."[54] The aim of the awarded damages is to make the "injured [party] . . . whole."[55] "The damage must be the natural result of the wrong inflicted, it must be real, and it must not be speculative."[56]

B. *Evidence*

The jury will determine the award for damages.[57] "A jury's award of damages is entitled to substantial deference." Appellate courts are reluctant to overturn the amount unless it is shown that "a proven element of damages was ignored, the verdict resulted from passion or prejudice, or the award bears no reasonable relationship to the loss suffered."[58] The burden is on the plaintiff to "establish a reasonable basis for computing damages."[59]

---

[50] Daly v. Bant, 258 N.E.2d 382, 386 (Ill. App. Ct. 1970); Murphy v. Chestnut Mountain Lodge, Inc., 464 N.E.2d 818, 821 (Ill. App. Ct. 1984).

[51] Beals v. Superior Welding Co., 653 N.E.2d 430, 437 (Ill. App. Ct. 1995).

[52] *Murphy*, 464 N.E.2d at 821.

[53] Kunz v. Little Co. of Mary Hosp. & Health Care Ctrs., 869 N.E.2d 328, 334 (Ill. App. Ct. 2007), *as modified on denial of reh'g* (May 25, 2007).

[54] Chi. Title & Trust Co. v. Walsh, 340 N.E.2d 106, 115 (Ill. App. Ct. 1975).

[55] Best v. Taylor Mach. Works, 689 N.E.2d 1057, 1076 (Ill. 1997).

[56] *Chi. Title & Trust Co.*, 340 N.E.2d at 115.

[57] Snover v. McGraw, 667 N.E.2d 1310, 1315 (Ill. 1996).

[58] *Id.*

[59] Gill v. Foster, 626 N.E.2d 190, 194 (Ill. 1993).

CHAPTER 15

INDIANA

INDIANA
Paul Petro[1]

I. Purpose of Tort Law

Indiana's negligence laws focus on a policy of preventing future injuries,[2] which is accomplished by promoting public safety through deterring negligent conduct.[3] The Indiana Supreme Court has explicitly stated that the purposes of tort law "include deterring negligent conduct and compensating the victims of those who act unreasonably."[4]

For example, in addressing questions of duty we encourage safe conduct by imposing liability against those whose actions cause foreseeable danger to others. "[L]iability for injury ordinarily depends upon the power to prevent injury."[5]

II. Duty to Exercise Ordinary Care

A. *Question of Law*

Indiana has adopted the classic elements of negligence: duty, breach, and a proximately caused harm.[6] The analysis starts with identifying a duty, because without a duty there can be no breach.[7] Duty is generally a question of law for the court to consider and will be found where one is well-established or—where one is not well-established—by balancing the three *Webb* factors, which are (1) the relationship between the parties, (2) the foreseeability of the harm, and (3) public policy concerns.[8]

In negligence cases, the standard of care is always reasonable care under the circumstances.[9] "The duty never changes, although the standard of conduct required to measure

---

[1] Attorney at Law, Fishers, I.N., Indiana University McKinney School of Law, 2009. paul@petrolaw.us.

[2] Gariup Const. Co., Inc. v. Foster, 519 N.E.2d 1224, 1227 (Ind. 1988) (citing PROSSER & KEETON ON TORTS § 53, at 357–59 (5th ed. 1984)).

[3] Hiatt v. Brown, 422 N.E.2d 736, 740 (Ind. Ct. App. 1981) (citing Johnson v. Equipment Specialist, Inc., 373 NE.2d 837 (Ill. Ct. App. 1978)).

[4] Hanson v. Saint Luke's United Methodist Church, 704 N.E.2d 1020, 1027 (Ind. 1998).

[5] Tibbs v. Huber, Hunt & Nichols, Inc., 668 N.E.2d 248, 250 (Ind. 1996).

[6] Yost v. Wabash College, 3 N.E. 3d 509, 515 (Ind. 2014) (sub-cites omitted).

[7] *Id.*

[8] *Id.* (citing Webb v. Jarvis, 575 N.E.2d 992,995 (Ind. 1991)).

[9] City of Gary v Smith & Wesson, 801 N.E.2d 1222, 1241 (Ind. 2003); City of Muncie v. Weidner, 831 N.E.2d 206, 211 (Ind. Ct. App. 2005) (sub-cites omitted).

up to that duty varies depending upon the particular circumstances."[10] Duty represents the normal expectations of civil society to take precautions against risk.[11]

This duty is not "owed to the world at large, but rather to those who might reasonably be foreseen as being subject to injury by the breach of the duty."[12] Stated slightly differently, duty is imposed "where a reasonably foreseeable victim is injured by a reasonably foreseeable harm. Thus, part of the inquiry into the existence of a duty is concerned with exactly the same factors as is the inquiry into proximate cause."[13]

Although touching on similar concerns as proximate cause, a court's determination of duty involves assessing the foreseeability of the *general* kind of harm. "In analyzing the foreseeability factor of duty, we focus on whether the injured person actually harmed was a foreseeable victim and whether the *type of harm* actually inflicted was reasonably foreseeable."[14] The Indiana Supreme Court recently reaffirmed the distinction between foreseeability as part of a duty analysis and foreseeability as part of a proximate cause analysis: "When foreseeability is part of the duty analysis, . . . involves an evaluation of (1) the broad type of plaintiff and (2) the broad type of harm."[15]

B. *Question of Fact*

i. Elements

The jury determines what constitutes "reasonable care under the circumstances."[16]

ii. Evidence

Safety rules that "bear upon issuable facts" may be used as evidence for or against a party.[17] Custom and practice are relevant to establish the standard of care required under the circumstances.[18] A statute or ordinance may be used to establish the standard of care required where the statute or ordinance (1) is intended to protect the class of persons which the plaintiff is a member, and (2) protects against the risk of the type of harm that resulted from its violation.[19]

---

[10] City of Muncie v. Weidner, 831 N.E.2d 206, 212 (Ind. Ct. App. 2005).

[11] Key v. Hamilton, 963 N.E.2d 573, 580 (Ind. Ct. App. 2012) (citing PROSSER AND KEATON ON TORTS, § 31 (5th ed. 1984)).

[12] *Key*, 963 N.E.2d 573, 580 (quoting Webb v. Jarvis, 575 NE.2d 992, 997 (Ind. 1991)).

[13] Campbell v. Eckman/Freeman & Assoc., 670 N.E.2d 925, 934 (Ind. Ct. App. 1996) (citing *Webb*, 575 N.E.2d at 997, and PROSSER AND KEATON ON TORTS § 53).

[14] M.S.D. of Martinsville v. Jackson, 9 N.E.3d 230, 244 (Ind. Ct. App. 2014) (emphasis added).

[15] *Rogers v. Martin*, 63 N.E.3d 316, 325 (Ind. 2016).

[16] Moore v. Moriarty, 415 N.E.2d 779, 782 (Ind. App. 1981).

[17] New York Cent. R. Co. v. Wyatt, 184 N.E.2d 657, 671 (Ind. App. 1962).

[18] Vann Duyn v. Cook-Teague Partnership, 694 N.E.2d 779, 782 (Ind. App. 1998).

[19] Brown v. City of Valparaiso, 67N.E.3d 652, 660 (Ind. App. 2016).

III. Breach of Duty

A. Elements

Negligence is conduct which shows a lack of reasonable care that an ordinary person would expect in the same or similar circumstances.[20] "The duty never changes, although the standard of conduct required to measure up to that duty varies depending upon the particular circumstances."[21] Because assessing breach of duty involves an evaluation of reasonableness under the circumstances, it is therefore usually a question of fact.[22] This factual assessment is accomplished by analyzing the defendant's conduct in reference to the duty owed.[23]

B. Evidence

Unless the defendant admits the allegations, a plaintiff bears the burden of proof on defendant's breach of duty.[24] A jury may infer negligence from proven facts, but may not infer the foundational facts themselves.[25] Qualitatively, evidence fails only where the proven facts will not support a logical inference of negligence.[26]

The factfinder may consider the foreseeability of an event when assessing the reasonableness of the defendant's actions.[27] Juries may also determine whether violation of a statute[28] or administrative regulation[29] constitutes negligence.

IV. Causation

A. Elements

Proximate cause is generally a question of fact,[30] and involves two main questions. First is the classic "but-for" causation: the injury would not have occurred but-for the defendant's negligence.[31] The second question is whether the harm was reasonably foreseeable as the natural and probable consequence of the negligence.[32] "Whether or not proximate cause exists is primarily a question of foreseeability."[33] The factfinder must evaluate whether

---

[20] Whitmore v. South Bend Pub. Trans. Corp., 7 N.E.2d 994, 997 (Ind. Ct. App. 2014).

[21] City of Muncie v. Weidner, 831 N.E.2d 206, 212 (Ind. Ct. App. 2005).

[22] Pfenning v. Lineman, 947 N.E.2d 392, 403 (Ind. 2011) (citing Kroger v. Plonski, 930 N.E.2d 1, 9 (Ind. 2010)).

[23] Patterson v. Seavoy, 822 N.E.2d 206, 213 (Ind. Ct. App. 2005).

[24] Peak v. Campbell, 578 N.E.2d 360, 361 (Ind. 1991).

[25] Wal-Mart Stores, Inc. v. Blaylock, 591 N.E.2d 624, 626 (Ind. Ct. App. 1992).

[26] Beckom v. Quigley, 824 N.E.2d 420, 424 (Ind. Ct. App. 2005).

[27] Patterson v. Seavoy, 822 N.E.2d 206, 213 (Ind. Ct. App. 2005).

[28] Larkins v. Kohlmeyer, 89 N.E.2d 896, 900 (Ind. 1951); Phoenix Natural Res. Inc. v. Messmer, 804 N.E.2d 842, 848 (Ind. Ct. App. 2004).

[29] Huffman v. Dexter Axle Co., 990 N.E.2d 947, 954 (Ind. Ct. App. 2013).

[30] Laycock v. Sliwkowski, 12 N.E.3d 986, 991 (Ind. Ct. App. 2014).

[31] Id.

[32] Id.

[33] Green v. Ford Motor Co., 942 N.E.2d 791, 795 (Ind. 2011) (quoting Control Techniques, Inc. v. Johnson, 762 N.E.2d 104, 109 (Ind. 2002)).

the injury is a natural and probable consequence which—under the totality of the circumstances—should have been foreseen.[34]

B. Evidence

To meet the burden of proof, a plaintiff "must present evidence of probative value based on facts, or inferences to be drawn from the facts, establishing both that the wrongful act was the cause-in-fact of the occurrence and that the occurrence was the cause-in-fact of her injury."[35] The evidence must be reasonably certain—mere speculation is insufficient.[36] "When an injury is objective in nature, the plaintiff is competent to testify as to the injury and such testimony may be sufficient for the jury to render a verdict without expert medical testimony."[37] More complicated questions involving permanent injuries or pre-existing conditions ordinarily require expert testimony.[38]

V. Damages

A. Elements

While "punitive damages may serve a dual purpose of punishment of the tortfeasor and deterrence to others,"[39] compensatory damages are not designed to punish, but to deter. "[D]eterrence . . . comes from exposure to regular civil damages."[40] Compensatory damages include medical expenses, lost wages, and pain and suffering. With sufficient proof, recovery for past, present, and future damages is permitted.

B. Evidence

Unless the defendant makes admissions, a plaintiff bears the burden of proof on all elements, including damages.[41] In tort actions, the jury's verdict does not need to reflect precise mathematical certainty.[42]

For over 100 years, Indiana has allowed tort compensation for "injury to business or profession, reputation or social position, and for physical suffering . . . and for mental trouble . . . all of which are considered compensatory."[43]

Special damages are not taken for granted, but must be shown with "specific proof to have been actually incurred as a natural and proximate consequence of the wrongful act."[44]

---

[34] *Id.* (sub-cites omitted)

[35] Mr. Bults, Inc. v. Orlando, 990 N.E.2d 1, 5 (Ind. Ct. App. 2013) (quoting Daub v. Daub, 629 N.E.2d 873, 877-78 (Ind. Ct. App. 1994)).

[36] *Id.*

[37] *Id.*

[38] *Id.*

[39] Crabtree *ex. rel.* Kemp v. Estate of Crabtree, 837 N.E.2d 135, 139 (Ind. 2005) (sub-cites omitted).

[40] Baker v. Westinghouse Elec. Corp., 637 N.E.2d 1271, 1274 (Ind. 1994).

[41] Peak v. Campbell, 578 N.E.2d 360 (Ind. 1991).

[42] Best Formed Plastics, LLC v. Shoun, 51 N.E.3d 345, 354 (Ind. Ct. App. 2016).

[43] Loparex, LLC v. MPI Release Technologies, *LLC*, 964 N.E.2d 806, 817 (Ind. 2012) (quoting State ex. rel. Scobey v. Stevens, 2 N.E. 214, 216 (Ind. 1885)).

[44] Levee v. Beeching, 729 N.E.2d 215, 223 (Ind. Ct. App. 2000).

CHAPTER 16

IOWA

IOWA

Jim Fitzsimmons[1]

I. Purpose of Tort Law

Iowa case law emphasizes compensating victims of wrongful behavior as the priority of tort law,[2] with a goal of fully compensating the victim "for all that he lost by the wrongful act."[3] The Iowa Supreme Court has long and consistently promulgated that the duty of exercising reasonable care for the safety of the public is absolute.[4] Continuing the focus on the safety of the public, Iowa law defines "negligence" as doing something a reasonably careful person would not do under similar circumstances, or failing to do something a reasonably careful person would do under similar circumstances for the protection of others against unreasonable risks of harm.[5] In a special concurrence, Justice Wiggins of the Iowa Supreme Court discussed the ability of the negligence doctrine to deter unreasonable conduct, and stated "the time has come to tip the balance in the direction of safety."[6]

In 2009, the Iowa Supreme Court, in *Thompson v. Kaczinski*, abrogated the traditional "Proximate Cause" approach by adopting the Restatement (Third) of Torts "Scope of Liability" standard.[7] In order to recover, a plaintiff has the burden to prove: (1) the existence of a duty of care, (2) the failure to exercise reasonable care, (3) factual cause, (4) physical harm, and (5) harm comes within the scope of liability (previously called "proximate cause").[8]

---

[1] Attorney, Fitzsimmons & Vervaecke Law Firm, PLC.

[2] Katko v. Briney, 183 N.W.2d 657, 671 (Iowa 1971).

[3] Hartley State Bank v. McCorkell, 60 N.W. 197, 199 (Iowa 1894).

[4] Connolly v. Des Moines Inv. Co., 105 N.W. 400, 401(Iowa 1905); Wiar v. Wabash R. Co., 144 N.W. 703, 706 (Iowa 1913); Koenig v. Koenig, 766 N.W.2d 635, 645 (Iowa 2009) (abandoning the distinction between invitees and licensees in premises liability cases describing that "[M]odern times demand a recognition that requiring all to exercise reasonable care for the safety of others is the more humane approach.").

[5] Thompson v. Kaczinski, 774 N.W.2d 829, 834 (Iowa 2009); Benham v. King, 700 N.W.2d 314, 317 (Iowa 2005); Knake v. King, 492 N.W.2d 416, 417 (Iowa 1992); Smith v. Shaffer, 395 N.W.2d 853, 855 (Iowa 1986); Seeman v. Liberty Mut. Ins. Co., 322 N.W.2d 35, 37 (Iowa 1982); Lewis v. State, 256 N.W.2d 181, 188 (Iowa 1977).

[6] Feld v. Borkowski, 790 N.W.2d 72, 92 (Iowa 2010).

[7] *Thompson*, 774 N.W. 2d at 836-39.

[8] *Id.*; *see also* Hill v, Damm, 804 N.W.2d 95, 99 (Iowa Ct. App. 2011).

II.   Duty to Exercise Ordinary Care

A.   *Question of Law*

Whether or not a duty exists under the particular circumstances of a case is a question of law for the court to determine.[9] The Iowa Supreme Court in *Thompson v. Kaczinski* adopted the *Restatement (Third) of Torts* duty analysis describing that an "actor ordinarily has a duty to exercise reasonable care when the actor's conduct creates a risk of physical harm."[10] The Court continued to discuss that "in most cases involving physical harm, courts ordinarily need not concern themselves with the existence or content of this ordinary duty. They may proceed directly to the elements of liability."[11] The Iowa Supreme Court has stated that "no-duty rulings should be limited to exceptional cases in which 'an articulated countervailing principal or policy warrants denying or limiting liability in a particular class of cases.'"[12]

III.   Breach of Duty

To recover with a claim of negligence, the plaintiff must prove that the applicable standard of care was breached.[13] The Iowa Supreme Court has adopted the *Restatement (Third) of Torts* standard which allocated the determination of the foreseeability of risk away from the courts and to the jury.[14] The "assessment of foreseeability should be allocated to the factfinder, as part of its determination of whether appropriate care has been exercised in any given scenario."[15]

A.   *Elements*

The Court noted in *Thompson v. Kaczinski* that:

> The assessment of the foreseeability of a risk is allocated by the *Restatement (Third)* to the factfinder, to be considered when the jury decides if the defendant failed to exercise reasonable care.
>
> Foreseeable risk is an element in the determination of negligence. In order to determine whether appropriate care was exercised, the factfinder must assess the foreseeable risk at the time of the defendant's alleged negligence. The extent of foreseeable risk depends on the specific facts of the case and cannot be usefully assessed for a category of cases; small changes in the facts may make a dramatic change in how much risk is foreseeable. . . . [C]ourts

---

[9] Hoyt v. Gutterz Bowl & Lounge L.L.C., 829 N.W.2d 772, 775 (Iowa 2013).

[10] *Thompson*, 774 N.W.2d at 834.

[11] *Thompson*, 774 N.W.2d at 835.

[12] *Hoyt*, 829 N.W.2d at 775 (citing *Thompson*).

[13] Alcala v. Marriott Int'l, Inc., 880 N.W.2d 699, 708 (Iowa 2016)

[14] *Thompson*, 774 N.W.2d at 835.

[15] *Hoyt*, 829 N.W.2d at 775.

should leave such determinations to juries unless no reasonable person could differ on the matter.

The drafters acknowledge that courts have frequently used foreseeability in no-duty determinations, but have now explicitly disapproved the practice in the *Restatement (Third)* and limited no-duty rulings to "articulated policy or principle in order to facilitate more transparent explanations of the reasons for a no-duty ruling and to protect the traditional function of the jury as factfinder." We find the drafters' clarification of the duty analysis in the *Restatement (Third)* compelling, and we now, therefore, adopt it.[16]

B. *Evidence*

The *Restatement (Third)* definition of negligence, adopted by the Iowa Court, describes three primary factors for the finder of fact to consider in ascertaining whether the person's conduct lacks reasonable care.[17] First, the foreseeable likelihood that the defendant's conduct will result in harm.[18] Second, the foreseeable severity of any harm that may ensue.[19] Third, the burden of precautions to eliminate or reduce the risk of harm.[20]

The Iowa Supreme Court has found statistics helpful to determine foreseeability.[21] Statistics give a norm as a frame of reference and allow a party to argue to the jury why a party would deviate from that norm.[22] In certain cases, statistics often demonstrate more than the testimony of many witnesses.[23] Courts can take judicial notice of statistics.[24]

Iowa Courts allow consideration of Safety Codes and Customs when determining whether conduct lacks reasonable care. When considering the issues of negligence and contributory negligence, evidence of custom in the performance of similar acts is generally admissible, but not conclusive.[25] Conformity with the custom is evidence of due care, and nonconformity with the custom is evidence of negligence.[26] Violation of an OSHA standard is negligence *per se* between employer and employee and evidence of negligence as to all others who are likely to be injured as a result of the violation.[27] A violation of the manual on uniform traffic devices is merely evidence of negligence.[28] The violation of a departmental rule is merely some evidence of negligence, but not negligence as a matter

---

[16] *Thompson*, 774 N.W.2d at 835 (citations omitted).

[17] Hill v, Damm, 804 N.W.2d 95, 99 (Iowa Ct. App. 2011).

[18] *Hill*, 804 N.W. 2d at 99.

[19] *Id.*

[20] *Id.*

[21] Galloway v. Bankers Trust Co., 420 N.W.2d 437, 440 (Iowa 1988).

[22] Gaza v. BNSF Ry. Co., 843 N.W.2d 713, 725 (Iowa 2014).

[23] Iron Workers Local No. 67 v. Hart, 191 N.W.2d 758, 769 (Iowa 1971).

[24] *In re* Marriage of Stamp, 300 N.W.2d 275, 281 (Iowa 1980); *Iron Workers Local No. 67,* 191 N.W.2d at 769.

[25] Langner v. Caviness, 28 N.W.2d 421, 423 (Iowa 1947).

[26] *Id.*

[27] Koll v. Mannatt's Transp. Co., 253 N.W.2d 265 (Iowa 1977); Adam v. T. I. P. Rural Elec. Co-op., 271 N.W.2d 896, 901 (Iowa 1978).

[28] Gipson v. State, 419 N.W.2d 369 (Iowa 1988).

of law.[29] The question of whether the violation of a statute will be construed as negligence *per se* or merely evidence of negligence "is to be decided in light of the purpose and intent of the pertinent statute or ordinance."[30] Violation of a statute or regulation may be used to establish negligence *per se* by showing the following: (1) the injury was caused by the violation of the rule; (2) the injury was the type intended to be prevented by the rule; and (3) the plaintiff was one of the class of people protected by the rule.[31] A violation of standards in private safety codes is evidence on the issue of negligence but not negligence *per se*.[32] When experts disagree, courts should instruct the jury to decide whether a standard in a private safety code applies.[33]

IV.   Causation

The jury must determine factual cause. The conduct of a party is a cause of damage when the damage would not have happened except for the conduct.[34] There can be more than one cause of an injury or damage.[35] In cases where there is an aggravation of a pre-existing condition, the jury should be instructed that the "conduct of a party is a cause of damage when the damage would not have happened except for the conduct or would not have happened as soon or as severe except for the conduct."[36]

The principle underlying allowing damages is that of compensation, the ultimate purpose being to place the injured party in as favorable a position as though no wrong had been committed.[37] The amount of direct injury or harm is compensated, whether the extent of that harm was contemplated by the parties or not.[38] An actor's liability is limited to the harms that result from the risks that made the actor's conduct negligent.[39]

The Iowa Supreme Court describes that "when scope of liability arises in a negligence case, the risks that make an actor negligent are limited to foreseeable ones, and the

---

[29] Porter v. Iowa Power & Light Co., 217 N.W.2d 221 (Iowa 1974).

[30] Rosenau v. City of Estherville, 199 N.W.2d 125 (Iowa 1972).

[31] Winger v. CM Holdings, LLC, 881 M.W.2d 433, 448 (Iowa 2016).

[32] Wiersgalla v. Garrett, 486 N.W.2d 290 (Iowa 1992); Jorgensen v. Horton, 206 N.W.2d 100, 102 (Iowa 1973).

[33] Alcala v. Marriott Int'l Inc., 880 N.W.2d 699, 710 (Iowa 2016).

[34] *Thompson*, 774 N.W.2d at 836-39.

[35] *Id.*; I.C.J.I.700.3 *Cause—Defined.*

[36] Becker v. D & E Distrib. Co., 247 N.W.2d 727, 731 (Iowa 1976), which provides, as follows:
The law is well settled that one predisposed to disease which is *aggravated or accelerated* by a negligent injury is entitled to recover damages necessarily resulting from such aggravation or acceleration. In other words, the previous condition of the person injured cannot be invoked by the defendant for the purpose of escaping the consequences of his own negligence. The duty of exercising care to avoid injury to the weak and infirm is precisely the same as toward the strong and healthy, and when that duty is violated the measure of damages is the injury inflicted, even though the injury might have been aggravated or might not have happened at all but-for the peculiar condition of the person injured. Hanson v. Dickinson, 188 Iowa 728, 824-25 (1920) (emphasis original).

[37] Adams v. Deur, 173 N.W.2d 100, 105 (Iowa 1969).

[38] Royal Indem. Co. v. Factory Mut. Ins. Co., 786 N.W.2d 839, 849 (Iowa 2010).

[39] *Id.*

factfinder must determine whether the type of harm that occurred is among those reasonably foreseeable potential harms that made the actor's conduct negligent."[40]

> To apply this rule requires consideration, "at an appropriate level of general-ity," of the risks that made the actor's conduct tortious and whether the harm for which recovery is sought was a result of any of those risks. [Restatement (Third) § 29 *cmt.* d, at 496.] Risk consists of "harm occurring with some probability." *Id.*
>
> The magnitude of the risk is the severity of the harm discounted by the probability that it will occur. For purposes of negligence, which requires foreseeability, risk is evaluated by reference to the foreseeable (if indefinite) probability of harm of a foreseeable severity.
>
> *Id.; see also id. cmt.* j, at 505 (discussing connection between the risk standard and foreseeability test used in proximate cause determinations). When defendants, as here, move for a determination that the plaintiff's harm is beyond the scope of liability as a matter of law, courts must initially con-sider all of the range of harms risked by the defendant's conduct that the jury *could* find as the basis for determining that conduct tortious. Then, the court can compare the plaintiff's harm with the range of harms risked by the defendant to determine whether a reasonable jury might find the former among the latter.*Id. cmt.* d, at 496 (*emphasis added*).[41]

The plaintiff's claimed harm is within the scope of defendant's liability if that harm arises from the same general types of danger that the defendants should have taken rea-sonable steps, or were obligated by other tort obligations such as the Rules of the Road, to avoid.[42]

To make the scope of liability determination, a jury must consider whether the repe-tition of a defendant's conduct, makes it more likely harm would happen to another person of the same type the plaintiff claims to have suffered.[43] "Those cases are left to the community judgment and common sense provided by the jury."[44] The limits imposed by applying scope of liability are important for creating appropriate incentives to deter tortious behavior and to address corrective-justice concerns.[45]

V. Damages

Negligent acts in and of themselves do not give rise to damages.[46] "There must be damage to a plaintiff as a result of defendant's wrongful act for there to be an accrued cause of

---

[40] *Id.*

[41] *Hill,* 804 N.W.2d at 100.

[42] *Thompson,* 774 N.W.2d at 839.

[43] *Id.*

[44] *Hill,* 804 N.W.2d at 101.

[45] *Royal Indemnity Co.*, 786 N.W.2d at 850-51.

[46] Uchtorff v. Dahlin, 363 N.W.2d 264, 266 (Iowa 1985).

action."[47] A negligent act in itself gives no right of action. The principle underlying an award of damages "is that of compensation, the ultimate purpose being to place the injured party in as favorable a position as though no wrong had been committed."[48]

A.   Evidence

In awarding damages for personal injuries, Iowa juries are instructed that the amount of damages "cannot be measured by any exact or mathematical standard. You must use your sound judgment based upon an impartial consideration of the evidence."[49]

---

[47] Wolfswinkel v. Gesink, 180 N.W.2d 452, 456 (Iowa 1970).

[48] Dealers Hobby, Inc. v. Marie Ann Realty Co., 255 N.W.2d 131, 134 (Iowa 1977).

[49] Iowa J.I. Civ. § 200.1

CHAPTER 17

KANSAS

KANSAS

Timothy Gatton[1]

I. Purpose of Tort Law

The Kansas Supreme Court has identified the purpose of Kansas tort law as being in line with the "Kansas common-law's reliance in part on protection of consumer expectations and a desire to fully compensate victims."[2] Furthermore, the court stated that "compensation of the victim and deterrence of negligent and worse conduct are, of course, general goals of tort law."[3] The Kansas Supreme Court has also stated that "[t]he aim of a tort action is to restore the plaintiff to the position he or she would have occupied had the injury not occurred."[4] The Kansas Court of Appeals reiterated this in 2010, by saying that "[t]he underlying purpose of any measure of damages in a tort action is to make the injured party whole again."[5] Kansas courts recognize that jurors represent the conscience of the community and are entitled to know the practical effects of their findings.[6]

II. Duty to Exercise Ordinary Care

A. *Question of Law*

In order to establish negligence, the plaintiff is required to show that "there is a duty owed by one person to another and a breach of that duty occurs and, if recovery is to be had for such negligence, the injured party must show a causal connection between the duty breached and the injury received, and that he or she was damaged by the negligence."[7] According to the Kansas Supreme Court, "[t]here first must be a duty owed before there can be negligence."[8] It is a question of law whether a duty exists.[9] According to the Kansas Court of Appeals:

---

[1] Head of Reference Services and Law Library Professor, Oklahoma City University School of Law, Chickasaw Nation Law Library.

[2] Gaumer v. Rossville Truck & Tractor Co., 257 P.3d 292, 304 (Kan. 2011).

[3] *Id.* (citing Kennedy v. City of Sawyer, 618 P.2d 788, 794 (1980); Restatement (Second) of Torts § 901 (1979)).

[4] Arche v. U.S. Dept. of Army, 798 P.2d 477, 481 (Kan. 1990) (citing Restatement (Second) of Torts § 901, comment *a* (1979)).

[5] Evenson v. Lilley, 228 P.3d 420, 422 (2010) (citing McBride v. Dice, 930 P.2d 631, 633 (1997)).

[6] Nail v. Doctor's Bldg., Inc., 708 P.2d 186, 188 (Kan. 1985) (*declined to follow on other grounds* Affiliated FM Ins. Co. v. Neosho Const. Co., 192 F.R.D. 662, 674 (D. Kan. 2000)).

[7] Akins ex rel. Akins v. Hamblin, 703 P.2d 771, 776 (Kan. 1985).

[8] *Id.*

[9] Major ex rel. Major v. Castlegate, Inc., 935 P.2d 225, 230 (1997) (citing Durflinger v. Artiles, 673 P.2d 86, 91 (1983)).

'[D]uty' has been defined as 'an obligation, to which the law will give recognition and effect, to conform to a particular standard of conduct toward
another.' . . . An act is wrongful, or negligent, only if a prudent person would
perceive the risk of damage. The risk to be perceived defines the duty to be
obeyed, and risk imports relation; it is risk to another or to others within
the range of apprehension. The existence of negligence in a given case will
depend upon the particular circumstances which surround the parties at the
time of the occurrence on which the controversy is based.[10]

B.   *Question of Fact*

i.   **Elements**

The elements that the plaintiff must prove are the existence of a duty, a breach of said
duty, an actual injury, and a causal connection between the duty that was breached and the
injury suffered by the plaintiff.[11] Whether the duty has been breached is a question of fact.[12]
"For negligence to exist there must be a duty owed by one person to another and a breach of
that duty. The injured party must show: (1) a causal connection between the duty breached
and the injury received and (2) damage from negligence."[13]

In the state of Kansas, there are three elements that must be satisfied in order to
establish a legal duty.[14] First, the plaintiff has to be foreseeable.[15] Secondly, the probability
of harm must also be foreseeable.[16] Finally, there cannot be any public policy that prohibits
imposing that duty on the defendant.[17] Whether the risk of harm is reasonably foreseeable
from the defendant's conduct is a question of fact for the jury.[18]

ii.   **Evidence**

According to the Kansas Supreme Court, a "plaintiff must be a foreseeable plaintiff and
. . . the probability of harm must be foreseeable."[19] That court defined a foreseeable plaintiff as "one that is 'within the range of apprehension.'"[20] The *Durflinger* court further stated
that "an act is wrongful, or negligent, only if the eye of vigilance, sometimes referred to as
the prudent person, perceives the risk of damage."[21] Generally, a finding of negligence is

---

[10] Schrader v. Great Plains Elec. Co-op. Inc., 868 P.2d 536, 538, *rev. denied*, 255 Kan. 1003 (1994).

[11] Norton Farms, Inc. v. Anadarko Petroleum Corp., 91 P.3d 1239, 1246 (2004).

[12] *Durflinger*, 673 P.2d at 91-92.

[13] Calwell v. Hassan, 925 P.2d 422, 428 (1996).

[14] Berry v. Nat'l Med. Servs., Inc. (*Berry I*), 205 P.3d 745, 749 (2009).

[15] *Id.*

[16] *Id.*

[17] *Id.*

[18] Shirley v. Glass, 241 P.3d 134, 147 (Kan. App. 2010) (*rev'd in part on other grounds* Shirley v. Glass, 308 P.3d 1 (2013).

[19] Berry v. Nat'l Med. Servs., Inc. (*Berry II*), 257 P.3d 287, 290 (2011).

[20] *Id.* (citing *Durflinger*, 673 P.2d at 91).

[21] *Id.*

something that "should be left to the trier of fact. Only when reasonable persons could not reach differing conclusions from the same evidence may the issue be decided as a question of law."[22] There are some special cases in which the actions are covered by approved, authoritative industry standards, and in those cases, the trial court might need to allow evidence of industry standards to be admitted and instruct the jury about these industry standards so that the jury can determine the duty owed to plaintiffs.[23] A statute or regulation may be used to establish the level of care required where the injured party was one of the particular group or class of persons protected by the statute.[24]

III.   Breach of Duty

A.   *Elements*

Negligence, according to the Kansas Judicial Council, is defined as "the lack of reasonable care. It is the failure of a person to do something that a reasonable person would do, or doing something that a reasonable person would not do, under the same circumstances."[25]

B.   *Evidence*

For a plaintiff to be successful in a negligence suit, he or she has the burden of proving that there is a duty, that duty was breached, there was an injury, and that there was a causal connection between the injury and the breached duty.[26] The Kansas Supreme Court has stated that:

> Negligence is not actionable unless it involves the invasion of a legally protected interest, the violation of a right. In every instance, before an act is said to be negligent, there must exist a duty to the individual complaining, the observance of which would have averted or avoided the injury. The plaintiff who sues his fellow man sues for a breach of duty owing to himself.[27]

Kansas does allow negligence to be shown through circumstantial evidence.[28] As the Kansas Supreme Court has held:

> In order for circumstantial evidence to be sufficient to establish negligence, 'such evidence need not rise to that degree of certainty which will exclude any and every other reasonable conclusion'—instead, '[i]t suffices that such evidence affords a basis for a reasonable inference by the court

---

[22] Gruhin v. City of Overland Park, 836 P.2d 1222, 1225 (1992).

[23] *See, e.g.,* Pullen v. West, 92 P.3d 584, 598-600 (2004).

[24] *Shirley*, 214 P.3d at 151.

[25] *Negligence Defined*, Pattern Inst. Kan. Civil 103.01.

[26] City of Andover v. Sw. Bell Tel., L.P., 153 P.3d 561, 565 (2007) (citing Reynolds v. Kansas Dep't of Transp., 43 P.3d 799, 800 Syl. ¶ 1 (2002)).

[27] Blackmore v. Auer, 357 P.2d 765, 771 (1960).

[28] Siruta v. Siruta, 348 P.3d 549, 558 (2015).

or jury,' even though 'some other inference equally reasonable might be drawn [from the evidence].'[29]

IV. Causation

A. Elements

As the Kansas Supreme Court stated, "[t]o find a legal duty to support a negligence claim, (1) the plaintiff must be a foreseeable plaintiff and (2) the probability of harm must be foreseeable."[30] The court in *Durflinger* defined a foreseeable plaintiff as "within the range of apprehension."[31] Also, the "injury must have been the direct and proximate result of some act or acts of negligence on the part of the one from whom recovery is sought. In other words, the negligent act or acts of the party against whom recovery is sought must have been the proximate cause of the injury and damage."[32] However, people are not held responsible for any possible consequence of their negligent actions, "only those consequences that are *probable* according to ordinary and usual experience."[33] Furthermore, the Kansas Supreme Court has also held that:

> [S]ince adoption of comparative negligence in 1974, Kansas courts compare the percentages of fault of all alleged wrongdoers. K.S.A. 60-258a. Proximate cause is not an obsolete concept in Kansas law, but when it has been mentioned by this court in recent years it typically has been in a criminal context. . . . With the adoption of comparative fault, Kansas has moved beyond the concept of proximate cause in negligence.[34]

Yet, the Kansas courts have not eliminated proximate cause from consideration, as evidenced by the Kansas Supreme Court stating in 2008 that "[t]his court has continued, however, to adhere to the common-law requirement of proximate cause."[35]

B. Evidence

To prove causation, a plaintiff must show that defendant's conduct created a foreseeable risk that some harm would likely result, although there is no requirement to prove that the specific harm that occurred was a likely result.[36] Determination of negligence is made by the trier of fact.[37] Negligence is to be determined by the jury and not by the court.[38]

---

[29] *Id.* at 768.

[30] *Berry*, 257 P.3d at 290 (citations omitted).

[31] *Durflinger*, 673 P.2d at 91.

[32] Hickert v. Wright, 319 P.2d 152, 159 (1957).

[33] Hale v. Brown, 197 P.3d 438, 440 (2008) (citing Aguirre v. Adams, 809 P.2d 8, 9 (1991)).

[34] *Reynolds*, 43 P.3d at 804.

[35] *Hale*, 328 Kan. at 323.

[36] *Shirley*, 241 P.3d at 148-49.

[37] *Gruhin*, 836 P.2d at 1225.

[38] Deal v. Bowman, 188 P.3d 941, 946 (2008).

V.   Damages

A.   Elements

Damages are awarded in negligence cases to "make a party whole by restoring that party to the position he or she was in prior to the injury."[39]

B.   Evidence

It is up to the plaintiff to prove the damages, and the trier of fact determines the amount of damages that a party receives.[40] The court has said that "[i]n a negligence action, recovery may be had only where there is evidence showing with reasonable certainty the damage was sustained as a result of the complained-of negligence. Recovery may not be had where the alleged damages are too conjectural or speculative to form a basis for measurement. To warrant recovery of damages, therefore, there must be some reasonable basis for computation which will enable the trier of fact to arrive at an estimate of the amount of loss."[41] The Kansas Supreme Court has held that "[d]amages for personal injuries cannot be definitely assessed by any single method of measurement or by any scientifically accurate combination of methods known to the legal profession, but all known methods which are helpful in determining actual loss or damage should be employed in aid of the judicial process, or effort, designed to render a reasonably just award."[42]

---

[39] Cerretti v. Flint Hills Rural Elec. Co-op. Ass'n, 251 Kan. 347, 360, 837 P.2d 330, 341 (1992).

[40] *Id.* at 362.

[41] *Id.* at 360-61 (citing Morris v. Francisco, 708 P.2d 498, 499 (1985)).

[42] Young v. Kansas City Pub. Serv. Co., 135 P.2d 551, 552 (1943).

CHAPTER 18

KENTUCKY

KENTUCKY
Timothy Gatton[1]

I. Purpose of Tort Law

Kentucky courts have held that the goal of tort law is "to compensate the injured, to spread the loss and to deter others from committing like wrongs."[2] While the Kentucky Supreme Court has stated that "[a] general goal of compensatory damages in tort cases is to put the victim in the same position he would have been prior to the injury or make him whole to the extent that it is possible to measure his injury in terms of money,"[3] the court has also been quite clear that double recovery is not the desired outcome.[4] As the court has stated, "[t]he object is not to place the plaintiff in a better position than he would have been had the wrong not been done."[5]

II. Duty to Exercise Ordinary Care

A. Question of Law

In Kentucky, in order to establish negligence, proof is required to show that "(1) the defendant owed the plaintiff a duty of care, (2) the defendant breached the standard by which his or her duty is measured, and (3) consequent injury."[6] According to the Kentucky Supreme Court, "[t]he existence of a duty is a question of law for the court . . . ."[7] There are various ways to identify duty, but "'[t]he most important factor in determining whether a duty exists is foreseeability.'"[8] The Kentucky Supreme Court stated that "[a]lthough *foreseeability* tends to be elusive in definition, perhaps most famously, Judge Cardozo stated on the subject of *duty* that '[t]he risk reasonably to be perceived defines the duty to be obeyed.'"[9] As a general rule, every individual "owes a duty to every other person to exercise ordinary care in his activities to prevent foreseeable injury."[10]

---

[1] Head of Reference Services and Law Library Professor, Oklahoma City University School of Law, Chickasaw Nation Law Library.

[2] City of Louisville v. Louisville Seed Co., 433 S.W.2d 638, 642 (Ky. 1968), overruled on other grounds by Gas Serv. Co. v. City of London, 687 S.W.2d 144 (Ky. 1985).

[3] Ky. Cent. Ins. v. Schneider, 15 S.W.3d 373, 374 (Ky. 2000).

[4] Hardaway Mgmt. Co. v. Southerland, 977 S.W.2d 910, 918 (Ky. 1998).

[5] *Schneider*, 15 S.W.3d at 374-75.

[6] Pathways, Inc. v. Hammons, 113 S.W.3d 85, 88 (Ky. 2003).

[7] Boland-Maloney Lumber Co. v. Burnett, 302 S.W.3d 680, 686 (Ky. Ct. App. 2009).

[8] *Id.* (citing DAVID J. LEIBSON, 13 KENTUCKY PRACTICE: TORT LAW §10.3, p. 113 (1995)).

[9] *Boland-Maloney*, 302 S.W.3d at 686 (citing Palsgraf v. Long Island R.R., 162 N.E. 99, 100 (N.Y. 1928)).

[10] Grayson Fraternal Order of Eagles, Aerie No. 3738, Inc. v. Claywell, 736 S.W.2d 328, 332 (Ky. 1987), *superseded by statute on other grounds as stated in* DeStock No. 14, Inc. v. Logsdon, 993 S.W.2d 952 (Ky. 1999).

B. Question of Fact

i. Elements

In Kentucky, the plaintiff is required to "prove the existence of a duty, breach thereof, causation, and damages."[11] Breach of that duty and any consequent injury would be questions of fact for a jury to consider.[12] Duty has been defined as having "two distinct elements: actual injury or harm to the plaintiff *and* legal causation between the defendant's breach and the plaintiff's injury."[13]

ii. Evidence

The Kentucky Supreme Court has stated that "the scope and character of a defendant's duty is largely defined by the foreseeability of the injury."[14] The Court has also held:

> Foreseeable risks are determined in part on what the defendant knew at the time of the alleged negligence. "The actor is required to recognize that his conduct involves a risk of causing an invasion of another's interest if a reasonable man would do so while exercising such attention, perception of the circumstances, memory, knowledge of other pertinent matters, intelligence, and judgment as a reasonable man would have." The term "knowledge of pertinent matters" is explained by *Restatement (Second) of Torts* §290, which states:
>
> > For the purpose of determining whether the actor should recognize that his conduct involves a risk, he is required to know (a) the qualities and habits of human beings and animals and the qualities, characteristics, and capacities of things and forces in so far as they are matters of common knowledge at the time and in the community; and (b) the common law, legislative enactments, and general customs in so far as they are likely to affect the conduct of the other or third persons.[15]

The Court has also stated that "[n]egligence may be inferred from circumstances properly adduced in evidence, provided those circumstances raise a fair presumption of negligence; and circumstantial evidence alone may authorize the finding of negligence."[16] If a company has safety rules which are not being followed, the Court has also held that "the failure of a company to enforce its own rules for employee safety is evidence of negligence

---

[11] *Boland-Maloney*, 302 S.W.3d at 686.

[12] *Id.*

[13] Pathways, Inc. v. Hammons, 113 S.W.3d 85, 89 (Ky. 2003).

[14] Lee v. Farmer's Rural Elec. Co-op Corp., 245 S.W.3d 209, 212 (Ky. Ct. App. 2007).

[15] *Pathways*, 113 S.W.3d at 90 (*internal citations omitted*) (citing RESTATEMENT (SECOND) OF TORTS § 289(a); Mitchell v. Hadl, 816 S.W.2d 183, 186 (Ky. 1991) (holding that liability for negligence is based on what the defendant was aware of at the time of the alleged negligent act and not on what the defendant should have known in hindsight)).

[16] Bruce v. Alley, 391 S.W.2d 678, 680 (Ky. Ct. App. 1965).

under Kentucky law."[17] A statute or regulation may be used to establish the level of care required where the injury was the type the statute was designed to prevent and the injured party was one of the class of persons protected by the statute.[18]

III. Breach of Duty

A. *Elements*

According to the Kentucky Supreme Court, "[i]n any negligence case, it is necessary to show that the defendant failed to discharge a legal duty or conform his conduct to the standard required."[19] Further, the Court has stated that "every person owes a duty to every other person to exercise ordinary care in his activities to prevent foreseeable injury."[20]

B. *Evidence*

In Kentucky negligence claims, "there must be a duty on the defendant's part, a breach of that duty, and consequent injury. In general, this court has adopted a "universal duty of care" which requires every person to exercise ordinary care in his activities to prevent foreseeable injury."[21] However, that "universal duty of care" is not without limits.[22] "The examination must be so focused as to determine whether a duty is owed, and consideration must be given to public policy, statutory and common law theories in order to determine whether a duty existed in a particular situation."[23] Additionally, the Court has stated that "the foreseeability of the risk of harm should be a question normally left to the jury under the breach analysis."[24]

The Supreme Court of Kentucky has affirmed the interpretive function of the jury in negligence cases.[25] This function is "an American tradition so fundamental" that it is enshrined in the Kentucky Constitution.[26] The Court has stated that "the conscience of the community speaks through the verdict of the jury, not the judge's view of the evidence. It may well be that deciding when to take a case away from the jury is a matter of degree, a line drawn in sand, but this is all the more reason why the judiciary should be careful not to overstep the line."[27]

---

[17] Wells v. Bottling Grp., LLC, 833 F. Supp. 2d 665, 671 (E.D. Ky. 2011) (citing Ray v. Hardee's Food Sys., Inc., 785 S.W.2d 519, 520 (Ky. Ct. App. 1990)).

[18] McCarty v. Covol Fuels No. 2, LLC, 476 S.W.3d 224, 227 (Ky. 2015).

[19] Mitchell v. Hadl, 816 S.W.2d 183, 185 (Ky. 1991) (citing W. PROSSER, LAW OF TORTS § 30 (1971)).

[20] Grayson Fraternal Order of Eagles, Aerie No. 3738, Inc. v. Claywell, 736 S.W.2d 328, 332 (Ky. 1987).

[21] T & M Jewelry, Inc. v. Hicks *ex rel.* Hicks, 189 S.W.3d 526, 530 (Ky. 2006).

[22] *Id.* at 531.

[23] Grand Aerie Fraternal Order of Eagles v. Carneyhan, 169 S.W.3d 840, 849 (Ky. 2005) (quoting Fryman v. Harrison, 896 S.W.2d 908, 909 (Ky. 1995)).

[24] Shelton v. Ky. Easter Seals Soc., Inc., 413 S.W.3d 901, 914 (Ky. 2013).

[25] Horton v. Union Light, Heat & Power Co., 690 S.W.2d 382, 385 (Ky. 1985).

[26] *Id.* (citing KY. CONST. Sec. 7).

[27] Horton, 690 S.W.2d at 385.

IV. Causation

A. Elements

According to the Kentucky Supreme Court, "[i]t is elemental that the negligence of a defendant be a proximate cause of the accident before liability attaches."[28] Furthermore, the court has held that:

> If the original negligent act set in force a chain of events which the original negligent actor might have reasonably foreseen would, according to the experience of mankind, lead to the event which happened, the original actor is not relieved of liability by the intervening act. If, however, the ultimate injury is brought about by an intervening act or force so unusual as not to have been reasonably foreseeable, the intervening act is considered as the superseding cause and the original actor is not liable.[29]

B. Evidence

It is not mandatory that a defendant "'foresee the particular consequences of [its] negligent acts' but only that its conduct would reasonably be anticipated to result in harm."[30] A defendant, therefore, would be held liable even if the results of that negligence were unexpectedly severe or even improbable.[31] While the court determines if there was any sort of duty owed, "questions regarding breach, injury, and causation are, generally, for the jury."[32]

V. Damages

A. Elements

In Kentucky, the purpose of awarding compensatory damages is "to make the injured party whole to the extent that it is possible to measure his injury in terms of money."[33] The court has stated that "the emphasis is not upon retribution but compensation."[34]

---

[28] Tillery v. Louisville & Nashville R.R., 433 S.W.2d 623, 624 (Ky. Ct. App. 1968).

[29] Hines v. Westerfield, 254 S.W.2d 728, 729 (Ky. Ct. App. 1953).

[30] CSX Transp., Inc. v. Moody, 313 S.W.3d 72, 83 (Ky. 2010) (citing Gallick v. Baltimore & Ohio R.R., 372 U.S. 108 (1963)).

[31] Id.

[32] Bartley v. Commonwealth, 400 S.W.3d 714, 726 (Ky. 2013).

[33] Ky. Cent. Ins. v. Schneider, 15 S.W.3d 373,374 (Ky. 2000).

[34] Paducah Area Pub. Library v. Terry, 655 S.W.2d 19, 23 (Ky. Ct. App. 1983).

B.   *Evidence*

If a defendant does not exercise ordinary care, then the defendant would be liable for damages.[35] Tort cases should be tried with the following goal:

> [P]rovide full recompense and nothing more . . . All cases are to be tried to these ends. The law recognizes the fundamental importance of the ability to earn, and therefore mandates that impairment of earning power shall be fully compensated. Likewise, the ability to live free of pain and suffering is essential to a meaningful life. If freedom from pain is lost through tortious injury, the law provides full compensation. In neither case, however, does the law provide a profit. To provide for full compensation for the tort victims and at the same time guard against oppressive retribution against wrongdoers is a salient objective of the trial court.[36]

---

[35] Dick's Sporting Goods, Inc. v. Webb, 413 S.W.3d 891, 898 (Ky. 2013).

[36] *Paducah,* 655 S.W.2d at 23.

CHAPTER 19

LOUISIANA

LOUISIANA
Timothy Gatton[1]

I. Purpose of Tort Law

In Louisiana, the purpose of tort law is spelled out in *Louisiana Civil Code,* article 2315: "Every act whatever of man that causes damage to another obliges him by whose fault it happened to repair it."[2] The Supreme Court of Louisiana has also weighed in on the purpose of tort law, by stating that "[i]t should be remembered that the main function of the law of torts is compensation and to a much lesser degree, deterrence."[3]

II. Duty to Exercise Ordinary Care

A. *Question of Law*

The Supreme Court of Louisiana has said that "[a] threshold issue in any negligence action is whether the defendant owed the plaintiff a duty. Whether a duty is owed is a question of law."[4] The *Lemann* court elaborated by saying that:

> In deciding whether to impose a duty in a particular case, the court must make a policy decision in light of the unique facts and circumstances presented. The inquiry is whether the plaintiff has any law (statutory, jurisprudential, or a rising from general principles of fault) to support the claim that the defendant owed him a duty.[5]

Additionally, the Court has stated that "[t]here is an almost universal duty on the part of the defendant in a negligence action to use reasonable care to avoid injury to another."[6]

---

[1] Head of Reference Services and Law Library Professor, Oklahoma City University School of Law, Chickasaw Nation Law Library.

[2] La. Civ. Code, art. 2315 (2001).

[3] State v. Chapman Dodge Ctr, Inc., 428 So.2d 413, 418 (La. 1983).

[4] Rando v. Anco Insulations Inc., 16 So.3d 1065, 1086 (La. 2009) (citing Lemann v. Essen Lane Daiquiris, Inc., 923 So.2d 627, 632-33 (La. 2006)).

[5] *Lemann*, 923 So.2d at 633.

[6] *Rando,* 16 So.3d at 1086 (citing Boykin v. La. Transit Co., 707 So.2d 1225, 1231 (La. 1998)).

B. Question of Fact

i. Elements

Louisiana uses a duty/risk analysis when looking at liability, which has the following four-prong inquiry:

(1)   Was the conduct in question a substantial factor in bringing about the harm to the plaintiff, *i.e.,* was it a cause-in-fact of the harm which occurred?

(2)   Did the defendant(s) owe a duty to the plaintiff?

(3)   Was the duty breached?

(4)   Was the risk, and harm caused, within the scope of protection afforded by the duty breached?[7]

It is a matter for the trier of fact to determine if the conduct of the defendant "was a substantial factor in bringing about the harm, and thus, a cause-in-fact of the injuries."[8]

There are five separate elements involved in the duty/risk analysis which must be proven by the plaintiff.[9] The elements are listed by the court as the following:

(1)   The defendants' conduct was a cause-in-fact of the plaintiffs' injuries,

(2)   The defendants had a duty to conform their conduct to a specific standard,

(3)   The defendants breached that duty to conform their conduct to a specific standard,

(4)   The defendants' conduct was the legal cause of the plaintiffs' injuries, and

(5)   Actual damages.[10]

ii. Evidence

The Louisiana Supreme Court has held that "[a] negative answer to any of the elements of the Duty/Risk analysis prompts a no-liability determination."[11] As far as the scope of any duty, the court has said that "[t]here is no 'rule' for determining the scope of the duty. Regardless if stated in terms of proximate cause, legal cause, or duty, the scope of the duty inquiry is ultimately a question of policy as to whether the particular risk falls within the scope of the duty."[12] A statute or regulation may be used to establish the level of care required where the injury was the type the statute was designed to prevent and the injured party was one of the class of persons protected by the statute.[13]

---

[7] *Rando,* 16 So.3d at 1085-86.

[8] England v. Fifth La. Levee Dist., 167 So.3d 1105, 1110 (La. Ct. App. 2015).

[9] Joseph v. Dickerson, 754 So.2d 912, 916 (La. 2000).

[10] *Id.*

[11] *Id.* (citing Stroik v. Ponseti, 699 So.2d 1072, 1077 (La. 1997)).

[12] Roberts v. Benoit, 605 So.2d 1032, 1044 (La. 1991).

[13] Savarese v. Bye, 398 So.2d 1276, 1278-79 (La. Ct. App. 1981).

III.   Breach of Duty

A.   Elements

According to *Louisiana Civil Jury Instructions*, "the basic standard is that the defendant must exercise the degree of care that we might reasonably expect from an ordinarily prudent person under the same or similar circumstances. The standard of care is not that of an extraordinarily cautious individual or an exceptionally skilled person, but that of a person of ordinary prudence."[14]

B.   Evidence

The Court of Appeal of Louisiana has held that "[i]n a negligence action the plaintiff must further prove that defendant had actual or constructive knowledge of the risk of harm presented by the condition of the thing and failed to take steps to remedy the condition or to warn persons of its existence. In a strict liability action, a plaintiff is relieved of the burden of proving that the defendant knew of the existence of the condition."[15]

IV.   Causation

A.   Elements

In Louisiana negligence actions, "the proper inquiry is whether the conduct in question was a substantial factor in bringing about the accident. Whether the defendant's conduct was a substantial factor in bringing about the harm, and thus, a cause-in-fact of the injuries, is a factual question to be determined by the factfinder."[16] The Louisiana Supreme Court has elaborated by stating that:

> The legal cause of the damage in question could be stated as part of the duty inquiry: was the defendant under a duty to protect each of the plaintiff's interests affected against the type of damage that did in fact occur? Such a form of statement is sometimes helpful because it is less likely than "proximate cause" to be interpreted as if it were policy free fact finding; thus, "duty" is more apt to direct attention to the policy issues which determine the extent of the original obligation and its continuance, rather than to the mechanical sequence of events which goes to make up causation in fact.[17]

---

[14] *Negligence—Breach*, 18 LA. CIV. L. TREATISE, CIVIL JURY INSTRUCTIONS §3:4 (3d ed.) (November 2016 update) (internal citations omitted).

[15] Buffinet v. Plaquemines Par. Comm'n Counsel, 645 So.2d 631, 635-36 (La. Ct. App. 1994).

[16] *England*, 167 So.3d at 1110.

[17] Pitre v. Opelousas Gen. Hosp., 530 So.2d 1151, 1155 (La. 1988).

B. *Evidence*

A plaintiff in a negligence action must prove that "the condition of the thing presented an unreasonable risk of harm, or was defective, and that this condition of the thing was a cause-in-fact of her injuries."[18] The Court of Appeal of Louisiana has elaborated by stating that:

> Cause-in-fact is a "but-for" analysis; if the plaintiff would not have sustained his injuries "but-for" the defendant's substandard conduct, then such conduct is a cause-in-fact of the plaintiff's harm. When multiple causes are present, a defendant's conduct is a cause-in-fact when it is a substantial factor in generating a plaintiff's harm. Causation is a fact-specific inquiry and the issue to be resolved is whether the factfinder's conclusion is a reasonable one.[19]

An important consideration is, as follows:

> In determining the limitation to be placed on liability for a defendant's substandard conduct—*i.e.*, whether there is a duty-risk relationship—we have found the proper inquiry to be how easily the risk of injury to plaintiff can be associated with the duty sought to be enforced. Restated, the ease of association inquiry is simply: "How easily does one associate the plaintiff's complained-of harm with the defendant's conduct? . . . Although ease of association encompasses the idea of foreseeability, it is not based on foreseeability alone."[20]

V. Damages

A. *Elements*

According to the *Louisiana Civil Code*:

> The owner or custodian of a thing is answerable for damage occasioned by its ruin, vice, or defect, only upon a showing that he knew or, in the exercise of reasonable care, should have known of the ruin, vice, or defect which caused the damage, that the damage could have been prevented by the exercise of reasonable care, and that he failed to exercise such reasonable care. Nothing in this Article shall preclude the court from the application of the doctrine of *res ipsa loquitur* in an appropriate case.[21]

---

[18] *Buffinet,* 645 So.2d at 635.

[19] Orthopaedic Clinic of Monroe v. Ruhl, 786 So.2d 323, 329-30 (La. Ct. App. 2001) (internal citations omitted).

[20] *Roberts*, 605 So.2d at 1045 (internal citations omitted).

[21] LA. CIV. CODE ANN. art. 2317.1 (2016).

B.   Evidence

In the state of Louisiana, "[i]t is well settled that the trier of fact has much discretion in awarding damages."[22] Also, it is noted that "[e]ach case is different, and the adequacy or inadequacy of the award should be determined by the facts or circumstances particular to the case under consideration."[23]

---

[22] *Ruhl,* 786 So.2d at 334.

[23] Youn v. Mar. Overseas Corp., 623 So.2d 1257, 1260 (La. 1993).

CHAPTER 20

MAINE

MAINE

Christine Iaconeta[1]

I. Purpose of Tort Law

The Supreme Judicial Court of Maine stated that "the law of torts has no higher purpose than to afford compensation for injuries sustained by one person as the result of the conduct of another."[2] The deterrent effect of tort liability is strengthened by holding wrong-doers accountable for the consequences of their actions.[3] The reason damages are awarded in torts claims is to "make the plaintiff whole by compensating him or her for any injuries or losses proximately caused by the defendant's negligence."[4]

II. Duty To Exercise Ordinary Care

A. *Question of Law*

The Supreme Judicial Court of Maine has held that "the existence of a duty, as an element of negligence, and the scope of that duty, are questions of law."[5] Furthermore, the Court has held that "duty refers to whether the defendant is under any obligation for the benefit of the particular plaintiff."[6]

B. *Question of Fact*

"The existence of a duty and the scope of that duty are questions of law."[7] "Duty involves the question of whether the defendant is under any obligation for the benefit of the particular plaintiff. When a court imposes a duty in a negligence case, the duty is always

---

[1] Law Library Director, Garbrecht Law Library, University of Maine School of Law. I would like to thank my colleagues in the library, Maureen Quinlan and Cindy Hirsch, for their help with this piece.

[2] Durepo v. Fishman, 533 A.2d 264, 266 (Me. 1987) (Nichols, J., dissenting) (citing Prosser and Keeton on Torts 6 (5th ed. 1984)).

[3] Bedard v. Greene, 409 A.2d 676, 677-78 (Me. 1979).

[4] Snow v. Villacci, 754 A.2d 360, 363 (Me. 2000) (citing SIMMONS, ZILLMAN & GREGORY, MAINE TORT LAW §9.01, 663 (1999). *See also* Reardon v. Lovely Dev., 852 A. 2d 66, 69 (Me. 2004).

[5] Gniadek v. Camp Sunshine at Sebago Law, Inc., 11 A.3d 308, 313 (Me. 2011) (citing Alexander v. Mitchell, 930 A.2d 1016, 1020 (Me. 2007)).

[6] *Gniadek*, 11 A.3d at 313 (citing Bryan R. v. Watchtower Bible & Tract Soc'y, Inc., 738 A.2d 839, 844 (Me. 1999)).

[7] Alexander v. Mitchell, 2007 ME 108, ¶ 14, 930 A.2d 1016, 1020 (Me. 2007). *See also* DONALD G. ALEXANDER, MAINE JURY INSTRUCTION MANUAL, 7-81 (2016) (discussing *Alexander*, 930 A.2d 1016 (Me. 2007)).

the same—to conform to the legal standard of reasonable conduct in the light of the apparent risk."[8] "Although the foreseeability of an injury is a foundational consideration, it is never the sole determinant of duty."[9] After considering "societal expectations regarding behavior and individual responsibility in allocating risks and costs," the courts will also "consider the hand of history, our ideals of morals and justice, the convenience of administration of the rule, and our social ideas as to where the loss should fall."[10]

III. Breach of Duty

A. Elements

Maine's courts have held, "the duty is always the same—to conform to the legal standard of reasonable conduct in the light of the apparent risk."[11] "Negligence is doing something that an ordinary careful person would not do or the failure to do something which an ordinary person would do in the same situation."[12] The jury decides if there has been a breach of duty. The Court holds "that if a duty exists, 'the question of whether there was a breach of the standard of care would ordinarily be a question for a factfinder, not susceptible' to summary judgment."[13]

"What constitutes a breach of duty of due care may factually vary according to circumstances."[14] "Whether a party has breached a duty of care to another is a question of fact."[15]

B. Evidence

Violation of a safety statute is evidence of negligence.[16] "The doctrine of *res ipsa loquitur* is applicable where (i) there has been an unexplained accident, (ii) the instrument that caused the injury was under the management or control of the defendant and (iii) in the

---

[8] Maravell v. R.J. Grondin & Sons, 2007 ME 1, ¶ 7, 914 A.2d. 709, 712 (2007) (quoting Searles v. Trs. of St. Joseph's Coll., 1997 ME 128, ¶ 5, 695 A.2d 1206, 1209 (1987) (quoting Trusiani v. Cumberland & York Distribs., Inc., 538 A.2d 258, 261 (Me. 1988)). For further discussion *see* JACK H. SIMMONS et al., MAINE TORT LAW MANUAL (2004).

[9] *Alexander*, 930 A.2d at 1020 (citing Cameron v. Pepin, 610 A.2d 279, 282 (Me. 1992)).

[10] *Id.* at 1020 (citing Decker v. New England Pub. Warehouse, Inc. & S.D. Warren Co., 2000 ME 76, ¶ 7, 749 A.2d at 765 (2000)).

[11] ANDREW M. HORTON AND PEGGY L. MCGHEE, MAINE CIVIL REMEDIES, 319 (4th ed. 2004); Beaulieu v. Beaulieu, 265 A.2d 610, 612 (Me. 1970) (quoting Levesque v. Pelletier, 131 Me. 266, 269, 161 A. 198 (Me. 1932)); Chaisson v. Williams, 130 Me. 341, 345, 156 A. 154 (Me. 1931).

[12] Carter v. Bangor Hydro-Elec. Co., 598 A.2d 739 (Me. 1991) (citing Fitts v. Cent. Maine Power Co., 562 A 2d 690, 692 (Me. 1989)). *See* also SIMMONS ET AL., *supra* note 3, at 7-11 (2004) (discussing *Fitts*, 562 A 2d at 692).

[13] Davis v. R C & Sons Paving, Inc., 2011 ME 88, 26 A.3d 787 (Me. 2011) (quoting *Alexander*, 930 A.2d at 1020).

[14] *See* HORTON AND MCGHEE, *supra* note 10, at 323 (discussing Stanton v. Univ. of Maine Sys., 773 A.2d 1045, 1049 (Me. 2001)).

[15] Feeney v. Hanover Ins. Co., 1998 ME 124, 711 A.2d 1296 (Me. 1998) (citing Welch v. McCarthy, 677 A.2d 1066, 1069 (Me. 1996)).

[16] Trusiani v. Cumberland & York Distributors, Inc., 538 A.2d 258, 263 (Me. 1988).

ordinary course of events, the accident would not have happened absent negligence on the part of the defendant."[17]

IV.   Causation

A.   Elements

A plaintiff in Maine first establishes duty and then "that a breach of that duty proximately caused an injury to the plaintiff."[18] What is proximate cause? It has been defined as "that cause which, in natural and continuous sequence, unbroken by an efficient intervening cause, produces the injury, and without which the result would not have occurred."[19] "A person's negligence is not the proximate cause of an injury which results from the intervention of a new and independent cause which is neither anticipated nor reasonably foreseeable by the person."[20]

B.   Evidence

Proximate cause is to be decided by the jury.[21] "In order to recover for damages in a cause of action for negligence or for any other tort, a plaintiff must establish that "there be some reasonable connection between the act or omission of the defendant and the damage which the plaintiff has suffered."[22]

"The question of whether a defendant's acts or omissions were the proximate cause of a plaintiff's injuries is generally a question of fact, and a judgment as a matter of law is improper if any reasonable view of the evidence could sustain a finding of proximate cause."[23] Evidence is sufficient to support a finding of proximate cause if the evidence and inferences that may reasonably be drawn from the evidence indicate that the negligence played

---

[17] Wellington Associates, Inc. v. Capital Fire Protection Co., Inc., 594 A.2d 1089 (Me. 1991) (citing Parker v. Harriman, 516 A.2d 549, 551 (Me. 1986)); Ginn v. Penobscot Co., 334 A.2d 874, 878 (Me. 1975). *See also*, JACK SIMMONS et al., MAINE TORT LAW, 7-32 - 7-33 (2004) (discussing *Wellington*, 594 A.2d 1089).

[18] Rowe v. Bennett, 514 A.2d 802, 804 (Me. 1986) (citing Macomber v. Dillman, 505 A.2d 810, 812 (Me. 1986)). For further discussion, *see also* JACK H. SIMMONS et al., MAINE TORT LAW MANUAL, 7-34 (2004).

[19] Merriam v. Wanger, 2000 ME 159, ¶8, 757 A.2d 778, 780 (2000) (quoting Webb v. Haas, 1999 ME 74, ¶ 20, 728 A.2d 1261, 1267 (1999)) (quoting Searles v. Trustees of St. Joseph's Coll., 1997 ME 128, ¶ 8, 695 A.2d 1206, 1209 (1997)). *See also*, ANDREW M. HORTON AND PEGGY L. McGHEE, MAINE CIVIL REMEDIES, 323-325 (4th ed. 2004), discussing *Merriam*, 757 A.2d at 780; *see also* JACK H. SIMMONS et al., MAINE TORT LAW MANUAL 7-33 to 7-37 (2004).

[20] Johnson v. Dubois, 256 A.2d 733, 735 (Me. 1969). *See also* ANDREW M. HORTON AND PEGGY L. McGHEE, MAINE CIVIL REMEDIES, 325 (4th ed. 2004) (discussing *Johnson*, 256 A.2d at 735).

[21] *Merriam*, 757 A.2d at 781 (citing Cyr v. Adamar Assocs., 2000 ME 110, ¶ 6, 752 A.2d 603 (Me. 2000)); Champagne v. Mid-Maine Med. Ctr., 1998 ME 87, ¶ 10, 711 A.2d 842, 845. *See also*, JACK H. SIMMONS et al., MAINE TORT LAW MANUAL, 7-34 (2004) (discussing Klingerman v. SOL Corp., 505 A.2d 474, 478 (Me. 1986); Schultz v. Gould Acad., 332 A2d 368 (Me. 1975).

[22] Houde v. Millett, 2001 ME 183, ¶ 10, 787 A.2d 757, 759 (Me. 2001) (citing Crowe v. Shaw, 2000 ME 136, ¶¶ 8-9, 755 A.2d 509, 512 (Me. 2001)) (quoting WILLIAM L. PROSSER, THE LAW OF TORTS § 41, at 236 (4th ed. 1971)). *See also* DONALD G. ALEXANDER, MAINE JURY INSTRUCTION MANUAL, 7-81 (2016) (discussing Addy v. Jenkins, 2009 ME 46, 969 A.2d 935 (Me. 2009)).

[23] *Houde*, 787 A.2d at 781 (citing Kaechele v. Kenyon Oil Co., 2000 ME 39, ¶ 17, 747 A.2d 167, 173 (Me. 2000)).

a substantial role in bringing about or causing the injury and the injury was a reasonably foreseeable consequence.[24] A consequence of negligence is reasonably foreseeable if the negligence has created a risk which might be expected to result in the injury or damage at issue, even if the exact nature of the injury is not foreseeable.[25] "A defendant is entitled to a summary judgment if there is so little evidence tending to show that the defendant's acts or omissions were the proximate cause of the plaintiff's injuries that the jury would have to engage in conjecture or speculation in order to return a verdict for the plaintiff."[26] "The mere possibility of such causation is not enough, and when the matter remains one of pure speculation or conjecture, or even if the probabilities are evenly balanced, a defendant is entitled to a judgment."[27]

V.   Damages

A.   Elements

"Tort damages, with the exception of punitive damages, are intended to make the plaintiff whole by compensating him or her for any injuries or losses proximately caused by the defendant."[28]

B.   Evidence

Assessment of compensatory damages is in the sole province of the factfinder; review is "highly deferential."[29] An award of damages must be supported by a rational basis. It will only be rejected if "there is no competent evidence in the record to support the award."[30] Damages that are "uncertain, contingent, or speculative" are not recoverable.[31] "[S]ome evidence of the amount of the loss sustained must support an award," but "damages need not be proved to a mathematical certainty."[32] The factfinder may also "act upon probable and inferential . . . proof in determining damages."[33] In proving damages, the plaintiff must "establish facts from which the loss may be determined to a probability."[34]

---

[24] *Merriam*, 757 A.2d at 780.

[25] *Id.* at 781.

[26] *Houde*, 787 A.2d at 781 (citing *Merriam*, 757 A.2d at 781).

[27] *Id.*

[28] Reardon v. Lovely Dev., Inc. 852 A.2d 66, 69 (Me. 2004) (citing *Snow*, 754 A.2d at 363) (distinguishing on other grounds, Lougee Conservancy v. CitiMortgage, Inc., 48 A.3d 774 (Me. 2012)).

[29] Rutland v. Mullen, 2002 ME 98, ¶ 20, 798 A.2d 1104, 1112 (Me. 2002).

[30] *Id.*

[31] Wood v. Bell, 2006 ME 98, ¶ 21, 902 A.2d 843, 851 (Me. 2006).

[32] Estate of Hoch v. Stifel, 16 A.3d 137, 150–51 (Me. 2011) (citing *Reardon*, 852 A.2d at 69) (*see also* Foss v. Ingeneri, 561 A.2d 498, 498–99 (Me. 1989)) (holding that plaintiff retains the burden of proving damages by a preponderance of the evidence following entry of default judgment); Decesere v. Thayer, 468 A.2d 597, 598 (Me. 1983) ("Damages must be grounded on established positive facts or on evidence from which their existence and amount may be determined to a probability.")

[33] *Estate of Hoch*, 16 A.3d at 150–51 (citing Tang of the Sea, Inc. v. Bayley's Quality Seafoods, Inc., 1998 ME 264, ¶ 10, 721 A.2d 648, 650 (Me. 1998)).

[34] Snow v. Villacci, 754 A.2d 360 (2000) (citing Currier v. Cyr, 570 A.2d 1205, 1210 (Me.1990)).

CHAPTER 21

MARYLAND

MARYLAND

Savanna L. Nolan[1]

I. Purpose of Tort Law

The Maryland Court of Appeals has held that an underlying purpose of tort law is "to discourage or encourage specific types of behavior by one party to the benefit of another party."[2] The court has extrapolated this purpose from the duty element of negligence, as duty is "an obligation, to which the law will give recognition and effect, to conform to a particular standard of conduct toward another."[3]

Maryland courts are concerned with both the deterrence and compensatory functions of tort law. Maryland common law has a strong "'prophylactic' policy of preventing future harm," as ideally individuals who witness the "admonition of the wrongdoer" will fear liability and be deterred from committing tortious actions.[4] This deterrence is accomplished by awarding a torts victim a monetary award "as compensation, indemnity, or restitution for harm sustained by him,"[5] thus fulfilling both the deterrence and compensatory purposes with the same action.

II. Duty to Exercise Ordinary Care

A. Question of Law

Maryland has long held that duty is an essential element of negligence.[6] As discussed above, Maryland defines duty as "an obligation, to which the law will give recognition and effect, to conform to a particular standard of conduct toward another."[7] The existence of a

---

[1] Reference Librarian, Georgetown University Law Center; J.D., University of Georgia; M.S.L.I.S., The Catholic University of America.

[2] Valentine v. On Target, Inc., 727 A.2d 947, 950 (Md. 1999).

[3] Ashburn v. Anne Arundel Cty., 510 A.2d 1078, 1083 (Md. 1986) (citing W. KEETON, PROSSER AND KEETON ON TORTS § 53 (5th ed. 1984)).

[4] Matthews v. Amberwood Assocs. Ltd. P'ship, Inc., 719 A.2d 119, 132 (1998) (quoting W. KEETON, PROSSER AND KEETON ON TORTS § 4 (5th ed. 1984)).

[5] Superior Const. Co. v. Elmo, 104 A.2d 581, 582 (Md. 1954).

[6] W. Virginia Cent. & Pittsburg Ry. Co. v. State, 54 A. 669, 671 (Md. 1903) ("Of course there can be no negligence where there is no duty that is due; for negligence is the breach of some duty that one person owes to another.").

[7] Dehn v. Edgecombe, 865 A.2d 603, 611 (Md. 2005) (quoting W. KEETON, PROSSER AND KEETON ON TORTS § 53 (5th ed. 1984)).

legal duty is a question of law,[8] and "represents a policy question of whether the specific plaintiff is entitled to protection from the acts of the defendant."[9]

Additionally, duty may be prescribed by statute or by a special relationship.[10] In order for a breach of statutory duty to be considered as evidence of negligence, the following must be established: (1) the plaintiff must be a member of the class of persons the statute was designed to protect; (2) the injury sustained must have been the type the statute was designed to prevent; and (3) the plaintiff must present legally sufficient evidence to demonstrate that the statutory violation was the proximate cause of the injury sustained.[11] A special relationship can be established in the three following manners: (1) by statute or rule; (2) by contractual or other private relationship; or (3) indirectly or impliedly by virtue of the relationship between the parties.[12]

There is no set formula for determining whether a duty exists,[13] though the court does examine the following seven factors:

(1)   the foreseeability of harm to the plaintiff;
(2)   the degree of certainty that the plaintiff suffered the injury;
(3)   the closeness of the connection between the defendant's conduct and the injury suffered;
(4)   the moral blame attached to the defendant's conduct;
(5)   the policy of preventing future harm;
(6)   the extent of the burden to the defendant and consequences to the community of imposing a duty to exercise care with resulting liability for breach; and
(7)   the availability, cost and prevalence of insurance for the risk involved.[14]

Foreseeability of harm is the most important variable when determining duty,[15] though the nature of the harm likely to result from a failure to exercise due care is also a major consideration.[16] Foreseeability is defined as "whether a reasonable person would or should know that the conduct would constitute an unreasonable risk of harm to another by reflecting current societal standards with respect to an acceptable nexus between the act and the ensuing harm."[17] It can also be established based on a "general field of danger which

---

[8] Doe v. Pharmacia & Upjohn Co., Inc., 879 A.2d 1088, 1092 (Md. 2005).

[9] Gourdine v. Crews, 955 A.2d 769, 783 (Md. 2008).

[10] Grimes v. Kennedy Krieger Inst., Inc., 782 A.2d 807, 846 (Md. 2001).

[11] Pahanish v. Western Trails, Inc., 517 A.2d 1122, 1132 (Md. 1986).

[12] Grimes, 782 A.2d at 842.

[13] Coates v. S. Md. Elec. Coop., Inc., 731 A.2d 931, 936 (Md. 1999).

[14] Ashburn v. Anne Arundel Cty., 510 A.2d 1078, 1083 (Md. 1986) (quoting Tarasoff v. Regents of Univ. of Cal., 551 P.2d 334, 342 (Ca. 1976)).

[15] Eisel v. Bd. of Educ. of Montgomery Cty., 597 A.2d 447, 452 (Md. 1991).

[16] Jacques v. First Nat. Bank of Maryland, 515 A.2d 756, 759 (Md. 1986).

[17] MD. CIVIL PATTERN JURY INSTR. 19:3 (4th ed.) (citing B.N. v. K.K., 312 Md. 135 (1988)).

should have been anticipated."[18] Foreseeability must be judged "by foresight, not in retrospect," and judged against how a reasonably prudent person would have apprehended the situation based on actual knowledge or the "opportunity by the exercise of reasonable care, prudence, and diligence to acquire knowledge."[19]

The court has emphasized that foreseeability is "simply intended to reflect current societal standards,"[20] and "the fact that a result may be foreseeable does not itself impose a duty."[21] The court must also consider the cost/benefit ratio of imposing the duty as a means of preventing future harm, including analysis of sub-factors such as the actions of third parties.[22] The court has explicitly limited foreseeability under the logic that the "concept that all persons owe a duty to all other persons to use reasonable care at all time to protect them from harm must be limited if we are to avoid liability for unreasonably remote consequences."[23]

B.   *Question of Fact*

i.   **Elements**

As discussed above, the existence of a legal duty is a question of law.[24] However, if the existence of a duty depends on a determination of material facts, the factfinder must first make that determination.[25] Additionally, determination of a special relationship between the parties that may give rise to a duty is to be done on a case by case basis, and, if properly pled, relies on the trier of fact.[26]

Duty is breached when there is "conduct that falls below the standard of care owed."[27] Maryland courts have used the terms "due care," "ordinary care," and "reasonable care" interchangeably to describe the standard of care owed.[28] The jury must evaluate whether the actions taken by the defendant were reasonable under all the circumstances, and this determination is the "essence of a negligence action."[29] What constitutes "due care" depends on the facts of the case, and "ordinary care varies with the nature of the undertaking."[30]

---

[18] Segerman v. Jones, 259 A.2d 794, 805 (Md. 1969) (quoting McLeod v. Grant Cty. Sch. Dist. No. 128, 255 P.2d 360, 363 (Wash. 1953)).

[19] Aleshire v. State to Use of Dearstone, 170 A.2d 758, 763 (Md. 1961).

[20] Henley v. Prince George's Cty., 503 A.2d 1333, 1340 (Md. 1986).

[21] Ashburn v. Anne Arundel Cty., 510 A.2d 1078, 1083 (Md. 1986).

[22] Valentine v. On Target, Inc., 686 A.2d 636, 639 (Md. Ct. Spec. App. 1996), *aff'd*, 727 A.2d 947 (Md. 1999).

[23] *Henley*, 503 A.2d at 1340.

[24] Doe v. Pharmacia & Upjohn Co., 879 A.2d 1088, 1092 (Md. 2005).

[25] Corinaldi v. Columbia Courtyard, Inc., 873 A.2d 483, 489 (Md. Ct. Spec. App. 2005).

[26] Grimes v. Kennedy Krieger Inst., Inc., 782 A.2d 807, 858 (Md. 2001).

[27] Moore v. Myers, 868 A.2d 954, 969 (Md. Ct. Spec. App. 2005).

[28] Baltimore Transit Co. v. Prinz, 137 A.2d 700 (Md. 1958).

[29] Brooks v. Lewin Realty III, Inc. 835 A.2d 616, 624 n.5 (Md. 2003).

[30] Martin G. Imbach, Inc. v. Tate, 100 A.2d 808, 813 (Md. 1953).

ii. Evidence

As with all other elements of a negligence claim in Maryland, the plaintiff has the burden of proof for establishing the standard of care.[31] Violation of a rule or regulation may be used to establish negligence by showing the following: (1) the injury was caused by the violation of the rule; (2) the injury was the type intended to be prevented by the rule; and (3) the plaintiff was one of the class of people protected by the rule.[32]

If the plaintiff claims negligence by a professional with specialized knowledge outside of the average layman's understanding, the court *generally* requires an expert witness to establish the appropriate standard of care.[33] The requirement of expert testimony developed in Maryland based on medical malpractice claims, has since expanded to include other professionals, including lawyers and banks.[34] The plaintiff must overcome the presumption that "due skill and care" were used by the professional.[35] If the plaintiff fails to meet this burden, the court may rule that there is not sufficient evidence, which may lead to summary judgment.[36] However, expert witness testimony is not required in negligence cases against a professional if the alleged negligence "would be so obviously shown that the trier of fact could recognize it without expert testimony, such as a case where a doctor amputates the wrong arm."[37] Expert testimony cannot be used to attempt to "establish liability for negligence where common knowledge shows that there was no danger so substantial that a man of ordinary prudence in the position of the defendant would have anticipated injury and guarded against it."[38]

Following the 1993 adoption of the *Maryland Rules of Evidence,* Rule 5-407, evidence of subsequent remedial measures, such as changing policies following an incident, is not admissible to show either what the applicable standard of care should have been, nor a deviation from that standard of care.[39]

Compliance with statutory standards are evidence of due care, but compliance with the standard does not preclude a finding of negligence.[40] However, Maryland common law permits a court to find that conforming with a statutory standard "amounts to due care as a matter of law" if there are no special circumstances that require extra caution.[41]

[31] Chesapeake & Potomac Tel. Co. v. Hicks, 337 A.2d 744, 756 (Md. Ct. Spec. App. 1975).

[32] *Brooks*, 835 A.2d at 621.

[33] Schultz v. Bank of Am., N.A., 990 A.2d 1078, 1086-87 (Md. 2010); Crockett v. Crothers, 285 A.2d 612, 614 (Md. 1972) (". . . generaly [sic] there must be produced expert testimony from which the trier of fact can determine the standard of skill and care ordinarily exercised by a professional man of the kind involved in the geographical area involved . . .").

[34] *Schultz*, 990 A.2d at 1086-87.

[35] *Crockett*, 285 A.2d at 614.

[36] Rodriguez v. Clarke, 926 A.2d 736, 755 (Md. 2007).

[37] *Schultz*, 990 A.2d at 1086-87.

[38] Long v. Joestlein, 66 A.2d 407, 411 (Md. 1949).

[39] Tuer v. McDonald, 701 A.2d 1101 (Md. Ct. Spec. App. 1997).

[40] Ellsworth v. Sherne Lingerie, Inc., 495 A.2d 348, 358 (Md. 1985) (citing W. KEETON, PROSSER AND KEETON ON TORTS § 36 (5th ed. 1984)).

[41] Beatty v. Trailmaster Prod., Inc., 625 A.2d 1005, 1014 (Md. 1993).

III.   Breach of Duty

A.   Elements

Negligence "necessarily involves the breach of some duty owed by a defendant to the plaintiff," and is "inconsistent with the exercise of ordinary care."[42]

B.   Evidence

Except for the determination of whether a duty exists, negligence claims in general are decided by a jury, and the plaintiff must prove negligence by a preponderance of the evidence.[43] More recently, courts have adapted the language that the jury must determine whether it is "'more likely than not' that [the] defendant's negligence caused [the] plaintiff's injuries."[44]

A plaintiff must "produce some evidence that the defendant violated some duty by his act or omission and thereby caused the injury."[45]

IV.   Causation

A.   Elements

A breach of duty alone is not sufficient for a negligence action, and a defendant's "negligence is actionable only if it is a proximate cause of damage."[46] Negligence is a proximate cause of an injury "when the injury is the natural and probable result or consequence of the negligent act or omission."[47]

In Maryland, there are two sub-parts to proximate cause. They are, as follows: (1) the negligence must be a "cause-in-fact" of the injury; and (2) the negligence must be a "legally cognizable" cause.[48] Causation in fact analyzes whether the defendant's conduct actually produced an injury.[49] The "legally cognizable" factor is a legal analysis that examines who should pay for the harmful consequences of the action.[50]

To prove causation in fact, the court applies either the "but-for" test or the "substantial factor" test; the "but-for" test is used when there is only one negligent act at issue, and the substantial factor test is used when two or more independent acts lead to the injury.[51] Under the "but-for" test, "to constitute actionable negligence, there must be not only causal connection

---

[42] Brown v. Dermer, 744 A.2d 47, 54 (Md. 2000), *overruled in part on other grounds by* Brooks v. Lewin Realty III, Inc., 835 A.2d 616 (Md. 2003).

[43] Potts v. Armour & Co., 39 A.2d 552, 554 (Md. 1944).

[44] Vito v. Sargis & Jones, Ltd., 672 A.2d 129, 134 (Md. Ct. Spec. App. 1996).

[45] Bauman v. Woodfield, 223 A.2d 364, 370 (Md. 1966).

[46] Cramer v. Hous. Opportunities Comm'n of Montgomery Cty., 501 A.2d 35, 39 (Md. 1985).

[47] Medina v. Meilhammer, 489 A.2d 35, 39 (Md. Ct. Spec. App. 1985), *cert denied*, 303 Md. 683 (1985).

[48] Sindler v. Litman, 887 A.2d 97 (Md. Ct. Spec. App. 2005).

[49] Peterson v. Underwood, 264 A.2d 851 (Md. 1970).

[50] Pittway Corp. v. Collins, 973 A.2d 771, 786 (Md. 2009).

[51] *Id.* at 786-87.

between the negligence complained of and the injury suffered, but the connection must be by a natural and unbroken sequence, without intervening efficient causes, so that, **but-for** the negligence of the defendants, the injury would not have occurred."[52] Maryland applies the substantial factor test as outlined in the *Restatement (Second) of Torts* § 433.[53]

The second factor of proximate cause, the legally cognizable element, focuses on "fairness or social policy as well as mere causation."[54] In determining this fairness, the court often focuses on whether the injury was foreseeable, following the definition of foreseeability outlined in the *Restatement (Second) of Torts* § 435.[55] Foreseeability of harm and manner of occurrence are the primary indicators of legal cause.[56]

B.   Evidence

Proximate cause is usually an issue for the trier of fact or jury, though it becomes a question of law if the circumstances are such that "reasoning minds cannot differ, or where uncontroverted evidence establishes an efficient intervening cause."[57] Additionally, if the "evidence, taken as a whole, does not rise above speculation, hypothesis, and conjecture," then the issue should not go to the jury and a motion for judgment or JNOV is appropriate.[58]

It is the plaintiff's burden to prove proximate cause,[59] and it must be shown that it is "'more likely than not' that the defendant's conduct was a substantial factor in producing the plaintiff's injuries."[60]

A plaintiff can prove causation through direct evidence, circumstantial evidence, or a mix of the two.[61] Circumstantial evidence may be used to prove causation as long as it creates a reasonable likelihood or possibility supporting a rational inference of causation and is not wholly speculative.[62] The courts have noted, "Maryland has gone almost as far as any jurisdiction we know of in holding that meager evidence of negligence is sufficient to carry the case to the jury."[63]

To prove causation in fact, the plaintiff can either use "lay testimony with reasonable inferences," or, if that alone is not sufficient, expert testimony showing that based on the evidence, "X was the efficient cause of the injury."[64]

---

[52] Maryland *ex rel.* Kalives v. Baltimore Eye, Ear & Throat Hosp., 10 A.2d 612, 616 (Md. 1940) (emphasis added).

[53] Yonce v. SmithKline Beecham Clinical Labs., Inc., 680 A.2d 569, 576 (Md. 1996).

[54] *Peterson*, 264 A.2d at 855.

[55] Asphalt & Concrete Servs., Inc. v. Perry, 108 A.3d 558, 574-75 (Md. 2015).

[56] Catler v. Arent Fox, LLP, 71 A.3d 155, 183 (Md. Ct. Spec. App. 2013).

[57] Segerman v. Jones, 259 A.2d 794, 806 (Md. 1969).

[58] Mallard v. Earl, 665 A.2d 287, 291 (Md. Ct. Spec. App. 1995).

[59] Rhaney v. Univ. of Maryland E. Shore, 880 A.2d 357, 364 (Md. 2005).

[60] Pittway Corp. v. Collins, 973 A.2d 771, 787 (Md. 2009).

[61] Hamilton v. Kirson, 96 A.3d 714, 730 (Md. 2014).

[62] *Id.* at 731.

[63] McSlarrow v. Walker, 467 A.2d 196, 200 (Md. Ct. Spec. App. 1983).

[64] Peterson v. Underwood, 264 A.2d 851, 855 (Md. 1970).

V.   Damages

A.   Elements

Maryland courts have both general (non-economic) damages and special (economic) damages.[65] Economic damages include medical expenses and lost earnings,[66] while noneconomic damages include personal injury, pain, suffering, disfigurement, or loss of consortium, and other damages.[67] Both economic and noneconomic damages are compensatory damages, and their purpose is to serve "as compensation, indemnity, or restitution for harm sustained" by the plaintiff.[68] Maryland has a long history of holding that compensatory damages should be "'precisely' commensurate with the injury; nothing more, nor less," and plaintiffs may not recover twice for the same injury.[69]

B.   Evidence

The plaintiff has the burden of proof and must prove each item of damage by the preponderance of the evidence.[70] The amount of damages does not need to be proven, but must be based on "some rational basis other than by pure speculation or conjecture."[71] In personal injury cases, the plaintiff must submit evidence of the extent and permanent or impermanent nature of the injury, and an expert opinion is not necessary if common knowledge would tell the jury that the injury is permanent.[72] However, an expert opinion is necessary in order for the plaintiff to introduce medical bills as evidence, as the amount of a bill does not necessarily establish the reasonable value of treatment.[73]

---

[65] MD. CODE ANN., CTS. & JUD. PROC. § 11-108 (West 2016); MD. CODE ANN., CTS. & JUD. PROC. § 11-109 (West 2016).

[66] CTS. & JUD. PROC. § 11-109.

[67] CTS. & JUD. PROC. § 11-108.

[68] Superior Const. Co. v. Elmo, 104 A.2d 581, 582 (Md. 1954).

[69] Exxon Mobile Corp. v. Albright, 71 A.3d 30, 89 (Md. 2013) (citing Baltimore Belt R.R. Co. v. Sattler, 102 Md. 595, 601 (1906)).

[70] MD. CIVIL PATTERN JURY INSTR. 10:1 (4th ed.).

[71] Brock Bridge Ltd. P'ship, Inc. v. Dev. Facilitators, Inc., 689 A.2d 622, 628-29 (1997) (quoting Ass'n of Maryland Pilots v. Baltimore & O. R.R. Co., 304 F. Supp. 548, 557 (D. Md. 1969)).

[72] Cluster v Upton, 168 A. 882 (Md. 1933).

[73] Desua v. Yokim, 768 A.2d 56, 58-59 (Md. Ct. Spec. App. 2013).

CHAPTER 22

MASSACHUSETTS

MASSACHUSETTS
Vicki Lawrence MacDougall[1]

I. Purpose of Tort Law

Tort law protects the right to a life "unhampered and unimpaired by damage negligently caused to the body or mind by another."[2] The requirement that a wrongdoer should be responsible for the harm that he or she causes fulfills the corrective justice policy behind tort law.[3] Conversely, the requirement that the plaintiff suffers harm at the hands of the defendant provides a "reasonable safeguard against false claims."[4] Thus, the provision of compensation for harm caused by the defendant's neglect is the main goal of tort law in Massachusetts, with deterrence of future wrongs serving a more secondary roll. "Tort law, especially that dealing with negligence does not concern itself with business decisions in the same way as does property and contract law: it would be unreasonable to assert that potential tortfeasors often reflect upon possible tort liability before embarking on a negligent course of conduct, or that they frequently are deterred from negligent conduct by the rules of tort law."[5] There is one behavior that clearly responds to the potential exposure to tort liability. The procurement of liability insurance results "tangentially" from reflecting upon the possibility of negligent behavior.[6]

However, deterrence of tortious behavior is still perceived as a justification for some rules of behavior or rules of compensation behind tort law.[7] To some degree, tort law promotes personal safety.[8] Although behavior modification might not be perceived as a primary goal of tort law in Massachusetts, failure to fashion behavior to meet society's expectations of reasonable behavior can still fulfill the underlying policy of providing compensation by the one who negligently caused the harm.

---

[1] Professor of Law, Director, Health Law Certificate Program, Law Review Faculty Advisor, Oklahoma City University School of Law, Member, California and Oklahoma Bar Associations.

[2] Payton v. Abbott Labs, 437 N.E.2d 171, 187 (Mass. 1982).

[3] *Id.* at 188.

[4] *Id.* at 180.

[5] *Id.* at 186.

[6] *Id.*

[7] Law v. Griffith, 930 N.E.2d 126, 132 (Mass. 2010).

[8] Lindsey v. Massios, 360 N.E.2d 631, 634 (Mass. 1977).

II.   Duty to Exercise Ordinary Care

A.   *Question of Law*

The negligence cause of action has four elements. They are duty, breach of duty, causation, and damages.[9] The issue of whether a duty exists is a question of law for the court,[10] although in most cases "every actor has a duty to exercise reasonable care to avoid physical harm to others."[11] Generally speaking, the other three elements are questions of fact reserved for deliberations by the jury.[12] The court decides if there is a duty of care "'by reference to existing social values and customs and appropriate social policy.'"[13] The court examines all circumstances "'based on the reasonable foreseeability of harm.'"[14] The linchpin of the duty determination is foreseeability of harm[15] and the most comprehensive statement of factors a court should examine in Massachusetts in determining the existence of a duty are, as follows:

> The concept of duty is not sacrosanct in itself, but is only an expression of the sum total of considerations of policy which lead the law to say that the plaintiff is entitled to protection. . . . No better general statement can be made than that the courts will find a duty where, in general, reasonable persons would recognize it and agree that it exists. . . . The assertion that liability must . . . be denied because defendant bears no duty to plaintiff begs the essential question—whether the plaintiff's interests are entitled to legal protection against the defendant's conduct. . . . A duty finds its source in existing social values and customs, . . . and thus imposition of a duty generally responds to changed social conditions.
>
> We have recognized that as a general principle of tort law, every actor has a duty to exercise reasonable care to avoid physical harm to others. . . . A precondition to this duty is, of course, that the risk of harm to another be recognizable or foreseeable to the actor. . . . Consequently, with some important exceptions, a defendant owes a duty of care to all persons who are foreseeably endangered by his conduct, with respect to all risks which make the conduct unreasonably dangerous. . . . To the extent that a legal standard

---

[9] Adams v. Cong. Auto Ins. Agency, Inc., 65 N.E.3d 1229, 1234 (Mass. App. Ct. 2016).

[10] *Id.*; *see also* Shea v. Caritas Carney Hosp., Inc., 947 N.E.2d 99, 103 (Mass. App. Ct. 2011).

[11] Judge v. Carrai, 934 N.E.2d 276, 279 (Mass. App. Ct. 2010).

[12] Adams v. Cong. Auto Ins. Agency, Inc., 65 N.E.3d 1229, 1234 (Mass. App. Ct. 2016).

[13] *Id.* (quoting Jupin v. Kask, 849 N.E.2d 829, 832 (Mass. 2006) (quoting Cremins v. Clancy, 612 N.E.2d 1183, 1185 (Mass. 1993))); *accord* Davis v. Westwood Grp., 652 N.E.2d 567, 569 (Mass. 1995).

[14] Adams v. Cong. Auto Ins. Agency, Inc., 65 N.E.3d 1229, 1235 (Mass. App. Ct. 2016) (quoting Whittaker v. Saraceno, 635 N.E.2d 1185, 1188 (Mass. 1994)).

[15] Judge v. Carrai, 934 N.E.2d 276, 279 (Mass. App. Ct. 2010). "A precondition to this duty is, of course, that the risk of harm to another be recognizable or foreseeable to the actor." *Id.* "The defendant had no obligation or duty to construct an impenetrable barrier surrounding its restaurant to prevent errant automobiles from entering the building as it is not reasonably foreseeable that such an incident will occur, resulting in such injuries as the plaintiffs suffered." Glick v. Prince Italian Foods of Saugus, Inc., 514 N.E.2d 100, 101 (Mass. App. Ct. 1987).

does exist for determining the existence of a tort duty . . ., it is a test of the reasonable foreseeability of the harm.[16]

A.   *Question of Fact*

Generally, there is no duty to control the behavior of a third party to prevent harm to a third party.[17] The exception to this rule is triggered if there is a special relationship between the parties. "In deciding whether a special relationship exists between a particular plaintiff and defendant, [the court's] foremost consideration is whether 'a defendant reasonably could foresee that he would be expected to take affirmative action to protect the plaintiff and could anticipate harm to the plaintiff from the failure to do so.'"[18] Examples of special relationships include the relationship "between a college and its students, . . . between a common carrier and its passengers, . . . and between a hotel and its guests."[19] Furthermore, in limited cases, "liability may be imposed if a defendant negligently failed to guard against the consequences of reasonably foreseeable criminal conduct."[20]

The duty to protect a third party is set forth statutorily in the limited circumstance of a mental health professional's duty to warn a third party of the dangerous propensities of his or her patient.[21] The duty of the mental health professional exists when the plaintiff establishes, the following: (1) a known history of physical violence; (2) a reasonable belief that "there is a clear and present danger the patient will attempt to kill or inflict serious bodily injury; and (3) a reasonably identifiable victim.[22]

In *Mounsey v. Ellard*,[23] the Supreme Judicial Court of Massachusetts abolished the common law categories of entrants upon land and discarded the distinction between invitees and licensees.[24] Because a distinction between invitee and licensee "no longer comport[s] with modern accepted values and common experience,"[25] the standard of due care is owed to

---

[16] Afarian v. Mass. Elec. Co., 866 N.E.2d 901, 905-906 (Mass. 2007) (internal citations and quotation marks omitted) (quoting Jupin v. Kask, 849 N.E.2d 829, 835-36 (Mass. 2006)).

[17] Adams v. Cong. Auto Ins. Agency, Inc., 65 N.E.3d 1229, 1234 (Mass. App. Ct. 2016).

[18] *Id.* at 1235 (quoting Irwin v. Ware, 467 N.E.2d 1292, 1300 (Mass. 1984)); *see also* O'Meara v. New England Life Flight, Inc., 842 N.E.2d 953, 954 (Mass. App. Ct. 2006).

[19] Whittaker v. Saraceno, 635 N.E.2d 1185, 1187 (Mass. 1994).

[20] Poskus v. Lombardo's of Randolph, Inc., 670 N.E.2d 383, 385 (Mass. 1996). Generally, however, "there is no duty to protect another from the criminal conduct of a third party." Lind v. Domino's Pizza LLC, 37 N.E.3d 1, 10 (Mass. App. Ct. 2015). "The previous occurrence of similar criminal acts on or near a defendant's premises is a circumstance to consider, but the foreseeability question is not conclusively answered in favor of a defendant . . . if there has been no prior similar criminal act." Whittaker v. Saraceno, 635 N.E.2d 1185, 1188 (Mass. 1994).

[21] Mass. Gen. Laws c. 123 § 36B; Shea v. Caritas Carney Hosp., Inc., 947 N.E.2d 99, 104 (Mass. App. Ct. 2011). "The legislature enacted the statute in response to Tarasoff v. Regents of the Univ. of Cal., 17 Cal.3d 425, 131 Cal.Rptr. 14, 551 P.2d 334 (1976), the landmark case on the subject of a mental health professional's duty to warn potential victims." *Shea*, 947 N.E.2d at 104 n.8.

[22] Shea v. Caritas Carney Hosp., Inc., 947 N.E.2d 99, 104 (Mass. App. Ct. 2011).

[23] Mounsey v. Ellard, 297 N.E.2d 43, 51 (Mass. 1973).

[24] *Id.* at 49.

[25] *Id.* "Modern values and the realities of urban living favor protection of personal safety over rights of absolute property control and demonstrate no logical basis for distinguishing among persons who enter private property

all lawful entrants.[26] Accordingly, a landowner owes a duty of reasonable care toward those invited onto the property "to maintain the premises in a reasonably safe condition and to warn her guests of any unreasonable dangers of which she was aware or should reasonably have been aware."[27] However, there is generally no duty to warn guests of risks "obvious to the ordinary person."[28]

In *Mounsey*, trespassers were excluded from its holding requiring landowners to use due care toward entrants upon the land.[29] In *Schofield v. Merrill*,[30] the court opined that reasonably prudent landowners would not generally exercise care to protect an adult trespasser.[31] The court observed that the lack of a legislative consensus made changing the no-duty owed to trespasser rule "unworkable."[32] A duty to use reasonable care is only owed to "lawful visitors, foreseeable child trespassers, and known helplessly trapped trespassers."[33] A duty to use reasonable care toward trespassing children is statutorily imposed in Massachusetts.[34] Although it is rare to adopt the attractive nuisance doctrine through a statutory enactment, the statute makes clear the landowner is only liable to the trespasser child for a failure to use reasonable care.[35] In comparison, the landowner only owes a duty to "refrain from willful, wanton or reckless disregard" for the adult trespasser's safety.[36] Furthermore, there is potential liability if the landowner fails to take reasonable actions to avoid further injury to the "trapped, imperiled and helpless trespasser."[37] The possessor of land cannot "ignore the plight of the trapped trespasser."[38]

---

for various legitimate purposes." Lindsey v. Massios, 360 N.E.2d 631, 634 (Mass. 1977).

[26] *Mounsey*, 297 N.E.2d at 49, 51; Davis v. Westwood Grp., 652 N.E.2d 567, 569 (Mass. 1995).

[27] Polak v. Whitney, 487 N.E.2d 213, 215 (Mass. App. Ct. 1985); Davis v. Westwood Grp., 652 N.E.2d 567, 569 (Mass. 1995); Monaco v. Vacation Camp Resorts Int'l, Inc., No. 14-P-141, 2014 WL 7189900, at *1 (Mass. App. Ct. Dec. 18, 2014). However, there is no duty to remove naturally occurring accumulation of ice. Higgins v. Gateway Motor Inn, No. 01-P-1528, 2003 WL 21976498, at *1 (Mass. App. Ct. Aug. 19, 2003).

[28] Polak v. Whitney, 487 N.E.2d 213, 216 (Mass. App. Ct. 1985). A party was held at the defendant's home for about 50 graduating high-school seniors. Parking was not provided and Schnepper parked his vehicle on the shoulder of a state highway adjacent to the property. Polak fell asleep in the back seat of the car and received fatal injuries when the Schnepper vehicle was struck by a car driven at a high rate of speed down the state highway. The defendant was sued, among other parties. The court stated that the "social host, we think, would not ordinarily be expected either to provide parking for all her guests on her premises or to warn them about the risks of parking along the streets or roadways adjacent to her property." Id. at 215. The risk was obvious. Id. at 216. See also Rainka v. Shing, No. 99WAD023, 2000 WL 869453, at *7 (Mass. App. Ct. June 23, 2000).

[29] Mounsey v. Ellard, 297 N.E.2d 43, 51 n.7 (Mass. 1973).

[30] Schofield v. Merrill, 435 N.E.2d 339, 345 (Mass. 1982).

[31] *Id.* at 342.

[32] *Id.*

[33] *Id.*

[34] M.G.L.A. c. 231, § 85Q; *see also* Mathis v. Mass. Elec. Co., 565 N.E.2d 1180, 1182 (Mass. 1991).

[35] M.G.L.A. c. 231, § 85Q(e); *see also* Mathis v. Mass. Elec. Co., 565 N.E.2d 1180, 1182 (Mass. 1991).

[36] Schofield v. Merrill, 435 N.E.2d 339, 340 (Mass. 1982).

[37] Pridgen v. Bos. Hous. Auth., 308 N.E.2d 467, 476 (Mass. 1974) (boy trapped in an elevator shaft).

[38] *Id.*

III.   Breach of Duty

A.   Elements

A breach of duty "is the failure of a responsible person, either by omission or by action, to exercise that degree of care, vigilance and forethought which . . . the person of ordinary caution and prudence ought to exercise under the particular circumstances."[39] Reasonable care, the standard of care required in a negligence cause of action, demands that "[o]ne is bound to anticipate and provide against what usually happens and what is likely to happen, but is not bound in a like manner to guard against what is . . . only remotely and slightly probable."[40] The plaintiff has the burden of proof to establish by a preponderance of the evidence how a "person of ordinary prudence would act in similar circumstances."[41] The likelihood and severity of the risk of harm and the burden to avoid the risk are factors to consider when deciding the issue of reasonable care under the circumstances.[42]

Children are liable for their torts; however, children are not "held to the same standard of care as adults."[43] A child is held to the standard of care "expected from a child of like age, intelligence, and experience."[44] Normally, children are not liable when the child is participating in games "customarily played by children and are usually harmless and free from danger to participants and bystanders."[45] Ultimately, whether a child conformed to the standard required is an issue for the jury to decide upon proper instructions regarding the appropriate children's standard of care.[46]

---

[39] Commonwealth v. Marshall, No. 15-P-900, 2016 WL 4009645, at *1 (Mass. App. Ct. July 22, 2016); *accord* Dahlquist v. Lydon Millwright Servs., Inc., No. 14-P-1875, 2016 WL 1238249, at *1 (Mass. App. Ct. March 30, 2016); Commonwealth v. Jules, No. 14-P-762, 2015 WL 3403545, at *2 (Mass. App. Ct. May 28, 2015). In certain select cases, the duty to use ordinary care is not the standard. For example, liability against an opposing coach or player for injuries occurring in a sporting event is "predicated on reckless disregard of safety." Dugan v. Thayer Acad., No. 14-1359-C, 2015 WL 3500385, at *2 (Mass. May 27, 2015) (quoting Gauvin v. Clark, 537 N.E.2d 94, 97 (Mass. 1989)) (citing Kavanagh v. Trustees of Boston Univ., 795 N.E.2d 1170, 1179 (Mass. 2003)). However, "the better authority indicates that a player's own coach must exercise that degree of care of a reasonably prudent coach." *Dugan*, 2015 WL 3500385, at *3. The duty owed to a partner engaged in consensual sexual relations is not to engage in wanton or reckless conduct. Wanton or reckless behavior is exposing someone to a markedly different degree of risk than simply negligent behavior. Doe v. Moe, 827 N.E.2d 240, 245 (Mass. App. Ct. 2005) (female partner changed her position during sexual intercourse and landed on her male partner in such a way to fracture his penis).

[40] Hebert v. Enos, 806 N.E.2d 452, 456 (Mass. App. Ct. 2004) (quoting Falk v. Finkelman, 168 N.E. 89, 90 (Mass.1929)).

[41] Frazzini v. Jiminy Peak Mountain Resort, LLC., No. 15-P-1061, 2016 WL 2755863, at *2 (Mass. App. Ct. May 12, 2016) (quoting LaClair v. Silberline Mfg. Co., 393 N.E.2d 867, 871 (Mass. 1979)); *see also* Donovan v. Phillip Morris USA, Inc., 914 N.E.2d 891, 899 (Mass. 2009).

[42] Bernier v. Smitty's Sports Pub, Inc., 59 N.E.3d 1192, 1195 (Mass. App. Ct. 2016) (citing Mounsey v. Ellard, 297 N.E.2d 43, 52 (Mass. 1973)).

[43] Mann v. Cook, 190 N.E.2d 676, 679 (Mass. 1963).

[44] Mathis v. Mass. Elec. Co., 565 N.E.2d 1180, 1184 (Mass. 1991) (citing Mann v. Cook, 190 N.E.2d 676, 679 (Mass. 1963)).

[45] Mann v. Cook, 190 N.E.2d 676, 679 (Mass. 1963).

[46] Mathis v. Mass. Elec. Co., 565 N.E.2d 1180, 1185 (Mass. 1991); Bartley v. Almeida, 76 N.E.2d 22, 24 (Mass. 1947); Brown v. Daley, 173 N.E. 545, 547 (Mass. 1930).

B. Evidence

The long-standing rule is that the plaintiff bears the burden to prove negligence or lack of ordinary care on the part of the defendant.[47] "Only when no rational view of the evidence warrants a finding that the defendant was negligent may the issues be taken from the jury."[48] One person's testimony regarding what he or she ordinarily recommends does not establish the standard of care required. For example, the testimony of a snowboarding instructor that "he typically recommends wrist guards is insufficient to establish the standard of care for a snowboarding instructor of ordinary caution and prudence. . . . '[T]he standard of care is based on the care that the average qualified [snowboarding instructor], no matter how skilled, would have taken.'"[49] If the standard of reasonable care is not within the common knowledge of the lay jury, the plaintiff may be required to present expert testimony to establish the standard of care.[50]

Custom evidence is admissible on the standard of care and whether reasonable care was used under the circumstances. However, the custom of an industry or business is not conclusive on the standard of care.[51] For example, the standard of care for a construction company should be that usually used by companies in its place; the standard "should be proved like any other such fact."[52] Indeed, "[i]f one does what others do in like circumstances, the inference that he is conforming to the community standard of reasonable conduct may be so strong in particular circumstances as to establish that the individual was not negligent."[53]

However, unlike other negligence cases, custom evidence is usually conclusive on the issue of the standard of care in medical negligence causes of action. The standard of care for a generalist is the degree of care and skill exercised by other qualified general practitioners.[54] A specialist is held to the standard of skill and care that other specialists in the same field would use.[55] The standard is based on the care the ordinary physician would provide under similar circumstances[56] "at the time of the alleged negligence."[57] Therefore, the care

---

[47] Adams v. Inhabitants of Carlisle, 21 Pick. 146, 147 (Mass. 1838); Lane v. Crombie, 12 Pick. 177, 182 (Mass. 1831).

[48] Irwin v. Town of Ware, 467 N.E.2d 1292, 1305 (Mass. 1984); accord Meesel v. Lynn & Bos. R.R., 8 Allen 234, 235, 1864 WL 3311, at *2 (Mass. 1864).

[49] Frazzini v. Jiminy Peak Mountain Resort, LLC., No. 15-P-1061, 2016 WL 2755863, at *2 (Mass. App. Ct. May 12, 2016) (citations omitted).

[50] Id. Expert testimony was required on the standard of care of snowboarding instructors because instruction of snowboarding was not within the common knowledge of the jury. Id. At times opinion testimony may be allowed from lay persons. For example, a lay person may testify from common experience that a person was intoxicated. Irwin v. Town of Ware, 467 N.E.2d 1292, 1310 (Mass. 1984).

[51] Upham v. Chateau DeVille Dinner Theater, Inc., 403 N.E.2d 384, 387 (Mass. 1980); Back v. Wickes Corp., 378 N.E.2d 964, 970 (Mass. 1978).

[52] Romano v. Rossano Constr. Co., 171 N.E.2d 853, 855 (Mass. 1961).

[53] Breault v. Ford Motor Co., 305 N.E.2d 824, 828 (Mass. 1973).

[54] Palandjian v. Foster, 842 N.E.2d 916, 920 (Mass. 2006).

[55] Id. (citing Brune v. Belinkoff, 235 N.E.2d 793, 798 (Mass. 1968)).

[56] Palandjian v. Foster, 842 N.E.2d 916, 920-921 (Mass. 2006). The duty of a physician may also include the duty to warn of the side effects of drugs prescribed and that duty may extend to "everyone foreseeably put at risk by his failure to warn of the side effects of his treatment." Coombes v. Florio, 877 N.E.2d 567, 570, 572 (Mass. 2007) (Ireland, J., concurring).

[57] Palandjian v. Foster, 842 N.E.2d 916, 926 (Mass. 2006).

that an *individual* physician would have provided under the circumstances is not probative of the customary practice.[58] Because the standard is the care customarily provided, the custom does not have to be proven effective.[59] In the typical medical negligence cause of action, the plaintiff must prove the applicable standard and demonstrate that the defendant doctor breached the standard which resulted in the plaintiff's harm.[60] Normally, expert testimony is required to establish the appropriate standard of care and the breach of the standard by the health care provider.[61] Experts are qualified if the expert has "sufficient 'education, training, experience and familiarity' with the subject matter of the testimony."[62] The medical expert does not necessarily have to be a specialist in the same field as the defendant to testify. It is within the discretion of the trial judge whether to qualify an expert and to allow, for example, the "opinions of a general practitioner in a case which related to specialized medical issues."[63]

Another type of medical negligence cause of action is failure to obtain informed consent. Expert testimony may be needed on some issues, but not on other issues, in an informed consent cause of action. As stated by the Supreme Judicial Court of Massachusetts in *Harnish v. Children's Hospital Medical Center:*

> [A] physician owes to his patient the duty to disclose in a reasonable manner all significant medical information that the physician possesses or reasonably should possess that is material to an intelligent decision by the patient whether to undergo a proposed procedure. The information a physician reasonably should possess is that information possessed by the average qualified physician or, in the case of a specialty, by the average qualified physician practicing that specialty. . . . What the physician should know involves professional expertise and can ordinarily be proved only through the testimony of expert. . . . However, the extent to which he must share that information with his patient depends upon what information he should reasonably recognize is material to the plaintiff's decision. . . . "Materiality may be said to be the significance a reasonable person, in what the physician knows or should know is his patient's position, would attach to the disclosed risk or risks in deciding whether to submit or not to submit to surgery or treatment." *The materiality determination is one that lay persons are qualified to make without the aid of an expert.*[64]

---

[58] *Id.* at 920-921 (emphasis added).

[59] *Id.* at 921.

[60] *Id.* at 920.

[61] *Id.* at 921.

[62] *Id.* (quoting Letch v. Daniels, 514 N.E.2d 675, 677 (Mass. 1987) (quoting Gill v. Northshore Radiological Assocs., 409 N.E.2d 248, 250 (Mass. App. Ct. 1980))).

[63] Letch v. Daniels, 514 N.E.2d 675, 677 (Mass. 1987).

[64] Harnish v. Children's Hosp. Med. Ctr., 439 N.E.2d 240, 243 (Mass. 1982) (emphasis added) (citations omitted). On the doctrine of informed consent, *see also* Feeley v. Baer, 679 N.E.2d 180 (Mass. 1997); Precourt v. Frederick, 481 N.E.2d 1144 (Mass. 1985); Halley v. Birbiglia, 458 N.E.2d 710 (Mass. 1983); Roukounakis v. Messer, 826 N.E.2d 777 (Mass. App. Ct. 2005); Benson v. Mass. Gen. Hosp., 731 N.E.2d 85 (Mass. App. Ct. 2000).

Violation of a criminal statute may be used as evidence of negligence. If the statute does not expressly create a private tort cause of action, "legislative intent determines whether a private right may be inferred"[65] and the violation used to set a standard of care. The doctrine of negligence *per se* is not utilized in Massachusetts; rather, the violation of the statute is only evidence of a failure to use reasonable care.[66] In other words, the jury may find the actor used reasonable care despite the statutory violation.[67] The harm must fall within the "consequences the statute was intended to prevent."[68] The existence of a duty must be established under common law principles, separate from the statutory obligation.[69] Further, there must be a causal link between the violation and the harm.[70]

Failure to use reasonable care may be shown through the use of circumstantial evidence. The doctrine of *res ipsa loquitur* is a form of circumstantial evidence that allows the plaintiff to show negligence without exact proof of the defendant's behavior.[71] "The rule of *res ipsa loquitur* merely permits the tribunal of fact, if it sees fit, in the absence of a finding of the specific cause of the occurrence, . . . to infer from the occurrence itself that it would not have happened unless in some respect the defendant had been negligent."[72] However, the burden of proof remains with the plaintiff.[73] The application of *res ipsa* hinges upon the circumstances of the accident being such that a "jury could reasonably find that the accident is of a kind that would not have happened in the ordinary course of events unless there was negligence by the defendant."[74] The defendant must have exclusive control.[75] Exclusive control is "where the

---

[65] Juliano v. Simpson, 962 N.E.2d 175, 179 (Mass. 2012).

[66] Bennett v. Eagle Brook Country Store, Inc., 557 N.E.2d 1166, 1168 (Mass. 1990); Scatena v Pittsburgh & New England Trucking, 319 N.E.2d 730, 731 (Mass. App. Ct. 1974).

[67] *Bennett*, 557 N.E.2d at 1168-1169. For example, the jury could properly find the defendant used reasonable care in serving alcoholic beverages despite the violation of the statute prohibiting the sale of alcohol to "drunkards." *Id.* Or, reasonable care can still be found on the part of a driver who crosses left of the center line. "One's presence on the wrong side of the street is excused when without fault on his part the machine skids across the center line." Herman v. Sladofsky, 17 N.E.2d 879, 881 (Mass. 1938).

[68] Juliano v. Simpson, 962 N.E.2d 175, 180 (Mass. 2012). For example, a statute mandating the installation of seat belts for the front seats does not create a duty to buckle up on the part of front-seat passengers in automobiles. Breault v. Ford Motor Co., 305 N.E.2d 824, 825 (Mass. 1973).

[69] Juliano, 962 N.E.2d at 180 (Mass. 2012). For example, whether a social host owes a duty to use reasonable care in serving underage guests must be established using common law principles "determined by reference to existing social values and customs and appropriate social policy." *Id.* The common law duty imposed upon social hosts is limited to "cases where the host had actually served alcohol or made it available." *Id.* at 181.

[70] Falvey v. Hamelburg, 198 N.E.2d 400, 403 (Mass. 1964). The defendant owned the car involved in the accident but the car was registered in his father's name. Thus, the car registration violated the law. *Id.* at 401. However, there was no causal connection "between the illegal registration and the accident." *Id.* at 403.

[71] Hemenway v. Shaw's Supermarket, Inc., No. 1115, 1998 WL 246663, at *4 (Mass. App. Ct. May 11, 1998).

[72] Roscigno v. Colonial Beacon Oil Co., 200 N.E. 883, 883 (Mass. 1936).

[73] Wilson v. Colonial Air Transp., Inc., 180 N.E. 212, 214 (Mass. 1932).

[74] Benzaquin v. Friendly Ice Cream Corp., No. 1469, 2003 WL 1901341, at *2 (Mass. App. Ct. April 15, 2003); Weldon v. Otis Elevator Co., No. 97 WAS 004, 1998 WL 51708, at *2 (Mass. App. Ct. Jan. 27, 1998). For example, "[u]nattended garage doors ordinarily do not fall or roll down from an open position, absent negligence." Wilson v. Honeywell, Inc., 569 N.E.2d 1011, 1014 (Mass. 1991).

[75] Wilson v. Honeywell, Inc., 569 N.E.2d 1011, 1013 (Mass. 1991).

direct cause of the accident and so much of the surrounding circumstances as were essential to its occurrence were within the sole control of the defendant."[76] However, the "concept of control is not applied rigidly."[77] Rather, the proper focus is on responsibility.[78] "Evidence of the defendant's exclusive control aids a jury in reaching the logical inference that no other party may have acted in a manner which caused the instrumentality to malfunction."[79] The ultimate question for the jury is if the defendant is "more likely responsible for the incident than someone else."[80] The doctrine is not applied if there were other probable causes for the accident besides the negligence of the defendant.[81] Every possible cause does not need to be excluded. "It is enough that the evidence makes it more probable than not that the defendant was negligent, and that [his or her] negligence was the cause of the injuries."[82]

IV. Causation

A. Elements

Proof of negligence is not sufficient to impose liability unless the plaintiff also shows by a preponderance of the evidence the existence of a causal connection.[83] "Negligence does not operate in a vacuum. Legal consequences result from it if, but only if, the negligence is causally related to the harm complained of."[84] For a negligent act to be considered a "cause" of the plaintiff's harm, the plaintiff must establish that his or her injury would not have occurred but-for the negligence of the defendant. If the injury would have occurred anyway, the defendant did not cause the harm. The plaintiff satisfies his or her burden by showing that "the harm suffered was more likely caused by the negligence of the defendant than for some other cause for which the defendant is not liable."[85] However, there can be more than one cause of an injury.[86]

Relaxed causation is allowed in a unique variety of medical negligence causes of action where the health care provider's negligence caused a reduction or eliminated the "patient's prospects for achieving a more favorable medical outcome" even if the patient had

---

[76] Wilson v. Colonial Air Transp., Inc., 180 N.E. 212, 214 (Mass. 1932).

[77] Wilson v. Honeywell, Inc., 569 N.E.2d 1011, 1013 (Mass. 1991).

[78] *Id.* at 1013. Exclusive control might be exhibited by having responsibility over "maintenance, inspection, and repair" and "proper use." *Id.*

[79] *Id.*

[80] *Id.* at 1014.

[81] Wilson v. Colonial Air Transp., Inc., 180 N.E. 212, 214 (Mass. 1932).

[82] Wilson v. Honeywell, Inc., 569 N.E.2d 1011, 1014 (Mass. 1991).

[83] Boucher v. Lowell Automatic Transmission, No. 9722, 2001 WL 920693, at *3 (Mass. App. Ct. Aug. 8, 2001).

[84] Falvey v. Hamelburg, 198 N.E.2d 400, 403 (Mass. 1964). Proof of causation in a legal malpractice action claiming an attorney negligently represented a criminal defendant requires the criminal defendant to prove his innocence. Glenn v. Aiken, 569 N.E.2d 783, 785 (Mass. 1991). Otherwise, the negligence of the attorney caused no harm. Arguably, a more accurate statement is that the defendant must prove his innocence or that an attorney using the care of a reasonable defense lawyer would have rendered a defense verdict or a lesser sentence.

[85] Delnegro v. Hampton, No. 00WAD005, 2001 WL 242210, at *3 (Mass. App. Ct. March 7, 2001).

[86] Solimene v. B. Grauel & Co., K.G., 507 N.E.2d 662, 667 (1987); *see also* No. 9722, 2001 WL 920693, at *3 (Mass. App. Ct. Aug. 8, 2001).

"less than even chance of recovery."[87] Loss chance cases still require the plaintiff to prove causation by a preponderance of the evidence. The causal link is established by showing the physician's negligence caused a diminished chance of a more favorable outcome.[88]

Although cause-in-fact is an essential prerequisite to the imposition of liability, cause-in-fact will not dictate liability without the added ingredient of proximate cause. In other words, the mere fact that there is an unbroken causal chain between the negligent act and the harm is not always sufficient for liability.[89] Both cause-in-fact and proximate, or legal, cause are required.[90]

Proximate cause is a cause that in a continuous sequence unbroken by any new cause, produces a result, and without which the result would not have occurred.[91] If the plaintiff's injury was a foreseeable result of the defendant's negligence, causation is generally established.[92] However, "[t]here must be limits to the scope or definition of reasonable foreseeability based on considerations of policy and pragmatic judgment."[93] For example, one could "envision a variety of foreseeable injuries arising out of a defective toilet, the electric shock to a neighbor when he touches a faucet outside the house is well beyond the 'range of reasonable apprehension' and therefore not foreseeable."[94]

An intervening cause is one that actively operates between the defendant's negligence and the plaintiff's injury.[95] The chain of causation is not broken by an intervening cause if the intervening cause was reasonably foreseeable.[96] It is a question of fact for the jury to determine whether an intervening cause is foreseeable.[97] For example, a jury could conclude that it was foreseeable that a victim would ask to be taken off a ventilator following a car accident negligently caused by the defendant.[98] Thus, the action of removal from life support was not "an independent occurrence but the final step in the continuous sequence of events that began with the defendant's negligent operation of her automobile. 'But-for' the negligence, the accident would not have occurred, and the victim would not have been forced

---

[87] Matsuyama v. Birnbaum, 890 N.E.2d 819, 823 (Mass. 2008).

[88] Id. at 832. The calculation of damages requires a specific mathematical formula. Id. at 840; Renzi v. Paredes, 890 N.E.2d 806, 813-814 (Mass. 2008).

[89] Hebert v. Enos, 806 N.E.2d 452, 457 (Mass. App. Ct. 2004).

[90] Kent v. Commonwealth, 771 N.E.2d 770, 777 (Mass. 2002).

[91] Solimene v. B. Grauel & Co., K.G. 507 N.E.2d 662, 667 (Mass. 1987).

[92] Adams v. Cong. Auto Ins. Agency, Inc., 65 N.E.3d 1229, 1237 (Mass. App. Ct. 2016).

[93] Poskus v. Lombardo's of Randolph, Inc., 670 N.E.2d 383, 386 (Mass. 1996); accord Hebert v. Enos, 806 N.E.2d 452, 456 (Mass. App. Ct. 2004).

[94] Hebert v. Enos, 806 N.E.2d 452, 456 (Mass. App. Ct. 2004) (quoting Palsgraf v. Long Island R.R., 162 N.E. 99, 101 (N.Y. 1928)). Another example is that a police officer slipping on ice following the officer interviewing the motorist is not a foreseeable consequence of a minor car accident. Whitman v. Sacchetti, No. 1347, 2001 WL 674671, at *2 (Mass. App. Ct. June 12, 2001).

[95] Fein v. Kahan, 635 N.E.2d 1, 1-2 (Mass. App. Ct. 1994).

[96] Id.; see also Adams v. Cong. Auto Ins. Agency, Inc., 65 N.E.3d 1229, 1237 (Mass. App. Ct. 2016); Delaney v. Reynolds, 825 N.E.2d 554, 557 (Mass. App. Ct. 2005).

[97] Commonwealth v. Carlson, 849 N.E.2d 790, 794-795 (Mass. 2006).

[98] Id. at 794.

into the position of having to make what was, in retrospect, a true life-or-death decision."[99] However, an intentional tort that intervenes will usually sever the causal chain.[100]

B.   Evidence

Normally, the jury decides questions of causation. However, causation may be decided as a matter of law where the connection between the negligent act and the resulting harm is not "rationally permissible."[101]

Examination of the risk of harm created by the original negligent act is a useful guide in ascertaining whether the harm that occurs will be considered foreseeable with resulting exposure to liability.[102] Only the "general character and probability of the injury" need to be foreseeable."[103] The plaintiff proves causation when the plaintiff establishes "that the defendant took a risk with respect to the plaintiff's safety that a person of ordinary prudence would not have taken, and that the plaintiff suffered a resulting injury that was within the foreseeable risk."[104] For example, a person who negligently "makes the theft of a motor vehicle possible," could be held liable for injuries caused by the "negligent operation of the stolen vehicle."[105] However, injuries inflicted upon a police officer by the thief resisting arrest one and a half hours after the car was stolen were not compensable.[106] The risk caused by the negligent act was harm caused by the operation of the vehicle. The risk did not include "harm caused when the thief resisted arrest, at least when that harm did not occur during flight from the scene of the theft."[107]

In *Leavitt v. Brockton Hospital, Inc.*,[108] the Supreme Judicial Court of Massachusetts expressed support for the *Restatement (Third) of Torts, Liability for Physical and Emotional Harm* (2010/2012) [hereinafter *Restatement (Third) PEH*]. Leavitt was a police officer who was responding to an emergency call when his cruiser was struck by a vehicle. Leavitt was seriously injured in this accident. The driver of the vehicle that struck Leavitt's cruiser is not a party to this litigation. Rather, the defendant in the current litigation is Brockton Hospital.[109] The hospital had allegedly allowed a patient to leave the hospital without an escort after receiving sedation. The patient was walking home after a colonoscopy and the resulting sedation when he was struck and killed by a car (not the same car that crashed into

---

[99] *Id.*

[100] Westerback v. Harold F. LeClair Co., 735 N.E.2d 1256, 1258 (Mass. App. Ct. 2000). (A bar who served a visibly intoxicated woman in violation of a statute is not liable for the customer's assault and rape when she left the bar, was walking down the street obviously intoxicated, and was offered a ride home by her assailants.)

[101] Falvey v. Hamelburg, 198 N.E.2d 400, 403 (Mass. 1964); *accord* Kent v. Commonwealth, 771 N.E.2d 770, 778 (Mass. 2002).

[102] Poskus v. Lombardo's of Randolph, Inc., 670 N.E.2d 383, 385 (Mass. 1996).

[103] Glick v. Prince Italian Foods of Saugus, Inc., 514 N.E.2d 100, 102 (Mass. App. Ct. 1987).

[104] Irwin v. Town of Ware, 467 N.E.2d 1292, 1305 (Mass. 1984).

[105] Poskus v. Lombardo's of Randolph, Inc., 670 N.E.2d 383, 385 (Mass. 1996).

[106] *Id.*

[107] *Id.* at 385-386.

[108] Leavitt v. Brockton Hosp., Inc., 907 N.E.2d 213, 216-17 (Mass. 2009).

[109] *Id.* at 214.

the cruiser).[110] Officer Leavitt was responding to the automobile/pedestrian accident when his cruiser was struck by the other vehicle. Leavitt sustained severe injuries as a result and brought suit against the hospital.[111] The argument was basically that the hospital had negligently allowed the pedestrian to leave without an escort, had it not been for the violation of that internal policy, the pedestrian would not have been hit by a car, Leavitt would not have been responding to the pedestrian/automobile accident, and his cruiser would not have been struck when he was in transit to the scene. The trial court held that the hospital did not owe Leavitt a duty and dismissed the cause of action.[112] The Supreme Judicial Court affirmed the dismissal.[113]

The court cited with approval the risk standard from the *Restatement (Third) PEH*.[114] The *Restatement (Third) PEH* uses the term "scope of liability" instead of the term proximate cause and utilizes the risk standard or risk test encompassed in *Section 29* as the test for the scope of liability (or proximate cause).[115] According to the court, "[l]iability for conduct obtains only where the conduct is both a cause-in-fact of the injury and where the resulting injury is within the scope of the foreseeable risk arising from the negligent conduct."[116] Applying the risk test to the facts at hand, the court concluded that the risk created by allowing a medicated patient to leave the hospital unsupervised would be the danger that the patient could injure himself or others.[117] The court acknowledged that a third party injured by a medicated patient driving an automobile upon leaving the hospital might be within the foreseeable risks created by the negligence of the hospital.[118] However, the foreseeable risks created by the hospital did not include a police officer being struck by an unrelated vehicle while attempting to respond to a pedestrian/automobile accident allegedly caused by the medicated condition of the pedestrian.[119]

This decision does apply the *Restatement (Third) PEH*. However, it is not clear if it adopted the approach of the *Restatement (Third) PEH* to the exclusion of prior case law. While the court did cite *Section 29* with approval and used the risk test or risk standard embodied within the *Restatement (Third) PEH,* it did not overrule existing case law. It observed that the risk approach and foreseeability approach were functionally consistent.[120] It would

---

[110] *Id.* at 215.

[111] *Id.* at 214.

[112] *Id.* at 215, 219.

[113] *Id.* at 221.

[114] *Id.* at 219-220.

[115] RESTATEMENT (THIRD) OF TORTS, LIABILITY FOR PHYSICAL AND EMOTIONAL HARM § 29 (2010/2012)

[116] *Leavitt*, 907 N.E.2d at 219.

[117] *Id.* at 220.

[118] *Id.*

[119] *Id.*

[120] The court cited with approval *comment j* to the *Restatement (Third) PEH,* Section 29, which provides, as follows: "Many jurisdictions employ a 'foreseeability' test for proximate cause, and in negligence actions such a rule is essentially consistent with the standard [of risk] set forth in this Section. . . . Properly understood, both the risk standard and a foreseeability test exclude liability for harms that were sufficiently unforeseeable at the time of the actor's tortious conduct that they were not among the risks—potential harms—that made the actor negligent. Negligence limits the requirement of reasonable care to those risks that are foreseeable. . . . Thus, when scope of

clearly appear that the "risk standard" is an appropriate test to employ in Massachusetts. However, prior case law, including the concept of proximate cause and foreseeability, were not explicitly overturned. The other controversial aspects of the *Restatement (Third) PEH* were not addressed.[121] A conservative interpretation is that generally Massachusetts supports use of the risk test and the risk test is superimposed over the existing case law, rather than superseding preexisting doctrine.

V.   Damages

A.   *Elements*

Plaintiff's recovery from the defendant whose negligent act caused the plaintiff's harm include compensation for pain and suffering, incurred expenses including medical expenses, and loss wages and diminution in earning capacity.[122] Recovery is allowed for these items of damages if "they are reasonably probable to continue in the future."[123] The goal is "fair compensation for the injury sustained."[124] The fact that fewer injuries would have been sustained if the victim was a younger or healthier person is not relevant; "the wrongdoer takes the victim as he or she finds him."[125] A wrongful death action may be maintained for the death of a viable fetus.[126] Recovery is also allowed for injuries tortiously caused to an unborn child "if the child is born alive."[127]

The amount of the verdict should only be set aside when the amount is so high or so low compared to the evidence that the jury was clearly "influenced by passion, partiality,

---

liability arises in a negligence case, the risks that make an actor negligent are limited to foreseeable ones, and the factfinder must determine whether the type of harm that occurred is among those reasonably foreseeable potential harms that made the actor's conduct negligent." *Leavitt*, 907 N.E.2d at 220 n.20 (quoting RESTATEMENT (THIRD) OF TORTS, LIABILITY FOR PHYSICAL AND EMOTIONAL HARM § 29 (2010/2012), *comment j*).

[121] For an overview of the *Restatement (Third) PEH*, see *Introduction, The Restatement (Third) and Foreseeability—"What Does It All Mean?," supra*. The approach of the *Restatement (Third) PEH* is to recommend the removal of foreseeability as a relevant consideration in the duty and/or proximate cause arena. Generally, there is no case-by-case determination of whether a duty of care is owed. There is a presumption that a duty is owed unless the case falls within a class of cases where no duty is owed to that particular category of cases. The *Restatement (Third)* attempts to eliminate the term proximate cause and the concept of the substantial factor test for cause-in-fact. The reception of the *Restatement (Third)* by the courts throughout the country is unclear. There is certainly not a landslide of cases running to adopt the controversial provisions of the *Restatement (Third)*. Most courts appear disinclined to overturn established case law in favor of uncertain novel approaches. An interesting aside is that the court in *Leavitt* affirmed the trial court's decision that the hospital did not owe Leavitt a duty of care. A finding of no duty based on the facts of an individual case is an approach specifically frowned upon by the *Restatement (Third) PEH*.

[122] 11 MASS. PRAC., MOTOR VEHICLE LAW AND PRACTICE § 16:1 (4th ed. 2016) [hereinafter MASS. PRAC.] (citing Rodgers v. Boynton, 52 N.E.2d 576, 577 (Mass. 1943)).

[123] *Id.*

[124] MASS. PRAC. (citing Daniels v. Celeste, 21 N.E.2d 1, 2 (Mass. 1939)); Mitchell v. Walton Lunch Co., 25 N.E.2d 151, 153 (Mass. 1939).

[125] Commonwealth v. Carlson, 849 N.E.2d 790, 796 (Mass. 2006).

[126] Remy v. MacDonald, 801 N.E.2d 260, 265 (Mass. 2004).

[127] Id. at 266.

prejudice or corruption."[128] A new trial on the amount of damages should only be allowed to avoid a miscarriage of justice.[129] For example, a new trial should be granted if the amount awarded is "greatly disproportionate to the injury proved."[130] On appeal, the action of the trial judge will only be set aside if there was an abuse of discretion,[131] "judicial action 'that no conscientious judge, acting intelligently, could honestly have taken.'"[132]

B.   Evidence

The plaintiff has the burden to prove each item of damages with as much certainty as the circumstances permit.[133] Pain and suffering may be inferred from the physical condition of the plaintiff.[134] "Proof of exacerbation or aggravation of injuries is more likely to require expert testimony."[135] Recovery is allowed for "the value of reasonable medical services required to treat the injury."[136] In order to prove medical expenses, copies of itemized medical bills are admissible as evidence.[137] The actual medical bill is admissible[138] even if the provider will accept a lesser amount in full payment of the account.[139] The wrongdoer is also liable for a "reasonable sum for estimated future necessary expenses."[140] Under the collateral source rule, a plaintiff's recovery is not reduced by insurance payments received from a third party (such as the injured party's health insurance company).[141] The policy behind the collateral source rule is that the wrongdoer should not receive a windfall by indirectly benefitting from premiums paid by the plaintiff to their insurance carrier.[142]

The plaintiff, "on proper proof, may properly recover reasonable compensation for loss [of] earning power in the future, as well as for such losses incurred prior to trial

---

[128] MASS. PRAC. § 16:14 (citing Downey v. Union Trust Co. of Springfield, 45 N.E.2d 373, 381 (Mass. 1942)); Clark v. Binney, 19 Mass. 113, 2 Pick. 113, 120 (Mass. 1824); Coffin v. Coffin, 4 Mass. 1, at *1 (Mass. 1808).

[129] MASS. PRAC. § 16:14 (citing Bartley v. Phillips, 57 N.E.2d 26, 29, 30 (Mass. 1944)); Davis v. Boston Elevated Ry., 126 N.E. 841, 843, 844 (Mass. 1920).

[130] MASS. PRAC. § 16:14 (citing Bartley v. Phillips, 57 N.E.2d 26, 29, 30 (Mass. 1944)); Bodwell v. Osgood, 3 Pick. 379, 385, 20 Mass. 379, 385 (Mass. 1825); Sampson v. Smith, 15 Mass. 365, 367 (Mass. 1819).

[131] MASS. PRAC. § 16:14 (citing Bartley v. Phillips, 57 N.E.2d 26, 29, 30 (Mass. 1944)).

[132] MASS. PRAC. § 16:14 (citing Shockett v. Akeson, 37 N.E.2d 1015, 1016, 1017 (Mass. 1941)); Kinnear v. Gen. Mills, 32 N.E.2d 263, 266 (Mass. 1941); Davis v. Bos. Elevated Ry., 126 N.E. 841, 846 (Mass. 1920).

[133] McElwain v. Capotosto, 122 N.E.2d 901, 902 (Mass. 1954). For recovery in lost chance cases, a category of medical negligence cases, the calculation of damages requires a specific mathematical formula. Matsuyama v. Birnbaum, 890 N.E.2d 819, 840 (Mass. 2008); Renzi v. Paredes, 890 N.E.2d 806, 813-814 (Mass. 2008).

[134] MASS. PRAC. § 16:7 (citing Choicener v. Walters Amusement Agency, 168 N.E. 918 (Mass. 1929)).

[135] Bailey v. Cataldo Ambulance Serv., Inc., 832 N.E.2d 12, 16 (Mass. App. Ct. 2005).

[136] Law v. Griffith, 930 N.E.2d 126, 129 (Mass. 2010).

[137] MASS. PRAC. § 16:8 (citing MASS. GEN. LAWS, c. 233, § 79G).

[138] Law v. Griffith, 930 N.E.2d 126, 130 (Mass. 2010) (citing MASS. GEN. LAWS, ch. 233, § 79G).

[139] MASS. PRAC. § 16:8 (citing MASS. GEN. LAWS, c. 233, § 79G).

[140] MASS. PRAC. § 16:8 (citing Cassidy v. Constantine, 168 N.E. 169, 170 (Mass. 1929)).

[141] Law v. Griffith, 930 N.E.2d 126, 131 (Mass. 2010).

[142] Id. at 132.

of his action."[143] A jury can decide future impairment of earning capacity "from evidence as to the nature and permanence of his disability, and opinions formed from his appearance or characteristics."[144] Admissible evidence includes statistical proof of the plaintiff's life expectancy.[145]

> The determination of damages for the impairment of earning capacity is not susceptible to arithmetical calculation, and its ascertainment must to a large degree depend on the practical sagacity, common knowledge and good sense of the jury in considering the plaintiff's age, skill, training, experience, and industry, extent of his injuries for which recovery is sought, wages commonly received by one pursuing a similar occupation in the vicinity of the plaintiff's employment and whatever other evidence is introduced to aid the jury in arriving at a just conclusion.[146]

Comparison of the wages the plaintiff earned before and after his or her injury is permissible.[147] A stay-at-home mother may recover damages for impairment for earning capacity because she could be employed earning money.[148] Punitive damages may be recoverable in wrongful death actions upon a showing of gross negligence on the part of the defendant.[149] "Gross negligence is substantially and appreciably higher in magnitude than ordinary negligence. . . . It is very great negligence, or the absence of slight diligence, or the want of even scant care. . . . Gross negligence is a manifestly smaller amount of watchfulness and circumspection than the circumstances require of a person of ordinary prudence."[150] One indicium of gross negligence is a "palpably negligent course of conduct over an appreciable period of time."[151]

---

[143] Mass. Prac. § 16:6 (citing Cross v. Sharaffa, 183 N.E. 838 (Mass. 1933); McCarthy v. Bos. Elevated Ry., 112 N.E. 235 (1916)).

[144] Mass. Prac. § 16:6 (citing Reckis v. Johnson & Johnson, 28 N.E.3d 445, 468 n.45 (Mass. 2015); Cross v. Sharaffa, 183 N.E. 838 (Mass. 1933)).

[145] Mass. Prac. § 16:6 (citing Foumier v. Zinn, 154 N.E. 268 (Mass. 1926); Banks v. Braman, 80 N.E. 799 (Mass. 1907)).

[146] Mass. Prac. § 16:6 (citing Solimene v. B. Grauel & Co., K.G., 507 N.E.2d 662, 671 (Mass. 1987); Griffin v. Gen. Motors Corp., 403 N.E.2d 402 (Mass. 1980); Mitchell v. Walton Lunch Co., 25 N.E.2d 151 (Mass. 1939); Doherty v. Ruiz, 18 N.E.2d 542, 543, 544 (Mass. 1939)).

[147] Mass. Prac. § 16:6 (citing Hendler v. Coffey, 179 N.E. 801 (Mass. 1932)).

[148] Mass. Prac. § 16:6 (citing Mass. Gen. Laws, c. 209, § 4; Matloff v. City of Chelsea, 31 N.E.2d 518 (Mass. 1941); Roselli v. Riseman, 182 N.E. 567 (Mass. 1932)).

[149] Williamson-Green v. Equip. 4 Rent, Inc., 46 N.E.3d 571, 575 (Mass. App. Ct. 2016) (citing Mass. Gen. Laws, ch. 229, § 2).

[150] *Williamson-Green*, 46 N.E.3d at 575.

[151] *Id.*

CHAPTER 23

MICHIGAN

MICHIGAN
Lee F. Peoples[1]

I. Purpose of Tort Law

The common law of the State of Michigan has defined tort as "a civil wrong, other than a breach of contract, for which the court will provide a remedy in the form of compensatory damages."[2] The primary purpose of tort law is to compensate persons injured by the negligence of another.[3] The Michigan Supreme Court has held that "the policy behind the law of torts is more than compensation of victims. It seeks also to encourage implementation of reasonable safeguards against risks of injury."[4] Encouraging tortfeasors to adopt corrective measures has been cited as another purpose of tort law.[5] Deterrence of harm and loss-allocation have been cited as additional purposes of tort law.[6]

When recognizing a tort cause of action, the Michigan Supreme Court explained that:

> [S]ociety stands with the victim, acknowledges the importance of the value that allegedly has been damaged, and fixes the responsibility of the tortfeasor. Thus, the law of torts is no more the mere adjustment of losses by the exchange of money damages than the criminal law is the taking of an eye for an eye or a tooth for a tooth. Certainly money damage is the principal tort remedy, just as punishment is the sanction for criminal behavior. But money damage is no more the purpose of tort law than punishment is the purpose of criminal law. The penalties are the imprecise analogies by which the law measures responsibility. The right recognized is the means by which society transmits the judgment that the value involved is worthy of protection.[7]

---

[1] Interim Dean and Frederick Charles Hicks Professor of Law, Oklahoma City University School of Law, Member of the Oklahoma Bar. Citations and other materials in this chapter were adapted from CHRISTINE M. GIMENO, ET AL., MICHIGAN CIVIL JURISPRUDENCE, Chapter 18 Negligence (2016).

[2] In re Bradley Estate, 494 Mich. 367, 384-85, 835 N.W.2d 545, 554-55 (Mich. 2013) (holding that the term "tort" as used in MCL 691.1407(1) is a non-contractual civil wrong for which a remedy may be obtained in the form of compensatory damages).

[3] Penwest Dev. Corp. v. Dow Chem. Co., 667 F. Supp. 436, 442 (E.D. Mich. 1987).

[4] Funk v. Gen. Motors Corp., 392 Mich. 91, 104, 220 N.W.2d 641, 646 (1974) (*overruled in part on other grounds in* Hardy v. Monsanto Enviro–Chem Sys., Inc., 414 Mich. 29; 323 NW2d 270 (Mich. 1982)).

[5] Holloway v. Gen. Motors Corp. Chevrolet Div., 403 Mich. 614, 626, 271 N.W.2d 777, 783 (Mich. 1978).

[6] Weymers v. Khera, 454 Mich. 639, 652, 563 N.W.2d 647, 654 (Mich. 1997).

[7] Sizemore v. Smock, 430 Mich. 283, 309, 422 N.W.2d 666, 678 (Mich. 1988) (Boyle, J., dissenting) (citing PROSSER & KEETON, TORTS (5th ed.), § 4, p. 21) (*superseded by statute on other grounds in* Roberts v. Williamson, 111 S.W.3d 113, 117 (Tex. 2003)).

II.   Duty to Exercise Ordinary Care

A.   *Question of Law*

To establish negligence, a plaintiff must prove that a defendant owed a legal duty to the plaintiff.[8] The duty has been described by the Court of Appeals of Michigan as "a legally recognized obligation to conform to a particular standard of conduct toward another so as to avoid unreasonable risk of harm."[9] Whether the defendant has a duty to exercise care is a question of law for the judge to decide.[10] The judge does not decide the standard of care to be exercised by a defendant in a specific case. The specific standard of care is determined by the jury.[11]

The court considers a variety of factors in determining whether a duty exists. The foreseeability of the risk is typically the first factor considered by the court.[12] Other factors considered include the relationship between the parties, the nature of the risk presented, and the burden of any duty on the defendant.[13] The Michigan Supreme Court has stated that a duty in a negligence case "arises out of the existence of a relationship 'between the parties of such a character that social policy justifies' its imposition."[14] Other factors considered by Michigan courts include the "degree of certainty of injury, closeness or connection between the conduct and the injury, moral blame attached to the conduct, policy of preventing future harm, and the burdens and consequences of imposing a duty and the resulting liability for breach."[15]

Considerations other than foreseeability may be more significant in determining if a duty exists. The Michigan Supreme Court has stated that "[w]here foreseeability fails as an adequate template for the existence of a duty, recourse must be had to the basic issues of policy underlying the core problem whether the plaintiff's interests are entitled to legal protection against the defendant's conduct."[16] In another case, the Michigan Supreme Court cited public policy as a mitigating factor against imposing a duty on a defendant in a negligence action. The Court stated that "social policy must intervene at some point to limit the extent of one's liability."[17]

---

[8] Fultz v. Union-Commerce Assocs., 470 Mich. 460, 683 N.W.2d 587 (Mich. 2004).

[9] Cummins v. Robinson Twp., 283 Mich. App. 677, 692, 770 N.W.2d 421, 433-34 (Mich. Ct. App. 2009).

[10] Foster v. Cone-Blanchard Mach. Co., 460 Mich. 696, 707, 597 N.W.2d 506, 512 (Mich. 1999).

[11] Case v. Consumers Power Co., 463 Mich. 1, 6, 615 N.W.2d 17, 20 (Mich. 2000).

[12] Buczkowski v. McKay, 441 Mich. 96, 102, 490 N.W.2d 330, 333 (Mich. 1992) (noting that considerations other than foreseeability may be more important and stating that, "Where foreseeability fails as an adequate template for the existence of a duty, recourse must be had to the basic issues of policy underlying the core problem whether the plaintiff's interests are entitled to legal protection against the defendant's conduct."). *See also,* Brown v. Brown, 478 Mich. 545, 553, 739 N.W.2d 313, 317 (Mich. 2007).

[13] Murdock v Higgins, 454 Mich. 46, 53; 559 N.W.2d 639 (Mich. 1997).

[14] Dyer v. Trachtman, 470 Mich. 45, 49, 679 N.W.2d 311, 314 (Mich. 2004) (quoting Prosser & Keeton, Torts (5th ed.), § 56, p 374).

[15] Gimeno, *supra* note 1, § 11. (citing Doe v. Johnson, 817 F. Supp. 1382 (W.D. Mich. 1993) (applying Michigan law); Rakowski v. Sarb, 269 Mich. App. 619, 713 N.W.2d 787 (Mich. Ct. App. 2006); Graves v. Warner Bros., 253 Mich. App. 486, 656 N.W.2d 195 (Mich. Ct. App. 2002)).

[16] *Buczkowski,* 490 N.W.2d at 333.

[17] Groncki v. Detroit Edison Co., 453 Mich. 644, 661, 557 N.W.2d 289, 296 (Mich. 1996).

B.   *Question of Fact*

i.   **Elements**

The jury determines the "specific standard of care that should have been exercised by a defendant in a given case."[18] Jurors are instructed that ordinary care is defined as "the care a reasonably careful person would use"[19] and that they will determine what "a reasonably careful person using ordinary care would do or not do under such circumstances."[20]

The Michigan Supreme Court has articulated that a "sliding scale" is used to determine the level of care required.[21] "The more severe the potential injury, the more resources a reasonable person will expend to try and prevent that injury. Similarly, the greater the likelihood that a severe injury will result, the greater the lengths a reasonable person will go to prevent it."[22]

There is no set definition of the level of reasonable care. Older jurisprudence defines the level of care using the "reasonably prudent man" standard.[23] More recent decisions employ a more situational definition. For example, the opinion in *Case v. Consumer Power Co.* articulates the level of care as:

> The terms 'ordinary care,' 'reasonable prudence,' and such like terms, as applied to the conduct and affairs of men, have a relative significance, and cannot be arbitrarily defined. What may be deemed ordinary care in one case may, under different surroundings and circumstances, be gross negligence. The policy of the law has relegated the determination of such questions to the jury, under proper instructions from the court. It is their province to note the special circumstances and surroundings of each particular case, and then say whether the conduct of the parties in that case was such as would be expected of reasonable, prudent men, under a similar state of affairs.[24]

What qualifies as ordinary care "may differ depending on the activity, trade, occupation, or profession."[25] The degree of care remains constant and has been defined as "what a reasonably careful person engaged in a particular activity, trade, occupation, or profession would do or would refrain from doing under the circumstances then existing."[26]

---

[18] Case v. Consumers Power Co., 463 Mich. 1, 7, 615 N.W.2d 17, 20 (Mich. 2000).

[19] MICHIGAN MODEL CIVIL JURY INSTRUCTIONS, § 10.02 (2016).

[20] *Id.*

[21] *Case,* 615 N.W.2d at 21.

[22] *Id.*

[23] Jones v. Grand Trunk W. R. Co., 303 Mich. 114, 120, 5 N.W.2d 676, 679 (Mich. 1942). *See also,* GIMENO, *supra* note 1, at Negligence § 2.

[24] *Case,* 615 N.W.2d at 21 (citing Grand Trunk Ry. Co. of Canada v. Ives, 144 U.S. 408, 417, 12 S. Ct. 679, 683, 36 L. Ed. 485 (1892). *See also,* McLaughlin v. Great Lakes Contracting Co. of Detroit, 82 Mich. App. 729, 732, 267 N.W.2d 489, 490 (Mich. Ct. App. 1978) (when determining the degree of care required the probability of risk must be considered along with the extent of the possible consequences caused by the risk).

[25] MICHIGAN MODEL CIVIL JURY INSTRUCTIONS, § 10.02 (2016).

[26] *Id.*

Typically, the jury determines the level of care in a negligence case. However, there are limited circumstances where the court may determine the "reasonableness of a defendant's conduct" when "overriding concerns of public policy" are involved.[27] When a duty arises out of a relationship between the parties and the facts surrounding the relationship are not clear, "the duty issue may be bifurcated for the court to determine the requisite elements of the relationship and for the jury to determine whether evidence establishes the elements of that relationship."[28]

ii.   Evidence

The plaintiff bears the burden of proof in a negligence action and must present evidence of the level of care.[29] Proof must be established by a preponderance of the evidence.[30] Evidence of the customary industry practice is relevant in determining whether the standard of care has been met.[31] Violations of statutes, rules, and regulations may be considered to impose a duty on a defendant in certain circumstances. The court will consider "whether the purpose of the statute was to prevent the type of injury and harm actually suffered, whether the plaintiff was within the class of persons which the statute was designed to protect"[32] and whether the ordinance was "designed to protect the class of persons in which plaintiff is included against the risk of the type of harm which has in fact occurred as the result of its violation before evidence of the ordinance may be introduced on the issue of negligence."[33] Workplace safety standards are admissible to prove the standard of care but standards do not impact a "worker's common-law duties or liabilities."[34]

III.   Breach of Duty

A.   Elements

To successfully establish a claim of negligence under Michigan law, a plaintiff must establish that the defendant breached a duty owed to the plaintiff.[35]

---

[27] GIMENO, *supra* n. 1, at § 161 (citing MacDonald v. PKT, Inc., 233 Mich. App. 395, 593 N.W.2d 176 (Mich. Ct. App. 1999), *rev'd on other grounds*, 464 Mich. 322, 628 N.W.2d 33 (Mich. 2001)).

[28] GIMENO, *supra* n. 1, at § 161 (citing Whiting v. Central Trux & Parts, Inc., 984 F. Supp. 1096 (E.D. Mich. 1997)).

[29] GIMENO, *supra* n. 1, at § 155.

[30] *Id.*

[31] Hill v. Husky Briquetting, Inc., 393 Mich. 136, 136, 223 N.W.2d 290, 291 (Mich. 1974).

[32] GIMENO, *supra* n. 1, at § 93 (citing Cipri v. Bellingham Frozen Foods, Inc., 235 Mich. App. 1, 596 N.W.2d 620 (Mich. Ct. App. 1999)).

[33] GIMENO, *supra* n. 1, at § 93 (citing Johnson v. Bobbie's Party Store, 189 Mich. App. 652, 473 N.W.2d 796 (Mich. Ct. App. 1991); McKnight v. Carter, 144 Mich. App. 623, 376 N.W.2d 170 (Mich. Ct. App. 1985); Webster v. WXYZ, 59 Mich. App. 375, 229 N.W.2d 460 (Mich. Ct. App. 1975)).

[34] Zalut v. Andersen & Assoc., Inc., 186 Mich. App. 229, 463 N.W.2d 236 (Mich. Ct. App. 1990). *But see* Co-Jo, Inc. v. Strand, 226 Mich. App. 108, 572 N.W.2d 251 (Mich. Ct. App. 1998) (refusing to allow workplace standards to establish the standard of care owed by an independent contractor to its customer in performing its services) (*superseded on other grounds as discussed in* Butler v. Michigan Consol. Gas Co., No. 278063, 2008 WL 2268308, at 1 (Mich. Ct. App. 2008)).

[35] *Case*, 615 N.W.2d at 20. *See also,* Dugan v. State Farm Mut. Auto. Ins., 845 F. Supp. 2d 803, 806 (E.D. Mich. 2012).

B.   Evidence

Breach of duty is normally a question of fact to be decided by the jury.[36] Summary disposition of breach of duty is not appropriate.[37] Breach of duty may be established by circumstantial evidence.[38]

IV.   Causation

A.   Elements

Michigan Appellate Courts have defined the proximate cause of an injury as:

> that which in a natural and continuous sequence, unbroken by any new, independent cause, produces the injury, and without which the injury would not have occurred, and involves a determination that the connection between the wrongful conduct and injury is of such a nature that it is socially and economically desirable to hold the wrongdoer liable.[39]

Proximate cause "incorporates both cause-in-fact and legal (or 'proximate') cause."[40] "Cause-in-fact requires a plaintiff to show that but-for the defendant's actions, the injury would not have occurred, while legal or proximate cause normally involves examining the foreseeability of consequences."[41] Foreseeability "requires that a reasonable person 'could anticipate the likelihood that a particular event would occur under certain conditions,' and that such an event would 'pose some sort of risk of injury to another person or his property.'"[42] Michigan jurors are instructed that proximate cause means "first, that the negligent conduct must have been a cause of plaintiff's injury, and second, that the plaintiff's injury must have been of a type that is a natural and probable result of the negligent conduct."[43]

---

[36] Latham v. Nat'l Car Rental Sys., 239 Mich. App. 330, 340, 608 N.W.2d 66, 72 (Mich. Ct. App. 2000).

[37] Spikes v. Banks, 231 Mich. App. 341, 354, 586 N.W.2d 106, 112 (Mich. Ct. App. 1998).

[38] Jakubiec v. VEI Friendly, L.L.C., No. 273579, 2008 WL 2667319, 4 (Mich. Ct. App. 2008) (citing Gadde v. Mich. Consol. Gas Co., 377 Mich. 117, 126; 139 NW2d 722 (Mich. 1966)).

[39] Gimeno, *supra* n. 1, at § 81 (citing McMillian v. Vliet, 422 Mich. 570, 374 N.W.2d 679 (Mich. 1985)); McKine v. Hamner, 387 Mich. 82, 194 N.W.2d 841 (Mich. 1972); Wiley v. Henry Ford Cottage Hosp., 257 Mich. App. 488, 668 N.W.2d 402 (Mich. Ct. App. 2003), *appeal denied*, 678 N.W.2d 439 (Mich. 2004); Ross v. Glaser, 220 Mich. App. 183, 559 N.W.2d 331 (Mich. 1996); Hobrla v. Glass, 143 Mich. App. 616, 372 N.W.2d 630 (Mich. Ct. App. 1985).

[40] Gimeno, *supra* n. 1, at § 85 (citing Mettler Walloon, L.L.C. v. Melrose Twp., 281 Mich. App. 184, 761 N.W.2d 293, 2008 Mich. App. LEXIS 1891 (Mich. Ct. App. 2008)).

[41] Mettler Walloon, L.L.C. v. Melrose Twp., 281 Mich. App. 184, 761 N.W.2d 293, 2008 Mich. App. LEXIS 1891 (Mich. Ct. App. 2008).

[42] Samson v. Sagniaw Prof'l Bldg, Inc., 393 Mich. 393, 406; 224 N.W.2d 843 (Mich. 1975).

[43] Michigan Model Civil Jury Instructions, § 15.01 (2016).

B. *Evidence*

Causation and proximate cause are generally left for the jury to decide.[44] The issue of proximate cause may be decided by the court "if reasonable minds could not differ regarding the proximate cause of the plaintiff's injury."[45]

Proof of causation cannot be based on mere speculation.[46] More than "a possibility of causation is required."[47] Proof of causation need not "negate all other possible causes, it must exclude other reasonable hypotheses with a fair amount of certainty."[48] Cause-in-fact may be shown with "substantial evidence from which a jury may conclude that more likely than not, but-for the defendant's conduct, the plaintiff's injuries would not have occurred."[49]

V. **Damages**

A. *Elements*

Damages should compensate the victim for the loss or injury sustained.[50] The Michigan Court of Appeals has stated that "a negligent defendant is liable for all injuries resulting directly from his or her wrongful act, whether foreseeable or not, if the damages were the legal and natural consequences of the defendant's conduct and might reasonably have been anticipated."[51]

B. *Evidence*

The plaintiff in a tort action must establish damages by a preponderance of the evidence.[52] Damages include "all the legal and natural consequences of the injury, i.e., the damages that naturally flow from the injury."[53] Damages are not limited to "those in fact already incurred, and future damages may be allowed if reasonably identified as to probability and ascertainable as to amount."[54]

---

[44] GIMENO, *supra* n. 1, at § 84, 160 (citing Ross v. Glaser, 220 Mich. App. 183, 559 N.W.2d 331 (Mich. Ct. App. 1996) and Helmus v. Michigan Dept. of Transp., 238 Mich. App. 250, 604 N.W.2d 793 (Mich. Ct. App. 1999)).

[45] GIMENO, *supra* n. 1, at § 160 (citing Hunley v. DuPont Auto., 341 F.3d 491 (6th Cir. 2003); Nichols v. Dobler, 253 Mich. App. 530, 655 N.W.2d 787 (Mich. Ct. App. 2002); Transp. Dep't v. Christensen, 229 Mich. App. 417, 581 N.W.2d 807 (1998)).

[46] Mettler Walloon, L.L.C. v. Melrose Twp., 281 Mich. App. 184, 218, 761 N.W.2d 293, 315 (Mich. Ct. App. 2008).

[47] Campbell v. Kovich, 273 Mich. App. 227, 233, 731 N.W.2d 112, 116 (Mich. Ct. App. 2006).

[48] *Id.*

[49] Badalamenti v. William Beaumont Hosp.-Troy, 237 Mich. App. 278, 285, 602 N.W.2d 854, 858 (Mich. Ct. App. 1999).

[50] Allison v. Chandler, 11 Mich. 542, 548, 1863 Mich. LEXIS 59 (Mich. 1863).

[51] State Auto Ins. Cos. v. Velazquez, 266 Mich. App. 726, 730, 703 N.W.2d 223, 226, 2005 Mich. App. LEXIS 1472 (Mich. Ct. App. 2005).

[52] Hannay v. Dep't of Transp., 497 Mich. 45, 79, 860 N.W.2d 67, 87 (Mich. 2014).

[53] *Id.*

[54] MICHIGAN CIVIL JURISPRUDENCE, HINSHAW AND KIMPFLEN, Chapter 7 Damages § 17 (2016) (citing McCurdy v. U.S. Hybrid Tree Co., 374 Mich. 388, 132 N.W.2d 169 (Mich. 1965)).

If multiple methods of estimating damages exist, the court should use the method "which best achieves the fundamental purpose of compensation to the injured person."[55] In establishing damages, "[t]he law does not require a greater degree of certainty when establishing tort damages than the nature of the case permits."[56] According to the Michigan Supreme Court, "[d]amages need not be calculated with absolute exactness. It is sufficient if a reasonable basis of computation be employed although the results be only approximate."[57]

---

[55] Leavitt v. Monaco Coach Corp., 241 Mich. App. 288, 299, 616 N.W.2d 175, 182 (Mich. Ct. App. 2000).

[56] HINSHAW AND KIMPFLEN, *supra* n. 54 (citing Matter of Green Charitable Trust, 172 Mich. App. 298, 431 N.W.2d 492 (Mich. Ct. App. 1988).

[57] Edmund W. Waskin Dev. Co. v. Weyn, 369 Mich. 121, 128, 119 N.W.2d 662, 665 (Mich. 1963).

CHAPTER 24

MINNESOTA

MINNESOTA

Lee F. Peoples[1]

I. Purpose of Tort Law

The deterrence and compensatory functions of tort law have been emphasized by the Minnesota Supreme Court.[2] The Court has stated that "[t]ort liability seeks to compensate the injured and to deter wrongdoing."[3] The Minnesota Court of Appeals has held that another purpose of tort law is to allocate losses arising out of human activities and to compensate victims "for injuries sustained as a result of another's conduct."[4]

II. Duty to Exercise Ordinary Care

A. *Question of Law*

The existence of a legal duty is one of the four elements of negligence under Minnesota law.[5] Duty has been defined as "an obligation to conform to a particular standard of conduct toward another."[6] A legal duty can be imposed by statute or common law.[7] Ordinances and regulatory standards can also impose a duty.[8] The existence of a duty is normally a question of law for the court to decide.[9] However, if the "foreseeability of a particular injury is in doubt, it may be permissible to submit the issue to the jury."[10]

Minnesota courts look at several factors in determining whether a duty exists. These factors include "the foreseeability of harm to the plaintiff, the connection between the defendant's conduct and the injury suffered, the moral blame attached to the defendant's conduct,

---

[1] Interim Dean and Frederick Charles Hicks Professor of Law, Oklahoma City University School of Law, Member of the Oklahoma Bar.

[2] Mike Steenson, *The Character of the Minnesota Tort System*, 33 Wm. Mitchell L. Rev. 239, 245 (2006) (citing Phelps v. Commonwealth Land Title Ins., 537 N.W.2d 271, 279 (Minn. 1995)).

[3] Pletan v. Gaines, 494 N.W.2d 38, 42 (Minn.1992) (citing Dickhoff ex rel. Dickhoff v. Green, 836 N.W.2d 321, 336 (Minn. 2013)).

[4] Larson v. Dunn, 449 N.W.2d 751, 756 (Minn. Ct. App. 1990) (*reversed in part on other grounds by* Larson v. Dunn, 460 N.W.2d 39 (Minn. 1990)).

[5] 4 Minn. Prac. Jury Instr. Guides Civil § 25.10 (6th ed.) (citing Domagala v. Rolland, 805 N.W.2d 14, 22 (Minn. 2011)).

[6] *Id.* (citing Vaughn v. Nw. Airlines, Inc., 558 N.W.2d 736, 742 (Minn. 1997)).

[7] *Id.* (citing Scott v. Indep. Sch. Dist. No. 709, 256 N.W.2d 485, 488 (Minn. 1977)).

[8] *Id.* (citing Pac. Indem. Co. v. Thompson-Yeager, Inc., 260 N.W.2d 548, 559 (Minn. 1977); Gray v. Badger Mining Co., 676 N.W.2d 268, 275 (Minn. 2004)).

[9] *Id.* (citing Molloy v. Meier, 679 N.W.2d 711, 716 (Minn. 2004)).

[10] *Id.* (citing Lundgren v. Fultz, 354 N.W.2d 25, 28 (Minn.1984)).

the policy of preventing future harm, and the burden to the defendant and community of imposing a duty to exercise care with resulting liability for breach."[11]

The Minnesota Supreme Court has stated that the "test for foreseeability as a threshold matter in determining duty is not whether the precise nature and manner of the plaintiff's injury was foreseeable, but whether the possibility of an accident was clear to the person of ordinary prudence."[12] In applying the test, courts focus "on whether it was objectively reasonable for a person of ordinary prudence to anticipate the danger."[13] Courts look to the conduct in question "and ask whether it was objectively reasonable to expect the specific danger causing the plaintiff's injury, not simply whether it was within the realm of any conceivable possibility."[14]

B. *Question of Fact*

i. **Elements**

The question of whether a duty is breached is normally a matter for the jury.[15] The jury will determine whether the defendant exercised reasonable care under the circumstances.[16] Courts have used the terms "ordinary care" and "reasonable care" interchangeably.[17] The level of care that is reasonable will vary with the circumstances. When danger increases, "the care that a reasonable person would use to respond to that increased danger will also change."[18]

ii. **Evidence**

Under Minnesota law, the level of care required is judged by an objective standard.[19] A defendant's own opinion about whether conduct met the standard is irrelevant.[20] Conduct will be judged against the "conduct of an ordinarily prudent person under the circumstances."[21] Direct evidence and circumstantial evidence are admissible to prove negligence.[22]

---

[11] *Domagala,* 805 N.W.2d at 26 (citing the RESTATEMENT (SECOND) OF TORTS § 321) (questioning some aspects of a duty arising out of a special relationship between the parties. Whebbe v. Beta Eta Chapter of Delta Tau Delta Fraternity, 2012 WL 5845171 (Dist. Ct. Minn. 2012)).

[12] 4 MINN. PRAC. JURY INSTR. GUIDES CIVIL § 25.10 (6th ed.) (quoting Domagala v. Rolland, 805 N.W.2d 14 (Minn. 2011)).

[13] *Id.*

[14] *Domagala,* 805 N.W.2d at 26 (quoting Whiteford ex rel. Whiteford v. Yamaha Motor Corp., 582 N.W.2d 916, 918 (Minn. 1998)).

[15] 4 MINN. PRAC. JURY INSTR. GUIDES CIVIL § 25 introductory note (6th ed.) (citing Canada v. McCarthy, 567 N.W.2d 496, 505 (Minn. 1997); Oakland v. Stenlund, 420 N.W.2d 248, 250 (Minn. Ct. App. 1988), *rev. denied* (Minn. April 20, 1988)).

[16] *Id.*

[17] Pogalz v. Kenna, 267 Minn. 340, 347, 126 N.W.2d 458, 463 (Minn. 1964).

[18] *Domagala,* 805 N.W.2d at 28.

[19] 4 MINN. PRAC. JURY INSTR. GUIDES CIVIL § 25.10 (6th ed.).

[20] *Id.*

[21] *Id.* (citing Olson v. Duluth, M. & I. R. Ry., 213 Minn. 106, 115, 5 N.W.2d 492, 496 (1942); Peterson v. Minnesota Power & Light Co., 206 Minn. 268, 271, 288 N.W. 588, 589 (1939)).

[22] *Id.*

Rules adopted by an institution are admissible as evidence of the standard of care.[23] Industry standards and codes are similarly admissible to demonstrate the standard of care.[24] Following or not following custom "does not necessarily amount to reasonable care or the lack of it, but it is admissible because it tends to show what a reasonably prudent person would do under the same or similar circumstances."[25] A defendant cannot avoid liability for a negligent act simply because the act was custom.[26] In certain situations the custom of the industry may in fact be negligent.[27] Violation of a rule or regulation may be used to establish negligence by showing the injury (1) was caused by the violation of the rule, (2) the injury was the type intended to be prevented by the rule, and (3) the plaintiff was one of the class of people protected by the rule.[28]

III.   Breach of Duty

A.   Elements

A plaintiff must prove breach of a legal duty to recover under a negligence claim.[29] Breach must be demonstrated by a preponderance of the evidence.[30]

B.   Evidence

The question of whether a duty is breached is generally for the jury to determine.[31]

IV.   Causation

A.   Elements

A plaintiff in a Minnesota negligence cause of action must prove that the defendant's failure to exercise due care caused injury.[32] Minnesota uses the term "direct cause" instead of

---

[23] Boland v. Garber, 257 N.W.2d 384, 386 (Minn. 1977) (holding that hospital rules can be used to show a standard of care); Murphy v. City of Minneapolis, 292 N.W.2d 751, 754 (Minn. 1980) (police department rules are admissible to show a standard of care).

[24] Stevens v. JDS Elec., No. C3-95-1244, 1996 WL 81496, 2 (Minn. Ct. App. 1996).

[25] 4 Minn. Prac. Jury Instr. Guides Civil § 25.47 (6th ed.) (citing Schmidt v. Beninga, 285 Minn. 477, 489–490, 173 N.W.2d 401, 408 (Minn. 1970); Hartmon v. National Heater Co., 240 Minn. 264, 277, 60 N.W.2d 804, 812 (Minn. 1953)).

[26] Id. (citing Tiemann v. Indep. Sch. Dist. No. 740, 331 N.W.2d 250, 251 (Minn. 1983); Scattergood v. Keil, 233 Minn. 340, 343, 45 N.W.2d 650, 653 (1951)).

[27] Id. (citing Gryc v. Dayton-Hudson Corp., 297 N.W.2d 727 (Minn. 1980), cert. denied, 449 U.S. 921, 101 S.Ct. 320, 66 L.Ed.2d 149 (1980)).

[28] Alderman's Inc., v. Shanks, 536 N.W.2d 4, 8 (Minn. 1995).

[29] Bjerke v. Johnson, 742 N.W.2d 660, 664 (Minn. 2007).

[30] Danielson v. City of Brooklyn Park, 516 N.W.2d 203, 205 (Minn. Ct. App. 1994).

[31] Lindrigan v. Arlt v. Duoos, No. C5-96-1773, 1997 WL 76477, 2 (Minn. Ct. App. Feb. 25, 1997) (citing Sauter v. Sauter, 244 Minn. 482, 486, 70 N.W.2d 351, 354 (1955)).

[32] 1-4 Pirsig on Minnesota Pleading § 4.453 (2016).

"proximate cause" in its jury instruction. While "'proximate' is a term that may be meaningful to lawyers because of familiarity with the concept, but it is not so understood by jurors. 'Proximate' often confuses, rather than enlightens, the trier of fact."[33]

The Minnesota Supreme Court expressly rejected the "but-for" test for causation.[34] The "substantial factor" test from the Restatement (Second) of Torts § 431 is used to determine if a cause is direct.[35] The Minnesota Jury Instructions define direct cause as a cause that had a "substantial part in bringing about the (collision) (accident) (event) (harm) (injury)."[36] Minnesota courts have also found a negligent act to be the proximate cause of an injury "where the party ought, in the exercise of ordinary care, to have anticipated that the act was likely to result in injury to others."[37] "If injury is foreseeable, then the party is liable for any injury proximately resulting from it, even though he could not have anticipated the particular injury which did happen."[38]

B. Evidence

Causation is generally an issue for the jury to determine.[39] A jury's causation finding will not be disturbed unless it is "manifestly and palpably contrary to the evidence viewed as a whole and in the light most favorable to the verdict. It is only where the evidence is so clear and conclusive as to leave no room for differences of opinion among reasonable [jurors] that the issue of causation becomes one of law to be decided by the court."[40]

V. Damages

A. Elements

Minnesota courts have defined both general and special damages. General damages "are the natural, necessary and usual result of the wrongful act or occurrence in question."[41]

---

[33] 4 Minn. Prac. Jury Instr. Guides Civil § 27.10 (6th ed.) (citing Staloch v. Belsaas, 271 Minn. 315, 327–28, 136 N.W.2d 92, 100 (Minn. 1965); Gardner v. Germain, 264 Minn. 61, 65–66, 117 N.W.2d 759, 762 (Minn. 1962); Strobel v. Chicago, R.I. & Pac. R.R., 255 Minn. 201, 204–207, 96 N.W.2d 195, 198–200 (Minn. 1959); W. Keeton, D. Dobbs, R. Keeton & D. Owen, Prosser and Keeton on the Law of Torts § 42 (5th ed. 1984)).

[34] Harpster v. Hetherington, 512 N.W.2d 585 (Minn. 1994).

[35] 4 Minn. Prac. Jury Instr. Guides Civil § 25 introductory note (6th ed.) (citing Flom v. Flom, 291 N.W.2d 914, 917 (Minn. 1980); Lestico v. Kuehner, 204 Minn. 125, 133, 283 N.W. 122, 127 (Minn. 1938); Peterson v. Fulton, 192 Minn. 360, 364, 256 N.W. 901, 903 (Minn. 1934). Under the "substantial factor" test, negligent conduct is the direct cause of harm to another if it is a substantial factor in bringing about the harm.).

[36] 4 Minn. Prac. Jury Instr. Guides Civil § 27.10 (6th ed.).

[37] Lennon v. Pieper, 411 N.W.2d 225, 228 (Minn. Ct. App. 1987).

[38] Id.

[39] 4 Minn. Prac. Jury Instr. Guides Civil § 27.10 (6th ed.) (citing Norberg v. Nw. Hosp. Ass'n, 270 N.W.2d 271, 274 (Minn. 1978)).

[40] Renswick v. Wenzel, 819 N.W.2d 198, 208-09 (Minn. Ct. App. 2012) (citing Vanderweyst v. Langford, 303 Minn. 575, 576, 228 N.W.2d 271, 272 (Minn.1975)).

[41] 4A Minn. Prac. Jury Instr. Guides Civil § 90 introductory note (6th ed.) (citing Ray v. Miller Meester Advert., Inc., 684 N.W.2d 404, 407 (Minn. 2004)).

"Special damages are those which are the natural, but not the necessary and inevitable result of the wrongful act."[42]

B.   *Evidence*

The plaintiff in a negligence action bears the burden of proving damages by a preponderance of the evidence.[43] When discussing the evidence required to prove damages the Minnesota Supreme Court stated that "it is not necessary that the evidence be unequivocal or that it establish future damages to an absolute certainty."[44] A plaintiff "is entitled to an instruction on future damages if he or she has shown that such damage is more likely to occur than not to occur."[45] The amount of damages to be awarded is left to the discretion of the jury.[46]

---

[42] *Id.*

[43] Rowe v. Munye, 702 N.W.2d 729, 735 (Minn. 2005).

[44] 4A MINN. PRAC. JURY INSTR. GUIDES CIVIL § 90.15 (6th ed.) (citing Pietrzak v. Eggen, 295 N.W.2d 504, 507 (Minn. 1980)).

[45] Pietrzak v. Eggen, 295 N.W.2d 504, 507 (Minn. 1980).

[46] Busch v. Busch Const., Inc., 262 N.W.2d 377, 396 (Minn. 1977) (*disagreed with on other grounds* Lippard v. Houdaille Indus., Inc., 715 S.W.2d 491 (Mo. 1986)); Krueger v. City of Faribault, 220 Minn. 89, 96, 18 N.W.2d 777, 780 (Minn. 1945).

CHAPTER 25

MISSISSIPPI

MISSISSIPPI

Lee F. Peoples[1]

I. Purpose

One purpose of tort law is to deter tortious behavior and the deterrent effect of tort recovery is useful to protect the public.[2] The general rule in Mississippi "provides that where an injury results from negligence, liability follows."[3] "For negligent or tortious conduct, liability is the rule. Immunity is the exception."[4] The Mississippi Court of Appeals has stated that "A state has an especial interest in exercising judicial jurisdiction over those who commit torts within its territory. This is because torts involve wrongful conduct which a state seeks to deter, and against which it attempts to afford protection, by providing that a tortfeasor will be liable for damages which are the proximate result of his tort."[5] Furthermore, the Supreme Court of Mississippi has acknowledged the deterrent effect of allowing "victims of gross negligence or intentional torts to recover damages above and beyond what is necessary to compensate them for their injuries."[6]

II. Duty to Exercise Ordinary Care

A. *Question of Law*

To establish liability for negligence, a defendant must be found to owe a duty to the plaintiff.[7] The Mississippi Supreme Court articulated the duty owed in negligence as:

> The standard of care applicable in cases of alleged negligent conduct is whether the party charged with negligence acted as a reasonable and prudent person would have under the same or similar circumstances. A defendant must only take reasonable measures to remove or protect against "foreseeable hazards" that he knows about or should know about in the exercise of due care. A defendant is obligated solely to safeguard against reasonable

---

[1] Interim Dean and Frederick Charles Hicks Professor of Law, Oklahoma City University School of Law, Member of the Oklahoma Bar.

[2] Standard Life Ins. Co. of Indiana v. Veal, 354 So.2d 239, 247 (Miss. 1977).

[3] Glaskox By & Through Denton v. Glaskox, 614 So.2d 906, 911 (Miss. 1992).

[4] *Id.*

[5] Miller v. Provident Adver. & Mktg., 155 So.3d 181, 193 (Miss. App. 2014)

[6] Sligh v. First Nat. Bank of Holmes Cty., 704 So.2d 1020, 1028 (Miss. 1997).

[7] Doe v. Cloverleaf Mall, 829 F. Supp. 866, 870 (S.D. Miss. 1993).

probabilities and is not charged with foreseeing all occurrences, even though such occurrences are within the range of possibility.[8]

Whether the defendant has a duty is a question of law for the judge to decide.[9] The jury is instructed as to the duty owed to the plaintiff and what standard of conduct the defendant is to be held.[10]

Generally, there is no duty to affirmatively act to aid or to protect others absent certain particular circumstances or special relationships.[11] Specific acts or omissions must form the basis of a negligence claim.[12] A duty does not exist, '[i]f the defendant could not reasonably foresee any injury as the result of his acts, or if his conduct was reasonable in the light of what he could anticipate' . . . The rationale behind this foreseeability requirement is that no one is expected to guard against events which are not reasonable to be anticipated or that are so unlikely that the risks would be commonly disregarded.[13] In determining whether a duty is owed, Mississippi courts ask "whether the plaintiff's interests are entitled to legal protection against the defendant's conduct rather than focusing solely on the level of relationship between the parties."[14] In a negligence case, "the standard for determining whether the actor should have foreseen the probability of harm from his conduct is an external one, from the point of view of the actor (Defendant) prior to the occurrence."[15]

In the case of Foster by Foster v. Bass, the Mississippi Supreme Court articulated several policy factors to be considered in determining whether a duty of care exists. "The policy factors which must be considered in determining whether a duty exists have been judicially defined as follows:

The foreseeability of harm;

The degree of certainty of injury;

The closeness of the connection between the defendant's conduct and the injury suffered;

The moral blame attached to the defendant's conduct;

The policy of preventing future harm;

The extent of the burden to the defendant and consequence to the community of imposing a duty to exercise care with resulting liability for breach, and; the availability, cost, and prevalence of insurance for the risk involved."[16]

---

[8] Donald v. Amoco Prod. Co., 735 So.2d 161, 174 (Miss. 1999).

[9] Id.

[10] ENCYCLOPEDIA OF MISS. LAW § 52:14 (2018).

[11] Higginbotham v. Hill Bros. Const. Co., 962 So.2d 46, 56 (Miss. Ct. App. 2006), cert. denied, 962 So.2d 38 (Miss. 2007); Jones v. James Reeves Contractors, Inc., 701 So.2d 774 (Miss. 1997).

[12] McWilliams By and Through Smith v. City of Pascagoula, 657 So.2d 1110, 1111 (Miss. 1995).

[13] Karpovs v. State, 663 F.2d 640, 649 (5th Cir. 1981); Gulledge v. Shaw, 880 So.2d 288 (Miss. 2004).

[14] Scafide v. Bazzone, 962 So.2d 585, 592 (Miss. Ct. App. 2006).

[15] Smith v. United States, 284 F.Supp. 259, 262 (S.D. Miss. 1967), aff'd 394 F.2d 482 (5th Cir. 1968).

[16] Foster by Foster v. Bass, 575 So.2d 967, 979 (Miss. 1990) (citations omitted).

B.   *The Question of Fact*

i.   Elements

Whether a breach of duty occurred is a question for the jury.[17] "The standard of care applicable in cases of alleged negligent conduct is whether the party charged with negligence acted as a reasonable and prudent person would have under the same or similar circumstances."[18]

ii.   Evidence

The plaintiff must present evidence that the defendant breached a duty owed to the plaintiff. Proof must be established by a preponderance of the evidence.[19] Negligence can be shown by demonstrating "the failure to exercise the standard of care that a reasonably prudent person would have exercised in a similar situation."[20] Plaintiffs in professional negligence typically establish the standard of care as what a reasonably prudent professional would have done in similar circumstances through expert testimony.[21]

A statutory violation may be found to be negligence *per se*, even when the statute does not impose civil liability for breach of the statute.[22] Negligence *per se* can be demonstrated with evidence of statutory violations.[23] Violation of a rule or regulation may be used to establish negligence by showing the injury was caused by the violation of the rule, and the plaintiff was one of the class of people protected by the rule.[24] Once conduct is determined to be negligent *per se*, a defendant cannot avoid liability "by attempting to prove that he or she acted reasonably under the circumstances."[25] Mississippi law has acknowledged exceptions to the establishment of negligence *per se* through statutory violations.[26] Exceptions are recognized when adherence to the statute would be absurd, when reasonable care is taken to comply with the statute, or when an actor doesn't know a statute is applicable.[27]

---

[17] Hankins Lumber Co. v. Moore, 774 So.2d 459, 464 (Miss. Ct. App. 2000).

[18] *Id.*

[19] Palmer v. Anderson Infirmary Benev. Ass'n, 656 So.2d 790, 795 (Miss. 1995).

[20] Willis v. Rehab Sols., PLLC, 82 So.3d 583, 587 (Miss. 2012) (citing Black's Law Dictionary 1061 (8th ed. 2004)).

[21] *Palmer,* 656 So.2d at 795. Miss. Law of Torts § 3:10 (2d ed.) (Expert testimony is not required "where a layman can observe and understand the negligence as a matter of common sense and practical experience.").

[22] Miss. Law of Torts § 3:11 (2d ed.) (citing Gallagher Bassett Servs., Inc. v. Jeffcoat, 887 So.2d 777, 787 (Miss. 2004), citing Snapp v. Harrison, 699 So.2d 567, 571 (Miss. 1997)). "To establish that a violation of a statute was negligence per se, a party must prove that he was a member of the class sought to be protected under the statute, that his injuries were of a type sought to be avoided, and that violation of the statute proximately caused his injuries." *Id.*

[23] Byrd v. McGill, 478 So.2d 302, 304–305 (Miss. 1985) Miss. Law of Torts § 3:12 (2d ed.).

[24] Palmer v. Anderson Infirmary Benevolent Ass'n, 656 So.2d 790,796 (Miss. 1995). *See also* Williams ex rel. Raymond v. Wal-Mart Stores East LP, 99 So.3d 112, 120 (Miss. 2012).

[25] Williams ex rel. Raymond v. Wal-Mart Stores East LP, 99 So.3d 112, 116 (Miss. 2012) (citing Rains v. Bend of the River, 124 S.W.3d 580, 589-90 (Tenn. App. 2003)).

[26] Miss. Law of Torts § 3:13 (2d ed.).

[27] Otto v. Specialties, Inc., 386 F. Supp. 1240, 1244 (N.D. Miss. 1974); Teche Lines, Inc., v. Danforth, 195 Miss.

III.   Breach of Duty

A.   Elements

Negligence is the failure to use reasonable care.[28] Reasonable care is that degree of care which a reasonably careful person would use under like or similar circumstances.[29] The duty to use reasonable care has similarly been explained as "the requirement to conform to a specific standard for the protection of others against the unreasonable risk of injury."[30]

B.   Evidence

Although the question of whether a duty exists is a question of law for the judge to decide, breach of duty is normally an issue resolved by the jury.[31] Evidence must be presented to show a breach of duty on the part of the defendant.[32] The plaintiff must specifically identify the act(s) amounting to a breach of duty by the defendant. The plaintiff must show that the defendant committed the act(s) and that the commission of the act(s) breached a duty to the plaintiff.[33] A breach of duty must be shown by a preponderance of the evidence.[34]

IV.   Causation

A.   Elements

A plaintiff must prove causation in fact and proximate cause to recover in a negligence action.[35] Cause-in-fact fact may be proven using the "but-for" causation test.[36] Cause in fact has been defined as "that cause which, in natural and continuous sequence unbroken by any efficient intervening cause, produces the injury and without which the injury would not have occurred."[37] Cause-in-fact may also be established using the substantial factor test.[38] Normally this test is used when multiple defendants are involved. When applying the substantial factor test the jury considers "whether the negligence of a particular tortfeasor was a substantial factor in bringing about the harm."[39]

[ ] 226, 12 So.2d 784 (Miss. 1943); Moore v. K & J Enters., 856 So.2d 621, 625 (Miss. Ct. App. 2003).

[28] Miss. Prac. Model Jury Instr. Civil § 14:1 (2d ed.) (citing Vaughn v. Ambrosino, 883 So.2d 1167 (Miss. 2004)).

[29] Id. See Doe ex rel. Doe v. Wright Sec. Servs., Inc., 950 So.2d 1076, 1081 (Miss. Ct. App. 2007).

[30] Clausell v. Bourque, 158 So.3d 384, 391 (Miss. Ct. App. 2015).

[31] Encyclopedia of Miss. Law § 52:14 (2018).

[32] Miss. Law of Torts § 3:9 (2d ed.).

[33] Id.

[34] Id. at § 3:10.

[35] Allen v. Choice Hotels Intern., 942 So.2d 817, 827 (Miss. Ct. App. 2006).

[36] Encyclopedia of Miss. Law § 52:20 (2018).

[37] Glenn v. Peoples, 185 So.3d 981, 986 (Miss. 2015) (quoting Glover ex rel. Glover v. Jackson State University, 968 So.2d 1267, 1277 (Miss. 2007)).

[38] Id.

[39] Encyclopedia of Miss. Law § 52:20 (citing Glenn v. Peoples, 185 So.3d 981, 986 (Miss. 2015)) (quoting Glover ex rel. Glover v. Jackson State University, 968 So.2d 1267, 1291 n.11, (Miss. 2007)).

Proximate cause is often referred to as legal cause or foreseeability.[40] To establish proximate cause the plaintiff must show "that the injury was a direct, foreseeable, natural (or some other such word) consequence of the negligent act."[41] "The test for determining issues of proximate cause is foreseeability."[42] This passage from a 1944 Mississippi Supreme Court case is frequently cited to define foreseeability. The passage is, as follows:

> The settled law in this state may be summarized in the form of a diagram, as follows: The area in which liability is imposed is that which is within the circle of reasonable foreseeability using the original point at which the negligent act was committed or became operative and thence looking in every direction as the semidiameters of the circle, and those injuries from which this point could or should have been reasonably foreseen as something likely to happen are within the field of liability, while those which, although foreseeable, were foreseeable only as remote possibilities, those only slightly probable, are beyond and not within the circle—in all of which time, place and circumstance play their respective and important parts.[43]

Recent appellate opinions have defined foreseeability in various ways, such as: "whether [an event] is likely to happen, even though the likelihood may not be sufficient to amount to a comparative probability;"[44] "whether [the injury] is the type of damage which reasonably should be anticipated (or foreseen before the fact) as a result of [the negligent act];"[45] and, "that a person of ordinary intelligence should have anticipated the dangers that his negligent act created for others."[46]

B. Evidence

Causation is a question of fact and is typically determined by the jury.[47] Foreseeability questions are to be determined by the jury "where reasonable minds may differ and sufficient evidence of negligence is presented."[48] Proximate cause may be established through "direct evidence or reasonable inference that such negligence proximately contributed to the damage."[49] The Supreme Court of Mississippi has "held consistently that it is solely within the

---

[40] Miss. Law of Torts § 3:17 (2d ed.) (citing Rolison v. City of Meridian, 691 So.2d 440 (Miss. 1997)).

[41] Miss. Law of Torts § 3:17 (2d ed.)

[42] Encyclopedia of Miss. Law § 52:45 (2016) (citing Marshall Durbin Inc. v. Tew, 362 So.2d 601, 603 (Miss. 1978)).

[43] Encyclopedia of Miss. Law § 52:45 (2016) (citing Wright v. Illinois Cent. R.R., 196 Miss. 150, 16 So.2d 381, 383 (Miss. 1944) (quoting Mauney v. Gulf Ref. Co., 193 Miss. 421, 9 So.2d 249, 9 So.2d 780, 781 (Miss. 1942)).

[44] *Gulledge,* 880 So.2d at 288.

[45] City of Jackson v. Estate of Stewart ex rel. Womack, 908 So.2d 703, 713 (Miss. 2005).

[46] Davis v. Christian Broth. Homes of Jackson, Mississippi, Inc., 957 So.2d 390 (Miss. Ct. App. 2007).

[47] *Doe ex rel. Doe*, 950 So.2d at 1085.

[48] Rhaly v. Waste Mgmt. of Mississippi, Inc., 43 So.3d 509, 514 (Miss. Ct. App. 2010).

[49] Barkley v. Miller Transporters, Inc., 450 So.2d 416, 418 (Miss. 1984)(citing Tombigbee Electric Power Ass'n v. Gandy, 216 Miss. 444, 452, 62 So.2d 567, 569 (1953)).

province of the jury to resolve vital evidentiary conflicts on issues of negligence."[50] In cases where a defendant admits liability the jury must still decide foreseeability and causation. A defendant's stipulation to the elements of duty and breach does not constitute a stipulation to causation and foreseeability.[51]

V.   Damages

A.   Elements

Damages in a negligence case include an amount of money that will compensate the plaintiff for her harm and injuries as a result of the defendant's negligence.[52] Compensatory damages are intended to "replace the loss caused by the wrong or injury" done to the plaintiff.[53]

B.   Evidence

Damages "must be reasonably ascertainable . . . and must be the proximate and reasonable result of the negligent act."[54] There is no pre-determined rule for determining damages. It is the primary province of the jury to determine the amount of damages to award.[55]

---

[50] Council v. Duprel, 250 Miss. 269, 291, 165 So.2d 134, 143 (Miss. 1964).

[51] Fisher v. Deer, 942 So.2d 217, 219, (Miss. App. 2006).

[52] MISS. PLAIN LANG. MODEL JURY INSTR. CIV. 5000 & 5007 (2015).

[53] Richardson v. Canton Farm Equip., Inc., 608 So.2d 1240, 1250 (Miss. 1992).

[54] Meridian Star v. Kay, 207 Miss. 78, 41 So.2d 30, 33 (1949), *error overruled*, 207 Miss. 78, 41 So.2d 746 (1949), (remanding for jury determination as to proper amount of damages).

[55] Teasley v. Buford, 876 So.2d 1070, 1083 (Miss. Ct. App. 2004).

CHAPTER 26

MISSOURI

MISSOURI

Lee F. Peoples[1]

I. Purpose of Tort Law

The Missouri Court of Appeals has stated that the "foremost policy of the tort law is to deter harmful conduct and to ensure that innocent victims of that conduct will have redress."[2] Principles of equity and economic efficiency underline the Court's policy "that the costs of the pervasive injury . . . shall be borne by those who can control the danger and make equitable distribution of the losses, rather than by those who are powerless to protect themselves."[3] In another case the Missouri Court of Appeals stated that the fundamental objectives of tort law is "concerned with the allocation of losses arising out of human activities. . . ."[4] The rules of liability established by the legislature and the courts "ought to function to promote care and punish neglect by placing the burden of their breach on the person who can best avoid the harm."[5] The Missouri Court of Appeals has stated "[a] primary function of tort law is to provide compensation to injured persons."[6]

II. Duty to Exercise Ordinary Care

A. Question of Law

To establish a case for negligence, a plaintiff must show "that the defendant had a duty to protect the plaintiff from injury."[7] The existence of a duty is dependent upon whether the risk of injury was foreseeable.[8] "The concept of foreseeability is paramount in determining whether a duty exists."[9] According to the Missouri Court of Appeals, "[a] duty of care arises out of circumstances in which there is a foreseeable likelihood that particular acts or

---

[1] Interim Dean and Frederick Charles Hicks Professor of Law, Oklahoma City University School of Law, Member of the Oklahoma Bar.

[2] Blanks v. Fluor Corp., 450 S.W.3d 308, 373 (Mo. Ct. App. 2014).

[3] Id.

[4] Lawrence v. Bainbridge Apartments, 957 S.W.2d 400, 404 (Mo. Ct. App. 1997).

[5] Id.

[6] Roedder v. Callis, 375 S.W.3d 824, 830 (Mo. Ct. App. 2012).

[7] Richey v. Philipp, 259 S.W.3d 1, 8 (Mo. Ct. App. 2008); Krause v. U.S. Truck Co., 787 S.W.2d 708, 710 (Mo. banc 1990).

[8] Lopez v. Three Rivers Elec. Co-op., 26 S.W.3d 151, 156 (Mo. 2000).

[9] Id.

omissions will cause harm or injury."[10] Foreseeability, according to the court, "is based on common sense perceptions of the risks created by various conditions and circumstances."[11]

Whether a duty exists is purely a question of law.[12] In determining whether a duty exists, the trial court must view the evidence in a light most favorable to the plaintiff.[13] A totality of the circumstances approach is used to determine when a duty exists.[14]

A duty may be created by statute, from the relationship between parties, or a party may agree to assume a duty.[15] When deciding if a duty exists, the court must consider "the foreseeability of the injury, the likelihood of the injury, the magnitude of the burden of guarding against it, and the consequences of placing that burden on the defendant."[16] The possibility of harm is insufficient to impose a duty. The test of whether a duty exists does not focus on "the balance of probabilities, but of the existence of some probability of sufficient moment to induce the reasonable mind to take the precautions which would avoid it."[17]

The Missouri Supreme Court and Missouri Legislature have noted the deterrent value of tort law as an important function in preventing negligence.[18] In this context, the Missouri Supreme Court has balanced the economic burden of imposing a duty against the magnitude of preventable injury.[19]

B. *Question of Fact*

i. Elements

It is for the jury to determine the degree of care required and whether a duty of care was breached.[20] Negligence is defined by the Missouri Civil Jury Instructions as "the failure to use ordinary care." Ordinary care is defined as "that degree of care that an ordinarily careful person would use under the same or similar circumstances."[21]

---

[10] Richardson v. QuikTrip Corp., 81 S.W.3d 54, 60 (Mo. Ct. App. 2002).

[11] *Id.* at 63.

[12] Aaron v. Havens, 758 S.W.2d 446, 447 (Mo. 1988) (en banc).

[13] Mo. Prac., Personal Injury and Torts Handbook § 2:5 (2015 ed.) (citing Parra v. Bldg. Erection Servs., 982 S.W.2d 278, 283 (Mo. Ct. App. W.D. 1998)).

[14] Richardson, 81 S.W.3d at 62. (discussing when a duty is owed by a business owner to an invitee to protect from criminal acts of unknown third parties).

[15] Mo. Prac., Personal Injury and Torts Handbook § 2:5 (2015 ed.) (citing Lumbermens Mut. Cas. Co. v. Thornton, 92 S.W.3d 259 (Mo. Ct. App. W.D. 2002)).

[16] *Id.*

[17] Lopez v. Three Rivers Elec. Co-op., 26 S.W.3d 151, 156 (Mo. 2000).

[18] State ex rel. D.M. v. Hoester, 681 S.W.2d 449, 452 (Mo. 1984).

[19] Bradley v. Ray, 904 S.W.2d 302, 310 (Mo. Ct. App. 1995).

[20] Keenan v. Miriam Found., 784 S.W.2d 298, 304 (Mo. Ct. App. 1990).

[21] Mo. Approved Jury Instr. (Civil) § 11.07 (7th ed.).

ii. Evidence

The burden is on the plaintiff to present evidence of the degree of care required.[22] Federal regulations are relevant and admissible to show the degree of care owed in a particular case.[23] State statutes and municipal ordinances may be used to define the standard of care.[24] Provisions of a building code can provide evidence of the standard of care.[25] Violation of a rule or regulation may be used to establish negligence by showing the injury (1) was caused by the violation of the rule, (2) the injury was the type intended to be prevented by the rule, and (3) the plaintiff was one of the class of people protected by the rule.[26] Although industry standards, custom, and usage are admissible to help determine the standard of care, they do not conclusively establish a legal standard of care.[27]

III.   Breach of Duty

A.   Elements

A plaintiff must establish that the defendant breached a duty of care by a preponderance of the evidence to prevail in a negligence case.[28] Breach has been defined by the Missouri Court of Appeals as "the commission or omission of an act that the actor should or should not have done in accordance with the relevant standard of care."[29] The jury must decide the issue of negligence "when there is conflicting evidence on the issue or where the facts being undisputed, reasonable minds could draw different conclusions therefrom."[30]

B.   Evidence

A breach of duty may be shown through evidence "of omission or affirmative act."[31] Evidence of industry standards, custom, or usage are admissible to show negligence.[32] Violations of relevant federal administrative law rules "may be hypothesized as evidence supporting a finding of negligence."[33]

---

[22] Saunders v. Baska, 397 S.W.3d 44, 49 (Mo. Ct. App. 2013).

[23] Giddens v. Kansas City S. Ry. Co., 29 S.W.3d 813 (Mo. 2000).

[24] Strong v. Am. Cyanamid Co., 261 S.W.3d 493, 517 (Mo. Ct. App. 2007) (*overruled on other grounds by* Badahman v. Catering St. Louis, 395 S.W.3d 29 (Mo. 2013)). *See* Fields v. Missouri Power & Light Co., 374 S.W.2d 17, 30 (Mo. 1963).

[25] Stacy v. Truman Med. Ctr., 836 S.W.2d 911 (Mo. 1992) (*abrogated on other grounds by* Southers v. City of Farmington, 263 S.W.3d 603 (Mo. 2008)).

[26] Blackwell v. CSF Props. 2 LLC, 443 S.W.3d 711, 716 (Mo. App., 2014).

[27] Basta v. Kansas City Power & Light Co., 456 S.W.3d 447, 453 (Mo. Ct. App. 2014); Robertson v. Clark Bros. Builders, 786 S.W.2d 602 (Mo. Ct. App. 1990).

[28] Mo. Prac., Personal Injury and Torts Handbook § 2:2 (2015 ed.).

[29] Ostrander v. O'Banion, 152 S.W.3d 333, 338 (Mo. Ct. App. 2004).

[30] Mo. Prac., Personal Injury and Torts Handbook § 2:3 (2015 ed.).

[31] Karnes v. Ray, 809 S.W.2d 738, 741 (Mo. Ct. App. 1999).

[32] Basta, 456 S.W.3d at 453.

[33] Vintila v. Drassen, 52 S.W.3d 28, 37 (Mo. Ct. App. 2001) (citing Giddens v. Kansas City S. Ry. Co., 29 S.W.3d 813, 821 (Mo.banc 2000)).

IV. Causation

A. *Elements*

A plaintiff in a negligence action must prove causation in fact and proximate cause.[34] The Missouri Supreme Court has defined proximate cause as:

> The practical test of proximate cause is generally considered to be whether the negligence of the defendant is that cause or act of which the injury was the natural or probable consequence. . . . Thus, from the essential meaning of proximate cause arises the principle that in order for an act to constitute the proximate cause of an injury, *some* injury, if not the precise one in question, must have been reasonably foreseeable. The cases discussing proximate cause contain the exasperating caveat that in deciding questions of proximate cause and efficient, intervening cause, each case must be decided on its own facts, and it is seldom that one decision controls another.[35]

"Mathematical certainty" is not required to prove foreseeability.[36] The plaintiff needs to show only that "the party charged knew or should have known there was an appreciable chance some injury would result."[37]

B. *Evidence*

Causation is an issue for the jury to determine.[38] According to the Missouri Court of Appeals "[t]he determination of proximate cause is dependent upon the particular facts of each case and is generally an issue reserved for the trier of fact."[39]

V. Damages

A. *Elements*

Damages are "but a single element, albeit a necessary one, of a tort."[40] The aim of the law "in every case is reasonable compensation to the injured party."[41] According to the

---

[34] Callahan v. Cardinal Glennon Hosp., 863 S.W.2d 852, 865 (Mo. banc 1993).

[35] Mo. Prac., Personal Injury and Torts Handbook § 2:7 (2015 ed.) (citing Krause v. U.S. Truck Co., 787 S.W.2d 708, 710 (Mo. 1990)).

[36] Shannon v. Wal-Mart Stores, Inc., 974 S.W.2d 588, 591 (Mo.App.1998).

[37] Jones v. Trittler, 983 S.W.2d 165, 168 (Mo. Ct. App. 1998).

[38] English v. Empire Dist. Elec. Co., 220 S.W.3d 849, 856 (Mo. Ct. App. 2007) (*distinguished on other grounds by* Bryan v. Peppers, 323 S.W.3d 70 (Mo.App. S.D. 2010); Coin Acceptors, Inc. v. Haverstock, Garrett & Roberts LLP, 405 S.W.3d 19 (Mo.App. E.D. 2013)).

[39] Id.

[40] Travelers Indem. Co. v. Chumbley, 394 S.W.2d 418, 422 (Mo. App. S.D. 1965).

[41] Mo. Damages § 1.2 (MoBar 3rd ed. 2012) (citing Dimick v. Noonan, 242 S.W.2d 599, 603 (Mo. App. W.D. 1951); DeSalme v. Union Elec. Light & Power Co., 102 S.W.2d 779, 782 (Mo. App. E.D. 1937)).

Missouri Court of Appeals "the ultimate test for damage is whether the award will fairly and reasonably compensate the plaintiff for the injuries."[42]

B. Evidence

It is within the province of the jury to assess damages.[43] "There is no exact formula to determine whether a jury's verdict for compensatory damages is excessive and each case must be decided on its own facts and merits."[44] The Missouri Supreme Court stated "[a] plaintiff is entitled to full compensation for past or present injuries that the plaintiff has shown by a preponderance of the evidence were caused by the defendant."[45] A plaintiff "only needs to produce the best evidence available to afford a reasonable basis for estimating the damages." "If the damages cannot be measured exactly, 'the law only requires that the evidence, with such certainty as [it] will permit, lay a foundation to enable the jury to make a fair and reasonable estimate.'"[46]

---

[42] Anderson v. Burlington N. R.R. Co., 700 S.W.2d 469, 476 (Mo. App. E.D. 1985) (*distinguished on other grounds by* Lindquist v. Scott Radiological Grp., 168 S.W.3d 635 (Mo. App. E.D. 2005)).

[43] Maldonado v. Gateway Hotel Holdings, L.L.C., 154 S.W.3d 303, 311 (Mo. Ct. App. E.D. 2003).

[44] MO. PRAC., PERSONAL INJURY AND TORTS HANDBOOK § 5:1 (2015 ed.) (citing Maldonado v. Gateway Hotel Holdings, L.L.C., 154 S.W.3d 303 (Mo. Ct. App. E.D. 2003)).

[45] MO. APPROVED JURY INSTR. CIVIL § 4.01 (7th ed.) (citing Swartz v. Gale Webb Transp. Co., 215 S.W.3d 127 (Mo. 2007)).

[46] MO. DAMAGES § 1.44 (MoBar 3rd ed. 2012) (quoting Weindel v. DeSoto Rural Fire Prot. Ass'n, 765 S.W.2d 712, 714 (Mo. App. E.D. 1989), *abrogated on other grounds by* Purcell Tire & Rubber Co. v. Exec. Beechcraft, Inc., 59 S.W.3d 505 (Mo. banc 2001)).

CHAPTER 27

MONTANA

MONTANA
Lee F. Peoples[1]

I. Purpose of Tort Law

According to the Montana Supreme Court, "the fundamental purpose of any tort remedy is to return the plaintiff to his or her rightful position, or the position or state the party *would have attained* had the wrong not occurred."[2] The Court has stated that "[t]he law of torts works to ensure that an award of damages restores an injured party as near as possible to the party's pre-tort position—no better, no worse."[3] A similar statement is found in a 2007 decision of the Montana Supreme Court. That statement is, as follows: "[t]he law of torts 'attempts primarily to put an injured person in a position as nearly as possible equivalent to his position prior to the tort.'"[4] Another Montana court has articulated the essential purposes of tort law as the "compensation of the victim, behavior alteration, deterrence of civil wrong doing, and moral accountability."[5]

II. Duty to Exercise Ordinary Care

A. *Question of Law*

To establish negligence, a plaintiff must prove that a "defendant owed the plaintiff a legal duty."[6] Whether or not a duty exists is a question of law to be determined by the court.[7] A court determines if a duty exists on a case-by-case basis.[8] However, "[a]t the most basic level, we all share the common law duty to exercise the level of care that a reasonable and prudent person would under the same circumstances."[9]

The existence of a legal duty "[d]epends largely on whether the allegedly negligent act was foreseeable."[10] Duty can be measured "by the scope of the risk which negligent

---

[1] Interim Dean and Frederick Charles Hicks Professor of Law, Oklahoma City University School of Law, Member of the Oklahoma Bar.

[2] Maloney v. Home & Inv. Ctr., 2000 MT 34, ¶ 48, 298 Mont. 213, 994 P.2d 1124.

[3] Lampi v. Speed, 2011 MT 231, ¶ 21, 362 Mont. 122, 261 P.3d 1000.

[4] Sunburst Sch. Dist. No. 2 v. Texaco, Inc., 2007 MT 183, ¶ 32, 338 Mont. 259, 165 P.3d 1079 (quoting Restatement (Second) of Torts § 901 cmt. a (Am. Law Inst. 1997)).

[5] Phillips ex rel. Byrd v. Gen. Motors Corp., 126 F. Supp. 2d 1328, 1329 (D. Mont. 2001), *vacated on other grounds*, 307 F.3d 1206 (9th Cir. 2002).

[6] Peterson v. Eichhorn, 2008 MT 250, ¶ 23, 344 Mont. 540, 189 P.3d 615.

[7] Gatlin-Johnson v. City of Miles City, 2012 MT 302, ¶ 11, 367 Mont. 414, 291 P.3d 1129.

[8] Goles v. Neumann, 2011 MT 11, ¶ 17, 359 Mont. 132, 247 P.3d 1089.

[9] Fisher v. Swift Transp. Co., 2008 MT 105, ¶ 16, 342 Mont. 335, 181 P.3d 601.

[10] Gourneau ex rel. Gourneau v. Hamill, 2013 MT 300, ¶ 12, 372 Mont. 182, 311 P.3d 760.

conduct foreseeably entails."[11] The Supreme Court of Montana has stated that "[d]uty turns primarily upon foreseeability, which depends upon whether or not the injured party was within the scope of risk created by the action of the alleged tortfeasor; that is, whether the injured party was a foreseeable plaintiff."[12] "However, there is no requirement that either the particular accident that ensues or the particular plaintiff need be foreseen."[13]

In analyzing foreseeability, Montana courts consider "the moral blame attached to the defendant's conduct, the prevention of future harm, the extent of the burden imposed, the consequence to the public of imposing duty, and the availability and cost of insurance."[14] Courts will also consider "whether the imposition of that duty comports with public policy, and whether the defendant could have foreseen that his conduct could have resulted in an injury to the plaintiff."[15]

B. *Question of Fact*

i. Elements

The jury determines whether the defendant met the requisite level of care.[16] The plaintiff "must establish the standard of care by which to measure the defendant's actions; in other words, she must establish the degree of prudence, attention, and caution the defendant must exercise in fulfilling that duty of care."[17] According to the Supreme Court of Montana "[w]hat is 'ordinary care' cannot be governed by arbitrary rules, but varies according to the exigencies which require attention and vigilance."[18] The duty of care is a duty to guard "against such dangers as can or ought to be anticipated or foreseen in the exercise of reasonable prudence and care."[19] Reasonable care "may indeed encompass the duty to employ foresight so as to anticipate problems which might result in the future from one's conduct."[20]

ii. Evidence

Industry custom and usage can be considered in determining a standard of care but are not controlling on negligence questions. Custom and usage "are merely one of the factors to be considered in determining whether or not ordinary care has been exercised."[21] However, custom can never "exonerate[ ] from the imputation of negligence."[22] Violation

---

[11] Busta v. Columbus Hosp. Corp., 276 Mont. 342, 363, 916 P.2d 122, 134 (1996).

[12] Gatlin-Johnson v. City of Miles City, 2012 MT 302, ¶ 13, 367 Mont. 414, 291 P.3d 1129.

[13] Emanuel v. Great Falls Sch. Dist., 2009 MT 185, ¶ 13, 351 Mont. 56, 209 P.3d 244 (citing *Fisher*, ¶ 26).

[14] *Gatlin-Johnson*, ¶ 11 (citing *Fisher*, ¶ 22).

[15] Newman v. Lichfield, 2012 MT 47, ¶ 29, 364 Mont. 243, 272 P.3d 625 (citing *Fisher*, ¶ 22).

[16] Gunnels v. Hoyt, 194 Mont. 265, 273, 633 P.2d 1187, 1192 (1981).

[17] Dulaney v. State Farm Fire & Cas. Ins. Co., 2014 MT 127, ¶ 12, 375 Mont. 117, 324 P.3d 1211.

[18] Brown v. Columbia Amusement Co., 91 Mont. 174, 188, 6 P.2d 874, 877 (1931).

[19] Gilligan v. City of Butte, 118 Mont. 350, 357, 166 P.2d 797, 801 (1946).

[20] Goles v. Neumann, 2011 MT 11, ¶ 17, 359 Mont. 132, 247 P.3d 1089.

[21] McCollum v. D & M Lumber Co., 156 Mont. 335, 338, 479 P.2d 458, 460 (1971).

[22] Surman v. Cruse, 57 Mont. 253, 262, 187 P. 890, 893 (1920).

of a statute or rule may be used to establish negligence if the plaintiff can demonstrate "(1) the defendant violated a particular statute; (2) the Legislature intended the statute to protect a specific class of persons; (3) the plaintiff is a member of that class; (4) the Legislature intended the statute to prevent plaintiff's injury; and (5) the Legislature intended the statute to regulate a member of defendant's class."[23]

III. Breach of Duty

A. Elements

The Montana Supreme Court has defined negligence as "breach of a legal duty resulting in actual loss or damage."[24] Without a breach of duty there can be no liability for negligence.[25] The question of breach is a question of fact for the jury to decide.[26] "At the most basic level, we all share the common law duty to exercise the level of care that a reasonable and prudent person would under the same circumstances."[27]

B. Evidence

In establishing a breach of duty by the defendant, the plaintiff does not have to demonstrate that the exact injury sustained was foreseeable.[28] It is enough that a "reasonably prudent defendant can or should foresee a danger of direct injury"[29] and "whether or not the injured party was within the scope of risk created by the action of the alleged tortfeasor; that is, whether the injured plaintiff was a foreseeable plaintiff."[30]

In determining whether a defendant breached a duty, the jury considers the defendant's conduct prospectively:

> [J]udges sometimes say that as danger increases, so does the duty. But judges do not mean by this that a duty of reasonable care suddenly becomes a duty of excessive care. Instead, they are using 'duty' in the sense of specific conduct and mean only that the duty remains the same—reasonable care under the circumstances—while circumstances of special danger show that reasonable care may be deemed by the trier of fact to require more precautions. In many such cases the words may be the words of duty, but the process of good decisionmaking requires a determination about what counts as ordinary care under the circumstances—the question of breach, not duty.[31]

---

[23] Olson v. Shumaker Trucking & Excavating Contractors, Inc., 2008 MT 378, ¶ 66, 347 Mont. 1, 196 P.3d 1265.

[24] Papich v. Quality Life Concepts, Inc., 2004 MT 116, ¶ 20, 321 Mont. 156, 91 P.3d 553.

[25] Rauh v. Jensen, 161 Mont. 443, 447, 507 P.2d 520, 522 (1973).

[26] Harrington v. Crystal Bar, Inc., 2013 MT 209, ¶ 10, 371 Mont. 165, 306 P.3d 342.

[27] Fisher v. Swift Transp. Co., Inc., 2008 MT 105, ¶ 16, 342 Mont. 335, 181 P.3d 601.

[28] Deeds v. United States, 306 F. Supp. 348, 361 (D. Mont. 1969).

[29] Newman ex rel. Newman v. Lichfield, 2012, MT 24, ¶ 31, 364 Mont. 243, 272 P.3d 625.

[30] Gatlin-Johnson v. City of Miles City, 2012 MT 302, ¶ 13, 367 Mont. 414, 291 P.3d 1129.

[31] Harrington v. Crystal Bar, Inc., 2013 MT 209, ¶ 14, 371 Mont. 165, 306 P.3d 342, n. 3 (quoting Dan B. Dobbs et al., The Law of Torts vol. 2, § 253, 7 (2d ed., West 2011)).

IV. Causation

A. *Elements*

Negligence on the part of the defendant "is the direct cause of the plaintiff's injury if there is an uninterrupted chain of events from the negligent act to the plaintiff's injury."[32] In cases where intervening causation is not an issue, "proof of causation is satisfied by proof that a party's conduct was a cause-in-fact of the damage alleged."[33] The Montana Supreme Court has held that "a party's act is the cause-in-fact of an event if 'the event would not have occurred but-for that conduct.'"[34]

In cases where intervening causation is alleged, a two-tiered analysis is employed. The trier of fact must first determine "whether the defendant's negligent act was a cause-in-fact of the plaintiff's injury."[35] In the context of intervening causation, "cause-in-fact is established by the 'substantial factor' test."[36] Furthermore, "[i]f two forces are actively operating, one because of the actor's negligence, the other not because of any misconduct on his part, and each of itself is sufficient to bring about harm to another, the actor's negligence may be found to be a substantial factor in bringing it about."[37]

Secondly, the court must determine "whether the defendant's act was a proximate cause of the plaintiff's injury."[38] Proximate cause in the context of intervening causation was discussed in the case of *Fisher v. Swift Transport* as follows:

> To establish proximate cause, the plaintiff must show that it was the "defendant's breach which 'foreseeably and substantially' caused his injury." Though foreseeability "is generally properly confined to the duty element of negligence under Montana law, where a dispute presents the issue of an intervening act of a third party . . . we address foreseeability in the proximate cause context as well."[39]

A foreseeable intervening act will not break the chain of causation.[40] As the Supreme Court of Montana has stated "if one of the reasons that makes a defendant's act negligent is a greater risk of a particular harmful result occurring, and that harmful result does occur, the defendant is generally liable. The test is based on foreseeability."[41]

---

[32] *Fisher*, ¶ 36 (citing Cusenbary v. Mortensen, 1999 MT 221, ¶ 26, 296 Mont. 25, 987 P.2d 351).

[33] Neal v. Nelson, 2008 MT 426, ¶ 32, 347 Mont. 431, 198 P.3d 819 (quoting Busta v. Columbus Hosp. Corp., 276 Mont. 342, 371, 916 P.2d 122, 139 (1996)).

[34] *Fisher*, ¶ 36 (quoting *Busta*, 276 Mont. at 371, 916 P.2d at 139).

[35] *Id.*, ¶ 39 (citing *Cusenbary*, ¶ 28).

[36] *Busta*, 276 Mont. at 364, 916 P.2d at 135.

[37] Christofferson ex rel. Christofferson v. City of Great Falls, 2003 MT 189, ¶ 66, 316 Mont. 469, 74 P.3d 1021 (quoting RESTATEMENT (SECOND) OF TORTS § 432(2) (1965)).

[38] *Fisher*, ¶ 39 (citing *Cusenbary*, ¶ 28).

[39] *Fisher*, ¶ 39 (citations omitted).

[40] *Cusenbary*, ¶ 25.

[41] *Id.*

B. *Evidence*

Causation is an issue to be determined by a jury.[42] The plaintiff bears the burden of presenting evidence of causation.[43] Evidence of the foreseeability of risks of harm in general and risks as they relate to a particular plaintiff are admissible.[44] Juries must have knowledge of what was foreseeable to a defendant "[i]n order to make an informed determination" in a negligence case.[45]

When juries analyze causation in a negligence action "the inquiry must be whether the defendant could have reasonably foreseen that his or her conduct could have resulted in an injury to the plaintiff. [t]he particular resulting injury need not have been foreseeable."[46]

IV.   Damages

A. *Elements*

In order to recover in a negligence action a plaintiff must show "actual loss or damage."[47] The measure of damages arising from obligations other than contract has been defined by the Montana Legislature as "the amount which will compensate for all the detriment proximately caused thereby, whether it could have been anticipated or not."[48] The Montana Supreme Court has held that "it is not necessary to show that [the wrongdoer] ought to have anticipated the particular injury which did result; but it is sufficient to show that he ought to have anticipated that some injury was likely to result as the reasonable and natural consequence of his negligence."[49]

Several cases have articulated the purpose of damage awards under Montana law. "It is the policy of the law that the injured party be put in the same condition he would have been if the tort had not been committed, so far as money can do it."[50] "[O]ne who is injured by the wrongful act of another, whether it be a negligent act or a breach of contract, has a right to recover such damages as will make him whole again."[51] "The law of torts works to ensure that an award of damages restores an injured party as near as possible to the party's pre-tort position—no better, no worse."[52]

---

[42] Prindel v. Ravalli County, 2006 MT 62, ¶ 65, 331 Mont. 338, 133 P.3d 165.

[43] Abraham v. Nelson, 2002 MT 94, ¶ 27, 309 Mont. 366, 46 P.3d 628.

[44] Newman v. Lichfield, 2012 MT 47, ¶ 35, 364 Mont. 243, 272 P.3d 625 (holding that evidence of previous similar problems are admissible *so long as they are predictable of the particular problem at issue* and the defendant was aware of these problems).

[45] *Id.* ¶ 32.

[46] Hinkle v. Shepherd Sch. Dist. No. 37, 2004 MT 175, ¶ 30, 322 Mont. 80, 93 P.3d 1239. *See also* Prindel v. Ravalli County, 2006 MT 62, ¶ 39, 331 Mont. 338, 133 P.3d 165.

[47] Papich v. Quality Life Concepts, Inc., 2004 MT 116, ¶ 20, 321 Mont. 156, 91 P.3d 553.

[48] Mont. Code Ann. § 27-1-317 (West).

[49] Mize v. Rocky Mountain Bell Tel. Co., 38 Mont. 521, 532, 100 P. 971, 973 (1909), *overruled on other grounds by* Dawson v. Hill & Hill Truck Lines, 206 Mont. 325, 333, 671 P.2d 589, 594 (1983).

[50] Quong v. McEvoy, 70 Mont. 99, 224 P. 266, 267 (1924) (citing 1 J. G. SUTHERLAND, A TREATISE ON THE LAW OF DAMAGES § 105 (2d ed. 1893)).

[51] Bos v. Dolajak, 167 Mont. 1, 6, 534 P.2d 1258, 1260 (1975).

[52] Lampi v. Speed, 2011 MT 231, ¶ 21, 362 Mont. 122, 261 P.3d 1000.

B. *Evidence*

It is the jury's function to make the factual determinations necessary to award damages.[53] In making a determination of damages the jury is "allowed a wide latitude."[54] The weight to be given to evidence relating to damages is for the jury to determine.[55] The Supreme Court of Montana has held that "[d]amages must be left to the enlightened consciences of the jurors, aided by the circumstances of each particular case."[56] The Court specifically addressed an award of damages in personal injury actions in *Sheehan v. DeWitt*, noting that "there is no measuring stick by which to determine the amount of damages to be awarded and each case must depend upon its own peculiar facts."[57]

---

[53] Seltzer v. Morton, 2007 MT 62, ¶ 94, 336 Mont. 225, 154 P.3d 561.

[54] McNair v. Berger, 92 Mont. 441, 461, 15 P.2d 834, 839 (1932).

[55] Nesbitt v. City of Butte, 118 Mont. 84, 94, 163 P.2d 251, 256 (1945).

[56] Waltee v. Petrolane, Inc., 162 Mont. 317, 322, 511 P.2d 975, 978 (1973).

[57] Sheehan v. DeWitt, 150 Mont. 86, 91, 430 P.2d 652, 655 (1967).

CHAPTER 28

NEBRASKA

NEBRASKA

Lee F. Peoples[1]

I. Purpose of Tort Law

The Nebraska Supreme Court has noted that a primary purpose of recovery in tort is just compensation for harm.[2] Tort actions are maintainable to give "compensation, indemnity or restitution for harms."[3] "The basic principle of the law of damages [in the context of torts] is that such compensation in money shall be allowed for the loss sustained as will restore the loser to the same value of property status as he occupied just preceding the loss."[4] The Court has held that "every person sustaining injury through [a wrongful act] is entitled to recover his loss."[5] One may be held answerable for an act that injures another, even if the act was done without malice.[6]

II. Duty to Exercise Ordinary Care

A. Question of Law

A plaintiff in a negligence case must establish that the defendant had a legal duty to protect the plaintiff from injury.[7] The Supreme Court of Nebraska discussed the essence of duty in a negligence case in *Holden v. Urban,* as follows:

> '[D]uty' is a question of whether the defendant is under any obligation for the benefit of the particular plaintiff, and in negligence cases, the duty is always the same—to conform to the legal standard of reasonable conduct in light of the apparent risk. . . .
>
> A duty, in negligence cases, may be defined as an obligation, to which the law will give recognition and effect, to conform to a particular standard of conduct toward another.[8]

---

[1] Interim Dean and Frederick Charles Hicks Professor of Law, Oklahoma City University School of Law, Member of the Oklahoma Bar. Citations and other materials in this chapter were adapted from Daniel A. Morris & Collin Mangrum, Nebraska Jury Instructions—Civil 2d. (2015).

[2] "L" Invs., Ltd. v. Lynch, 212 Neb. 319, 326-27, 322 N.W.2d 651, 656 (1982).

[3] *Id.* at 326, 322 N.W.2d at 656 (quoting Restatement (Second) of Torts § 901 (1979)).

[4] Davenport v. Intermountain Ry., Light & Power Co., 108 Neb. 387, 393, 187 N.W. 905, 907 (1922).

[5] Hindmarsh v. Sulpho Saline Bath Co., 108 Neb. 168, 173, 187 N.W. 806, 808 (1922).

[6] Newman v. Christensen, 149 Neb. 471, 476, 31 N.W.2d 417, 419-20 (1948).

[7] Holden v. Urban, 224 Neb. 472, 474, 398 N.W.2d 699, 701 (1987).

[8] *Id.* at 474-75, 398 N.W.2d at 701 (quoting W. Page Keeton et al., Prosser and Keeton on the Law of Torts § 53 (5th ed. 1984)).

Whether the defendant owes a plaintiff a legal duty is a question of law and is "dependent on the facts in a particular situation."[9] The question of whether a duty exists is to be determined by the court.[10]

In determining the existence of a duty, Nebraska "abandoned the risk-utility test and adopted the duty analysis set forth in the Restatement (Third) of Torts" in *A.W. v. Lancaster City School District*.[11] The Restatement approach "examines the defendant's conduct, not in terms of whether he had a 'duty' to take particular actions, but, rather, in terms of whether his conduct breached the duty to exercise the care that would be exercised by a reasonable person under the circumstances."[12]

The Nebraska Supreme Court held that "foreseeability is not a factor to be considered by courts when making determinations of duty."[13] However, the jury considers what is reasonable care under the circumstances when determining foreseeability.[14] The court may determine the issue of foreseeability only "when no reasonable person could differ on the matter."[15]

The existence of a duty is a policy determination.[16] As the Supreme Court of Nebraska explained in *Kimminau v. City of Hastings*,

> A no-duty determination, then, is grounded in public policy and based upon
> legislative facts, not adjudicative facts arising out of the particular circum-
> stances of the case. And such ruling should be explained and justified based
> on articulated policies or principles that justify exempting these actors from
> liability or modifying the ordinary duty of reasonable care.[17]

If the court determines that a duty exists, the court must then "define the scope and extent of the duty. In other words, the necessary complement of duty—the standard of care— must be ascertained."[18] The determination of the standard of care is a question of law.[19] In most negligence cases the standard of care will be "the reasonably prudent person standard, or some variation thereof; i.e., what a reasonable person of ordinary prudence would have done in the same or similar circumstances."[20]

A different standard is applied when the defendant "possesses special knowledge, skill, training, or experience pertaining to the conduct in question that is superior to that of

---

[9] *Id.*

[10] MORRIS & MANGRUM, *supra* note 1, at § 3.02.

[11] *Id.*

[12] Riggs v. Nickel, 281 Neb. 249, 256-57, 796 N.W.2d 181, 187 (2011).

[13] A.W. v. Lancaster Cty. Sch. Dist. 0001, 280 Neb. 205, 218, 784 N.W.2d 907, 918 (2010).

[14] Hodson v. Taylor, 290 Neb. 348, 362, 860 N.W.2d 162, 175 (2015).

[15] *A.W.*, 280 Neb. at 212, 784 N.W.2d at 914.

[16] *Id.* at 215, 784 N.W.2d at 916.

[17] Kimminau v. City of Hastings, 291 Neb. 133, 148, 864 N.W.2d 399, 412 (2015).

[18] Cerny v. Cedar Bluffs Junior/Senior Pub. Sch., 262 Neb. 66, 73, 628 N.W.2d 697, 703 (2001) (citing W. PAGE KEETON ET AL., PROSSER AND KEETON ON THE LAW OF TORTS § 37 (5th ed. 1984)).

[19] *Id.* at 74, 628 N.W.2d at 704 (citing DAN B. DOBBS, THE LAW OF TORTS § 122 (2000)).

[20] *Id.* at 73, 628 N.W.2d at 703-04.

the ordinary person."[21] These types of defendants are held "to a standard consistent with his or her specialized knowledge, skill, and other qualities."[22]

B. *Question of Fact*

In defining the standard of care, "the law resorts to formulae which state the standard in broad terms without attempt to fill it in in detail."[23] The standard "must be measured against a particular set of facts and circumstances"[24] because "negligence and the duty to use care do not exist in the abstract."[25] In determining the standard of care, the court "must determine what conduct the standard of care would require under the particular circumstances presented by the evidence and whether the conduct of the alleged tortfeasor conformed with the standard."[26] The violation of a rule or regulation is admissible to demonstrate negligence along with other evidence.[27]

III. **Breach of Duty**

A. *Elements*

Negligence in the state of Nebraska is defined as "doing something that a reasonably careful person would not do under similar circumstances, or failing to do something that a reasonably careful person would do under similar circumstances."[28] The Nebraska Supreme Court held that the issue of breach in a negligence case is to be decided by the jury.[29]

B. *Evidence*

The plaintiff must present evidence that the defendant breached a legal duty owed to the plaintiff.[30] Nebraska case law "has placed foreseeability in the context of breach and as a factor in determining whether there was a breach of the duty of reasonable care."[31] Nebraska has expressly adopted the position of the Restatement (Third) of Torts regarding breach of duty, which provides:

> A person acts negligently if the person does not exercise reasonable care under all the circumstances. Primary factors to consider in ascertaining

---

[21] *Id.* at 73, 628 N.W.2d at 704.

[22] *Id.* (citing Restatement (Second) of Torts § 290 cmt. f (Am. Law Inst. 1965)).

[23] *Id.* at 74, 628 N.W.2d at 704.

[24] *Id.*

[25] *Id.*

[26] *Id.* (citing Restatement (Second) of Torts § 328C cmt. b (Am. Law Inst. 1965)).

[27] *See* Scheele v. Rains, 292 Neb. 974, 982, 874 N.W.2d 867, 873 (2016).

[28] Morris & Mangrum, *supra* note 1, at § 3.02.

[29] Hodson v. Taylor, 290 Neb. 348, 362, 860 N.W.2d 162, 176 (2015).

[30] *Id.*

[31] *Id.* at 361-62, 860 N.W.2d at 175.

whether the person's conduct lacks reasonable care [include] the foreseeable likelihood that the person's conduct will result in harm, the foreseeable
severity of any harm that may ensue, and the burden of precautions to eliminate or reduce the risk of harm.[32]

The Nebraska Supreme Court explained that under this approach, foreseeability is analyzed as a fact-specific inquiry into the circumstances that
might have placed the defendant on notice of the possibility of injury. Stated
another way, the foreseeability analysis requires us to ask what the defendants knew, "when they knew it, and whether a reasonable person would
infer from those facts that there was a danger." Small changes in the facts
may make a dramatic change in how much risk is foreseeable. The law does
not require precision in foreseeing the exact hazard or consequence which
happens; it is sufficient if what occurs is one of the kinds of consequences
which might reasonably be foreseen.[33]

IV. Causation

A. Elements

A plaintiff must show damages "proximately resulting from [defendant's] undis-
charged duty."[34] Nebraska law defines proximate cause as "a cause that produces a result in
a natural and continuous sequence, and without which the result would not have occurred."[35]
According to the Nebraska Supreme Court, "[t]here are three basic requirements that must
be met to establish causation: (1) that 'but-for' the defendant's negligence, the injury would
not have occurred; (2) that the injury is the natural and probable result of the negligence; and
(3) that there is no efficient intervening cause."[36]

The first requirement for proving causation is the 'but-for' requirement which has
also been referred to as causation in fact.[37] The Nebraska Supreme Court has used both the
'substantial factor' and 'but-for' tests in determining causation in fact.[38] While a "proximate
cause must be a cause-in-fact of the damage" it does not have to be the only cause.[39] In cases
where the acts of several parties cause harm, courts use the substantial factor test. This rule
was "developed primarily for cases in which application of the but-for rule would allow each
defendant to escape responsibility because the conduct of one or more others would have
been sufficient to produce the same result."[40]

---

[32] *Id.*

[33] *Id.* at 362, 860 N.W.2d at 175-76.

[34] Brown ex rel. Watts v. Soc. Settlement Ass'n, 259 Neb. 390, 393, 610 N.W.2d 9, 11 (2000).

[35] MORRIS & MANGRUM, *supra* note 1, at § 3.41.

[36] World Radio Labs., Inc. v. Coopers & Lybrand, 251 Neb. 261, 276-77, 557 N.W.2d 1, 11 (1996).

[37] MORRIS & MANGRUM, *supra* note 1, at § 3.41.

[38] Travelers Indem. Co. v. Ctr. Bank, 202 Neb. 294, 299, 275 N.W.2d 73, 76 (1979).

[39] MORRIS & MANGRUM, *supra* note 1, at § 3.41.

[40] Reimer v. Surgical Servs. of Great Plains, P.C., 258 Neb. 671, 677, 605 N.W.2d 777, 781 (2000).

The second element of causation requires "the damage sued upon must have been the natural, probable, and reasonable consequence of the negligent act sued upon."[41] In determining whether an injury is the natural and probable result of the negligence, the injury must "be of such a character as an ordinarily prudent person could have known, or would or ought to have foreseen might probably occur as the result."[42] It is the "foreseeability of an injury that results from a negligent act [that] determines whether that injury is the 'natural and probable result' of the act."[43] "The law does not require precision in foreseeing the exact hazard or consequence which happens. It is sufficient if what occurs is one of the kind of consequences which might reasonably be foreseen."[44]

B.   *Evidence*

Causation issues are questions of fact and are to be determined by the jury.[45] The jury must be provided with instructions on proximate cause when it is an issue in the case.[46] However, when "under the facts of the case, the legal causation is clear, obvious and unmistakable," instructing the jury on probable cause is not required.[47] To prevail in a negligence action, a plaintiff must demonstrate causation by a preponderance of the evidence.[48] Proof may be shown through direct or circumstantial evidence.[49]

V.   Damages

A.   *Elements*

In negligence cases the correct measure of damages "is that which will place the aggrieved party in the position in which he or she would have been had there been no negligence."[50] Damages are intended "to place the injured party in the same position, so far as money can do it."[51] The Nebraska Supreme Court has held that "the amount of damages to be awarded is a determination solely for the factfinder."[52] A factfinder does not have to "accept a party's [damage] evidence at face value, even [when it is] not contradicted by evidence adduced by the [opposing] party."[53] An award of damages "will not be disturbed on appeal

---

[41] MORRIS & MANGRUM, *supra* note 1, at § 3.41.

[42] Becerra v. Sulhoff, 21 Neb. App. 178, 191, 837 N.W.2d 104, 114 (2013) (citing Heatherly v. Alexander, 421 F.3d 638, 645 (8th Cir. 2005)).

[43] *Id.*

[44] *Id.*

[45] Dolberg v. Paltani, 250 Neb. 297, 301, 549 N.W.2d 635, 638 (1996).

[46] *See* Enyeart v. Swartz, 218 Neb. 425, 426, 355 N.W.2d 786, 788 (1984).

[47] Danielsen v. Eickhoff, 159 Neb. 374, 380, 66 N.W.2d 913, 916 (1954) (quoting Kielley v. McCauley, 139 Neb. 60, 64, 296 N.W. 437, 439 (1941)).

[48] Meyer v. Platte Valley Const. Co., 147 Neb. 860, 863-64, 25 N.W.2d 412, 415 (1946).

[49] C.E. v. Prairie Fields Family Med. P.C., 287 Neb. 667, 676, 844 N.W.2d 56, 63 (2014).

[50] World Radio Labs., Inc. v. Coopers & Lybrand, 251 Neb. 261, 280, 557 N.W.2d 1, 13 (1996).

[51] J.D. Warehouse v. Lutz Co., 263 Neb. 189, 195, 639 N.W.2d 88, 92 (2002).

[52] Richardson v. Children's Hosp., 280 Neb. 396, 410, 787 N.W.2d 235, 246 (2010).

[53] O'Connor v. Kaufman, 260 Neb. 219, 233, 616 N.W.2d 301, 312 (2000).

NEBRASKA   215

if it is supported by the evidence and bears a reasonable relationship to the elements of the damages proved."[54]

B. *Evidence*

Plaintiffs in negligence cases must prove general and special damages to a level of reasonable certainty.[55] In defining 'reasonable certainty,' the Nebraska Supreme Court has stated the rule is "not whether there is any competent evidence in the record to show that the damages are capable of mathematically exact measurement, but whether there is sufficient evidence and data to enable the trier of fact, the jury, with a reasonable degree of certainty and exactness to estimate the actual damages."[56] Whether damages have been proven to the level of 'reasonable certainty' is a question of law.[57]

---

[54] Eicher v. Mid Am. Fin. Inv. Corp., 275 Neb. 462, 468, 748 N.W.2d 1, 8 (2008).

[55] World Radio Labs., Inc., 251 Neb. at 280, 557 N.W.2d at 13 (citing Patterson v. Swarr, May, Smith & Anderson, 238 Neb. 911, 473 N.W.2d 94 (1991)).

[56] Midlands Transp. Co. v. Apple Lines, Inc., 188 Neb. 435, 438, 197 N.W.2d 646, 648 (1972).

[57] *See* Griffith v. Drew's L.L.C., 290 Neb. 508, 515, 860 N.W.2d 749, 758 (2015).

CHAPTER 29

NEVADA

NEVADA
Matthew Granda[1]

I. Purpose of Tort Law

"Perhaps no field of the law comes closer to the lives of so many families in this country than does the law of negligence. . . ."[2] With this understanding, the Nevada Supreme Court has stated that the purpose of tort law is "to secure the protection of all citizens from the danger of physical harm" and "to enforce standards of conduct" that are "imposed by society."[3] The overriding policy of tort law in Nevada is to promote safety[4] and to protect "the weak from the insults of the stronger. . . ."[5]

Another recognized principle of tort law is to "afford compensation for injuries sustained by one person as the result of the conduct of another."[6] Compensation is appropriate where the law considers it to be "properly (and morally) required."[7]

The Nevada Supreme Court has also recognized that deterrence is an important public policy consideration that underlies tort liability.[8] This consideration furthers the goal of tort law, which is to "encourage[ ] citizens to avoid causing physical harm to others"[9] and to "enforc[e] those laws by which rights are defined and wrongs punished."[10] Deterrence is also evident in the Court's decision not to impose tort liability for purely economic losses where no accompanying physical injury or property damage exists—the

---

[1] Partner, Claggett & Sykes Law Firm, Member of the Nevada Bar.

[2] Greco v. United States, 111 Nev. 405, 407, 893 P.2d 345, 346 (1995) (quoting Justice Frankfurter in Tiller v. Atl. Coast Line R.R., Co., 318 U.S. 54, 73 (1943)).

[3] Calloway v. City of Reno, 116 Nev. 250, 260, 993 P.2d 1259, 1265 (2000) (emphasis omitted), *overruled on other grounds*, Olson v. Richard, 120 Nev. 240, 89 P.3d 31 (2004).

[4] *Id.* at 261 n.3, 993 P.2d 1266, 1269 n.3.

[5] K Mart Corp. v. Ponsock, 103 Nev. 39, 45-46, 732 P.2d 1364, 1368 (1987).

[6] *Greco*, 111 Nev. at 412, 893 P.2d at 349-50 (quoting W. PAGE KEETON ET AL., PROSSER AND KEETON ON THE LAW OF TORTS § 2, at 6 (5th ed. 1984)); *see Ponsock*, 103 Nev. at 49, 732 P.2d at 1371 (tort damages serve to make the injured party whole).

[7] Szekeres v. Robinson, 102 Nev. 93, 97, 715 P.2d 1076, 1078 (1986).

[8] Sadler v. PacificCare of Nev., Inc., 340 P.3d 1264, 1270 (Nev. 2014) (recognizing a cause of action for negligence with medical monitoring as a remedy based upon a review of other authorities that recognize, among other things, the public policy consideration of deterrence); *see Greco*, 111 Nev. at 417, 893 P.2d at 353 (Shearing & Rose, J.J., concurring in part and dissenting in part) (noting that the "public policy objectives of tort law [are] to compensate injured parties and to deter future wrongful conduct").

[9] *Sadler*, 340 P.3d at 1268 (quoting Terracon Consultants W., Inc. v. Mandalay Resort Grp., 125 Nev. 66, 72-73, 206 P.3d 81, 86 (2009)).

[10] *Ponsock*, 103 Nev. at 45-46, 732 P.2d at 1368 (quoting 2 WILLIAM BLACKSTONE, COMMENTARIES ON THE LAW OF ENGLAND bk. 3, at 2 (Lippencott & Co. 1860)).

economic loss doctrine.[11] The law cuts off tort liability at the point where only economic loss is at stake, and in the absence of accompanying physical injury or property damage, in order to "provide . . . incentives and disincentives to engage in economic activity and to make it safer."[12]

II.   Duty to Exercise Ordinary Care

A.   *Question of Law*

To establish a claim for negligence, the plaintiff must prove that the defendant "owed a duty of care to the plaintiff."[13] Duty is "an expression of . . . those policy considerations which cause the law to conclude that protection is owed."[14] "In negligence cases, the duty is invariably the same, one must 'conform to the legal standard of reasonable conduct in light of the apparent risk.'"[15] Whether a person is guilty of negligence is a question for the jury.[16]

Whether a defendant owes a plaintiff a duty of care is a generally a question of law[17] that focuses on whether the law should "safeguard the plaintiff from the consequences of the defendant's conduct."[18] "[L]iability is not without limitation,"[19] and "[f]oreseeability of harm is a predicate to establishing the element of duty, and thus is of prime importance in every case."[20] Duty requires an analysis of "foreseeability and gravity of harm, and the feasibility and availability of alternative conduct that would have prevented the harm."[21] Foreseeability of harm is determined by viewing the totality of the circumstances.[22]

Generally, "no duty is owed to control the dangerous conduct of another."[23] "However, Nevada recognizes an exception to this general rule, and a duty of care arises when

---

[11] *See Terracon Consultants W., Inc.*, 125 Nev. at 73, 206 P.3d at 86.

[12] *Terracon Consultants W., Inc.*, 125 Nev. at 76, 206 P.3d at 88 (quoting Barber Lines A/S v. M/V Donau Maru, 764 F.2d 50, 55 (1st Cir. 1985)).

[13] Scialabba v. Brandise Constr. Co., 112 Nev. 965, 968, 921 P.2d 928, 930 (1996).

[14] Merluzzi v. Larson, 96 Nev. 409, 412, 610 P.2d 739, 742 (1990), *overruled in part on other grounds by* Smith v. Clough, 106 Nev. 568, 570, 796 P.2d 592, 594 (1990).

[15] *Id.* (quoting W. PROSSER, LAW OF TORTS, § 53, at 324 (4th ed. 1971)).

[16] *E.g.*, Solen v. Virginia & Truckee R.R., Co., 13 Nev. 106, 127 (1878) (stating it would have been clearly erroneous for district judge to decide that the plaintiff was "guilty of negligence" and this "was a question for the jury to decide").

[17] *Scialabba*, 112 Nev. at 968, 921 P.2d at 930 (citing Dubus v. Dresser Indus., 649 P.2d 198, 202 (Wyo. 1982)); Turner v. Mandalay Sports Entm't, L.L.C., 124 Nev. 213, 220-21, 180 P.3d 1172, 1177 (2008).

[18] Turpel v. Sayles, 101 Nev. 35, 39, 692 P.2d 1290, 1292 (1985) (quoting Clarke v. O'Connor, 435 F.2d 104, 106 (D.C. Cir. 1970).

[19] *Merluzzi*, 96 Nev. at 412, 610 P.2d at 742 (citing Rupert v. Stienne, 90 Nev. 397, 528 P.2d 1015 (1974); Palsgraf v. Long Island R.R., 248 N.Y. 339, 16 N.E. 99 (1928)).

[20] *Merluzzi*, 96 Nev. at 414, 610 P.2d at 742 (citations omitted).

[21] Foster v. Costco Wholesale Corp., 291 P.3d 150, 156 (Nev. 2012) (quoting Coln v. City of Savannah, 966 S.W.2d 34, 43 (Tenn. 1998), *overruled on other grounds by* Cross v. City of Memphis, 20 S.W.3d 642, 644 (Tenn. 2000)) (citing RESTATEMENT (THIRD) OF TORTS: PHYS. & EMOT. HARM § 51 cmt. i (2012)).

[22] *Scialabba*, 112 Nev. at 970, 921 P.2d at 931.

[23] Sparks v. Alpha Tau Omega Fraternity, Inc., 127 Nev. 287, 255 P.3d 238, 244 (2011) (quoting Sanchez v. Wal-Mart Stores, Inc., 125 Nev. 818, 824, 221 P.3d 1276, 1280-81 (2009)).

(1) a special relationship exists between the parties . . ., and (2) the harm created by the defendant's conduct is foreseeable.[24] Special relationships include, but are not limited to, "innkeeper-guest, teacher-student, employer-employee," and "restaurateur and . . . patron."[25]

B. Question of Fact

i. Elements

"Foreseeability of harm is a predicate to establishing the element of duty."[26] The question of foreseeability is generally one for the jury. Foreseeable, in this context, "means a level of probability which would lead a prudent person to take effective precautions."[27] The reasonable person standard is an objective standard and the conduct at issue must be measured "by a standard of behavior likely to have been adopted by other persons of common prudence."[28]

The standard of care is graduated according to the danger.[29] As the level of risk increases, individuals must exercise greater care.[30] Ultimately, the question is what a person of ordinary prudence would have done under all existing circumstances and in view of the probable danger of injury.[31]

ii. Evidence

The plaintiff must present evidence of the level of care required and the jury is responsible for stating the level of care owed.[32] In some cases, expert evidence is generally required to establish the breach of care.[33] However, where the breach of duty is so apparent and within the ordinary knowledge and experience of the layman, expert testimony is unnecessary.[34] The violation of a statutory rule establishes the elements of duty and breach "when the injured party is in the class of persons whom the statute is intended to protect and the injury is of the type against which the statute is intended to protect."[35]

---

[24] *Id.*

[25] *Sparks*, 127 Nev. at 299, 255 P.3d at 246 (quoting Lee v. GNLV Corp., 117 Nev. 291, 295-96, 22 P.3d 209, 212 (2001)).

[26] Dakis v. Scheffer, 111 Nev. 817, 820, 898 P.2d 116, 118 (1995) (citing Merluzzi v. Larson, 96 Nev. 409, 414, 610 P.2d 739, 742 (1990), *overruled in part on other grounds by* Smith v. Clough, 106 Nev. 568, 570, 796 P.2d 592, 594 (1990)).

[27] Wood v. Safeway, Inc., 121 Nev. 724, 740 n.53, 121 P.3d 1026, 1036 n.53 (2005) (quoting Rodgers v. Kemper Constr. Co., 50 Cal. App. 3d 608, 124 Cal. Rptr. 143, 148-49 (1975) (citations omitted)).

[28] *Solen*, 13 Nev. at 127.

[29] Early v. N.L.V. Casino Corp., 100 Nev. 200, 204, 678 P.2d 683, 685 (1984).

[30] *Solen*, 13 Nev. at 123 (citing Grippen v. New York Cent. R.R. Co., 40 N.Y. 34, 42 (N.Y. 1869) (discussing the need for railroad companies to increase care and prudence as they move from inhabited country to towns, villages, and cities)).

[31] *Id.*

[32] NEV. J.I. 4.10.

[33] *See, e.g.*, Allyn v. McDonald, 112 Nev. 68, 71, 910 P.2d 263, 266 (1996) (stating general principle in legal malpractice action);

[34] *See, e.g., Allyn*, 112 Nev. at 72, 910 P.2d at 266 (noting that an attorney allowing a statute of limitation to run is the type of negligence so apparent as to make expert testimony unnecessary).

[35] Sanchez ex rel. Sanchez v. Wal-Mart Stores, Inc., 125 Nev. 818, 828, 221 P.3d 1276, 1283 (2009).

III. Breach of Duty

A. Elements

If a legal duty exists, reasonable care must be exercised to protect against reasonably foreseeable harm.[36] Whether a defendant's conduct was reasonable under a given set of facts is generally an issue for the jury to decide.[37]

Breach of a duty may result from the commission of an act or the omission of an act.[38] The role of the jury is to determine whether or not the evidence presented demonstrates that the conduct of the defendant has or has not conformed to what "the community requires."[39] In determining reasonable care, the totality of circumstances must be considered.[40] The totality of the circumstances includes the likelihood of injury to others, the probable seriousness of such injuries, and the burden of reducing or avoiding the risk.[41]

B. Evidence

The plaintiff must present proof that the defendant breached the duty of care owed.[42] A plaintiff may prove breach of duty through circumstantial or direct evidence.[43]

Statutes, administrative regulations, company rules, and other laws which protect peoples' safety serve as evidence of the duty of care owed by a defendant[44] and may create a duty of reasonable care that can be enforced in a legal action.[45] The violation of a duty created by a statute that was intended to protect the public establishes the duty and breach elements of negligence when the injured party is in the class of persons whom the statute is intended to protect and the injury is the type against which the statute is intended to protect.[46] This is negligence *per se*.[47]

---

[36] Lee v. GNLV Corp., 117 Nev. 291, 296, 22 P.3d 209, 212 (2001) (citing Sims v. Gen. Tel. & Elec., 107 Nev. 516, 526-27, 815 P.2d 151, 157-58 (1991) (*overruled on other grounds by* Tucker v. Action Equip. & Scaffold Co., 113 Nev. 1349, 951 P.2d 1027 (1997)); *Merluzzi*, 96 Nev. at 412, 610 P.2d at 742 (citing *Palsgraf*, 16 N.E. 99)).

[37] *Solen*, 13 Nev. at 123.

[38] Ferguson v. Virginia & T.R.R., 13 Nev. 184, 187 (1878).

[39] *GNLV Corp.*, 117 Nev. at 296-97, 22 P.3d at 212-13.

[40] Joynt v. California Hotel & Casino, 108 Nev. 539, 543-44, 835 P.2d 799, 802 (1992) (citing Chance v. Lawry's, Inc., 374 P.2d 185 (Cal. 1962); Calerich v. Cudahy Packing Co., 460 P.2d 801 (Colo. 1967); Ottis v. Brough, 409 P.2d 95 (Idaho 1965); Autry v. Walls I.G.A. Foodliner, Inc., 497 P.2d 303 (Kan. 1972); Todd v. Harr, Inc., 417 P.2d 945 (Wash. 1966)).

[41] *Turpel*, 101 Nev. at 38, 692 P.2d at 1292 (quoting Sargent v. Ross, 308 A.2d 528, 534 (N.H. 1973)).

[42] *Foster*, 291 P.3d at 153 (citing DeBoer v. Sr. Bridges of Sparks Fam. Hosp., 282 P.3d 727, 732 (Nev. 2012)).

[43] Otis Elevator Co. v. Reid, 101 Nev. 515, 521, 706 P.2d 1378, 1381 (1985).

[44] Stalk v. Mushkin, 125 Nev. 21, 28 n.2, 199 P.3d 838, 843 n.2 (2009) (noting that Nevada Rules of Professional Conduct "serve as evidence of the duty of care owed by an attorney to his or her client") (citing Mainor v. Nault, 120 Nev. 750, 769, 101 P.3d 308, 321 (2004)); *see also* Auckenthaler v. Grundmeyer, 110 Nev. 682, 689, 877 P.2d 1039, 1043 (1994) (whether defendant followed rules of the game in the context of recreational activities or sporting events is relevant to determining breach of standard of care).

[45] *Sanchez*, 125 Nev. at 828, 221 P.3d at 1283 (citing Torrealba v. Kesmetis, 124 Nev. 95, 178 P.3d 716 (2008)).

[46] *Id.* at 828-29, 221 P.3d at 1283-84 (citing Ashwood v. Clark County, 113 Nev. 80, 86, 930 P.2d 740, 744 (1997)).

[47] *Id.* (citing Torrealba v. Kesmetis, 124 Nev. 95, 178 P.3d 716 (2008)).

Proof of deviation from safety rules and regulations is relevant to whether a defendant is negligent,[48] but deviation does not establish negligence *per se* because regulations lack the force and effect of a substantive legislative enactment.[49] On the other hand, proof of compliance is not proof of due care, but rather, evidence of the care taken.[50]

Evidence of whether or not a person conformed to a custom of a given locality or business is also relevant and ought to be considered.[51] The jury may also consider the rules of a defendant company to determine whether a duty of care was breached.[52]

In closing argument, counsel may remind the jury that they act as the "conscience of the community"[53] in determining whether the defendant acted reasonably and may ask the jury to "send a message" that, based on the evidence, the defendant's conduct was not reasonable.[54]

IV. Causation

A. *Elements*

A plaintiff must prove that the defendant's conduct more probably than not caused the plaintiff's injury.[55] Causation consists of actual cause and proximate cause.[56] To demonstrate actual cause, the plaintiff must prove that but-for the defendant's conduct, the plaintiff's injury would not have occurred.[57] Proximate cause of an injury is a policy consideration that limits a defendant's liability to foreseeable consequences that have a reasonably close connection with both the defendant's conduct and the harm that conduct created.[58]

---

[48] Lightenburger v. Gordon, 81 Nev. 553, 583, 407 P.2d 728, 744 (1965) (Thompson, J., concurring) (citing Dragash v. W. Pac. Ry. Co., 161 Cal. App. 2d 233, 326 P.2d 649 (1958)); *see also* Griffin v. Old Republic Ins. Co., 122 Nev. 479, 484-85 (2006) (stating that federal aviation safety regulations are a legitimate means of insuring safe flight and "designed to promote safe conduct of air traffic"); Price v. Sinnott, 85 Nev. 600, 605, 460 P.2d 837, 840 (1969) (discussing deviation from administrative regulation as being evidence of negligence, not negligence *per se*).

[49] *Price*, 85 Nev. at 605, 460 P.2d at 840 (citing Major v. Waverly & Ogden, Inc., 165 N.E.2d 181, 184 (N.Y. 1960); Prosser on Torts, 3d ed., p. 203)).

[50] *Id.*

[51] NEV. J.I. 4.10.

[52] *See, e.g.*, Burch v. S. Pac. Co., 32 Nev. 75, 98, 104 P. 225, 226 (1909) (discussing the jury's role in determining duty of care by reviewing evidence of company rules and whether employees habitually disregard those rules) (*abrogated on other grounds in part by* Boonsang Jitnan v. Oliver, 254 P.3d 623 (Nev. 2011)).

[53] El Dorado Hotel, Inc. v. Brown, 100 Nev. 622, 691 P.2d 436 (1984) (referring expressly to the jury in a tort action as "acting as the conscience of the community").

[54] *See* Gunderson v. D.R. Horton Inc., 130 Nev. Adv. Rep. 9, 319 P.3d 606, 614 (2014) (en banc) (distinguishing between proper use of phrase "send a message" when based upon the evidence and improper use of "send a message" when not based on the evidence).

[55] Perez v. Las Vegas Med. Ctr., 107 Nev. 1, 4, 805 P.2d 589, 591 (1991) (citing Orcutt v. Miller, 95 Nev. 408, 411-12, 595 P.2d 1191, 1193 (1979)).

[56] Goodrich & Pennington Mortg. Fund, Inc. v. J.R. Woolward, Inc., 120 Nev. 777, 784, 101 P.3d 792, 797 (2004) (quoting Dow Chem. Co. v. Mahlum, 114 Nev. 1468, 1481, 970 P.2d 98, 107 (1998)).

[57] *Id.*

[58] *Id.*

To recover, a plaintiff must prove it was foreseeable that someone in the plaintiff's position could suffer some type of injury from the defendant's conduct.[59] The defendant does not have to foresee the extent of harm or the manner in which the harm occurred to the specific plaintiff; only that the conduct could cause a particular variety of harm to a person in a similar position as the plaintiff.[60] A defendant is responsible for all foreseeable consequences of his or her negligent act.[61]

B. Evidence

Proximate cause and foreseeability are questions of fact for the jury.[62] The plaintiff must show that "it is more probable than not that the injury resulted from defendant's breach of duty."[63] In establishing foreseeability, evidence of injuries to other persons is a relevant factor.[64]

V. Damages

A. Elements

Tort damages serve to make the injured party whole.[65] Damages in a negligence case are to compensate for injuries that constitute the foreseeable consequences proximately caused by the defendant's breach of duty.[66] Actual or compensatory damages are to compensate for a proven injury or loss and may include tangible or intangible losses.[67]

B. Evidence

Damages must be reasonable and fair.[68] The plaintiff has the burden to prove that he or she has suffered harm of a kind legally compensable by damages.[69] In terms of intangible losses, like pain or suffering, no legal rule of measurement exists by which to calculate

---

[59] Hammerstein v. Jean Dev. West, 111 Nev. 1471, 1476, 907 P.2d 975, 978 (1995) (citing *Sims*, 107 Nev. 516, 815 P.2d 151, 157 (1991)).

[60] *Id.* (citing *Sims*, 107 Nev. 516, 815 P.2d 151, 157).

[61] *Sims*, 107 Nev. at 525, 815 P.2d at 156 (quoting Taylor v. Silva, 96 Nev. 738, 741, 615 P.2d 970, 971 (1980)).

[62] White v. Demetelin, 84 Nev. 430, 433, 442 P.2d 914, 915 (1968).

[63] Am. Elevator Co. v. Briscoe, 93 Nev. 665, 669, 572 P.2d 534, 537 (1977).

[64] *Mahlum*, 114 Nev. at 1484, 970 P.2d at 109 (finding jury's determination of foreseeability proper based upon evidence of prior testing that showed silicone used in breast implants would migrate throughout the body and was probably harmful to women) (*overruled in part on other grounds by* GES, Inc. v. Corbitt, 117 Nev. 265, 21 P.3d 11 (2001)).

[65] *Greco*, 111 Nev. at 412, 893 P.2d at 350 (citing *Ponsock*, 103 Nev. at 49, 732 P.2d at 1371).

[66] NRS 41.130; NEV J.I. 10.00; *Dakis*, 111 Nev. at 820, 898 P.2d at 118 (citing *Silva*, 96 Nev. at 741, 615 P.2d at 971); Grosjean v. Imperial Palace, Inc., 125 Nev. 349, 371, 212 P.3d 1068, 1083 (2009).

[67] Betsinger v. D.R. Horton, Inc., 232 P.3d 433, 436 (Nev. 2010).

[68] NEV J.I. 10.00.

[69] *Szekeres*, 102 Nev. at 95 n.1, 715 P.2d at 1076 n.1 (1986) (quoting RESTATEMENT (SECOND) OF TORTS, § 328A (1965)).

damages.[70] Instead, because the elements of pain and suffering are subjective, these damages are peculiarly within the province of the jury.[71] The jury is also given wide latitude in awarding special damages.[72] So long as special damages are supported by an evidentiary basis, the amount need not be mathematically exact.[73] The jury is allowed to draw reasonable inferences from the evidence to support an award of damages.[74]

Damages cannot be based upon passion or prejudice.[75] The mere fact a verdict is large, however, is not conclusive that it is the result of passion, prejudice, sympathy, or other consideration,[76] and a damage award will not be revisited unless flagrantly improper.[77]

[70] Canterino v. Mirage Casino-Hotel, 16 P.3d 415, 418 (Nev. 2001) (citing Stackiewicz v. Nissan Motor Corp., 100 Nev. 443, 454, 686 P.2d 925, 932 (1984)).

[71] Id. (citing Stackiewicz, 100 Nev. at 454, 686 P.2d at 932).

[72] Wyeth v. Rowatt, 244 P.3d 765, 782 (2010).

[73] Bahena v. Goodyear Tire & Rubber, Co., 235 P.3d 592, 601 (2010) (citing Countrywide Home Loans, Inc. v. Thitchener, 124 Nev. 725, 737, 192 P.3d 243, 251 (2008)).

[74] Id.

[75] Hernandez v. Salt Lake, 100 Nev. 504, 507-08, 686 P.2d 251, 253 (1984); Canterino, 16 P.3d 415 418 (citing Stackiewicz, 100 Nev. at 454-55, 686 P.2d at 932).

[76] Wells, Inc. v. Shoemake, 64 Nev. 57, 74, 177 P.2d 451, 460 (1947).

[77] Canterino, 16 P.3d at 418 (citing Stackiewicz, 100 Nev. at 454-55, 686 P.2d at 932).

CHAPTER 30

NEW HAMPSHIRE

NEW HAMPSHIRE
Matthew C. Kane[1]

I.   Purpose of Tort Law

In New Hampshire, the "first principles" of the state law of negligence are (1) to deter negligent conduct, and (2) to compensate the victims from those who act unreasonably.[2] Tort law is not focused on "a law of wrongs," but rather "for the creation and protection of rights—a method for providing compensation for harm caused another."[3] Courts should apply tort law to give financial protection to those who are injured.[4] The New Hampshire Supreme Court has further noted that tort law is not "static but dynamic, as the law grows and changes to meet new social and economic conditions."[5]

II.   Duty to Exercise Ordinary Care

A.   *Question of Law*

Claims for negligence "rest primarily upon a violation of some duty owed by the offender to the injured party."[6] Absent a duty, there is no negligence.[7] Whether a duty exists in a particular case depends on what risks, if any, are reasonably foreseeable.[8] "[W]hether a defendant's conduct creates a sufficiently foreseeable risk of harm to others sufficient to charge the defendant with a duty to avoid such conduct is a question of law."[9]

"The general rule of tort liability . . . is that a defendant will not be held liable for negligence if he could not reasonably foresee that his conduct would result in an injury or if his

---

[1] Director, Ryan, Whaley, Coldiron, Jantzen, Peters & Weber, Adjunct Professor, Oklahoma City University School of Law and Oklahoma College of Law.

[2] Smith v. Cote, 128 N.H. 231, 242, 513 A.2d 341, 348 (1986).

[3] Briere v. Briere, 107 N.H. 432, 434, 224 A.2d 588, 590 (1966) (citing SEAVEY, COGITATIONS ON TORTS, pp. 5, 6 (1954)).

[4] Johnson v. Johnson, 107 N.H. 30, 32, 216 A.2d 781, 783 (1966).

[5] *Briere*, 224 A.2d at 590.

[6] Walls v. Oxford Mgmt. Co., 137 N.H. 653, 656-57, 633 A.2d 103, 104-05 (1993) (quoting Guitarini v. Macallen Co., 98 N.H. 118, 118, 95 A.2d 784, 785 (1953)).

[7] *Id.*

[8] Goodwin v. James, 134 N.H. 579, 583-84, 595 A.2d 504, 507 (1991) (citing McLaughlin v. Sullivan, 123 N.H. 335, 342, 461 A.2d 123, 127 (1983)).

[9] Kellner v. Lowney, 145 N.H. 195, 197, 761 A.2d 421, 423 (2000) (quoting Manchenton v. Auto Leasing Corp., 135 N.H. 298, 304, 605 A.2d 208, 213 (1992)); *see Walls*, 633 A.2d at 104-05 (whether a duty exists is a question of law) (citing *Manchenton*, 605 A.2d at 213); *see Goodwin*, 595 A.2d at 506-07; *see* Paquette v. Joyce, 117 N.H. 832, 837, 379 A.2d 207, 210 (1977).

conduct was reasonable in light of what he could anticipate."[10] The test of due care is what reasonable prudence would require under similar circumstances.[11] Duty and foreseeability are inextricably bound together; the manner in which foreseeability is defined will determine whether a duty exists.[12] "The risk reasonably to be perceived defines the duty to be obeyed."[13] A person may be liable only to those who are foreseeably endangered by his or her conduct and only with respect to those risks or hazards whose likelihood made the conduct unreasonably dangerous.[14] The scope of the duty, therefore, is limited to those risks that are reasonably foreseeable.[15]

> In some cases, a party's *actions* give rise to a duty. A party who does not otherwise have a duty, but who voluntarily renders services for another, has been held to a duty of reasonable care in acting. In other cases, a duty *to act* exists based on a special relationship between two parties. In either case, the scope of the duty imposed is limited by what risks, if any, are reasonably foreseeable. As a general rule, a defendant will not be held liable for negligence if he could not reasonably foresee that his conduct would result in an injury or if his conduct was reasonable in light of what he could anticipate.[16]

Additionally, a statute may create, either explicitly or implicitly, a cause of action for violation of its standard of conduct or, if a cause of action already exists at common law, "the standard of conduct to which a defendant will be held may be defined as that required by statute, rather than as the usual reasonable person standard."[17] However "[t]he doctrine of negligence *per se* . . . plays no role in the creation of common law causes of action" and "in many cases, the common law may fail to recognize liability for failure to perform affirmative duties that are imposed by statute. If no common law duty exists, the plaintiff cannot maintain a negligence action, even though the defendant has violated a statutory duty."[18]

---

[10] *Goodwin*, 595 A.2d at 507 (citing Vincent v. Pub. Serv. Co. of New Hampshire, 129 N.H. 621, 624, 529 A.2d 397, 398 (1987)); RESTATEMENT (SECOND) OF TORTS § 289 (1965). Moreover, "[w]hen charged with determining whether a duty exists in a particular case, we necessarily encounter the broader, more fundamental question of 'whether the plaintiff's interests are entitled to legal protection against the defendant's conduct.'" *Walls*, 633 A.2d at 104-05; Libbey v. Hampton Water Works Co., 118 N.H. 500, 502, 389 A.2d 434, 435 (1978) (quotation omitted).

[11] State v. Exxon Mobil Corp., 168 N.H. 211, 235, 126 A.3d 266, 287 (2015), *cert. denied sub nom.* Exxon Mobil Corp. v. New Hampshire, No. 15-933, 2016 WL 309800 (U.S. May 16, 2016); Carignan v. New Hampshire Int'l Speedway, Inc., 151 N.H. 409, 414, 858 A.2d 536, 541 (2004).

[12] Corso v. Merrill, 119 N.H. 647, 651, 406 A.2d 300, 303 (1979).

[13] *Id.* (quoting Palsgraf v. Long Island R.R., 248 N.Y. 339, 344, 162 N.E. 99, 100 (1928)). *See also,* Macie v. Helms, 156 N.H. 222, 225, 934 A.2d 562, 565 (2007) (noting that New Hampshire concepts of duty are predicated on the majority opinion in *Palsgraf*); *accord* Kellner v. Lowney, 145 N.H. 195, 197, 761 A.2d 421, 423 (2000); Goodwin v. James, 134 N.H. 579, 583-84, 595 A.2d 504, 507 (1991).

[14] *Corso*, 406 A.2d at 303 (quoting 2 F. HARPER & F. JAMES, THE LAW OF TORTS § 18.2 at 1018 (1956).

[15] *Macie*, 934 A.2d at 565.

[16] Walls v. Oxford Mgmt. Co., 137 N.H. 653, 656-57, 633 A.2d 103, 104-05 (1993) (internal citations and quotations omitted); *e.g.,* Remsburg v. Docusearch, Inc., 149 N.H. 148, 153, 816 A.2d 1001, 1006 (2003); *e.g., Kellner*, 761 A.2d at 424.

[17] Gauthier v. Manchester Sch. Dist., 168 N.H. 143, 147, 123 A.3d 1016, 1019 (2015); Marquay v. Eno, 139 N.H. 708, 720, 662 A.2d 272, 281 (1995).

[18] Marquay v. Eno, 139 N.H. 708, 720, 662 A.2d 272, 281 (1995).

B. Question of Fact

i. Elements

Whether to impose a duty of care "rests on a judicial determination that the social importance of protecting the plaintiff's interest outweighs the importance of immunizing the defendant from extended liability."[19] The decision to impose liability ultimately rests on "a judicial determination that the social importance of protecting the plaintiff's interest outweighs the importance of immunizing the defendant from extended liability."[20] The court's balancing of factors considers: (1) the severity of the risk, (2) the likelihood of occurrence, (3) the relationship between the parties, and (4) the burden on the defendant.[21] The violation of a statute will result in liability "when the plaintiff is in a class the statute is designed to protect and the injury is of the type that the statute is intended to prevent."[22]

ii. Evidence

The plaintiff has the burden to prove facts upon which the law imposes a duty of care.[23]

III. Breach of Duty

A. Elements

Only after a court has determined that a defendant owed a plaintiff a duty, and identified the standard of care imposed by that duty, may a jury consider the separate question of whether the defendant breached that duty. Whether the defendant breached the duty of care is a question for the trier of fact.[24]

B. Evidence

The burden is on the plaintiff to establish that a breach of duty occurred.[25] While proof of actual knowledge of unsafe conditions is not necessary to establish a breach of duty,

---

[19] Sisson v. Jankowski, 148 N.H. 503, 506, 809 A.2d 1265, 1267 (2002) (quoting Walls v. Oxford Mgmt. Co., 137 N.H. 653, 657, 633 A.2d 103, 105 (1993)); see Goodwin v. James, 134 N.H. 579, 583, 595 A.2d 504, 506-07 (1991) ("'whether the defendants' conduct created such a foreseeable risk of harm to the . . . plaintiff that defendants were under a duty to avoid it' is a question of law to be determined in the first instance by the trial court").

[20] Walls v. Oxford Mgmt. Co., 137 N.H. 653, 656-57, 633 A.2d 103, 104-05 (1993) (citing Libbey v. Hampton Water Works Co., 118 N.H. 500, 502, 389 A.2d 434, 435 (1978)) (quotations and brackets omitted). *See generally* Keeton, *supra* § 54, at 358 (duty not sacrosanct in itself, but only expression of sum total of policy considerations).

[21] *Sisson*, 809 A.2d at 1267 (citing Hungerford v. Jones, 143 N.H. 208, 211, 722 A.2d 478, 480 (1998)).

[22] Island Shores Estates Condo. Ass'n v. City of Concord, 136 N.H. 300, 307, 615 A.2d 629, 633 (1992).

[23] Yager v. Clauson, No. 2015-0463, 2016 WL 1576713, at *2 (N.H. Apr. 19, 2016) (citing North Bay Council, Inc. v. Bruckner, 131 N.H. 538, 542, 563 A.2d 428, 430 (1989)); Witte v. Desmarais, 136 N.H. 178, 182, 614 A.2d 116, 117 (1992). Generally, plaintiff has the burden of proof as to all elements of negligence. Anglin v. Kleeman, 140 N.H. 257, 261, 665 A.2d 747, 750 (1995).

[24] Carignan v. New Hampshire Int'l Speedway, Inc., 151 N.H. 409, 414, 858 A.2d 536, 541 (2004) (quoting Young v. Clogston, 127 N.H. 340, 343, 499 A.2d 1007, 1009 (1985).

[25] *See* Douglas v. Connor, 108 N.H. 443, 445, 237 A.2d 686, 688 (1968); Apr. v. Peront, 88 N.H. 309, 188 A. 457, 458 (1936).

such evidence is admissible to establish that the defendant was aware of the need to investigate and repair.[26]

IV. Causation

A. Elements

Causation is comprised of two elements: cause-in-fact and legal/proximate cause.[27] Conduct is the cause-in-fact of an injury if the injury would not have occurred without the negligent conduct.[28] Legal cause requires a plaintiff to establish that the negligent conduct was a substantial factor in bringing about the harm.[29] Although the negligent conduct need not be the sole cause of the injury, to establish proximate cause a plaintiff must prove that the defendant's conduct caused or contributed to cause the harm.[30]

B. Evidence

The plaintiff "must produce evidence sufficient to warrant a reasonable juror's conclusion that the causal link between the negligence and the injury probably existed."[31] "The plaintiff need only show with reasonable probability, not mathematical certainty, that but-for the defendant's negligence, the harm would not have occurred."[32] Specifically, courts have stated that the question of legal cause is generally for the trier of fact to resolve.[33] Expert testimony is required, however, to aid the jury "whenever the matter to be determined is so distinctly related to some science, profession, business or occupation as to be beyond the ken of the average layman."[34] In particular, expert testimony is necessary to preclude the jury from engaging in idle speculation "if any inference of the requisite causal link must depend [upon] observation and analysis outside the common experience of jurors."[35]

---

[26] Dowling v. L. H. Shattuck, Inc., 91 N.H. 234, 17 A.2d 529, 534 (1941).

[27] As a point of caution, different New Hampshire cases use the term "proximate cause" as either the overarching causal concept, comprised of (1) cause-in-fact and (2) legal cause, or as the legal cause element itself (which must also be accompanied by "cause-in-fact").

[28] Estate of Joshua T. v. State, 150 N.H. 405, 407-08, 840 A.2d 768, 771-72 (2003) (citing Bronson v. Hitchcock Clinic, 140 N.H. 798, 801, 677 A.2d 665, 668 (1996)); North Bay Council, Inc. v. Bruckner, 131 N.H. 538, 548, 563 A.2d 428, 434 (1989); W. KEETON et al., PROSSER AND KEETON ON THE LAW OF TORTS § 41, at 266 (5th ed. 1984); Carignan v. New Hampshire Int'l Speedway, Inc., 151 N.H. 409, 414, 858 A.2d 536, 541-42 (2004).

[29] Estate of Joshua T., 840 A.2d at 771-72; Brookline Sch. Dist. v. Bird, Inc., 142 N.H. 352, 354-55, 703 A.2d 258, 260 (1997); see In re Haines, 148 N.H. 380, 382, 808 A.2d 72, 75 (2002) (legal cause refers to substantial factor test); Carignan, 858 A.2d at 541-42.

[30] Carignan, 858 A.2d at 541-42; Estate of Joshua T., 840 A.2d at 771-72; Brookline Sch. Dist., 703 A.2d at 260.

[31] Estate of Joshua T., 840 A.2d at 771-72 (quoting Bronson, 677 A.2d at 668); see also Carignan, 858 A.2d at 541-42; Martin v. Wentworth-Douglass Hosp., 130 N.H. 134, 136, 536 A.2d 174, 176 (1987).

[32] Goudreault v. Kleeman, 158 N.H. 236, 246, 965 A.2d 1040, 1049-50 (2009).

[33] Estate of Joshua T., 840 A.2d at 771; Brookline Sch. Dist., 703 A.2d at 260.

[34] Estate of Joshua T., 840 A.2d at 771-72; Powell v. Catholic Med. Ctr., 145 N.H. 7, 14, 749 A.2d 301, 306 (2000).

[35] Estate of Joshua T., 840 A.2d at 771-72 (citing Thorpe v. State, Dept. of Corrs., 133 N.H. 299, 304, 575 A.2d 351, 353 (1990)).

V. Damages

A. Elements

As damages are an essential element to any negligence claim, a verdict for the plaintiff cannot result without them.[36] "The usual rule of compensatory damages in tort cases requires that the person wronged receive a sum of money that will restore him as nearly as possible to the position he would have been in if the wrong had not been committed."[37]

B. Evidence

"The defendant's liability is not confined merely to damages for injuries which an ordinary man might have expected would follow from the negligence proved, but includes damages for such injuries as are the direct and natural result thereof, as disclosed by the evidence."[38] "It seems to be settled, that he is entitled to recover one compensation for all his injuries, past and prospective, in consequence of the defendants' wrongful or negligent acts. Damages are presumed to embrace indemnity for actual nursing and medical expenses, also loss of time or loss from inability to perform ordinary labor, or capacity to earn money. Plaintiff is to have a reasonable satisfaction for loss of both bodily and mental powers, or for actual suffering both of the body and mind, which are shown to be the immediate and necessary consequences of the injury wrongfully received."[39] Such damages may be very broad, including, for instance, mental distress associated with the "apprehension of insanity."[40] If there is a finding of liability but the damages are grossly inadequate, the court should order additur, or, if the defendant does not consent to additur, a new trial on damages.[41]

---

[36] Kravitz v. Beech Hill Hosp., L.L.C., 148 N.H. 383, 391, 808 A.2d 34, 42 (2002). Consequently, "[c]auses of action for negligence do not arise at the occurrence of the negligent act but rather when the damages result." Deschamps v. Camp Dresser & McKee, Inc., 113 N.H. 344, 346, 306 A.2d 771, 773 (1973) (citing White v. Schnoebelen, 91 N.H. 273, 18 A.2d 185 (1941)).

[37] Smith v. Cote, 128 N.H. 231, 243, 513 A.2d 341, 348 (1986).

[38] Challis v. Lake, 71 N.H. 90, 51 A. 260, 262-63 (1901). Thus, "if the defendants were liable in the action, the plaintiff was entitled to recover, as part of his damages, compensation for his loss of physical and mental capacity, so far as proved to have been caused solely by the defendants' negligence; that there was no rule of law that one man was or was not exactly like another; that it was a question of fact for the jury, what injury the plaintiff had suffered by the defendants' negligence, not what any other man had suffered; that the evidence of his occupation and capacity was admissible only in order to enable the jury to judge of the injury to his capacity; that this was an action for an injury to the man, and not for interfering with his business, and the damages must be limited to the personal injury to him, occasioned by the defendants' negligence." Holyoke v. Grand Trunk Ry., 48 N.H. 541, 541-42, 1869 WL 2788, *1-2 (1869).

[39] Holyoke v. Grand Trunk Ry., 48 N.H. 541, 545, 1869 WL 2788, *5 (1869).

[40] Young v. Abalene Pest Control Servs., Inc., 122 N.H. 287, 293, 444 A.2d 514, 517-18 (1982).

[41] Kravitz v. Beech Hill Hosp., L.L.C., 148 N.H. 383, 390, 808 A.2d 34, 42 (2002).

CHAPTER 31

NEW JERSEY

NEW JERSEY

Connie Calvert[1]

I. Purpose of Tort Law

Tort law is an expression of society's shared beliefs regarding the fundamental rules governing others' conduct.[2] Its primary purpose is to compensate plaintiffs for their injuries wrongfully suffered at the hands of others.[3] Those responsible should bear the cost of their tortious conduct.[4]

> Other policies underlie this fundamental purpose. Imposing liability on defendants for their negligent conduct discourages others from similar tortious behavior, fosters safer products to aid our daily tasks, vindicates reasonable conduct that has regard for the safety of others, and, ultimately, shifts the risk of loss and associated costs of dangerous activities to those who should be and are best able to bear them. . . . [W]e strive to ensure that the application of negligence doctrine advances the fundamental purpose of tort law and does not unnecessarily or arbitrarily foreclose redress based on formalisms or technicalisms.[5]

New Jersey recognizes that tort law should encourage reasonable conduct while also discouraging conduct creating unreasonable risks of injury to others.[6] Thus, a key goal of tort law is deterring personal injuries and wrongful conduct.[7] This deterrent goal is effectuated by imposing both a duty of reasonable care and the corresponding liability for a duty's breach.[8]

---

[1] Calvert Talent Consulting LLC; Member of the Oklahoma Bar Association.

[2] Estate of Desir ex rel. Estiverne v. Vertus, 69 A.3d 1247, 1260 (N.J. 2013).

[3] Berman v. Allan, 404 A.2d 8, 11-12 (N.J. 1979), *abrogation recognized in* Hummel v. Reiss, 608 A.2d 1341, 1346 (N.J. 1992); D.J.L. v. Armour Pharm. Co., 704 A.2d 104, 114 (N.J. 1997) ("The very essence of tort law is to protect those to whom a duty of care is owed against injury.").

[4] People Exp. Airlines, Inc. v. Consol. Rail Corp., 495 A.2d 107, 111 (N.J. 1985).

[5] *Id.* at 111.

[6] Sciarrotta v. Glob. Spectrum, 944 A.2d 630, 637 (N.J. 2008) (quoting Gantes v. Kason Corp., 679 A.2d 106, 111 (N.J. 1996)).

[7] Lewis v. Am. Cyanamid Co., 715 A.2d 967, 983 (N.J. 1998) (noting purpose of tort law as a deterrent to causing personal injuries).

[8] *Sciarrotta*, 944 A.2d at 637 (quoting *Gantes*, *supra* note 5, at 111).

II. Duty to Exercise Ordinary Care

A. Question of Law

Negligence requires plaintiff prove defendant owed him or her a duty of protection from injury.[9] The general rule is that every person must exercise the same care as that of a reasonably vigilant, prudent, and cautious person under the same or similar circumstances.[10] New Jersey's tort law has always recognized—that as a matter of justice—the burden of loss should fall on the party at fault.[11] The existence of a duty and its scope are questions of law,[12] and the failure to meet that duty is proved as fact.[13] The jury determines the standard of care by comparing the defendant's conduct with that of a reasonably prudent person in defendant's position.[14] "The jury thus must formulate an unformulated community standard of conduct and match the defendant's acts against it."[15]

While foreseeability is the foundational element[16] for imposing a duty, the court also considers the following fairness factors: (1) the parties' relationship; (2) the nature of the risk; (3) the ability to exercise care; and (4) public policy considerations.[17] Foreseeability of harm requires finding both that the plaintiff was a foreseeable victim of some harm, and that the harm was within the types of harm foreseeable. However, the law does not require foreseeing the exact manner in which the harm manifests.[18] In this way, the defendant's conduct establishes a foreseeable "zone of danger."[19]

Foreseeability of harm creates a duty to prevent that harm and to protect others from risk, including third parties or strangers.[20] This blend of foreseeability and fairness ensures proper furtherance of deterrence principles.[21] "In effect, a primary policy of tort law is

---

[9] Fernandes v. DAR Dev. Corp., 119 A.3d 878, 885 (N.J. 2015).

[10] McKinley v. Slenderella Sys., Inc., 165 A.2d 207, 212 (N.J. Super. Ct. App. Div. 1960).

[11] Franklin Mut. Ins. v. Jersey Cent. Power & Light Co., 902 A.2d 885, 887 (N.J. 2006).

[12] Badalamenti v. Simpkiss, 27 A.3d 191, 195-96 (N.J. Super. Ct. App. Div. 2011) (quoting Wlasiuk v. McElwee, 760 A.2d 829, 832 (N.J. Super. Ct. App. Div. 2000)).

[13] Scully v. Fitzgerald, 843 A.2d 1110, 1118 (N.J. 2004).

[14] Sanzari v. Rosenfeld, 167 A.2d 625, 628 (N.J. 1961).

[15] Id. (quoting Clarence Morris, *The Relation of Criminal Statutes to Tort Liability*, 46 HARV. L. REV. 453, 454 (1933)).

[16] J.S. v. R.T.H., 714 A.2d 924, 928 (N.J. 1998).

[17] Hopkins v. Fox & Lazo Realtors, 625 A.2d 1110, 1116 (N.J. 1993).

[18] Wlasiuk v. McElwee, 760 A.2d 829, 833 (N.J. Super. Ct. App. Div. 2000).

[19] Taylor by Taylor v. Cutler, 703 A.2d 294, 298, 300 (N.J. Super. Ct. App. Div. 1997), *aff'd in part and cert. order vacated per curiam*, 724 A.2d 793 (N.J. Super. Ct. App. Div. 1999) (citing Palsgraf v. Long Island R.R., 162 N.E. 99, 103 (N.Y. 1928)).

[20] Chomatopoulous v. Roma De Notte Soc. Club, 515 A.2d 296, 298 (N.J. Super Ct. Law Div. 1985).

[21] Kuzmicz v. Ivy Hill Park Apts., 688 A.2d 1018, 1030 (N.J. 1997); *see also* Weinberg v. Dinger, 524 A.2d 366, 375 (N.J. 1987), *limited on other grounds by* Bongo v. N.J. Bell Tel. Co., 595 A.2d 557, 563 (N.J. Super. Ct. Law Div. 1991) (limiting Weinberg's immunity holding to its specific facts) ("Moreover, forcing tortfeasors to pay for the harm they have wrought provides proper incentive for reasonable conduct.").

to conform conduct."[22] New Jersey's Constitution also supports this fundamental tenant by guaranteeing injured parties the right of redress for another's tortious conduct.[23]

The "zone of danger" is limited only by the foreseeability of harm.[24] A defendant's duty is established when it was or should have been foreseeable to him or her that an act or omission would cause another harm.[25] The duty to exercise care is not always based on the parties' relationship.[26] The court determines foreseeability by objectively analyzing the totality of the circumstances.[27]

B. *Question of Fact*

i. **Elements**

The court imposes a duty and its scope as a matter of law;[28] and the jury, competent to determine what precautions a reasonably prudent man in the defendant's position would have taken, establishes the applicable standard of conduct.[29] Thus, the plaintiff need not provide evidence of the standard of care, but need only show what the defendant did and what the circumstances were.[30] However, when negligence involves conduct beyond the jury's collective experience, the plaintiff must establish the standard of care and the defendant's deviation from that standard through reliable expert testimony.[31]

ii. **Evidence**

The jury and court's objective determinations are based, in part, on all factors a reasonably prudent person would consider.[32] This may include evidence for how others would act under similar circumstances and evidence as to the harm's foreseeable frequency and severity.[33] The law permits methods, practices, or rules to aid the jury in comparing the defendant's

---

[22] Taylor by Taylor v. Cutler, 703 A.2d 294, 300 (N.J. Super. Ct. App. Div. 1997), *aff'd in part and cert. order vacated per curiam*, 724 A.2d 793 (N.J. Super. Ct. App. Div. 1999).

[23] Berkowitz v. Soper, 128 A.3d 1159, 1170 (N.J. Super. Ct. App. Div. 2016) (quoting Johnson v. Scacetti, 927 A.2d 1269, 1282 (N.J. 2007), *overruled in part on other grounds by* Cuevas v. Wentworth, 144 A.3d 890, 903 (N.J. 2016)) (quoting N.J. Const. art. I, para. 9; *Id.* ("The right of trial by jury shall remain inviolate.")).

[24] *Taylor*, 703 A.2d at 298.

[25] *Id.*

[26] *Id.* at 296, 299 ("While New Jersey courts have generally followed common law tort principles, our courts have shown disfavor in determining legal responsibility based simply on the relationship among the parties.").

[27] Badalamenti v. Simpkiss, 27 A.3d 191, 196 (N.J. Super. Ct. App. Div. 2011).

[28] Wlasiuk v. McElwee, 760 A.2d 829, 832 (N.J. Super. Ct. App. Div. 2000).

[29] Fernandes v. DAR Dev. Corp., 119 A.3d 878, 886 (N.J. 2015) (quoting Davis v. Brickman Landscaping, Ltd., 98 A.3d 1173, 1179 (N.J. 2014)).

[30] *Davis*, *supra* note 28, 98 A.3d at 1179 (first quoting *Sanzari*, *supra* note 13, 167 A.2d at 628, then quoting Giantonnio v. Taccard, 676 A.2d 1110, 1115 (N.J. Super. Ct. App. Div. 1996), then quoting *Sanzari*, 167 A.2d at 628; then quoting *Giantonnio*, 676 A.2d at 1115).

[31] Fernandes v. DAR Dev. Corp., 119 A.3d 878, 886 (N.J. 2015).

[32] Badalamenti v. Simpkiss, 27 A.3d 191, 196 (N.J. Super. Ct. App. Div. 2011).

[33] J.S. v. R.T.H., 714 A.2d 924, 928, 929 (N.J. 1998).

conduct with the required conduct of normal or reasonable prudence.[34] These safety standards act as a parameter of conduct for the jury's consideration when determining the actions of a reasonably prudent person in the defendant's circumstance.[35]

The jury may consider the violation of a statute as evidence of reasonable care.[36] Evidence of remedial measures made after manufacture but before an accident are admissible as evidence of the standard of care.[37] An industry's safety codes, practices, or rules are also admissible as evidence of a reasonable person's conduct when in the defendant's situation.[38] Other common sources of admissible safety standards include legislative codes, agency regulations, and industry standards or professional organizations' standards.[39] Elements from text books and treatises may be introduced through expert witnesses.[40] The court may take judicial notice of all agency regulations and rules having the effect of law.[41]

III. Breach of Duty

A. Elements

The jury decides whether the defendant breached the duty.[42] Defendant's act or failure to act constitutes negligence when an ordinary person under similar circumstances acting with ordinary care could reasonably foresee the possibility of some harm and, in response, would have adjusted his or her conduct to prevent the harm.[43] By definition, negligence is the departure from the standard of care of an ordinary prudent person in the same or similar circumstance to prevent an appreciable risk of harm to others.[44]

---

[34] McComish v. DeSoi, 200 A.2d 116, 121 (N. J. 1964); *but see* Swank v. Halivopoulos, 260 A.2d 240, 243 (N.J. Super. Ct. App. Div. 1969) (distinguished from *McComish* as the standards did not contain specific "how to" directions but only general "recommendations" for a clinician's use combined with his or her clinical opinion); Maussner v. Atlantic City Country Club, Inc., 691 A.2d 826, 836-37 (N.J. Super. Ct. App. Div. 1997).

[35] *Maussner*, 691 A.2d at 836-37.

[36] *Badalamenti*, 27 A.3d at 201.

[37] Molino v. B.F. Goodrich Co., 617 A.2d 1235, 1244 (N.J. Super. Ct. App. Div. 1992); *see also* Shatz v. TEC Tech. Adhesives, 415 A.2d 1188, 1192 (N.J. Super. Ct. App. Div. 1980) ("[W]e perceive of no social policy furthered by allowing a defendant to keep from the jury evidence of remedial conduct undertaken before an accident."); Harris v. Peridot Chem., Inc., 712 A.2d 1181, 1198 (N.J. Super. Ct. App. Div. 1998) ("[E]vidence of such subsequent remedial conduct may [also] be admitted as to other issues." (quoting N.J.R.E. 407)).

[38] *McComish*, 200 A.2d at 121-22; *Maussner*, 691 A.2d at 836-37.

[39] Fernandes v. DAR Dev. Corp., 119 A.3d 878, 886 (N.J. 2015) ("The standard of care is derived from many sources, including codes adopted by the Legislature, regulations adopted by state and federal agencies, and standards adopted by professional organizations.").

[40] Kaplan v. Skoloff & Wolfe, P.C., 770 A.2d 1258, 1263 (N.J. Super. Ct. App. Div. 2001) (quoting Taylor by Taylor v. DeLosso, 725 A.2d 51, 54 (N.J. Super. Ct. App. Div. 1999)).

[41] Canal Ins. v. F.W. Clukey Trucking Co., 684 A.2d 953, 959 (N.J. Super. Ct. App. Div. 1996).

[42] Scully v. Fitzgerald, 843 A.2d 1110, 1118 (N.J. 2004).

[43] Lynch v. Scheininger, 162 N.J. 209, 232, 744 A.2d 113, 127 (N.J. 2000) (quoting Hill v. Yaskin, 380 A.2d 1107, 1109 (N.J. 1977)).

[44] McKinley v. Slenderella Sys., Inc., 165 A.2d 207, 212 (N.J. Super. Ct. App. Div. 1960).

B. Evidence

Evidence of defendant's conduct or other circumstances may be direct or circumstantial.[45] Evidence of defendant's actions is admissible as to whether the defendant breached a duty.[46] The jury may consider all evidence presented when determining whether the defendant breached a duty.[47]

IV. Causation

A. Elements

To recover in negligence, the plaintiff must also prove that the defendant's breach of duty was the proximate cause of the harm suffered.[48] Again, foreseeability is the cornerstone of this analysis; however, unlike *duty* foreseeability, *proximate-cause* foreseeability turns on whether the plaintiff's harm reasonably flowed from the defendant's breach.[49] Proximate cause is established when the injury is a reasonably foreseeable result of the negligent act.[50] It is not necessary that all possible harms be foreseeable, only that the harm suffered be within the realm of foreseeability for types of harm risked by the defendant's negligence.[51] Even remote risks can give rise to a duty.[52] And a proximate cause need not be the sole cause of the plaintiff's harm but only a substantial contributing factor.[53] Nor is recovery cut off when more than one defendant is the proximate cause of injury; all defendants proximately causing

---

[45] Simpson v. Duffy, 88 A.2d 520, 523 (N.J. Super. Ct. App. Div. 1952) (quoting Hansen v. Eagle-Picher Lead Co., 84 A.2d 281, 285 (N.J. 1951), *superseded by statute on other grounds by* Richard J. Biunno, *Current N.J. Rules of Evidence*, comment 1 on *Evid.R.* 63(9) (1993), *as recognized in* Reisman v. Great Am. Recreation, Inc., 628 A.2d 801, 807 (N.J. Super. Ct. App. Div. 1993)).

[46] Davis v. Brickman Landscaping, Ltd., 98 A.3d 1173, 1180-81 (N.J. 2014).

[47] *Simpson*, 88 A.3d at 523.

[48] Scafidi v. Seiler, 543 A.2d 95, 97 (N.J. Super. Ct. App. Div. 1988), *abrogated on other grounds by* Scafidi v. Seiler, 574 A.2d 398, 399-400 (N.J. 1990).

[49] Doe v. XYC Corp., 887 A.2d 1156, 1170 (N.J. Super. Ct. App. Div. 2005) (quoting Clohesy v. Food Circus Supermarkets, 694 A.2d 1017, 1021 (N.J. 1997)).

[50] Braitman v. Overlook Terrace Corp., 332 A.2d 212, 214 (N.J. Super. Ct. App. Div. 1974), *aff'd*, 346 A.2d 76 (N.J. 1975).

[51] Conklin v. Hannoch Weisman, 678 A.2d 1060, 1072-73 (N.J. 1996) ("[I]f conduct creates an unreasonable risk of foreseeable harm, it matters not that the precise injury which occurred was not foreseen. If it is within the realm of foreseeability that some harm might result, negligence may be found.") (quoting Koenig v. Gen. Foods Corp., 403 A.2d 36, 39 (N.J. Super. Ct. App. Div. 1979); then quoting Chomatopoulous v. Roma De Notte Soc. Club, 515 A.2d 296, 300 (N.J. Super Ct. Law Div. 1985)).

[52] Maussner v. Atlantic City Country Club, Inc., 691 A.2d 826, 832 (N.J. Super. Ct. App. Div. 1997) (noting a wrongdoing found to be an efficient and cooperative cause of the harm is combined with an independent or foreseeable intervening cause also leading to the harm does not relieve wrongdoer from liability by proof that an act of God was a concurring cause) (quoting Andreoli v. Nat. Gas Co., 154 A.2d 726, 732 (N.J. Super. Ct. App. Div. 1959)).

[53] *Conklin*, 678 A.2d at 1072 (quoting Scott v. Salem Cty. Mem'l Hosp., 280 A.2d 843, 845 (N.J. Super. Ct. App. Div. 1971)).

the plaintiff's harm may be held liable.[54] Even if, on its own, one risk would not bring the above factor; and therefore, a proximate cause of the plaintiff's harm.[55]

B.   Evidence

Proximate cause can be established with evidence that a reasonable person would foresee the consequences of the negligent act.[56] The jury determines the credibility of evidence and makes inferences from it in order to decide if the defendant breached a duty proximately causing the plaintiff's injury.[57] The plaintiff must show it is more likely than not that the defendant's conduct was a cause-in-fact of the harm.[58] Evidence or reasonable inferences from evidence must establish a proximate cause relation between the defendant's negligence and the plaintiff's injury.[59] The jury determines proximate cause issues based upon the evidence of harm caused by the defendant's breach of duty.[60]

V.   Damages

A.   Elements

Predating any constitution, common-law negligence provided for money damages as redress for tortious conduct.[61] When a defendant's negligent conduct is a substantial factor in bringing about a plaintiff's injuries, the defendant is generally held liable for the injuries that in the ordinary course of events arose from the defendant's negligent conduct.[62] It is essential in protecting society from unreasonable risks of harm to provide recovery for damages stemming from negligent acts.[63] Damage recovery is limited to the value of the legal interest invaded.[64]

---

[54] Kubert v. Best, 75 A.3d 1214, 1222 (N.J. Super. Ct. App. Div. 2013).

[55] Reynolds v. Gonzalez, 798 A.2d 67, 75 (N.J. 2002) (quoting *Scott*, 280 A.2d at 845).

[56] Braitman v. Overlook Terrace Corp., 332 A.2d 212, 214 (N.J. Super. Ct. App. Div. 1974), *aff'd*, 346 A.2d 76 (N.J. 1975).

[57] Scully v. Fitzgerald, 843 A.2d 1110, 1119 (N.J. 2004).

[58] *Braitman*, 332 A.2d at 215 ("Proof of causality need not be established to a certainty. The test as to whether defendants' act caused damage or loss is one of probability or likelihood.").

[59] Doe v. XYC Corp., 887 A.2d 1156, 1169 (N.J. Super. Ct. App. Div. 2005) (quoting Germann v. Matriss, 260 A.2d 825, 831 (N.J. 1970)); Scafidi v. Seiler, 574 A.2d 398, 408 (N.J. 1990) (quoting Joseph H. King, Jr., *Causation, Valuation, and Chance in Personal Injury Torts Involving Preexisting Conditions and Future Consequences*, 90 Yale L.J. 1353, 1356 (1981)).

[60] *Doe*, 887 A.2d at 1169 (quoting *Germann*, 260 A.2d at 831).

[61] Jersey Cent. Power & Light Co. v. Melcar Util. Co., 59 A.3d 561, 568 (N.J. 2013).

[62] Komlodi v. Picciano, 89 A.3d 1234, 1254 (N.J. 2014) (quoting Brown v. U.S. Stove Co., 484 A.2d 1234, 1243 (N.J. 1984)).

[63] Hopkins v. Fox & Lazo Realtors, 625 A.2d 1110, 1120 (N.J. 1993) (noting that preventing accidents and providing redress to injured parties are of equal importance in tort law) (quoting Richard A. Posner, Economic Analysis of Law 78 (1972)).

[64] Reynolds v. Gonzalez, 798 A.2d 67, 77 (N.J. 2002) (quoting Scafidi v. Seiler, 574 A.2d 398, 408 (N.J. 1990)).

B. *Evidence*

The factfinder makes liability and damage determinations.[65] It is the plaintiff's burden to prove by a preponderance of the evidence each damage item claimed and to show the damages were a natural and probable consequence of the defendant's negligent conduct.[66] The jury's damage verdict is "cloaked with a presumption of correctness."[67] As such, courts give juries broad latitude to determine damage amounts.[68] "That is so because in our constitutional system of civil justice, the jury—not a judge—is charged with the responsibility of deciding the merits of a civil claim and the quantum of damages to be awarded plaintiff."[69]

---

[65] Cuevas v. Wentworth Grp., 144 A.3d 890, 901 (N.J. 2016) ("The drafters of our Constitution placed their trust in ordinary men and women of varying experiences and backgrounds, who serve as jurors, to render judgments concerning liability and damages." (citation omitted) (internal quotation marks omitted)) (quoting Johnson v. Scacetti, 927 A.2d 1269, 1282 (N.J. 2007), *overruled in part on other grounds by* Cuevas v. Wentworth, 144 A.3d 890, 903 (N.J. 2016)).

[66] *Reynolds*, 798 A.2d at 82 (quoting W. Page Keeton et al., Prosser & Keeton on the Law of Torts § 41, 269 (5th ed. 1984)).

[67] *Cuevas*, 144 A.3d at 902 (internal quotation marks omitted) (quoting Baxter v. Fairmont Food Co., 379 A.2d 225, 230 (N.J. 1977) ("In the American system of justice the presumption of correctness of a verdict by a jury has behind it the wisdom of centuries of common law merged into our constitutional framework.")).

[68] Caicedo v. Caicedo, 110 A.3d 969, 977 (N.J. Super. Ct. App. Div. 2015); *see also Cuevas*, 144 A.3d at 902 ("A judge may not substitute his judgment for that of the jury merely because he would have reached the opposite conclusion; he is not a . . . decisive juror.") (quoting *Baxter*, 379 A.2d at 230).

[69] *Cuevas*, 144 A.3d at 901; *see also* Anderson v. Sammy Redd & Assocs., 650 A.2d 376, 379 (N.J. Super. Ct. App. Div. 1994) (explaining that questions of breach of duty, foreseeability, and proximate cause are jury determinations).

CHAPTER 32

NEW MEXICO

NEW MEXICO

Matthew C. Kane[1]

I. Purpose of Tort Law

The primary purposes of tort law are compensation of the victim and deterrence of the tortfeasor.[2] Courts should also keep in mind that one of the policies behind the law of torts is the encouragement of reasonable safeguards against risks of harm.[3] Thus, "[i]n New Mexico, negligence encompasses the concepts of foreseeability of harm to the person injured and of a duty of care toward that person."[4]

II. Duty to Exercise Ordinary Care

A. *Question of Law*

"It is thoroughly settled in New Mexico, of course, that whether the defendant owes a duty to the plaintiff is a question of law."[5] The question of duty "must be decided as a matter of law by the judge, using established legal policy."[6] Duty may be based on common law,

---

[1] Director, Ryan, Whaley, Coldiron, Jantzen, Peters & Webber, Adjunct Professor, Oklahoma City University School of Law and Oklahoma College of Law.

[2] Padilla v. Wall Colmonoy Corp., 2006-NMCA-137, 140 N.M. 630, 634, 145 P.3d 110, 114, *as revised* Oct. 31, 2006; *see also* Beavers v. Johnson Controls World Servs., Inc., 1994-NMSC-094, 118 N.M. 391, 399-400, 881 P.2d 1376, 1384-85 (citing Folz v. State, 110 N.M. 457, 467, 797 P.2d 246, 256 (1990) ("Under our fault system, there is a policy of deterrence associated with responsibility for compensatory damages."); *Id.* at 261 (Montgomery, J., specially concurring) ("[O]ur tort law has the dual objectives of compensating victims and deterring negligence.") (citing, inter alia, RESTATEMENT (SECOND) OF TORTS § 901 (1977))).

[3] Enriquez v. Cochran, 1998-NMCA-157, 126 N.M. 196, 222, 967 P.2d 1136, 1162; Saiz v. Belen Sch. Dist., 1992-NMSC-018, 113 N.M. 387, 398, 827 P.2d 102, 113.

[4] Herrera v. Quality Pontiac, 2003-NMSC-018, 134 N.M. 43, 48, 73 P.3d 181, 186 (quoting Ramirez v. Armstrong, 1983-NMSC-104, 100 N.M. 538, 541, 673 P.2d 822, 825, *overruled on other grounds by Folz*, 797 P.2d at 249).

[5] Solon v. WEK Drilling Co., 1992-NMSC-023, 113 N.M. 566, 571, 829 P.2d 645, 650 (citing Bober v. N.M. State Fair, 1991-NMSC-031, 111 N.M. 644, 650, 808 P.2d 614, 620 (citing Schear v. Board of Cty. Comm'rs, 1984-NMSC-079, 101 N.M. 671, 672, 687 P.2d 728, 729)); Tafoya v. Rael, 2008-NMSC-057, 145 N.M. 4, 7, 193 P.3d 551, 554.

[6] *Herrera*, 73 P.3d at 186 (quoting Calkins v. Cox Estates, 1990-NMSC-044, 110 N.M. 59, 61, 792 P.2d 36, 38); *see also* Torres v. State, 1995-NMSC-025, 119 N.M. 609, 612, 894 P.2d 386, 389 ("Policy determines duty."); *Saiz*, 827 P.2d at 113 (citing Ramirez, 673 P.2d at 825 (It is a "policy determination that the obligation of the defendant is one to which the law will give recognition and effect.")); *Schear*, 687 P.2d at 729.

statutory law, or general negligence standards.[7] The primary source for determining policy is the legislature, as it serves as the "voice of the people."[8]

B.   *Question of Fact*

i.   **Elements**

Where the legislature has not articulated a statutory duty, the courts then consider whether common law supports the imposition of a duty under the circumstances of the case.[9] Such a determination cannot be predicated on a foreseeability analysis; rather, "courts must articulate specific policy reasons, unrelated to foreseeability considerations, when deciding whether a defendant does or does not have a duty or that an existing duty should be limited."[10] "[T]he existence and scope of a defendant's duty of care . . . depends on the nature of the [activity] in question, the parties' general relationship to the activity, and public policy considerations."[11] The New Mexico Supreme Court has looked to *Prosser & Keeton* to address the evolving nature of the concept of duty:

> Changing social conditions lead constantly to the recognition of new duties. No better general statement can be made, than that the courts will find a duty where, in general, reasonable men would recognize it and agree that it exists.[12]

The New Mexico Supreme Court has further articulated: "By reference to existing statutes, rules of court, judicial precedent, and other principles comprising the law, we must determine whether the public policy of New Mexico supports a duty that runs [from defendant to plaintiff]."[13] The court must conduct a "careful balancing . . . 'tak[ing] into account

---

[7]   Thompson v. Potter, 2012-NMCA-014, 268 P.3d 57, 63 (citing Lessard v. Coronado Paint & Decorating Ctr., Inc., 2007-NMCA-122, ¶ 30, 142 N.M. 583, 168 P.3d 155); *see also,* Spencer v. Health Force, Inc., 2005-NMSC-002, ¶ 11, 137 N.M. 64, 107 P.3d 504 (noting statutory and common law sources of duty).

[8]   *Torres*, 894 P.2d at 389 ("The judiciary, however, is not as directly and politically responsible to the people as are the legislative and executive branches of government. Courts should make policy in order to determine duty only when the body politic has not spoken and only with the understanding that any misperception of the public mind may be corrected shortly by the legislature."); *Herrera*, 73 P.3d at 188; *see Thompson*, 268 P.3d at 66 (discussing negligence *per se*).

[9]   *Herrera*, 73 P.3d at 188; Vigil v. State Auditor's Office, 2005-NMCA-096, ¶ 16, 138 N.M. 63, 116 P.3d 854.

[10]   Rodriguez v. Del Sol Shopping Ctr. Assocs., L.P., 2014-NMSC-014, 326 P.3d 465, 474.

[11]   *Thompson*, 268 P.3d at 63 (quoting Edward C. v. City of Albuquerque, 2010-NMSC-043, ¶ 14, 148 N.M. 646, 241 P.3d 1086).

[12]   Wilschinsky v. Medina, 1989-NMSC-047, 108 N.M. 511, 513, 775 P.2d 713, 715 (quoting W. PAGE KEETON, PROSSER & KEETON ON THE LAW OF TORTS, § 53, at 359 (5th ed. 1984)).

[13]   Lester *ex rel.* Mavrogenis v. Hall, 1998-NMSC-047, 126 N.M. 404, 407, 970 P.2d 590, 593 (quoting Leyba v. Whitley, 120 N.M. 768, 771, 907 P.2d 172, 175 (1995)); *Thompson*, 268 P.3d at 63 (quoting Estate of Haar v. Ulwelling, 2007-NMCA-032, ¶ 15, 141 N.M. 252, 154 P.3d 67 ("To impose a duty, a relationship must exist that

the likelihood of injury, the magnitude of the burden of guarding against it and the conse-quences of placing that burden upon the defendant.'"[14]

Thus, for example, the New Mexico Supreme Court has indicated that, as a matter of social policy (closely tied to but distinct from the concept of foreseeability) based primarily on prior case law, New Mexico does not recognize a loss of consortium claim brought by parents upon the death of their adult child resulting from the defendant's negligence.[15]

Notably, the existence of a duty for purposes of a negligence action cannot be pred-icated on a duty imposed by contract.[16] However, in limited circumstances (for example, an agreement between attorney and client to act to benefit a third party), the existence of the contract establishes the existence of the intent necessary for a duty to be imposed as a matter of law.[17]

ii. Evidence

The plaintiff has the burden to prove facts upon which the law imposes a duty of care; without presenting such evidence, the court need not rule on the existence or scope of the alleged duty.[18] Violation of a statute may be used to establish negligence by showing (1) that the "statute 'prescribes certain actions or defines a standard of conduct, either explicitly or implicitly,' (2) the defendant 'violate[d] the statute,' (3) the plaintiff is 'in the class of persons sought to be protected by the statute,' and (4) the plaintiff's 'harm or injury . . . must generally be of the type the [l]egislature through the statute sought to prevent.'"[19]

III. Breach of Duty

A. *Elements*

Only after a court has determined that a defendant owed a plaintiff a duty may a jury consider the separate question of whether the defendant breached that duty.[20] Thus, "[w]hile the existence of a duty is a legal determination for the court, '[w]hether a duty has been violated . . .

---

legally obligates a defendant to protect a plaintiff's interest, and in the absence of such a relationship, there exists no general duty to protect others from harm.")).

[14] *Wilschinsky*, 775 P.2d at 715 (quoting Kirk v. Michael Reese Hosp. & Med. Ctr., 117 Ill.2d 507, 526, 111 Ill. Dec. 944, 953, 513 N.E.2d 387, 396 (1987)).

[15] *Solon*, 829 P.2d at 650.

[16] Cottonwood Enters. v. McAlpin, 1991-NMSC-044, 111 N.M. 793, 795-96, 810 P.2d 812, 814-15 (citing Stern v. Farah Bros., 17 N.M. 516, 529, 133 P. 400, 404 (1913)).

[17] *Leyba*, 907 P.2d at 177, n. 2.

[18] *Thompson*, 268 P.3d at 64; Gillin v. Carrows Rests., Inc., 1994-NMCA-089, 118 N.M. 120, 123, 879 P.2d 121, 124.

[19] Paez v. Burlington N. Santa Fe Ry., 2015-NMCA-112, 362 P.3d 116, 127.

[20] *Herrera*, 73 P.3d at 186 (quoting *Schear*, 687 P.2d at 729 ("Negligence is generally a question of fact for the jury. A finding of negligence, however, is dependent upon the existence of a duty on the part of the defendant. Whether a duty exists is a question of law for the courts to decide.")).

is a factual issue to be resolved by the factfinder.'"[21] The New Mexico Supreme Court has further addressed the role of the jury as follows:

> Under the definitions of "negligence" and "ordinary care" in UJI Civil 1601 and 1603, the responsibility for determining whether the defendant has breached a duty owed to the plaintiff entails a determination of what a reasonably prudent person would foresee, what an unreasonable risk of injury would be, and what would constitute an exercise of ordinary care in light of all the surrounding circumstances. This is a factual determination or, perhaps, a mixed determination of law and fact, involving as it does the application of precepts of duty to the historical facts as found by the fact finder.[22]

B. *Evidence*

The burden is on the plaintiff to establish that a breach of duty occurred.[23] The trier of fact weighs all the evidence to make a determination as to whether the defendant breached the duty owed to the plaintiff.[24]

IV. Causation

A. *Elements*

New Mexico adheres to traditional causation elements: cause-in-fact and proximate cause.[25] Thus, "[t]o establish liability [for negligence], there must be a chain of causation initiated by some negligent act or omission of the defendant, which in legal terms is the cause-in-fact or the "but-for" cause of plaintiff's injury."[26] However, the cause-in-fact requirement seemingly receives less attention than in the jurisprudence of other states. Cause-in-fact is most often addressed in the context of a potential intervening cause.[27] Cause-in-fact does not

---

[21] *Gillin*, 879 P.2d at 123 (quoting Lopez v. Ski Apache Resort, 1992-NMCA-047, 114 N.M. 202, 209, 836 P.2d 648, 655); *see also Bober*, 808 P.2d at 620 (quoting Knapp v. Fraternal Order of Eagles, 106 N.M. 11, 13, 738 P.2d 129, 131 (Ct.App.1987) ("[E]very person has a duty to exercise ordinary care for the safety of others. Whether or not defendant breached th[at] dut[y] is a question of the reasonableness of its conduct, and thus a fact question.")).

[22] *Bober*, 808 P.2d at 620.

[23] McMillan v. Allstate Indem. Co., 2004-NMSC-002, 135 N.M. 17, 23, 84 P.3d 65, 71; Tanuz v. Carlberg, 1996-NMCA-076, 122 N.M. 113, 116-17, 921 P.2d 309, 312-13.

[24] *Tanuz,* 921 P.2d at 316; Davila v. Bodelson, 1985-NMCA-072, 103 N.M. 243, 249, 704 P.2d 1119, 1125.

[25] Romero v. Giant Stop-N-Go of New Mexico, Inc., 2009-NMCA-059, 146 N.M. 520, 522, 212 P.3d 408, 410 (citing *Herrera*, 73 P.3d at 186-87).

[26] Chamberland v. Roswell Osteopathic Clinic, Inc., 2001-NMCA-045, 130 N.M. 532, 536, 27 P.3d 1019, 1023.

[27] *Chamberland*, 27 P.3d at 1022. For instance, "the independent intervening cause instruction presupposes causation in fact and comes into play only if the evidence shows (1) negligence by a defendant that is a cause-in-fact, or "but-for" cause, of the plaintiff's injury, see UJI 13-305, and (2) the intervention of an independent, unforeseeable event that "interrupts and turns aside" the normal progression of that causation in fact, see UJI 13-306. Without causation in fact, there can be no independent intervening cause." *Id.* at 1024.

have a stand-alone jury instruction. However, one opinion has found that the cause-in-fact requirement is contained within the proximate cause instruction.[28]

In its simplest terms, proximate or "legal" cause is a reasonably "close causal connection between the conduct and the resulting injury."[29] "The proximate causation element . . . is concerned with whether and to what extent the defendant's conduct foreseeably and substantially caused the specific injury that actually occurred. [It] is part of the much more specific *factual* requirement that must be proved to win the case once the courthouse doors are open."[30] The New Mexico Court of Appeals has recently provided the following, significantly detailed analysis (which seemingly subsumes a cause-in-fact determination):

> We have defined the element of "proximate cause" to be that which, in a natural or continuous sequence, produces the injury and without which the injury would not have occurred. Proximate cause encompasses whether and to what extent the defendant's conduct foreseeably and substantially caused the specific injury that actually occurred. . . . An act or omission may be deemed a "proximate cause" of an injury if it contributes to bringing about the injury, if the injury would not have occurred without it, and if it is reasonably connected as a significant link to the injury. Absent the element of proximate cause, a claim for negligence fails regardless of the presence of the remaining elements of the cause of action.[31]

B. Evidence

The question of foreseeability on the issue of causation is generally for the trier of fact.[32] "The argument before the jury when it is determining whether breach occurred is whether the foreseeable likelihood and severity of injuries that might have occurred due to the defendant's conduct warranted the additional precautions argued by the plaintiff."[33] Circumstantial evidence produced by the plaintiff may be sufficient to raise the issue of actual cause.[34] Moreover, submitting evidence to support an inference in favor of the plaintiff regarding proximate cause may also give rise to a jury question.[35]

---

[28] *Id.* at 1023 (citing to UJI 13-305 "encompassing cause-in-fact within our instruction on proximate cause, defining it as 'that . . . without which the injury would not have occurred.'").

[29] Holland v. Lawless, 1981-NMCA-004, 95 N.M. 490, 495, 623 P.2d 1004, 1009 (citing W. PROSSER, LAW OF TORTS § 30 (4th ed. 1971)).

[30] *Herrera*, 73 P.3d at 186.

[31] Paez v. Burlington N. Santa Fe Ry., 2015-NMCA-112, 362 P.3d 116, 121-22 (internal citations and quotations omitted).

[32] *Id.*

[33] *Rodriguez*, 326 P.3d at 468 (citing Ford v. Bd. of Cty. Comm'rs, 1994-NMSC-077, ¶ 12, 118 N.M. 134, 879 P.2d 766).

[34] Richards v. Upjohn Co., 1980-NMCA-062, 95 N.M. 675, 678, 625 P.2d 1192, 1195.

[35] *Tafoya*, 890 P.2d at 804; *see also* Deakin v. Putt, 1979-NMCA-053, 93 N.M. 58, 61, 596 P.2d 271, 274, Hepp v. Quickel Auto & Supply Co., 37 N.M. 525, 25 P.2d 197 (1933).

The necessity of an expert witness to establish causation varies based on the nature of the case. For instance:

- To prove causation in a toxic tort case, a plaintiff must first show that a suspected cause actually is capable of causing a particular injury or condition in the general population. After establishing such general causation, the plaintiff must then demonstrate specific causation: that the suspected cause did actually cause the plaintiff's injury. [36]
- Expert testimony is generally required to show causation in professional malpractice cases . . . However, where negligence on the part of the doctor is demonstrated by facts which can be evaluated by resort to common knowledge, expert testimony is not required."[37]

If expert testimony is sufficient to support reasonable inferences that the plaintiff's injuries were the proximate result of the defendant's conduct, the question remains one for the trier-of-fact.[38] However, where an "expert fail[s] to provide the jury with sufficient evidence on the element of causation, such that a reasonable jury would have a legally sufficient evidentiary basis to find for Plaintiff," then the defendant prevails as a matter of law.[39]

In sum:

[P]roximate cause becomes an issue of law when the facts are undisputed and the reasonable inferences from those facts are plain and consistent. In order to determine that a breach of duty did not legally cause the alleged damages, the district court must conclude that no reasonable jury would find that the breach of duty by the defendant legally caused the damages suffered by the plaintiff. [Courts] may still decide whether a defendant did or did not breach the duty of ordinary care as a matter of law, or that the breach of duty did not legally cause the damages alleged in the case.[40]

V. Damages

A. Elements

While the fact that one is injured does not itself establish liability,[41] damages are a necessary element of a negligence claim.[42]

---

[36] Conception & Rosario Acosta v. Shell W. Expl. & Prod., Inc., 2016-NMSC-012, 370 P.3d 761, 767 (citations and quotations omitted).

[37] Am. Mech. Sols., L.L.C. v. Northland Process Piping, Inc., No. CV 13-1062 JB/SCY, 2016 WL 3124633, at *22 (D.N.M. Apr. 30, 2016).

[38] Berlangieri v. Running Elk Corp., 2002-NMCA-060, 132 N.M. 332, 340, 48 P.3d 70, 78.

[39] Lopez v. Martinez, No. 32,085, 2014 WL 7187065, at *1 (N.M. Ct. App. Nov. 17, 2014).

[40] Paez v. Burlington N. Santa Fe Ry., 2015-NMCA-112, 362 P.3d 116, 121-22 (internal citations omitted).

[41] Archibeque v. Homrich, 1975-NMSC-066, 88 N.M. 527, 531, 543 P.2d 820, 824 (citing Waterman v. Ciesielski, 87 N.M. 25, 528 P.2d 884 (1974)).

[42] Lopez v. Maez, 1982-NMSC-103, 98 N.M. 625, 630, 651 P.2d 1269, 1274; Goffe v. Pharmaseal Labs., Inc., 1976-NMCA-123, 90 N.M. 764, 767, 568 P.2d 600, 603 (quoting WILLIAM L. PROSSER, HANDBOOK OF THE LAW OF TORTS, § 30, at 143-44 (4th ed. 1971)), rev'd in part on other grounds by 90 N.M. 753, 568 P.2d 589 (1977); Alberts v. Schultz, 1999-NMSC-015, 126 N.M. 807, 975 P.2d 1279, 1284; Tafoya, 890 P.2d at 805.

Once the existence of damage is established, the question then turns to the amount of damages. The proper measure of damages should be the difference between what the plaintiff would have owed absent the negligence and what the plaintiff paid because of the negligence, plus incidental damages. We believe that this measure of damages most closely comports with the purpose of compensatory damages, which is to fully compensate a plaintiff, or restore [the] plaintiff to his [or her] rightful position.[43]

This includes application of the "thin skull" rule.[44] "The theory of damages is to make an injured person whole . . . The rules for measuring damages are not inflexible, the object is to afford just compensation for the injuries received."[45] Such compensatory damages are recoverable if they "proximately result" from the defendant's culpable conduct.[46] Using slightly different terms, "consequential damages," defined as "reasonable foreseeable damage resulting from [the defendant's] negligence," may be recovered.[47]

New Mexico requires an award of damages that "will reasonably and fairly compensate" the plaintiff for her injuries.[48] Compensable damages include, among others: value of lost earnings (including awards to minors for earnings after reaching the age 18),[49] medical expenses—present and future,[50] non-medical expense (such as caretaking expenses, although inconvenience is insufficient)—present and future,[51] nature, extent and duration of the injury (including disfigurement),[52] and pain and suffering.[53]

In *Lovelace Med. Ctr. v. Mendez*, the New Mexico Supreme Court addressed the issue of damages in the context of a "wrongful birth" case:

> We particularly agree with Judge Alarid that the fundamental question on the merits issue in this appeal is a question as to measure of damages. Given that a tort has occurred (the doctor's negligence in performing the sterilization operation and failing to inform the mother of the unsuccessful outcome) and given that an injury has resulted from this tort (the mother's continued fertility, despite her desire and effort to be sterilized), what is the measure of damages to compensate her for the injury she has suffered? As Judge Alarid points out, it is virtually undisputed that *some* elements

---

[43] Maese v. Garrett, 2014-NMCA-072, 329 P.3d 713, 718, *cert. denied sub nom.* Maese v. Garret, 2014-NMCERT-006, 328 P.3d 1187 (citations and quotations omitted).

[44] "[A]lthough the condition may contribute to the injury, as long as Defendant's conduct can be said to have proximately caused the injury, he will be held liable for the resulting injuries. The eggshell plaintiff theory of liability prevents the defendant from escaping liability when his conduct precipitates a more severe injury than a person of normal health would typically suffer." Salopek v. Friedman, 2013-NMCA-087, 308 P.3d 139, 148.

[45] Topmiller v. Cain, 1983-NMCA-005, 99 N.M. 311, 314, 657 P.2d 638, 641.

[46] *Id.*

[47] *Id.* at 642.

[48] N.M.U.J.I. 13-916.

[49] N.M.U.J.I. 13-1803.

[50] N.M.U.J.I. 1804.

[51] N.M.U.J.I. 1805.

[52] N.M.U.J.I. 1806.

[53] N.M.U.J.I. 1807.

of damages are compensable for this tort—*e.g.,* Mrs. Mendez's pain and suffering associated with her pregnancy and Joseph's birth; the cost of a subsequent sterilization; and her expenses, including lost wages, associated with the pregnancy and the birth. To be sure, the most controversial item of claimed damage—the cost of raising Joseph to adulthood—is the critical issue in this case; but it is an issue primarily involving quantification of the plaintiff's loss.[54]

B. *Evidence*

New Mexico case law reveals little as to the specific evidence necessary to support a damages award. However, the following passage shows various categories of damages as well as the use of experts to establish a basis for the award:

> As to the proof of damages, the record discloses the following: Appellee was a plumber, drawing $1.87 per hour at the time, and had a life expectancy of 21.63 years. The accident occurred January 3, 1953, and appellee did not regain complete consciousness for some months thereafter. He had an injured knee cap and a broken hip; his chest was crushed; his face was lacerated; his left lung was injured and most of his ribs were broken; his right arm and collar bone were broken; he had a serious head injury; his leg was broken and placed in a cast for several months, and finally in June following, it was amputated; his right arm, fingers, and shoulders are stiff. He suffered pain and continues to do so. He was hospitalized for several months. Medical experts testified that his injuries are permanent and that he never again will be able to perform manual labor. There were hospital, ambulance, surgical, medical, and nurse expenses; and his 1952 automobile was a total loss. We deem this evidence substantial.[55]

Generally, courts will not disturb an award of damages on appeal "except where it appears to have resulted from passion, prejudice, partiality, sympathy, undue influence, or some corrupt cause or motive, where there has been palpable error, or the measure of damages has been mistaken."[56] Whether or not a damage award is excessive must be determined based on the evidence in that case; comparing the award to awards in other cases is improper.[57] "A remittitur may only be ordered when the issue of damages is separable and

---

[54] Lovelace Med. Ctr. v. Mendez, 1991-NMSC-002, 111 N.M. 336, 342, 805 P.2d 603, 609.

[55] Burkhart v. Corn, 1955-NMSC-032, 59 N.M. 343, 347-48, 284 P.2d 226, 229, *holding modified by* Madrid v. Shryock, 1987-NMSC-106, 106 N.M. 467, 745 P.2d 375; *see also* Robinson v. Mem'l Gen. Hosp., 1982-NMCA-167, 99 N.M. 60, 64, 653 P.2d 891, 895 ("The damage items on which the jury was instructed included present and future medical expense, pain and suffering, the aggravation of a pre-existing physical condition, and the nature, extent and duration of the injury. The evidence supporting each of the damage items is substantial and supports the jury's determination of the total amount of plaintiff's damage.").

[56] Hammond v. Blackwell, 1966-NMSC-258, 77 N.M. 209, 212, 421 P.2d 124, 126.

[57] *Robinson*, 653 P.2d at 895.

distinct from the issues of liability, contributory negligence and where all issues other than the one of damages have been fully and fairly decided by a jury."[58] If the court grants a remittitur, "the plaintiff is given the option of remitting the excess and having affirmance of the judgment for the remainder" or a new trial on damages will be conducted.[59] New Mexico also acknowledges the potential for "additur . . . [an] order, issued usu[ally] with the defendant's consent, that increases the jury's award of damages to avoid a new trial on grounds of inadequate damages," albeit predicated on its general analysis of the propriety of disturbing a damages award on appeal.[60]

---

[58] Vivian v. Atchison, T. & S.F. Ry. Co., 1961-NMSC-093, 69 N.M. 6, 12, 363 P.2d 620, 624.

[59] *Id.* ("However, whereas here the issues of liability and contributory negligence have been fairly decided by a jury, if the plaintiff should elect not to remit in accordance with the option granted, those issues should not be relitigated in the absence of other controlling reasons even though a new trial is required on the issue of damages.").

[60] Hicks v. Eller, 2012-NMCA-061, 280 P.3d 304, 312 (quoting Black's Law Dictionary 44 (9th ed. 2009)).

CHAPTER 33

NEW YORK

NEW YORK

Margaret (Meg) Butler[1]

I. Purpose of Tort Law

New York tort law has several purposes. They include holding responsible "those who cause socially unreasonable injuries" and deterring similar conduct.[2] Another purpose is compensating the injured or wronged party.[3] When awarding compensatory damages, the purpose is "to make the injured [party] whole."[4] The courts consider "the larger social consequences of our decisions" and thus apportion risks and assign the burden of loss to control the degree of legal consequences for wrongs.[5] Though the courts do not seek to provide "a windfall opportunity" for a plaintiff "to fare better as a result" of the negligence than he would have fared if reasonable care had been exercised,[6] "the liability to make reparation for an injury rests not upon the consideration of any reciprocal obligation, but upon an original moral duty enjoined upon every person so to conduct himself, or exercise his own rights as not to injure another."[7]

---

[1] Associate Director for Public Services, Georgia State University College of Law Library

[2] 5th Ave. Chocolatiere, Ltd. v. 540 Acquisition Co., 272 A.D. 2d 23, 28, 712 N.Y.S.2d 8, 12 (N.Y. App. Div. 2000), *rev'd sub nom.* 532 Madison Ave. Gourmet Foods, Inc. v. Finlandia Ctr., Inc., 96 N.Y.2d, 727 N.Y.S.2d 49, 750 N.E.2d 1097 (N.Y. 2001) (citing PROSSER AND KEETON, THE LAW OF TORTS 1-6 (5th ed. 1984).

[3] *Id.*

[4] *See* McKenna v. Forsyth & Forsyth, 280 A.D.2d 79, 83, 720 N.Y.S.2d 654, 657 (N.Y. App. Div. 2001) (quoting Campagnola v. Muholland, Minon & Roe, 76 N.Y.2d 38, 42, 556 N.Y.S.2d 239, 241, 555 N.E.2d 611, 613 (N.Y. 1990)).

[5] Landon v. Kroll Lab. Specialists, Inc., 91 A.D.3d 79, 86-87, 934 N.Y.S.2d 183, 191 (N.Y. App. Div. 2011), *aff'd*, 22 N.Y.3d 1, 999 N.E.2d 1121 (N.Y. 2013); *see also* Waters v. New York City Hous. Auth., 69 N.Y.2d 225, 229, 513 N.Y.S.2d 356, 505 N.E.2d 922 (N.Y. 1987) (In determining the existence of a duty, "not only logic and science, but policy play an important role. The common law of torts is, at its foundation, a means of apportioning risks and allocating the burden of loss. While moral and logical judgments are significant components of the analysis, we are also bound to consider the larger social consequences of our decisions and to tailor our notion of duty so that the legal consequences of wrongs are limited to a controllable degree.) (citations and internal quotation marks omitted); *Id.,* 69 N.Y.2d at 229, 513 N.Y.S.2d at 358, 505 N.E.2d at 923-24.

[6] *See* Rudolf v. Shayne, Dachs, Stanisci, Corker, & Sauer, 31 A.D.3d 418, 422, 818 N.Y.S.2d 153, 156 (N.Y. App. Div. 2006), *aff'd as modified*, 8 N.Y. 3d 438, 867 N.E.2d 385 (N.Y. 2007).

[7] Rich v. New York Cent. & Hudson Riv. R.R., 87 N.Y. 382, 398 (N.Y. 1882) (citing Kerwhacker v. Cleveland, Columbus & Cincinnati R.R., 3 Ohio St. 172, 188 (Ohio 1854)).

II.   Duty to Exercise Ordinary Care

A.   *Question of Law*

Before an act can give rise to negligence, there must be a duty of care to the claimant, "the observance of which would have averted or avoided the injury."[8] The duty to avoid causing injury to others is imposed by law.[9] The courts determine whether a duty exists as a question of law.[10] Early New York cases found that when a duty exists, it may exist "as to all the world."[11] The Court of Appeals has more recently required instead "a duty running directly to the injured person . . . however careless the conduct or foreseeable the harm."[12] The scope of the duty owed to the plaintiff "is defined by the risk of harm reasonably to be perceived."[13] The harm must be "within the class of reasonably foreseeable hazards" for liability to attach.[14]

Foreseeability is one consideration that helps determine the scope of a duty determined to exist.[15] In determining whether a duty exists, courts consider the relationship of the parties, "whether the plaintiff was within the zone of foreseeable harm, and whether the consequences were reasonably foreseeable."[16]

Since Palsgraf, the historic question used to assess foreseeability and duty has been whether "every one of ordinary sense who did think" would recognize the danger of injury to a foreseeable party arising from the failure to use ordinary care and skill.[17] In other words, the duty arises when a foreseeable harm injures a foreseeable person due to the failure of a defendant to use ordinary care. No person would be expected to guard against events that would be commonly disregarded as so unlikely.[18] New York has adopted the zone of danger

---

[8] Palsgraf v. Long Island R.R., 248 N.Y. 339, 342, 162 N.E. 99, 99-100 (N.Y. 1928) (citing West Virginia Cent. & P. Ry. v. State, 96 Md. 652, 656, 54 A. 669, 671 (Md. 1903)). The requirement of a duty of care is axiomatic. Kennedy-McInnis v. Biomedical Tissue Servs., Ltd., 178 F. Supp. 3d 97 (W.D.N.Y. 2016) (citing Kimmell v. Schaefer, 89 N.Y.2d 257, 263, 652 N.Y.S.2d 715, 675 N.E.2d 450 (N.Y. 1996)).

[9] New York Univ. v. Cont'l Ins., 87 N.Y.2d 308, 316, 639 N.Y.S.2d 283, 287, 662 N.E.2d 763, 765 (N.Y. 1995).

[10] *Kimmell*, 675 N.E.2d at 454.

[11] *See* Kain v. Smith, 80 N.Y. 458, 466 (N.Y. 1880) (citations omitted).

[12] Lauer v. City of New York, 95 N.Y.2d 95, 100, 733 N.E.2d 184, 187 (N.Y. 2000).

[13] Sanchez v. State of New York, 99 N.Y.2d, 247, 252, 754 N.Y.S.2d 621, 624, 784 N.E.2d 675, 678 (N.Y. 2002).

[14] *Id.*

[15] Hamilton v. Beretta U.S.A. Corp., 96 N.Y.2d 222, 232, 727 N.Y.S.2d 7, 13, 750 N.E.2d 1055, 1060 (N.Y. 2001), *opinion after certified question answered*, 264 F.3d 21 (2d Cir. 2001); *see also* Galasso v. Wegmans Food Mkts., Inc., 53 A.D.3d 1145, 1145, 862 N.Y.S.2d 246, 246 (N.Y. App. Div. 2008) (citations omitted).

[16] Dance Magic, Inc. v. Pike Realty, Inc., 85 A.D.3d 1083, 1089, 926 N.Y.S.2d 588, 593 (N.Y. App. Div. 2011) (citations omitted).

[17] Havas v. Victory Paper Stock Co., 49 N.Y.2d 381, 386, 402 N.E.2d 1136, 1138 (N.Y. 1980) (citing *Palsgraf*, 248 N.Y. at 344 (quoting Heaven v. Prender, 11 Q.B.D. 503, 509, Britt. M.R. (1883)).

[18] Lafontant v. U-Haul Co. of Florida, 48 A.D.3d 757, 759, 854 N.Y.S.2d 405, 406 (N.Y. App. Div. 2008) (quoting DiPonzio v. Riordan, 89 N.Y.2d 578, 583, 657 N.Y.S.2d 377, 380, 679 N.E.2d 616, 619 (N.Y. 1997) (quoting PROSSER AND KEETON, LAW OF TORTS § 31, at 170 (5th ed.))).

rule, so that a plaintiff who has observed the serious injury or death of an immediate family member may recover "damages for injuries suffered in consequence of the observation" so long as the plaintiff was also endangered "by the negligence of the defendant."[19]

A determination of the scope of the duty of care owed to a plaintiff is a complex question of law, requiring courts to balance sometimes competing public policy considerations.[20] Due to the policy nature of the analysis of whether a duty exists and the scope of any duty, there is no bright-line rule,[21] nor can it be "derived or discerned from an algebraic formula."[22] Factors considered include "logic, science, weighty competing socioeconomic policies and sometimes contractual assumptions of responsibility."[23] Further factors balanced include "the reasonable expectations of parties and society generally, the proliferation of claims, the likelihood of unlimited or insurer-like liability, disproportionate risk and reparation allocation, and public policies affecting the expansion or limitation of new channels of liability' . . . [.] Thus, in determining whether a duty exists, 'courts must be mindful of the precedential, and consequential, future effects of their rulings, and 'limit the legal consequences of wrongs to a controllable degree.'"[24] Courts are cautioned that the imposition of a legal duty where none had existed must be made with extreme care, "for legal duty imposes liability."[25]

The standard of care is the "reasonable and prudent" person test.[26] "Negligence involves the failure to exercise the degree of care that a reasonably prudent person would exercise in the same circumstances."[27] The standards of the community may also be factored into expectations for the reasonable person.[28] Ordinary care should be exercised "in proportion to the danger to be avoided and the consequences that might reasonably be anticipated."[29]

---

[19] Bovsun v. Sanperi, 61 N.Y.2d 219, 231, 473 N.Y.S.2d 357, 362-63, 461 N.E.2d 843, 848-49 (N.Y. 1984) (adopting the zone-of danger rule discussed in RESTATEMENT (SECOND) OF TORTS § 436 (1965)).

[20] Espinal v. Melville Snow Contractors, Inc., 98 N.Y.2d 136, 138, 746 N.Y.S.2d 120, 122, 773 N.E.2d 485, 487 (N.Y. 2002) (citing Palka v. Servicemaster Mgmt. Servs. Corp., 83 N.Y.2d 579, 586, 611 N.Y.S.2d 817, 821, 634 N.E.2d 189, 193 (N.Y. 1994); Eaves Brooks Costume Co. v. Y.B.H. Realty Corp., 76 N.Y.2d 220, 226-27, 557 N.Y.S.2d 286, 289, 556 N.E.2d 1093, 1096 (N.Y. 1990)); see also Alfaro v. Wal-Mart Stores, Inc., 210 F.3d 111, 114 (2d Cir. 2011) (citing Palka, 634 N.E.2d at 192).

[21] Espinal, 773 N.E.2d at 487. The Court of Appeals notes that in some circumstances a party to a service contract may assume a duty of care to third persons. Id.

[22] Palka, 634 N.E.2d at 192.

[23] In re Sept. 11 Litig., 905 F. Supp. 2d 547, 552 (S.D.N.Y. 2012) (quoting Alfaro, 219 F.3d at 114).

[24] Church ex rel. Smith v. Callanan Indus. Inc., 285 A.D.2d 16, 20, 729 N.Y.S.2d 545, 548 (N.Y. App. Div. 2001), aff'd, 99 N.Y.2d 104, 752 N.Y.S.2d 254, 782 N.E.2d 50 (N.Y. 2002) (quoting Hamilton v. Beretta U.S.A. Corp., 96 N.Y.2d 222, 232, 727 N.Y.S.2d 7, 750 N.E.2d 1055 (N.Y. 2001)).

[25] Pulka v. Edelman, 40 N.Y.2d 781, 786, 390 N.Y.S.2d 393, 397, 358 N.E.2d 1019, 1022 (N.Y. 1976).

[26] Sadowski v. Long Island R.R., 292 N.Y. 448, 454, 55 N.E.2d 497, 499 (N.Y. 1944) (citing Tiller v. Atl. Coast Line R.R., 318 U.S. 54, 67 (1943)).

[27] Cooper v. Burt's Reliable, Inc., 105 A.D.3d 886, 887, 964 N.Y.S.2d 195, 197 (N.Y. App. Div. 2013) (quoting Bello v. Transit Auth. of N.Y. City, 12 A.D.3d 58, 60, 783 N.Y.S.2d 648 (N.Y. App. Div. 2004)); see N.Y. Pattern Jury Instr.—Civil 2:10 (Dec. 2015); RESTATEMENT (SECOND) OF TORTS § 299) (1964).

[28] Shannahan v. Empire Eng'g Corp., 204 N.Y. 543, 550, 98 N.E. 9, 11 (N.Y. 1912). "We have said that 'ordinarily what everybody does is all that anybody need do.'" Id.

[29] Sadowski, 55 N.E.2d at 500 (citing Baltimore & Potomac R.R. v. Jones, 95 U.S. 439 (1913)); Bailey v. Cent. Vt. Ry., 319 U.S. 350 (1943).

In the context of dangerous activities, the analysis of foreseeability and duty requires a second step. In evaluating whether a duty exists, and the scope of that duty, the court must examine the "plaintiff's reasonable expectations of the care owed him by others."[30] A plaintiff who understands and accepts the risk of danger and participates anyway cannot recover for an injury as a result of those risks.[31]

B. Question of Fact

i. Elements

Whether a duty to exercise ordinary care exists is a determination of law for the court,[32] rather than fact for the jury. The jury considers the facts and determines whether there has been a lack of ordinary care.[33]

ii. Evidence

The plaintiff bears the burden of establishing a duty owed by the defendants.[34] Further, the plaintiff must demonstrate breach and injury to establish a prima facie case of negligence.[35] Violation of an administrative rule or safety regulation, in and of itself, can be considered as some evidence of negligence.[36] A plaintiff may establish negligence by showing violation of "a statute without an adequate excuse and the violation causes the harm that the statute was created to prevent."[37]

III. Breach of Duty

A. Elements

A defendant must breach a duty owed to a plaintiff to be liable in negligence.[38] When considering whether there has been a breach of duty, the factfinder answers the question whether the defendant acted as a reasonable person would have acted under the same circumstances, considering the foreseeable risk.[39] In evaluating whether there was a breach of duty,

---

[30] Turcotte v. Fell, 68 N.Y.2d 432, 437, 510 N.Y.S.2d 49, 52, 502 N.E.2d 964, 967 (N.Y. 1986).

[31] Id.

[32] N. Assur. Co. v. Nick, 203 A.D.2d 342, 343, 610 N.Y.S.2d 307, 308-09 (N.Y. App. Div. 1994) (citing Eiseman v. State of New York, 70 N.Y.2d 175, 187, 518 N.Y.S.2d 608, 613, 511 N.E.2d 1128, 1134 (N.Y. 1987)).

[33] See Quinlan v. Cecchini, 41 N.Y.2d 686, 690, 394 N.Y.S.2d 872, 875, 363 N.E.2d 578, 581 (N.Y. 1977) (citations omitted); Seeger v. Marketplace, 101 A.D. 3d 1691, 1692, 956 N.Y.S.2d 770, 772 (N.Y. App. Div. 2012).

[34] Solomon v. City of New York, 66 N.Y.2d 1026, 1027, 499 N.Y.S.2d 392, 489 N.E.2d 1294, 1294-95 (N.Y. 1985) (citing Akins v. Glens Falls City Sch. Dist., 53 N.Y.2d 325, 333, 441 N.Y.S.2d 644, 648, 424 N.E.2d 531, 535 (N.Y. 1981)) (citing PROSSER AND KEETON THE LAW OF TORTS §30 at 143 (4th ed.)).

[35] Id.

[36] Cruz v. Long Island R.R., 22 A.D.3d 451, 453, 803 N.Y.S.2d 91, 94 (N.Y. App. Div. 2005); Black v. City of Schenectady, 21 A.D.3d 661, 662, 800 N.Y.S.2d 240, 242 (N.Y. App. Div. 2005).

[37] Lowell v. Peters, 3 A.D.3d 778, 780, 770 N.Y.S.2d 796, 798-99 (N.Y. App. Div. 2004).

[38] Strauss v. Belle Realty Co., 65 N.Y.2d 399, 402, 492 N.Y.S.2d 555, 557, 482 N.E.2d 34, 36 (N.Y. 1985).

[39] Sadowski, 55 N.E.2d at 499 (citations omitted).

or negligence, the factfinder considers foreseeability of possible harm and its severity as well as the burden of precautions.[40] The factfinder also considers the circumstances in existence, or known, when the defendant was allegedly negligent, not subsequent acts.[41] Negligence is described as "a matter of time, place, and circumstance."[42]

B.   Evidence

The jury normally determines whether a breach of duty has occurred[43] as well as the extent of the breach.[44] The plaintiff bears the burden of establishing the breach.[45] The plaintiff may prove negligence by direct evidence or clear inferences. Liability cannot rest on conjecture.[46] To establish a prima facie case, the plaintiff must show "facts and conditions from which defendant's negligence and causation of accident by such negligence may be reasonably inferred."[47] Although circumstantial evidence may be sufficient to establish a prima facie case of negligence,[48] inferences must be reasonably drawn from circumstantial evidence.[49]

When proving breach, the plaintiff may offer evidence regarding compliance with an organization's internal rules, administrative code provisions, and statutes. Note that the failure to comply with internal company rules that require more care than that required by the reasonable person standard is not evidence of negligence.[50] Similarly, a jury may consider evidence of common usage and custom, but the evidentiary worth is determined by the circumstances of the case.[51] An administrative agency regulation "is merely some evidence to be considered on the question of a defendant's negligence."[52] For agency regulations to be considered by the jury, "the actual injury must have been a consequence against which the

---

[40] Korean Air Lines Co. v. McLean, 118 F. Supp. 3d 471, 486 (E.D.N.Y. 2015) (citation omitted).

[41] Alfieri v. Carmelite Nursing Home, Inc., 29 Misc.3d 509, 511, 907 N.Y.S.2d 577, 579 (N.Y. Civ. Ct. 2010) (citing Quinn v. City of New York, 145 A.D. 195, 197, 129 N.Y.S. 1028 (N.Y. App. Div. 1911); Dougan v. Champlain Transp. Co., 56 N.Y. 1, 8 (N.Y. 1873)).

[42] Levine v. City of New York, 309 N.Y. 88, 92, 127 N.E.2d 825, 826 (N.Y. 1955).

[43] Di Benedetto v. Pan Am. World Serv., Inc., 359 F.3d 627, 630 (2d Cir. 2004) (citing Stagle v. Delta Airlines, 52 F.3d 463, 469 (2d Cir.1995)).

[44] Evarts v. Pyro Eng'g, Inc., 117 A.D.3d 1148, 1150, 985 N.Y.S.2d 179, 181 (N.Y. App. Div. 2014) (citing Grant v. Nembhard, 94 A.D.3d 1397, 1398, 943 N.Y.S.2d 272 (N.Y. App. Div. 2012)).

[45] Krull v. U.S., 9 F. Supp. 3d 298, 302 (W.D.N.Y. 2015) (quoting *Stagle*, 52 F.3d at 467 (2d Cir. 1995)).

[46] Halverson v. 562 West 149th St. Corp., 290 N.Y. 40, 43, 47 N.E.2d 685, 687 (N.Y. 1943) (quoting Holland House Co. v. Baird, 169 N.Y. 136, 142, 62 N.E. 149, 151 (N.Y. 1901)).

[47] Ingersoll v. Liberty Bank of Buffalo, 278 N.Y. 1, 7, 14 N.E.2d 828, 830 (N.Y. 1938) (citing Stubbs v. City of Rochester, 226 N.Y. 516, 526, 124 N.E. 137, 140 (N.Y. 1919)).

[48] Wurtzel v. Starbucks Coffee Co., 257 F. Supp. 2d 520, 526 (E.D. N.Y. 2003).

[49] *Id.* (quoting Bradish v. Tank Tech Corp., 216 A.D.2d 505, 506, 628 N.Y.S.2d 807, 809 (N.Y. App. Div. 1995)).

[50] Gilson v. Metro. Opera, 5 N.Y.3d 574, 577, 807 N.Y.S.2d 588, 590, 841 N.E.2d 747, 749 (N.Y. 2005) (Justice Smith filed a dissenting opinion) (quoting Sherman v. Robinson, 80 N.Y.2d 483, 489, 591 N.Y.S.2d 974, 978, 606 N.E.2d 1365, 1369 (N.Y. 1992)).

[51] Trembley v. Coca-Cola Bottling Co., 285 A.D. 539, 540-41,138 N.Y.S.2d 332, 334 (N.Y. App. Div. 1955) (citing Saglimbeni v. W. End Brewing Co., 274 App. Div. 201, 204, 80 N.Y.S.2d 635, 637 (N.Y. App. Div. 1948)).

[52] Juarez v. Wavecrest Mgmt. Team Ltd., 88 N.Y.2d 628, 645, 649 N.Y.S.2d 115, 121, 672 N.E.2d 135, 141 (N.Y. 1996) (citations omitted).

regulation was intended to protect."[53] Regulatory statutes, which contain no reference to civil remedies, may be admissible on the question of negligence.[54] The Noseworthy doctrine may apply to reduce the burden of proof on claims for amnesiacs, decedents, and others who are unable to recall or testify regarding the alleged negligence.[55] In Noseworthy v. City of New York,[56] the Court of Appeals of New York held that in some cases, such as wrongful death actions, the plaintiff is entitled to an instruction that "the plaintiff is not held to the high degree of proof required in a case where the injured party may take the stand and give his version of the happening of the accident."[57] Statistical evidence and methods may be used to establish liability, especially in the context of mass torts.[58]

IV. Causation

A. Elements

Causation is the "essential link between negligent conduct and its consequences,"[59] and causation must be proven to sustain a claim.[60] This means that the plaintiff must demonstrate that the alleged injury was "more likely" or "more reasonabl[y]" caused by the defendant than some other party.[61] A defendant remains liable for all normal and foreseeable consequences of his acts.[62] Foreseeability is viewed "as of the time the damage was done," rather than at the time of the tortious act or omission.[63] The precise manner in which the accident happened and the extent of the injuries need not have been foreseeable.[64] Foreseeability may be limited to the "natural" or "probable" results of actions, with attenuated consequences

---

[53] O'Leary v. Am. Airlines, 100 A.D.2d. 959, 960, 475 N.Y.S.2d 285, 288 (N.Y. App. Div. 1999) (citing Chester Litho v. Palisades Interstate Park Comm., 33 A.D.2d 202, 205, 305 N.Y.S.2d 682, 686 (N.Y. App. Div. 1969), aff'd., 27 N.Y.2d 323, 317 N.Y.S.2d 761, 266 N.E.2d 229 (N.Y. 1971)).

[54] See Dance v. Town of Southampton, 95 A.D.2d 442, 448-49, 467 N.Y.S.2d 203, 208 (N.Y. App. Div. 1983).

[55] Lynn v. Lynn, 216 A.D.2d 194, 194-95, 628 N.Y.S.2d 667, 668 (N.Y. App. Div. 1995).

[56] Noseworthy v. City of New York, 298 N.Y. 76, 80, 80 N.E.2d 744, 745 (N.Y. 1948).

[57] Id.

[58] Blue Cross & Blue Shield of New Jersey, Inc. v. Philip Morris, Inc., 113 F. Supp. 2d 345, 372 (E.D.N.Y. 2000) (citing In re Chevron U.S.A., Inc., 109 F.3d 1016, 1019-20 (5th Cir. 1997)).

[59] Sewar v. Gagliardi Bros. Serv., 51 N.Y.2d 752, 758-59, 432 N.Y.S.2d 367, 371, 411 N.E.2d 786, 790 (N.Y. 1980) (Fuchsberg, J., concurring).

[60] See Boudreau-Grillo v. Ramirez, 74 A.D. 3d. 1265, 1267, 904 N.Y.S.2d 485, 487 (N.Y. App. Div. 2010); Grant v. L & J. Stickley, Inc., 20 A.D. 3d 506, 507, 799 N.Y.S.2d 123, 124 (N.Y. App. Div. 2005).

[61] Gayle v. City of New York, 92 N.Y.2d 936, 937, 680 N.Y.S.2d 900, 901, 703 N.E.2d 758, 759 (N.Y. 1998) (quoting Schneider v. Kings Highway Hosp. Ctr., 67 N.Y.2d 743, 745, 500 N.Y.S.2d 95, 96, 490 N.E.2d 1221, 1222 (N.Y. 1986)) (quoting Wragge v. Lizza Asphalt Constr. Co., 17 N.Y.2d 313, 321, 270 N.Y.S.2d 616, 622, 217 N.E.2d 666, 670 (N.Y. 1966)).

[62] Mack v. Altmans Stage Lighting Co., 98 A.D.2d 468, 471, 470 N.Y.S.2d 664, 667 (N.Y. App. Div. 1984) (citing Nallan v. Helmsley-Spear, Inc., 50 N.Y.2d 507, 520-521, 429 N.Y.S.2d 606, 614, 407 N.E.2d 451, 459 (N.Y. 1980)).

[63] Sewar, 411 N.E.2d at 790; Mack, 98 A.D.2d at 471, 470 N.Y.S.2d at 667.

[64] Derdiarian v. Felix Contracting Corp., 51 N.Y.2d 308, 315, 434 N.Y.S.2d 166, 169, 414 N.E.2d 666, 670 (N.Y. 1980) (citing RESTATEMENT (SECOND) TORTS, § 435, subd. 2 (1965)).

or intervening actions insulating a defendant.[65] The substantial cause test is generally used to evaluate causation. The factfinder should consider the factors involved that contributing toward the harm and the factors' effect. The jury decides whether the defendant "created a continuous force active up to the time of harm," or whether others forces outside of the defendant's control had a role. Lapse of time is also an appropriate consideration.[66]

B.   *Evidence*

A plaintiff must offer evidence to establish a prima facie case of negligence; speculation about causation is insufficient.[67] The plaintiff bears the burden of proving causation in a negligence action.[68] The plaintiff must establish that the defendant's negligence proximately caused the claimed injuries.[69] Causation is a matter for the factfinder to determine,[70] as it raises questions of foreseeability, what is normal, and may be the subject of varying inferences.[71]

The plaintiff meets the burden of proof so long as the jury can reach its verdict based on logical inferences based on the evidence, rather than speculation.[72]

V.   Damages

A.   *Elements*

To recover in negligence, a plaintiff must have experienced some physical harm or injury.[73] The award of damages is meant to compensate the victim and return the victim, "to the extent possible, to the position that would have been occupied had the wrong not occurred."[74] The purpose of compensatory damages is to make the victim whole, rather than to punish the tortfeasor and deter similar wrongdoing.[75] The focus on compensation has limited the application of the common-law collateral source rule.[76]

---

[65] Laidlaw v. Sage, 158 N.Y. 73, 99, 52 N.E. 679, 688 (N.Y. 1899).

[66] *Mack*, 98 A.D.2d at 470-71, 470 N.Y.S.2d at 667 (citing Restatement (Second) Torts, § 433 (1965); N.Y. Pattern Jury Instr., Civil 2:70).

[67] Mandel v. 370 Lexington Ave., LLC., 32 A.D.3d 302, 303, 820 N.Y.S.2d 249, 251 (N.Y. App. Div. 2006) (quoting Segretti v. Shorenstein Co., 256 A.D.2d 234, 235, 682 N.Y.S.2d 176, 178 (N.Y. App. Div. 1998)).

[68] *See* DeCicco v. Roberts, 202 A.D.2d 165, 607 N.Y.S.2d 946 (N.Y. App. Div. 1994).

[69] Burgos v. Aqueduct Realty Corp., 92 N.Y.2d 544, 550, 684 N.Y.S.2d 139, 141, 706 N.E.2d 1163, 1165 (N.Y. 1998).

[70] *Derdiarian*, 414 N.E.2d at 668.

[71] *Id.* at 670.

[72] *Burgos*, 706 N.E.2d at 1165 (citations omitted).

[73] Caronia v. Philip Morris USA, Inc., 22 N.Y.3d 439, 446, 982 N.Y.S.2d 40, 43, 5 N.E.3d 11, 14 (N.Y. 2013) (citations omitted).

[74] McDougald v. Garber, 73 N.Y.2d 246, 253, 538 N.Y.S.2d 937, 939, 536 N.E.2d 372, 374 (N.Y. 1989).

[75] Ross v. Louise Wise Servs., Inc., 8 N.Y.3d 478, 489, 836 N.Y.S.2d 509, 516, 868 N.E.2d 189, 196 (N.Y. 2007).

[76] Oden v. Chemung Cty. Indus. Dev. Agency, 87 N.Y.2d 81, 88, 637 N.Y.S.2d 670, 673, 661 N.E.2d 142, 145 (N.Y. 1995).

The plaintiff bears the burden of proof regarding compensatory damages.[77] The plaintiff must demonstrate that damages directly resulted from the defendant's wrong and also that the damages were proximately caused by the defendant's wrong.[78] Although damages may not be contingent, uncertain, or speculative, they may be recoverable even if they cannot be measured with "absolute mathematical certainty."[79] Damages may be recovered for physical and mental injuries,[80] pecuniary losses,[81] and pain and suffering or loss of enjoyment of life.[82] There may be alternate ways to measure damages, but the plaintiff seeking damages need only establish the damages under one measure.[83] Damages may be based on lost profits.[84]

B. Evidence

The plaintiff has the burden of proof regarding damages.[85] This includes establishing a causal connection between the alleged negligence and claimed injury.[86] General damages are presumed to flow from the alleged injury, and thus do not need to be pleaded specifically.[87] Special damages must be specifically pleaded with particularity and indicating the causal relationship to the misconduct.[88]

The jury "may not abandon analysis for sympathy for a suffering plaintiff and treat an injury as though it were a winning lottery ticket," although the jury does have broad discretion in assessing damages.[89] On review, a jury's damage award may be set aside if it "materially deviates from what would be reasonable compensation."[90] A jury's damage award is afforded considerable deference, since the assessment of the award is primarily a question of fact.[91]

---

[77] Yarrow v. United States, 309 F. Supp. 922, 931 (S.D. N.Y. 1970) (citations omitted).

[78] Idrees v. Am. Univ. of the Caribbean, 546 F. Supp. 1342, 1350 (S.D.N.Y. 1982) (citing Steitz v. Gifford, 280 N.Y. 15, 20, 19 N.E.2d 661, 664 (N.Y. 1939)) (citing Sands v. Abelli, 290 F. Supp. 677, 681 (S.D.N.Y. 1968)).

[79] *Steitz*, 19 N.E.2d at 664.

[80] Battalla v. State, 10 N.Y.2d 237, 239, 219 N.Y.S.2d 34, 35, 176 N.E.2d 729, 730 (N.Y. 1961) (overruling Mitchell v. Rochester Ry., 151 N.Y. 107, 45 N.E. 354 (N.Y. 1896)).

[81] Dombrowski v. Bulson, 19 N.Y.3d 347, 352, 948 N.Y.S2d 208, 210, 971 N.E.2d 338, 340 (N.Y. 2012) (legal malpractice limited to pecuniary damages).

[82] *McDougald*, 536 N.E.2d at 376.

[83] Jenkins v. Etlinger, 55 N.Y.2d 35, 38, 447 N.Y.S.2d 696, 697, 432 N.E.2d 589, 590 (N.Y. 1982).

[84] *Steitz*, 19 N.E.2d at 664.

[85] *See* Gaida-Newman v. Holtermann, 34 A.D. 634, 635, 825 N.Y.S.2d 503, 505 (N.Y. App. Div. 2006); Molony v. Boy Comics Publishers, 227 A.D. 166, 172, 98 N.Y.S.2d 119, 125 (N.Y. App. Div. 1950); Lynch v. Gibson, 254 A.D. 47, 52, 3 N.Y.S.2d 672, 677 (N.Y. App. Div. 1938).

[86] Miranda v. City of New York, 256 A.D.2d 605, 607, 683 N.Y.S.2d 129, 130 (N.Y. App. Div. 1998).

[87] Arett Sales Corp. v. Island Garden Ctr. Queens, Inc., 25 A.D.2d 546, 546, 267 N.Y.S.2d 623, 627 (N.Y. App. Div. 1966) (citations omitted).

[88] Beck v. Gen. Tire & Rubber Co., 98 A.D.2d 756, 758, 469 N.Y.S.2d 785, 787 (N.Y. App. Div. 1983) (citations omitted).

[89] Scala v. Moore McCormack Lines, Inc., 985 F.2d 680, 684 (2d Cir. 1993) (citations omitted).

[90] Inya v. Ide Hyundai, Inc., 209 A.D.2d 1015, 619 N.Y.S.2d 440 (N.Y. App. Div. 1994) (citations omitted).

[91] Duncan v. Hillebrandt, 239 A.D.2d 811, 813-14, 657 N.Y.S.2d 538, 540 (N.Y. App. Div. 1997) (citations omitted).

CHAPTER 34

NORTH CAROLINA

NORTH CAROLINA

Vernon Sumwalt[1]
Narendra K. Ghosh[2]
Brian Davis[3]
Jon Moore[4]
Paige L. Pahlke[5]

I. Purpose of Tort Law

Under North Carolina law, compensatory damages serve the purpose of deterring negligent conduct in addition to making the victim whole.[6] Counsel has the right to explain the law to the jury, including reading passages from reported cases.[7] The deterrent function of tort liability exists regardless of punitive damages.[8]

---

[1] Partner, The Sumwalt Law Firm, N.C. State Bar Board of Certified Specialist in Workers Compensation and Appellate Practice.

[2] Partner, Patterson Harkavy, LLP, Chapel Hill, North Carolina.

[3] Managing Partner, Davis Law Group, P.A., Asheville, N.C., Member American Association for Justice, Member North Carolina Advocates for Justice, Member, Best Lawyers in America, Wake Forest University School of Law, 1991, University of North Carolina at Chapel Hill, 1987.

[4] Partner, Brown Moore & Associates, PLLC, Charlotte, North Carolina.

[5] Associate, Brown Moore & Associates, PLLC, Charlotte, North Carolina.

[6] Rabon v. Rowan Mem'l Hosp., Inc., 152 S.E.2d 485 (N.C. 1967). In *Rabon,* the North Carolina Supreme Court recognized that ordinary damages in negligence cases deters unsafe conduct, holding: "Requiring hospitals to respond in damages for the carelessness of its employees provides the penalty which will insure the installation of safety methods and the enforcement of strict supervision over hospital personnel." In imposing tort liability on hospitals, and abolishing charitable immunity, the *Rabon* court further stated that requiring payment of "damages for negligent injury serves a two-fold purpose, for it both assures payment of an obligation to the person injured *and gives warning that justice and the law demand the exercise of care.*" The court then more fully explained: "There can be little doubt that immunity fosters neglect and breeds irresponsibility, while liability promotes care and caution." The public "is interested in having any hospital open to it safely equipped and properly conducted by carefully selected employees who perform their duties with due care." Accordingly, "the primary interest and welfare of the public requires that one person should not suffer an injury to his or her life or limb without recompense."

[7] N.C. GEN. STAT. § 7A-97; State v. Gardner, 342 S.E.2d 872, 876 (N.C. 1986).

[8] DiDonato v. Wortman, 358 S.E.2d 489, 491, 494 (N.C. 1987); *see* Woodson v. Rowland, 407 S.E.2d 222, 229 (N.C. 1991) (explaining that the imposition of tort liability on employers for certain workplace injuries "serv[es] as a deterrent" for employer wrongdoing and "promot[es] safety in the workplace"); Pleasant v. Johnson, 325 S.E.2d 244, 250 (N.C. 1985) (explaining that the imposition of tort liability on co-employees for certain workplace misconduct "will help to deter such conduct in the future").

Leading treatises on torts and damages have also recognized the deterrent purpose of compensatory damages.[9] Because deterrence of negligent conduct is a recognized purpose of compensatory damages, it is entirely proper for counsel to explain this purpose in arguments made to the jury.[10] The North Carolina Supreme Court states that "encouraging the jury to act as the voice and conscience of the community is proper and is one of the very reasons for the establishment of the jury system."[11]

II. Duty to Exercise Ordinary Care

A. *Question of Law*

"The essence of negligence is behavior creating an unreasonable danger to others."[12] "To state a claim for common law negligence, a plaintiff must allege: (1) a legal duty; (2) a breach thereof; and (3) injury proximately caused by the breach."[13] Whether a defendant owes a duty of care is a question of law.[14] "The law imposes upon every person who enters upon an active course of conduct the positive duty to exercise ordinary care to protect others from harm, and calls a violation of that duty negligence."[15] "The duty of ordinary care is no more than a duty to act reasonably . . . [and that] duty does not require perfect prescience, but instead extends only to causes of injury that were reasonably foreseeable and avoidable through the exercise of due care."[16] The requisite duty of care is owed to every person for whom, under the circumstances, injury to that person is "reasonably foreseeable."[17]

---

[9] *See, e.g.*, RESTATEMENT (THIRD) OF TORTS: *Liability for Physical and Emotional Harm*, § 6(d) (2005) ("Another justification for imposing liability for negligence is to give actors appropriate incentives to engage in safe conduct."); 1 DAN B. DOBBS et al., THE LAW OF TORTS § 14, at 29 (2d ed. 2011) ("Courts and writers almost always recognize that another aim of tort law is to deter certain kinds of conduct by imposing liability when the conduct causes harm."); DAN B. DOBBS, DOBBS LAW OF REMEDIES, Vol. 1, at 282 (2d ed. 1993) ("Even if the defendant is not subject to punitive damages, an ordinary 'compensatory' damages judgment can provide an appropriate incentive to meet the appropriate standard of behavior."); 1 STUART M. SPEISER ET AL., THE AMERICAN LAW OF TORTS, § 1:3, at 12 (2013) ("The deterrent goal of the tort laws is effectuated through the recognition of a duty to exercise reasonable care and the imposition of liability for the breach of such a duty"); RESTATEMENT (SECOND) OF CONFLICT OF LAWS, § 36 comment (c) (1971) ("[T]orts involve wrongful conduct which a state seeks to deter, and against which it attempts to afford protection, by providing that a tortfeasor shall be liable for damages which are the proximate result of his tort.").

[10] *See Gardner*, 342 S.E.2d at 876 (holding that counsel has "the right to argue the law to the jury which includes the authority to read and comment on reported cases and statutes").

[11] State v. Erlewine, 403 S.E.2d 280, 284 (N.C. 1991); *see also* State v. Phillips, 711 S.E.2d 122, 144, 153 (N.C. 2011).

[12] Bolkhir v. N.C. State Univ., 365 S.E.2d 898, 900 (N.C. 1988).

[13] Stein v. Asheville City Bd. of Educ., 626 S.E.2d 263, 267 (N.C. 2006).

[14] Huntley v. Howard Lisk Co., 573 S.E.2d 233, 236 (N.C. Ct. App. 2002).

[15] Fussell v. N.C. Farm Bureau Mut. Ins., 695 S.E.2d 437, 440 (N.C. 2010) (quoting Council v. Dickerson's, Inc., 64 S.E.2d 551, 553 (N.C. 1951)).

[16] Fussell v. N.C. Farm Bureau Mut. Ins., 695 S.E.2d 437, 440 (N.C. 2010) (citing Palsgraf v. Long Island R.R., 162 N.E. 99, 100 (N.Y. 1928)).

[17] Carsanaro v. Colvin, 716 S.E.2d 40, 46 (N.C. Ct. App. 2011) (holding that the duty owed by a defendant with a sexually transmitted disease also extends to the spouse of the infected person's sexual partner); Estate of Mullis by Dixon v. Monroe Oil Co., 505 S.E.2d 131, 137 (N.C. 1998) (holding that a duty is owed to another person if one would reasonably recognize that the failure to use due care "would cause danger of injury to the person or

B.   *Question of Fact*

i.   **Elements**

The required level of care depends on the extent of danger that is foreseeable.[18] Therefore, greater care is required if the odds of harm are higher or if the threatened harm is more severe.[19] Foreseeability of harm is usually a question of fact for the jury.[20]

ii.   **Evidence**

A plaintiff must show that a person exercising reasonable care might have foreseen that defendant's conduct would result in some injury, "or that consequences of a generally injurious nature might have been expected."[21] Evidence to establish the foreseeability of who could have been harmed by the defendants' conduct, the foreseeable types of injuries that could result from defendants' conduct, the likelihood of foreseeable harm resulting from defendants' conduct, or the foreseeable severity of the injuries from defendants' conduct is probative and admissible on the issue of the level of care required.[22]

North Carolina recognizes that "safety rules" are another way to describe the standard of care in negligence actions. Because "wide latitude is given to counsel in addressing

---

property of the other" (quoting Dail v. Taylor, 66 S.E. 135, 136 (N.C. 1909)); *see also* Hairston v. Alexander Tank & Equip. Co., 311 S.E.2d 559, 568 (N.C. 1984) (concluding that the plaintiff's death fell within the "area of risk created by the negligence" of the defendant); Hart v. Ivey, 420 S.E.2d 174, 178 (N.C. 1992) (holding that social hosts "were under a duty to the people who travel on the public highways not to serve alcohol to an intoxicated individual who was known to be driving").

[18] Estate of Mullis, 505 S.E.2d at 137 ("The risk reasonably to be perceived defines the duty to be obeyed." "The orbit of the danger as disclosed to the eye of reasonable vigilance is the orbit of the duty." (quoting *Palsgraf*, 162 N.E. at 100)).

[19] *See* Rea v. Simowitz, 35 S.E.2d 871, 874 (N.C. 1945) ("But a prudent man increases his watchfulness as the possibility of danger mounts. So then the degree of care required of one whose breach of duty is very likely to result in serious harm is greater than when the effect of such breach is not nearly so great."); *see also* Nance v. Parks, 146 S.E.2d 24, 28 (N.C. 1966) (concluding that duty of care existed because danger to others increased when the defendant left his car running with a mechanic working near the accelerator); Pulley v. Rex Hosp., 392 S.E.2d 380, 385 (N.C. 1990) (noting that to determine the duty of care, a jury could treat "a fault in a sidewalk leading into a hospital emergency room" differently than "an identical fault in an ordinary sidewalk" given that "people entering emergency rooms are frequently and foreseeably very distracted from their ordinary behavior"); Cobb *ex rel.* Knight v. Town of Blowing Rock, 713 S.E.2d 732, 741 (N.C. 2011) (Stroud, J., dissenting), dissent adopted *per curiam* by 722 S.E.2d 479 (N.C. 2012) (holding that "foreseeable characteristics of lawful visitors" is relevant to determining the duty of care for a landowner).

[20] Carsanaro v. Colvin, 716 S.E.2d 40, 45 (N.C. Ct. App. 2011).

[21] *Id.*

[22] *See* Murrow v. Daniels, 364 S.E.2d 392, 397 (N.C. 1988) (holding that evidence of criminal acts occurring near the premises in question may be relevant to the question of foreseeability in a case concerning a motel's failure to maintain adequate security measures); Screaming Eagle Air, Ltd. v. Airport Comm'n of Forsyth Cty., 387 S.E.2d 197, 203 (N.C. Ct. App. 1990) (admitting evidence of the number of dog sightings by airport personnel over a five-year period as "clearly relevant to foreseeability" of harm posed by dogs to aircraft taking off regardless of the remoteness in time of some of the sightings).

the jury,"[23] even during its selection,[24] counsel's use of the phrase "safety rules" is accurate and helps the jury understand the concept of a standard of care. A standard of care "may arise specifically by mandate of statute, or it may arise generally by operation of law . . . which imposes on every person engaged in the prosecution of any undertaking an obligation to use due care, or to so govern his actions as not to endanger the person or property of others."[25] North Carolina courts recognize that a particular event in controversy is "reasonably foreseeable" if statistical evidence shows a positive correlation between a general set of circumstances and other events that are similar to the one in controversy.[26]

Violation of a statute or ordinance may be used to establish negligence by showing "(1) a duty created by a statute or ordinance; (2) that the statute or ordinance was enacted to protect a class of persons which includes the plaintiff; (3) a breach of the statutory duty; (4) that the injury sustained was suffered by an interest which the statute protected; (5) that the injury was of the nature contemplated in the statute; and, (6) that the violation of the statute proximately caused the injury."[27]

III.   Breach of Duty

A.   Elements

The issue of breach of duty (i.e. whether defendant exercised reasonable care under the circumstances) is for the finder of fact.[28]

B.   Evidence

A plaintiff must show that the defendant violated the duty to use ordinary care to protect others from injury to establish negligence.[29] A plaintiff must submit "substantial evidence" of negligence. Substantial evidence is such relevant evidence that a reasonable mind might accept as adequate to support a conclusion.[30] Evidence creating a mere possibility or conjecture is not sufficient.[31] Evidence presented by the plaintiff may be direct or circumstantial.[32]

---

[23] Cuthrell v. Greene, 50 S.E.2d 525, 529 (N.C. 1948); *see also* State v. Johnson, 259 S.E.2d 752, 761 (N.C. 1979).

[24] *See* State v. Prevatte, 570 S.E.2d 440, 467 (N.C. 2002).

[25] Pinnix v. Toomey, 87 S.E.2d 893, 897 (N.C. 1955).

[26] *See* Lea Co. v. N.C. Bd. of Transp., 304 S.E.2d 164, 174 (N.C. 1983) (citing statistical evidence to distinguish between "Acts of God" and "reasonably foreseeable events"); Hutchens v. Hankins, 303 S.E.2d 584, 598 (N.C. Ct. App. 1983) ("[t]his reasonable foreseeability of harm is evidence by the statistics of auto accidents and carnage on our highways") (quoting and endorsing the dissenting opinion in *Garcia v. Hargrove,* 176 N.W.2d 566, 572-573 (Wis. 1970)). *Cf. also,* Foster v. Winston-Salem Joint Venture, 281 S.E.2d 36 (N.C. 1981) (J. Carlton, dissenting) (citing crime statistics to show the foreseeability of larceny).

[27] Davis v. Hulsing Enters., LLC, 783 S.E.2d 765, 771 (N.C. Ct. App. 2016).

[28] Stein v. Asheville City Bd. Of Educ., 626 S.E.2d 263, 269 (N.C. 2006).

[29] Carsanaro v. Colvin, 716 S.E.2d 40, 45 (N.C. Ct. App. 2011).

[30] Asfar v. Charlotte Auto Auction, Inc., 490 S.E.2d 598, 600 (N.C. Ct. App. 1997).

[31] Maye v. Gorrlieb, 482 S.E.2d 750, 751 (N.C. Ct. App. 1997).

[32] Johnson v. Williams, 198 S.E.2d 192, 194 (N.C. Ct. App. 1973).

IV. Causation

A. Elements

A negligent act must have a causal relationship with an injury before it can be considered a proximate cause of an injury.[33] Negligence alone will not establish liability without a showing of proximate cause.[34] Proximate cause is a cause which (1) in a natural and continuous sequence unbroken by any new and independent cause, (2) which produces the plaintiff's injuries, (3) without which the injuries would not have occurred, and (4) which a person of ordinary prudence could have reasonably foreseen that such a result or consequences of an injurious nature were likely to occur.[35] Foreseeability is a required element of demonstrating proximate cause.[36] The test of foreseeability, however, does not mean that a plaintiff must show the defendant should have foreseen—or had the ability to foresee—the exact injury which occurred.[37] Rather, a plaintiff must demonstrate simply that the defendant might have foreseen some injury or consequence of a generally injurious nature would result from an act or omission of the defendant.[38]

B. Evidence

"To establish foreseeability, the plaintiff must prove that defendant, in the exercise of reasonable care, might have foreseen that its actions would cause some injury."[39] Whether the harm was foreseeable depends on the particular facts of the case.[40] "Questions of proximate cause and foreseeability are questions of fact to be decided by the jury."[41] "The test of proximate cause is whether the risk of injury, not necessarily in the precise form in which it actually occurs, is within the reasonable foresight of the defendant."[42] Finally, as with the relationship of foreseeability to duty of care, foreseeability for proximate cause is relevant as to whether *some* type of injury is foreseeable, not whether the precise type of injury that

---

[33] Ingold v. Carolina Power & Light Co., 181 S.E.2d 173, 174 (N.C. Ct. App. 1971).

[34] King v. Allred, 305 S.E.2d 554, 557 (N.C. 1983).

[35] Hairston v. Alexander Tank & Equip. Co., 311 S.E.2d 559, 565 (N.C. 1984).

[36] Taylor v. Interim Healthcare of Raleigh-Durham, Inc., 574 S.E.2d 11, 15 (N.C. Ct. App. 2002).

[37] *Hairston*, 311 S.E. 2d at 565.

[38] *Id.*

[39] Bolkhir v. N.C. State Univ., 365 S.E.2d 898, 901 (N.C. 1988); *see also* Martishius v. Carolco Studios, Inc., 562 S.E.2d 887, 896 (N.C. 2002) (concluding that electrocution injury was a foreseeable type of injury from the placement of a movie studio set); Collingwood v. Gen. Elec. Real Estate Equities, Inc., 376 S.E.2d 425, 429 (N.C. 1989) ("Rational jurors could find that the jumping of residents trapped in their apartments by the spreading of the fire was readily foreseeable."); Wallen v. Riverside Sports Ctr., 618 S.E.2d 858, 860 (N.C. Ct. App. 2005) (concluding that injury was foreseeable where defendant's failure to maintain his property resulted in a tree falling and paralyzing the plaintiff during a storm); Clemons v. Williams, 300 S.E.2d 873, 876 (N.C. Ct. App. 1983) (concluding that injury was foreseeable when defendant driver failed to respond to the flashing headlights of another car by slowing down or stopping, and instead simply avoided the vehicle, thereby striking the plaintiff who was lying on the highway 15 feet behind the vehicle).

[40] Fussell v. N.C. Farm Bureau Mut. Ins., 695 S.E.2d 437, 440 (N.C. 2010).

[41] Acosta v. Byrum, 638 S.E.2d 246, 251 (N.C. Ct. App. 2006).

[42] Williams v. Carolina Power & Light Co., 250 S.E.2d 255, 258 (N.C. 1979).

occurred is foreseeable.[43] Accordingly, any evidence on the foreseeability of harm from the defendant's conduct is probative and admissible on the issue of proximate cause.

V.   Damages

A.   Elements

The objective of compensatory damages is to restore the plaintiff to his or her original condition had the injury not occurred, or to "make them whole."[44] In North Carolina, general damages and special damages are different, even though they combine to make up the broader class of actual or compensatory damages.[45] General damages are allowed even when "no actual pecuniary loss ha[s] in fact resulted" and the injury, even though "a real one," is "not susceptible of being accurately measured in dollars and cents. . . ."[46] General damages thus address "injury to feelings, mental anguish," "physical inconvenience," and "mental suffering."[47] On the other hand, "[s]pecial damages are usually synonymous with pecuniary loss. "Medical and hospital expenses . . . are regarded as special damages in personal-injury cases."[48] While evidence of medical and hospital expenses is important when measuring special damages, it has no significance to general damages. This evidence is, therefore, irrelevant to how those damages are measured.

B.   Evidence

Evidence is "relevant" if it has "any tendency to make the existence of any fact that is of consequence to the determination of the action more probable or less probable than it would be without the evidence."[49] "Evidence which is not relevant is not admissible."[50] The assessment of damages rests within the sound discretion of the jury.[51]

---

[43] *See* Hairston v. Alexander Tank & Equip. Co., 311 S.E.2d 559, 565 (N.C. 1984); *see also* Fussell v. N. Carolina Farm Bureau Mut. Ins., 695 S.E.2d 437, 440 (N.C. 2010).

[44] Watson v. Dixon 532 S.E.2d 175, 178 (N.C. 2000).

[45] Ringgold v. Land, 193 S.E. 267, 268 (N.C. 1937). Special and general damages are a part of the broader class of "compensatory" or "actual" damages. *See, e.g.,* NCPIs *Civil* 810.04-810.04D and *Civil* (MV) 106.02, which are mutually exclusive to "punitive" damages, *see* NCPIs *Civil* 810.90-810.98 and *Civil* (MV) 106.96. *See generally* Carmichael v. S. Bell Tel. & Tel. Co., 72 S.E. 619, 620 (N.C. 1911).

[46] Osborn v. Leach, 47 S.E. 811, 813 (N.C. 1904); *see also* NCPI *Civil* 810.08 (For pain and suffering as damages in personal injury actions, "[t]here is no fixed formula for placing a value on physical pain and mental suffering. You will determine what is fair compensation by applying logic and common sense to the evidence.").

[47] Ammons v. S. Ry., 52 S.E. 731, 733 (N.C. 1905) (J. Hoke, concurring); *see also Ringgold*, 212 N.C. at 371, 193 S.E. at 268. For this reason, plaintiffs must plead special damages in enough detail, but do not need to plead general damages with numerical precision. *See* Conrad v. Shuford, 94 S.E. 424, 425 (N.C. 1917) (in discussing noneconomic damages for pain, stating that "[t]he pleader is not required by the rule to go into an account of minute details and to specify every muscle that ached and every nerve that throbbed, every contusion or fracture, and every racking pain").

[48] Iadanza v. Harper, 611 S.E.2d 217, 221 (N.C. Ct. App. 2005).

[49] N.C. Gen. Stat. § 8C-1, Rule 401.

[50] N.C. Gen. Stat. § 8C-1, Rule 402.

[51] E-B Grain Co. v. Denton, 325 S.E.2d 522, 529 (N.C. Ct. App. 1985).

CHAPTER 35

NORTH DAKOTA

NORTH DAKOTA

Casey D. Duncan[1]

I. Purpose of Tort Law

To recover in an action for negligence in North Dakota, the plaintiff must establish a duty, a breach of that duty, an injury proximately caused by the breach, and damages.[2] The determination of whether a duty exists is the paramount concern as there can be no actionable negligence without a duty.[3] Two statutes in the North Dakota Century Code establish duties relevant to tort actions. One creates a general duty to avoid inflicting injury on the person or property of another,[4] while the other imposes responsibility and liability for negligent acts that harm another.[5] An additional statute provides that the appropriate measure of damages "is the amount which will compensate for all the detriment proximately caused thereby, whether it could have been anticipated or not."[6] This statute is clearly based on the common law principle that damages in tort are primarily designed to compensate for the loss or injury proximately caused by a negligent act.[7]

A final relevant statute establishes "that there is not common law in any case in which the law is declared by statute."[8] Because of the longevity[9] of these statutes, courts in North Dakota have had few occasions to expound at length upon the purposes underlying tort liability. In an early personal injury case, the Territorial Supreme Court held when a statute was intended to adopt the common law, rather than to change it, that enactment "cannot give it any more force than it had before such enactment."[10] On appeal before the U.S. Supreme

---

[1] Director of the Law Library and Assistant Professor of Law, University of Wyoming College of Law.

[2] Palmer v. 999 Quebec, Inc., 2016 ND 17, ¶ 9, 874 N.W.2d 303, 309; Rogstad v. Dakota Gasification Co., 2001 ND 54, ¶ 12, 623 N.W.2d 382, 385; Diegel v. City of W. Fargo, 546 N.W.2d 367, 370 (N.D. 1996).

[3] *Palmer*, 874 N.W.2d at 309; *Rogstad*, 623 N.W.2d at 385; *Diegel*, 546 N.W.2d at 370.

[4] N.D. CENT. CODE § 9-10-01 (Lexis Advance).

[5] N.D. CENT. CODE § 9-10-06 (Lexis Advance).

[6] N.D. CENT. CODE § 32-03-20 (Lexis Advance).

[7] Johnson v. Monsanto Co., 303 N.W. 2d 86, 93 (N.D. 1981); Schmeet v. Schumacher, 137 N.W. 2d 789, 791 (N.D. 1965).

[8] N.D. CENT. CODE § 1-01-06 (Lexis Advance).

[9] Prior to statehood, the Dakota Territory was one of the first of a handful of western states and territories to adopt a complete civil code. William B. Fisch, *Civil Code: Notes for an Uncelebrated Centennial*, 43 N.D. L. REV. 485, 485-86 (1966) (noting that many provisions from the territorial code were carried over into the consolidated Century Code). *See also* Robert Vogel, *Looking Back on a Century of Complete Codification of the Law*, 53 N.D. L. REV. 225 (1976) (arguing that Georgia and Dakota Territory "were the first jurisdictions in the English-speaking world to codify their entire body of law").

[10] Herbert v. N. Pac. R.R., 13 N.W. 349, 352 (Dakota Terr. 1882), *aff'd*, 116 U.S. 642 (1886).

Court, Justice Field upheld the Territorial Supreme Court's decision and held that the code section in question did not prevent courts from looking to the common law as "[t]he declaration by the Code of a general rule, which is conformable to existing law, does not prevent the courts from looking to those cases for explanation any more than it prevents them from looking into the dictionary for the meaning of words."[11]

In short, the North Dakota statutory provisions regarding duty and tortious liability are specific enough that courts will rarely need to engage in a detailed discussion regarding the purposes and policies underlying tort liability, but still leave sufficient room for courts to evaluate and apply broader common law principles when necessary.[12]

II. Duty to Exercise Ordinary Care

A. Question of Law

In North Dakota, a plaintiff must show the defendant owed a duty to protect the plaintiff from injury,[13] because "[i]f no duty exists, there is no negligence."[14] Once established, however, a duty extends to all reasonably foreseeable injuries and results of a negligent act or failure to act in accordance with the duty.[15]

Generally, whether a duty exists is a preliminary question of law for the court to determine,[16] and negligence actions are "ordinarily not appropriate for summary judgment."[17] The question of whether a duty of care exists, however, is "considered within the framework of [North Dakota] law on summary judgment," and "if the court determines that there is no duty by the defendant to the plaintiff, then summary judgment dismissal is appropriate"[18] "before allowing a jury to hear evidence concerning a breach of that duty and proximate cause."[19] Conversely, when a determination regarding whether a duty exists depends on the resolution of factual issues, the factual issues are to be resolved by the trier of fact.[20]

In North Dakota, a duty may be imposed by statute, and, in those instances, "there is no common law in any case in which the law is declared by the code."[21] The North Dakota

---

[11] N. Pac. R.R. v. Herbert, 116 U.S. 642, 654 (1886).

[12] *See, e.g.*, Vogel v. Marathon Oil Co., 2016 ND 104, ¶ 30, 879 N.W.2d 471, 482 ("[T]he common law remains relevant when there is no conflict between the statutory and common law.").

[13] Rogstad v. Dakota Gasification Co., 2001 ND 54, ¶ 12, 623 N.W.2d 382, 385.

[14] *Rogstad*, 623 N.W.2d at 385; Pechtl v. Conoco, Inc., 1997 ND 161, ¶ 7, 567 N.W.2d 813, 816.

[15] Hoff v. Elkhorn Bar, 613 F. Supp. 2d 1146, 1154 (D.N.D. 2009); Nelson v. Gillette, 1997 ND 205, ¶ 40, 571 N.W.2d 332, 340; Moum v. Maercklein, 201 N.W.2d 399, 403 (N.D. 1972).

[16] *Rogstad*, 623 N.W.2d at 385; Hurt v. Freeland, 1999 ND 12, ¶ 9, 589 N.W.2d 551, 555; Barsness v. Gen. Diesel & Equip. Co., 383 N.W.2d 840, 843 (N.D. 1986) (case citations omitted) (citing § 328B, RESTATEMENT (SECOND) OF TORTS (1965)).

[17] *Hurt*, 589 N.W.2d at 555.

[18] Holter v. City of Sheyenne, 480 N.W.2d 736, 737-38 (N.D. 1992).

[19] DeLair v. LaMoure Cty., 326 N.W.2d 55, 58 (N.D. 1982).

[20] *Pechtl*, 567 N.W.2d at 816.

[21] N.D. CENT. CODE § 1-01-06 (Lexis Advance). *See also* Manitoba Pub. Ins. v. Dakota Fire Ins., 2007 ND 206, ¶ 19, 743 N.W.2d 788, 793 ("The North Dakota Legislature, however, has forbidden such common-law treatment. 'In this state there is no common law in any case in which the law is declared by the code.' N.D. CENT. CODE § 1–01–06.").

statutes further provide that individuals are responsible for the results of their own willful acts as well as for injuries resulting "to another by the person's want of ordinary care or skill in the management of the person's property or self."[22] More generally, another statute states "Every person is bound without contract to abstain from injuring the person or property of another or infringing upon any of that person's rights."[23] North Dakota courts have also independently held that "[e]very person has a duty to act reasonably to protect others from harm."[24]

Thus, courts will determine whether a duty existed as a matter of law in cases where the existence of the duty does not hinge upon the resolution of factual issues. This may occur by examination of those statutorily imposed duties, as well as prior cases interpreting the scope of those duties or other duties that exist at common law.[25] The North Dakota Supreme Court has interpreted "the standard for analyzing the potential coexistence of common law and statutory provisions under N.D. Cent. Code § 1-01-06: 'to mean that statutory enactments take precedence over and govern conflicting common law doctrines.'"[26] The Court went on to clarify that the "common thread in the cases applying the language of N.D. Cent. Code § 1-01-06 is '[t]here cannot be two rules of law on the same subject contradicting each other.'"[27]

B. Questions of Fact

i. Elements

In North Dakota, actionable negligence "'consists of a duty on the part of an allegedly negligent person to protect the plaintiff from injury, a failure to discharge the duty, and a resulting injury proximately caused by the breach of the duty.'"[28] The North Dakota Pattern Jury Instructions define "negligence" as a lack of ordinary care and diligence as required by the circumstances,[29] while "ordinary care" is defined as "the care a person of ordinary prudence usually exercises about one's own affairs of ordinary importance."[30]

---

[22] N.D. Cent. Code § 9-10-06 (Lexis Advance).

[23] N.D. Cent. Code § 9-10-01 (Lexis Advance).

[24] Dinger ex rel. Dinger v. Strata Corp., 2000 ND 41, ¶ 16, 607 N.W.2d 886, 891 (quoting Barsness v. Gen. Diesel & Equip. Co., 383 N.W.2d 840, 845 n. 5 (N.D. 1986)) (relying on Restatement (Second) of Torts § 388 (1965)).

[25] See, e.g., Vogel v. Marathon Oil Co., 2016 ND 104, ¶ 30, 879 N.W.2d 471, 482 ("[T]he common law remains relevant when there is no conflict between the statutory and common law."); Norby v. Estate of Kuykendall, 2015 ND 232, ¶ 19, 869 N.W.2d 405, 411 (Sandstrom, J., concurring) ("This Court's opinions . . . appear to have resolved the question here . . . limiting the statute's application . . . [a]lthough this interpretation adds words not in the statute, the opinions have stood for half a century without judicial or legislative correction . . . the doctrines of stare decisis and legislative acquiescence apply, and the interpretation persists.").

[26] Finstad v. Ransom-Sargent Water Users, Inc., 2014 ND 146, ¶ 12, 849 N.W.2d 165, 170 (quoting Vandall v. Trinity Hosps., 2004 ND 47, ¶¶ 14-15, 676 N.W.2d 88).

[27] Finstad, 849 N.W.2d at 170 (quoting N. Pac. R.R. v. Herbert, 116 U.S. 642, 654 (1886)).

[28] Hurt, 589 N.W.2d at 555 (quoting Diegel v. City of W. Fargo, 546 N.W.2d 367, 370 (N.D. 1996)); Rogstad v. Dakota Gasification Co., 2001 ND 54, ¶ 12, 623 N.W.2d 382, 385; Gullickson v. Torkelson Bros., 1999 ND 155, ¶ 7, 598 N.W.2d 503, 505; Rawlings v. Fruhwirth, 455 N.W.2d 574, 576 (N.D. 1990); Carlson Homes, Inc. v. Messmer, 307 N.W.2d 564, 566 (N.D. 1981).

[29] ND. J.I. Civ. § C - 2.05 (Lexis Advance).

[30] ND. J.I. Civ. § C - 2.05 (Lexis Advance).

What constitutes ordinary care will vary according to the actual circumstances and dangers.[31] Numerous decisions have noted that "[t]he term 'negligence' is a relative one,[32] 'and its application depends on the situation of the parties, and the degree of care and vigilance which the circumstances reasonably impose.'"[33] The pattern jury instructions likewise indicate that danger is a relevant factor in the duty to use ordinary care, measured by the actual knowledge of danger or what should have been reasonably foreseeable under the circumstances.[34] In addition to knowledge of danger, the duty of care in the totality of circumstances also "necessarily includes" any specialized knowledge or skills of the person owing the duty.[35]

ii. Evidence

In a negligence action, the plaintiff bears the burden of proof to establish negligence[36] by demonstrating that a duty was owed,[37] as "[w]hen a duty does not exist, there is no negligence."[38] Generally, the existence of a duty is a question of law for the court.[39] If the determination regarding whether a duty existed depends on resolving factual issues, however, those facts must be resolved by the trier of fact.[40] The Supreme Court of North Dakota has recognized the RESTATEMENT (SECOND) OF TORTS, § 413 position that "'where there is a foreseeable risk of harm to others unless precautions are taken,' it is the duty of one who employs another to do work to exercise reasonable care in selecting a contractor "and to provide, in the contract or otherwise, for such precautions as reasonably appear to be called for."[41] Violation of a statute or regulation is admissible as evidence of negligence.[42]

---

[31] Glatt v. Feist, 156 N.W.2d 819, 829 (N.D. 1968) (citing 65 C.J.S. *Negligence* § 11(3)); Chi., Milwaukee, St. Paul & Pac. RR. v. Johnston's Fuel Liners, Inc., 122 N.W.2d 140, 146 (N.D. 1963) (quoting 65 C.J.S. *Negligence* § 11).

[32] Halverson v. Zimmerman, 232 N.W. 754, 757 (N.D. 1930) (quoting COOLEY ON TORTS 1324 (3d ed.). *See also, e.g.,* Zerr v. Sommer, 179 N.W.2d 330, 333 (N.D. 1970) (citing *Halverson*, 232 N.W. 754 (N.D. 1930); Kreidt v. Burlington N. R.R., 2000 ND 150, ¶ 10, 615 N.W.2d 153, 156; Rittenour v. Gibson, 2003 ND 14, ¶ 60, 656 N.W.2d 691, 707.

[33] *Halverson*, 232 N.W. at 757 (quoting COOLEY ON TORTS 1324 (3d ed.)); Moum v. Maercklein, 201 N.W.2d 399, 402 (N.D. 1972) (citing *Halverson*, 232 N.W. 754 (N.D. 1930)).

[34] ND. J.I. CIV. § C - 2.05 (Lexis Advance)

[35] Tom Beuchler Const., Inc. v. City of Williston, 392 N.W.2d 403, 405 (N.D. 1986).

[36] Mikkelson v. Risovi, 141 N.W.2d 150, 152 (N.D. 1966).

[37] Inv'rs Real Estate Tr. Props., Inc. v. Terra Pac. Midwest, Inc., 2004 ND 167, ¶ 7, 686 N.W.2d 140, 144.

[38] Azure v. Belcourt Pub. Sch. Dist., 2004 ND 128, ¶ 9, 681 N.W.2d 816, 820. *See also* Mikkelson v. Risovi, 141 N.W.2d 150, 152 (N.D. 1966).

[39] *Azure*, 681 N.W.2d at 819.

[40] *Id.* at 820.

[41] McLean v. Kirby Co., 490 N.W.2d 229, 234 (N.D. 1992).

[42] Gonzalez v. Tounjian, 2003 ND 121, ¶ 19, 665 N.W.2d 705, 713.

III.   Breach of Duty

A.   *Elements*

In a negligence action, the plaintiff bears the burden of demonstrating that a breach of a duty occurred.[43] Negligence must be affirmatively proved by the plaintiff, and, while it may not be presumed from the mere occurrence of an accident or injury, it may be proved by circumstantial evidence.[44] The burden is that of a "fair preponderance of the evidence."[45] The burden remains with the plaintiff throughout the case, but, once a prima facie case has been established, the "burden of evidence" shifts to the defendant.[46]

B.   *Evidence*

In a negligence action, the plaintiff bears the burden of proof to establish negligence[47] by demonstrating that a duty was owed and there was a breach of that duty.[48] The violation of a statutory or regulatory duty is evidence of negligence, but is not negligence *per se*.[49] Compliance or non-compliance with a statute may be considered by the trier of fact as evidence tending to show that reasonable care was or was not exercised in the circumstances.[50] In a 1986 case that was subsequently abrogated on other grounds,[51] the Court stated "before the violation of an ordinance may be considered as evidence of negligence, the court must determine that a purpose of the ordinance was to protect the class of persons injured against the type of injury and harm suffered."[52]

---

[43] Inv'rs Real Estate Tr. Props., Inc. v. Terra Pac. Midwest, Inc., 2004 ND 167, ¶ 7, 686 N.W.2d 140, 144; Farmers Home Mut. Ins. of Medelia, Minn. v. Grand Forks Implement Co., 55 N.W.2d 315, 317 (N.D. 1952) (citing 38 Am.Jur., *Negligence*, §§ 285, 975; 65 C.J.S., *Negligence*, §§ 208, 209).

[44] Victory Park Apartments, Inc. v. Axelson, 367 N.W.2d 155, 158 (N.D. 1985) (citing Prosser & W. Keeton, Law of Torts 242 (5th ed. 1984)); Nw. Equip., Inc. v. Cudmore, 312 N.W.2d 347, 352 (N.D. 1981); Foerster v. Fischbach-Moore, Inc., 178 N.W.2d 258, 262 (N.D. 1970).

[45] Mertz v. Weibe, 180 N.W.2d 664, 667 (N.D. 1970) (citing McKenzie v. Hanson, 143 N.W.2d 697, 703 (N.D. 1966); Farmers' Mercantile Co. v. N. Pac. Ry., 146 N.W. 550, 555 (N.D. 1914); 38 Am.Jur., *Negligence*, § 285).

[46] *McKenzie*, 143 N.W.2d at 703.

[47] Mikkelson v. Risovi, 141 N.W.2d 150, 152 (N.D. 1966).

[48] Inv'rs Real Estate Tr. Props., Inc. v. Terra Pac. Midwest, Inc., 2004 ND 167, ¶ 7, 686 N.W.2d 140, 144; Grewal v. N.D. Ass'n of Ctys. & Nw. Contracting, Inc., 2003 ND 156, ¶ 9, 670 N.W.2d 336, 339; Pechtl v. Conoco, Inc., 1997 ND 161, ¶ 7, 567 N.W.2d 813, 816.

[49] Larson v. Kubisiak, 1997 ND 22, ¶ 8, 558 N.W.2d 852, 854 (quoting Ebach v. Ralston, 510 N.W.2d 604, 611 (N.D. 1994)); Praus *ex rel.* Praus v. Mack, 2001 ND 80, ¶ 35, 626 N.W.2d 239, 250.

[50] ND. J.I. Civ. § C - 2.05 (Lexis Advance).

[51] Keyes v. Amundson, 391 N.W.2d 602, 608 (N.D. 1986), *abrogated by* State v. Putney, 2016 ND 59, 877 N.W.2d 28.

[52] *Keyes*, 391 N.W.2d at 608 ("The appropriate approach in determining whether or not a plaintiff's injury is of the kind that an ordinance was intended to prevent requires interpreting the purpose of the ordinance to include all risks that may reasonably be anticipated as likely to follow from its violation." *Id.* (citing Prosser, Law of Torts, pp. 192-97 (4th ed. 1971)).

Evidence of general custom or usage may be considered by the trier of fact to determine whether "conduct meets the standard of reasonable care under the circumstances,"[53] but "not for the purpose of establishing a set standard on the basis of which the conduct is to be held negligent or not negligent."[54] In one case, the North Dakota Supreme Court indicated that evidence of the failure to comply with hortatory but otherwise non-enforceable standards "is admissible to show knowledge of existence of risk and a measure of actions of a reasonable man, or of custom."[55]

IV. Causation

A. Elements

Negligence and proximate cause are separate elements and must each be proved separately.[56] The North Dakota Supreme Court has stated that it is "hornbook law" that a negligent act must be the proximate cause of the alleged damages to sustain an action for negligence.[57] Courts in North Dakota frequently define proximate cause as "a cause which, in natural and continuous sequence, produces the injury and without which the injury would not have occurred."[58]

For a causal act to be proximate, it must play a substantial part in bringing about an injury immediately or through a chain of sequential events.[59] Proximate cause "embodies the requirement of 'causation in fact,' which asks whether the conduct of the defendant caused the plaintiff's harm."[60] As part of the determination as to whether factual causation exists, North Dakota courts have "incorporated the 'but-for' rule in their definition of proximate cause," which requires that an injury would not have occurred without the defendant's conduct.[61] A proximate cause need not be the last or sole cause of the injury so long as it was an essential event without which the injurious result would not have occurred.[62] For a

---

[53] Wanner v. Getter Trucking, Inc., 466 N.W.2d 833, 837 (N.D. 1991) (citing Tom Beuchler Const., Inc. v. City of Williston, 392 N.W.2d 403, 405 (N.D. 1986); Besette v. Enderlin Sch. Dist. No. 22, 310 N.W.2d 759, 761 (N.D. 1981)).

[54] Schmitt v. N. Imp. Co., 115 N.W.2d 713, 720 (N.D. 1962) (collecting cases).

[55] Falkenstein v. City of Bismarck, 268 N.W.2d 787, 790 (N.D. 1978), *disagreed with on other grounds by* Minto Grain, LLC v. Tibert, 2009 ND 213, 776 N.W.2d 549 (citing RESTATEMENT (SECOND) OF TORTS § 288B(2)).

[56] Jim's Hot Shot Serv., Inc. v. Cont'l W. Ins., 353 N.W.2d 279, 283 (N.D. 1984); Knorr v. K-Mart Corp., 300 N.W.2d 47, 50 (N.D. 1980).

[57] Rued Ins. v. Blackburn, Nickels & Smith, Inc., 543 N.W.2d 770, 773 (N.D. 1996).

[58] Perius v. Nodak Mut. Ins., 2010 ND 80, ¶ 13, 782 N.W.2d 355, 360 (quoting Klimple v. Bahl, 2007 ND 13, ¶ 5, 727 N.W.2d 256); *Rued Ins.*, 543 N.W.2d at 773.

[59] ND. J.I. CIV. § C - 2.15 (Lexis Advance)

[60] Dick v. Lewis, 506 F. Supp. 799, 805 (D.N.D. 1980), *aff'd*, 636 F.2d 1168 (8th Cir. 1981) (citing PROSSER, LAW OF TORTS § 41 (1971)).

[61] *Dick*, 506 F. Supp. at 805.

[62] Froemke v. Otter Tail Power Co., 276 N.W. 146, 148 (N.D. 1937); Chi., Milwaukee, St. Paul & Pac. RR. v. Johnston's Fuel Liners, Inc., 122 N.W.2d 140, 148 (N.D. 1963).

specific negligent act to be the proximate cause of an injury, "the injury must be the natural and probable result of the conduct and must have been foreseen or reasonably anticipated by that person as a probable result of the conduct."[63] A party is not liable for all possible consequences of a negligent act but "only for the consequences which are probable according to the ordinary, usual experiences of mankind."[64]

B. *Evidence*

In most cases, the trier of fact determines questions as to causation and proximate cause.[65] Conversely, when reasonable men can draw but one conclusion from the facts presented, questions of negligence become a matter of law for the court to decide.[66] In order for the trier of fact to find that an injury was proximately caused by an alleged tortfeasor, the plaintiff has the burden of proof to present some affirmative evidence that the negligent conduct caused the injury.[67] Mere speculation is insufficient to prove proximate cause.[68] Instead, the evidence presented must permit a reasonable inference as to the likely cause of the injury, and, "at the same time exclude equally reasonable inferences of other causes for which the defendant is not responsible."[69] "In establishing proximate cause, the plaintiff must adduce evidence that shows plaintiff's theory of causation is reasonably probable, not merely possible, and more probable than any other theory based thereon."[70]

V. Damages

A. *Elements*

By statute, the measure of damages for tort actions "is the amount which will compensate for all the detriment proximately caused thereby, whether it could have been anticipated or not."[71] At least one North Dakota Supreme Court opinion has noted that this statutory language "is merely a restatement of the common-law rule."[72] There is, however, "no certain or definite rule by which the amount of damages can be measured, and each case

---

[63] Kimball v. Landeis, 2002 ND 162, ¶ 7, 652 N.W.2d 330, 334; Jones v. Ahlberg, 489 N.W.2d 576, 581 (N.D. 1992); Moum v. Maercklein, 201 N.W.2d 399, 402 (N.D. 1972).

[64] *Moum*, 201 N.W.2d at 402.

[65] Leno v. Ehli, 339 N.W.2d 92, 96 (N.D. 1983); F-M Potatoes, Inc. v. Suda, 259 N.W.2d 487, 491 (N.D. 1977).

[66] *Leno*, 339 N.W.2d at 96; Rawlings v. Fruhwirth, 455 N.W.2d 574, 577 (N.D. 1990); Morrison v. Grand Forks Hous. Auth., 436 N.W.2d 221, 229 (N.D. 1989) (citing Mikkelson v. Risovi, 141 N.W.2d 150 (N.D. 1966)).

[67] Inv'rs Real Estate Tr. Props., Inc. v. Terra Pac. Midwest, Inc., 2004 ND 167, ¶ 9, 686 N.W.2d 140, 145.

[68] *Id.*

[69] *Id.* (quoting Leno v. Ehli, 339 N.W.2d 92, 96 (N.D. 1983)).

[70] Dick v. Lewis, 506 F. Supp. 799, 806 (D.N.D. 1980), *aff'd,* 636 F.2d 1168 (8th Cir. 1981).

[71] N.D. Cent. Code § 32-03-20 (Lexis Advance); Johnson v. Monsanto Co., 303 N.W.2d 86, 93 (N.D. 1981); Schmeet v. Schumacher, 137 N.W.2d 789, 791 (N.D. 1965); *see also* Carpenter v. Vill. of Dickey, 143 N.W. 964, 967 (N.D. 1913) ("the measure of damages is the amount which will reasonably and fairly compensate the injured person for the detriment suffered as a proximate result of the injuries.").

[72] Needham v. H.S. Halverson & Co., 135 N.W. 203, 204 (N.D. 1912).

must be determined on its merits."[73] In cases where the amount of damages is difficult to ascertain or prove, it is for the finder of fact to determine the appropriate amount.[74] As the determination of damages "is largely within the jury's discretion," courts "will sustain an award of damages when it is within the range of evidence presented."[75] In one opinion, the North Dakota Supreme Court noted, however, "[t]he measure of damages in tort is broader than that in contract."[76]

B.   *Evidence*

Damages may not be based on speculation or conjecture.[77] Instead, the trier of fact must be provided with evidence and data sufficient to determine appropriate damages.[78] Evidence that is imprecise as to the amount of damages, however, will not preclude recovery.[79] While damages must be proved, neither difficulty in proving them,[80] nor mathematical uncertainty as to the proper amount, will preclude recovery.[81] In those cases where the amount of damages are difficult to determine with precision, "the amount of damages is to be left to the sound discretion of the finder of facts."[82] The Supreme Court of North Dakota has stated that determining damages for pain and suffering "is not susceptible of arithmetical calculation; rather, its ascertainment must, to a large degree, depend upon the common knowledge, good sense and practical judgment of the jury."[83]

---

[73] Carpenter v. Rohrer, 2006 ND 111, ¶ 8, 714 N.W.2d 804, 810 (quoting Vallejo v. Jamestown Coll., 244 N.W.2d 753, 759 (N.D. 1976)).

[74] Langer v. Bartholomay, 2008 ND 40, ¶ 27, 745 N.W.2d 649, 659; *Vallejo*, 244 N.W.2d at 759.

[75] Westby v. Schmidt, 2010 ND 44, ¶ 18, 779 N.W.2d 681, 687.

[76] Delzer v. United Bank, 1997 ND 3, ¶ 17, 559 N.W.2d 531, 536 (quoting Twentieth Century–Fox Film Corp. v. Harbor Ins., 85 Cal.App.3d 105, 149 Cal.Rptr. 313, 318 n. 8 (Cal. Ct. App. 1978) and noting that the California statute at issue was "the same, effectively" as N.D. Cent. Code § 32-03-20). Numerous North Dakota statutes, including N.D. Cent. Code § 32-03-20, were "derived from the California Civil Code." Note, *General Damages for Pain and Suffering in A Personal Tort Action*, 39 N.D. L. Rev. 80, 80 (1963). *See also* William B. Fisch, *The Dakota Civil Code: More Notes for an Uncelebrated Centennial*, 45 N.D.L. Rev. 9, 37-38 (1968) (noting that the Dakota Territory Civil Code was "by no means a slavish copy of the California Code, but in most particulars substantially identical").

[77] United Power Ass'n v. Heley, 277 N.W.2d 262, 268 (N.D. 1979); Johnson v. Monsanto Co., 303 N.W.2d 86, 95 (N.D. 1981).

[78] *Johnson*, 303 N.W.2d at 95.

[79] Keller v. Bolding, 2004 ND 80, ¶ 21, 678 N.W.2d 578, 584; State v. Gendron, 2008 ND 70, ¶ 8, 747 N.W.2d 125, 128 (quoting Keller v. Bolding, 678 N.W.2d 578); Red River Wings, Inc. v. Hoot, Inc., 2008 ND 117, ¶ 42, 751 N.W.2d 206, 223 (quoting Keller v. Bolding, 678 N.W.2d 578).

[80] Langer v. Bartholomay, 2008 ND 40, ¶ 27, 745 N.W.2d 649, 659; SolarBee, Inc. v. Walker, 2013 ND 110, ¶ 26, 833 N.W.2d 422, 429.

[81] *SolarBee*, 833 N.W.2d at 429.

[82] *Keller*, 678 N.W.2d at 585 (quoting B.W.S. Invs. v. Mid–Am Rests., Inc., 459 N.W.2d 759, 764 (N.D. 1990)).

[83] Stoner v. Nash Finch, Inc., 446 N.W.2d 747, 753 (N.D. 1989).

CHAPTER 36

OHIO

OHIO

Joseph A. Custer[1]

I. Purpose of Tort Law

The Court of Appeals of Ohio has stated that "the purpose of tort law and litigation is to allow the injured party to recover damages and to achieve a desirable social result."[2] The Ohio Supreme Court reinforced the role of equity in tort law. Tort law "is designed to redress losses suffered by breach of a duty imposed by law to protect societal interests."[3] In addition, the state supreme court has ~~also~~ stated the purpose of tort law is to provide "a means of redress to individuals for damages suffered as a result of tortious conduct." [4]

II. Duty to Exercise Ordinary Care

A. Question of Law

Foreseeability of injury needs to be present for a duty to exist. The Ohio Supreme Court has stated "injury is foreseeable if a defendant knew or should have known that his act was likely to result in harm to someone."[5] The test for foreseeability is "whether a reasonably prudent person would have anticipated that an injury was likely to result from the performance or nonperformance of an act."[6]

The existence of a duty in a negligence action is a question of law for the court to determine.[7] There is no express formula for determining whether or not a duty exists.[8] In Ohio, in determining whether a duty exists, the trial court must view the evidence in a light most favorable to the non-moving party.[9] A totality of the circumstances standard is used to determine whether a duty exists.[10]

---

[1] Associate Professor of Law & Director, Judge Ben C. Green Law Library.

[2] Gates v. Brewer, 2 Ohio App. 3d 347, 349, 442 N.E. 2d 72, 75 (10th Dist. 1981).

[3] Corporex Dev. & Constr. Mgt., Inc. v. Shook, 106 Ohio St. 3d 412, 414, 2005-Ohio-5409, 835 N.E. 2d 701, 704 (Ohio 2005).

[4] Fred Siegel Co., L.P.A. v. Arter & Hadden, 85 Ohio St. 3d 171, 178, 707 N.E. 2d 853, 859 (1999).

[5] Huston v. Konieczny, 52 Ohio St. 3d 214, 217, 556 N.E. 2d 505, 508 (1990).

[6] Menifee v. Ohio Welding Products, Inc., 15 Ohio St. 3d 75, 77, 472 N.E. 2d 707, 710 (1984).

[7] Mussivand v. David, 45 Ohio St. 3d 314, 318, 544 N.E. 2d 265, 270 (1989).

[8] Id.

[9] Uddin v. Embassy Suites Hotel, 165 Ohio App. 3d 699, 716, 2005-Ohio-6613, 848 N.E. 2d 519, 532 (2005).

[10] Reitz v. May Co. Dept. Stores, 66 Ohio App. 3d 188,193, 583 N.E. 2d 1071, 1075 (1990).

A duty may be created by statute,[11] from the relationship between the parties,[12] or a party may agree to assume a duty.[13] The determination of the duty question requires the court to weigh several factors, such as "the foreseeability of the occurrence, the likelihood of injury, the magnitude of the burden against guarding against it and the consequences of placing that burden upon the plaintiff."[14] The Ohio Supreme Court has stated "any number of considerations may justify the imposition of duty in particular circumstances, including the guidance of history, our continually refined concepts of morals and justice, the convenience of the rule, and social judgment as to where the loss should fall."[15] Courts also consider "the moral blame attached to the defendant's conduct and the policy of preventing future harm" in deciding to impose a duty.[16] The test of whether a duty exists focuses on "whether a reasonable person under the prevailing attendant circumstances would have expected and discovered the danger, and taken precautions to avoid it."[17]

In Ohio, "the tort system exists, in part, to encourage and discourage certain behaviors. Owing to this deterrent purpose and effect, tort law must be as clear and certain as possible so that it may serve its function in regulating how persons deal with and treat one another."[18] It is settled law in Ohio that "[w]here a legislative enactment imposes upon any person a specific duty for the protection of others," the failure to perform that duty is negligence *per se*.[19] "The distinction between negligence and 'negligence *per se*' in Ohio is the means and method of ascertainment. The former must be found by the jury from the facts, the conditions, and circumstances disclosed by the evidence; the latter is a violation of a specific requirement of law or ordinance, the only fact for determination by the jury being the commission or omission of the specific act inhibited or required."[20] Negligence *per se* may be excused in certain situations. "Negligence *per se* is different from strict liability, in that a negligence-*per-se* violation will not preclude defenses and excuses, unless the statute clearly contemplates such a result."[21]

B. *Question of Fact*

i. **Elements**

It is for the jury to determine the degree of care required[22] and whether a duty of care was breached.[23] As stated above, negligence must be found by the jury from the facts, the

---

[11] Goldberg v. Agudath B'nai Israel Congregation, 66 Ohio App. 379, 382, 34 N.E. 2d 73, 74 (3rd Dist. 1940).

[12] Jackson v. Forest City Ent., Inc., 111 Ohio App. 3d 283, 285, 675 N.E. 2d 1356, 1358 (8th Dist. 1996).

[13] Cooper v. Roose, 151 Ohio St. 316, 324, 85 N.E. 2d 545, 549 (1949).

[14] Simon v. Zipperstein, No. 9655, 1986 WL 8531 (Ohio Ct. App. July 29, 1986), *rev'd on other grounds*, Simon v. Zipperstein, 32 Ohio St. 3d 74, 512 N.E. 2d 636 (1987).

[15] Wallace v. Ohio Dep't of Commerce, 96 Ohio St. 3d 266, 274, 2002-Ohio-4210, ¶ 24 274, 773 N.E. 2d 1018, 1026.

[16] Childs v. Charske, 2004-Ohio-7331, ¶ 27, 129 Ohio Misc. 2d 50, 52, 822 N.E. 2d 853, 859.

[17] Ellington v. JCTH Holdings, Inc., 2015 WL 1019458 (Ohio Ct. App. Mar. 2, 2015).

[18] Roe *ex rel.* Roe v. Heap, 2004 WL 1109849 (Ohio Ct. App. May 11, 2004).

[19] Marich v. Bob Bennett Constr. Co., 116 Ohio St. 3d 553, 561, 880 N.E. 2d 906, 916 (2008).

[20] Swoboda v. Brown, 129 Ohio St. 512, 513, 196 N.E. 274, 278 (1935).

[21] Robinson v. Bates, 112 Ohio St. 3d 17, 24, 857 N.E. 2d 1195, 1201 (2006).

[22] Cranon v. Toledo Area Regional Transit Authority, 1988 WL 30501 (Ohio Ct. App. Mar. 11, 1988).

[23] Texler v. D.O. Summers Cleaners & Shirt Laundry Co., 81 Ohio St. 3d 677, 681, 693 N.E. 2d 271, 274 (1988).

conditions, and circumstances disclosed by the evidence.[24] In determining whether ordinary care was used, the jury is instructed that they will consider whether the defendant ought to have foreseen from the circumstances presented that "the natural and probable result of an act or a failure to act would cause some injury."[25] Ordinary care is "that degree of care that a reasonably careful and prudent person would use under like or similar circumstances."[26]

ii. Evidence

In Ohio, the "burden of persuading the jury or court is ultimately upon the plaintiff to show that the defendant was not in the exercise of the degree of care required."[27] Federal regulations can be relevant and admissible in certain cases to show the degree of care owed.[28] State statutes, regulations, and local ordinances can prescribe the standard or duty of care.[29] Violation of a building code may serve as strong evidence that the condition at issue was dangerous and defendant breached the attendant duty of care by not rectifying the problem. However, the violation is mere evidence of negligence and does not raise an irrefutable presumption of it.[30] A plaintiff may establish duty and breach by "merely showing that the defendant committed or omitted a specific act prohibited or required by statute."[31]

III. Breach of Duty

A. Elements

In order to prevail, the plaintiff must prove, by a preponderance of the evidence, that the defendant owed him a duty which the defendant breached through his or her act or omission which the defendant should or should not have done in accordance with the standard of care[32] and the defendant's breach proximately caused the plaintiff's injuries.[33] Where there is conflicting evidence as to the issues in a case of negligence, submission of the case to the jury is proper in order for the jury to decide whether the evidence supported the element(s).[34]

B. Evidence

A breach of duty may be shown "by the failure or omission to do some particular thing or things" that a reasonable person would have done under like or similar conditions and

---

[24] Becker V. Shaull, 62 Ohio St. 3d 480, 483, 584 N.E. 2d 684, 686 (1992).

[25] Richard v. St. Denis Council, Knights of Columbus, No. 1756, 1986 WL 13237 (Ohio Ct. App. Nov. 20, 1986).

[26] Goldfuss v. Davidson, 79 Ohio St. 3d 116, 119, 679 N.E. 2d 1099, 1101 (1997).

[27] Agricultural Ins. Co. v. Constantine, Ohio App., 40 Ohio Law Abs. 569, 56 N.E. 2d 687, 693 (1943).

[28] Gable v. Gates Mills, 151 Ohio App. 3d 480, 491, 784 N.E. 2d 739, 747 (2003), *rev'd on other grounds*, Gable v. Gates Mills, 103 Ohio St. 3d 449, 816 N.E. 2d 1049 (2004).

[29] Wolfe v. Great Atlantic & Pacific Tea Co., 143 Ohio St. 643, 647, 28 Ohio Op. 520, 56 N.E. 2d 230, 232 (1944).

[30] Lang v. Holly Hill Motel, Inc., 122 Ohio St. 3d 120, 124, 909 N.E. 2d 120, 125 (2009).

[31] Webster v. Shaw, 2016-Ohio-1484, ¶ 10, 63 N.E. 3d 677, 680 (2016).

[32] Pisani v. Pisani, 1997 WL 767452 (Ohio Ct. App. Dec.11,1997).

[33] Strother v. Hutchinson, 67 Ohio St. 2d 282, 423 N.E. 2d 467 (1981).

[34] Briere v. Lathrop Co., 22 Ohio St. 2d 166, 175, 258 N.E. 2d 597, 603 (1970).

circumstances.[35] Courts may let a jury determine whether government or industry standards are relevant.[36] The Ohio Court of Appeals determined that a jury question existed when the evidence showed that either an original design defect or a substantial alteration proximately caused the plaintiff's injuries.[37] Violation of an administrative rule does not constitute negligence *per se* in Ohio as does a violation of a "legislative enactment." However, the violation of an administrative rule may be admissible as evidence of negligence.[38]

IV.   Causation

A.   *Elements*

A plaintiff in a negligence action must prove causation in fact and proximate cause.[39] Foreseeability must be found in order to establish proximate cause.[40] The Ohio Supreme Court has defined proximate cause as follows:

> For an act to be the proximate cause of an injury, it must appear that the injury was the natural and probable consequence of such act.[41] To find that an injury was the natural and probable consequence of an act, it must appear that the injury complained of could have been foreseen or reasonably anticipated from the alleged negligent act.[42]

There may be more than one proximate cause of an injury in Ohio. The negligence of each party can be a cause of the injury when a negligent act or the failure to act of one party combines with the negligence of another to produce an injury.[43] It is for the trier of fact to determine proximate cause and to assess the comparative negligence of the parties in causing the injuries.[44]

If an injury is the natural and probable consequence of a negligent act in Ohio, it is not necessary that the defendant should have anticipated the particular injury. It is sufficient that his act is likely to result in an injury to someone.[45]

---

[35] Powell v. Hawkins, 175 Ohio App. 3d 138, 142, 885 N.E. 2d 958, 961 (2007).

[36] Bruni v. Tatsumi, 46 Ohio St. 2d 127, 346 N.E. 2d 673, 675 (1976).

[37] Cox v. Oliver Machinery Co., 41 Ohio App. 3d 28, 29, 534 N.E. 2d 855, 857 (1987).

[38] Chambers v. St. Mary's School, 82 Ohio St. 3d 563, 566, 697 N.E. 2d 198, 201 (1998).

[39] Snyder v. Department of Transp., 2002 WL 233519 (Ohio Ct. App. Feb. 19, 2002).

[40] Cromer v. Children's Hosp. Med. Ctr. of Akron, 142 Ohio St. 3d 257, 271, 2015-Ohio-229, ¶ 50, 29 N.E. 3d 921, 935.

[41] Foss-Schneider Brewing Co. v. Ulland, 97 Ohio St. 210, 218, 119 N.E. 454, 457 (1918).

[42] Ross v. Nutt, 177 Ohio St. 113, 114, 203 N.E. 2d 118, 120 (1964).

[43] Berk v. Matthews, 53 Ohio St. 3d 161,164, 559 N.E. 2d 1301, 1304 (1990).

[44] Darling v. Fairfield Med. Ctr., 142 Ohio App. 3d 682, 688, 756 N.E. 2d 754, 758 (2001).

[45] Estate of Graves v. Circleville, 179 Ohio App. 3d 479, 495, 902 N.E. 2d 535, 547 (2008).

B.   *Evidence*

Causation is an issue for the jury to determine.[46] A question as to the proximate cause of an injury is for the trier of fact to determine. If reasonable minds cannot determine that the condition is unreasonably dangerous or what the proximate cause of the injury is, the trial court should not permit the trier of fact to make a determination.[47]

V.   Damages

A.   *Elements*

The Court of Appeals of Ohio has stated that "the purpose of tort law and litigation is to allow the injured party to recover damages and to achieve a desirable social result."[48] The Ohio Supreme Court, citing *Prosser and Keeton*, stated that tort law "is directed toward the compensation of individuals . . . for losses which they have suffered within the scope of their legally recognized interests . . . where the law considers that compensation is required."[49]

B.   *Evidence*

The jury normally assesses damages. "It is primarily the province of the jury to assess damages and that determination should not be disturbed unless it appears to have been the result of passion or prejudice, or is such as to shock the sense of fairness or justice."[50] In a tort action "whether the trier of fact is a jury or the court, if the trier of fact determines that any defendant is liable for punitive or exemplary damages, the amount of those damages shall be determined by the court."[51]

---

[46]   Roberts v. Ohio Permanente Med. Group, Inc., 76 Ohio St. 3d 483, 486-487, 668 N.E. 2d 480, 483 (1996).

[47]   Gartland v. Garcia, 153 Ohio App. 3d 523, 526, 795 N.E. 2d 59, 61 (2003).

[48]   *Gates*, 442 N.E. 2d at 75.

[49]   Floor Craft Floor Covering, Inc. v. Parma Community General Hosp. Ass'n., 54 Ohio St. 3d 1, 13, 560 N.E. 2d 206, 216 (1990) (citing PROSSER & KEETON, LAW OF TORTS § 1, 5-6 (5th ed. 1984)).

[50]   Glover v. Massey, 1990 WL 1328 (Ohio Ct. App. Jan. 11, 1990).

[51]   Villella v. Waikem Motors, Inc., 45 Ohio St. 3d 36, 46, 543 N.E. 2d 464, 474 (1989).

CHAPTER 37

OKLAHOMA

OKLAHOMA

Gregg W. Luther[1]

I. Purpose of Tort Law

The Oklahoma Supreme Court has stated that the purpose of Oklahoma's common law is to protect every person against wrongful acts of others.[2] This purpose has never changed.[3] The policy of Oklahoma's common law is to protect people's safety, the safety of families, and the safety of the general public.[4] Public safety and individual responsibility are a reasonable basis for imposing tort liability.[5] Tort liability has been imposed to protect public policy, deter wrongdoing, and compensate those injured by violations of public policy.[6] It is the "statutorily established public policy" in Oklahoma to deter wrongdoing through civil actions.[7]

II. Duty to Exercise Ordinary Care

A. *Question of Law*

To establish negligence, a plaintiff must prove that a defendant owed them a "*duty to protect* them from injury."[8] As a general rule a "defendant owes a duty of care to all persons who are foreseeably endangered by his conduct with respect to all risks which make the conduct unreasonably dangerous."[9] The duty to prevent harm to others is embodied within statute.[10] Whether the defendant has a duty to exercise care is a question of law.[11] The court, however, does not decide the scope of the duty to exercise ordinary care. The jury must decide how a reasonably careful person must act in the same (or similar) circumstances.[12]

---

[1] Oklahoma City University Law Review and School of Law alumni.

[2] Schonwald v. Ragains, 122 P. 203, 210 (Okla. 1912).

[3] Wilspec Tech. v. Dunan Holding Group, 2009 OK 12, ¶ 11, 204 P.3d 69, 73.

[4] Darrow v. Integris Health, Inc., 2008 OK 1, ¶ 17, 176 P.3d 1204, 1215.

[5] Thomas v. EZ Mart Stores, Inc., 2004 OK 82, ¶ 13, 102 P.3d 133, 137.

[6] MacDonald v. Corporate Integris Health, 2014 OK 10, ¶ 6, 321 P.3d 980, 983.

[7] Copeland v. Anderson, 707 P.2d 560, 568 (Okla. Civ. App. 1985).

[8] Iglehart v. Bd. of County Comm'rs of Rogers County, 60 P.3d 497, 502 (Okla. 2002) (emphasis in original).

[9] Wofford v. E. State Hosp., 795 P.2d 516, 519 (Okla. 1990) (citations omitted).

[10] 76 O.S. (2011) § 1. Section 1 was enacted in 1910 and provides, as follows: "Every person is bound, without contract, to abstain from injuring the person or property of another, or infringing upon any of his rights."

[11] *Iglehart,* 60 P.3d at 502.

[12] Oklahoma Uniform Jury Instruction—Civil § 9.2 provides as follows: "Since this lawsuit is based on the theory of negligence, you must understand what the terms 'negligence' and 'ordinary care' mean in the law with reference to this case. 'Negligence' is the failure to exercise ordinary care to avoid injury to another's person

The court looks at six factors to determine whether a duty to exercise care exists. These are: (1) foreseeability of the harm; (2) degree of certainty of the harm; (3) the moral blame attached to the defendant's conduct; (4) the need to prevent future harm; (5) the extent of the burden to the defendant and consequences to the community of imposing a duty on the defendant; and (6) the availability of insurance for the risk.[13] Of these six factors, foreseeability of harm is the most important consideration.[14] With regard to foreseeability of harm, a court must determine: (1) if the plaintiff was a foreseeable "victim" of some harm; and (2) if the harm suffered was foreseeable from the perspective of the defendant, prior to the act or failure to act. Foreseeability of harm establishes a "zone of risk" created by the defendant's conduct.[15]

Foreseeability of those put at risk of harm creates the duty to prevent harm and protect those put at risk, including strangers and/or third parties.[16] Imposing a duty to prevent foreseeable harm serves the deterrent function of tort law.[17] The "zone of risk" is limited only by those foreseeably at risk of harm. Where the public is in the "zone of risk" created by a defendant's conduct, a duty will be imposed to exercise ordinary care to protect all members of the public.[18] A defendant's duty is established when it can be said that it was foreseeable that his act or omission to act may cause harm to someone.[19] The duty to exercise care is not always based on the relationship of the parties.[20] Whether a defendant

---

or property. 'Ordinary care' is the care which a reasonably careful person would use under the same or similar circumstances. The law does not say how a reasonably careful person would act under those circumstances. That is for you to decide. Thus, under the facts in evidence in this case, if a party failed to do something which a reasonably careful person would do, or did something which a reasonably careful person would not do, such party would be negligent."

[13] Lowery v. Echostar Satellite Corp., 2007 OK 38, ¶ 14, 160 P.3d 959, 967, n.4.

[14] "The *threshold question* for negligence suits is whether a defendant owes a plaintiff a duty of care. We recognize the traditional common-law rule that whenever one person is by circumstances placed in such a position with regard to another, that, if he (she) did not use ordinary care and skill in his (her) own conduct, he would cause danger of injury to the person or property of the other, a duty arises to use ordinary care and skill to avoid such danger. Among a number of factors used to determine the existence of a duty of care, *the most important consideration is foreseeability . . . Foreseeability establishes a "zone of risk,"* which is to say that it forms a basis for assessing whether the conduct "creates a generalized and foreseeable risk of harming others." *Iglehart,* 60 P.3d at 502 (emphasis added).

[15] *Id.*

[16] Delbrel v. Doenges Bros. Ford, Inc., 913 P.2d 1318, 1321 (Okla. 1996).

[17] McKellips v. St. Francis Hosp., Inc., 741 P.2d 467, 474 (Okla. 1987).

[18] *Delbrel,* 913 P.2d at 1322.

[19] *Wofford,* 795 P.2d at 520 (citing Schuster v. Altenberg, 424 N.W.2d 159, 164 (Wis.1988)).

[20] In *Wofford,* the court also found sound reasoning from the Washington Supreme Court, where a released mental health patient caused a car accident which injured the plaintiff. *Id.* That court found that the defendant had a "duty to take reasonable precautions to protect anyone who might foreseeably be endangered by the patient's drug-related mental problems. . . . We have long recognized that without regard to the relationship of the parties, a person owes a duty of care to another person whenever the circumstances place the one person in a position towards the other person such that an ordinary prudent person would recognize that if he or she did not act with ordinary care and skill in regard to the circumstances, he or she may cause danger of injury to the other person. We have explained that a duty of care may arise from a set of circumstances which would require the defendant to foresee the particular harm to the plaintiff." *Id.*

should realize that his conduct could put another in danger of harm is judged by the ordinary prudent person standard.[21]

B.   *Question of Fact*

i.   **Elements**

The jury determines what level of care is required to satisfy the duty to exercise ordinary care under the circumstances.[22] When the circumstances are such that an ordinary prudent person would understand that the conduct will place another in danger of harm, the duty to exercise ordinary care arises.[23] The duty to exercise care is dependent upon the foreseeable frequency and severity of the harm.[24]

ii.   **Evidence**

The plaintiff must present evidence of the level of care required.[25] Evidence of how others would act in the same or similar circumstances is admissible to establish the level of care required.[26] Evidence of the foreseeable frequency and severity of the harm is also admissible to determine the level of care required.[27] In closing, counsel may remind the jury that they are "setting a standard" for everyone, or "sending a message" to a class of defendants, when they determine how a reasonably careful person would have acted under the circumstances.[28]

Rules and regulations are "highly material and relevant" to the issue of the level of care required.[29] Statutes, rules and regulations, safety codes, and other laws which protect people's safety create a duty of reasonable care which can be enforced in a common law negligence action.[30]

---

[21] "One of the most important considerations in establishing a duty is foreseeability. Foreseeability is critical as it determines (1) to whom a duty is owed and (2) the extent of the duty. A defendant owes a duty of care only to foreseeable plaintiffs. As for the extent of the duty, it too is determined in great part by the foreseeability of the injury. Whenever the circumstances attending a situation are such that an ordinarily prudent person could reasonably apprehend that, as the natural and probable consequences of his act, another person will be in danger of receiving an injury, a duty to exercise ordinary care to prevent such injury arises." Woods v. Mercedes Benz of Oklahoma City, 2014 OK 68, ¶ 7, 336 P.3d 457, 459-60 (citations omitted).

[22] Oklahoma Uniform Jury Instruction—Civil § 9.2, *supra,* n.11.

[23] Woodis v. OG&E, 704 P.2d 483, 487 (Okla. 1985).

[24] *Id.*

[25] Myers v. Lutrell, 373 P.2d 22, 25 (Okla. 1961).

[26] Boyles v. Oklahoma Natural Gas Co., 619 P. 2d 613, 619 (Okla. 1980).

[27] Woodis v. OG&E, 704 P.2d 483, 486-87 (Okla. 1985).

[28] Covel v. Rodriguez, 2012 OK 5, ¶¶ 21-22, 272 P.3d 705, 713-14; English v. Wal-Mart Stores, Inc., 2001 OK CIV APP 5, ¶ 16, 16 P.3d 1136, 1142; Bays Exploration, Inc., v. Jones, 2007 OK CIV APP 111, ¶ 24, 172 P.3d 217, 223.

[29] Howard v. Zimmer, 2013 OK 17, ¶ 15, 299 P.3d 463, 468.

[30] *Id.* (federal statutes regulating manufacturing are admissible to establish level of care owed); Covel v. Rodriguez, 2012 OK 5, ¶¶ 24-26, 272 P.3d 705, 714-15 (Federal Motor Carrier Safety Rules are admissible to show level of due care); Bittle v. Bahe, 2008 OK 10, ¶¶ 43-44, 192 P.3d 810, 824 (statutes that protect the safety of the people

Rules and regulations enacted by administrative agencies and boards pursuant to the powers delegated to them have the force and effect of law, and are relevant to the applicable standard of care.[31] Oklahoma Courts must take judicial notice of any such rules.[32] Violation of a rule or regulation may be used to establish negligence by showing the injury (1) was caused by the violation of the rule, (2) the injury was the type intended to be prevented by the rule, and (3) the plaintiff was one of the class of people protected by the rule.[33]

Safety rules are also relevant and admissible to show the level of care required.[34] Safety rules have the same legal function as other non-legislative safety standards.[35] Safety rules in textbooks and literature are admissible through an expert witness to establish the standard of care.[36] Recommendations of a manufacturer are proper evidence for the factfinder to consider in determining the standard of care.[37] Company policies of the defendant are also proper evidence as proof of the level of care required.[38]

III.   Breach of Duty

A.   *Elements*

Negligence is the lack of due care required in a certain setting.[39] The degree of care that an ordinary prudent person would exercise in the situation is decided by the jury.[40]

B.   *Evidence*

Evidence must be presented to show a breach of duty on the part of the defendant.[41] The actions taken by the defendant in the situation is proper evidence for the jury to consider in determining whether the defendant exercised due care in the situation.[42] Evidence of

---

of this state are admissible to establish the level of care owed); Tomlinson v. Love's Country Store, 854 P.2d 910, 917 (Okla. 1993) (statute which protects the safety of third parties is admissible to establish the level of care owed); Woodis v. OG&E, 704 P.2d 483, 486-7 (Okla. 1985) (National Electric Safety Code is admissible to establish the level of care owed); Boyles v. Oklahoma Natural Gas Co., 619 P. 2d 613, 618 (Okla. 1980) (custom and safety practices are admissible to establish level of care owed); Shoopman v. Travelers Ins., 518 P.2d 1108, 1111 (Okla. 1974) (Oklahoma's statutory rules of the road are proper evidence of the level of care required); Claborn v. Plains Cotton Co-Op., 2009 OK CIV APP 39, ¶ 9, 211 P.3d 915, 919 (OSHA is proper evidence of due care).

[31] Johnson v. Hillcrest Health Center, Inc., 2003 OK 16, ¶ 14, 70 P.3d 811, 817-18.

[32] 75 O.S. (2011) § 252(A).

[33] Boyles v. Oklahoma Natural Gas Co., 619 P.2d 613, 618 (Okla. 1980).

[34] Jackson v. Oklahoma Mem'l Hosp., 909 P.2d 765, 775 (Okla. 1995).

[35] *Id.*

[36] 12 O.S. (2011) § 2803(18); Nail v. Okla. Children's Mem'l Hosp., 710 P.2d 755, 762 (Okla. 1985).

[37] Grayson v. Children's Hosp. of Oklahoma, 838 P.2d 546, 549 (Okla. Civ. App. 1992).

[38] Harder v. F.C. Clinton, Inc., 948 P.2d 298, 308 (Okla. 1997); Strubhart v. Perry Mem'l Hosp. Trust Auth., 903 P.2d 263, 277 n.14 (Okla. 1995); Scribner v. Hillcrest Med. Ctr., 866 P.2d 437, 441 (Okla. Civ. App. 1992).

[39] Wetsel v. Indep. Sch. Dist., 670 P.2d 986, 990 (Okla. 1983).

[40] *Id.*

[41] Myers v. Lutrell, 373 P.2d 22, 25 (Okla. 1961).

[42] Wetsel v. Indep. Sch. Dist., 670 P.2d 986, 991 (Okla. 1997).

breach of duty can be direct or circumstantial.[43] The jury may consider all evidence presented in determining whether the defendant breached the duty of care.[44]

IV. Causation

A. Elements

A plaintiff must prove that his or her injuries were proximately caused by the defendant's failure to exercise due care.[45] To recover, the plaintiff must show that some injury (not the exact injury sustained) to someone in the plaintiff's position was foreseeable.[46] Foreseeability for proximate cause is the specific factual showing that establishes the conduct as the cause of the injury.[47] Whether the injurious consequences could have been reasonably foreseen is a jury question, as long as such a conclusion can be reasonably drawn from the facts.[48]

B. Evidence

The question of foreseeability on the issue of causation is for the trier of fact.[49] Evidence of the foreseeability of harm from the defendant's conduct is probative on the issue of causation and admissible.[50] The jury decides the weight to be given evidence of foreseeability of harm in determining whether the breach of duty caused the harm.[51]

V. Damages

A. Elements

The damages in a negligence case are the amount that will compensate the plaintiff for all harm caused by defendant's failure to exercise ordinary care.[52] Compensation is the remedy for a violation of private rights and the means for securing the observance of private rights.[53]

---

[43] Dumas v. Waggoner, 304 P. 2d 991, 993-94 (Okla. 1956).

[44] Boxberger v. Martin, 552 P.2d 370, 373-74 (Okla. 1976).

[45] McKellips v. St. Francis Hosp., Inc., 741 P.2d 467, 470 (Okla. 1987).

[46] Bradford Sec. v. Plaza Bank & Trust, 653 P.2d 188, 191 (Okla. 1982).

[47] Delbrel v. Doenges Bros. Ford, Inc., 913 P.2d 1318, 1322 (Okla. 1996).

[48] Woodis v. OG&E, 704 P.2d 483, 488 (Okla. 1985).

[49] Graham v. Keuchel, 847 P.2d 342, 367 (Okla. 1993).

[50] 12 O.S. (2011) § 2401-2.

[51] Tomlinson v. Love's Country Store, 854 P.2d 910, 917 (Okla. 1993); Brewer v. Murray, 2012 OK CIV APP 109, ¶ 27, 292 P.3d 41, 53.

[52] 23 O.S. (2011) § 61.

[53] 23 O.S. (2011) § 1.

B. Evidence

Damages are to be reasonable and fair.[54] Jurors must be able to award full and fair damages as shown by the evidence.[55] The damages recoverable are those which flow naturally and foreseeably from the defendant's negligent acts.[56] Assessment of the compensatory damages proven by plaintiff lies squarely in the jury's province.[57] A wide latitude of discretion is left to the good sense of the jury in determining damages.[58]

---

[54] Walker v. St. Louis-San Francisco Ry. Co., 646 P.2d 593, 599 (Okla. 1982).

[55] Rhodes v. Lamar, 292 P. 335, 338-39 (Okla. 1930).

[56] Stroud v. Arthur Anderson, 2001 OK 76, ¶ 14, 37 P.3d 783, 788-89 (Okla. 2001).

[57] Id.

[58] Shebester, Inc. v. Ford, 361 P.2d 200, 205 (Okla. 1961).

CHAPTER 38

OREGON

OREGON

Margaret (Meg) Butler[1]

I. Purpose of Tort Law

The right to a remedy for an injury to person, property, or reputation is constitutionally protected in Oregon.[2] The protection arising from the remedy clause is "not tied to a particular point in time but instead continue[s] to evolve to meet changing needs."[3] The Oregon Supreme Court noted that the principles of tort law[4] embody the public interest,[5] including deterring negligent conduct.[6] Although some may believe that the primary function of tort law is the compensation for losses, the Oregon Supreme Court has explained that it may be "more accurate to describe the primary function as one of determining when compensation is to be required."[7] Further, the preventative, or prophylactic, goal of preventing future harm raises concerns "not only with compensation of the victim, but with admonition of the wrongdoer."[8] "Public policy favors the deterrence of negligent conduct,"[9] and does so through criminal, administrative, and civil sanctions.[10]

Negligent conduct is that which "foreseeably poses an unreasonable risk of harm."[11] Where there is a foreseeable risk of harm, a person should avoid the conduct.[12] "[T]he predicate [for negligence] is blameworthiness in some sense; the actor being regarded as blameworthy if his conduct is, according to community standards, generally considered as creating a danger to persons in the situation in which the plaintiff finds himself. . . . 'Thus the standard

---

[1] Margaret (Meg) Butler, Associate Director for Public Services, Georgia State University College of Law Library.

[2] Or. Const. art. I, § 10; *see also* Horton v. Or. Health Sci. Univ., 376 P.3d 998, 1006 (Or. 2016).

[3] *Horton*, 376 P.3d at 1007 (overruling Smothers v. Gresham Transfer, Inc., 23 P.3d 333 (Or. 2001) (regarding the purpose of the remedy clause).

[4] "Tort" is defined and codified in the Oregon Tort Claim Act (OTCA): "'Tort' means the breach of a legal duty that is imposed by law, other than a duty arising from contract or quasi-contract, the breach of which results in injury to a specific person or persons for which the law provides a civil right of action for damages or for a protective remedy." Or. Rev. Stat. Ann. § 30.260(8) (West 2016).

[5] Bagley v. Mt. Bachelor, Inc., 340 P.3d 27, 34 (Or. 2014).

[6] *Id.* at 45.

[7] *Id.*

[8] *Id.* at 551 (changes in original) (quoting W. Page. Keeton, Prosser and Keeton on the Law of Torts § 4, 20-25 (5th ed. 1984)).

[9] *Bagley,* 340 P.3d at 45 (citing 2 Farnsworth on Contracts § 5.2, 9-12 (3d ed 2004)).

[10] A-1 Sandblasting & Steamcleaning Co. v. Baiden, 643 P.2d 1260, 1263 (Or. 1982).

[11] Cain v. Rijken, 717 P.2d 140, 145 (Or. 1986).

[12] *Id.*

represents the general level of moral judgment of the community, what it feels ought ordinarily be done, and not necessarily what is ordinarily done, although in practice the two would very often come to the same thing.'"[13]

When considering whether a defendant is negligent, the social utility of the defendant's conduct is a factor.[14] However, a defendant's negligence may not be exonerated by a jury on the basis of the social utility of his conduct.[15] "It is the court, not the jury that weights such general values and sets the general standards of conduct."[16]

II.   Duty to Exercise Ordinary Care

A.   *The Question of Law*

Duty is firmly embedded in negligence.[17] Traditionally, common-law negligence required a plaintiff to plead and prove duty, breach of that duty, and resultant damages.[18] The Oregon Supreme Court has stated, "It is well established that actionable negligence arises only from the breach of a duty owed by one person to another, and that to state a cause of action for negligence the complaint must state the duty imposed or facts from which the law will imply a duty."[19] Oregon law has shifted, with the Oregon Supreme Court noting that "'[Duty]' is not sacrosanct in itself, but is only an expression of the sum total of those considerations of policy which lead the law to say that the plaintiff is entitled to protection."[20]

The Court's more recent cases establish that duty is not always a required element of a negligence case. The duty-breach analysis of an ordinary negligence action has been subsumed by "the question whether the defendant's conduct resulted in a foreseeable and unreasonable risk of harm of the kind that the plaintiff suffered."[21] On an ordinary negligence claim,

---

[13] Stewart v. Jefferson Plywood Co., 469 P.2d 783, 785-86 (Or. 1970) (quoting 2 HARPER & JAMES, THE LAW OF TORTS, p. 903 (1956)).

[14] Furrer v. Talent Irr. Dist., 466 P.2d 605, 612-13 (Or. 1970).

[15] *Id.*

[16] *Id.*

[17] Buchler v. State ex rel. Or. Corr. Div., 853 P.2d 798, 810-11 (Or. 1993) (Peterson, J., concurring).

[18] Chapman v. Mayfield, 361 P.3d 566, 571 (Or. 2015) (citing Brennen v. City of Eugene, 591 P.2d 719 (Or. 1979)):

"To adequately plead a negligence claim, a complaint 'must allege facts from which a factfinder could determine (1) that defendant's conduct caused a foreseeable risk of harm, (2) that the risk is to an interest of a kind that the law protects against negligent invasion, (3) that defendant's conduct was unreasonable in light of the risk, (4) that the conduct was a cause of plaintiff's harm, and (5) that plaintiff was within the class of persons and plaintiff's injury was within the general type of potential incidents and injuries that made defendant's conduct negligent.'"

Horton v. Or. Health & Sci. Univ., 373 P.3d 1158, 1161-62 (Or. Ct. App. 2016) (citing Solberg v. Johnson, 760 P.2d 867, 870 (Or. 1988) (abrogated on another issue)).

[19] Klerk v. Tektronix, Inc., 415 P.2d 510, 512 (Or. 1966) (citing Hendricks v. Sanford, 337 P.2d 974, 979 (Or. 1959)).

[20] *Buchler,* 853 P.2d at 810-11 (Peterson, J., concurring).

[21] Towe v. Sacagawea, Inc., 347 P.3d 766, 775 (Or. 2015). Premises liability is an example of status (invitee, licensee, or trespasser) determining scope of liability. *Id.*

there is no need to prove that the plaintiff was owed a duty because everyone owes a general duty "to act reasonably in light of foreseeable risks of harm."[22] Liability is assessed against a defendant who, as an ordinary reasonable person, should have foreseen that his conduct would unreasonably harm another; liability is imposed due to the foreseeability of harm.[23]

Foreseeability can be seen as referring to both duty and proximate cause, as the concepts are understood in other jurisdictions.[24] Under the foreseeability test for negligence, "one is negligent only if he, as an ordinary reasonable person, ought reasonably to foresee that he will expose another to an unreasonable risk of harm."[25] This reasonable person, reasonably foreseeable, standard, corresponds with the historical standard for negligence; the one who inflicts the injury "is bound by what he knew, or might have known by the exercise of ordinary care and diligence."[26] Reasonableness modifies the foreseeability test such that a precise forecast of specific harm to a particular person is not required for liability.[27] Instead, a "generalized risk of the types of incidents and injuries that occurred" is sufficient.[28] A negligence claim may rest on negligent action by a defendant as well as negligent inaction, "when the lack of action creates a foreseeable unreasonable risk of harm."[29] "[T]he critical issue is whether plaintiff's. . . losses were a reasonably foreseeable result of defendant's wrongful conduct."[30]

Duty is a required part of the negligence analysis if the parties "invoke a status, a relationship, or a particular standard of conduct that creates, defines, or limits the defendant's duty."[31] "[T]he nature and scope of the duty owed by the defendant to the plaintiff can be created, defined, or limited based on, among other things, the relationship between or status of the parties."[32] "A special relationship between the parties creates a heightened duty on the defendant's part."[33] Such a special relationship can be established in several ways.

A plaintiff may assert a statutory tort claim, based on a statute imposing a legislated duty (so long as the statute does not include an alternate enforcement mechanism).[34] The Oregon Supreme Court has recognized statutory torts in situations where there is no common law duty, rather, a statute or an ordinance created a special duty.[35] The duty typically arises from either "the status of the parties or the relationship between them."[36]

---

[22] *Id.*

[23] Kirby v. Sonville, 594 P.2d 818, 822 (Or. 1979). The negligence defendant's blameworthiness is "subsumed in the concept of foreseeability." *Id.*

[24] State v. Ramos, 368 P.3d 446, 454 (Or. 2016). Just as proximate cause and duty serve to limit general liability in tort, so does foreseeability. *Id.*

[25] Stewart v. Jefferson Plywood Co., 469 P.2d 783, 786 (Or. 1970).

[26] Cerrano v. Portland Ry., Light & Power Co., 126 P. 37, 40 (Or. 1912).

[27] Piazza v. Kellim, 377 P.3d 492, 505 (Or. 2016).

[28] *Id.* (quoting Fazzolari ex rel. Fazzolari, v. Portland Sch. Dist. No. 1J, 734 P.2d 1326, 1326 (Or. 1987)).

[29] Fuhrer v. Gearhart-By-The-Sea, Inc., 760 P.2d 874, 877 (Or. 1988).

[30] Or. Steel Mills, Inc. v. Coopers & Lybrand, LLP, 83 P.3d 322, 330 (Or. 2004).

[31] Fazzolari ex rel. Fazzolari, v. Portland Sch. Dist. No. 1J, 734 P.2d 1326, 1336 (Or. 1987).

[32] *Piazza,* 377 P.3d at 500 (citing Towe v. Sacagawea, Inc., 347 P.3d 766, 775 (Or. 2015)).

[33] Jernigan v. Alderwoods Grp., Inc., 489 F. Supp. 2d 1180, 1204 (D. Or. 2007) (citing Lowe v. Philip Morris USA, Inc., 142 P.3d 1079 (Or. Ct. App. 2006)).

[34] *See* Scovill ex rel. Hubbard v. City of Astoria, 921 P.2d 1312, 1319 (Or. 1996).

[35] *Id.*

[36] *Id.* (quoting Nelson v. Lane Cty., 743 P.2d 692 (Or. 1987)).

Duty must also be established when the plaintiff asserts liability that caused a purely economic harm. The claim "must be predicated on some duty of the negligent actor to the injured party beyond the common law duty to exercise reasonable care to prevent foreseeable harm."[37]

Oregon law specifically imposes a duty of care to prevent foreseeable harm upon professionals toward their clients.[38] The professionals include lawyers and physicians, as well as engineers and architects if the contract for service "incorporates a general standard of skill or care to which the professional would be bound."[39]

Relationships having a heightened duty of care include principal-agent, trustees, pledgees exercising a power of sale, shippers, bailors, and liability insurers who have undertaken a duty to defend the insured.[40] When a negligence claim arises from an alleged breach of contract, "a tort duty must exist 'independent of the contract and without reference to the specific terms of the contract.'"[41] Whether an enhanced duty of care arises from a particular relationship is a question of law.[42]

However, foreseeability may serve to limit the scope of duty, and thus a defendant's liability, even if the plaintiff alleges a special relationship.[43] A defendant may also assert that no duty exists as a way to deny "legal liability for conduct that might be found, in fact, to have unreasonably caused a foreseeable risk of harm to an interest of the kind for which the plaintiff claims damages."[44]

B. The Question of Fact

i. Elements

The Uniform Civil Jury Instructions, though not the law themselves, state clearly the test for foreseeability. "First, the plaintiff must be within the general class of persons that one would reasonably anticipate might be threatened by the defendant's conduct. Second, the harm suffered must be within the general class of harms that one reasonably would anticipate might result from the defendant's conduct."[45] The Oregon Supreme Court describes the foreseeability determination "as a blended factual and normative—that is, value-laden—inquiry."[46] The plaintiff must show the "generalized risk of the types of incidents and injuries that occurred, rather than the predictability of the actual sequence of events."[47]

---

[37] Or. Steel Mills, Inc. v. Coopers & Lybrand, LLP, 83 P.3d 322, 328 (Or. 2004) (citing Onita Pac. Corp. v. Trs. of Bronson, 843 P.2d 890, 896 (Or. 1992)).

[38] Conway v. Pac. Univ., 924 P.2d 818, 823-24 (Or. 1996).

[39] Id.

[40] Id.

[41] Conway, 924 P.2d at 822 (citing Georgetown Realty v. Home Ins., 831 P.2d 7, 14 (Or. 1992)).

[42] Country Mut. Ins. v. Pittman, 910 F.Supp.2d 1233, 1237 (D. Oregon 2012).

[43] Stewart v. Kids Inc. of Dallas, OR, 261 P.3d 1272, 1277-78 (Or. Ct. App. 2011) (quoting Or. Steel Mills, Inc. v. Coopers & Lybrand, LLP, 83 P.3d 322, 328 (Or. 2004) (footnote omitted in original).

[44] Donaca v. Curry Cty., 734 P.2d 1339, 1340 (Or. 1987).

[45] Oregon State Bar Committee on Uniform Civil Jury Instructions, *Oregon Jury Instructions for Civil Cases*, § 20.03 (Or. State Bar Dec. 2015).

[46] Piazza v. Kellim, 377 P.3d 492, 499 (Or. 2016).

[47] Id. at 506 (quoting Fazzolari ex rel. Fazzolari, v. Portland Sch. Dist. No. 1J, 734 P.2d 1326, 1333 (Or. 1987)).

If disputed, foreseeability is ordinarily a jury question, "depend[ing] on the facts of a concrete situation."[48] The jury applies community standards to determine whether a particular outcome is a foreseeable result of conduct.[49] In determining the foreseeability of a defendant's actions, "'foreseeable' is modified explicitly or implicitly by 'reasonably.'"[50] In extreme cases, the court may decide that no reasonable factfinder could find the risk foreseeable or that the defendant's conduct fell below acceptable standards.[51]

ii.   Evidence

"[W]hen a claim for common-law negligence is premised on general principles of foreseeability, the plaintiff must plead and prove that the defendant's conduct created a foreseeable and unreasonable risk of legally cognizable harm to the plaintiff and that the conduct in fact caused that kind of harm to the plaintiff."[52] Once the plaintiff has met the initial burden of proof in a negligence action, the defendant may rebut an inference of negligence by demonstrating "good reasons why it did not in fact take a precaution that, according to plaintiff's proof, it might reasonably have taken."[53]

Plaintiff's evidence to meet the foreseeability test should demonstrate that "the relevant risk of harm must be reasonably foreseeable."[54] The plaintiff's description of the "injury-producing factual circumstances" is central to the question of whether a jury issue is raised regarding foreseeability in the context of the plaintiff's theory of the negligence claim.[55] Thus, proof of foreseeability will differ depending on the circumstances and the claimed negligence.[56] On a claim arising from an alleged sexual assault at a restaurant, the Oregon Court of Appeals required the plaintiff to present "specific factual support—as opposed to relying on generalized abstractions about the existence of criminal activity" to demonstrate the foreseeability of the assault.[57] Generally the plaintiff is not required, however, to prove foreseeability of the "'actual sequence of events' that caused the harm."[58]

When pursuing a claim of negligence against a professional person, expert testimony is used to establish the reasonable practice in the community and sets the standard used to judge the conduct of the defendant.[59]

---

[48] *Piazza*, 377 P.3d at 499 (quoting *Fazzolari*, 734 P.2d at 1328).

[49] *Piazza*, 377 P.3d at 512-13. "Exceptions exist only for harm resulting from 'the concatenation of highly unusual circumstances.'" *Id.*

[50] *Id.* at 499 (quoting Walter Probert, *Torts and Language*, 48 Fla. L. Rev. 841, 854-55 (1996)).

[51] Donaca v. Curry Cty., 734 P.2d 1339, 1344 (Or. 1987).

[52] Chapman v. Mayfield, 361 P.3d 566, 572 (Or. 2015).

[53] Hall v. State, 619 P.2d 256, 262 (Or. 1980).

[54] *Piazza*, 377 P.3d at 503.

[55] *Id.*

[56] Piazza ex rel. Piazza v. Kellim, 354 P.3d 698, 708 (Or. Ct. App. 2015), *affirmed by* Piazza v. Kellim, 377 P.3d 492 (Or. 2016).

[57] *Id.* The Court of Appeals notes that the proof of foreseeability differs when the alleged negligence is the "failure to protect against the risk of harm posed by criminals in general" as compared with negligence "based on the foreseeability of criminal activity at large." *Id.* In the latter case, the courts more broadly define the class of harm against which the defendant has allegedly failed to protect the plaintiff. *Id.*

[58] *Id.* at 710.

[59] Gretchell v. Mansfield, 489 P.2d 953, 955 (Or. 1971).

On a general negligence claim, however, a statute, regulation, or industry standards could "be used to establish the proper standard of care and to show that the defendant met or failed to meet this standard."[60] Advisory safety standards, on the other hand, may be used as evidence of "what a reasonable person in a particular industry would do," which can be useful for a jury attempting to determine whether the standard of care was met.[61]

A plaintiff may establish negligence by showing that: "(1) a statute imposed a duty on the defendant; (2) the legislature expressly or impliedly intended to create a private right of action for violation of the duty; (3) the defendant violated the duty; (4) the plaintiff is a member of the group that the legislature intended to protect by imposing the duty; and (5) the plaintiff suffered an injury that the legislature intended to prevent by creating the duty."[62]

III.   Breach of Duty

A.   Elements

Whether a defendant has breached a duty of care to a plaintiff is a question that arises when there exists a relationship or status between the parties imposing the duty.[63] The issue of duty also arises when a plaintiff asserts a claim for purely economic losses.[64] The plaintiff must allege "that the defendant acted unreasonably during or after the creation of an actual and foreseeable risk to a foreseeable plaintiff of the same type as the present plaintiff."[65] The scope of the duty arising from a special relationship or status may be limited by common-law principles including foreseeability.[66]

B.   Evidence

The plaintiff bears the burden of proof that "the defendant did not meet an applicable standard of due care under the circumstances."[67] Expert testimony is typically required to support a claim that a professional has breached a standard of care, as the jury is not expected to know what would be reasonable conduct for the professional.[68] The weight of expert evidence regarding the standard of care may be determined by the jury, following cross-examination of the witness.[69]

A statute may be used to show the standard of care, that the defendant did not meet the standard of care, or that the defendant should have considered a particular risk.[70] Safety

---

[60] Bixby v. KBR, Inc., 893 F.Supp.2d 1067, 1095 (D. Or. 2012).

[61] Hansen v. Abrasive Eng'g & Mfg., Inc., 856 P.2d 625, 628 (Or. 1993).

[62] Deckard v. Bunch, 370 P.3d 478, 482 (Or. 2016).

[63] Piazza v. Kellim, 377 P.3d 492, 500 (Or. 2016).

[64] Or. Steel Mills, Inc. v. Coopers & Lybrand, LLP, 83 P.3d 322, 328 (Or. 2004).

[65] Bellikka v. Green, 762 P.2d 997, 1008 (Or. 1988).

[66] Or. Steel Mills, Inc., 83 P.3d at 328.

[67] Shahtout ex rel. Shahtout v. Emco Garbage Co., 695 P.2d 897, 899 (Or. 1985).

[68] Gibson v. Bankofier, 365 P.3d 568, 586 (Or. Ct. App. 2015).

[69] Trees v. Ordonez, 311 P.3d 848, 857 (Or. 2013).

[70] Bellikka, 762 P.2d at 1009-10.

rules may also be considered by the factfinder after the court determines the purpose of the rule and the nature and circumstances of the risk addressed by the rule.[71]

IV. Causation

A. Elements

The concepts of proximate and legal cause have been disregarded by the Oregon Supreme Court;[72] the issue of causation in fact in a negligence action is "determined as a purely factual matter."[73] There are two standards for causation: substantial factor and "but-for" or "reasonable probability standard."[74] The more commonly used "but-for" test requires the plaintiff prove that the defendant's negligence "more likely than not caused the plaintiff's harm."[75] The substantial factor test, used in determining the liability of multiple defendants, assess whether the negligence of each defendant "was a substantial factor in producing the complained of harm."[76]

B. Evidence

There is no presumption of negligence based on "the mere fact that an accident happened."[77] Circumstantial evidence, expert testimony, or common knowledge may all be proffered to prove causation.[78] Questions of causation are ordinarily for the trier of fact.[79]

V. Damages

A. Elements

Damage is the gravamen of an action for negligence.[80] "A guiding principle of tort law is to compensate the injured."[81] Liability is imposed on tortfeasors by applying community standards based on the foreseeability of harm to persons like the plaintiff.[82] The measure of damages for an injured party will fully compensate for the loss of time, loss of money,

---

[71] *Shahtout ex rel. Shahtout*, 695 P.2d at 901-02.

[72] McEwen v. Ortho Pharm. Corp., 528 P.2d 522, 528 n.7 (Or. 1974).

[73] Lasley v. Combined Transp., Inc., 261 P.3d 1215, 1219 (Or. 2011).

[74] Joshi v. Providence Health Sys. of Or. Corp., 149 P.3d 1164, 1169 (Or. 2006).

[75] *Id.*

[76] *McEwen*, 528 P.2d at 543.

[77] Cain v. Bovis Lend Lease, Inc., 817 F. Supp. 2d 1251, 1280 (D. Or. 2011).

[78] Two Two v. Fujitec Am., Inc., 325 P.3d 707, 714 (Or. 2014).

[79] Babler Bros., Inc. v. Pac. Intermountain Exp. Co., 415 P.2d 735, 737-38 (Or. 1966) (overruling Or. Mut. Fire Ins. v. Mayer, 316 P.2d 805 (Or. 1957)).

[80] Hall v. Cornett, 240 P.2d 231, 235 (Or. 1952).

[81] Granewich v. Harding, 945 P.2d 1067, 1074 (Or. Ct. App. 1997), *rev'd in part on other grounds*, 985 P.2d 788 (Or. 1999).

[82] Fazzolari ex rel. Fazzolari, v. Portland Sch. Dist. No. 1J, 734 P.2d 1326, 1333 (Or. 1987).

bodily pain, or permanent bodily injury.[83] Personal injury damages for medical treatment and medicine must be reasonable.[84] An owner may recover for real property damage.[85] Economic losses, absent a personal injury, are recoverable if the parties have a special relationship or another duty outside the contract.[86]

B.   *Evidence*

Compensatory damages are a factual issue for the jury.[87] The court makes a determination of liability only when the defendant's conduct either clearly meets or clearly falls below the standard of reasonable conduct set by the community.[88] A plaintiff must establish the reasonableness of medical expenses claimed as damages.[89] A medical bill alone is insufficient to raise a jury question as to reasonableness.[90] A claim for medical charges cannot be limited to the amount that a third party, such as an insurer, pays on behalf of the plaintiff.[91]

---

[83] Oliver v. N. Pac. Transp. Co., 3 Or. 84, 88, 1869 WL 590, at *3 (Or. Cir. 1869).

[84] Tuohy v. Columbia Steel Co., 122 P. 36, 38 (Or. 1912) (citing Int'l & G.N.R. Co. v. Boykin, 74 S.W.93 (Tex. Civ. App. 1903); Amann v. Chi. Consol. Traction Co., 90 N.E. 673 (Ill. 1909); Wheeler v. Tyler, S.E. Ry., 43 S.W. 876 (Tex. 1898)).

[85] Abraham v. T. Henry Const., Inc., 249 P.3d 534, 540 (Or. 2011) (quoting Harris v. Suniga, 180 P.3d 12 (Or. 2008)).

[86] *Id.*

[87] Horton v. Or. Health Sci. Univ., 376 P.3d 998, 1033 (Or. 2016) (citing Oberg v. Honda Motor Co., 851 P.2d 1084 (Or. 1993), *rev'd and remanded on other grounds,* Honda Motor Co. v. Oberg, 512 U.S. 415 (1994); Van Lom v. Schneiderman, 210 P.2d 461, 470-71 (Or. 1949)).

[88] Fazzolari ex rel. Fazzolari, v. Portland Sch. Dist. No. 1J, 734 P.2d 1326, 1336 (Or. 1987) (quoting Stewart v. Jefferson Plywood Co., 469 P.2d 783, 785 (Or. 1970)).

[89] Ellington v. Garrow, 162 P.3d 328, 330 (Or. 2007).

[90] *Id.* at 331.

[91] White v. Jubitz Corp., 219 P.3d 566, 579 (Or. 2009).

CHAPTER 39

PENNSYLVANIA

PENNSYLVANIA

Joseph A. Custer[1]

I. Purpose of Tort Law

The Pennsylvania Supreme Court has stated the purpose of tort law is to "put an injured person in a position as near as possible to his position prior to the tort."[2] The high court in Pennsylvania clarified the objectives of tort law as follows:

> The compensation of one injured because of the negligence of another is merely a reflection of the American sense of justice. If one citizen through inadvertence or carelessness causes damage to another it is appropriate to require the offending party to restore the victim as near as possible to his or her prior state. Tort law was never intended to unjustly enrich, or to provide the occasion for the fulfillment of all fanciful aspirations.[3]

The object of Pennsylvania's tort law is to modify behavior by imposing the financial risk on the party in the best position to prevent the harm.[4] Although a tort action "is not fully capable of providing a sufficient deterrent incentive to achieve perfect safety goals," such a limitation does not justify restricting a wrongdoer's duty.[5]

II. Duty to Exercise Ordinary Care

A. Question of Law

To establish a case for negligence, a plaintiff must show that the defendant had a duty to protect the plaintiff from injury.[6] The existence of a duty is dependent upon whether the risk of injury was foreseeable.[7] The Pennsylvania Supreme Court has stated that the test of negligence is whether "the wrongdoer could have anticipated and foreseen the likelihood of harm resulting from his act or omission."[8] Further, before an act can be held as negligent it "must reasonably be foreseen that the doing of it is attended with such probabilities of injury

---

[1] Associate Professor of Law & Director, Judge Ben C. Green Law Library.

[2] Tincher v. Omega Flex, Inc., 628 Pa. 296, 404, 104 A.3d 328, 423 (2014).

[3] Amadio v. Levin, 509 Pa. 199, 231, 501 A.2d 1085, 1101 (1985).

[4] Excavation Technologies v. Columbia Gas, 604 Pa. 50, 57, 985 A.2d 840, 844 (2009).

[5] Tincher v. Omega Flex, Inc., 628 Pa. 296, 404, 104 A.3d 328, 423 (2014).

[6] Malinder v. Jenkins Elevator & Mach. Co., 371 Pa. Super. 414, 433, 538 A.2d 509, 519 (1988).

[7] Truax v. Roulhac, 2015 PA Super 217, 126 A.3d 991, 997 (2015).

[8] Paulscak v. Hoebler, 330 Pa. 184, 192, 198 A. 646, 650 (1938).

to another that a duty arises either to refrain from the act altogether, or to do it in such manner that harm does not result. It is well settled that conduct is negligent only if the harmful consequences thereof could reasonably have been foreseen and prevented."[9]

The first element of a negligence cause of action, the existence of a duty, is a question of law for the court to decide.[10] The examination of the evidence needs to be in a light most favorable to plaintiffs, giving them the benefit of every inference of fact pertaining to the issues involved, which may reasonably be deduced from the evidence.[11] A totality of the circumstances approach is used to determine when a duty exists.[12]

A duty may be created by statute or from the relationship between parties.[13] A party may also agree to assume a duty.[14] The Pennsylvania Supreme Court has asserted that "[i]n determining whether to impose a duty, this Court must consider the risk, foreseeability, and likelihood of injury weighed against the social utility of the actor's conduct, the magnitude of the burden of guarding against the injury and the consequences of placing that burden on the actor."[15] In deciding whether to impose a duty, the Pennsylvania Supreme Court has adopted a five-factor test, "focusing upon: (1) the relationship between the parties; (2) the utility of the defendant's conduct; (3) the nature and foreseeability of the risk in question; (4) the consequences of imposing the duty; and (5) the overall public interest in the proposed solution.[16]

B.   *The Question of Fact*

i.   Elements

It is for the jury to determine whether the defendant exercised the degree of care to be expected of an ordinarily prudent man under the circumstances.[17] The jury also determines whether a duty of care was breached.[18] Negligence is defined as the absence of care under the circumstances.[19] The "test of negligence" is whether the wrongdoer could have anticipated and foreseen from his act the likelihood of harm to the injured person.[20]

ii.   Evidence

In order to hold a defendant liable for negligence, the plaintiff must prove the following four elements: (1) a legally recognized duty that the defendant conform to a standard of care;

---

[9] Venzel v. Valley Camp Coal Co., 304 Pa. 583, 590, 156 A. 240, 242 (1931).

[10] R.W. v. Manzek, 585 Pa. 335, 345, 888 A.2d 740, 746 (2005).

[11] Kolb v. Isenberg, 150 Pa. Super. 482, 484, 28 A.2d 729, 730 (1942).

[12] Com. v. Hughes, 575 Pa. 447, 458, 836 A.2d 893, 899 (2003).

[13] Moses v. McWilliams, 379 Pa. Super. 150, 180, 549 A.2d 950, 965 (1988).

[14] Reider v. Martin, 359 Pa. Super. 586, 592-93, 519 A.2d 507, 511 (1987).

[15] Althaus ex rel. Althaus v. Cohen, 562 Pa. 547, 552-53, 756 A.2d 1166, 1168-69 (some citations omitted) (2000).

[16] R.W. v. Manzek, 585 Pa. 335, 347, 888 A.2d 740, 747 (2005).

[17] Susser v. Wiley, 350 Pa. 427, 432, 39 A.2d 616, 619 (1944).

[18] Ford v. Jeffries, 474 Pa. 588, 595, 379 A.2d 111, 114 (1977).

[19] Helm v. South Penn Oil Co., 382 Pa. 437, 441, 114 A.2d 909, 911 (1955).

[20] Brusis v. Henkels, 376 Pa. 226, 230, 102 A.2d 146, 148 (1954).

(2) the defendant breached that duty; (3) causation between the conduct and the resulting injury; and (4) actual damage to the plaintiff.[21] A plaintiff may establish negligence by showing a violation of a statute by proving: "(1) The purpose of the statute must be, at least in part, to protect the interest of a group of individuals, as opposed to the public generally; (2) The statute or regulation must clearly apply to the conduct of the defendant; (3) The defendant must violate the statute or regulation; (4) The violation of the statute or regulation must be the proximate cause of the plaintiff's injuries."[22]

III. Breach of Duty

A. Elements

To successfully establish a claim of negligence under Pennsylvania law, a plaintiff must establish that the defendant breached a duty owed to the plaintiff.[23] Any "breach of duty, neglect, error, misstatement, misleading statement, omission or other act done or wrongfully attempted" by the defendant is defined as a wrongful act.[24] It is up to the jury to apply the appropriate standard of care and decide the issue of negligence.[25]

B. Evidence

It has long been established in Pennsylvania law that "no legal liability is imposed upon the defendant unless there be evidence to warrant a finding there was a breach of some legal duty by its act or omission."[26] Whether injuries were foreseeable from the defendant's conduct is relevant to the determination of breach of the duty of care.[27] Evidence of industry standards and regulations is generally relevant and admissible on the issue of negligence.[28] Safety rules are also admissible to establish the level of care and its breach.[29]

IV. Causation

A. Elements

The plaintiff has the burden of proving that the defendant's negligence was the proximate cause of her injury.[30] The doctrine of proximate cause is defined by the Pennsylvania Supreme Court as: "That which, in a natural and continuous sequence, unbroken by any

---

[21] Truax v. Roulhac, 2015 PA Super 217, 126 A.3d 991, 997 (2015).

[22] Ramalingam v. Keller Williams Realty Grp., Inc., 2015 PA Super 172, 121 A.3d 1034, 1042-43 (2015).

[23] Truax v. Roulhac, 2015 PA Super 217, 126 A.3d 991 at 997.

[24] Hunt v. National Union Fire Ins. Co. of Pittsburgh, P.A., 2005 WL 3003471 (2005).

[25] Dunn v. Teti, 280 Pa. Super. 399, 401, 421 A.2d 782, 783 (1980).

[26] Milligan v. Bell Tel. Co., 62 Pa. Super. 197, 200, 1916 WL 4391 (1915).

[27] McCloy v. Penn Fruit Co., 245 Pa. Super. 251, 255-256, 369 A.2d 389, 391 (1976).

[28] Birt v. Firstenergy Corp., 2006 Pa. Super. 11, 891 A.2d 1281, 1290 (2006).

[29] Jones v. Port Auth. of Allegheny Cty., 136 Pa. Cmmw. 445, 450, 583 A.2d 512, 515 (1990).

[30] Cuthbert v. City of Philadelphia, 417 Pa. 610, 614, 209 A.2d 261, 263 (1965).

efficient intervening cause, produces the injury, and without which the result would not have occurred."[31]

The element of causation consists of two separate and essential concepts: cause-in-fact and legal, or proximate, cause.[32] The Pennsylvania Supreme Court has defined 'cause-in-fact' in the 'but-for' sense, explaining that a "defendant's allegedly wrongful act is a cause-in-fact if the plaintiff proves that the harm he sustained would not have happened, but-for the defendant's act."[33] Likewise, the Pennsylvania Supreme Court has "defined 'legal' or 'proximate' cause as that point at which legal responsibility should attach to the defendant as a matter of fairness because the plaintiff has demonstrated (in addition to cause-in-fact) that the defendant's act was a 'substantial factor' or a 'substantial cause,' as opposed to an 'insignificant cause' or a 'negligible cause,' in bringing about the plaintiff's harm."[34]

The Restatement (Second) of Torts (1965) and many jurisdictions do not regard foreseeability as a relevant factor in determining proximate or legal cause.[35] Pennsylvania ascribes to this view, and "it has long been the law of this state that foreseeability is not a relevant consideration to a determination of proximate cause."[36] However, the determination of whether an intervening cause breaks the causal chain and supercedes liability depends on the foreseeability of the intervening cause.[37]

B.   *Evidence*

According to the Pennsylvania Supreme Court, "the element of causation is normally a question of fact for the jury; the question is to be removed from the jury's consideration only where it is clear that reasonable minds could not differ on the issue.[38] A plaintiff must present evidence to justify the inference that the defendant's negligence was the cause of the injury by a preponderance.[39] Circumstantial evidence alone may be sufficient to establish such preponderance.[40]

---

[31] Coyne v. Pittsburgh Railways Co., 393 Pa. 326, 334, 141 A.2d 830, 835 (1958).

[32] Estate of Flickinger v. Ritsky, 452 Pa. 69, 74, 305 A.2d 40, 43 (1973).

[33] Reott v. Asia Trend, Inc., 618 Pa. 228, 253, 55 A.3d 1088, 1103 (2012).

[34] *Id.*

[35] RESTATEMENT (SECOND) OF TORTS § 435 (1965). Section 435 (1) provides that "the fact that the actor neither foresaw nor should have foreseen the extent of the harm or the manner in which it occurred does not prevent him from being liable." The first part of § 435 (1) references fairly established law regarding the extent of damages (you are liable for all damages caused once liability is established) even if the extent of the damages was not foreseen, commonly referred to as the eggshell-skull theory or "you take your plaintiff as you find them." The next part of § 435 (1) sets forth a fairly universal rule that an actor does not have to foresee the exact manner in which an accident occurs to be held liable for the consequences of her neglect. Section 425 (2) does not use the term foreseeability; however, it does use an arguably interchangeable concept when it provides that an actor may not be liable for harm "where after the event and looking back from the harm to the actor's negligent conduct, it appears to the court highly extraordinary that it should have brought about the harm." *Id.*

[36] McCloy v. Penn Fruit Co., 245 Pa. Super. 251, 255-256, 369 A.2d 389, 391 (1976).

[37] *Id.*

[38] Hamil v. Bashline, 481 Pa. 256, 266, 392 A.2d 1280, 1285 (1978).

[39] Lewis v. U.S. Rubber Co., 414 Pa. 626, 630, 202 A.2d 20, 22-3 (1964).

[40] *Id.*

V. Damages

A. Elements

Damages should compensate the victim for the loss or injury sustained. By the adoption of uninsured and underinsured motorist insurance coverage, "the General Assembly has articulated a remedial public policy that promotes the recovery of damages for innocent victims of accidents" when motorists who cause accidents cannot adequately compensate their victims for their injuries.[41] "[A] tortfeasor is liable for all injuries resulting directly from his wrong acts, irrespective of whether they could have been foreseen by him, provided the damages are the legal and natural consequences of the wrong action imputed to the defendant."[42]

B. Evidence

The duty to assess damages is squarely within the province of the jury, who, as the finders of fact, weigh the veracity and credibility of the witnesses and their testimony.[43] The Pennsylvania Supreme Court stated that "the plaintiff has the burden of establishing, by a preponderance of the evidence that the defendant engaged in conduct that deviated from the general standard of care expected under the circumstances, and that this deviation proximately caused actual harm."[44] The Pennsylvania high court stated "[a]lthough the factfinder is not entitled to base a judgment on speculation or guesswork, the jury may make a just and reasonable estimate of the damage based on relevant data, and render its verdict accordingly."[45]

---

[41] Williams v. GEICO Gov't Emps. Ins. Co., 613 Pa. 113, 140, 32 A.3d. 1195, 1212 (2011).

[42] Speck v. Finegold, 268 Pa. Super. 342, 361, 408 A.2d 496, 506 (1979) (partially aff'd and partially re'v on other grounds, Speck v. Finegold, 497 Pa. 77, 439 A.2d 110 (1981)).

[43] Dranzo v. Winterhalter, 395 Pa. Super. 578, 584, 577 A.2d 1349, 1352 (1990).

[44] Martin v. Evans, 551 Pa. 496, 503, 711 A.2d 458, 462 (1998).

[45] Samuel-Bassett v. Kia Motors America, Inc., 613 Pa. 371, 438, 34 A.3d 1, 41 (2011).

CHAPTER 40

RHODE ISLAND

RHODE ISLAND

Vicki Lawrence MacDougall[1]

I. Purpose of Tort Law

Recovery for negligence requires proof that the defendant owes a legal duty to the plaintiff to "refrain from negligent activities," a breach of that duty by the defendant, the breach proximately causes the plaintiff's injury, and "actual loss or damage resulting."[2] There are three main goals that are served by the award of damages caused by tortious conduct. The goals are to provide compensation for harm,[3] "to settle disputes as to rights," and "to punish wrongdoers."[4] Inherent in any award of compensatory damages is deterrence of future bad behavior.[5] Indeed, the United States Supreme Court acknowledges that an award of damages "compensate[s] victims of wrongdoing and deter[s] tortious conduct."[6] However, the goal of tort law is only to restore the plaintiff, to the extent possible through an award of monetary damages, to "his or her pre-injury position, not to grant . . . a windfall."[7]

Corrective justice is omnipresent throughout tort law. Tort law encompasses "ideals of righting wrongs, or . . . ideas about accountability or personal responsibility for harm-causing conduct."[8] Many torts involve "morally faulty conduct."[9] As stated by Professor Dobbs: "The defendant's fault is a wrong that has harmed the plaintiff in some recognizable way; tort liability, by requiring the wrongdoer to compensate the plaintiff, can put the accounts right between the parties."[10]

---

[1] Professor of Law, Director Health Law Certificate Program, Law Review Faculty Advisor, Oklahoma City University School of Law, Member, California and Oklahoma Bar Associations.

[2] Splendorio v. Bilray Demolition Co., Inc., 682 A.2d 461, 466 (R.I. 1996); *see also* Williams v. Alston, 154 A.3d 456, 459 (R.I. 2017).

[3] Vallinoto v. DiSandro, 688 A.2d 830, 849 (R.I. 1997). "Indeed, The very purpose of tort law is to compensate those persons injured as a result of another's tortious acts." *Id.*

[4] RESTATEMENT (FIRST) OF TORTS § 901 (1939) (updated March 2017).

[5] Carey v. Piphus, 435 U.S. 247, 256-57, 98 S.Ct. 1042, 1048-49 (1978). *See also* Palmisano v. Toth, 624 A.2d 314, 317-18 (R.I. 1993).

[6] United States v. Stanley, 483 U.S. 669, 695, n. 13, 107 S.Ct. 3054, 3070, n. 13 (1987).

[7] Morabit v. Hoag, 80 A.3d 1, 18 (R.I. 2013).

[8] DAN B. DOBBS, THE LAW OF TORTS 13 (2000).

[9] *Id.* at 14.

[10] *Id.* at 15.

II. Duty to Exercise Ordinary Care

A. *Question of Law*

Whether a legal duty exists is a question of law and the court makes this "determination on a case-by-case basis."[11] Factors such as "the relationship between the parties, the scope and burden of the obligation to be imposed upon the defendant, public policy considerations, and the foreseeability of harm to the plaintiff" are all considered.[12] Notions of fairness,[13] "the closeness of the connection between the defendant's conduct and the injury suffered," "the consequences to the community," and "preventing future harm" are also considered.[14] However, the "linchpin" in determining whether the defendant owed a legal duty to the plaintiff is the ability of the defendant to foresee the risk of harm to the plaintiff.[15] "The 'risk reasonably to be perceived defines the duty to be obeyed, and risk imports relation; it is risk to another or to others within the range of apprehension.'"[16] Foreseeability "plays a variety of roles in tort doctrine" and "it is part of the calculus to which a court looks in defining the boundaries of 'duty.'"[17] As stated by the Rhode Island Supreme Court, "[a]s it pertains to the determination of duty, the foreseeability inquiry considers generally whether 'the category of negligent conduct at issue is sufficiently likely to result in the kind of harm experienced that liability may appropriately be imposed on the negligent party.'"[18]

Although the question of whether a duty exists is for the court, "it is still the function of the jury to determine the existence of those predicate facts that trigger the presence of a legal duty."[19] And, the court should not determine such facts "under the guise of deciding what legal duty (if any) is owed to the plaintiff."[20]

---

[11] Martin v. Marciano, 871 A.2d 911, 915 (R.I. 2005).

[12] *Martin*, 871 A.2d at 915. *See also* Carlson v. Town of South Kingstown, 131 A.3d 705, 709 (R.I. 2016). The court held that a little league baseball team did not owe a duty to a spectator to maintain the premises where the game took place because the team did not "own, operate, or have control over the park where the plaintiff's alleged injury occurred." *Carlson*, 131 A.3d at 709.

[13] Volpe v. Gallagher, 821 A.2d 699, 705 (R.I. 2003).

[14] Gushlaw v. Milner, 42 A.3d 1245, 1256-57 (R.I. 2012).

[15] *Splendorio*, 682 A.2d at 466. *Accord* Terry v. Central Auto Radiators, Inc., 732 A.2d 713, 718 (R.I. 1999); Banks v. Bowen's Landing Corp., 522 A.2d 1222, 1225 (R.I. 1987). However, foreseeability is considered "in tandem with all factors germane to the duty analysis" and the question is not simply if an event was foreseeable. Gushlaw v. Milner, 42 A.3d 1245, 1261 (R.I. 2012).

[16] *Splendorio*, 682 A.2d at 467 (quoting Builders Specialty Co. v. Goulet, 639 A.2d 59, 60 (R.I. 1994)) (quoting Palsgraf v. Long Island Railroad Co., 248 N.Y. 339, 344, 162 N.E. 99, 100 (1928)).

[17] Martin v. Marciano, 871 A.2d 911, 917 (R.I. 2005); *accord* Banks v. Bowen's Landing Corp., 522 A.2d 1222, 1226 (R.I. 1987).

[18] *Martin*, 871 A.2d 911 at 917 (quoting Banks v. Bowen's Landing Corp., 522 A.2d 1222, 1225 (R.I. 1987)) (quoting Ballard v. Uribe, 41 Cal. 3d 564, 224 Cal. Rptr. 664, 715 P.2d 624, 628, n. 6 (1986)).

[19] Volpe v. Gallagher, 821 A.2d 699, 705 (R.I. 2003).

[20] *Id.*

B.   *Question of Fact*

In Rhode Island, the common law status of an entrant upon land as either an invitee or licensee is not determinative of the duty of care owed.[21] Rhode Island rejects the common law categories; instead, "the question to be resolved will be whether the owner has used reasonable care for the safety of all persons reasonably expected to be upon his premises."[22] The status of the entrant as an invitee may still be one factor to be considered.[23] However, Rhode Island maintains the common law "no-duty rule" toward a trespasser and the owner or occupier of land owes no duty to the trespasser other than restraint from willful and wrongful injury.[24] The duty to avoid willful and wanton behavior only applies if the trespasser is in a known position of danger.[25]

Furthermore, Rhode Island historically held a landowner to the same level of care (the no-duty rule) toward a trespassing adult as well as a trespassing child.[26] In 1971, however, Rhode Island adopted the attractive nuisance doctrine as embodied within the *Restatement (Second) of Torts* § 339.[27] The rule imposes potential liability on the owner or possessor of land for maintaining an artificial condition on the land that poses an unreasonable risk toward trespassing children. Liability is imposed if the following is established by the trespassing child:

> (a) the possessor knows or has reason to know that young children are likely to trespass where the condition exists; (b) the condition is one which he knows or has reason to know and which he realizes or should realize involves an unreasonable risk of death or serious injury to such children; (c) the

---

[21] Mariorenzi v. Joseph DiPonte, Inc., 333 A.2d 127, 133 (1976).

[22] *Id.* Rhode Island adopts the "Connecticut Rule." Unless there are "unusual circumstances, a business "is given reasonable time after the storm has ceased to remove the accumulation of any snow or ice or to take some such measures as will make the owner's premises 'safe from the hazards arising from such a condition.'" Terry v. Central Auto Radiators, Inc., 732 A.2d 713, 716-17 (R.I. 1999) (citing Fuller v. The Housing Authority of Providence, 108 R.I. 770, 774, 279 A.2d 438, 441 (1971)). Such an "unusual" circumstance might be directing a patron across patches of ice to retrieve the patron's car following repairs by the occupier of the premises. *Terry*, 732 A.2d at 717.

[23] *Mariorenzi*, 333 A.2d at 133. An important consideration is also the area of invitation and if the landowner does not want an entrant to go into a portion of the premises, the "invitor must make the limitation apparent to the invitee either expressly or by obstructing or otherwise segregating the limited portion." Goyette v. Sousa, 153 A.2d 509, 512-13 (R.I. 1959).

[24] Haddad v. First National Stores, Inc., 280 A.2d 93, 95 (R.I. 1971); *accord* Hill v. National Grid, 11 A.3d 110, 113 (R.I. 2011). Rhode Island rejects the RESTATEMENT (SECOND) OF TORTS § 334 (1965), also known as the "beaten path exception," which would impose a duty toward frequent trespassers on the limited area of the land that they frequent. Cain v. Johnson, 755 A.2d 156, 160-161 (R.I. 2000). The Rhode Island Supreme Court in rejecting the doctrine, stated that there was "no legal duty imposed on defendant to anticipate the presence of plaintiffs' son as a trespasser on its property." *Id.* at 162.

[25] Hill v. National Grid, 11 A.3d 110, 113 (R.I. 2011); Cain v. Johnson, 755 A.2d 156, 160 (R.I. 2000). An entrant into a city park after closing is a trespasser to whom no duty is owed. *Cain*, 755 A.2d at 159-160; Bennett v. Napolitano, 746 A.2d 138 (R.I. 2000); Brindamour v. City of Warwick, 697 A.2d 1075 (R.I. 1997).

[26] *Haddad*, 280 A.2d at 96. The historic view (one held by only seven states in 1971) was originally followed by Rhode Island and was represented by the Rhode Island Supreme Court stating that it "could find no satisfactory reason to make a distinction between the duty owed by a landowner to a trespasser be he a child or an adult." *Id.*

[27] *Id.* (citing RESTATEMENT (SECOND) OF TORTS § 339 (1965)); *accord Hill*, 11 A.3d at 113.

child because of his youth does not discover the condition or realize the risk involved in intermeddling with it or coming within the area made dangerous by it; (d) the utility to the possessor of maintaining the condition is slight as compared to the risk to the children; and (e) the possessor fails to exercise reasonable care to eliminate the danger or otherwise protect the children.[28]

The approach by the *Restatement* provides a good balance between the "landowner's unrestricted right to use of his land and society's interest in the protection of the life and limb of its young."[29]

Under Rhode Island law, owners and occupiers of land owe an affirmative duty "to exercise reasonable care for the safety of persons reasonably expected to be on the premises . . . includ[ing] an obligation to protect against the risks of a dangerous condition existing on the premises, provided the landowner knows of, or by the exercise of reasonable care would have discovered, the dangerous condition."[30] Compliance with this duty is a question for the "jury's factual determination."[31] However, the possessor has no duty to protect against or warn about obvious dangers.[32] Nor does an "owner of premises abutting a public way [have] a duty to control traffic on a public way."[33]

Generally, a landlord does not owe a tenant an affirmative duty to repair the leasehold. However, "where a landlord reserves control of a passageway outside the demised premises for the common use of all tenants and invitees, he has the duty of maintaining such common passageway in a reasonably safe condition consistent with the prospective use thereof."[34]

Furthermore, "a landowner has no duty to protect another from harm caused by the dangerous or illegal acts of a third party," unless there exists a special relationship between the plaintiff and the defendant.[35] Accordingly, a social host is not liable for injuries caused to an innocent third party by an intoxicated guest operating a motor vehicle.[36] But, a social host who serves alcohol to underage guests may owe a duty to protect the other guests.[37] This duty can even extend to a duty to protect the guest from physical attacks if the host has "created an atmosphere that could lead to violence."[38]

---

[28] Haddad v. First National Stores, Inc., 280 A.2d 93, 96 (R.I. 1971) (citing RESTATEMENT (SECOND) OF TORTS § 339 (1965)).

[29] Hill v. National Grid, 11 A.3d 110, 113 (R.I. 2011).

[30] Kurczy v. St. Joseph Veterans Ass'n, 820 A.2d 929, 935 (R.I. 2003) (quoting Tancrelle v. Friendly Ice Cream Corp., 756 A.2d 744, 752 (R.I. 2000)) (citing Cutroneo v. F. W. Woolworth Co., 112 R.I. 696, 698, 315 A.2d 56, 58 (1974)).

[31] *Kurczy*, 820 A.2d 929 at 943.

[32] Bucki v. Hawkins, 914 A.2d 491, 496 (R.I. 2007).

[33] Ferreira v. Strack, 636 A.2d 682, 686 (R.I. 1994).

[34] Lawton v. Vadenais, 122 A.2d 138, 141 (R.I. 1956).

[35] Martin v. Marciano, 871 A.2d 911, 915 (R.I. 2005).

[36] *Martin*, 871 A.2d 911 at 916 (citing Ferreira v. Strack, 652 A.2d 965, 967 (R.I. 1995)). *See also* Gushlaw v. Milner, 42 A.3d 1245, 1252 (R.I. 2012); Willis v. Omar, 954 A.2d 126, 130-131 (R.I. 2008).

[37] *Martin*, 871 A.2d at 916.

[38] *Id.* at 916.

The possessor of property has a duty to use reasonable care in conducting activities upon the land to avoid injury to people outside the premises.[39] In some circumstances, this duty may extend to a duty to control the activities of a third party conducted on the property,[40] if possessors, "(1) know or have reason to know that they have the ability to control the person(s) using their land, and (2) know or should know of the necessity and opportunity for exercising such control."[41] In order to determine if injury to others is foreseeable by the activities of a third party, including criminal or intentional activities, the court should look to the totality of the circumstances approach and not the "prior similar incidents" rule.[42] Although "previous conduct is one factor to weigh when assessing foreseeability," landowners or occupiers of land "should not obtain the benefit of one free act of negligence merely because the foreseeable consequences of their negligence did not materialize in the precise form and manner of the particular injury in question until the occurrence of the injury-causing incident itself."[43]

An employer may owe a duty to a third party "who [is] injured by acts of unfit, incompetent, or unsuitable employees."[44] A duty to the third party arises if the third party is exposed to an unreasonable risk of harm from failure to use reasonable care in selecting an employee that the employer "knew or should have known was unfit or incompetent for employment."[45]

The general rule is that there is "no duty to control the conduct of a third party to prevent injury to another person unless 'a defendant has a special relationship with either the person whose conduct needs to be controlled or with the intended victim of the conduct.'"[46]

---

[39] Volpe v. Gallagher, 821 A.2d 699, 705 (R.I. 2003).

[40] *Id.* at 705.

[41] *Id.* at 706.

[42] *Id.* at 716.

[43] *Id.* "Otherwise, possessors of residential property would have carte blanche to allow third-party users of their property, including those who are mentally ill or unstable, to engage in such inherently dangerous activities as possessing guns and ammunition, playing with fire, storing dynamite and other explosives, experimenting with volatile chemicals such as nitroglycerin, harboring poisonous snakes or other deadly or potentially life-threatening animals, or undertaking any number of other unreasonably dangerous activities on the possessors' property, and thereby needlessly exposing their neighbors and other innocent parties to wrack and ruin, let alone serious bodily injury and death. Such a rule of law would be intolerable in a civilized society." *Volpe* dealt with a mother who allowed her mentally ill adult son to live on her premises. The son shot and killed a neighbor. The mother contended she did not know the son had guns on the property. *Id.* at 702-703. The Rhode Island Supreme Court held that the mother could be potentially liable for the violent act. *Id.* at 718. A vigorous dissent contended that the majority assumed that the mother had the ability to control her son because she allowed her son to live in her home. *Id.* at 718 (Shea, J., Ret., dissenting opinion). Normally, a parent is deprived of the right to control a child when the child reaches 18. *Id.* at 721 (Shea, J., Ret., dissenting opinion). The dissent criticized the majority opinion because "[a]lthough couched in a theory of landowner liability, the majority effectively has created a new cause of action allowing tort liability for parents who fail to control the conduct of their adult offspring." *Id.* at 720 (Shea, J., Ret., dissenting opinion).

[44] Welsh Mfg., Div. of Textron, Inc. v. Pinkerton's Inc., 474 A.2d 436, 438 (R.I. 1984).

[45] *Id.* at 440.

[46] Gushlaw v. Milner, 42 A.3d 1245, 1257 (R.I. 2012); Santana v. Rainbow Cleaners, Inc., 969 A.2d 653, 658 (R.I. 2009).

As previously mentioned, a social host/guest is not such a special relationship even if the social host "agrees to transport the intoxicated individual to his automobile."[47] The relationship between an out-patient mental health center and a patient voluntarily seeking treatment does not, standing alone without other circumstances, create a special relationship that would give rise to a duty to control the behavior of the patient.[48]

Rhode Island accepts the gratuitous undertaking theory whereby a duty is created if an actor voluntarily assumes a duty.[49] A duty to use reasonable care is created even if there was not a duty prior to the assumption of the undertaking.[50] Liability is imposed if the action increases the risk of harm or if harm is suffered as a result of reliance upon the undertaking.[51]

III.   Breach of Duty

A.   Elements

The standard of care that an actor must exercise is the care that a "person of ordinary prudence exercises under the circumstances."[52] The degree of care varies with the perceived risk. "The greater the danger the higher the degree of care required to constitute ordinary care."[53] However, a child is not held to the same standard of care as an adult. "The degree of care to be exercised by children of tender years . . . is that degree of care which children of the same age, education and experience would be expected to exercise in similar circumstances."[54]

Although whether a duty exists is a question of law for the court to decide, whether the duty was breached; *i.e.*, whether the defendant conformed to the standard of care that the law requires under the circumstances of the case, is a "question for the factfinder."[55] Whether the behavior of the defendant was negligence, or whether he breached the duty owed, is a question of law only "if the facts suggest only one reasonable inference."[56]

B.   Evidence

A plaintiff who seeks to recover monetary damages from the defendant based on a negligence theory "has the burden to 'establish a standard of care and prove, by a preponderance of the

---

[47] *Gushlaw*, 42 A.3d 1245, 1257-1258 (citing McGee *by and through* McGee v. Chalfant, 248 Kan. 434, 806 P.2d 980, 985 (1991)).

[48] Santana v. Rainbow Cleaners, Inc., 969 A.2d 653, 665 (R.I. 2009). "Based on the record before us, defendant possessed neither the legal authority nor the opportunity to exercise such control." *Id.*

[49] Gushlaw v. Milner, 42 A.3d 1245, 1258-59 (R.I. 2012).

[50] *Id.* at 1259.

[51] *Id.* at 1259 (citing RESTATEMENT (SECOND) OF TORTS § 324A (1965)), *rejecting* RESTATEMENT (SECOND) OF TORTS §§ 323, 324 (1965).

[52] Lawton v. Vadenais, 122 A.2d 138, 141 (R.I. 1956).

[53] *Id.*; *accord* Welsh Manufacturing, Div. of Textron, Inc. v. Pinkerton's Inc., 474 A.2d 436, 440 (R.I. 1984).

[54] Haddad v. First National Stores, Inc., 280 A.2d 93, 96 (R.I. 1971).

[55] O'Connell v. Walmsley, 93 A.3d 60, 66 (R.I. 2014).

[56] Williams v. Alston, 154 A.3d 456, 459 (R.I. 2017) (quoting Berard v. HCP, Inc., 64 A.3d 1215, 1218 (R.I. 2013)). "Of the four well-worn elements of negligence, only duty is a question of law. On the other hand, 'the remaining three element of a negligence claim . . . are fact-based.'" *Id.*

evidence, that the defendant deviated from that standard of care.'"[57] To aid in that burden of proof, evidence of "customary practices in [an] industry or past practices of [the] defendant" may be admissible to establish the standard of care under the circumstances of a case.[58]

In medical negligence causes of action, the plaintiff must establish the standard of care required and the departure from that standard "through the use of expert testimony, unless the breach of a duty of care would be obvious to a lay person."[59] Rhode Island "repudiated the 'same or similar' communities test in favor of a national standard and hold[s] that a physician is under a duty to use the degree of care and skill that is expected of a reasonably competent practitioner in the same class to which he or she belongs, acting in the same or similar circumstances."[60] An expert is qualified to testify if the physician has "knowledge of or familiarity with the procedure, acquired through experience, observation, association, or education."[61] Normally, a physician who has earned board certification is "presumptively qualified to render an opinion" within his or her area of expertise.[62]

A physician also has an obligation to obtain informed consent. The "doctrine of informed consent imposes a duty upon a doctor which is completely separate and distinct from his responsibility to skillfully diagnose and treat the patient's ills."[63] This duty requires disclosure of material risks[64] including "what [is] to be done, the risk involved and the alternatives to the contemplated treatment."[65] In some cases, expert testimony might not be required for the jury to determine whether the physician disclosed "enough information to enable the patient to make an intelligent choice."[66]

Failure to comply with a traffic regulation or statue is admissible. However, violation of a statute is not negligence *per se* in Rhode Island. Rather, it is admissible as evidence of negligence.[67] The violation of "a penal statute . . . may be considered by the jury to be evidence of negligence only as respects persons whom the statute was designed to protect." For example, a statute requiring a driver to stop when a school bus is stopped and the bus'

---

[57] Medeiros v. Sitrin, 984 A.2d 620, 625 (R.I. 2009) (quoting Riley v. Stone, 900 A.2d 1087, 1095 (R.I. 2006)) (citing Morales v Town of Johnston, 895 A.2d 721, 732 (R.I. 2006)).

[58] Scittarelli v. Providence Gas Co., 415 A.2d 1040, 1043 (R.I. 1980).

[59] Gianquitti v. Atwood Medical Associates, 973 A.2d 580, 594 (R.I. 2009); Wilkinson v. Vesey, 295 A.2d 676, 682 (R.I. 1972). Similar criteria exists to pursue a cause of action for legal malpractice. Ahmed v. Pannone 779 A.2d 630 (R.I. 2001).

[60] Sheeley v. Memorial Hosp., 710 A.2d 161, 167 (R.I. 1998). However, medical laboratories may be held to simply a standard of ordinary care. Ho-Rath v. Rhode Island Hosp., 89 A.3d 806 (R.I. 2014). The court in *Ho-Rath* concluded that cases against medical laboratories were not medical malpractice claims. *Id.*, 89 A.3d at 812.

[61] Sheeley v. Memorial Hosp., 710 A.2d 161, 166 (R.I. 1998).

[62] *Id.*

[63] Wilkinson v. Vesey, 295 A.2d 676, 685 (R.I. 1972). *Accord* Flanagan v. Wesselhoeft, 712 A.2d 365, 370-71 (R.I. 1998). The policy behind this doctrine is that "the patient's right to make his decision in the light of his own individual value judgment is the very essence of his freedom of choice." *Wilkinson.* 295 A.2d at 687.

[64] *Wilkinson*, 295 A.2d 676, 689 (R.I. 1972).

[65] *Id.* at 685.

[66] *Id.* at 688.

[67] Paquin v. Tillinghast, 517 A.2d 246, 248 (R.I. 1986); Salcone v. Bottomley, 129 A.2d 635, 637 (R.I. 1957); Audette v. New England Transp. Co., 46 A.2d 570, 573 (R.I. 1946).

lights are flashing was intended to protect school children and "not to protect adult motorist in vehicles further down the road."[68] Furthermore, the injury that occurs must be the type of harm that was foreseeable from breach of the statutory enactment.[69] For example, the owner of a liquor store who illegally sold grain alcohol to minors could be liable for injuries caused by consumption of the alcohol but could not be held liable for injuries caused by igniting the alcohol.[70] "The statutes regulating alcohol and minors reflect a public policy against under-age drinking and not incendiary behavior."[71] Additionally, a violation of the statute must be shown to have caused the injury before it can be used as evidence. In other words, the statute may not be used unless it is shown that "the injuries and death would have been prevented."[72]

The mere fact that an accident occurred does not infer negligence.[73] However, a plaintiff may rely on the doctrine of *res ipsa loquitur* to establish the standard of care owed and its breach so long as the plaintiff establishes "that the accident was one that in the ordinary course of events occurs when someone is negligent and that at the time of the accident defendant exclusively controlled the instrument of plaintiff's injury."[74] However, the "critical inquiry is not control, but whether a particular defendant is the responsible cause of the [plaintiff's] injury."[75] Further, "the event must not have been due to any voluntary act or contribution on the part of the plaintiff."[76] The jury uses its "common sense" in applying the *res ipsa* doctrine. The plaintiff does not have to set forth that she plans to use *res ipsa* in her pleadings. However, the complaint ought to set out basic facts that would support the application of the doctrine."[77] The inference of negligence drawn from the use of *res ipsa* "casts upon a defendant the burden of rebutting the same to the satisfaction of the jury."[78]

Web pages and e-mails must be properly authenticated to be admissible.[79] Authentication of a printout of a web page must establish that the printout reflects the image of the page when the image was made, "when or by whom the documents . . . were accessed," the

---

[68] *Paquin*, 517 A.2d 246, 248 (R.I. 1986).

[69] Selwyn v. Ward, 879 A.2d 882, 887 (R.I. 2005).

[70] *Id.* at 888.

[71] *Id.*

[72] Sitko v. Jastrzebski, 27 A.2d 178, 179 (R.I. 1942) (Even though the landlord violated an ordinance that required a fire escape on the building, there was no evidence that the presence of a fire escape would have prevented the injuries or death that occurred in *this* fire.).

[73] Martinelli v. Hopkins, 787 A.2d 1158, 1169 (R.I. 2001).

[74] Scittarelli v. Providence Gas Co., 415 A.2d 1040, 1044-1045 (R.I. 1980). The mere fact that an explosion occurred in a gas stove, without additional facts, is not sufficient evidence to allow the use of *res ipsa. Id.* at 1045.

[75] Cruz v. Daimlerchyrsler Motors Corp., 66 A.2d 446, 452 (R.I. 2013) (quoting Parrillo v. Giroux Co., 426 A.2d 1313, 1320 (R.I. 1981)). In *Cruz*, the Rhode Island Supreme Court made clear its adherence to *Parrillo* and the RESTATEMENT (SECOND) OF TORTS § 328D (1965).

[76] Montuori v. Narragansett Elec. Co., 418 A.2d 5, 13 (R.I. 1980).

[77] *Id.* at 13.

[78] Cruz v. Daimlerchyrsler Motors Corp., 66 A.2d 446, 451 (R.I. 2013).

[79] O'Connor v. Newport Hosp., 111 A.3d 317, 323 (R.I. 2015). Rhode Island Rules of Evidence, Rule 901(a) states, as follows: "The requirement of authentication or identification as a condition precedent to admissibility is satisfied by evidence sufficient to support a finding that the matter in question is what its proponent claims."

entity that controls the website, and that the author of the web page is attributable to the site.[80] The most direct method to authenticate an e-mail is "through the testimony of a witness with personal knowledge that the proffered exhibit is what it is claimed to be, such as the author or recipient of the email."[81] However, because expert testimony "plays a 'pivotal role'" in the determination if the health care provider conformed to customary practice[82] in a medical negligence cause of action, web pages or e-mails regarding qualifications for board certification offered to impeach an expert's credibility are inadmissible hearsay.[83]

IV. Causation

A. Elements

There are two elements regarding causation in Rhode Island. "A plaintiff must not only prove that a defendant is the cause-in-fact of an injury, but also must prove that a defendant proximately caused the injury."[84] In order to establish causation, the jury must find "that the harm would not have occurred but-for the [act] and that the harm [was a] natural and probable consequence of the [act]."[85] Causation in most cases is "established by showing that but-for the negligence of the tortfeasor, injury to the plaintiff would not have occurred."[86] The defendant's misbehavior does not need to be the sole cause of the plaintiff's harm. In other words, the negligence of the defendant does not have to be *the* proximate cause, it must only be *a* proximate cause.[87]

B. Evidence

Although 'proximate cause may not be established by conjecture or speculation," circumstantial evidence may be used to establish causation.[88] Direct evidence is not always necessary.[89] If expert testimony is relied upon to establish causation, the opinion must be of "substantial probative value."[90] "Absolute certainty, of course, is not required. In those cases where expert testimony is relied on to show that out of several potential causes a given result came from one specific cause, the expert must report that the result in question 'most

---

[80] *O'Connor*, 111 A.3d at 324 (citing CHRISTOPHER B. MUELLER AND LAIRD C. KIRKPATRICK, 5 FEDERAL EVIDENCE § 9:9 (4th ed.)); 2 KENNETH S. BROUN ET AL., McCORMICK ON EVIDENCE § 227 at 74 (6th ed. 2006).

[81] *O'Connor*, 111 A.3d at 325.

[82] *Id.* at 328.

[83] *Id.* at 326.

[84] Almonte v. Kurl, 46 A.3d 1, 18 (R.I. 2012).

[85] *Almonte*, 46 A.3d at 18 (quoting Pierce v. Providence Retirement Board, 15 A.3d 957, 964 (R.I. 2011)).

[86] Martinelli v. Hopkins, 787 A.2d 1158, 1169 (R.I. 2001).

[87] *Id.* at 1170 (emphasis added).

[88] Gianquitti v. Atwood Medical Associates, 973 A.2d 580, 592 (R.I. 2009); Seide v. State, 875 A.2d 1259, 1268 (R.I. 2005); Martinelli v. Hopkins, 787 A.2d 1158, 1169 (R.I 2001).

[89] Seide v. State, 875 A.2d 1259, 1268 (R.I. 2005).

[90] Montuori v. Narragansett Elec. Co., 418 A.2d 5, 10 (R.I. 1980).

probably' came from the cause alleged."[91] Every other possible cause need not be excluded.[92] Ultimately, the issue of proximate cause is for the jury to resolve.[93]

Normally, causation must be established by a preponderance of the evidence. The defendant's behavior more likely than not caused the plaintiff's harm.[94] The exception is the loss of chance doctrine in medical malpractice cases. Loss chance is "an alternative to conventional notions of causation."[95] Loss of chance is a "relaxed causation" doctrine whereby the plaintiff need only prove that the negligence of the defendant was "a proximate cause of the lost chance to avoid the ultimate harm."[96]

The intervention of an outside force or actor may relieve the defendant of liability. An intervening act is a secondary act that occurs after the alleged tortfeasor's negligence.[97] However, it is "well established that an intervening act will not insulate a defendant from liability if his [or her] negligence was a concurring proximate cause which had not been rendered remote by reason of the secondary cause which intervened."[98] Normally, the intervention of intentional or criminal action will relieve the original tortfeasor from liability with the caveat that the criminal or intentional intervening act must not be foreseeable.[99] "[T]he test in these cases must be whether the intervening act could reasonably have been foreseen as a natural and probable result of the original act of negligence of the defendant."[100] The intervening cause "becomes the sole proximate cause of injury" when the intervening cause is an "independent and intervening or secondary act of negligence" that renders the original act of negligence "totally inoper[able] as a cause of the injury."[101]

Whether an intervening cause supercedes liability is a question of fact for the jury. The question may become one for the court if the facts do not "permit even an inference of proximate cause," such as where the intervening actions violate contractual and criminal provisions designed to protect the safety of others.[102] However, there are a few reoccurring cases

---

[91] *Montuori*, 418 A.2d 5, 10-11 (quoting Sweet v. Hemingway Transport, Inc., 114 R.I. 348, 355, 333 A.2d 411, 415 (1975)) (citing Tabuteau v. London Guar. & Accident Co., 351 Pa. 183, 40 A.2d 396 (1945)).

[92] *Gianquitti*, 973 A.2d at 593; *Seide*, 875 A.2d at 1269; *Martinelli*, 787 A.2d at 1169.

[93] *Gianquitt*, 973 A.2d 580, 593 (R.I. 2009); *accord* Berman v. Sitrin, 101 A.3d 1251, 1267 (R.I. 2014).

[94] Mandros v. Prescod, 948 A.2d 304, 310 (R.I. 2008).

[95] *Id.*

[96] *Id.* (quoting Contois v. Town of West Warwick, 865 A.2d 1019, 1023 (R.I. 2004)) (quoting Mead v. Adrian, 670 N.W.2d 174, 186 (Iowa 2003)) (Cady, J., concurring).

[97] Seide v. State, 875 A.2d 1259, 1270 (R.I. 2005).

[98] Martin v. Marciano, 871 A.2d 911, 918 (R.I. 2005) (quoting Denisewich v. Pappas, 97 R.I. 432, 435-37, 198 A.2d 144, 147-48 (1964)).

[99] *Martin*, 871 A.2d at 918.

[100] *Id.* (quoting Aldcroft v. The Fidelity & Casualty Co. of N.Y., 106 R.I. 311, 314, 259 A.2d 408, 411 (1969)). It was a question of fact for the jury to determine whether an assault with a baseball bat at a party was foreseeable. The host rented a tent and served alcohol to over 70 underage drinkers. A fight had previously broken out among the guests. Therefore, a jury could find that the attack with a baseball bat was a foreseeable intervening cause. *Martin*, 871 A.2d at 919.

[101] Seide v. State, 875 A.2d 1259, 1270 (R.I. 2005); *see also* Contois v. Town of West Warwick, 865 A.2d 1019, 1027 (R.I. 2004) (quoting Hueston v. Narragansett Tennis Club, Inc., 502 A.2d 827, 830 (R.I. 1986)).

[102] Splendorio v. Bilray Demolition Co., Inc., 682 A.2d 461, 467 (R.I. 1996).

dealing with intervening causes where the facts repeat with sufficient frequency that the court's reaction to the intervening cause is more predictable. Negligent conduct that results in the plaintiff committing suicide is generally not a compensable wrong. The intervening act of suicide by the plaintiff will supercede liability unless the plaintiff was overcome by an "uncontrollable impulse."[103] Another frequent category of reoccurring cases are cases where the intervening cause alleged is a rescue attempt. "The rescue doctrine assigns the party who negligently creates a dangerous situation with responsibility for any rescuer injured in a reasonable rescue attempt. The party creating the danger is by law charged with foreseeing all nonreckless rescue attempts."[104]

V.   Damages

A.   Elements

"A person injured by the tort of another is entitled to recover damages from him for all harm, past, present and prospective, legally caused by the tort."[105] An award may include medical bills, lost wages, pain and suffering, and property damages.[106] However, in Rhode Island, there are "no discrete categories that limit the amount or the type of damages that a plaintiff alleging negligence may recover. Rather victims of a negligent tortfeasor are ordinarily permitted to recover for all the injuries and damages that can be proven to have been reasonably foreseeable and proximately caused by the tortfeasor's negligence."[107]

Punitive damages are only awarded when there is proof that the defendant acted with "intent to cause harm" or "with malice or in bad faith."[108] The plaintiff must produce "evidence of such willfulness, recklessness or wickedness, on the part of the party at fault, as amount[s] to criminality, which for the good of society and warning to the individual, ought to be punished."[109] As a matter of statutory construction, punitive damages are not recoverable in wrongful death actions in Rhode Island.[110]

---

[103]   Clift v. Narragansett Television L.P., 688 A.2d 805, 809 (R.I. 1996). The court recognized and apparently adopted the RESTATEMENT (SECOND) OF TORTS § 808 (1965). The difference between an act of suicide that would not cut off liability and one that would was explained, as follows: "[W]here the negligent wrong only causes a mental condition in which the injured person is able to realize the nature of the act of suicide and has the power to control it if he so desires, the act then becomes an independent intervening force and the wrongdoer cannot be held liable for the death. On the other hand, if the negligent wrong causes mental illness which results in an uncontrollable impulse to commit suicide, then the wrongdoer may be held liable for the death." *Id.* at 808 (quoting Tate v. Canonica, 180 Cal. App. 2d 898, 5 Cal. Rptr. 28, 40 (1960)).

[104]   Ouellette v. Carde, 612 A.2d 687, 693 (R.I. 1992). The rescue doctrine also prohibits the charge of contributory negligence against one who sees an imperiled person in imminent danger and is injured in a rescue attempt so long as it is "a nonreckless attempt to rescue the imperiled person." *Id.* at 689. This doctrine was founded based on the policy to "encourage rescue." *Id.*

[105]   RESTATEMENT (FIRST) OF TORTS, § 910 (1939) (updated March 2017).

[106]   Hayhurst v. LaFlamme, 441 A.2d 544, 545 (R.I. 1982).

[107]   Flanagan v. Wesselhoeft, 712 A.2d 365, 371 (R.I. 1998).

[108]   Palmisano v. Toth, 624 A.2d 314, 318 (R.I. 1993).

[109]   *Id.*

[110]   Simeone v. Charron, 762 A.2d 442, 444-45 (R.I. 2000).

Damages for wrongful birth, such as when a physician negligently performs a sterilization procedure, would be recoverable under the "limited recovery" rule if the child that resulted was a healthy child. The damages would include compensation for "medical expenses of the ineffective sterilization procedure, for the medical and hospital costs of the pregnancy, for the expense of a subsequent sterilization procedure, for loss of wages, and sometimes for emotional distress arising out of the unwanted pregnancy and loss of consortium to the spouse arising out of the unwanted pregnancy. They also generally include medical expenses for prenatal care, delivery, and post-natal care."[111] Child-rearing costs are not available when the cause of action deals with the birth of a healthy child.[112] However, recovery of extraordinary expenses, or increased costs, associated with raising a disabled child is allowed if the case involves a disabled child. Furthermore, the entire cost of raising the child would be borne by the physician if the doctor was on notice that the parents feared the birth of an impaired infant. The damages for care would not end when the child reaches 18. Also, the parents could potentially recover damages for resulting emotional distress.[113]

B. Evidence

"The task of assessing compensatory damages is peculiarly within the province of the jury."[114] Substantial latitude should be given to the jury in setting the amount of damages and any jury award should be sustained unless the award is "so grossly excessive as to shock the conscience or if the jury was clearly influenced by passion or prejudice or proceeded in a clearly erroneous fashion in arriving at the award."[115] For example, testimony that the plaintiff suffered from "persistent headaches, loss of sleep, [and] a degree of emotional disturbance" that interfered with employment was sufficient evidence to sustain an award of $18,000.[116] The plaintiff "need not prove damages with 'mathematical exactitude[.] [A]ll that is required is that they are based on reasonable and probable estimates."[117]

A single uniform measure of damages is not necessarily used in destruction of property.[118] Replacement cost at the time of the injury, diminution in the fair market value, or restoration costs may all be appropriate alternative methods of calculating damages depending on the facts of an individual case.[119]

It is properly within the discretion of the jury to decide the amount of money awarded for pain and suffering. Generally, there is not a "particular formula or rule of thumb" available to compute pain and suffering.[120] However, attorneys are allowed to use the *per diem*

---

[111] Emerson v. Magendantz, 689 A.2d 409, 412 (RI 1997).

[112] *Id.* at 413.

[113] *Id.* at 414.

[114] Paquin v. Tillinghast, 517 A.2d 246, 249 (R.I. 1986); *see also* Morabit v. Hoag, 80 A.3d 1, 15 (R.I. 2013).

[115] *Id.* at 249.

[116] Paquin v. Tillinghast, 517 A.2d 246, 249 (R.I. 1986).

[117] Morabit v. Hoag, 80 A.3d 1, 15 (R.I. 2013) (quoting Butera v. Boucher, 798 A.2d 340, 350 (R.I. 2002)) (citing Rhode Island Tpk. & Bridge Auth. v. Bethlehem Steel Corp., 119 R.I. 141, 167-68, 379 A.2d 344, 358 (1977)).

[118] *Morabit*, 80 A.3d at 17.

[119] *Morabit*, 80 A.3d at 14, 16-17. *Morabit* dealt with the negligent removal of "rare and historic" trees. *Id.* at 5.

[120] Worsley v. Corcelli, 377 A.2d 215, 217 (R.I. 1977).

method of arguing for the amount the jury will calculate.[121] An attorney asks the jury to consider how much it would be worth to suffer similar pain on a daily basis and then asks the jury to arrive at an award by multiplying that amount by the number of days the plaintiff endured the suffering. Rhode Island adopts the *per diem* rule and "permits counsel for the plaintiff, if he or she chooses, to use in summation to the jury the *per diem* method under proper instructions from the trial justice."[122]

---

[121] *Id.* at 219.

[122] *Id.*

CHAPTER 41

SOUTH CAROLINA

SOUTH CAROLINA

Allan Galbraith[1]

I. Purpose of Tort Law

Tort law undertakes to compensate plaintiffs for injuries they have suffered as the result of wrongful conduct of another.[2] In doing so, the tort system seeks to apportion fault among the various actors involved in the event[3] while at the same time being fair to all parties.[4] The concept of fairness requires the wrongdoer to restore the injured party, as nearly as possible through the payment of money, to the same position he occupied before the wrongful injury occurred.[5] There is an important caveat to this proposition which illustrates that the tort system also seeks to facilitate social policy goals. The tort system requires that the wrongdoer pay full compensation for all of the harms caused, even if that results in a windfall to the injured party.[6] Thus, tort law seeks to further broader social purposes, such as: (a) it "seeks to protect safety interests and is rooted in the concept of protecting society as a whole from physical harm to person or property."[7]; and (b) acts as a means of deterring negligent conduct in the future.[8]

II. Duty to Exercise Ordinary Care

A. Question of Law

An essential element of every claim for negligence is the existence of a duty of care owed by the defendant to the plaintiff.[9] Whether a duty exists in a particular case is determined as a question of law by the court.[10] Duty has been defined by the South Carolina Supreme Court as "the obligation to conform to a particular standard of conduct toward

---

[1] Attorney, The Keenan Law Firm, Palm Desert, California, Member, Georgia and California Bars.

[2] Willis v. Wu, 362 S.C. 146, 607 S.E.2d 63 (2004).

[3] Davenport v. Cotton Hope Plantation Horizontal Prop. Regime, 333 S.C. 71, 508 S.E.2d 565 (1998).

[4] Fabian v. Lindsay, 410 S.C. 475, 765 S.E.2d 132 (2014).

[5] Clark v. Cantrell, 339 S.C. 369, 378, 529 S.E.2d 528, 533 (2000).

[6] Dixon v. Besco Eng'g, Inc., 320 S.C. 174, 463 S.E.2d 636 (S.C. App. 1995).

[7] Sapp v. Ford Motor Co., 386 S.C. 143, 687 S.E.2d 47 (2009).

[8] Ashley II of Charleston, L.L.C. v. PCS Nitrogen, Inc., 409 S.C. 487, 763 S.E.2d 19 (2014); Harrison v. Bevilacqua, 354 S.C. 129, 580 S.E.2d 109 (S.C., 2003).

[9] Huggins v. Citibank, N.A., 355 S.C. 329, 585 S.E.2d 275 (2003); Bass v. Gopal, Inc., 395 S.C. 129, 716 S.E.2d 910 (2011).

[10] Sharpe v. S.C. Dep't of Mental Health, 292 S.C. 11, 354 S.E.2d 778 (S.C. Ct. App. 1987).

another."[11] The existence of a duty is based upon the concept that an individual (or entity) should not suffer a harm to his person or property which is foreseeable and which the defendant might have avoided through the exercise of reasonable care.[12]

South Carolina additionally recognizes that duty is a flexible concept and "it seeks to balance the degree of foreseeability of harm against the burden of the duty imposed."[13] However, foreseeability of injury standing alone is insufficient to support a duty.[14] The existence of a duty arises from the relationship between the alleged tortfeasor and the injured party.[15] Duty may be "created by statute, a contractual relationship, status, property interest, or some other special circumstance."[16] In determining whether a duty is owed in a particular case, multiple policy considerations are evaluated to determine whether a particular plaintiff is entitled to protection.[17] These factors include, but are not limited to, the policy of deterring future tortfeasors and the moral culpability of the tortfeasor.[18]

B. *Question of Fact*

i. **Elements**

The degree of care owed is generally phrased as ordinary care or reasonable care.[19] This is the degree of care that an ordinarily prudent person would exercise under the circumstances.[20] Once the Court has determined that a duty of care exists, it is usually for the jury to determine whether the standard of care has been met in a particular case.[21]

ii. **Evidence**

The plaintiff has the burden of producing evidence that the defendant's conduct was unreasonable given the risks involved.[22] Multiple sources of evidence are admissible for the purpose of making the requisite showing. Evidence of industry standards, customs, and

---

[11] Hubbard v. Taylor, 339 S.C. 582, 588, 529 S.E.2d 549, 552 (2000).

[12] Snow v. The City of Columbia, 305 S.C. 544, 409 S.E.2d 797 (S.C. Ct. App. 1991).

[13] Bass v. Gopal, Inc., 395 S.C. 129, 716 S.E.2d 910 (2011). The *Bass* Court goes on to say, "In adopting a balancing approach, we do not alter this duty, but merely elucidate how to determine (1) if a crime is foreseeable, and (2) given the foreseeability, determine the economically feasible security measures required to prevent such harm. The optimal point at which a dollar spent equals a dollar's worth of prevention will not always be apparent, but may be roughly ascertained with the aid of an expert, or some other testimony." This serves to illustrate that on occasion, South Carolina courts conflate the concepts of duty and standard of care, which is a factual question of whether a duty which has been legally determined to exist has been breached. *See* Part II.B. *infra*.

[14] Nelson v. Piggly Wiggly Cent., Inc., 390 S.C. 382, 701 S.E.2d 776 (S.C. Ct. App. 2010).

[15] South Carolina Ports Auth. v. Booz-Allen & Hamilton, Inc., 289 S.C. 373, 346 S.E.2d 324 (1986).

[16] McCullough v. Goodrich & Pennington Mortg. Fund, Inc., 373 S.C. 43, 644 S.E.2d 43 (2007).

[17] Araujo v. Southern Bell Tel. & Tel. Co., 291 S.C. 54, 351 S.E.2d 908 (S.C. Ct. App. 1986).

[18] *Id.*

[19] Dorrell v. S.C. Dep't of Transp., 361 S.C. 312, 605 S.E.2d 12 (2004).

[20] Eargle v. Sumter Lighting Co., 110 S.C. 560, 96 S.E. 909 (1918).

[21] Miller v. City of Camden, 317 S.C. 28, 451 S.E.2d 401 (S.C. Ct. App. 1994).

[22] *Bass,* 395 S.C. at 142.

practices is relevant and probative for defining the standard of care.[23] Privately established safety standards and rules are similarly admissible for the same purpose.[24] A defendant's internal operating rules and procedures may also be used as evidence of the standard of care.[25] Statutes and governmental agency regulations are also admissible.[26]

III.   Breach of Duty

A.   Elements

In order to recover, the plaintiff is required to establish that the defendant breached the duty of care owed to the plaintiff.[27] A breach of duty exists when it is foreseeable that a person's conduct is likely to cause injury to a person to whom a duty is owed.[28] Whether a breach of duty exists under the circumstances of the case is an issue for jury determination.[29]

B.   Evidence

South Carolina does not recognize the doctrine of *res ipsa loquitor*: it is therefore necessary that the plaintiff come forward with some evidence of negligence other than simply the fact of the occurrence itself.[30] However, circumstantial evidence may be sufficient to meet this burden.[31] If in consideration of all conditions and circumstances of the event, a reasonable inference can be drawn that the defendant did not observe ordinary care, then the issue of breach is for jury determination.[32] Other similar occurrences involving the same defendant in the same time frame may be admissible and sufficient to raise an inference of breach of duty.[33]

IV.   Causation

A.   Elements

Plaintiff also has the burden of showing that the defendant's breach of duty proximately caused the damages claimed.[34] This entails proof of both causation in fact and legal cause.[35] As to causation in fact, a "but-for" standard is used which is generally phrased as

---

[23] Elledge v. Richland/Lexington Sch. Dist. Five, 352 S.C. 179, 573 S.E.2d 789 (2002).

[24] *Id.*

[25] Tidwell v. Columbia Ry., Gas & Elec. Co., 109 S.C. 34, 95 S.E. 109 (1918); Caldwell v. K-Mart Corporation, 306 S.C. 27, 410 S.E.2d 21 (1991).

[26] Madison v. Babcock Ctr., Inc., 370 S.C. 42, 634 S.E.2d 275 (2006).

[27] Bishop v. S.C. Dep't. of Mental Health, 331 S.C. 79, 502 S.E.2d 78 (1998).

[28] Vinson v. Hartley, 324 S.C. 389, 477 S.E.2d 715 (S.C. Ct. App. 1996).

[29] Stallings v. Ratliff, 292 S.C. 349, 356 S.E.2d 414 (S.C. Ct. App. 1987).

[30] Eickhoff v. Beard-Laney, Inc., 199 S.C. 500, 20 S.E.2d 153 (1942).

[31] *Id.*

[32] Boyd v. Marion Coca-Cola Bottling Co., 240 S.C. 383, 126 S.E.2d 178 (1962).

[33] *Id.*

[34] *Bishop*, 331. S.C. at 88.

[35] *Id.*

requiring proof that "the injury would not have occurred 'but-for' the defendant's negligence."[36] However, in some other cases, the South Carolina Supreme Court has stated that the plaintiff's burden is to show that the defendant's conduct was a substantial factor in causing the harm to the plaintiff.[37] The defendant's conduct need not be the sole cause of the injury.[38]

Legal cause is established by showing foreseeability.[39] "The touchstone of proximate cause in South Carolina is foreseeability."[40] Foreseeability is determined by looking to the natural and probable consequences of the conduct complained of.[41] It is not necessary that the defendant anticipate the exact event that occurred; proof of causation is sufficient if the defendant "should have foreseen that his negligence would probably cause injury to something or someone."[42] Foreseeability is not determined in hindsight, rather the events are viewed from the defendant's perspective at the time of the alleged breach.[43]

B. *Evidence*

Generally, the question of causation is to be resolved by the jury.[44] The question of causation may be removed from jury consideration only on the rare occasion when the evidence is susceptible to a single inference, or interpretation.[45] If there can be a fair difference of opinion regarding the cause of the injury, the case must be submitted to the jury for determination.[46]

V. Damages

A. *Elements*

Actual damages are given "to make the injured party whole, to put him in the same position he was in prior to the damages received insofar as this is monetarily possible."[47] They are given in satisfaction of the loss the plaintiff has sustained.[48] Actual damages include compensation for all injuries which were proximately caused by the defendant's wrongful conduct.[49] Pain and suffering, mental anguish, and loss of enjoyment of life are compensable

---

[36] *Id.*

[37] Baggerly v. CSX Transp., Inc., 370 S.C. 362, 635 S.E.2d 97 (2006).

[38] *Id.*

[39] Hurd v. Williamsburg Cty., 353 S.C. 596, 579 S.E.2d 136 (S.C. Ct. App. 2003).

[40] Koester v. Carolina Rental Ctr., Inc., 313 S.C. 490, 443 S.E.2d 392 (1994).

[41] Young v. Tide Craft, Inc., 270 S.C. 453, 242 S.E.2d 671 (1978).

[42] McQuillen v. Dobbs, 262 S.C. 386, 204 S.E.2d 732 (1974).

[43] Parks v. Characters Night Club, 345 S.C. 484, 548 S.E.2d 605 (2001).

[44] Small v. Pioneer Mach., Inc., 329 S.C. 448, 494 S.E.2d 835 (S.C. Ct. App. 1997).

[45] *Id.*

[46] *Hurd,* 353 S.C. at 614.

[47] Clark v. Cantrell, 339 S.C. 369, 529 S.E.2d 528 (2000).

[48] Barnwell v. Barber-Colman Co., 301 S.C. 534, 393 S.E.2d 162 (1989).

[49] Rogers v. Florence Printing Co., 233 S.C. 567, 578, 106 S.E.2d 258, 264 (1958).

as separate items of damage.[50]

B. *Evidence*

Generally evidence of damages has to be such to allow the jury to determine such damages with reasonable certainty, though mathematical certainty is not required.[51] To recover future damages, the plaintiff must show that such damages are reasonably certain to occur.[52] However, the standard for admissibility of evidence on future damages is "any evidence which tends to establish the nature, character, and extent of injuries which are the natural and proximate consequences of the defendant's acts."[53] The assessment of damages is uniquely a function of the jury and the jury's assessment of damages is not to be interfered with unless the "amount of the verdict is so grossly inadequate or excessive that it shocks the conscience of the court and clearly indicates the amount was the result of passion, caprice, prejudice, partiality, corruption or some other improper motives."[54] The courts recognize that the evaluation of actual damages in a personal injury case is a difficult task that is best left to the consideration of the jury under appropriate instructions from the court.[55]

---

[50] Boan v. Blackwell, 343 S.C. 498, 541 S.E.2d 242 (2000).

[51] Whisenant v. James Island Corp., 277 S.C. 10, 281 S.E.2d 794 (1981).

[52] Haltiwanger v. Barr, 258 S.C. 27, 186 S.E.2d 819 (1982).

[53] Pearson v. Bridges, 344 S.C. 366, 544 S.E.2d 617 (2001).

[54] Green v. Fritz, 356 S.C. 566, 590 S.E.2d 39 (2002).

[55] Mickle v. Blackmon, 252 S.C. 202, 166 S.E.2d 173 (1969).

CHAPTER 42

SOUTH DAKOTA

SOUTH DAKOTA

Vicki Lawrence MacDougall[1]

I. Purpose of Tort Law

There are three interrelated elements that must be satisfied under South Dakota law in order to recover for negligence. The elements are, as follows: "(1) A duty on the part of the defendant; (2) a failure to perform that duty; and (3) an injury to the plaintiff resulting from such a failure."[2] Once the prima facie case is established, the primary goal of allowing recovery based on negligence is to make the injured party whole.[3] The "*primary objective of an award of damages* in a civil action, and the fundamental principle on which it is based, are *just compensation* . . . for the loss or injury sustained by the complainant, *and no more*."[4] Corrective justice also demands that the actor should be responsible for the injuries caused by "want of ordinary care or skill."[5] Another goal of tort law is the belief that an award of damages, particularly punitive damages, helps to deter future tortious behavior.[6]

II. Duty to Exercise Ordinary Care

A. *Question of Law*

There must be a legal duty before liability attaches in a negligence cause of action. Thus, duty is the threshold issue in any torts case.[7] "Negligence is the breach of a legal duty. It is immaterial whether the duty is one imposed by the rule of the common law requiring the exercise of ordinary care or skill not to injure another, or is imposed by a statute designed for the benefit of a class of persons which included the one claiming to have been injured as the result of nonperformance of the statutory duty."[8]

---

[1] Professor of Law, Director Health Law Certificate Program, Law Review Faculty Advisor, Oklahoma City University School of Law, Member, California and Oklahoma Bar Associations.

[2] Leslie v. City of Bonesteel, 303 N.W.2d 117, 119 (S.D. 1981); *accord* Kuehl v. Horner (J.W.) Lumber Co., 2004 SD 48, ¶ 10, 678 N.W.2d 809, 812.

[3] Papke v. Harbert, 2007 SD 87, ¶ 66, 738 N.W.2d 510, 532.

[4] *Papke*, 2007 SD 87, ¶ 75, 738 N.W.2d 510, 534 (emphasis in original) (quoting Hanif v. Hous. Auth., 200 Cal. App. 3d 635, 640-41, 246 Cal. Rptr. 192 (Cal. Ct. App. 1988) (quoting Mozzetti v. City of Brisbane, 67 Cal. App. 3d 565, 576, 136 Cal. Rptr.751 (Cal. Ct. App. 1977))).

[5] SDCL § 20-9-1.

[6] Schaffer v. Edward D. Jones & Co., 1996 SD 94, ¶ 25, 552 N.W.2d 801, 809.

[7] E.P. v. Riley, 1999 SD 163, ¶ 24, 604 N.W.2d 7, 14.

[8] Peterson v. Spink Elec. Co-op., Inc., 1998 SD 60, ¶ 13, 578 N.W.2d 589, 592 (quoting Westover v. E. River Elec. Power Coop. Inc., 488 N.W.2d 892, 898 (S.D. 1992) (citing Ward v. LaCreek Elec. Ass'n, 83 S.D. 584, 163 N.W.2d 344, 347 (S.D. 1968))).

The determination of duty depends on "whether 'a relationship exists between the parties such that the law will impose upon the defendant a legal obligation of reasonable conduct for the benefit of the plaintiff.'"[9] It is a question of law for the court to determine if a duty of care is owed under the facts of an individual case.[10] As such, the determination of the issue of duty is subject to *de novo* review.[11] Moreover, injury must be anticipated before a duty is imposed by the court.[12] "Whether a common-law duty exists depends on the foreseeability of injury;"[13] there is no duty unless injury is reasonably anticipated.[14] "Foreseeability is the touchstone of the determination of the existence of a duty."[15] In addition, however, "[p]ublic policy is a major consideration in identifying a legal duty."[16]

B. *Question of Fact*

South Dakota adopts the "rescue doctrine" which holds a negligent party liable for injuries caused to the would-be-rescuer as well as the victim of the negligent act. The premise of the rescue doctrine is "that the defendant's negligence in placing another in a position of imminent peril is not only a wrong to that person, but also to the rescuing plaintiff."[17]

There is generally no duty to control the conduct of a third person to prevent the third person from injuring another unless there exists a special relationship between the actor and the third person or the actor and the other person.[18] The duty to control a third party may also spring from having actual control over the third person and foreseeing that injury could occur without reasonable care being used to exercise control over the third party.[19]

Medical professionals have the duty to obtain informed consent from their patients prior to medical treatments or procedures.[20] The physician must discuss the risks and

---

[9] Casillas v. Schubauer, 2006 SD 42, ¶ 14, 714 N.W.2d 84, 88 (quoting In re Estate of Shuck v. Perkins Cty., 1998 SD 32, ¶ 8, 577 N.W.2d 584, 586); *accord* Zerfas v. Amco Ins., 2015 SD 99, ¶ 10, 873 N.W.2d 65, 69.

[10] Casillas v. Schubauer, 2006 SD 42, ¶ 14, 714 N.W.2d 84, 88.

[11] Poelstra v. Basin Elec. Power Co-op, 1996 SD 36, ¶ 9, 545 N.W.2d 823, 825; *accord* Kuehl v. Horner (J.W.) Lumber Co., 2004 SD 48, ¶ 10, 678 N.W.2d 809, 812.

[12] *Casillas*, ¶ 15, 714 N.W.2d at 88-89. The owner of a bull only owed a duty to keep the bull confined if the owner could have anticipated that injury to the users of the highway could result from the roaming bull. *Id.*

[13] *Poelstra*, ¶ 16, 545 N.W.2d at 826.

[14] *Id.* at ¶¶ 16 & 17, 545 N.W.2d at 826-27.

[15] Johnson v. Straight's, Inc., 288 N.W.2d 325, 327 (S.D. 1980).

[16] Kirlin v. Halverson, 2008 SD 107, ¶ 52, 758 N.W.2d 436, 453. There was no duty on the part of an employer to refuse to hire or terminate employment of an employee with *some* evidence of a violent past because of the strong public policy that employers would be hesitant to hire such individuals if there was potential liability. Such a result would impede employment opportunities and be contra to the concept of rehabilitation. *Id.* at 453-54.

[17] Thompson v. Summers, 1997 SD 103, ¶ 14, 567 N.W.2d 387, 392.

[18] Small v. McKennan Hosp., 403 N.W.2d 410, 413 (S.D. 1987) (citing RESTATEMENT (SECOND) OF TORTS § 315 (1965)).

[19] E.P. v. Riley, 1999 SD 163, ¶¶ 24, 26, 31, 32, 604 N.W.2d 7, 14-16.

[20] Veith v. O'Brien, 2007 S.D. 88, ¶ 60, 739 N.W.2d 15, 32.

potential complications of a medical procedure.[21] The duty of disclosure under the doctrine of informed consent is a personal duty of the physician and liability remains for a violation of this duty even if the doctor attempted to delegate the duty to subordinates.[22]

The common law categories of entrants upon land still dictate the scope of potential liability and the extent of the duty owed to the entrant upon land in South Dakota.[23] There are three categories: trespasser, licensee, and invitee.[24]

> These categories make out a sliding standard, where, as the legal status of the visitors improves, the landowner owes him or her a higher standard of care. At the top of the scale, the possessor of land owes the invitee "the duty of exercising reasonable or ordinary care for his safety and is liable for the breach of such duty." On the other hand, the licensee and trespasser "take the property as the visitors find it."[25]

However, licensees, or social guests, as compared to a trespasser, are owed the duty of warning of concealed dangers.[26] Heightened duties are owed to the invitee, or business visitor.[27]

The underlying philosophy of the common law is that "premises liability is based on possession and control."[28] "The possessor of land owes an invitee the duty of exercising reasonable care for the benefit of the invitee's safety" including maintaining the property in a reasonably safe condition.[29] The duty to use reasonable care for the benefit of invitees includes a duty to warn of concealed dangers on the land[30] and includes a duty to use care in the active operations on the land.[31] The duty to warn is tempered by the requirement that the owner of land must know of the dangerous concealed condition on the land.[32] Businesses, such as a hospital or shopping mall, owe a duty to protect entrants against criminal attacks of third parties if the attacks are foreseeable based upon the "totality of the circumstances" test,[33] not the "prior similar acts" rule.[34]

---

[21] *Veith,* ¶ 63, 739 N.W.2d at 33. Unless medically contraindicated, a surgeon has the obligation under the doctrine of informed consent to tell a patient that the surgeon believes a foreign object has been left inside the patient. Alberts v. Giebink, 299 N.W.2d 454, 456 (S.D. 1980).

[22] *Veith,* ¶ 61, 739 N.W.2d at 32.

[23] Andrushchenko v. Silchuk, 2008 SD 8, ¶ 22, 744 N.W.2d 850, 857-58.

[24] Musch v. H-D Elec. Co-op., Inc., 460 N.W.2d 149, 151 (S.D. 1990).

[25] *Id.* at 151-152 (citations omitted).

[26] *Andrushchenko,* ¶ 22, 744 N.W.2d at 858.

[27] *Id.*

[28] Englund v. Vital, 2013 S.D. 71, ¶ 12, 838 N.W.2d 621, 627.

[29] Johnson v. Matthew J. Batchelder Co., 2010 SD 23, ¶ 9, 779 N.W.2d 690, 693; *see also* Urban v. Wait's Supermarket, Inc., 294 N.W.2d 793, 795 (S.D. 1980).

[30] Mitchell v. Ankney, 396 N.W.2d 312, 313-14 (S.D. 1986).

[31] Pierce v. City of Belle Fourche, 2001 SD 41, ¶ 11, 624 N.W.2d 353, 355.

[32] Janis v. Nash Finch Co., 2010 SD 27, ¶ 12, 780 N.W.2d 497, 501.

[33] Kirlin v. Halverson, 2008 SD 107, ¶¶ 38, 40, 758 N.W.2d 436, 451.

[34] Small v. McKennan Hosp., 403 N.W.2d 410, 413 (S.D. 1987); *accord* Walther v. KPKA Meadowlands Ltd. Partner., 1998 SD 78, ¶ 46, 581 N.W. 2d 527, 536 (S.D. 1998).

A two-tier test must be meet before liability is extended for the criminal actions of others. The two factors are the existence of a special relationship and the foreseeability of the criminal attack.[35] Normally, there is no such special relationship between a lessor and lessee to require protection from criminal attacks[36] unless the affirmative acts by the landlord create a "high risk of harm from crime"[37] or there exists numerous prior incidents to put the landlord "on notice that there was probable danger to the tenants."[38]

The doctrine of gratuitous duty is accepted in South Dakota. Even if a duty of care was not owed originally, a duty of care is created by an actor who voluntarily undertakes a service toward another person that the actor should know is necessary to protect the other person. Failure to use reasonable care may create liability for the resulting damages if the actor increases the risk of harm or the other party relies on the undertaking.[39]

III. Breach of Duty

A. Elements

The "care an actor is required to exercise is that which a reasonable person should recognize is necessary to prevent his acts from creating an unreasonable risk of harm to another."[40] In order to fail to live up to the standard of care required by the law, an actor must fail to anticipate and guard against foreseeable risks from the standpoint of the ordinary person.[41] "Common law duty depends on foreseeability of the injury. The risk defines the duty to be obeyed. A person is not required to take measures against a risk which would not be anticipated by a reasonable person."[42] "[O]nce a duty is established, whether a breach of that duty occurred is for the finder of fact, not for the court."[43] Generally, breach of duty is shown by the failure to exercise ordinary care which places "another at risk of physical injury."[44] Generally, no liability is imposed for a failure to act; however, "once having acted, [one] must proceed without negligence."[45] The jury determines

---

[35] Walther v. KPKA Meadowlands Ltd. P'ship, 1998 SD 78, ¶ 41, 581 N.W.2d 527, 535; *accord Kirlin*, ¶ 31, 758 N.W.2d at 449.

[36] *Walther*, ¶ 42, 581 N.W.2d at 535. *See also* Smith *ex rel.* Ross v. Lagow Constr. & Developing Co., 2002 SD 37, 642 N.W.2d 187, wherein the court held that the landlord created a heightened duty by the manner in which locks to the apartments were changed. "If landlords insist on the exclusive right to change locks, then they may have some duty to change them when the locks are no longer effective [to protect] against foreseeable criminal activity." *Lagow*, ¶ 31, 642 N.W.2d at 194.

[37] Englund v. Vital, 2013 S.D. 71, ¶ 21, 838 N.W.2d 621, 629.

[38] *Id.* at ¶ 21, 838 N.W.2d at 630.

[39] Andrushchenko v. Silchuk, 2008 SD 8, ¶ 24, 744 N.W.2d 850, 858 (quoting RESTATEMENT (SECOND) OF TORTS § 323 (1965)).

[40] Johnson v. Straight's, Inc., 288 N.W.2d 325, 327 (S.D. 1980).

[41] Janis v. Nash Finch Co., 2010 SD 27, ¶ 15, 780 N.W.2d 497, 502-503.

[42] Pierce v. City of Belle Fourche, 2001 SD 41, ¶ 12, 624 N.W.2d 353, 355.

[43] Johnson v. Matthew J. Batchelder Co., 2010 SD 23, ¶ 10, 779 N.W.2d 690, 694; *see also* Pexa v. Clark, 176 N.W.2d 497, 500 (S.D. 1970).

[44] Zerfas v. Amco Ins., 2015 SD 99, ¶ 12, 873 N.W.2d 65, 70.

[45] Tipton v. Town of Tabor, 1997 SD 96, ¶ 13, 567 N.W.2d 351, 358.

whether the actor meets the standard of acting as the "ordinary prudent man would under similar circumstances."[46]

A child is held to a different standard than the adult standard unless the child is engaged in an adult activity, an activity "normally only undertaken by adults."[47] Once the minor is engaged in an adult activity, then the minor is held to the standard of a reasonable person under the circumstances.[48] Absent engagement in an adult activity, a minor is held to a "special (subjective) standard."[49] The child is held to the standard of care that another child of the same age, intelligence, experience, and capacity would exercise under similar circumstances.[50] Even if the child's behavior violates a safety statute, the violation is only a factor to consider in determining if the child complied with this "special standard," unless the minor is engaged in an adult activity.[51]

B. Evidence

The "unexcused violation of a statute enacted to promote safety constitutes negligence *per se.*"[52] However, the standard of care remains a jury issue if the actor offers evidence that his or her behavior was reasonable despite the violation of a safety statute.[53] The statute must be designed to protect or benefit a class of people that includes the injured party[54] and prevent the type of risk that has occurred.[55] However, proof of a violation is not sufficient to establish negligence absent proof that the statutory violation caused the injury.[56]

Res ipsa loquitur may be used in appropriate cases to infer negligence and establish a breach of the standard of care. However, it should be used "sparingly," when the "demands of justice make its application essential."[57] *Res ipsa* is a doctrine based on the "absence of specific proof."[58] Use of the doctrine of *res ipsa* is accordingly inappropriate when there is direct proof of the facts and the cause of the accident.[59] There are "three essential elements" that

---

[46] Baddou v. Hall, 2008 SD 90, ¶ 23, 756 N.W.2d 554, 560 (citing Weber v. Bernard, 349 N.W.2d 51, 53-54 (S.D. 1984)).

[47] Wittmeier v. Post, 105 N.W.2d 65, 68 (S.D. 1960).

[48] Alley v. Siepman, 214 N.W.2d 7, 10 (S.D. 1974).

[49] *Id.*

[50] *Id.*

[51] *Id.* at 11.

[52] Hertz Motel v. Ross Signs, 2005 SD 72, ¶ 9, 698 N.W.2d 532, 535. The National Electric Code (NEC) was "enacted to protect the public from personal injuries and property damage resulting from the improper installation of neon lighting systems." *Id.* at ¶ 12, 698 N.W.2d at 535. *See also* Thompson v. Summers, 1997 SD 103, ¶ 13, 567 N.W.2d 387, 393.

[53] Baddou v. Hall, 2008 SD 90, ¶ 27, 756 N.W.2d 554, 561.

[54] Peterson v. Spink Elec. Co-op., Inc., 1998 SD 60, ¶ 17, 578 N.W.2d 589, 592 (quoting Lovell v. Oahe Elec. Co-op., 382 N.W.2d 396, 398 (S.D. 1986) (citing Albers v. Ottenbacher, 116 N.W.2d 529, 531 (S.D. 1962)).

[55] Lovell v. Oahe Elec. Co-op., 382 N.W.2d 396, 398 (S.D. 1986).

[56] *Hertz Motel,* ¶ 13, 698 N.W.2d at 535; *see also* Fritz v. Howard Twp., 1997 SD 122, ¶ 17, 570 N.W.2d 240, 243.

[57] Shipley v. City of Spearfish, 235 N.W.2d 911, 913 (S.D. 1975).

[58] Malloy v. Commonwealth Highland Theaters, Inc., 375 N.W.2d 631, 636 (S.D. 1985).

[59] *Id.* at 637.

must be established before the doctrine of *res ipsa* may be used. They are, as follows: "(1) the instrumentality which caused the injury must have been under the full management and control of the defendant or his servants; (2) the accident was such that, according to knowledge and experience, does not happen if those having management or control had not been negligent; and (3) the plaintiff's injury must have resulted from the accident."[60] However, in medical negligence cases an expert normally must testify that the accident is not one that would occur in the medical setting "in the absence of a hospital's or physician's negligence."[61]

A defendant's own internal standards may be considered by the jury in determining the standard of care.[62] However, public policy encourages higher standards of care than the care commonly employed.[63] As a result, internal standards are not determinative of the standard of care particularly when there is evidence that the policy was above the normal standard of care.[64] Similarly, standards of an industry, governmental bodies, or customs of a community "are factors to be taken into account, but are not controlling where a reasonable man would not follow them."[65] Custom is relevant because it is behavior that the "community deems as proper under the circumstances," unless the custom violates a safety statute.[66]

In medical negligence causes of action, the standard of care is whether the health care provider complied with the accepted standards of the medical profession.[67] Normally, physicians and hospitals are judged by the customary practice of other professionals or facilities in the same or similar circumstances practicing in the same or similar localities.[68] However, medical specialists are held to a national, not local, standard of care. The standard is how others in the same speciality would have performed.[69]

---

[60] Wuest *ex rel.* Carver v. McKennan Hosp., 2000 S.D. 151, ¶18, 619 N.W.2d 682, 688 (quoting Van Zee v. Sioux Valley Hosp., 315 N.W.2d 489, 492 (S.D. 1982) (other citations omitted).

[61] *Wuest*, ¶¶ 18, 29, 619 N.W.2d at 688. For example, the fact that a patient commits suicide doesn't infer negligence under *res ipsa* because an expert testified that suicides can occur even when reasonable care is used. *Id.* If the accident falls within the common knowledge rule, one that a layperson would know only occurs as a result of negligence, then expert testimony is not required. *Id.*

[62] *Id.* at ¶18, 619 N.W.2d at 688-89.

[63] *Id.* at ¶19, 619 N.W.2d at 689.

[64] *Id.* For example, the hospital policy required the bathroom door to be locked when not in use. That policy was not determinative on the issue of whether reasonable care required a locked door because there was testimony that the "bathroom door policy was above the required community standard of care." *Id.*

[65] Zacher v. Budd Co., 396 N.W.2d 122, 133-34 (S.D. 1986).

[66] Alley v. Siepman, 214 N.W.2d 7, 11 (S.D. 1974).

[67] Veith v. O'Brien, 2007 S.D. 88, ¶¶ 47 & 49, 739 N.W.2d 15, 29.

[68] Wuest *ex rel.* Carver v. McKennan Hosp., 2000 S.D. 151, ¶¶ 15 & 23, 619 N.W.2d 682, 687-88, 689 (citing Shamburger v. Behrens, 418 N.W.2d 299, 306 (S.D. 1988), *overruled on other grounds by* Russo v. Takata Corp., 2009 S.D. 83, 774 N.W.2d 441).

[69] Veith v. O'Brien, 2007 S.D. 88, ¶ 49, n. 23, 739 N.W.2d 15, 29, n. 23 (citing Shamburger v. Behrens, 418 N.W.2d 299 (S.D. 1988)).

IV.   Causation

A.   *Elements*

Most states require both cause-in-fact and proximate cause as two distinct requirements to establish liability for negligence. South Dakota does not recognize the distinction
between the two doctrines. "While there may be an academic difference between legal cause
and factual cause, the current law on proximate cause in South Dakota does not note the distinction."[70] South Dakota adopts the "substantial factor" test of causation[71] and it is improper
to use the "but-for" test.[72] However, use of either the "substantial factor" test or the "foreseeability" approach is permissible.[73]

Proximate cause has been described as a "cause that produces a result in a natural
and probable sequence *and without which the result would not have occurred.*"[74] A proximate
cause "must be a substantial factor in bringing about the harm."[75] Further, the harm must be
foreseeable for proximate cause to exist.[76] South Dakota distinguishes the use of foreseeability in causation as compared with foreseeability as applied to the concept of duty. "As to
causation, foreseeability is a fact question and is examined at the time the damage was done.
By contrast, 'foreseeability in defining the boundaries of a duty is always a question of law'
and is examined at the time the act or omission occurred."[77]

However, a cause does not have to be the sole cause in order for liability to attach
thereto.[78] Concurrent causes exist where two forces combine to produce the result; the mere
fact other causes contribute to the result does not absolve the tortfeasor from liability.[79]

B.   *Evidence*

Absolute certainty is not required to prove causation. The plaintiff "has the burden of
establishing that there is sufficient evidence for the factfinder 'to reasonably' conclude, without resort to speculation, that the preponderance favors liability."[80] Reasonable people should
be able to conclude that the defendant's conduct was the cause of the plaintiff's harm.[81]

---

[70] Musch v. H-D Co-op., Inc., 487 N.W.2d 623, 624 (S.D. 1992).

[71] *Id.*

[72] *Id.* at 625.

[73] *Id.* at 626.

[74] Hertz Motel v. Ross Signs, 2005 SD 72, ¶ 19, 698 N.W.2d 532, 537 (emphasis in original) (quoting First
Premier Bank v. Kolcraft Enters., Inc., 2004 SD 92, ¶ 62, 686 N.W.2d 430, 454).

[75] Leslie v. City of Bonesteel, 303 N.W.2d 117, 119 (S.D. 1981).

[76] *Id.*

[77] Zerfas v. Amco Ins., 2015 SD 99, ¶ 14, 873 N.W.2d 65, 70 (quoting Johnson v. Hayman & Assocs., Inc., 2015
S.D. 63, ¶ 13, 867 N.W. 698, 702 (quoting Braun v. New Hope Twp., 2002 S.D. 67, ¶ 9, 646 N.W.2d 737, 740).

[78] *Leslie,* 303 N.W.2d at 120; *see also* Wierzbicki v. U.S., 32 F. Supp. 3d 1013, 1025 (D.S.D. 2014); State v.
Mollman, 2003 SD 150, ¶ 9, 674 N.W.2d 22, 26.

[79] *Leslie,* 303 N.W.2d at 120; *see also* Carver v. McKennan Hosp., 2000 S.D. 151, ¶ 24, 619 N.W.2d 682, 689;
Rumbolz v. Wipf, 82 S.D. 327, 145 N.W.2d 520 (S.D. 1966); Rowan v. Becker, 73 S.D. 273, 41 N.W.2d 836 (S.D.
1950); Krumvieda v. Hammond, 71 S.D. 544, 27 N.W.2d 583 (S.D. 1947).

[80] *Leslie,* 303 N.W.2d at 119.

[81] *Id.*

Normally, it is the jury who decides whether proximate cause is present under the facts of any given case.[82] The following jury instruction has been endorsed by the Supreme Court of South Dakota regarding causation:

> When the expression "proximate cause" is used, it means an immediate cause of any injury, which, in natural or probable sequence, produces the injury complained of. Without the proximate cause, the injury would not occur. The proximate cause need not be the only cause, nor the last or nearest cause. It is sufficient if it concurs with some other cause acting at the same time, which in combination with it causes the injury.
>
> For proximate cause to exist, you must find that the harm suffered was a foreseeable consequence of the act complained of.[83]

An intervening cause may supersede the liability of a negligent actor. A superseding cause occurs when "the natural and continuous sequence of causal connection between the negligent conduct and the injury is interrupted by a new and independent cause, which itself products the injury, that intervening cause operates to relieve the original wrongdoer of liability."[84] In order for an intervening cause to become a superceding cause, the intervening cause "must so entirely supersede the operation of the defendant's negligence that it alone . . . produces the injury."[85] The appropriate inquiry is whether the original actor's liability should extend to the consequences that result from the intervention of the outside cause.[86] Many factors are considered in determining whether an intervening cause is a superceding one. Two of the most important factors are the relationship between the parties and foreseeability.[87]

V. Damages

A. Elements

Recoverable damages include compensation for loss wages, including loss earning capacity in the future, medical expenses, both already incurred and that will be incurred in the future, and pain and suffering.[88] The award for pain and suffering includes the nature, extent, and duration of the pain and suffering including any "mental anguish and loss of capacity of the enjoyment of life she experienced."[89] The amount of pain and suffering is

---

[82] Hertz Motel v. Ross Signs, 2005 SD 72, ¶ 22, 698 N.W.2d 532, 538.

[83] Wuest *ex rel.* Carver v. McKennan Hosp., 2000 S.D. 151, ¶ 24, 619 N.W.2d 682, 689; *accord* Musch v. H-D Co-op Inc., 487 N.W.2d 623, 625 (S.D. 1992).

[84] Braun v. New Hope Twp., 2002 SD 67, ¶ 10, 646 N.W.2d 737, 740.

[85] *Id.*

[86] *Id.* at ¶ 11, 646 N.W.2d at 740.

[87] *Id.* at ¶ 14, 646 N.W.2d at 741.

[88] Reinfeld v. Hutcheson, 2010 SD 42, ¶ 17, 783 N.W.2d 284, 289-90.

[89] *Id.*

usually left to the "good judgment of the jury"[90] because there is no means of evaluating it's measure with mathematical certainty.[91]

Medical expenses sustained and pain and suffering endured prior to death may be recovered provided that the decedent was conscious and endured the pain and suffering.[92] The designated class of beneficiaries may also bring an independent cause of action for wrongful death.[93]

The measure of damages for damage to real property is generally the lesser of the following amounts: "The difference between the reasonable value of the house [or condition on the land] immediately before and immediately after its injury, or [t]he reasonable expense of repair if the house [or condition] can thereby be substantially restored to its former condition."[94]

B.   Evidence

The amount of damages is typically a question for the jury to decide and the amount of the verdict will only be set aside in unique cases where there exists proof that the verdict was the result of passion or prejudice by the jury.[95] If the amount of the verdict can be explained based on the evidence adduced at trial, then the verdict should be affirmed.[96] Furthermore, an award for medical bills without an accompanying award for pain and suffering is sustainable if there is evidence that "the plaintiff's injuries were not related to the defendant's negligence."[97] A simple prayer for recovery of damages for the loss of enjoyment of life does not render the plaintiff's mental or emotional state relevant.[98]

Payments received by the plaintiff from a collateral source do not reduce the damages that are recovered from the wrongdoer. "No reason in law, equity or good conscience can be advanced why a wrongdoer should benefit from part payment from a collateral source of damages caused by his wrongful act. If there must be a windfall certainly it is more just that the injured person shall profit therefrom, rather than the wrongdoer shall be relieved of his full responsibility for his wrongdoing."[99] Thus, the collateral source rule precludes admission into evidence of "amounts 'written off' by medical care providers because of

---

[90] Plank v. Heirigs, 156 N.W.2d 193, 204 (S.D. 1968).

[91] *Id.* at 203.

[92] *Id.* at 196, 200-201.

[93] *Id.* at 196.

[94] Ward v. LaCreek Elec. Assoc., 163 N.W.2d 344, 349 (S.D. 1968).

[95] Waldner v. Berglund, 2008 SD 75, ¶ 14, 754 N.W.2d 832, 836; *see also* Stoltz v. Stonecypher, 336 N.W.2d 654, 657 (S.D. 1983).

[96] *Waldner,* ¶ 14, 754 N.W. 2d at 837; *accord* Andreson v. Black Hills Power & Light Co., 1997 SD 12, ¶¶ 7 & 8, 559 N.W.2d 886, 888; Nelson v. Rahman, 219 N.W.2d 474, 476 (S.D. 1974).

[97] Reinfeld v. Hutcheson, 2010 SD 42, 783 N.W.2d 284, 290 (for example, if the plaintiff has a preexisting injury that could have caused the pain and suffering); *but see* Morrison v. Mineral Palace, 1998 SD 33, 576 N.W.2d 869, 871 (a verdict for medical bills without an award of pain and suffering is generally considered inadequate).

[98] Kostel v. Schwartz, 2008 SD 85, ¶ 83, 756 N.W.2d 363, 388.

[99] Papke v. Harbert, 2007 SD 87, ¶ 62, 738 N.W.2d 510, 531 (quoting Grayson v. Williams, 256 F.2d 61, 65 (10th Cir. 1958)).

contractual agreements" with third party payors of health care services, such as Medicare or Medicaid.[100]

Punitive damages may be awarded for misbehavior that amounts to "oppression, fraud, deceit, misrepresentation, malice, willful and wanton misconduct, or reckless disregard of plaintiff's rights."[101] They are awarded to punish the defendant and to deter similar future behavior.[102] The following five factors are considered in determining the amount of punitive damages: "(1) the amount allowed in compensatory damages, (2) the nature and enormity of the wrong, (3) the intent of the wrongdoer, (4) the wrongdoer's financial condition, and (5) all of the circumstances attendant to the wrongdoer's actions."[103] Compensatory damages must be awarded before an award of punitive damages is considered appropriate in South Dakota.[104] Even malicious or reprehensible conduct does not warrant punishment unless it causes injury.[105] Otherwise, there would be "an incentive to bring 'petty outrages' to court."[106] Furthermore, there must be a reasonable relationship between the punitive and compensatory award for the punitive award to withstand judicial scrutiny.[107]

---

[100] *Papke*, ¶ 80, 738 N.W.2d at 536; *see also* Kostel v. Schwartz, 2008 SD 85, ¶ 89, 756 N.W.2d 363, 389.

[101] Schaffer v. Edward D. Jones & Co., 1996 SD 94, ¶ 15, 552 N.W.2d 801, 806-07 n.3.

[102] *Id.* at ¶ 25, 552 N.W.2d at 809.

[103] *Id.* at ¶ 27, 552 N.W.2d at 810.

[104] Henry v. Henry, 2000 SD 4, ¶ 5, 604 N.W.2d 285, 288.

[105] *Id.*

[106] *Id.* (quoting PROSSER AND KEETON, THE LAW OF TORTS, § 2 (5th ed. 1984)).

[107] Henry v. Henry, 2000 SD 4, ¶ 5, 604 N.W.2d 285, 288.

CHAPTER 43

TENNESSEE

TENNESSEE

Danny Ellis[1]
Gary Massey Jr.[2]
Josh Ward[3]

I. Purpose of Tort Law

The Supreme Court of Tennessee has stated that the purpose of tort law is to protect people from another's act or conduct.[4] The court has also stated that "some deterrent is required to assure that due care will be exercised by providers of avoidance techniques, which deterrence is one of the operative policies of tort law."[5] Deterrence is promoted by liability for personal injury.[6] Further, they have stated that "compensation for an injury to a legally protected interest is another tort policy involved."[7]

II. Duty to Exercise Ordinary Care

A. *Question of Law*

In order to establish negligence, a plaintiff must prove that there was "a duty of care owed by defendant to plaintiff."[8] Generally, all persons have a broad duty to exercise reasonable care to avoid causing foreseeable injury to others.[9] The question is whether, based on the facts, "such a relation exists between the parties that the community will impose a legal obligation upon one for the benefit of others—or, more simply, whether the interest of the plaintiff which has suffered invasion was entitled to legal protection at the hands of the defendant."[10] This "reflects society's contemporary policies and social requirements concerning the right of individuals and the general public to be protected from another's acts or conduct."[11] The court must weigh the foreseeable risk and gravity of the harm against the burden placed on the defendant to engage in alternative conduct which would have prevented the

---

[1] Attorney, Massey & Associates, PC, Member of the Tennessee and Georgia Bar Associations.

[2] Attorney, Massey & Associates, PC, Member of the Tennessee Bar Association.

[3] Attorney, Massey & Associates, PC, Member of the Tennessee Bar Association.

[4] Bradshaw v. Daniel, 854 S.W.2d 865, 870 (Tenn. 1993).

[5] Smith v. Gore, 728 S.W.2d 738, 748 (Tenn. 1987).

[6] Lincoln Gen. Ins. v. Detroit Diesel Corp., 293 S.W.3d 487, 491 (Tenn. 2009).

[7] *Id.*

[8] McCall v. Wilder, 913 S.W.2d 150, 153 (Tenn. 1995).

[9] Draper v. Westerfield, 181 S.W.3d 283, 291 (Tenn. 2005).

[10] Lindsey v. Miami Dev. Corp., 689 S.W.2d 856, 858-59 (Tenn. 1985).

[11] Nichols v. Atnip, 844 S.W.2d 655 (Tenn. Ct. App. 1992).

harm.[12] The "degree" of foreseeability required to establish duty "decreases in proportion" as the gravity of the harm increases.[13] The "balancing factors" used to determine whether a duty of care exists are: (1) the foreseeable probability of the harm or injury occurring; (2) the possible magnitude of the potential harm or injury; (3) the importance or social value of the activity engaged in by the defendant: (4) the usefulness of the conduct to the defendant; (5) the feasibility of alternative conduct that is safer; (6) the relative costs and burdens associated with the safer conduct; (7) the relative usefulness of the safer conduct: and (8) the relative safety of the alternative conduct.[14]

B. *Question of Fact*

i. **Elements**

Once duty is established, the scope of the duty of care is a question of fact for the jury.[15] The line between "duty as law" and "scope of duty as fact" is difficult to see, and often cannot be distinguished.[16] Foreseeability is the test for negligence.[17] The inquiry is whether defendant's conduct created an unreasonable risk of harm to the plaintiff.[18] The injury sustained must be within the foreseen reasonable range of risks created by defendant's conduct.[19]

ii. **Evidence**

Generally, evidence of custom, usage, and practice is admissible on the issue of due care required under the circumstances.[20] Safety rules and/or policies the defendant is aware of are admissible as evidence for determining the scope of due care,[21] but do not have the same effect of statutes or municipal ordinances which establish the level of care required.[22] Negligence as a matter of law may be demonstrated with evidence of violation of a statute when a plaintiff belongs to a class of persons a statute was designed to protect and when a plaintiff's injury is of the type that the statute was designed to prevent.[23]

---

[12] Friedenstab v. Short, 174 S.W.3d 217, 225 (Tenn. 2004).

[13] Pittman v. Upjohn Col, 890 S.W.2d 425, 433 (Tenn. 1994).

[14] Satterfield v. Breeding Insulation Co., 266 S.W.3d 347, 367 (Tenn. 2008).

[15] Dooley v. Everett, 805 S.W.2d 380, 384 (Tenn. Ct. App. 1990).

[16] Friedenstab v. Short, 174 S.W.3d 217, 225 (Tenn. 2004).

[17] Lancaster v. Montesi, 390 S.W.2d 217, 220 (Tenn. 1965).

[18] *Id.*

[19] *Id.*

[20] Merchs. & Mfrs. Transfer Co. v. Johnston, 403 S.W.2d 106 (Tenn. 1966).

[21] Gross v. Nashville Gas Co., 608 S.W.2d 860, 867-9 (Tenn. Ct. App. 1980).

[22] Snider v. Snider, 855 S.W.2d 588, 591 (Tenn. Ct. App. 1993).

[23] Rains v. Bend of the River, 124 S.W.3d 580, 591 (Tenn. Ct. App. 2003). Watkins v. Affiliated Internists, P.C., 2012 WL 4086139, at 5 (Tenn. Ct. App. 2012).

III.   Breach of Duty

A.   *Elements*

Duty of care is a legal obligation owed by defendant to plaintiff to conform to a reasonable person standard of care for protection against unreasonable risks of harm.[24] Once the court has determined that the defendant owes a duty to the plaintiff, the questions of whether the defendant has breached his duty are matters to be determined by the jury.[25]

B.   *Evidence*

Material evidence must be presented to show a breach of duty on the part of the defendant.[26] Conduct taken by the defendant in the situation is proper evidence for this determination.[27] Evidence for all elements of negligence, including breach of duty, can be direct, circumstantial, or a combination of the two.[28]

IV.   Causation

A.   *Elements*

Causation and proximate cause are distinct elements of negligence, and both must be proven by the plaintiff by a preponderance of the evidence.[29] "Causation" means the harm would not have happened "but-for" the defendant's negligent conduct.[30] Tennessee applies a three-prong test for proximate cause: (1) the defendant's conduct must have been a substantial factor in bringing about the harm; (2) there is no rule or policy that relieves the wrongdoer from liability; and (3) the actual harm could have reasonably been foreseen or anticipated by a person of ordinary intelligence or prudence.[31] There is no requirement that defendant's conduct be the "sole cause" of the injury, provided it is a substantial factor in producing the result.[32] The plaintiff must show that the injury was a reasonably foreseeable probability, not just a remote possibility, and that some action within the defendant's control more probably than not would have prevented the injury.[33] Foreseeability must be determined as of the time of the acts or omissions claimed to be negligent.[34] "Where an act is one which a reasonable [person] would recognize as involving a risk of harm to another, the risk is unreasonable and the act is negligent if the risk is of such

---

[24] McClung v. Delta Square Ltd. Partn., 937 S.W.2d 891, 894 (Tenn. 1996).

[25] Patterson-Khoury v. Wilson World Hotel-Cherry Rd., Inc., 139 S.W.3d 281, 285 (Tenn. App. 2003).

[26] Doe v. Linder Const. Co., 845 S.W.2d 173, 183 (Tenn. 1992).

[27] Burton v. Warren Farmers Co-op., 129 S.W.3d 513, 523 (Tenn. App. 2002).

[28] *Id.*

[29] Kilpatrick v. Bryant, 868 S.W.2d 594, 598 (Tenn. 1993).

[30] *Id.*

[31] McClenahan v. Cooley, 806 S.W.2d 767, 775 (Tenn. 1991).

[32] *Id.*

[33] Doe v. Linder Const. Co., 845 S.W.2d 173, 178 (Tenn. 1992).

[34] *Id.*

magnitude as to outweigh what the law regards as the utility of the act or of the particular manner in which it is done."[35]

B.   Evidence

Proof of foreseeability is of critical importance in a negligence case to establish causation.[36] To satisfy the foreseeability requirement, the plaintiff need only show that some harm to someone was reasonably foreseeable.[37] Plaintiff need not prove that the defendant should have foreseen the exact manner in which the harm occurred.[38] The plaintiff must introduce evidence which affords a reasonable basis for the conclusion that it is more likely than not that the conduct of the defendant was a cause-in-fact of the result.[39] Where the plaintiff has introduced evidence that the defendant's conduct was a substantial factor in causing the injury, it is a question of fact for the jury.[40] Causation in fact and proximate causation are both jury questions.[41]

V.   Damages

A.   Elements

The damages in a negligence case are the amount that will compensate the plaintiff for all harm caused and make the plaintiff whole again.[42] Under the modified comparative fault system adopted in Tennessee, the plaintiff may recover so long as the plaintiff's negligence remains less than the defendant's negligence.[43]

B.   Evidence

To support an award of damages, the plaintiff must establish proof of damages within a reasonable degree of certainty.[44] Compensatory damages compensate for the actual loss.[45] The amount of damages is for the determination of the jury.[46]

---

[35] McCall v. Wilder, 913 S.W.2d 150, 153 (Tenn. 1995).

[36] Rathnow v. Knox County, 209 S.W.3d 629, 633 (Tenn. Ct. App. 2006).

[37] McClenahan v. Cooley, 806 S.W.2d 767, 775 (Tenn. 1991).

[38] *Id.*

[39] Kilpatrick v. Bryant, 868 S.W.2d 594, 602 (Tenn. 1993).

[40] Hale v. Ostrow, 166 S.W.3d 713, 719 (Tenn. 2005).

[41] McClenahan v. Cooley, 806 S.W.2d 767, 775 (Tenn. 1991).

[42] Goff v. Elmo Greer & Sons Const. Co., 297 S.W.3d 175, 187 (Tenn. 2009).

[43] McIntyre v. Balentine, 833 S.W.2d 52, 57 (Tenn. 1992).

[44] Airline Const. Inc., v. Barr, 807 S.W.2d 247, 256 (Tenn. Ct. App. 1990).

[45] Johnson v. Woman's Hosp., 527 S.W.2d 133, 142 (Tenn. Ct. App. 1975).

[46] Transps., Inc., v. Perry, 414 S.W.2d 1, 5 (Tenn. 1967).

CHAPTER 44

TEXAS

TEXAS

Michael Panesar[1]

I. Purpose of Tort Law

Safety of life and limb from the foreseeable mayhem of unreasonable human activity is at the heart of Texas tort law.[2] "The fundamental purposes of our tort system are to deter wrongful conduct, shift losses to responsible parties, and fairly compensate deserving victims."[3] One objective of tort litigation is to modify the defendant's behavior—and the behavior of others who want to engage in the same conduct—by deterring conduct considered after the fact to be unreasonable.[4] Courts have always sought to reflect and adapt to changes in society acting to balance both individual and societal interests. Our courts have always recognized and used tort law's unique ability to deter wrongdoing as a means of social policy.[5] This concept has, in fact, become a part of Texas law.[6]

II. Duty to Exercise Ordinary Care

A. *Elements*

The elements of a negligence cause of action consist of the "existence of a legal duty, a breach of that duty, and damages *proximately caused* by the breach."[7] Duty is a threshold

---

[1] Panesar Law Firm, Houston, Texas.

[2] Beaty v. Mo., Kan. & Tex. Ry. Co., 185 S.W. 298, 301 (Tex. 1916) (tracing history of railway company liability for passenger safety). A plaintiff prevailed in claim against a railway company for violation of a well-known "safety rule" designed to prevent this type of crash. Tex. & Pac. Ry. Co. v. Mallon, 65 Tex. 115 (Tex. 1885). Plaintiff cannot recover unless from the evidence the jury finds that the defendant was guilty of negligence in failing to provide a reasonably safe engine, or a reasonably safe track. Hous. & Tex. Cent. R.R. Co. v. Ray, 28 S.W. 256 (Tex. Civ. App. 1894).

[3] Ritchie v. Rupe, 443 S.W.3d 856, 889 (Tex. 2014); Roberts v. Williamson, 111 S.W.3d 113, 118 (Tex. 2003).

[4] Macmillan v. Redman Homes, Inc., 818 S.W.2d 87, 95-96 (Tex. App. 1991) (citing F. HARPER, F. JAMES, & O. GRAY, THE LAW OF TORTS §§ 12.4 & 25.22 (2d ed. 1986); PROSSER AND KEETON, THE LAW OF TORTS §4 (5th ed. 1984).

[5] RESTATEMENT (SECOND) OF TORTS § 901 (1965); *see also* Golden Spread Council, Inc. v. Akins, 926 S.W.2d 287, 293 (Tex. 1996) (Cornyn, J., concurring) (citing PROSSER AND KEETON, THE LAW OF TORTS §4 (5th ed. 1984) (referring to the "prophylactic" purpose of tort law)).

[6] *See, e.g.,* McKisson v. Sales Affiliates, Inc., 416 S.W.2d 787 (Tex. 1967) (recognizing strict products liability); Leal v. C.C. Pitts Sand & Gravel, Inc., 419 S.W.2d 820 (Tex. 1967) (finding an unborn child is able to recover); Otis Eng'g Corp. v. Clark, 668 S.W.2d 307 (Tex. 1983) (holding an employer could be liable for the negligence of a drunken off-duty employee); *see also* Nelson v. Krusen, 678 S.W.2d 918, 932 (Tex. 1984) (Kilgarlin, J., concurring & dissenting).

[7] Gharda USA, Inc. v. Control Sols., Inc., 464 S.W.3d 338, 352 (Tex. 2015).

question of law.[8] It is fundamental that the existence of a legally cognizable duty is a prerequisite to all tort liability.[9] If there is no legal duty, there is no liability for negligence.[10]

Duties are found in common law, statute or rule, contract, and sometimes as a result of a special relationship.[11] In the absence of a specific legally prescribed duty, Texas law imposes a general duty on all persons to exercise ordinary care to avoid foreseeable injury to others.[12] A person owes another the duty to act as a reasonably prudent person would act under the same or similar circumstances regarding a reasonably foreseeable risk.[13] A duty to act reasonably, therefore, turns on the foreseeability of the risk, or what a person should, under the circumstances, reasonably anticipate as a consequence of his conduct.[14]

There is no general duty in Texas to control others, but a special relationship may sometimes give rise to a duty to aid or protect others.[15] Texas law may impose a duty to act in the case of an employer/employee relationship, where the employer has a right to control the employee, who caused the harm.[16] The Texas Supreme Court defined the parameters of the duty in the employer/employee context in *Pagayon v. Exxon Mobil*. One convenience store employee started a fistfight with another employee and that employee's father. The father was knocked to the ground, and taken to the hospital. Twenty-three days later, the father died. Pagayon sued Exxon Mobil for failing to control and supervise the employee that started the fight. The Court held that Texas does not recognize the duty set out in Section 317 of the Restatement (Second) of Torts because it imposes too great a

---

[8] Nabors Drilling, U.S.A., Inc. v. Escolo, 288 S.W.3d 401, 404 (Tex. 2009); Centeq Realty, Inc. v. Siegler, 899 S.W.2d 195, 197 (Tex. 1995); Greater Hous. Transp. Co. v. Phillips, 801 S.W.2d 523, 525 (Tex. 1990); El Chico Corp. v. Poole, 732 S.W.2d 306, 311 (Tex. 1987); Otis Eng'g Corp. v. Clark, 668 S.W.2d 307, 312 (Tex. 1983); Pagayon v. Exxon Mobil Corp., No. 15-0642, 2017 WL 2705530, at *3 (Tex. June 23, 2017).

[9] Graff v. Beard, 858 S.W.2d 918, 919 (Tex. 1993).

[10] Thapar v. Zezulka, 994 S.W.2d 635, 637 (Tex. 1999).

[11] Midwest Emps. Cas. Co. v. Harpole, 293 S.W.3d 770, 776 (Tex. App. 2009) (common law); Perry v. S.N., 973 S.W.2d 301, 306-07 (Tex. 1998) (civil statutes); Nixon v. Mr. Prop. Mgmt. Co., 690 S.W.2d 546, 549 (Tex. 1985) (city ordinance); Carter v. William Sommerville & Son, Inc., 584 S.W.2d 274, 279 (Tex. 1979) (criminal statute); Continental Oil Co. v. Simpson, 604 S.W.2d 530, 534 (Tex. App. 1980) (administrative rules and regulations); Pagayon v. Exxon Mobil Corp., No. 15-0642, 2017 WL 2705530, at *3 (Tex. June 23, 2017) (employer/employee). In legal and CPA malpractice cases, plaintiff must prove a contractual relationship. Kennedy v. Gulf Coast Cancer & Diagnostic Ctr. at Se., Inc., 326 S.W.3d 352, 357 (Tex. App. 2010); Greenstein, Logan & Co. v. Burgess Mktg., Inc., 744 S.W.2d 170, 185 (Tex. App. 1987).

[12] El Chico Corp. v. Poole, 732 S.W.2d 306, 311 (Tex. 1987); *but see* Torrington Co. v. Stuzman, 46 S.W.3d 829, 837 (Tex. 2000) ("no duty to take action or prevent harm to others absent certain special relationships or circumstances").

[13] Colvin v. Red Steel Co., 682 S.W.2d 243, 245 (Tex. 1984).

[14] Texas Home Mgmt., Inc. v. Peavy, 89 S.W.3d 30, 36 (Tex. 2002).

[15] Pagayon v. Exxon Mobil Corp., No. 15-0642, 2017 WL 2705530, at *3 (Tex. June 23, 2017).

[16] Humble Sand & Gravel, Inc. v. Gomez, 146 S.W.3d 170 (Tex. 2004); Pagayon v. Exxon Mobil Corp., No. 15-0642, 2017 WL 2705530, at *3 (Tex. June 23, 2017).

burden on the employment relationship.[17] The employer in this situation owed no duty as a matter of law.[18]

When a duty has not been recognized in a particular circumstance, the question then becomes whether a duty should be imposed for the defined class of cases.[19] In such circumstances, the following factors must be analyzed before recognizing a duty:

> The considerations include social, economic, and political questions and their application to the facts at hand. We have weighed the risk, foreseeability, and likelihood of injury against the social utility of the actor's conduct, the magnitude of the burden of guarding against the injury, and the consequences of placing the burden on the defendant. Also among the considerations are whether one party would generally have superior knowledge of the risk or a right to control the actor who caused the harm.

When the factors for finding a duty are disputed, such as, when the risk and foreseeability are controverted, the question of fact cannot be determined as a matter of law and must be resolved by the factfinder. However, such cases are unusual.[20] To impose a duty, the factual situation must be evaluated in the broader context of similarly situated actors. The court must consider the "defined class of cases," and go beyond the specific case in front of the court. Further, the material fact questions for these elements are either undisputed or can be viewed in the light required by the procedural posture of the case. In *Pagayon v. Exxon Mobil Corp.*, the Court viewed the facts in favor of the verdict, making the question a matter of law. When the question of imposing a duty is one of policy (social, economic, or political), including the nature of the covered risks and general foreseeability,[21] the court considers these issues as a matter of law.

Most cases concerning whether a duty exists center around whether the risk is foreseeable.[22] Chief Judge Benjamin Nathan Cordoza, writing the four-to-three majority opinion in *Palsgraf*, inked the concept of foreseeability and zone of danger into the tort analysis, limiting an actor's duty to those foreseeably harmed by negligence, thus denying Ms. Palsgraf's

---

[17] "A master is under a duty to exercise reasonable care so to control his servant while acting outside the scope of his employment as to prevent him from intentionally harming others or from so conducting himself as to create an unreasonable risk of bodily harm to them, if (a) the servant (i) is upon the premises in possession of the master or upon which the servant is privileged to enter only as his servant, or (ii) is using a chattel of the master, and (b) the master (i) knows or has reason to know that he has the ability to control his servant, and (ii) knows or should know of the necessity and opportunity for exercising such control." RESTATEMENT (SECOND) OF TORTS § 317 (1965).

[18] Pagayon v. Exxon Mobil Corp., No. 15-0642, 2017 WL 2705530, at *8 (Tex. June 23, 2017).

[19] Pagayon v. Exxon Mobil Corp., No. 15-0642, 2017 WL 2705530, at *3–4 (Tex. June 23, 2017) (citing Humble Sand & Gravel, Inc. v. Gomez, 146 S.W.3d 170 (Tex. 2004)).

[20] Pagayon v. Exxon Mobil Corp., No. 15-0642, 2017 WL 2705530, at *4 (Tex. June 23, 2017).

[21] This line in the opinion contradicts the obvious example of foreseeability being a fact question for the trier of fact. If "general foreseeability" relates to the policy of foreseeability, then the court is reviewing a social, legal policy question. If the foreseeability of a plaintiff and injury from the defendant's negligence is in question, then that can only be a fact question. The policy has already been decided to hold wrongdoers responsible.

[22] Greater Houston Transp. Co. v. Phillips, 801 S.W.2d 523, 525 (Tex. 1990).

recovery.[23] The three dissenting members of the court contended that everyone owes to the world at large the duty to refrain from acts that may reasonably threaten the safety of others.[24] While Texas does not go as far as the dissent, Texas does depart from the strict, i.e., limited, foreseeability analysis of *Palsgraf* when analyzing the concept of duty.[25]

B.   *Evidence*

When the factors for duty turn on facts that cannot be determined as a matter of law, then the factual disputes must be resolved by the factfinder.[26] Expert testimony is generally not necessary to establish the applicable standard of care when the alleged negligence is of such a nature as to be within the common experience of laymen.[27] In determining whether expert testimony is necessary to establish negligence, Texas courts have considered whether the conduct at issue involves the use of specialized equipment and techniques unfamiliar to the ordinary person.[28] When expert testimony is necessary, the expert must establish the requisite standard of care and skill, the departure from that standard, and the causal link between the plaintiff's damages and the negligent act.[29]

III.   Breach of Duty

A.   *Elements*

The Texas Pattern Jury Charge (PJC) defines negligence as the failure to use ordinary care, that is, failing to do that which a person of ordinary prudence would have done under the same or similar circumstances or doing that which a person of ordinary prudence would not have done under the same or similar circumstances. "Ordinary care" means that degree of care that would be used by a person of ordinary prudence under the same or similar circumstances. The concept of ordinary care is so elastic that it can meet all emergencies, and the amount of care to be applied will depend on the circumstances presented.[30]

---

[23] Palsgraf v. Long Island R.R. Co., 162 N.E. 99 (N.Y. 1928).

[24] 248 N.Y. at 350, 162 N.E. at 103.

[25] Brown v. Edwards Transfer Co., 764 S.W.2d 220 (Tex. 1988) (Kilgarlin, J., concurring) (citing Kilgarlin & Sterba-Boatwright, *The Recent Evolution of Duty in Texas*, 28 S. Tex. L.J. 241, 306 (1986)); Powers, *Judge and Jury in the Texas Supreme Court*, 75 Tex. L. Rev. 1699, 1702-03 (1997) (explaining that Dean Keeton's approach to duty and proximate cause, in which questions about whether a defendant's liability extends to a particular type of plaintiff are questions of proximate cause and not duty, has prevailed in Texas); *Mellon Mortg. Co. v. Holder*, 5 S.W.3d 654, 655 (Tex. 1999) (plurality opinion) (*Palsgraf* teaches that the duty question properly considers the foreseeability of the injured party.).

[26] Pagayon v. Exxon Mobile Corp., No. 15-0642, 2017 WL 2705530, at *3 (Tex. June 23, 2017).

[27] FFE Transp. Serv., Inc. v. Fulgham, 154 S.W.3d 84, 90 (Tex. 2004).

[28] *Id.*

[29] *Id.*

[30] Prather v. Brandt, 981 S.W.2d 801, 811 (Tex. App. 1998).

B.   *Evidence*

The question of whether a defendant breached a standard of care is for the jury to decide.[31] When a duty requires a nonprofessional to exercise ordinary care, the defendant's standard of care is defined as what a person of ordinary prudence would or would not have done under the same or similar circumstances.[32] A professional breaches the professional's standard of care, when the profession does or fails to do what a professional of ordinary prudence in that particular field in the same or similar circumstances would have done.[33]

IV.   Causation

"Proximate cause" includes both cause-in-fact, meaning that "the act or omission was a substantial factor in bringing about the injuries, and without it, the harm would not have occurred" (cause-in-fact), and foreseeability.[34] Proximate cause is normally a question of fact, unless the evidence is undisputed and only one reasonable inference can be drawn.[35]

A.   *Elements*

i.   Cause-in-Fact

Cause-in-fact, but-for causation, requires proof "that an act or omission was a substantial factor in bringing about injury which would not otherwise have occurred."[36] Cause-in-fact is not established where a defendant's actions do no more than furnish a condition which makes the injuries possible.[37] In such a case, the defendant's conduct is too attenuated from the resulting injuries to be a substantial factor in bringing about the harm.[38]

ii.   Foreseeability

To be a proximate cause, the act or omission complained of must be such that a person using ordinary care would have foreseen that the event, or some similar event, might

---

[31] Brown v. Goldstein, 685 S.W.2d 640, 641-42 (Tex. 1985).

[32] Colvin v. Red Steel Co., 682 S.W.2d 243, 245 (Tex. 1984); Texas Pattern Jury Charges—General Negligence & Intentional Torts, PJC 2.1.

[33] Cosgrove v. Grimes, 774 S.W.2d 662, 664 (Tex. 1989) (attorney); Texas Pattern Jury Charges—Malpractice, Premises & Products, PJC 50.1.

[34] IHS Cedars Treatment Ctr., Inc. v. Mason, 143 S.W.3d 794, 798-99 (Tex. 2004); Ryder Integrated Logistics, Inc. v. Fayette Cty., 453 S.W.3d 922, 929 (Tex. 2015). *See also* Texas Pattern Jury Charge, PJC 2.4.

[35] Ambrosio v. Carter's Shooting Ctr., Inc., 20 S.W.3d 262, 266 (Tex. App. 2000).

[36] Prudential Ins. Co. of Am. v. Jefferson Assocs., Ltd., 896 S.W.2d 156, 161 (Tex. 1995); Transcon. Ins. Co. v. Crump, 330 S.W.3d 211, 222-23 (Tex. 2010).

[37] Givens v. M&S Imaging Partners, L.P., 200 S.W.3d 735, 738 (Tex. App. 2006).

[38] *Id.*; *see also* Providence Health Ctr. v. Dowell, 262 S.W.3d 324, 328-29 (Tex. 2008) (holding that the discharge of patient from emergency room, when patient had presented to emergency room with self-inflicted cut on wrist and then committed suicide thirty-three hours after discharge, "was simply too remote from his death in terms of time and circumstances" and, thus, plaintiffs presented insufficient evidence of proximate cause).

reasonably result therefrom.[39] The Texas Supreme Court uses a two-prong test for foresee-ability: (1) that the injury be of such a general character as might reasonably have been antic-ipated (anticipated injury); and (2) that the injured party should be so situated with relation to the wrongful act that injury to him or one similarly situated might reasonably have been foreseen (foreseeable plaintiff).[40] "Stated more broadly, we determine both the foreseeability of the general danger and the foreseeability that a particular plaintiff—or one similarly situated—would be harmed by that danger."[41]

The question of whether an injury or damage is foreseeable involves a practical in-quiry based on "common experience applied to human conduct."[42] It asks whether the injury might reasonably have been anticipated as a result of the defendant's conduct.[43] It is not neces-sary that the exact path leading to injury be anticipated as long as the general danger surround-ing the event is appreciated.[44] However, foreseeability requires more than someone, viewing the facts in retrospect, theorizing an extraordinary sequence of events whereby the defendant's conduct brings about the injury.[45] Foreseeability turns on "the risk and likelihood of injury" to a plaintiff, viewed from the standpoint of what the defendant knew or should have known.[46]

B.   Evidence

Cause-in-fact must be proven by either direct or circumstantial evidence, not mere conjecture, guess, or speculation.[47] The evidence must be sufficient for the jury to determine within a reasonable probability that the plaintiff's injury would not have occurred but-for the defendant's negligence.[48] To prove the foreseeability element of proximate cause, the plaintiff must put on evidence that a person of ordinary intelligence would have anticipated the danger created by the defendant's conduct.[49] The evidence must satisfy the two-part test of foreseeable plaintiff and foreseeable injury.

---

[39] Texas Pattern Jury Charges—General Negligence, PJC 2.4.

[40] The Texas cases cited for the two-prong foreseeability analysis discuss foreseeability only in the context of proximate cause, not duty. Nixon v. Mr. Prop. Mgmt. Co., 690 S.W.2d 546, 549-50 (Tex. 1985); Texas Cities Gas Co. v. Dickens, 168 S.W.2d 208, 212 (Tex. 1943); Carey v. Pure Distrib. Corp., 124 S.W.2d 847, 849-50 (Tex. 1939); San Antonio & Aransas Pass Ry. v. Behne, 231 S.W. 354, 356 (Tex. 1921). Moving the determination of whether harm to a certain class of potential plaintiffs is foreseeable from the proximate cause analysis to the duty analysis shifts the allocation of power in such cases. Powers, *Judge and Jury in the Texas Supreme Court*, 75 TEX. L. REV. 1699, 1703. Traditionally, duty is a threshold legal issue the court properly decides. Walker v. Harris, 924 S.W.2d 375, 377 (Tex. 1996); Powers, *Judge and Jury in the Texas Supreme Court*, 75 TEX. L. REV. 1699, 1703. Proximate cause is usually a jury issue. Clark v. Waggoner, 452 S.W.2d 437, 440 (Tex. 1970).

[41] Mellon Mortg. Co. v. Holder, 5 S.W.3d at 655.

[42] City of Gladewater v. Pike, 727 S.W.2d 514, 518 (Tex. 1987); Doe v. Boys Clubs of Greater Dallas, Inc., 907 S.W.2d 472, 477 (Tex. 1995); Read v. Scott Fetzer Co., 990 S.W.2d 732, 737 (Tex. 1998).

[43] City of Gladewater, 727 S.W.2d at 517.

[44] Trinity River Auth. v. Williams, 689 S.W.2d 883, 886 (Tex. 1985).

[45] Boys Clubs of Greater Dallas, 907 S.W.2d at 478.

[46] Del Lago Partners, Inc. v. Smith, 307 S.W.3d 762, 770 (Tex. 2010).

[47] Excel Corp. v. Apodaca, 81 S.W.3d 817, 820 (Tex. 2002).

[48] Lenger v. Physician's Gen. Hosp., Inc., 455 S.W.2d 703, 706 (Tex. 1970).

[49] Holloway v. Texas Elec. Utility Const., Ltd., 282 S.W.3d 207, 212 (Tex. App. 2009) (citing Nixon v. Mr. Prop. Mgmt. Co., 690 S.W.2d 546, 549-50 (Tex. 1985).

V. Damages

A. *Elements*

To establish causation in a personal injury case, a plaintiff must prove that the defendant's conduct caused an event and that the event caused the plaintiff to suffer compensable injuries.[50] The typical remedy in a civil case is an award of money damages sufficient to compensate the injured plaintiff.[51] Compensatory damages are intended to make the plaintiff "whole" for any losses resulting from the defendant's interference with the plaintiff's rights.[52] The primary purpose of awarding compensatory damages in civil actions is to fairly compensate the injured plaintiff.[53] Compensable injuries include past and future physical pain, mental anguish, disfigurement, physical impairment, medical expenses, loss of earning capacity, loss of consortium, and loss of services.[54]

B. *Evidence*

Under Texas law, "whether to award damages and how much is uniquely within the factfinder's discretion."[55] Thus, a jury thus has broad discretion to award damages within the range of evidence presented at trial.[56] Damages awarded must be fair and reasonable.[57] When the evidence supports a range of damages to be awarded, an award of damages within that range is an appropriate exercise of the jury's discretion.[58]

---

[50] Burroughs Wellcome Co. v. Crye, 907 S.W.2d 497, 499 (Tex. 1995).

[51] Cavnar v. Quality Control Parking, Inc., 696 S.W.2d 549, 552 (Tex. 1985); Reaugh v. McCollum Exploration Co., 139 Tex. 485, 163 S.W.2d 620, 621 (1942).

[52] *Cavnar*, 696 S.W.2d at 552; W. PAGE KEETON, ET AL., PROSSER AND KEETON, THE LAW OF TORTS §§ 1, 4 (5th ed. 1984); Transp. Ins. Co. v. Moriel, 879 S.W.2d 10, 16 (Tex. 1994).

[53] Enter. Prods. Partners, L.P. v. Mitchell, 340 S.W.3d at 482; Torrington Co. v. Stutzman, 46 S.W.3d 829, 848 (Tex. 2000).

[54] Texas Pattern Jury Charges—General Negligence & Intentional Personal Torts, PJC 15.1-15.12.

[55] Golden Eagle Archery, Inc. v. Jackson, 116 S.W.3d 757, 772 (Tex. 2003).

[56] City of Houston v. Harris Cty. Outdoor Adver. Ass'n, 879 S.W.2d 322, 334 (Tex. App. 1994).

[57] Saenz v. Fid. & Guar. Ins. Underwriters, 925 S.W.2d 607, 614 (Tex. 1996).

[58] Hani v. Jimenez, 264 S.W.3d 881, 888 (Tex. App. 2008).

CHAPTER 45

UTAH

UTAH

Andrew G. Deiss[1]

I. Purpose of Tort Law

Tort law in Utah serves the general objective of placing an individual who is harmed in the same position that he or she would have occupied had the harm never occurred.[2] By providing compensation to the injured and requiring individuals whose conduct causes harm to others to bear the full costs of their actions, tort law in Utah is aimed at protecting the health and safety of the public while deterring harmful behavior[3] and preventing future harm.[4]

II. Duty

A. Question of Law

To establish a claim of negligence, a plaintiff must establish that a defendant owed them a duty of care.[5] In Utah, duty is a question of law[6] and as a general rule, everyone has "a duty to exercise care when engaging in affirmative conduct that creates a risk of physical harm to others."[7] A duty is a legal obligation "to conform to a particular standard of conduct toward another."[8]

Utah courts look to several factors to determine whether a duty exists: "(1) whether the defendant's allegedly tortious conduct consists of an affirmative act or merely an omission, (2) the legal relationship of the parties, (3) the foreseeability or likelihood of injury, (4) public policy as to which party can best bear the loss occasioned by the injury, and (5) other general policy considerations."[9] However, these factors are not equally weighted in every case.[10]

With regard to duty, foreseeability is determined on a broad categorical level, and relates to the general relationship between the alleged tortfeasor and the victim and the

---

[1] Andrew G. Deiss is an attorney with Deiss Law PC in Salt Lake City, Utah. Mr. Deiss is a graduate of Yale University and the University of Chicago Law School.

[2] Kilpatrick v. Wiley, Rein & Fielding, 2001 UT 107, ¶ 97, 37 P.3d 1130, 1150.

[3] Scott v. Universal Sales, Inc., 2015 UT 64, ¶ 48, 356 P.3d 1172, 1185.

[4] Hill v. Superior Prop. Mgmt. Servs., Inc., 2013 UT 60, ¶ 17, 321 P.3d 1054, 1058; *see also* Higgins v. Salt Lake Cnty., 855 P.2d 231, 237 (Utah 1993).

[5] MacFarlane v. Applebee's Rest., 2016 UT App 158, ¶ 8, 378 P.3d 1286, 1288.

[6] B.R. *ex rel.* Jeffs v. West, 2012 UT 11, ¶ 25, 275 P.3d 228, 235.

[7] *Id.* at 234.

[8] *Id.*

[9] *Id.*

[10] *Id.*

general foreseeability of harm.[11] "The appropriate foreseeability question for duty analysis is whether a category of cases includes individual cases in which the likelihood of some type of harm is sufficiently high that a reasonable person could anticipate a general risk of injury to others."[12]

For example, Utah courts have recognized that healthcare providers have a duty to non-patients to exercise reasonable care when prescribing medication to patients in part because the harm to non-patients is a foreseeable result of improperly prescribing medication.[13] In *West,* the Utah Supreme Court reasoned that while "[s]ome negligent prescription cases may very well involve little foreseeable risk of injury" such as "a patient that has a rare violent reaction to ibuprofen. . . other cases may involve highly foreseeable risks, as where a physician mistakenly prescribes a high dose of a potent narcotic to an active airline pilot instead of the mild antibiotic the pilot needed."[14] Thus "[b]ecause the class of cases includes some in which a risk of injury to third parties is reasonably foreseeable," the foreseeability factor weighed "in favor of imposing a duty on healthcare providers to exercise care in prescribing medications so as to refrain from affirmatively causing injury to non-patients."[15] Similarly, Utah courts have recognized that gun owners owe a duty to exercise reasonable care in supplying their guns to others whom they know, or should know, are likely to use the gun in a manner that creates a foreseeable risk of injury to themselves or third parties.[16] Supplying others with a gun—an intoxicated individual for instance—clearly creates a foreseeable risk of harm to others and as such the foreseeability factor weighs in favor of imposing a duty.[17]

Notably, Utah courts may find a duty of care exists even where the parties do not have a legal relationship when other factors, including foreseeability, support a finding of duty.[18] For example, in *West*, the second factor in the duty analysis—the legal relationship of the parties—played no role in the court finding a duty because there is no "special relationship or physician-patient relationship" between a healthcare provider and a non-patient.[19]

III.   Standard of Care

The standard of care that applies to a given case and governs a given tortfeasor's conduct is analyzed by Utah courts as a stand-alone element that effectively bridges the duty

---

[11] Foreseeability is a factor in three of the four elements of negligence: duty, breach, and proximate cause. Foreseeability has a different connotation depending on the elements to which it is applied. With respect to the duty analysis, "foreseeability does not question the specifics of the alleged tortious conduct such as the specific mechanism of the harm. . . . [but] instead relates to the general relationship between the alleged tortfeasor and the victim and the general foreseeability" of harm. *Id.* at 234. (internal quotation marks and citations omitted).

[12] Buu Nguyen v. IHC Med. Servs., Inc., 2012 UT App 288, ¶ 14, 288 P.3d 1084, 1091 (citing *Jeffs*, 275 P.3d 228, 235-36).

[13] B.R. *ex rel.* Jeffs v. West, 2012 UT 11, ¶ 28, 275 P.3d 228, 236.

[14] *Id.*

[15] *Id.*

[16] Herland v. Izatt, 2015 UT 30, ¶ 10, 345 P.3d 661, 665.

[17] *Id.*

[18] *Id.*

[19] B.R. *ex rel.* Jeffs v. West, 2012 UT 11, ¶ 25, 275 P.3d 228, 235; *see generally* Benjamin C. Zipursky, *Foreseeability in Breach, Duty, and Proximate Cause,* 44 WAKE FOREST L.REV. 1247 (2009).

and breach elements.[20] However, some case law in Utah analyzes standard of care under the breach element alone.[21]

A. Elements

In a negligence action, the standard of care that a tortfeasor is required to conform to depends on the circumstances of the case and on the extent of the foreseeable danger involved.[22] In Utah, the standard of care is typically a question of fact to be resolved by the jury[23,24] although "the applicable standard of care in a given case may be established, as a matter of law, by legislative enactment or prior judicial decision."[25]

B. Evidence

Unless the standard of care has been determined as a matter of law, the plaintiff must present evidence of the required level of care.[26] Evidence of industry standards,[27] or what a reasonable person would do in same or similar circumstances, is probative of the level of care required.[28] Evidence of the foreseeable frequency and severity of the harm is also admissible to determine the level of care required.[29] Rules and regulations may be admitted as a "legitimate source for determining the standard of reasonable care."[30] Finally, in cases where the standard of care is not "within the common knowledge of the lay juror, testimony from relevant experts is generally required in order to ensure that factfinders have adequate knowledge upon which to" determine the appropriate standard of care.[31]

IV. Breach of Duty

A. Elements

Breach of a duty by the defendant is a necessary element of a negligence action.[32] Indeed, it is the very essence of a negligence claim.[33] "The issue of . . . breach of a legal duty

---

[20] Graves v. N. E. Servs., Inc., 2015 UT 28, ¶¶ 37-43, 345 P.3d 619, 627-28.

[21] B.R. *ex rel.* Jeffs v. West, 2012 UT 11, ¶¶ 26-28, 275 P.3d 228, 235-36.

[22] Rose v. Provo City, 2003 UT App 77, ¶ 9, 67 P.3d 1017, 1020-21.

[23] B.R. *ex rel.* Jeffs v. West, 2012 UT 11, ¶ 37, 275 P.3d 228, 238; Callister v. Snowbird Corp., 2014 UT App 243, ¶ 12, 337 P.3d 1044, 1048.

[24] Callister v. Snowbird Corp., 2014 UT App 243, ¶ 12, 337 P.3d at 1048 (*quoting* Wycalis v. Guardian Title, 780 P.2d 821, 825 (Utah Ct. App. 1989)).

[25] *Wycalis*, 780 P.2d at 825.

[26] *Compare* Wycalis v. Guardian Title, 780 P.2d 821, 825 (Utah Ct. App. 1989), *cert. denied*, 789 P.2d 33 (Utah 1990), *with* Cooper Enters., PC v. Brighton Title Co., 2010 UT App 135, ¶ 11, 233 P.3d 548, 551.

[27] Mitchell v. Pearson Enters., 697 P.2d 240, 244 (Utah 1985).

[28] Graves v. N.E. Servs., Inc., 2015 UT 28, ¶¶ 40-41, 345 P.3d 619, 627-28.

[29] Price v. Smith's Food & Drug Ctrs., Inc., 2011 UT App 66, ¶ 18, 252 P.3d 365, 369.

[30] Slisze v. Stanley-Bostitch, 1999 UT 20, ¶ 18, 979 P.2d 317, 321.

[31] Bowman v. Kalm, 2008 UT 9, ¶ 7, 179 P.3d 754, 755.

[32] Proctor v. Costco Wholesale Corp., 2013 UT App 226, ¶ 20, 311 P.3d 564, 572.

[33] Reeves v. Gentile, 813 P.2d 111, 116 (Utah 1991), *overruled on other grounds by* Red Flame, Inc. v. Martinez, 2000 UT 22, 996 P.2d 540.

is normally a question of fact for the jury."[34] In making the determination, the jury considers whether the injury that occurred was the type that fell within the zone of risk created by the defendant's negligent conduct.[35]

B. Evidence

A plaintiff must offer some proof of breach to prevail at trial.[36] "A defendant's subjective reasons for acting or failing to act are relevant to the analysis of whether the defendant breached its duty of care."[37] Testimony regarding similar past occurrences is admissible, where prior occurrences took place under similar conditions as those that gave rise to the plaintiff's injury.[38] The length of time a hazard exists prior to an injury is also relevant to determine breach.[39] Actions taken by the defendant or their employees are admissible in determining whether due care was exercised.[40] While Utah law prohibits jurors from speculating as to possibilities, it empowers them to make justifiable inferences from circumstantial evidence to find negligence.[41] Circumstantial evidence is sufficient to establish a prima facie case of negligence if reasonable minds could conclude the probability of the conduct having proximately caused the injury is greater than not.[42] Violation of a safety law also serves as evidence of negligence unless the violation is excused.[43]

V.   Causation

A.   Elements

Plaintiffs must prove the defendant's failure to exercise due care was the proximate cause of their injuries.[44] Utah courts require plaintiffs to demonstrate two elements in order to prove proximate cause:

> "(1) the person's act or failure to act produced the harm directly or set in motion events that produced the harm in a natural and continuous sequence; and (2) the person's act or failure to act could be foreseen by a reasonable person to produce a harm of the same general nature."[45]

---

[34] Kitchen v. Cal Gas Co., Inc., 821 P.2d 458, 461 (Utah Ct. App. 1991); Rose v. Provo City, 2003 UT App 77, ¶ 9, 67 P.3d 1017.

[35] *Rose*, 67 P.3d at 1020.

[36] Kitchen v. Cal Gas Co., Inc., 821 P.2d 458, 462 (Utah Ct. App. 1991); Rand v. KOA Campgrounds, 2014 UT App 246, ¶ 6, 338 P.3d 222.

[37] Kerr v. City of Salt Lake, 2013 UT 75, ¶ 47, 322 P.3d 669, 681.

[38] Erickson v. Wasatch Manor, Inc., 802 P.2d 1323, 1326 (Utah Ct. App. 1990).

[39] Price v. Smith's Food & Drug Ctrs., Inc., 2011 UT App 66, ¶ 18, 252 P.3d 365, 369.

[40] *Id.*

[41] Lindsay v. Gibbons & Reed, 497 P.2d 28, 31 (Utah 1972).

[42] *Id.*

[43] MUJI 2d, CV212 (Utah State Bar 2016), https://www.utcourts.gov/resources/muji/.

[44] Proctor v. Costco Wholesale Corp., 2013 UT App 226, ¶ 9, 311 P.3d 568-69.

[45] MUJI 2d, CV209 (Utah State Bar 2016), https://www.utcourts.gov/resources/muji/.

In the context of proximate cause, "foreseeability is not concerned with categorical inquiries such as whether 'a reasonable person could anticipate a *general risk of injury* to others.'"[46] Foreseeability is an element of proximate cause that requires an inquiry into the specifics of the alleged tortious conduct.[47] Whether the injury and mechanism of harm was foreseeable is generally an issue for the jury to decide, although a trial court may rule as a matter of law if there is no evidence establishing a causal connection or where no reasonable person could find causation.[48]

B.   *Evidence*

Questions of foreseeability on the issue of causation are for the trier of fact to decide.[49] The appropriate inquiry focuses on specifics such as whether the *specific mechanism* of the harm could be foreseen.[50] Evidence related to the foreseeability of the injury, or of superseding causes of injury, are relevant to determine the existence of proximate cause, and are admissible.[51]

VI.   Damages

A.   *Elements*

As a general matter, a "plaintiff is entitled to recover for all harm that is proximately caused by a defendant's negligence, including aggravation of a preexisting condition."[52] "Damages" is commonly defined as the estimated money equivalent for detriment or injury sustained.[53] The "[f]undamental aim in deciding damages is to restore the injured party to the position he would have been in had it not been for the wrong of the other party."[54]

B.   *Evidence*

Juries in Utah are allowed wide discretion in determining the amount of damages.[55] Utah "[c]ourts must defer to the jury's determination of damages unless (1) the jury disregarded competent evidence, (2) the award is so excessive beyond rational justification as to indicate the effect of improper factors in the determination, and (3) the award was rendered under a misunderstanding."[56] Damages are based on fault and "are generally limited only by the findings and conscience of the jury."[57]

---

[46] Dee v. Johnson, 2012 UT App 237, ¶ 5, 286 P.3d 22, 23 (citing B.R. *ex rel.* Jeffs v. West, 2012 UT 11, ¶ 27, 275 P.3d 228).

[47] Proctor v. Costco Wholesale Corp., 2013 UT App 226, ¶ 11, 311 P.3d 564, 569.

[48] Bansasine v. Bodell, 927 P.2d 675, 676 (Utah Ct. App. 1996).

[49] Mackay v. 7-Eleven Sales Corp., 2000 UT 15, ¶ 12, 995 P.2d 1233, 1236.

[50] Dee v. Johnson, 2012 UT App 237, ¶ 5, 286 P.3d 22, 23.

[51] Proctor v. Costco Wholesale Corp., 2013 UT App 226, ¶¶ 10-14, 311 P.3d 564, 569-71.

[52] Gines v. Edwards, 2017 UT App 47, ¶ 35, 397 P.3d 612, 620, *cert. denied*, 398 P.3d 52 (Utah 2017).

[53] Eleopulos v. McFarland & Hullinger, LLC, 2006 UT App 352, ¶ 13, 145 P.3d 1157, 1159.

[54] Harris v. ShopKo Stores, Inc., 2013 UT 34, ¶ 25, 308 P.3d 449, 456.

[55] Brown v. Richards, 840 P.2d 143, 153 (Utah Ct. App. 1992).

[56] *Id.*

[57] Aris Vision Inst., Inc. v. Wasatch Prop. Mgmt., Inc., 2006 UT 45, ¶ 16, 143 P.3d 278, 282.

CHAPTER 46

VERMONT

VERMONT

Vicki Lawrence MacDougall[1]

I. Purpose of Tort Law

A legal duty owed by the defendant to the plaintiff, a breach of that duty by the defendant, and the breach of the duty both causing and proximately causing the plaintiff's injury must all be established to prevail in a negligence cause of action.[2] One clear goal of tort law is to compensate the plaintiff for injuries. "It is the responsibility of the courts to balance competing interests and to allocate losses arising out of human activities. One of the principal purposes of the law of torts is to compensate people for injuries they sustain as a result of the negligent conduct of others."[3] The "only workable way that our legal system has found to ease the injured party's tragic loss" is the arguable poor substitute of a monetary award of damages.[4]

Deterrence of negligent behavior is another goal of tort law.[5] However, an accident is not sufficient reason to require compensation; rather, the injury must result from a failure to use reasonable care.[6] Recovery for injuries caused by negligent behavior reflects "the value we place on human health and safety."[7] The creation of any new cause of action should be done cautiously after proper consideration of the need to provide justice to a new class of plaintiffs.[8] However, the common law is dynamic[9] and should adapt to changing needs.[10] "That court best serves the law which recognizes that the rules of law which grew up in a remote generation may, in the fullness of experience, be found to serve another generation badly, and which discards the old rule when it finds that another rule of law represents what should be according to established and settled judgment of society."[11]

---

[1] Professor of Law, Director Health Law Certificate Program, Law Review Faculty Advisor, Oklahoma City University School of Law, Member, California and Oklahoma Bar Associations.

[2] Long Trail House Condo. Ass'n v. Engelberth Const., Inc., 2012 VT 80, ¶ 26, 59 A.3d 752, 760 (Vt. 2012).

[3] Hay v. Med. Ctr. Hosp. of Vermont, 145 Vt. 533, 541, 496 A.2d 939, 944 (Vt. 1985).

[4] *Id.,* 145 Vt. at 541, 496 A.2d at 944.

[5] Young v. Bioran, No. 15-1-96, 1999 WL 34841343, at *5, *8 (Vt. Super. Ct. Apr. 30, 1999).

[6] Mattison v. Smalley, 122 Vt. 113, 117, 165 A.2d 343, 347 (Vt. 1960).

[7] Demag v. Better Power Equip., Inc., 2014 VT 78, ¶ 24, 197 Vt. 176, 185, 102 A.3d 1101, 1109 (Vt. 2014).

[8] *Hay,* 145 Vt. at 539, 496 A.2d at 943. *See, e.g.,* Knight v. Rower, 742 A. 2d 1237, 1241, 1245 (Vt. 1999), wherein the court held that sufficient policy reasons did not exist to expand liability of the social host. The social host can only be liable if the social host serves a minor or serves someone visibly intoxicated and the social host should foresee that the imbiber will drive. *Knight,* 742 A. 2d at 1241, 1245.

[9] *Hay,* 145 Vt. at 544, 496 A.2d at 945.

[10] *Id.,* 145 Vt. at 541, 496 A.2d at 944.

[11] *Id.* 145 Vt. at 542, 496 A.2d at 944-45 (citing B. CARDOZO, THE NATURE OF THE JUDICIAL PROCESS 151-52 (1921)) (quoting Dwy v. Connecticut Co., 89 Conn. 74, 99, 92 A. 883, 891 (1915)) (Wheeler, J., concurring).

II.   Duty to Exercise Ordinary Care

A.   *Question of Law*

The actor must owe a duty of care to the injured party or liability cannot be imposed for negligence and whether there exists a duty hinges, in part, upon the relationship between the parties.[12] Without a duty, any cause of action for negligence will fail.[13] Although a duty to act as a reasonably prudent person is imposed by the common law, "whether there is a cognizable legal duty that supports a [particular] tort action depends on a variety of public policy considerations and relevant factors."[14] Those factors include considerations of fairness, the relationship between the parties, the likelihood and severity of the risk of harm, "the public interest at stake, and the foreseeability of the harm."[15] Also included in the factors that are utilized in determining whether a duty exists are "the degree of certainty that plaintiff suffered injury, the closeness of the connection between defendant's conduct and plaintiff's injury, the moral blame attached to defendant's conduct, the policy of preventing future harm, the burden to the defendant, the consequences to the community of finding a duty, and the availability and cost of insurance."[16] "Duty is 'an expression of the sum total of those considerations of policy which lead the law to say that the plaintiff is entitled to protection.'"[17] The determination of whether a duty owed in a particular case is a question of law for the court.[18]

B.   *Question of Fact*

Generally speaking, there is no duty to warn about obvious dangers, as compared with latent or hidden dangers, nor is there a duty to correct the patent danger.[19] However, there is a duty to warn a third party of the danger of contracting a contagious disease from the actor if the actor knows or should know that he or she has the disease.[20] Further, the psychiatric profession has a *Tarasoff*[21] duty to warn about the dangerous propensities of a patient.[22]

---

[12] Lavallee v. Pratt, 166 A.2d 195, 197 (Vt. 1960).

[13] Deveneau v. Wielt, 144 A.3d 324, 326 (Vt. 2016). Absentee landowner had no duty to motorist who was struck by the tenant's horse because the landowner had no previous knowledge that the horse was likely to escape. It was the tenant's duty to care for the fence and the horses. *Id.*

[14] *Id.* at 326.

[15] *Id.* at 326; *see also* Long Trail House Condo. Ass'n v. Engelberth Const., Inc., 2012 VT 80, ¶ 16, 192 Vt. 322, 330, 59 A.3d 752, 757 (Vt. 2012).

[16] O'Connell v. Killington, Ltd., 164 Vt. 73, 77, 665 A.2d 39, 42 (Vt. 1995). Another factor can be in appropriate cases whether the plaintiff seeks compensation for physical harm or economic loss. Generally, there is no duty to "prevent purely economic loss" or "protect another's economic litigation interest." *Id. See also* Lenoci v. Leonard, 189 Vt. 641, 643, 21 A.3d 694, 698 (Vt. 2011).

[17] Endres v. Endres, 185 Vt. 63, 968 A.2d 336, 340 (Vt. 2008) (quoting W. PROSSER & W. KEETON, THE LAW OF TORTS § 53, at 358 (5th ed. 1984). *See also* Sorge v. State, 171 Vt. 171, 178, 762 A.2d 816, 821 (Vt. 2000).

[18] Deveneau v. Wielt, 144 A. 3d 324, 326 (Vt. 2016).

[19] Green v. Sherburne Corp., 403 A.2d 278, 279 (Vt. 1979) (finding no duty to warn of utility pole on ski slope).

[20] *Endres*, 968 A.2d at 340, 342 (recognizing potential liability of a husband for transmission of an STD to his wife).

[21] Tarasoff v. Regents of Univ. of California, 17 Cal. 3d 425, 131 Cal. Rptr. 14, 551 P.2d 334 (Cal. 1976).

[22] Peck v. Counseling Serv. of Addison Cty., Inc., 146 Vt. 61, 499 A.2d 422 (Vt. 1985).

In Vermont, the duty to warn extends beyond "identifiable victims" and includes a duty to warn all those in the "zone of danger."[23]

Generally, there is "no duty to control the conduct of a third person as to prevent" the third person from injuring another unless there exists a special relationship.[24] Furthermore, there is no duty to act affirmatively for the positive benefit of another nor is there a general duty to rescue someone in danger.[25] However, there is a limited duty to rescue in Vermont, unlike most other jurisdictions, under the *Duty to Aid the Endangered Act*.[26] The *Act* provides, as follows:

> A person who knows that another is exposed to grave physical harm shall, to the extent that the same can be rendered without danger or peril to himself or without interference with important duties owed to others, give reasonable assistance to the exposed person unless that assistance or care is being provided by others.[27]

The statute does not require assistance in all instances, such as intervention in a fist fight where the would-be rescuer would be exposed to danger.[28]

Where a duty does not normally exist, the defendant can create a duty to protect the plaintiff if the defendant voluntarily undertakes services and his or her failure to exercise reasonable care increases the risk of harm to the plaintiff or the plaintiff relies upon the undertaking.[29] A duty can also be created by exercising control over a helpless plaintiff.[30] Liability attaches for failure to use reasonable care to assure the safety of the helpless plaintiff.

Until 1970, Vermont was one of the few states to have a guest/passenger statute which stated that the driver of an automobile only owed a duty to a passenger to avoid gross negligence.[31] The repeal of the statute modified the duty to the standard one of ordinary care under the circumstances.[32]

---

[23] Kuligoski v. Brattleboro Retreat, 2016 VT 54A, ¶ 37, 156 A.3d 436, 450 (Vt. 2016).

[24] Knight v. Rower, 742 A. 2d 1237, 1242 (Vt. 1999); *see also* Lenoci v. Leonard, 189 Vt. 641, 643, 21 A.3d 694, 698 (Vt. 2011) (concluding that there is no duty for an eighteen-year-old friend to control a minor friend's behavior); Sorge v. State, 174 Vt. 171, 178, 762 A. 2d 816, 821 (Vt. 2000) (finding a rehabilitative program had no duty to control the behavior of a juvenile placed in the program's custody when the juvenile assaulted a delivery person).

[25] Buxton v. Springfield Lodge No. 679, 2014 VT 52, ¶ 8, 196 Vt. 486, 490, 99 A.3d 171, 174 (Vt. 2014). The plaintiff must prove "sins of commission rather than omission." Murphy v. Sentry Ins., 196 Vt. 92, 102, 95 A.3d 985, 992 (Vt. 2014).

[26] State v. Joyce, 139 Vt. 638, 641, 433 A.2d 271, 273 (Vt. 1981).

[27] 12 V.S.A. § 519 (a).

[28] *Joyce*, 433 A.2d at 273 (Vt. 1981); *accord* Kane v. Lamothe, 182 Vt. 241, 936 A.2d 1303, n. 4 (Vt. 2007).

[29] Collins v. Thomas, 2007 VT 92, ¶ 13, 182 Vt. 250, 256, 938 A.2d 1208, 1213 (Vt. 2007) (quoting RESTATEMENT (SECOND) OF TORTS, § 323 (1964). *See also* Murphy v. Sentry Ins., 196 Vt. 92, 102, 104, 95 A.3d 985, 992, 993-994 (Vt. 2014).

[30] *Collins*, ¶ 13, 182 Vt. at 256, 938 A. 2d at 1213 (quoting RESTATEMENT (SECOND) OF TORTS, § 324 (1964); *see also* Buxton v. Springfield Lodge No. 679, 2014 VT 52, ¶ 8, 196 Vt. 486, 490, 99 A.3d 171, 174 (Vt. 2014).

[31] 23 V.S.A. § 1491 (repealed 1969). *See, e.g.,* Chamberlain v. Delphia, 103 A.2d 94 (Vt. 1954).

[32] *Collins*, 938 A. 2d at 1213.

Prior to 2014, Vermont followed the common law rules that varied the duty that a occupier of land owed to an entrant upon land by the status of the entrant as an invitee, licensee or trespasser.[33] In 2014, Vermont overturned its common law in *Demag v. Better Power Equipment, Inc.*[34] and held that a "landowner owes the same duty of care to a licensee as to an invitee"; *i.e.*, the duty to use reasonable care under the circumstances.[35] Whether the entrant is a licensee or invitee is still a factor that may be considered in ascertaining if the landowner recognized a foreseeable risk of harm; however, the status is not determinative.[36] The Vermont Supreme Court believed that overturning the traditional common law rule was appropriate because the common law rules were arbitrary and rigid[37] and did not reflect our "modern social norms and humanitarian values."[38] As stated by the court, "considerations of human safety within an urban community dictate that the landowner's relative immunity, which is primarily supported by values of the agrarian past, be modified in favor of negligence principles of landowner liability."[39] There is one important caveat. The court made clear that it was not addressing or changing the no-duty rule toward trespassers. The court explicitly stated that the no-duty rule—"a landowner owes no duty to protect a trespasser from injury caused by unsafe or dangerous conditions—remains good law in Vermont."[40]

III. Breach of Duty

A. Elements

"Foresight of harm lies at the foundation of negligence."[41] The standard of conduct needed to discharge a duty of care" is measured by the "avoidance of reasonably foreseeable risks" in any given situation.[42] Breach of duty is "failure to take reasonable steps to address a foreseeable hazard."[43] An actor is not judged by how the situation appeared to the actor; rather, the "proper test is how it would have appeared to an ordinarily prudent person."[44] The

---

[33] *See, e.g.,* Lomberg v. Renner, 157 A.2d 222 (Vt. 1960).

[34] Demag v. Better Power Equip., Inc., 2014 VT 78, ¶ 26, 197 Vt. 176, 186, 102 A.3d 1101, 1110 (Vt. 2014).

[35] *Id.* at ¶ 24, 197 Vt. at 185, 102 A.3d at 1109.

[36] *Id.* at ¶ 26, 197 Vt. at 187, 102 A.3d at 1110; *see also* Ainsworth v. Chandler, 197 Vt. 541, 546, 107 A.3d 905, 909 (2014).

[37] *Demag,* ¶ 20, 197 Vt. at 184, 102 A.3d at 1108.

[38] *Id.* at ¶ 24, 197 Vt. at 185, 102 A.3d at 1109.

[39] *Id.* at ¶ 24, 197 Vt. at 186, 102 A.3d at 1109-10.

[40] *Id.* at ¶ 26, 197 Vt. at 186, 102 A.3d at 1110.; *accord* Keegan v. Lemieux Sec. Servs., Inc., 177 Vt. 575, 576, 861 A.2d 1135, 1138 (Vt. 2004).

[41] Lenoci v. Leonard, 189 Vt. 641, 644, 21 A.3d 694, 699 (Vt. 2011).

[42] Green v. Sherburne Corp., 403 A.2d 278, 280 (Vt. 1979); *see also* Endres v. Endres, 185 Vt. 63, 968 A.2d 336, 340-341 (2008).

[43] Malaney v. Hannaford Bros. Co., 2004 VT 76, ¶ 19, 177 Vt. 123, 132, 861 A.2d 1069, 1075 (Vt. 2004). A self-service method of selling loose produce, such as grapes, creates a foreseeable hazard in the produce department of a grocery store. Accordingly, a jury could find the store liable when a customer slipped on a grape and fell. *Id.*

[44] State v. Graves, 122 A.2d 840, 846 (Vt. 1956); *see also* LaFaso v. LaFaso, 126 Vt. 90, 93-94, 223 A.2d 814, 818-819 (Vt. 1966).

obligation of the prudent person increases commensurate with the foreseeable risk.[45] The reasonable person standard varies with the facts and circumstances of the individual case. "What is prudence in one case may be negligence in another, recklessness in another, and downright foolhardiness in still another."[46]

B.   *Evidence*

Breach of duty is one for the trier of fact[47] and judgment as a matter of law is not appropriate if there is evidence that supports all the elements of the claim.[48] Negligence is only a question of law if it is clear that the defendant has not been diligent.[49] It is a truism that the "test of liability is not whether the injury was accidental, but whether the defendant was at fault."[50] It is appropriate to consider if the defendant was confronted with a sudden emergency in trying to ascertain if the defendant was negligent[51] so long as the peril was not caused by the defendant.[52] The "law recognizes that a prudent man so brought face to face with an unexpected danger may fail to use the best judgment, may omit some precaution he could have taken or may not choose the best available method of meeting the dangers of the situation."[53] Some accidents may not be avoidable; however, the claim of an unavoidable accident is simply a "denial by the defendant of negligence, or a contention that his negligence, if any, was not the proximate cause of the accident."[54]

The trial judge may allow the jury to view the scene of an accident to make the evidence offered at trial more understandable to the jury.[55] Furthermore, breach of duty may be established through the creation of a dangerous situation that is activated by a third person to injure the plaintiff.[56]

If children are afoot, the actor must "anticipate the ordinary behavior of children."[57] Furthermore, the "duty to avoid injury to children increases with their inability to protect themselves and with their childish indiscretions, instincts and impulses; the caution required must be measured in all cases according to the maturity and capacity of the infant."[58]

Breach of duty can be established through the doctrine of *res ipsa loquitur*. In Vermont, the elements of *res ipsa* are, as follows: (1) The defendant owes a legal duty in connection

---

[45] Green v. Sherburne Corp., 403 A.2d 278, 280 (Vt. 1979).

[46] Farrell v. Greene, 2 A.2d 194, 196 (Vt. 1938).

[47] Morway v. Trombly, 789 A.2d 965, 971 (Vt. 2001).

[48] Lasek v. Vermont Vapor, Inc., 95 A.3d 447, 453 (Vt. 2014).

[49] Tyrrell v. McDonald, 340 A.2d 99, 100 (Vt. 1975).

[50] Mattison v. Smalley, 165 A.2d 343, 347 (Vt. 1960).

[51] *Id.*; *see also* Kremer v. Fortin, 119 Vt. 1, 7, 117 A.2d 245, 249 (Vt. 1955).

[52] State v. Graves, 122 A.2d 840, 846 (Vt. 1956). A situation that calls for quick action is not necessarily a sudden emergency if it could have been anticipated. *Id. See also* Chamberlain v. Delphia, 103 A.2d 94, 95 (Vt. 1954).

[53] Stevens v. Nurenburg, 97 A.2d 250, 256 (Vt. 1953).

[54] *Mattison*, 165 A.2d at 347.

[55] *Stevens*, 97 A.2d at 259.

[56] Bessette v. Humiston, 121 Vt. 325, 326, 157 A.2d 468, 470 (Vt. 1960).

[57] LaFaso v. LaFaso, 126 Vt. 90, 95, 223 A.2d 814, 818 (Vt. 1966).

[58] *Id.*

with the instrumentality in question to prevent the occurrence; (2) the instrumentality must be under the control and management of the defendant so that "there can be no serious question concerning the defendant's responsibility for the misadventure of the instrument;" (3) the instrument must cause the injury; and (4) the injury is one that would not have happened without negligence on the part of the defendant.[59] "The doctrine of *res ipsa loquitur* allows an inference of negligence in certain cases, not causation. Established causation is a prerequisite to the application of the doctrine."[60] Generally, *res ipsa* is only used when there is a void in the evidence and "some facts are left to inference."[61] The permissible inference avoids a directed verdict.[62]

Violation of a safety statute or a regulation may be used to establish negligence provided it is determined that the statute was intended to encompass the following:

> (a) to protect a class of persons which includes the one whose interest is invaded, and (b) to protect the particular interest which is invaded, and (c) to protect that interest against the kind of harm which has resulted, and (d) to protect that interest against the particular hazard from which the harm results.[63]

Normally, violation of a statute is considered negligence *per se*. In Vermont, however, violation of a statute creates a prima facie case of negligence.[64] The burden of production[65] shifts to produce such evidence "fairly and reasonably tending to show that the fact is not as presumed."[66] Then, the rebuttable presumption disappears.[67] Safety rules, as compared with safety statutes, are not "hard and fast;" rather, safety rules are "guides" to whether "the actor's conduct meets the standard required of a prudent man under the circumstances."[68] OSHA regulations are also "properly admissible as evidence of a standard of care."[69]

---

[59] Lasek v. Vermont Vapor, Inc., 2014 VT 33, ¶ 16, 196 Vt. 243, 252, 95 A.3d 447, 454 (Vt. 2014) (quoting Cyr v. Green Mountain Power Corp., 145 Vt. 231, 235-236, 485 A.2d 1265, 1268 (1985)). Because the cause of fires is generally unknown and fires can commonly start without negligence, *res ipsa* is usually not applicable to fire cases. *Lasek*, ¶ 17, 196 Vt. at 252, 95 A.3d at 454.

[60] *Id.*

[61] Morway v. Trombly, 789 A.2d 965, 972 (Vt. 2001).

[62] *Cyr*, 485 A.2d at 1268 (allowing a *res ipsa* instruction against power company for electrocution of dairy cows when there was evidence tending to show problem with power lines was in the control of the power company).

[63] Estate of Kelley v. Moguls, Inc., 160 Vt. 531, 534, 632 A.2d 360, 362 (Vt. 1993). For example, the class of person protected by a regulation that prohibits the provision of alcohol to an intoxicated patron protects both a victim injured by the intoxicated patron as well as the imbiber himself/herself. *Id.*, 160 Vt. at 535, 632 A.23d at 363.

[64] Barber v. LaFromboise, 2006 VT 77, ¶ 21, 180 Vt. 150, 162, 908 A.2d 436, 445 (Vt. 2006).

[65] Smith v. Grove, 119 Vt. 106, 112, 119 A.2d 880, 883 (Vt. 1956).

[66] *Id.*; *accord* Barber v. LaFromboise, 908 A.2d 436, 445 (Vt. 2006); Kremer v. Fortin, 119 Vt. 1, 4, 117 A.2d 245, 248 (Vt. 1955). The courts tend to use the terms "presumption" of negligence and "prima facie evidence" of negligence interchangeably in this arena. *Id.*

[67] Smith v. Grove, 119 A.2d 880, 883 (Vt. 1956).

[68] Smith v. Blow & Cote, Inc. 124 Vt. 64, 69, 196 A.2d 489, 493 (Vt. 1963).

[69] Marzec-Gerrior v. D.C.P. Indus., Inc., 164 Vt. 569, 571, 674 A.2d 1248, 1249 (Vt. 1996).

Professional negligence must generally be shown by expert testimony and the expert must establish the proper standard for the profession, that the defendant's conduct departed from the customary practice, and that the defendant's departure caused the plaintiff's harm.[70] For example, "the standard of care by which an attorney is held in rendering professional services is the degree of care, skill, diligence, and knowledge commonly possessed and exercised by a reasonable, careful, and prudent attorney practicing in the jurisdiction of Vermont."[71] Unless a professional fails to use the care that other similarly situated professionals would use under the circumstances, a mere error in judgment is not enough to establish liability.[72]

IV.   Causation

A.   Elements

Liability for negligence requires more than proof of a duty and breach of duty. Causation must be established as well.[73] Causation requires proof of both cause-in-fact and proximate causation. The "but-for" test is used to establish cause-in-fact. "But-for" the actor's conduct, the harm would not have occurred.[74] For example, a defendant who left a hole in the ice unguarded was not liable for horses who ran into the hole and drowned if the speed of the horses was so fast that a reasonable fence or guard would not have prevented the accident.[75] The substantial factor test has also been utilized in Vermont particularly where the actor creates a risk of harm that comes to fruition through the intervention of an outside force. The original actor is still considered a substantial factor and cause of the plaintiff's harm.[76] Further, "more than one act of negligence . . . may combine to produce an injury" and both acts may be considered the cause-in-fact of the injury.[77]

Proximate cause centers on whether the conduct of the defendant was legally sufficient to result in liability.[78] "Proximate cause is the law's method of keeping the scope of liability for a defendant's negligence from extending by ever-expanding causal links."[79] Generally, liability attaches for all consequences of a negligent act unless an efficient intervening cause diverts liability[80] or "the force set in motion by the negligent act has so far spent itself as to be too small for the law's notice."[81] Intervening causes that are not foreseeable

---

[70] Estate of Fleming v. Nicholson, 724 A.2d 1026, 1028 (Vt. 1998).

[71] *Id.*

[72] Hartnett v. Med. Ctr. Hosp. of Vermont, 503 A.2d 1134, 1138 (Vt. 1985).

[73] Lasek v. Vermont Vapor, Inc., 2014 VT 33, 95 A.3d 447, 453 (Vt. 2014).

[74] Collins v. Thomas, 2007 VT 92, ¶ 8, 182 Vt. 250, 253, 938 A.2d 1208, 1211 (Vt. 2007).

[75] Sowles v. Moore, 65 Vt. 322, 26 A. 629 (Vt. 1893).

[76] Lussier v. Bessette, 2010 VT 104, ¶ 14, 189 Vt. 95, 104, 16 A.3d 580, 586 (Vt. 2010).

[77] Tufts v. Wyand, 536 A.2d 541, 542 (Vt. 1987); *accord* Estate of Kelley v. Moguls, Inc., 160 Vt. 531, 535, 632 A.2d 360, 363 (Vt. 1993).

[78] *Collins*, ¶ 8, 182 Vt. at 253, 938 A. 2d at 1211.

[79] *Id.*

[80] *Id.*

[81] Isham v. Dow's Estate, 41 A. 585, 586 (Vt. 1898); *see also* Bennett v. Robertson, 177 A. 625, 628 (Vt. 1935).

will sever the causal chain.[82] Whether a new independent force will break the causal chain depends if the original actor could have foreseen or anticipated the intervening cause.[83] It must be a new and independent cause.[84] The actor "cannot take refuge behind the doctrine of intervening cause" if he should have anticipated it occurring as a result of his negligence.[85]

B.   Evidence

Normally, proximate cause is a question of fact for the jury. However, "it may be decided as a matter of law where 'the proof is so clear that reasonable minds cannot draw different conclusions or where all reasonable minds would construe the facts and circumstances one way.'"[86] For example, voluntary suicide is generally considered "an independent intervening act that breaks the causal chain and severs potential liability."[87] Prior similar accidents may be offered as evidence that a risk of harm was foreseeable.[88] There is one important caveat to the limitation to liability provided by proximate cause. If the action is proven to be wanton, the defendant is "liable for all the consequences, however remote, because the act is *quasi* criminal in its character, and the law conclusively presumes that all the consequences were foreseen and intended."[89]

In a medical negligence cause of action, a plaintiff must show that there was more than a 50% chance of a different outcome (more likely than not) had it not been for the negligence of the health care provider in order to establish liability.[90] A Vermont Superior Court rejected the loss of chance doctrine[91] that allows recovery if negligence "deprived the decedent of a significant chance of survival, albeit one that had odds of less than 50%."[92]

Liability in certain cases can be imposed without the presence of cause-in-fact. If a group acts in concert, or by implicit or explicit agreement, to commit a tortious act, then each member of the group faces liability for the damage even if only one tortfeasor caused-in-fact

---

[82] Lussier v. Bessette, 2010 VT 104, ¶ 14, 189 Vt. 95, 104, 16 A.3d 580, 586 (Vt. 2010) Although the plan of a group of hunters to "push" or "drive" deer toward a shooter could create a risk of harm, the action of pointing a high power rifle without the safety on at a tractor was an unforeseeable intervening cause relieving the other hunters from liability for the death of the farmer who was on the tractor when the rifle accidentally discharged. *Id.*

[83] Edson v. Barre Supervisory Union No. 61, 182 Vt. 157, 161, 162, 933 A.2d 200, 204, 205 (Vt. 2007) (concluding premeditated murder committed by a third party was not foreseeable and broke the causal chain).

[84] Johnson v. Cone, 29 A.2d 384, 388 (Vt. 1942).

[85] Paton v. Sawyer, 134 Vt. 598, 601, 370 A.2d 215, 217 (Vt. 1976).

[86] Collins v. Thomas, 2007 VT 92, ¶ 8, 182 Vt. 250, 254, 938 A.2d 1208, 1211 (Vt. 2007) (quoting Estate of Sumner v. Dep't of Soc. & Rehab. Servs., 162 Vt. 628, 619, 649 A.2d 1034, 1036 (Vt. 1994)).

[87] Lenoci v. Leonard, 189 Vt. 641, 644, 21 A.3d 694, 699 (Vt. 2011).

[88] Cole v. N. Danville Coop. Creamery Ass'n, 151 A. 568, 572 (Vt. 1930) (finding prior evidence of frightened "horses of ordinary gentleness" relevant on whether it was a foreseeable risk that escaping steam at a creamery would frighten a horse).

[89] Isham v. Dow's Estate, 70 Vt. 588, 41 A. 585, 585 (Vt. 1898).

[90] Young v. Bioran, No. 15-1-96, 1999 WL 34841343, at *6, *8 (Vt. Super. Ct. Apr. 30, 1999).

[91] *Id.* The Vermont Supreme Court has yet to decide whether to adopt or reject the loss of chance doctrine. *Id.* at *4, *8.

[92] *Id.* at *3, *8.

the loss.[93] "Liability of an individual defendant will not depend upon whether he actually [inflicted the plaintiff's harm]; *participation in the concerted activity* is equivalent to participation in the accident resulting in the injury."[94]

V. Damages

Vermont requires that the plaintiff suffers an actual injury, not simply exposed to a potential risk of harm, before the plaintiff can recover.[95] Actual physical damages must be shown.

A. *Elements*

Damages awarded in a negligence cause of action include medical bills, pain and suffering, including the permanency of any disability, and loss of earning.[96] However, the economic loss rule precludes recovery for stand-alone economic losses, losses that result pursuant to a contract.[97] Tort actions are to recover for "unanticipated physical injury."[98]

Loss of consortium damages are available to either spouse.[99] Vermont also allows recovery of damages for loss of parental consortium when the "parent has been rendered permanently comatose" because such a recovery was perceived to be in the "best interests of justice" and the citizens of Vermont.[100] The court allowed recovery of loss of parental consortium because "[a]lthough monetary damages may be an inadequate compensation for the loss of a parent, we are satisfied that monetary damages can help to ease the loss, and should therefore be made available."[101] Recovery for negligent infliction of emotional distress is only permissible when there is a "direct relation between the tortfeasor and the victim."[102]

Damage to property considers the "doctrine of economic waste." The difference in the fair market value of the property is a better guide to the calculation of damages when the cost of repair is excessive considering the value of the property. The damage rule is particularly true when the damage is "permanent and beyond full repair."[103] The reduction in value to the property "affords the better guide to a just award."[104]

---

[93] Lussier v. Bessette, 2010 VT 104, ¶ 6, 189 Vt. 95, 100, 16 A.3d 580, 583 (Vt. 2010) (citing RESTATEMENT (SECOND) OF TORTS § 876 (1979)).

[94] *Lussier*, ¶ 15, 189 Vt. at 105, 16 A.3d at 587 (emphasis added) (quoting Herman v. Wesgate, 94 A.D.2d 938, 464 N.Y.S.2d 315, 316 (1983)).

[95] Long Trail House Condo. Ass'n v. Engelberth Const., Inc., 2012 VT 80, ¶ 26, 192 Vt. 322, 333, 59 A.3d 752, 760 (Vt. 2012).

[96] Mattison v. Smalley, 165 A.2d 343, 348 (Vt. 1960).

[97] *Long Trail House Condo. Ass'n*, ¶ 10, 192 Vt. at 327, 59 A.3d at 755-56.

[98] *Id.*, ¶ 10, 192 Vt. at 327, 59 A.3d at 756.

[99] Hay v. Med. Ctr. Hosp. of Vermont, 145 Vt. 533, 537, 496 A.2d 939, 942 (Vt. 1985).

[100] *Id.*, 145 Vt. at 546, 496 A.2d at 946.

[101] *Id.*, 145 Vt. at 541, 496 A.2d at 944.

[102] *Id.*, 145 Vt. at 539, 496 A.2d at 942.

[103] Langlois v. Town of Proctor, 2014 VT 130, ¶ 41, 198 Vt. 137, 157, 113 A.3d 44, 57 (Vt. 2014) (citing Bean v. Sears, Roebuck & Co., 129 Vt. 278, 282, 276 A.2d 613, 616 (1971)).

[104] *Langlois*, ¶ 41, 198 Vt. at 157, 113 A.3d at 57.

B. *Evidence*

Damages must be proven by a preponderance of the evidence.[105] Vermont's "touchstone for determining damages . . . is reasonableness."[106] A claim for future medical expenses must be accompanied by "competent expert medical testimony."[107] A bare allegation of damage is insufficient. "In negligence cases, as is well known, the amount of damages alleged in the complaint is ordinarily in excess of the sum which the plaintiff expects to recover, and is certainly not a standard for estimating the damages. It is not evidence, nor proof of the amount due a plaintiff."[108] Evidence is permissible to establish that the plaintiff could have minimized his or her damages through the exercise of reasonable care after the accident. The plaintiff has a duty to mitigate damages. Accordingly, recovery is reduced by the avoidable amount.[109]

---

[105] Hebert v. Stanley, 124 Vt. 205, 210, 201 A.2d 698, 702 (Vt. 1964) (concluding damages must be shown by reasonable probability or reasonable certainty); *see also Langlois*, ¶ 43, 198 Vt. at 158, 113 A.3d at 58.

[106] *Langlois*, ¶ 43, 198 Vt. at 158, 113 A.3d at 58.

[107] *Hebert*, 124 Vt. at 210, 201 A.2d at 703; LaFaso v. LaFaso, 126 Vt. 90, 97-98, 223 A.2d 814, 820 (Vt. 1966).

[108] Mattison v. Smalley, 165 A.2d 343, 347 (Vt. 1960).

[109] *Langlois*, ¶ 22, 198 Vt. at 149, 113 A.3d at 51.

Chapter 47

Virginia

VIRGINIA

Lee F. Peoples[1]

I. Purpose of Tort Law

The common law of the State of Virginia guarantees that an aggrieved party with adequate legal standing has a right to recover damages from a third party for injuries sustained.[2] The Supreme Court of Virginia has stated that the purpose of Virginia's tort law is to protect every person against injurious acts of others.[3] This purpose springs from the duty "owed to mankind" which requires every person to exercise due care to avoid injuring others, or exposing others to peril.[4]

The policy of Virginia's common law is to protect people's safety, the safety of families, and the safety of the general public.[5] The public policy of Virginia generally encompasses a matter which is "injurious to the interests of the public, contravenes some established interest of society, violates some public statute, is against good morals, tends to interfere with the public welfare or safety, or, as it is sometimes put, if it is at war with the interests of society and is in conflict with the morals of the time."[6]

---

[1] Interim Dean and Frederick Charles Hicks Professor of Law, Oklahoma City University School of Law, Member of the Oklahoma Bar.

[2] Virginia Mun. Grp. Self-Ins. Ass'n v. Crawford, No. CH03-59, 2004 WL 3132010, at *3 (Va. Cir. Nov. 24, 2004); VA. CODE ANN. § 1-200 (West).

[3] Filak v. George, 267 Va. 612, 618, 594 S.E.2d 610, 613 (2004); Worrell v. Worrell, 174 Va. 11, 29, 4 S.E.2d 343, 350 (1939).

[4] RGR, LLC v. Settle, 288 Va. 260, 275-76, 764 S.E.2d 8, 16-17 (2014); Cline v. Dunlora S., LLC, 284 Va. 102, 107, 726 S.E.2d 14, 17 (2012); Dudley v. Offender Aid & Restoration of Richmond, Inc., 241 Va. 270, 278, 401 S.E.2d 878, 882-83 (1991) (quoting RESTATEMENT (SECOND) OF TORTS § 281; Blake Const. Co. v. Alley, 233 Va. 31, 34-35, n.3, 353 S.E.2d 724, 726 (1987); Overstreet v. Sec. Storage & Safe Deposit Co., 148 Va. 306, 317, 138 S.E. 552, 555 (1927); Louisville & Nashville R.R. Co. v. O'Neil, 119 Va. 611, 627, 89 S.E. 862, 866 (1916); Standard Oil Co. v. Wakefield's Adm'r, 102 Va. 824, 47 S.E. 830, 832 (1904); CHARLES E. FRIEND, PERSONAL INJURY LAW IN VIRGINIA § 1.1.1., at 2 (3rd ed. 2003); 2 DAN B. DOBBS, THE LAW OF TORTS § 251, at 2-3 (2d ed. 2011)).

[5] Sensenbrenner v. Rust, Orling & Neale, 236 Va. 419, 425, 374 S.E.2d 55 (1988); Blake Construction Co., Inc. v. Alley, 233 Va. 31, 34-35, 353 S.E.2d 724, 726 (1987); Kamlar Corp. v. Haley, 224 Va. 699, 706, 299 S.E.2d 514, 517 (1983); Gonella v. Lumbermens Mut. Cas. Co., No. 216138., 2004 WL 836031, at *5 (Va. Cir. Mar. 15, 2004).

[6] Taxson v. Taxson, No. 114910, 1993 WL 946187, at *3 (Va. Cir. Aug. 10, 1993) (quoting 17A AM.JUR.2d § 263, p. 267-69 (citing RESTATEMENT OF CONTRACTS 2d § 178) (citing 4B M.J. Contracts § 115; Wallihan v. Hughes, 196 Va. 117, 124-25, 82 S.E.2d 553, 558 (1954)).

Tort liability has been imposed to protect the broad interests of social policy, deter wrongdoing and compensate those injured by violations of public policy.[7] It is also the public policy in Virginia to deter wrongdoing and promote proper conduct through civil actions.[8]

II. Duty to Exercise Ordinary Care

A. *Question of Law*

In a negligence action, a plaintiff must prove "that the defendant owed the plaintiff a duty to use reasonable and ordinary care toward the plaintiff, and protect the plaintiff against unreasonable risks."[9] The Supreme Court of Appeals of Virginia has stated "this duty to be careful does not grow out of a contractual relation; it arises from that basic and necessary regulation of civilization which forbids any person, because of his own convenience, to recklessly, heedlessly, or carelessly injure another."[10]

The existence of a duty of care is purely a question of law and will be decided by the court.[11] The Supreme Court of Appeals of Virginia has recognized "a duty owed to mankind generally . . . not to do any act which a person of ordinary prudence could reasonably apprehend, as a natural and probable consequence thereof, would subject [another person] to peril."[12] A general duty to not injure others "arises whenever a defendant's conduct creates a risk of harm to others."[13] Thus, "whenever one person is by circumstances placed in such a position with regard to another . . . that if he did not use ordinary care and skill in his own conduct with regard to those circumstances, he would cause danger of injury to the person or the property of the other, a duty arises to use ordinary care and skill to avoid such injury."[14]

The duty to exercise ordinary care is imposed by the common law and does not depend on statutory law.[15] The only relationship between the parties that must exist for the duty to exist is "a sufficient juxtaposition of the parties in time and space to place the plaintiff in danger from the defendant's acts"[16]

---

[7] Sensenbrenner v. Rust, Orling & Neale, Architects, Inc., 236 Va. 419, 425, 374 S.E.2d 55, 58 (1988) (quoting Kamlar Corp. v. Haley, 224 Va. 699, 706, 299 S.E.2d 514, 517 (1983).

[8] Marshall v. City of Richmond, Va., No. LL-2883-3, 1988 WL 619129, at *2 (Va. Cir. Feb. 22, 1988).

[9] Va. Prac. Tort and Personal Injury Law § 3:1 (2017).

[10] Louisville & Nashville R.R. Co. v. O'Neil, 119 Va. 611, 627, 89 S.E. 862, 866 (1916).

[11] Va. Prac. Tort and Personal Injury Law § 3:2 (2017) (citing Fox v. Custis, 236 Va. 69, 74, 372 S.E.2d 373, 375 (1988)).

[12] RGR, LLC v. Settle, 288 Va. 260, 275, 764 S.E.2d 8, 16 (2014) (citing Overstreet v. Sec. Storage & Safe Deposit Co., 148 Va. 306, 317, 138 S.E. 552, 555 (1927)).

[13] *RGR, LLC*, 288 Va. at 275, 764 S.E.2d at 16 (citing Charles E. Friend, Personal Injury Law in Virginia § 1.1.1., at 2 (3rd ed. 2003)).

[14] *RGR, LLC*, 288 Va. at 276, 764 S.E.2d at 17.

[15] 1-1 Personal Injury Law In Virginia § 1.1 (2017) (citing Rice v. Turner, 191 Va. 601, 62 S.E.2d 24 (1950)).

[16] 1-1 Personal Injury Law In Virginia § 1.1 (2017) (citing *RGR, LLC*, 288 Va. at 279, 764 S.E.2d at 19).

B. *Question of Fact*

i. **Elements**

As explained by the Supreme Court of Virginia, "[t]he law determines the duty, and the jury, upon the evidence, decides whether the duty has been performed."[17] What level of care constitutes ordinary or reasonable care will vary depending on the circumstances of each case.[18] The jury will be guided in making its determination of whether the standard of care has been breached by the following instruction:

> "Reasonable care" or "Ordinary care" is a relative term, and varies with the nature and character of the situation to which it is applied. The amount or degree of diligence and caution that is necessary to constitute reasonable or ordinary care depends upon the circumstances and the particular surroundings of each specific case. The test is the degree of care that an ordinarily prudent person would exercise under the same or similar circumstances to avoid injury to another.[19]

ii. **Evidence**

The plaintiff must present evidence of the level of care required.[20] The Supreme Court of Virginia has held, as follows:

> Whether reasonable care was exercised depends upon what a reasonably prudent person, with knowledge of the circumstances, ought to have foreseen in regard to the consequences of his act or omission. However, the precise nature of the consequences need not be foreseen. It is enough if the act [or omission] is such that the party ought to have anticipated that it was liable to result in injury to others.[21]

It is proper to consider foreseeability as an element of the duty of care.[22] The Supreme Court of Virginia articulated the following approach: "When circumstances, reasonably discernible, create a hazard, reasonably foreseeable, the standard of care the law imposes is that degree of care an ordinarily prudent person would exercise under similar conditions."[23]

The reasonably prudent person used for the negligence standard of conduct "is based on an *objective* and *external* standard, rather than being based upon an individual's

---

[17] Commonwealth v. Peterson, 286 Va. 349, 749 S.E. 2d 307 (Va. 2013) (citing Acme Markets, Inc. v. Remschel, 181 Va. 171, 178, 24 S.E.2d 430, 434 (1943)).

[18] 1-2 PERSONAL INJURY LAW IN VIRGINIA § 2.1 (2017).

[19] VA. PRAC. JURY INSTRUCTION § 11:2 (2017).

[20] *Id.*

[21] RGR, LLC v. Settle, 288 Va. 260, 282, 764 S.E.2d 8, 20 (2014).

[22] 1-3 PERSONAL INJURY LAW IN VIRGINIA § 3.2 (2017) (citing Trail v. White, 221 Va. 932, 275 S.E.2d 617 (1981)).

[23] Trail v. White, 221 Va. 932, 934, 275 S.E.2d 617, 619 (1981).

subjective judgment."[24] The reasonable person "is a mythical creation, and is entirely a concoction of the common law."[25] The reasonable person "possesses those attributes that a jury decides represent the community norm"[26] and "is the personification of a community ideal of reasonable behavior, determined by the jury's social judgment."[27] The person "must know the habits of human beings and animals, and the qualities, characteristics, and capacities of things and forces insofar as they are matters of common knowledge in the community."[28] The reasonable person is assumed to have knowledge of "commonly understood dangers."[29]

Industry custom and practice are admissible to demonstrate "a reasonable standard of care."[30] However, custom and practice do not control "when a reasonable person would not follow such custom and practice."[31] The Supreme Court of Virginia has held that private safety rules are not admissible to show the standard of care owed to others.[32]

Violation of a statute may be used to establish negligence by showing, the following:

> "First, the plaintiff must prove that the defendant violated a statute enacted for public safety. Second, the plaintiff must belong to the class of persons for whose benefit the statute was enacted, and demonstrate that the harm that occurred was of the type against which the statute was designed to protect. Third, the statutory violation must be a proximate cause of plaintiff's injury."[33]

III.   Breach of Duty

A.   *Elements*

The plaintiff must show that the defendant breached a legal duty to prevail with a case of negligence.[34] The question of breach is a question of fact and the jury determines whether the defendant breached the duty of care.[35] The court will decide the issue of breach only when reasonable persons could not differ on the issue of breach.[36]

---

[24] VA. PRAC. TORT AND PERSONAL INJURY LAW § 3:3 (2017).

[25] *Id.*

[26] *Id.*

[27] *Id.*

[28] VA. PRAC. TORT AND PERSONAL INJURY LAW § 3:3 (2017) (citing RESTATEMENT (SECOND) OF TORTS § 290A (1965)).

[29] VA. PRAC. TORT AND PERSONAL INJURY LAW § 3:3 (2017) (citing Robbins v. Old Dominion Power Co., 204 Va. 390, 131 S.E.2d 274 (1963)).

[30] VA. PRAC. TORT AND PERSONAL INJURY LAW § 3:3 (2017) (citing RESTATEMENT (SECOND) OF TORTS § 295A (1965)).

[31] *Id.*

[32] Pullen v. Nickens, 226 Va. 342, 350, 310 S.E.2d 452, 456 (1983).

[33] Collett v. Cordovana, 290 Va. 139, 148, 772 S.E.2d 584, 589 (2015).

[34] RGR, LLC v. Settle, 288 Va. 260, 281, 764 S.E.2d 8, 20 (2014).

[35] Brown v. Koulizakis, 229 Va. 524, 531, 331 S.E.2d 440, 445 (1985).

[36] Hadeed v. Medic-24, Ltd., 237 Va. 277, 285, 377 S.E.2d 589, 593 (1989).

B. *Evidence*

The plaintiff must demonstrate the negligence of the defendant by a preponderance of the evidence.[37] Direct or circumstantial evidence is admissible to prove negligence.[38] Evidence of failing to follow custom does not, by itself, establish negligence.[39]

IV. **Causation**

A. *Elements*

Proof of duty and breach are not sufficient to establish negligence. The plaintiff must also prove that the actions of the defendant caused plaintiff's injuries.[40] Causation in Virginia law consists of both cause-in-fact and legal causation. These two categories are often combined into the single requirement of proximate cause. Proximate cause is defined by the Virginia Jury Instructions, as follows:

> (1) The proximate cause of an event is that act or omission that, in natural and continuous sequence, unbroken by an efficient intervening cause, produces the event, and without which that event would not have occurred. (2) The "proximate cause" of an event is a cause that, in natural and continuous sequence, unbroken by any efficient intervening cause, produces the event, and without which the event would not have occurred. It is an act or omission that immediately causes or fails to prevent the event; an act or omission occurring or concurring with another act, without which the event would not have occurred; provided such event could reasonably have been anticipated by a prudent man in the light of attendant circumstances.[41]

Foreseeability is relevant to proximate cause. The Supreme Court of Virginia has stated:

> [T]o establish proximate cause the plaintiff is not required to prove an injury was certain to occur as a result of the defendant's negligence; "it is [not] necessary . . . that the precise occurrence be foreseen." . . . Rather, the plaintiff must only show that "a reasonably prudent person under similar circumstances ought to have anticipated 'that an injury might probably result from the negligent acts.'" . . . Thus, reasonable foreseeability is sufficient; clairvoyance is not required.[42]

---

[37] Doe v. Terry, 273 Va. 3, 8, 639 S.E.2d 197, 200 (2007).

[38] Clark v. Lang, 124 Va. 544, 98 S.E. 673, 673 (1919).

[39] Filkins v. McAllister Bros., 695 F. Supp. 845, 848 (E.D. Va. 1988).

[40] Va. Prac. Tort and Personal Injury Law § 3:17 (2017) (citing Carolina, Clinchfield & Ohio R.R. Co. v. Mullins, 207 Va. 207, 148 S.E.2d 752 (1966)).

[41] Va. Prac. Jury Instruction § 11:10 (2017).

[42] Virginia Elec. & Power Co. v. Winesett, 225 Va. 459, 468, 303 S.E.2d 868, 874 (1983).

B. Evidence

The question of causation is ordinarily determined by the jury.[43] Only when reasonable persons could not differ on the question of causation will a court decide the issue of causation.[44] The Virginia Jury Instructions state:

> The burden is upon the plaintiff not only to prove by a preponderance of the evidence that the defendant was negligent but also to prove by a preponderance of the evidence that any such negligence was a proximate cause of the occurrence complained of; that is, that the occurrence was a natural and probable consequence of any such negligence. A person is not charged with foreseeing that which could not reasonably be expected to happen, nor for casualties which, though possible, were wholly improbable. Therefore, even though you may believe from a preponderance of the evidence that the defendant was negligent, yet unless you further believe from a preponderance of the evidence that any such negligence was a proximate cause of the occurrence, you must find your verdict in favor of the defendant.[45]

V. Damages

A. Elements

Proof of damages is essential to any claim of negligence.[46] The Virginia Supreme Court has stated that "[d]amages are awarded in tort actions to compensate the plaintiff for all losses suffered by reason of the defendant's breach of some duty imposed by law to protect the broad interests of social policy."[47] The purpose of awarding damages is to put "the injured plaintiff in the same position that he would have been if the injury had not occurred."[48]

B. Evidence

The Virginia Jury Instructions provide, as follows:

> Damages are not to be presumed nor may they be based on speculation, but they must be proven. The burden is on the plaintiff to prove by a preponderance of the evidence any item or element of damage claimed and that it is properly attributable to the accident. Unless such item or element is proven by a preponderance of the evidence, then the plaintiff cannot recover for such item or element.[49]

---

[43] Brown v. Koulizakis, 229 Va. 524, 531, 331 S.E.2d 440, 445 (1985).

[44] Hadeed v. Medic-24, Ltd., 237 Va. 277, 285, 377 S.E.2d 589, 593 (1989).

[45] Va. Prac. Jury Instruction § 12:13 (2017).

[46] Va. Prac. Tort and Personal Injury Law § 3:33 (2017).

[47] Kamlar Corp. v. Haley, 224 Va. 699, 706, 299 S.E.2d 514, 517 (1983).

[48] 1-13 Personal Injury Law In Virginia § 13.1 (2017) (citing Lehigh Portland Cement Co. v. Virginia S.S. Co., 132 Va. 257, 111 S.E. 104 (1922)).

[49] Va. Prac. Jury Instruction § 23:10 (2017).

The plaintiff bears the burden of proving damages by a preponderance of the evidence. Damages do not have to be proven "with mathematical precision" but the plaintiff must "furnish evidence of sufficient facts and circumstances to permit an intelligent and probable estimate thereof."[50]

---

[50] Va. Prac. Jury Instruction § 23:4 (2017).

CHAPTER 48

WASHINGTON

WASHINGTON

Justin R. Huckaby[1]

I. Purpose of Tort Law

The Supreme Court of Washington has noted that "[the] underlying purpose of tort law is to provide for public safety through deterrence."[2] Tort law "protects society's interests in freedom from harm."[3] The Washington Supreme Court has stated that tort actions will be maintainable "to compensate injured parties; to determine parties' rights; to punish wrongdoers and deter wrongful conduct; and to vindicate parties and deter retaliation."[4] In some variation, all tort rules are "designed to both deter other wrongdoers and to compensate the injured person."[5] Absent a legislative provision or compelling public policy, it is a fundamental precept that "the law should not immunize tortfeasors or deny remedy to their victims."[6]

II. Duty to Exercise Ordinary Care

A. Question of Law

To establish a negligence action, a plaintiff must show "the existence of a duty owed."[7] As stated by the Supreme Court of Washington, "it is well settled that [the legal duty] is an essential element in any negligence [claim]."[8] The Second Division of the Court of Appeals of Washington has noted that, "[w]hether a legal duty exists is a question of law."[9]

The court looks to three components to determine "the existence of a legal duty which the defendant owes to the plaintiff." The three components are: "(1) By whom is this duty owed? (2) To whom is it owed? (3)What is its nature?"[10] The third question can also be answered by determining "what is the standard of care?"[11] These questions are questions

---

[1] Research, Instructional Services, and Circulation Librarian, Mississippi College School of Law Library.

[2] Davis v. Baugh Indus. Contractors, Inc., 150 P.3d 545, 548 (Wash. 2007) (quoting Johnson v. Equip. Specialists, Inc., 373 N.E.2d 837, 843 (Ill. App. Ct. 1978)).

[3] Alejandre v. Bull, 153 P.3d 864, 868 (Wash. 2007).

[4] Ford v. Trendwest Resorts, Inc., 43 P.3d 1223, 1227 (Wash. 2002).

[5] Barr v. Interbay Citizens Bank of Tampa, Fla., 635 P.2d 441, 444 (Wash. 1981), *amended by* Barr v. Interbay Citizens Bank of Tampa, Fla., 649 P.2d 827 (Wash. 1982).

[6] Freehe v. Freehe, 500 P.2d 771, 777 (Wash. 1972), *overruled on other grounds by* Brown v. Brown, 675 P.2d 1207 (Wash. 1984).

[7] Lee v. Willis Enters., Inc., 377 P.3d 244, 248 (Wash. Ct. App. 2016).

[8] Petersen v. State, 671 P.2d 230, 236 (Wash. 1983).

[9] *Lee*, 377 P.3d at 248.

[10] Schooley v. Pinch's Deli Mkt., Inc., 912 P.2d 1044, 1046 (Wash. Ct. App. 1996).

[11] *Id.*

of law and should be "answered generally without reference to the facts or parties in a particular case."[12]

A duty may be created through statute or through common law principles of negligence.[13] It can also be created through administrative rules and regulations.[14] When deciding if "the law imposes a duty of care," and determining "the duty's measure and scope," courts weigh "considerations of logic, common sense, justice, policy, and precedent."[15]

Foreseeability defines "the scope of [that] duty owed" to the plaintiff.[16] Foreseeability limits the scope of the duty owed to others because "actors are responsible only for the foreseeable consequences of their acts."[17] Foreseeability is normally decided by the trier of fact, and it should only be decided by a court as a matter of law "where reasonable minds could not differ."[18] Foreseeability is established when "the harm sustained [is] reasonably perceived as being within the general field of danger covered by the specific duty owed by the defendant."[19] It must be determined if "the duty imposed by the risk embraces the conduct which resulted in injury to [the] plaintiff."[20] If the defendant could "not reasonably foresee any injury" resulting from his or her conduct, "there is no negligence and no liability."[21]

B. *The Question of Fact*

i. Elements

The jury determines what level of care is required to satisfy the duty owed to the plaintiff. Absent a statutory standard, the "jury is to measure a party's liability by the common law principles of negligence."[22] Negligence is defined by the *Washington Pattern Jury Instructions—Civil* as "the failure to exercise ordinary care."[23] Ordinary care is defined as "the care a reasonably careful person would exercise under the same or similar circumstances."[24]

ii. Evidence

The plaintiff must present evidence of negligence and the level of care required of the defendant.[25] Statutes, regulations, or other similar rules "may help define the scope of the

---

[12] *Id.*

[13] Bernethy v. Walt Failor's Inc., 653 P.2d 280, 282 (Wash. 1982).

[14] Doss v. ITT Rayonier, Inc., 803 P.2d 4, 7 (Wash. Ct. App. 1991).

[15] Affiliated FM Ins. v. LTK Consulting Servs., Inc., 243 P.3d 521, 526 (Wash. 2010) (quoting Snyder v. Med. Serv. Corp. of E. Wash., 35 P.3d 1158, 1164 (Wash. 2001)).

[16] Schooley v. Pinch's Deli Mkt., Inc., 951 P.2d 749, 753 (Wash. 1998).

[17] *Id.* at 754.

[18] Minahan v. W. Wash. Fair Ass'n, 73 P.3d 1019, 1028 (Wash. Ct. App. 2003).

[19] Hansen v. Friend, 824 P.2d 483, 487 (Wash. 1992) (quoting Christen v. Lee, 780 P.2d 1307, 1313 (Wash. 1989)).

[20] Maltman v. Sauer, 530 P.2d 254, 258 (Wash. 1975) (quoting Rikstad v. Holmberg, 456 P.2d 355, 358 (Wash. 1969)).

[21] Strong v. Terrell, 195 P.3d 977, 983 (Wash. Ct. App. 2008).

[22] Mina v. Boise Cascade Corp., 710 P.2d 184, 190-91 (Wash. 1985).

[23] Wash. Pattern Jury Instr. Civ. WPI 10.01 (6th ed.).

[24] Wash. Pattern Jury Instr. Civ. WPI 10.02 (6th ed.).

[25] Andersen v. Seattle Auto. Co., 265 P. 162, 165 (Wash. 1928).

duty or the standard of care [owed]."[26] Statutes may impose a duty in addition to, or different from, the traditional duty to exercise ordinary care. This occurs when the statute's purposes is: "(1) to protect a class of persons that includes the person whose interest is invaded; (2) to protect the particular interest invaded; (3) to protect the interest against the kind of harm that resulted; and (4) to protect that interest against the particular hazard from which the harm resulted."[27] Internal directives, department policies, and other similar directives "may provide evidence of the standard of care."[28] When such policies are provided as evidence, *Washington Pattern Jury Instruction—Civil* 60.03 should be provided to the jury "which clarifies that a violation is not negligence per se."[29] Counsel may inform the jury in closing argument that they serve as the conscience of the community in deciding the level of care required under the circumstances.[30]

III. Breach of Duty

A. *Elements*

In order to establish negligence, a plaintiff must show a "breach of the duty owed to the person injured."[31] The plaintiff must show: "(1) that the defendant is a member of the class of persons that owes the duty; (2) that the plaintiff is a member of the class of persons to whom the duty is owed; and (3) that the defendant violated the applicable standard of care."[32] A breach of duty is ordinarily a question of fact to be decided by the jury unless reasonable minds could not differ.[33]

B. *Evidence*

The plaintiff must present evidence to meet his burden that the defendant breached his duty owed to the plaintiff.[34] The subjective belief or subsequent actions of a defendant cannot be entered into evidence as proof of the objective determination that a breach of duty owed to the plaintiff has actually occurred.[35] Evidence of a "violation of a statute or administrative regulation is only evidence of negligence" and not evidence of negligence *per se*.[36] Likewise, a violation of safety rules "may afford some evidence of negligence," but it does not constitute negligence as a matter of law.[37]

---

[26] Owen v. Burlington N. & Santa Fe R.R., 108 P.3d 1220, 1223 (Wash. 2005).

[27] Schwartz v. Elerding, 270 P.3d 630, 635 (Wash. Ct. App. 2012).

[28] Joyce v. State Dep't of Corr., 119 P.3d 825, 834 (Wash. 2005).

[29] *Id.*

[30] Miller v. Kenny, 325 P.3d 278, 300 (Wash. Ct. App. 2014).

[31] Walker v. King Cty. Metro, 109 P.3d 836, 838 (Wash. Ct. App. 2005).

[32] Gall v. McDonald Indus., 926 P.2d 934, 940 (Wash. Ct. App. 1996).

[33] *Id.*

[34] Howell v. Spokane & Inland Empire Blood Bank, 818 P.2d 1056, 1059 (Wash. 1991).

[35] Bartlett v. Hantover, 526 P.2d 1217, 1219-20 (Wash. 1974).

[36] Williams v. Leone & Keeble, Inc., 285 P.3d 906, 916 (Wash. Ct. App. 2012).

[37] Engen v. Arnold, 379 P.2d 990, 994 (Wash. 1963).

IV. Causation
A. Elements

In a negligence action, the plaintiff must prove that the defendant's actions were the proximate causation of the plaintiff's injuries. In order to prove proximate causation, the plaintiff must meet the two required elements of: "(1) cause-in-fact and (2) legal causation."[38] Cause-in-fact "refers to the 'but-for' consequences of [the] act—the physical connection between [the] act and [the] injury."[39] Determining the cause-in-fact is generally a question for the jury."[40] The Supreme Court of Washington has recognized that the "issues regarding whether duty and legal causation exist are intertwined."[41] Legal causation is "grounded in the determination of how far the consequences of a defendant's act should extend."[42] It must be determined if the plaintiff's injury was foreseeable[43] or was it "too remote or attenuated to impose liability."[44] Legal causation is a question of law as it deals primarily with policy concerns.[45]

B. Evidence

Proximate causation is "a question for the trier of fact under usual circumstances."[46] The jury "must weigh . . . factors, values, facts and circumstances presented in a given case" when deciding proximate cause.[47]

V. Damages
A. Elements

To establish a negligence claim, the plaintiff must show that damages exist as a result of the actions of the defendant.[48] Where a defendant's negligence causes injury, the defendant is liable for "any and all foreseeable damages."[49] Washington law "favors just compensation of [injured] victims."[50] Damages "must be compensatory of a pecuniary loss."[51] In personal

---

[38] *Schooley*, 951 P.2d at 754.

[39] Hartley v. State, 698 P.2d 77, 83 (Wash. 1985).

[40] Doherty v. Municipality of Metro. Seattle, 921 P.2d 1098, 1101 (Wash. Ct. App. 1996).

[41] *Schooley*, 951 P.2d at 755.

[42] M.H. v. Corp. of Catholic Archbishop of Seattle, 252 P.3d 914, 920 (Wash. Ct. App. 2011).

[43] Kim v. Budget Rent A Car Sys., Inc., 15 P.3d 1283, 1289-90 (Wash. 2001).

[44] Dewar v. Smith, 342 P.3d 328, 337 (Wash. Ct. App. 2015).

[45] Almquist v. Finley Sch. Dist. No. 53, 57 P.3d 1191, 1197 (Wash. Ct. App. 2002).

[46] Everett v. Diamond, 638 P.2d 605, 607 (Wash. Ct. App. 1981).

[47] Hosea v. City of Seattle, 393 P.2d 967, 970 (Wash. 1964).

[48] Wuth *ex rel.* Kessler v. Lab. Corp. of Am., 359 P.3d 841, 854 (Wash. Ct. App. 2015).

[49] Lindquist v. Dengel, 581 P.2d 177, 180 (Wash. Ct. App. 1978).

[50] Stottlemyre v. Reed, 665 P.2d 1383, 1386 (Wash. Ct. App. 1983), *disagreed with on other grounds by* Bennett v. Shinoda Floral, Inc., 717 P.2d 1379 (Wash. Ct. App. 1986).

[51] Adams v. State, 429 P.2d 109, 120 (Wash. 1967).

injury cases, plaintiffs should not include a "statement of the damages sought but [should include] a prayer for damages as shall be determined" in their complaint.[52]

B. Evidence

The damages amount should be left to "the discretion of the jury."[53] There is "no precise formula for [determining] an award."[54] Awards "can be substantial (citing authorities) but not out of proportion to actual damages."[55] Courts should not "interfere with the conclusion of the jury, when fairly made."[56] The amount should be "supported by substantial evidence" admitted in the record.[57] Although damages are difficult to prove through "mathematical certainty," the damage amount should be "[justified] in light of the evidence" so as not to "shock the [court's] sense of justice and sound judgment."[58]

---

[52] Wash. Rev. Code § 4.28.360.

[53] Aronson v. City of Everett, 239 P. 1011, 1015 (Wash. 1925).

[54] Estes v. Bevan, 395 P.2d 44, 45 (Wash. 1964).

[55] *Adams*, 429 P.2d at 120.

[56] Kellerher v. Porter, 189 P.2d 223, 231-32 (Wash. 1948).

[57] Terrell v. Hamilton, 358 P.3d 453, 463 (Wash. Ct. App. 2015) (quoting Bunch v. King Cty. Dept. of Youth Serv., 116 P.3d 381, 387 (Wash. 2005)).

[58] *Adams*, 429 P.2d at 120.

CHAPTER 49

WEST VIRGINIA

WEST VIRGINIA

Savanna L. Nolan[1]

I. Purpose of Tort Law

In West Virginia, the Supreme Court of Appeals has held that the "primary unifying principle of tort law is one of corrective justice," focusing on repairing the damage done to the victim,[2] usually by an attempt to make the victim whole again.[3] West Virginia has a strong public policy of allowing victims of negligence to recover under tort law.[4] This policy has also been framed as an "original moral duty, enjoined upon every person, so to conduct himself, or exercise his own rights, as not to injure another."[5]

Though it is less firmly established, West Virginia has also recognized the deterrent aspect of tort law.[6]

II. Duty to Exercise Ordinary Care

A. Question of Law

Under West Virginia law, the threshold question in all negligence actions is whether the defendant owed the plaintiff a duty.[7] Duty has been defined as "a question of whether the defendant is under any obligation for the benefit of the particular plaintiff; and in negligence cases, the duty is always the same, to conform to the legal standard of reasonable conduct in light of the apparent risk."[8]

A duty can be imposed by statute,[9] but it can also be imposed by the common law, especially as duty is "not absolute, but is always relative to some circumstance of time, place, manner, or person."[10] Whether the defendant owed the plaintiff a legal duty is a question of

---

[1] Reference Librarian, Georgetown University Law Center; J.D., University of Georgia; M.S.L.I.S., The Catholic University of America.

[2] Kenney v. Liston, 760 S.E.2d 434, 445 (W. Va. 2014).

[3] Brooks v. City of Huntington, 768 S.E.2d 97, 102 (W. Va. 2014).

[4] Paul v. Nat'l Life, 352 S.E.2d 550, 556 (W. Va. 1986).

[5] Robertson v. LeMaster, 301 S.E.2d 563, 567 (W. Va. 1983) (quoting Blaine v. Chesapeake & O. R.R. Co., 9 W. Va. 252, 254 (1876)).

[6] Hannah v. Heeter, 584 S.E.2d 560, 566 (W. Va. 2003).

[7] Strahin v. Cleavenger, 603 S.E.2d 197, 203 (W. Va. 2004).

[8] *Robertson,* 301 S.E.2d at 567 (quoting W. Prosser, The Law of Torts, § 53 (4th ed. 1971)).

[9] Schaffer v. Acme Limestone Co. 524 S.E.2d 688 (W. Va. 2005).

[10] *Strahin,* 603 S.E.2d at 206 (quoting Dicken v. Liverpool Salt & Coal Co., 23 S.E. 582 (W. Va. 1895)).

law to be determined by the court.[11] However, when facts concerning foreseeability are disputable, those facts are to be determined by a jury, and the court's findings concerning duty are conditioned on those determinations.[12] Additionally, though the court decides whether a duty existed, the jury determines the scope of the "due care" owed because of that duty under the circumstances.[13]

West Virginia courts consider two aspects when determining duty: foreseeability and "policy considerations underlying the core issue of the scope of the legal system's protections," such as the likelihood of injury, the magnitude of the defendant's burden to prevent the injury, and the consequences of placing that burden on the defendant.[14] Between the two factors, the courts have held that foreseeability is the "ultimate test of the existence of duty."[15]

Foreseeability, or "reasonable anticipation of the consequences of an act" is the core consideration for negligence in West Virginia.[16] The test for foreseeability is whether an ordinary person in the defendant's position, "knowing what he knew or should have known," would have anticipated that the "harm of the general nature of that suffered was likely to result."[17] Conversely, if the danger could not have been reasonably apprehended or guarded against, then there is no duty and therefore no negligence.[18]

Negligence liability and the duty to exercise reasonable care extend to the maintenance of areas within the defendant's control as well as the repercussions of a specific act.[19]

B. *Question of Fact*

i. **Elements**

Negligence and what constitutes "due care" under the circumstances are questions of fact for the jury to decide, provided that differing conclusions can be drawn from the facts presented.[20] West Virginia uses the terms "due care," "reasonable care," and "ordinary care" interchangeably to mean the level of care that an ordinarily prudent person would use under the same or similar circumstances.[21] Since this standard varies and is based on the situation,

---

[11] Aiken v. Debow, 541 S.E.2d 576, 580 (W. Va. 2000).

[12] *Strahin*, 603 S.E.2d at 207.

[13] Waugh v. Traxler, 412 S.E.2d 756, 759 (W. Va. 1991).

[14] Robertson v. LeMaster, 301 S.E.2d 563, 567-68 (W. Va. 1983).

[15] *Aiken*, 541 S.E.2d at 581 (quoting Sewell v. Gregory, 371 S.E.2d 82, 85 (W. Va. 1988)).

[16] State *ex rel*. Cox v. Sims, 77 S.E.2d 151, 159-60 (W. Va. 1997).

[17] *Sewell*, 371 S.E.2d at 85 (W. Va. 1988).

[18] *Cox*, 77 S.E.2d at159 (W. Va. 1997) (citing 1 SHEARMAN & REDFIELD ON NEGLIGENCE § 24) ("Reasonable anticipation is that expectation created in the mind of the ordinarily prudent and competent person as the consequence of his reaction to any given set of circumstances. If such expectation carries recognition that the given set of circumstances is suggestive of danger, then failure to take appropriate safety measures constitutes negligence. On the contrary, there is no duty to guard when there is no danger reasonably to be apprehended. Negligence is gauged by the ability to anticipate. Precaution is a duty only so far as there is reason for apprehension.").

[19] Durm v. Heck's, Inc. 401 S.E.2d 908, 911 (W. Va. 1991) ("We have generally adhered to the principle that liability results either from control of the subject area or from a specific wrongful act.").

[20] Waugh v. Traxler, 412 S.E.2d 756, 759 (W. Va. 1991).

[21] Koontz v. Whitney, 153 S.E. 797, 798 (W. Va. 1930).

it allows for higher degrees of care in riskier circumstances, such as handling electricity or firearms. The standard becomes "ordinary care" under those riskier circumstances.[22]

ii.   Evidence

The plaintiff must prove by a preponderance of the evidence that the defendant owed him a legal duty,[23] and the plaintiff "must establish a prima facie case of negligence against the defendant in order to warrant jury consideration."[24] Though this is a lesser standard than the reasonable doubt standard, the court has held that there must be more than a "mere scintilla of evidence" in order to put the case before a jury.[25] Evidence that "invites speculation, conjecture, and random judgment" is insufficient evidence to find that the defendant owed a duty to the plaintiff.[26] It is well settled in West Virginia jurisprudence that the evidence in a negligence case can be circumstantial or direct evidence.[27] However, the courts have ruled that a witness may not opine on whether the defendant in a negligence case acted with due care, as that is a vital issue for the jury to resolve based on the facts presented.[28] Violation of a statute can provide prima facie evidence of negligence.[29]

As the level of ordinary care is based upon the specific circumstances, the common usage and practices of the parties is a test for the level of ordinary care, but it is not a conclusive or controlling test, especially when the negligent act at issue violates a statute.[30] West Virginia Rule of Evidence 406 allows for the introduction of evidence concerning the habits of an individual, "shown to be a regularly repeated response to similar factual situations," or the routine practices of an organization to prove that the conduct at the time of the injury conformed to that habit; this evidence is admissible even without eyewitness corroboration.[31]

Rules and regulations may be used as evidence of an accepted standard of conduct for the community in question.[32] However, the statute or regulation creates a floor for the level of due care; the specific circumstances may require greater care.[33] Expert testimony is not required to establish a standard of care if the acts in question are simple enough for the average juror to understand.[34]

---

[22] *Id.*

[23] Webb v. Brown & Williamson Tobacco Co., 2 S.E.2d 898, 899 (W. Va. 1939).

[24] Smith v. Edward M. Rude Carrier Corp., 151 S.E.2d 738, 744 (W. Va. 1966).

[25] David v. Cross, 164 S.E.2d 899, 904 (W. Va. 1968).

[26] Culberson v. McCloud, 315 S.E.2d 219, 221 (W. Va. 1984).

[27] *Smith*, 151 S.E.2d at 744.

[28] Hendricks v. Monongahela W. Penn Pub. Serv. Co., 163 S.E. 411, 415 (W. Va. 1932).

[29] Marcus v. Staubs, 736 S.E.2d 360, 368 (W. Va. 2012).

[30] Schaffner v. Nat'l Supply Co., 92 S.E. 580, 589 (W. Va. 1917).

[31] Rodgers v. Rodgers, 399 S.E.2d 664, 668, 675-76 (W. Va. 1990).

[32] Finch v. Inspectech, LLC, 727 S.E.2d 823, 833-35 (W. Va. 2012).

[33] Miller v. Warren, 390 S.E.2d 207, 209 (W. Va. 1990) (citing RESTATEMENT (SECOND) OF TORTS, § 288C (1965)).

[34] Adkins v. Slater, 298 S.E.2d 236, 242 (W. Va. 1982).

III.   Breach of Duty

A.   *Elements*

A plaintiff must prove that the defendant committed "some act or omission in violation of a duty owed to the plaintiff."[35] It has long been established in West Virginia that "where there is no duty broken there can be no negligence."[36] Unlike Virginia, in West Virginia the violation of a statute creates a rebuttable assumption of prima facie negligence, and not negligence *per se*.[37]

B.   *Evidence*

The plaintiff must prove a breach of duty by a preponderance of the evidence.[38]

IV.   Causation

A.   *Elements*

A plaintiff in a West Virginia negligence action must prove that his injuries were proximately caused by the defendant's breach of duty.[39] A breach of duty on its own is not actionable unless the plaintiff can also present evidence that the defendant's breach proximately caused the injury.[40] West Virginia courts have rules that proximate cause can be loosely defined as "cause, which, in natural and continuous sequence, unbroken by any efficient intervening causes, produces the injury, and without which the result would not have occurred."[41] However, the courts have also held that there cannot be a single "yardstick" test for proximate cause, and that each fact situation must be examined and determined "based on logic, common sense, justice and precedent."[42]

Proximate cause is a question of fact for the jury to decide.[43] To establish proximate cause, the plaintiff must show two factors: that the "doing or the failure to do an act which a person of ordinary prudence could foresee might naturally or probably produce an injury," and that the act or omission actually did produce an injury.[44] The foreseeability factor is vital

---

[35] Parsley v. Gen. Motors Acceptance Corp., 280 S.E.2d 703, 706 (W. Va. 1981).

[36] Uthermohlen v. Bogg's Run Min. & Mfg. Co., 40 S.E. 410, 411 (W. Va. 1901).

[37] Waugh v. Traxler, 412 S.E.2d 756, 759 (W. Va. 1991).

[38] Webb v. Brown & Williamson Tobacco Co., 2 S.E.2d 898, 899 (W. Va. 1939).

[39] *Id.*

[40] Louk v. Isuzu Motors, Inc., 479 S.E.2d 911, 923 (W. Va. 1996).

[41] Evans v. Farmer, 133 S.E.2d 710, 715 (W. Va. 1963).

[42] *Id.*

[43] Waugh v. Traxler, 412 S.E.2d 756, 759 (W. Va. 1991).

[44] Matthews v. Cumberland & Allegheny Gas Co., 77 S.E.2d 180, 189 (W. Va. 1953).

to establishing proximate cause and the negligence claim overall; if an injury was not foreseeable, then there was no negligence.[45]

As with foreseeability within the context of establishing a duty, foreseeability for the purposes of determining proximate cause is defined as "reasonably expected to produce an injury" or "reasonable anticipation that some injury might result."[46] The courts have tested foreseeability by asking whether an act or omission "might have been reasonably expected to produce an injury."[47]

B. Evidence

Proximate cause is a question of fact for the jury as long as there are either conflicting facts or undisputed facts that could lead reasonable individuals to draw different conclusions.[48] The plaintiff must prove by a preponderance of the evidence that his injuries were proximately caused by the defendant's breach of duty.[49]

V. Damages

A. Elements

West Virginia recognizes both general and special damages. General damages have been defined as "damages which necessarily flow from the act or omission complained of," while special damages are "damages which are not the necessary results, though they may be the natural and proximate consequence of the act or omission."[50] Both of these types of damages are compensatory, and are intended to "measure the actual loss, and are given as amends therefor."[51] A plaintiff can only recover damages once for one injury; double recovery is not permitted for two legal theories of the same injury.[52]

B. Evidence

Determining the amount of damages in a negligence case is a question of fact reserved for a jury.[53] The common law has established that an appellate court will not set aside a jury's damages determination "unless the verdict is monstrous and enormous, at first blush beyond

---

[45] Puffer v. Hub Cigar Store, 84 S.E.2d 145, 153 (W. Va. 1954) ("Foreseeable injury is a requisite of proximate cause, and proximate cause is a requisite for actionable negligence, and actionable negligence is a requisite for recovery in an action for personal injury negligently inflicted."), *overruled on other grounds*, Mallet v. Pickens, 522 S.E.2d 436 (W. Va. 1999).

[46] *Matthews*, 77 S.E.2d at 188.

[47] Haddox v. Suburban Lanes, Inc, 349 S.E.2d 910, 914 (W. Va. 1986).

[48] *Waugh*, 412 S.E.2d at 759.

[49] Webb v. Brown & Williamson Tobacco Co., 2 S.E.2d 898, 899 (W. Va. 1939).

[50] Raines v. Faulkner, 48 S.E.2d 393, 399 (W. Va. 1947).

[51] Talbott v. West Virginia Cent. & Pittsburgh Ry. Co., 26 S.E. 311, 311 (W. Va. 1896).

[52] Harless v. First Nat'l Bank in Fairmont, 289 S.E.2d 692, 705 (W. Va. 1982).

[53] Bressler v. Mull's Grocery Mart, 461 S.E.2d 124, 128 (W. Va. 1995).

all measure, unreasonable and outrageous, and such manifestly shows jury passion, partiality, prejudice, or corruption."[54] Similarly, a jury award for either pain and suffering or non-permanent injuries "will generally not be disturbed because of the small amount awarded."[55] However, the courts will overturn a jury's findings if "there is uncontroverted evidence that there was a substantial injury" and the jury does not award damages in any amount.[56]

---

[54] Roberts v. Stevens Clinic Hosp., Inc., 345 S.E.2d 791, 800 (W. Va. 1986) (quoting Addair v. Majestic Petroleum Co., Inc., 232 S.E.2d 821, 825 (W. Va. 1977)).

[55] Keiffer v. Queen, 189 S.E.2d 842, 845 (W. Va. 1972).

[56] *Id.*

CHAPTER 50

WISCONSIN

WISCONSIN

Gregg W. Luther[1]

I. Purpose of Tort Law

Tort law serves three broad social purposes in Wisconsin: (1) to shift the losses caused by personal injury to the one at fault; (2) to deter unsafe behavior; and (3) to compensate the victim, tort law creates a mechanism to distribute losses widely. The distribution is effected through liability insurance premiums, consumer prices, etc.[2] "[W]isconsin negligence law has not only a compensatory aspect, but also an admonitory and deterrent aspect."[3]

"Tort law . . . serves the 'prophylactic' purpose of preventing future harm . . . payment of damages provides a strong incentive to prevent the occurrence of harm."[4] Tort law is designed to "protect society against the unreasonable risk of harm from accidental and unexpected injury."[5]

"Tort law offers more than a minimal financial safety net."[6] It provides the opportunity for a person who is harmed by another to recover damages to make that person whole.[7] Wisconsin has a "significant interest in fully compensating victims of ordinary negligence."[8]

II. Duty to Exercise Ordinary Care

A. Question of Law

To maintain a cause of action for negligence under Wisconsin law, the plaintiff must prove: (1) A duty of care on the part of the defendant; (2) a breach of that duty; (3) a causal connection between the conduct and the injury; and (4) actual loss or damage as a result of the injury. "Even if these elements are met, public policy considerations may . . . preclude imposing liability on the defendant."[9] Negligence, like all facts, can be proven by direct or circumstantial evidence.[10]

---

[1] Oklahoma City University Law Review and School of Law alumnus.

[2] CLL Assocs. Ltd. P'ship v. Arrowhead Pac. Corp., 174 Wis. 2d 604, 610, 497 N.W.2d 115, 117 (1993) (citing John G. Flemming, *The Law of Torts* 7-10 (7th ed. 1987)).

[3] State Farm Mut. Auto. Ins. Co. v. Gillette, 2002 WI 31, ¶ 64, 251 Wis. 2d 561, 593, 641 N.W.2d 662, 678 (2002).

[4] Merten v. Nathan, 108 Wis. 2d 205, 211-12, 321 N.W.2d 173, 177 (1982).

[5] Grams v. Milk Prod., Inc., 2005 WI 112, ¶18, 283 Wis. 2d 511, 699 N.W.2d 167, 172 (2005) (quoting Ins. Co. of N. Am. v. Cease Elec. Inc., 2004 WI 139, ¶ 39, 276 Wis. 2d 361, 377, 688 N.W.2d 462, 470 (2004)).

[6] Teschendorf v. State Farm Ins. Cos., 2006 WI 89, ¶ 60, 293 Wis. 2d 123, 155, 717 N.W.2d 258, 273 (2006).

[7] Jones v. Dane County, 195 Wis. 2d 892, 918, 537 N.W.2d 74 (Ct. App. 1995).

[8] State Farm Mut. Auto. Ins. Co. v. Gillette, 2002 WI 31, ¶ 65, 251 Wis. 2d 561, 593, 641 N.W.2d 662, 678 (2002).

[9] Miller v Wal-Mart Stores, Inc., 219 Wis. 2d 250, 260, 580 N.W.2d 233, 238 (1998).

[10] Lambrecht v. Estate of Kaczmarczyk, 2001 WI 25 ¶ 3, 623 N.W.2d 751, 756 (2001).

"The duty of any person is the obligation of due care to refrain from any act which will cause a foreseeable harm to others even though the nature of that harm and the identity of the harmed person or harmed interest are unknown at the time of the act."[11] "A defendant's duty is established when it can be said that it was foreseeable that his or her act or omission to act may cause harm to someone. The duty is to refrain from such act or omission."[12] Whether a duty exists and the scope of a duty are questions of law for the court.[13]

B. *Question of Fact*

i. Elements

The level of care required to satisfy "ordinary care" is decided by the jury.[14] "Ordinary care is the care which a reasonable person would use in similar circumstances."[15] When a person's conduct is such that a reasonable person would recognize the conduct creates an unreasonable risk of injury to another, it is appropriate for the jury to find that a person is not using ordinary care.[16] "Ordinary care involves the concept of foreseeability, in that a reasonable person exercising ordinary care would have foreseen injury as a consequence of his act."[17] In most cases, "foreseeability of harm" is left to the jury.[18] Ordinary care becomes a question of law where the court finds that no reasonable jury could find that the injury was a foreseeable consequence.[19]

ii. Evidence

A statute or previous judicial decision may set a standard of care.[20] The court can determine that a violation of a safety statute represents negligence *per se* if (1) the harm inflicted was the type of harm that the statute was intended to prevent; (2) the person injured was within the class of persons the statute intended to protect; and (3) there is some indication that the legislature intended the statute to serve as a basis for civil liability.[21] Safety rules adopted by most of an industry are admissible.[22] The violation of a safety statute can be

---

[11] *Miller,* 219 Wis. 2d at 260, 580 N.W.2d at 238 (citations omitted).

[12] *Id.* (citations omitted).

[13] Hoida, Inc. v. M & I Midstate Bank, 2006 WI 69, ¶ 23, n.12, 291 Wis. 2d 283, 302, 717 N.W.2d 17, 27 (2006).

[14] *Id.,* ¶ 71, n.3, 291 Wis. 2d at 325, 717 N.W.2d at 38. "A person is negligent when [he/she] fails to exercise ordinary care. Ordinary care is the care which a reasonable person would use in similar circumstances. A person is not using ordinary care and is negligent, if the person, without intending to do harm, does something (or fails to do something) that a reasonable person would recognize as creating an unreasonable risk of injury or damage to a person or property." Wis. JI-CIVIL 1005 ("Negligence: Defined").

[15] *Id.*

[16] *Id.*

[17] *Id.,* ¶ 30, 291 Wis. 2d at 306, 717 N.W.2d at 29.

[18] Tesar v. Anderson, 2010 WI App 116, ¶ 11, n.13, 329 Wis. 2d 240, 252, 789 N.W.2d 351, 357 (2010).

[19] *Id.*

[20] Osborne v. Montgomery, 203 Wis. 223, 240, 234 N.W. 372, 378 (1931).

[21] Antwaun A. *ex rel.* Muwonge v. Heritage Mut. Ins. Co., 228 Wis. 2d 44, 66-67, 596 N.W.2d 456, 466 (1999).

[22] Johnson v. Misericordia Cmty. Hosp., 97 Wis. 2d 521, 510, 294 N.W.2d 501, 538 (1980).

excused in cases of emergency.[23] Custom or practice in an industry, trade, or community may be introduced and considered as evidence of whether or not the defendant exercised ordinary care, but that evidence does not establish ordinary care as a matter of law.[24]

III. Breach of Duty

A. *Elements*

A person is negligent when, without intending to do any harm, he does something or fails to do something under circumstances where a reasonable person would foresee "some injury might probably result from his conduct."[25] A person is negligent when they fail to exercise ordinary care.[26] The existence of negligence, as a general rule, is a jury question.[27] "In most cases, whether a defendant breached a duty is a question of fact that is submitted to the jury . . ."[28] However, the court can find that the defendant was not negligent as a matter of law if it determines that no reasonable person could find that the defendant was negligent,[29] that a particular risk was not foreseeable,[30] or that no duty to take a specific precaution existed under the facts of the case.[31]

B. *Evidence*

A plaintiff must present evidence of the defendant's breach of the duty to exercise ordinary care.[32]

---

[23] Totsky v. Riteway Bus Serv., Inc., 2000 WI 29, ¶¶ 29-31, 233 Wis. 2d 371, 391-94, 607 N.W.2d 637, 645-47 (2000) (citing RESTATEMENT (SECOND) OF TORTS §288A).

[24] Victorson v. Milwaukee & Suburban Transport Co., 70 Wis. 2d 336, 351-352, 234 N.W.2d 332 (1975) (abrogated on other grounds). *See* Wis. JI-CIVIL 1019.

[25] Osborne v. Montgomery, 203 Wis. 223, 242, 234 N.W. 372, 379 (1931); Miller v Wal-Mart Stores, Inc., 219 Wis. 2d 250, 261-62, 580 N.W.2d 233, 238 (1998).

[26] In 2009, Wis. JI-CIVIL 1005 ("Negligence: Defined") was amended to read:

"A person is negligent when (he) (she) fails to exercise ordinary care. Ordinary care is the care which a reasonable person would use in similar circumstances. A person is not using ordinary care and is negligent, if the person, without intending to do harm, does something (or fails to do something) that a reasonable person would recognize as creating an unreasonable risk of injury or damage to a person or property."

[27] Morgan v. Pennsylvania Gen. Ins. Co., 87 Wis. 2d 723, 732, 275 N.W.2d 660, 664-65 (1979).

[28] Behrendt v. Gulf Underwriters Ins. Co., 2009 WI 71, ¶ 4, 318 Wis. 2d 622, 628, 768 N.W.2d 568, 571 (2009).

[29] *Id.*, 318 Wis. 2d at 637, 768 N.W.2d at 575-76.

[30] Univ. Dodge, Inc. v. Drott Tractor Co., 55 Wis. 2d 396, 400, 198 N.W.2d 621, 623 (1972) (finding no negligence because the risk was not foreseeable); Hoida, Inc. v. M & I Midstate Bank, 2006 WI 69, ¶¶ 28-30, 40, 46, 291 Wis. 2d 283, 717 N.W.2d 17 (concluding there was no breach because the duty did not include an unforeseeable risk); *Behrendt*, ¶¶ 3, 15-31, 318 Wis. 2d at 627, 633-42, 768 N.W.2d at 571, 574-78 (finding no breach of the duty of ordinary care because the risk was not foreseeable).

[31] Rockweit by Donohue v. Senecal, 197 Wis. 2d 409, 421, 541 N.W.2d 742, 748 (1995); Hocking v. City of Dodgeville, 2009 WI 70, ¶¶ 10-13, 318 Wis. 2d 681, 689-91, 768 N.W.2d 552, 555-56 (2009).

[32] Milwaukee Area Technical College v. Frontier Adjusters of Milwaukee, 752 N.W. 2d 396, 405, 2008 WI App. ¶ 23.

IV. Causation

A. Elements

There must be a causal connection between the defendant's negligent conduct and the injury. The test for cause-in-fact is whether the negligence of the defendant was a substantial factor in producing the injury.[33] "The phrase 'substantial factor' denotes that the defendant's conduct has such an effect in producing the harm as to lead the trier of fact, as a reasonable person, to regard it as a cause, using that word in the popular sense."[34] Foreseeability is not an element of cause-in-fact.[35]

Public policy considerations may preclude imposing liability in a specific case if the jury determines that the defendant breached a duty and that the defendant's negligent conduct caused injury in fact to the plaintiff. Whether public policy factors operate to limit liability in a particular case is a question of law, but do involve inquiry into the concepts of "foreseeability of harm" and "range of harms/scope of risk."[36] However, "[l]iability is the rule and relief for public policy reasons is the exception."[37]

B. Evidence

Once negligence is established, the defendant is responsible for all consequences, both foreseen and unforeseen, for which the defendant's act was a substantial factor.[38] There can be more than one substantial factor contributing to the same result and thus more than one cause-in-fact.[39] If reasonable people could differ on whether the defendant's negligence was a cause-in-fact of the plaintiff's injuries, the question is one for the jury.[40] The determination of cause-in-fact is a question for the court only if reasonable people could not disagree.[41]

Causation cannot be a matter of speculation or conjecture. A mere possibility of causation is not sufficient. There must be sufficient credible evidence for the jury to conclude that the harm was the result of the defendant's negligent conduct.[42]

---

[33] Morgan v. Pennsylvania Gen. Ins. Co., 87 Wis. 2d 723, 735, 275 N.W.2d 660, 666 (1979).

[34] Merco Distrib. Corp. v. Commercial Police Alarm Co., 84 Wis. 2d 455, 458-59, 267 N.W.2d 652, 654 (1978).

[35] Stewart v. Wulf, 85 Wis. 2d 461, 469, 271 N.W.2d 79, 83 (1978) (citations omitted).

[36] Miller v. Wal-Mart Stores, Inc., 219 Wis. 2d 250, 264-65, 580 N.W.2d 233, 240 (1998). "Some of the public policy reasons for not imposing liability despite a finding of negligence as a substantial factor producing injury are: (1) The injury is too remote from the negligence; or (2) the injury is too wholly out of proportion to the culpability of the negligent tortfeasor; or (3) in retrospect it appears too highly extraordinary that the negligence should have brought about the harm; or (4) because allowance of recovery would place too unreasonable a burden on the negligent tortfeasor; or (5) because allowance of recovery would be too likely to open the way for fraudulent claims; or (6) allowance of recovery would enter a field that has no sensible or just stopping point." Id.

[37] Tesar v. Anderson, 2010 WI App 116, ¶ 9, 329 Wis. 2d 240, 250, 789 N.W.2d 351, 356 (2010).

[38] Pfiefer v. Standard Gateway Theater, 262 Wis. 229, 235-36, 55 N.W.2d 29, 32 (1952); A. E. Inv. Corp. v. Link Builders, Inc., 62 Wis. 2d 479, 484, 214 N.W.2d 764, 766 (1974).

[39] Morgan v. Pennsylvania Gen. Ins. Co., 87 Wis. 2d 723, 735, 275 N.W.2d 660, 666 (1979).

[40] Merco Distrib. Corp. v. Commercial Police Alarm Co., 84 Wis. 2d 455, 459, 267 N.W.2d 652, 654 (1978).

[41] Morgan, 87 Wis. 2d at 735-6, 275 N.W.2d at 666.

[42] Merco, 84 Wis. 2d at 460, 267 N.W.2d at 655.

V. Damages

A. *Elements*

"In Wisconsin[,] compensatory damages are given to make whole the damage or injury of the injured party."[43] A defendant is responsible for all consequences of their negligent conduct, both foreseen and unforeseen.[44]

B. *Evidence*

"[D]amages must be proven with reasonable certainty"[45] and cannot be based on speculation or guesswork.[46] "[W]here, from the nature of the case, the extent of the injury and the amount of damage are not capable of exact and accurate proof . . . the evidence . . . [must] lay a foundation which will enable the trier of fact to make a fair and reasonable estimate."[47] The amount of damages is a question of fact within the discretion of the jury.[48]

---

[43] White v. Benkowski, 37 Wis. 2d 285, 290, 155 N.W.2d 74, 77 (1967).

[44] Pfiefer v. Standard Gateway Theater, 262 Wis. 229, 235-36, 55 N.W.2d 29, 32 (1952); A. E. Inv. Corp. v. Link Builders, Inc., 62 Wis. 2d 479, 484, 214 N.W.2d 764, 766 (1974).

[45] Cutler Cranberry Co. v. Oakdale Elec. Co-op., 78 Wis. 2d 222, 233, 254 N.W.2d 234, 240 (1977) (citing Caygill v. Ipsen, 27 Wis. 2d 578, 589-90, 135 N.W.2d 284 (1965)).

[46] Kuhlman, Inc. v. G. Heileman Brewing Co., 83 Wis. 2d 749, 767, 266 N.W.2d 382, 391 (1978).

[47] *Cutler Cranberry Co.*, 78 Wis. 2d at 234, 254 N.W.2d at 240.

[48] Jones v. Fisher, 42 Wis. 2d 209, 217, 166 N.W.2d 175, 179 (1969).

CHAPTER 51

WYOMING

WYOMING

Casey D. Duncan[1]

I. Purpose of Tort Law

A fundamental theory of tort law is "that one should pay for the harm which he causes when he is at fault."[2] While the Wyoming Supreme Court has never provided "an all-inclusive definition" of what constitutes a tort, it has generally defined a tort as an "unlawful act injurious to another, independent of contract."[3] The Court has also noted that the most common aims of tort law are "(1) compensation of injured persons and (2) deterrence of undesirable behavior,"[4] and that the "controlling policy consideration underlying tort law is . . . the protection of persons and property from losses resulting from injury."[5]

Similarly, the Court has noted that the legislative objectives underlying statutorily created tort claims, namely "deterrence, compensation and regulating or cost-spreading," are closely related to traditional elements of common law-based negligence claims.[6] Finally, the Court has also affirmed that it "is at liberty to recognize new common law torts when appropriate to meet society's changing needs," in addition to traditional common law torts and those created by legislative enactment.[7]

II. Duty to Exercise Ordinary Care

A. Question of Law

Tort liability in Wyoming is premised upon the existence of a duty and a failure to perform that duty.[8] A duty, while "not sacrosanct in itself," may generally be expressed as "the sum total of those considerations of policy which lead the law to say that the plaintiff is

---

[1] Director of the Law Library and Assistant Professor of Law, University of Wyoming College of Law.

[2] Fraley v. Worthington, 385 F. Supp. 605, 609 (D. Wyo. 1974).

[3] Price v. State Highway Comm'n, 62 Wyo. 385, 396, 167 P.2d 309, 312 (1946); ABC Builders, Inc. v. Phillips, 632 P.2d 925, 934 (Wyo. 1981).

[4] Greenwalt v. Ram Rest. Corp. of Wyoming, 2003 WY 77, ¶ 13, 71 P.3d 717, 724 (Wyo. 2003) (quoting DAN B. DOBBS, THE LAW OF TORTS § 8, at 12 (2000)).

[5] Rissler & McMurry Co. v. Sheridan Area Water Supply Joint Powers Bd., 929 P.2d 1228, 1235 (Wyo. 1996) (quoting Sensenbrenner v. Rust, Orling & Neale, Architects, Inc., 236 Va. 419, 374 S.E.2d 55, 58 (1988)).

[6] Greenwalt, ¶ 56, 71 P.3d 717, 737 (acquiescing with party's characterization of legislative objectives for legislatively created tort claims).

[7] Sorensen v. State Farm Auto. Ins. Co., 2010 WY 101, ¶ 19, 234 P.3d 1233, 1239 (Wyo. 2010) (citing Greenwalt, ¶ 12, 71 P.3d at 723).

[8] Hines v. Sweeney, 28 Wyo. 57, 201 P. 1018, 1021 (1921); Danculovich v. Brown, 593 P.2d 187, 195 (Wyo. 1979); ABC Builders, Inc. v. Phillips, 632 P.2d 925, 931 (Wyo. 1981).

entitled to protection."[9] A duty may be imposed "by statute, by common law, or by virtue of a contract relationship."[10] A duty may also be imposed "'when the relationship of the parties is such that the law imposes an obligation on the defendant to act reasonably for the protection of the plaintiff,'"[11] or by virtue of a duty that has been voluntarily assumed,[12] such as in a "Good Samaritan context."[13]

Whether a duty to exercise care exists is a question of law.[14] The determination of whether a duty exists is "determined by reference to the body of statutes, rules, principles and precedents which make up the law; and it must be determined only by the court."[15] The question to be answered by the court is "[w]hether, upon the facts in evidence, such a relation exists between the parties that the community will impose a legal obligation upon one for the benefit of the other."[16] Whether a duty will be found to exist hinges on a number of considerations, "including the magnitude of the risk involved in defendant's conduct, the burden of requiring defendant to guard against that risk, and the consequences of placing that burden upon the defendant."[17]

While foreseeability is the foremost consideration,[18] Wyoming courts balance a number of factors when determining the existence and scope of a duty. Most consistently, these factors are recited as follows:

> (1) the foreseeability of harm to the plaintiff, (2) the closeness of the connection between the defendant's conduct and the injury suffered, (3) the degree of certainty that the plaintiff suffered injury, (4) the moral blame attached to the defendant's conduct, (5) the policy of preventing future harm, (6) the

---

[9] Shafer v. TNT Well Serv., Inc., 285 P.3d 958, 965 (Wyo. 2012) (quoting Killian v. Caza Drilling, Inc., 2006 WY 42, ¶ 8, 131 P.3d 975, 979-80 (Wyo. 2006)). *See also* Sorensen v. State Farm Auto. Ins. Co., 234 P.3d 1233 (Wyo. 2010).

[10] Brubaker v. Glenrock Lodge Int'l Order of Odd Fellows, 526 P.2d 52, 58 (Wyo. 1974).

[11] Lucero v. Holbrook, 2012 WY 152, ¶ 8, 288 P.3d 1228, 1232 (Wyo. 2012) (citing *Killian*, ¶ 8, 131 P.3d at 980) (quoting Hamilton v. Natrona Cty. Educ. Ass'n, 901 P.2d 381, 384 (Wyo. 1995)).

[12] *See, e.g.,* WYOMING CIVIL PATTERN JURY INSTRUCTIONS § 3.11 ("Any duty that is voluntarily assumed must be performed with reasonable care even when no duty previously existed.").

[13] Wyoming has adopted the RESTATEMENT (SECOND) OF TORTS' view as to liability arising from the voluntary undertaking of a duty. *See* Rice v. Collins Commc'n, Inc., 2010 WY 109, ¶ 11, 236 P.3d 1009, 1014 (Wyo. 2010); Berry v. Tessman, 2007 WY 175, ¶ 13, 170 P.3d 1243, 1246 (Wyo. 2007); RESTATEMENT (SECOND) OF TORTS § 324A (1965).

[14] Lee v. LPP Mortg. Ltd., 2003 WY 92, ¶ 20, 74 P.3d 152, 160 (Wyo. 2003).

[15] *Lee*, ¶ 19, 74 P.3d at 160 (quoting PROSSER, LAW OF TORTS § 37 (5th ed. 1984)).

[16] Caterpillar Tractor Co. v. Donahue, 674 P.2d 1276, 1280 (Wyo. 1983) (quoting PROSSER, LAW OF TORTS, § 37 (4th ed. 1971)). *See also* Thomas By Thomas v. S. Cheyenne Water & Sewer Dist., 702 P.2d 1303, 1307 (Wyo. 1985) (quoting *Caterpillar Tractor Co.*, 674 P.2d at 1280); Killian v. Caza Drilling, Inc., 2006 WY 42, ¶ 8, 131 P.3d 975, 980 (Wyo. 2006) (quoting *Thomas By Thomas*, 702 P.2d at 1307); Shafer v. TNT Well Serv., Inc., 285 P.3d 958, 966 (Wyo. 2012) (quoting *Killian*, ¶ 8, 131 P.3d at 980).

[17] Borns *ex rel.* Gannon v. Voss, 2003 WY 74, ¶ 31, 70 P.3d 262, 273 (Wyo. 2003).

[18] Glenn v. Union Pac. R.R. Co., 2011 WY 126, ¶ 34, 262 P.3d 177, 193 (Wyo. 2011) (quoting the Tenth Circuit Court of Appeals in *Beugler v. Burlington N. & Santa Fe Ry.*, 490 F.3d 1224 (10th Cir. 2007) for the proposition that "[m]any factors inform the duty analysis, but the most important consideration is foreseeability").

extent of the burden upon the defendant, (7) the consequences to the community and the court system, and (8) the availability, cost and prevalence of insurance for the risk involved.[19]

The element of foreseeability establishes a "zone of risk" that forms a basis for assessing whether given conduct creates a general and foreseeable risk of harm for others.[20] Under a "zone of risk" assessment, it is not necessary to anticipate the precise injury resulting from a negligent act; it is only necessary that some resulting injury could be reasonably anticipated.[21]

Neither is it required that the tortfeasor have foreseen the likelihood, extent, or manner of occurrence of a particular injury.[22] Rather, "it is only necessary that he should have anticipated that some injury or harm might result from his conduct."[23] Once a duty exists, it imposes an obligation to do whatever a reasonable person would have done in order to avoid both the negligent act itself and the resulting harm.[24] This is true in all instances when a duty has been found to exist, including when a duty has been voluntarily assumed,[25] subject to a few statutory exceptions.[26]

B. *Question of Fact*

i. **Elements**

In Wyoming, the "law of negligence is predicated upon that which is required of a reasonable person in the light of all the circumstances."[27] The *Wyoming Civil Pattern Jury Instructions* define negligence as the failure to use ordinary care.[28] Ordinary care is then

---

[19] Gates v. Richardson, 719 P.2d 193, 196 (Wyo. 1986); Rice v. Collins Commc'n, Inc., 2010 WY 109, ¶ 13, 236 P.3d 1009, 1014-15 (Wyo. 2010) (stating that "[t]he eight factors utilized to determine the existence of a duty are: . . ."); Glenn v. Union Pac. R.R. Co., 2011 WY 126, ¶ 34, 262 P.3d 177, 193 (Wyo. 2011) (quoting *Gates*, 719 P.2d at 196); Lucero v. Holbrook, 2012 WY 152, ¶ 10, 288 P.3d 1228, 1233 (Wyo. 2012) (quoting *Gates*, 719 P.2d at 196).

[20] Sperry v. Fremont Cty. Sch. Dist., 84 F. Supp. 3d 1277, 1288 (D. Wyo. 2015) (quoting Glenn v. Union Pacific R.R. Co., 2011 WY 126, ¶34, 262 P.3d 177, 193 (Wyo. 2011)).

[21] ABC Builders, Inc. v. Phillips, 632 P.2d 925, 937 (Wyo. 1981); Daily v. Bone, 906 P.2d 1039, 1043 (Wyo. 1995).

[22] Endresen v. Allen, 574 P.2d 1219, 1222 (Wyo. 1978) (quoting 57 Am.Jur.2d, *Negligence* § 59, p. 411).

[23] *Endresen*, 574 P.2d at 1222 (quoting Swearngin v. Sears Roebuck & Co., 376 F.2d 637, 642 (10 Cir. 1967)).

[24] Jeffers v. Offe, 598 P.2d 450, 451 (Wyo. 1979).

[25] *See* Wyoming Civil Pattern Jury Instructions § 3.11, *supra*, note 11 and discussion of Restatement (Second) of Torts, *supra* note 12.

[26] *See* Wyo. Stat. Ann. § 1-1-120 (granting immunity to persons attempting to render emergency assistance), Wyo. Stat. Ann. § 1-1-125 (granting immunity to non-profit volunteers and volunteer firefighters), and Wyo. Stat. Ann. § 1-1-129 (granting immunity for civil liability to volunteer health care professionals).

[27] Fegler v. Brodie, 574 P.2d 751, 755 (Wyo. 1978).

[28] Wyoming Civil Patten Jury Instructions § 3.02 (2015). Courts have also provided the instruction using the term "ordinary negligence." *See, e.g.,* Hannifan v. Am. Nat'l Bank of Cheyenne, 2008 WY 65, ¶ 28, 185 P.3d 679, 690 (Wyo. 2008).

defined as "the degree of care that . . . should reasonably be expected of the ordinary careful person under the same or similar circumstances."[29] The concept of ordinary care is "commensurate with the danger" and "accommodates all circumstances so that the degree of care varies with the circumstances."[30] The conduct of the reasonable person "varies not only with standard of ordinary care, but also with his ability to avoid injuries to others, as well as the consequences of his conduct."[31]

ii. Evidence

The Wyoming Supreme Court has stated that "[n]egligence occurs when one fails to act as would a reasonable person of ordinary prudence under like circumstances."[32] To establish negligence, the plaintiff must show:

(1) The defendant owed the plaintiff a duty to conform to a specified standard of care, (2) the defendant breached the duty of care, (3) the defendant's breach of the duty of care proximately caused injury to the plaintiff, and (4) the injury sustained by the plaintiff is compensable by money damages.[33]

The plaintiff must prove the elements of negligence by a preponderance of the evidence.[34] This includes establishing the existence of a duty and the breach of that duty.[35] Establishing a *prima facie* case of negligence does not shift the burden of proof from the plaintiff, but "the burden of going forward with the evidence shifts to the defendant."[36]

---

[29] WYOMING CIVIL PATTEN JURY INSTRUCTIONS § 3.02 (2015). While the wording may vary, essentially the same definition is provided time and again for common negligence actions in Wyoming. *See, e.g.*, Fegler v. Brodie, 574 P.2d 751, 755 (Wyo. 1978); Ruhs v. Pac. Power & Light, 671 F.2d 1268, 1271 (10th Cir. 1982); Keehn v. Town of Torrington, 834 P.2d 112, 114 (Wyo. 1992).

[30] Wyrulec Co. v. Schutt, 866 P.2d 756, 762 (Wyo. 1993). In *Cervelli v. Graves*, 661 P.2d 1032, 1036 (Wyo. 1983), the Wyoming Supreme Court noted that this view of negligence is "in accord with the general view," referencing THE RESTATEMENT (SECOND) OF TORTS § 283 and PROSSER AND KEETON ON THE LAW OF TORTS § 32 (4th ed. 1971) for support.

[31] Cervelli v. Graves, 661 P.2d 1032, 1036 (Wyo. 1983) (quoting 1 DOOLEY, MODERN TORT LAW § 3.08 (1982 Rev.)).

[32] Lucero v. Holbrook, 2012 WY 152, ¶ 7, 288 P.3d 1228, 1232 (Wyo. 2012). In an earlier case, the Wyoming Supreme Court approved of language found in AM.JUR.2D *Negligence* § 58, stating that "[T]he broad test of negligence is what a reasonably prudent person would foresee and would do in the light of this foresight under the circumstances." Endresent v. Allen, 574 P.2d 1219, 1221 (Wyo. 1978).

[33] *Lucero*, ¶ 7, 288 P.3d at 1232 (quoting Hatton v. Energy Elec. Co., 2006 WY 151, ¶ 10, 148 P.3d 8, 13 (Wyo. 2006)).

[34] WYOMING CIVIL PATTERN JURY INSTRUCTIONS § 3.01 (2015). Preponderance of the evidence is defined as "the amount of evidence, taken as a whole, that leads the jury to find that the existence of a disputed fact is more probable than not." WYOMING CIVIL PATTERN JURY INSTRUCTIONS § 2.03 (2015).

[35] Maxted v. Pac. Car & Foundry Co., 527 P.2d 832, 835 (Wyo. 1974); Pine Creek Canal No. 1 v. Stadler, 685 P.2d 13, 16 (Wyo. 1984).

[36] Sky Aviation Corp. v. Colt, 475 P.2d 301, 304 (Wyo. 1970).

The plaintiff may rely on the violation of a statute as evidence of negligence.[37] It is for the court, however, to determine whether a statute that is silent as to whether it does in fact create a new duty has nevertheless created one.[38] While the burden of proof for a plaintiff relying on a duty of care derived from a statute is the same as for a common law duty,[39] the precise effect of the violation of a statute, regulation, or ordinance establishing a standard of conduct are to be resolved by application of sections from the *Restatement (Second) of Torts*.[40]

Custom and practice may also serve as evidence as to whether given conduct meets the general standard of reasonable care, but custom and practice are not alone dispositive of what constitutes a reasonable standard of care, nor whether negligence occurred.[41] Similarly, a long-standing and established practice or custom that falls short of affording reasonable protection against foreseeable injuries does not relieve those with a duty of care from liability for negligently caused harm.[42]

III.   Breach of Duty

A.   Elements

The essential elements of a negligence claim are the existence of a duty on behalf of the defendant, a failure to perform that duty, which resulted in an actual injury or loss, proximately caused by the failure to perform that duty.[43] A breach of duty may occur by "nonfeasance, malfeasance, or misfeasance."[44] Once the existence of the duty has been determined as a matter of law, the subsequent determination as to whether there was a breach of that duty is a question for the trier of fact.[45] This is true in both cases of negligence and contributory negligence[46] and in cases where there is "no great disagreement about the evidentiary facts,

---

[37] Hester v. Coliseum Motor Co., 41 Wyo. 345, 285 P. 781, 784 (1930); Zanetti Bus Lines, Inc. v. Logan, 400 P.2d 482, 484 (Wyo. 1965).

[38] Merrill v. Jansma, 2004 WY 26, ¶ 39, 86 P.3d 270, 287 (Wyo. 2004).

[39] Distad v. Cubin, 633 P.2d 167, 180 (Wyo. 1981).

[40] *Distad*, 633 P.2d at 175. The pertinent sections of the RESTATEMENT (SECOND) OF TORTS include §§ 286, 287, 288, 288A, 288B, and 288C.

[41] Johnson v. Dale C. & Helen W. Johnson Family Revocable Tr., 2015 WY 42, ¶ 21, 345 P.3d 883, 889 (Wyo. 2015) (citing RESTATEMENT (SECOND) OF TORTS § 295A *cmt*. B (updated Mar. 2015)). The standard is always one of reasonable care and neither the presence nor the absence of custom alters that standard; custom merely assists in the determination of what constitutes due care. Pan Am. Petroleum Corp. v. Like, 381 P.2d 70, 76 (Wyo. 1963). *See also* WYOMING CIVIL PATTERN JURY INSTRUCTIONS § 3.08 (2015).

[42] Rocky Mountain Trucking Co. v. Taylor, 79 Wyo. 461, 475, 335 P.2d 448, 451 (1959).

[43] Andersen v. Two Dot Ranch, Inc., 2002 WY 105, ¶ 11, 49 P.3d 1011, 1014 (Wyo. 2002); Turcq v. Shanahan, 950 P.2d 47, 51 (Wyo. 1997); Daily v. Bone, 906 P.2d 1039, 1043 (Wyo. 1995); ABC Builders, Inc. v. Phillips, 632 P.2d 925, 931 (Wyo. 1981); Danculovich v. Brown, 593 P.2d 187, 195 (Wyo. 1979).

[44] Price v. State Highway Comm'n, 62 Wyo. 385, 396, 167 P.2d 309, 312 (1946).

[45] Lucero v. Holbrook, 2012 WY 152, ¶ 10, 288 P.3d 1228, 1233 (Wyo. 2012); Lee v. LPP Mortg. Ltd., 2003 WY 92, ¶ 20, 74 P.3d 152, 160 (Wyo. 2003); John Q. Hammons Inc. v. Poletis, 954 P.2d 1353, 1356 (Wyo. 1998) (citing PROSSER AND KEETON ON THE LAW OF TORTS § 37 (5th ed. 1984), and RESTATEMENT (SECOND) OF TORTS § 328C *cmt*. b (1965)).

[46] Fitzsimonds v. Cogswell, 405 P.2d 785, 786 (Wyo. 1965).

but the evidence is subject to conflicting interpretations or reasonable minds might differ as to its significance."[47] This is not necessarily the rule, however, in those cases[48] when there is but one conclusion that can be reasonably inferred from the undisputed facts.[49]

B.   Evidence

It is for the plaintiff[50] to prove the elements of a negligence case by a preponderance of the evidence.[51] Evidence of custom and industry practice is admissible to show negligence.[52] Conduct that is in violation of statute, ordinance, or regulation may also be submitted as evidence to support a finding of negligence, but the decision to adopt a standard of care as established by a statute or regulation is a discretionary decision by courts in Wyoming requiring special consideration.[53] To help guide this decision, the Wyoming Supreme Court has adopted provisions from the *Restatement (Second) Torts* "as guidelines for addressing negligence claims premised on duties created by statutes, regulations or ordinances."[54]

IV.   Causation

A.   Elements

Wyoming tort actions must be premised on a theory that the tortious act proximately caused the injury at issue.[55] For an act to proximately cause an injury, the injury must result as a "natural and probable consequence of the act of negligence."[56] Multiple proximate causes may exist for a single injury.[57] A cause does not have be the last, or nearest, proximate cause

---

[47] Foote v. Simek, 2006 WY 96, ¶ 16, 139 P.3d 455, 462 (Wyo. 2006) (quoting Roussalis v. Wyoming Med. Ctr., Inc., 4 P.3d 209, 229 (Wyo. 2000)).

[48] Brockett v. Prater, 675 P.2d 638, 640 (Wyo. 1984); DeWald v. State, 719 P.2d 643, 651 (Wyo. 1986).

[49] *Brockett*, 675 P.2d at 640.

[50] WYOMING CIVIL PATTERN JURY INSTRUCTIONS § 3.01 (2015).

[51] Maxted v. Pac. Car & Foundry Co., 527 P.2d 832, 835 (Wyo. 1974); Pine Creek Canal No. 1 v. Stadler, 685 P.2d 13, 16 (Wyo. 1984).

[52] Johnson v. Dale C. & Helen W. Johnson Family Revocable Tr., 2015 WY 42, ¶ 21, 345 P.3d 883, 889 (Wyo. 2015) (citing RESTATEMENT (SECOND) OF TORTS § 295A cmt. B (updated Mar. 2015)); Pan Am. Petroleum Corp. v. Like, 381 P.2d 70, 76 (Wyo. 1963); WYOMING CIVIL PATTERN JURY INSTRUCTIONS § 3.08 (2015); Rocky Mountain Trucking Co. v. Taylor, 79 Wyo. 461, 475, 335 P.2d 448, 451 (1959).

[53] Landsiedel v. Buffalo Props., LLC, 2005 WY 61, ¶ 23, 112 P.3d 610, 616 (Wyo. 2005).

[54] Dubray v. Howshar, 884 P.2d 23, 27 (Wyo. 1994) (citing Distad v. Cubin, 633 P.2d 167 (Wyo. 1981). The court in *Distad* expressly adopted RESTATEMENT (SECOND) OF TORTS §§ 286, 287, 288, 288A, 288B, and 288C. *Distad*, 633 P.2d at 175.

[55] Allmaras v. Mudge, 820 P.2d 533, 536 (Wyo. 1991); Beard v. Brown, 616 P.2d 726 (Wyo. 1980).

[56] Turcq v. Shanahan, 950 P.2d 47, 51 (Wyo. 1997) (quoting Bettencourt v. Pride Well Serv., Inc., 735 P.2d 722, 726 (Wyo. 1987); *accord* Nat. Gas Processing Co. v. Hull, 886 P.2d 1181, 1186 (Wyo. 1994); *accord* Lynch v. Norton Const., Inc., 861 P.2d 1095, 1099 (Wyo. 1993)).

[57] Nat. Gas Processing Co. v. Hull, 886 P.2d 1181, 1186 (Wyo. 1994). Multiple proximate causes arise in situations of so-called "concurrent negligence," which "involves acts of negligence of two or more people that, although not working in concert, combine to produce a single injury." *Id.*

so long as it joins in a natural or probable way with other acts or events to cause the claimed injury.[58] In these circumstances, each concurrent cause constitutes a proximate cause.[59]

In order for a proximate cause to also qualify as a legal cause, the causal act must be a "substantial factor" in the chain of events that brought about the resulting injury.[60] Conduct is a substantial factor when, "in the natural and continuous sequence, unbroken by a sufficient intervening cause," it produced an injury which would not have otherwise resulted.[61] An intervening cause is defined as a cause "that comes into being after a defendant's negligent act has occurred,"[62] and is sufficiently significant to break the causal chain necessary for a proximate or legal cause.[63] The Wyoming Supreme Court has stated that "the notion of intervening cause is an 'alternative method' for explaining the concepts of legal or proximate cause and the 'substantial factor' test."[64] An intervening cause, however, will only insulate a tortfeasor from liability if the intervening cause was itself a foreseeable event.[65]

B.   Evidence

The foreseeability of an injury has been called the "ultimate test" for determining proximate cause.[66] The exact nature or extent of the harm need not itself have been foreseeable so long as a reasonable person in similar circumstances would have anticipated that an injury might result.[67] The Wyoming Supreme Court has held that proximate cause "addresses the scope of a defendant's liability and is a question of fact for the factfinder, and

---

[58] WYOMING CIVIL PATTERN JURY INSTRUCTIONS § 3.05 (2015).

[59] Nat. Gas Processing Co. v. Hull, 886 P.2d 1181, 1186 (Wyo. 1994).

[60] Turcq v. Shanahan, 950 P.2d 47, 51 (Wyo. 1997); Killian v. Caza Drilling, Inc., 2006 WY 42, ¶ 20, 131 P.3d 975, 985 (Wyo. 2006) (quoting *Turcq*, 950 P.2d at 51); Foote v. Simek, 2006 WY 96, ¶ 22, 139 P.3d 455, 463 (Wyo. 2006) (quoting *Turcq*, 950 P.2d at 51); WYOMING CIVIL PATTERN JURY INSTRUCTIONS § 3.04 (2015).

[61] *Turcq*, 950 P.2d at 51; *Killian*, ¶ 20, 131 P.3d at 985 (*Turcq*, 950 P.2d at 51); Johnson v. Allis-Chalmers Corp. Prod. Liab. Tr., 11 F. Supp. 3d 1119, 1129 (D. Wyo. 2014).

[62] Buckley v. Bell, 703 P.2d 1089, 1092 (Wyo. 1985).

[63] "[T]his court first defined proximate cause as '[t]hat which, in a natural and continuous sequence, unbroken by any efficient intervening cause, produces the injury, and without which the result would not have occurred.'" *Killian*, ¶ 20, 131 P.3d at 985 (quoting Lemos v. Madden, 28 Wyo. 1, 200 P. 791, 793 (1921)); Johnson v. Allis-Chalmers Corp. Prod. Liab. Tr., 11 F. Supp. 3d 1119, 1129 (D. Wyo. 2014) (quoting *Killian*, ¶ 20, 131 P.3d at 985).

[64] Glenn v. Union Pac. R.R. Co., 2011 WY 126, ¶ 40, 262 P.3d 177, 195 (Wyo. 2011); Buckley v. Bell, 703 P.2d 1089, 1092 (Wyo. 1985).

[65] *Buckley*, 703 P.2d at 1092. An intervening cause is reasonably foreseeable "if it is a probable consequence of the defendant's wrongful act or is a normal response to the stimulus of the situation created thereby." *Id.*

[66] Turcq v. Shanahan, 950 P.2d 47, 51 (Wyo. 1997); Foote v. Simek, 2006 WY 96, ¶ 22, 139 P.3d 455, 464 (Wyo. 2006) (quoting *Turcq*, 950 P.2d at 51); Killian v. Caza Drilling, Inc., 2006 WY 42, ¶ 20, 131 P.3d 975, 985 (Wyo. 2006) (quoting *Turcq*, 950 P.2d at 51); Collings v. Lords, 2009 WY 135, ¶ 6, 218 P.3d 654, 656 (Wyo. 2009) (quoting *Foote*, ¶ 22, 139 P.3d at 464).

[67] WYOMING CIVIL PATTERN JURY INSTRUCTIONS § 3.06 (2015). The note accompanying this instruction states, as follows: "The Wyoming Supreme Court has discussed a foreseeability requirement in conjunction with both the duty and the causation elements of a negligence claim. This instruction addresses foreseeability in the context of the causation element. Instruction 3.02 impliedly addresses foreseeability as it relates to the duty element."

less appropriate for a summary judgment action."[68] This is the usual rule, and is true in cases where "different inferences may fairly be drawn even though the evidence is undisputed."[69] Conversely, this is not the rule in cases in which reasonable persons cannot disagree as to those inferences.[70] The question of whether proximate cause exists "is to be determined on the facts of each case, and is to be answered in accordance with common sense and common understanding."[71]

V. Damages

A. Elements

Ultimately, the question of liability in a negligence action "is irrelevant if there are no damages."[72] In Wyoming tort cases, the measure of damages is that amount which will provide compensation for the damage proximately caused by a tortfeasor's breach of duty.[73] Wyoming courts have consistently stated that the goal in awarding damages "is to make the injured party whole to the extent that it is possible to measure an injury in terms of money."[74] To be made whole, an injured party should be placed in the same financial position he or she would have been if the injury had never happened.[75] The goal is that "the person injured shall receive a compensation commensurate with his loss and no more."[76]

Wyoming has also adopted the "economic loss rule" specifically as a means to distinguish between damages in contract and tort disputes.[77] The rule "bars recovery in tort when a plaintiff claims purely economic damages unaccompanied by physical injury to persons or property."[78] The determination of whether a given intentional tort claim "is simply a repackaged contract claim requires consideration of the conduct alleged, its relationship to the contractual duties of the parties, the source of the tort duty alleged to have been breached, and the nature of the damages claimed."[79]

---

[68] Lucero v. Holbrook, 2012 WY 152, ¶ 7, 288 P.3d 1228, 1232 (Wyo. 2012) (citing RESTATEMENT (THIRD) OF TORTS § 7 (2010)).

[69] O'Mally v. Eagan, 43 Wyo. 233, 2 P.2d 1063, 1066 (1931).

[70] Buckley v. Bell, 703 P.2d 1089, 1092 (Wyo. 1985) (collecting cases).

[71] Burgert v. Tietjens, 499 F.2d 1, 5 (10th Cir. 1974).

[72] Serda v. Dennis, 2004 WY 141, ¶ 6, 100 P.3d 860, 861 (Wyo. 2004).

[73] Atlas Const. Co. v. Slater, 746 P.2d 352, 359 (Wyo. 1987); Hagar v. Mobley, 638 P.2d 127, 139 (Wyo. 1981).

[74] Lieberman v. Mossbrook, 2009 WY 65, ¶ 49, 208 P.3d 1296, 1310-11 (Wyo. 2009); Alcaraz v. State, 2002 WY 57, ¶ 15, 44 P.3d 68, 73 (Wyo. 2002) (citing 22 AM.JUR.2d *Damages* § 26 (1988)).

[75] *Lieberman*, 208 P.3d at 1310-11; *Alcaraz*, 44 P.3d at 68.

[76] Hunt v. Thompson, 19 Wyo. 523, 120 P. 181, 184 (1912); Walton v. Atl. Richfield Co., 501 P.2d 802, 805 (Wyo. 1972); Reynolds v. Tice, 595 P.2d 1318, 1324 (Wyo. 1979).

[77] Level 3 Commc'ns, LLC v. Liebert Corp., 535 F.3d 1146, 1162 (10th Cir. 2008); Rissler & McMurry Co. v. Sheridan Area Water Supply Joint Powers Bd., 929 P.2d 1228, 1234-35 (Wyo. 1996).

[78] *Rissler & McMurry Co.*, 929 P.2d at 1234-35.

[79] Excel Const., Inc. v. HKM Eng'g, Inc., 2010 WY 34, ¶ 31, 228 P.3d 40, 48 (Wyo. 2010).

B.   *Evidence*

In Wyoming, damages must be proven with a reasonable degree of certainty,[80] and the party seeking recovery of damages holds the burden of proof.[81] Proof as to an exact amount of damages is not required,[82] so long as they are "proven with a reasonable degree of certainty so that the factfinder, in turn, can determine the amount with a measurable degree of certainty."[83] Although an exact amount of damages need not be proven, theoretical, conjectural, and speculative damages are not permitted.[84]

As stated above, the overriding goal in Wyoming is "is to make the injured party whole to the extent that it is possible to measure an injury in terms of money."[85] Courts have also consistently stated that "[i]n computing damages, the primary objective is to determine the amount of loss, applying whatever rule is best situated to that purpose."[86] In calculating reasonable and adequate compensatory damages, the trier of fact is to base the awarded amount on the evidence heard in the case as well as "knowledge, observation, and experience in life."[87] Likewise, the fact that an injured party does not provide expert testimony as to the monetary value of an alleged injury does not prevent the trier of fact from determining an amount to award,[88] because "the amount to be assessed for damages suffered by a plaintiff as a result of personal injuries is a matter within the sound discretion of the trier of fact."[89]

---

[80] Goforth v. Fifield, 2015 WY 82, ¶ 40, 352 P.3d 242, 250 (Wyo. 2015); Knight v. TCB Const. & Design, LLC, 2011 WY 27, ¶ 17, 248 P.3d 178, 184 (Wyo. 2011); Wyoming Steel Prods., Inc. v. Wyoming Steel Fabricators & Erectors, Inc., 2007 WY 80, ¶ 19, 158 P.3d 651, 655 (Wyo. 2007). While the Wyoming Supreme Court continues to invoke the language "reasonable degree of certainty" as the standard for proving damages in tort actions, in 1989 the court held "that the words 'reasonable probability' should more precisely be the standard employed in civil personal injury jury instructions to avoid confusion." Hashimoto v. Marathon Pipe Line Co., 767 P.2d 158, 165 (Wyo. 1989).

[81] Cottonwood Valley Ranch, Inc. v. Roberts, 874 P.2d 897, 899 (Wyo. 1994).

[82] *Wyoming Steel Prods., Inc.*, ¶ 19, 158 P.3d at 655; Goforth v. Fifield, 2015 WY 82, ¶ 40, 352 P.3d 242, 250 (Wyo. 2015); Reposa v. Buhler, 770 P.2d 235, 238 (Wyo. 1989).

[83] *Reposa*, 770 P.2d at 238.

[84] *Id.*

[85] Lieberman v. Mossbrook, 2009 WY 65, ¶ 49, 208 P.3d 1296, 1310-11 (Wyo. 2009); Alcaraz v. State, 2002 WY 57, ¶ 15, 44 P.3d 68, 73 (Wyo. 2002) (citing 22 Am.Jur.2d *Damages* § 26 (1988)).

[86] *Lieberman*, 208 P.3d at 1310-11; *Alcaraz*, 44 P.3d at 68.

[87] Wyoming Civil Pattern Jury Instructions § 4.02 (2015).

[88] Mariner v. Marsden, 610 P.2d 6, 13 (Wyo. 1980) (holding that the lack of expert medical testimony was not "fatal to the award for past pain and suffering").

[89] Buttrey Food Stores Div. v. Coulson, 620 P.2d 549, 555 (Wyo. 1980).

INDEX